FINANCIAL ACCOUNTING THEORY

ISSUES AND CONTROVERSIES

THIRD EDITION

Edited by

Stephen A. Zeff, Ph.D.
Rice University

Thomas F. Keller, Ph.D., C.P.A.
Duke University

McGraw-Hill, Inc.

New York St. Louis San Francisco Auckland Bogotá Caracas Hamburg
Lisbon London Madrid Mexico Milan Montreal New Delhi Paris
San Juan São Paulo Singapore Sidney Tokyo Toronto

This book was set in Times Roman by Publication Services.
The editor was Jim DeVoe;
the production supervisor was Marietta Breitwieser.
The cover was designed by Scott Chelius.
Project supervision was done by Publication Services.
R. R. Donnelley & Sons Company was printer and binder.

FINANCIAL ACCOUNTING THEORY

Issues and Controversies

4 5 6 7 DOC/DOC 9 9 8 7 6 5 4 3 2 1

ISBN 0-07-072791-0

Library of Congress Cataloging in Publication Data
Main entry under title:

Financial accounting theory.

   Rev. ed. of : Financial accounting theory I.   2nd ed.
c1973.
   Bibliography: p.
   1. Accounting—Addresses, essays, lectures.
I. Zeff, Stephen A.   II. Keller, Thomas F.   III. Title:
Financial accounting theory I.
HF5635.F533   1985   657   84-19398
ISBN 0-07-072791-0

CONTENTS

PREFACE

The aim of this collection is to provide institutional and historical perspective to contemporary financial accounting controversies, as well as supply a lively dialogue on accounting theory for future accounting professionals and others interested in corporate financial reporting. The need for such a volume is even greater than it was in 1964 when our first edition appeared. The number and complexity of accounting pronouncements have multiplied, and the trend in accounting curricula has been to devote more time to the numerous utterances of the FASB and other standard-setting bodies and correspondingly less time to the theory of the field. In such circumstances, accounting graduates could be more aptly described as technicians than accounting thinkers. Accounting standards change, and we believe that a proper professional education is one that attends not only to the details of recommended practice but also to conceptual knowledge, research findings, and the historical and institutional factors that collectively set the stage for today's accounting debates.

Several changes in the literature have occurred since the appearance of our second edition a dozen years ago. Much more attention has been given to the standard-setting process itself, especially the motivations lying behind the lobbying efforts of companies, government departments, accounting firms, and other interested parties. A corollary has been the alleged "economic consequences" that are said to flow from changes in particular accounting standards. There seems to be little doubt that the actions of standard setters in several countries have been influenced by arguments—as well as by the political force used to buttress such arguments—inspired by the magnitude and seriousness of economic consequences that are associated with proposed standards.

A second development has been the unremitting search for a Conceptual Framework. Not only in the United States, but also in the United Kingdom and Ireland, Australia, and Canada, the leaders of the accounting profession have, at various times in the 1970s, professed a strong desire to lay a theoretical foundation for accounting standards. Articles and monographs have dealt with the strategic importance of a Conceptual Framework in the profession's program of establishing accounting standards.

A third trend has been the expansion of accounting disclosures. In such diverse areas as segment reporting and social responsibility accounting, disclosures have multiplied in the annual reports of major North American and European companies. In the United States, the SEC has called for a greater range of both interpretive and factual information to assist readers in understanding the uncertain corporate world. Demands continue to be expressed for an enlargement of the scope of financial reporting, and the literature reflects these developments.

Finally, the argument has been made on several fronts that accrual accounting should be displaced, or at least complemented, by cash flow accounting. It has been contended that financial statements, based on the arbitrary allocations inherent in conventional accrual accounting, contain information not calculated to assist decision makers. At the very least, critics argue that the funds statement should be redefined in terms of cash flows instead of movements in working capital.

In this edition, we devote a section to each of these trends. Moreover, articles appearing in other sections address similar concerns in the context of specific controversies.

About half of the articles in this collection relate to specific problem areas in the balance sheet and income statement. They may be assigned in an intermediate course as the relevant textbook chapters are taken up; in an accounting theory seminar, they will challenge students to think beyond the confines of authoritative pronouncements.

Nearly 40 percent of the articles address the strategic and tactical factors (some of which are known as economic consequences) that have impelled company managers, bankers, and government policy makers to lobby for or against particular accounting practices, or, in the case of company managers, to prefer one accounting practice to another in their published financial statements.

None of the contents of this third edition has been carried over from the second edition. With one minor exception, every article was originally published in 1973 or later, and two-thirds of the articles are as recent as 1979. Most of the articles appeared in the *Journal of Accountancy* or *The Accounting Review,* but others were published in such journals as *CAmagazine, Financial Analysts Journal, Journal of Accounting Research, Journal of Accounting, Auditing and Finance* and *The Bell Journal of Economics.* Several articles were drawn from the financial press, including *Fortune, The Wall Street Journal, Forbes, Business Week,* and *The New York Times.* Most of the authors are accounting academics, but a number are practicing accountants and financial journalists.

We have prepared introductions to each of the sections (and, in Section 7, to each of the subsections). The purpose of the introductions is to place the areas of controversy into perspective. Historical backgrounds are sketched, and the international dimensions are outlined. Following all but two of the sections and subsections, we have provided Bibliographical Notes containing highly selected and annotated references to other useful writings on the subject. The references are not limited to North American authors but include many works written by British, Australian, New Zealand, and Continental European authors. These are intended to guide students in their research for term papers, and to assist others who would pursue their inquiries beyond these pages.

We have given the current affiliation of the authors of articles in this collection, but where the affiliation at the time of the article is pertinent, we have included it as well.

We wish to thank our colleagues for their suggestions. In particular, George Foster, Bala G. Dharan, Richard Macve, and Philip W. Bell should be mentioned. We also wish to thank Edna Hodges for her tireless efforts in preparing the manuscript. We hope that instructors and students alike find the contents of this volume to be a valuable part of the accounting curriculum.

Stephen A. Zeff
Thomas F. Keller

ISSUES IN THE STANDARD-SETTING PROCESS

Prior to the 1970s, few academics paid much attention to the standard-setting process in accounting. Little research was done on the subject. Beginning in the 1970s, however, it became clear that standard setting was a fascinating process that had become intertwined with the economic self-interests of affected parties. In the 1960s, managers had "discovered" the standard setters and together with government had sought on several occasions to influence the deliberations of the Accounting Principles Board. It was not until the 1970s that many students of the subject began to study how the standard-setting process actually worked, and they came to the realization that accounting standard setting was, despite the best efforts of the standard setters themselves, an integral part of the American political process.

Currently, standard-setting boards or committees are active in a number of countries, including the United States, Canada, United Kingdom, Australia, New Zealand, Mexico, the Netherlands, Argentina, Japan, South Africa, and Sweden. Securities commissions are particularly powerful in the United States, France, and Canada. In the Netherlands, there is an Accounting Court.[1] The International Accounting Standards Committee, whose members represent the accounting bodies of some 65 countries, is active at the international level; and the Fourth and Seventh Directives of the European Economic Community, issued in 1978 and 1983, respectively, deal with accounting matters and will eventually be adopted by the legislatures of the ten EEC countries.

The ostensible purpose of each of these standard-setting organizations is to promote the dissemination of timely and useful financial information to investors

---

[1]For a discussion of the nature and role of the Dutch accounting court, see Jan Klaassen, "An Accounting Court: The Impact of the Enterprise Chamber on Financial Reporting in the Netherlands," *The Accounting Review* (April 1980), pp. 327–341.

and certain other parties having an interest in companies' economic performance. Standard setters disagree over just what information is likely to be "useful." Differences in the institutions, traditions, and legal systems from one country to another give rise to differences in international accounting standards. But even within a single country, such as the United States or the United Kingdom, leading accountants disagree profoundly on what information is "useful." In the United States, the Financial Accounting Standards Board, now in its second decade of operations, is still struggling to produce a completed conceptual framework. (More about this in Section 2.)

Formal standard setting has had a longer history in the United States than in any other country. As early as 1932–1934, the American Institute of Accountants (today known as the American Institute of Certified Public Accountants) collaborated with the New York Stock Exchange in the formulation of five "rules or principles" of accounting. These were intended to be followed by companies listed on the Stock Exchange. The next standard-setting initiative occurred in 1938–1939, when the Institute—in response to pressure from the Securities and Exchange Commission—authorized its Committee on Accounting Procedure to issue "Accounting Research Bulletins." The bulletins were not binding on Institute members, but since they were in most instances endorsed by the SEC, their influence on the accounting practices of major American corporations was considerable.

Between 1939 and 1959, the Committee on Accounting Procedure issued 51 Accounting Research Bulletins. In 1953, Bulletin 43 codified and superseded those of the first 42 bulletins that dealt with accounting principles (several of the earlier bulletins discussed terminology). Today, Bulletins 43 to 51, as modified by subsequent pronouncements, are still in effect.

In 1959, the Institute established the Accounting Principles Board to supplant the Committee on Accounting Procedure. The new Board was to invest heavily in research so as to provide a solid conceptual base for its "Opinions." One of the charges to the Board was to resolve accounting controversies that had perplexed and divided leaders of the accounting profession during the 1940s and 1950s. Examples were: the "current operating performance" versus "all-inclusive" conception of income, price-level accounting, income tax allocation, and accounting for business combinations and intercorporate investments. As it turned out, the Board's early research initiatives only intensified the controversy and hence failed to unite the Board on conceptual grounds. Nonetheless, the Board addressed a number of the most difficult accounting issues in a series of major Opinions during the middle and later 1960s. Opinion 8 raised the standard of accounting for pensions, Opinion 9 pleased the SEC by supporting the all-inclusive conception of income, and Opinion 11 (in a sharply divided Board) endorsed comprehensive income tax allocation. In Opinions 14 (treatment of convertible debt and detachable warrants), 15 (earnings per share), 16 (business combinations), 17 (goodwill), 18 (intercorporate investments), and in Statement 2 (segmental reporting), the Board wrestled with complex issues arising out of the wave of conglomerate mergers during the 1960s. In the end, the Board was defeated by the actions of company managements, government, and the financial community to shape accounting standards in a manner furthering their own special interests. As we have noted, the Board's research program did not fulfill the grandiose expectation that it furnish the Board with a theoretical underpinning for difficult pronouncements. Whether an effective research program would have enabled the Board to counter the pressures of special interest groups cannot be known, but it seems likely that the interest groups would have held considerable sway in any event.

In 1973 the Financial Accounting Standards Board replaced the Accounting Principles Board after the latter had issued 31 opinions and 4 statements. Unlike its predecessor, the FASB was not a committee of the Institute. It was set up under the new Financial Accounting Foundation, an entity largely independent of the Institute and which was responsible for financing the FASB and choosing its members. Paul A. Pacter in his article, "The FASB after Ten Years: History and Emerging Trends," discusses the FASB's first decade from the vantage point of a member of the Board's staff whose responsibilities have been more administrative than concerned with the drafting of statements.

Pacter does not mention "economic consequences" by name, but he does allude to them by the term "cost/benefit" tradeoffs. In order to understand the pressurized environment in which the standard-setting process takes place, one must become aware of the possible economic consequences of the standard-setter's actions. Stephen A. Zeff, in his review of the standard-setting process from the 1940s to the 1970s, notes the several points at which economic consequences considerations have intervened. These are the special pleadings by parties who have an interest in how the proposed standard might affect people's actions—regardless of the inherent accounting merits of the standard. David Solomons, in a widely quoted article, argues that accounting standards should be "neutral." He believes that standard setters should not allow economic consequences to influence the manner in which accounting information is conveyed in financial reports.

Charles T. Horngren, who was a member of the APB in its final years, examines the highly politicized environment in which the APB had operated, and he counsels the FASB that it will need to lobby for acceptance of its standards. "The aim of such a strategy," he writes, "would be to convince Congress, the SEC and other powerful forces that the FASB is the premier group of experts on accounting standards." Horngren uses the controversy over accounting for marketable securities to illustrate how "widespread industry hostility" to a proposed standard can effectively kill it. He also argues that the APB acts in a subordinate role to the SEC, contrary to the SEC Chief Accountant's assertion that the Commission and the APB were "in partnership." Horngren's frustrations as a private-sector standard setter are evident throughout the article.

John C. Burton was the SEC chief accountant who said that he visualized the relation between the SEC and the APB as a partnership. He was chief accountant from 1972 to 1976, and in the final article in this section he styles the SEC as a "creative irritant" that prods the profession into action on accounting standards. Burton contends that the SEC, representing the investor, endeavors to counteract the "preparer bias that institutionally exists in the [accounting] standard-setting process." Burton and Horngren present two very different views of the relationship between the SEC and the accounting standard setter.

In two chapters taken from his book, *The SEC and Corporate Disclosure: Regulation in Search of a Purpose,* Homer Kripke, a nationally respected securities lawyer and law professor who has spoken out frequently on accounting questions, criticizes the SEC for delegating its statutory authority over accounting standards to the committees and boards established under the sponsorship of the accounting profession. "Determining what accounting means," writes Kripke, "is the responsibility not only of accountants, but, also, of such users of accounting data as financial analysts and other securities professionals, as well as the representatives of the issuers." Accountants—the "technicians," according to Kripke—should not be in control of the SEC's disclosure policies. Prior to the 1970s, the SEC prevented the accounting profession from "breaking the shackles of the stewardship concept.... The Commission's failure to consider the purposes and nature of financial accounting led to forty years' stagnation of accounting thought within the practicing profession." Kripke believes that the SEC should reassert itself decisively in the field of accounting standards and should respond to the needs of the serious investor.

BIBLIOGRAPHICAL NOTES

Much has been written in the last fifteen years about the standard-setting process. Works collecting the views and research of a number of authors are as follows:

Articles appearing in the Winter 1970 issue of the *Journal of Business Finance.*

Sterling, Robert R. (ed.): *Institutional Issues in Public Accounting* (Lawrence, KS: Scholars Book Co., 1974).

Adbel-khalik, A. Rashad (ed.): *Government Regulation of Accounting Information,* Accounting Series Number 11 (Gainesville, FL: University Presses of Florida, 1980).

Buckley, John W. and J. Fred Weston (eds.): *Regulation and the Accounting Profession* (Belmont, CA: Lifetime Learning Publications—Wadsworth, 1980).

Burton, John C. (ed.): *The International World of Accounting: Challenges and Opportunities,* 1980 Proceedings of the Arthur Young Professors' Roundtable (Reston, VA: The Council of Arthur Young Professors, 1981).

Leach, Sir Ronald and Edward Stamp (eds.): *British Accounting Standards: The First Ten Years* (Cambridge, England: Woodhead-Faulkner Ltd., 1981).

"Studies on Standardization of Accounting Practices: An Assessment of Alternative Institutional Arrangements," 1981 Supplement to the *Journal of Accounting Research.*

Bromwich, Michael and Anthony G. Hopwood (eds.): *Accounting Standards Setting: An International Perspective* (London: Pitman Books Limited, 1983).

Historical studies of the standard-setting process may be found in the following works:

Storey, Reed K.: *The Search for Accounting Principles: Today's Problems in Perspective* (New York: AICPA, 1964).

Carey, John L.: *The Rise of the Accounting Profession: From Technician to Profession, 1896–1936* (AICPA, 1969), Chaps. 5–6 and 9–11.

Carey, John L.: *The Rise of the Accounting Profession: To Responsibility and Authority, 1937–1939* (AICPA, 1970), Chaps. 1 and 4–6.

Zeff, Stephen A.: *Forging Accounting Principles in Five Countries: A History and an Analysis of Trends* (Champaign, IL: Stipes Publishing Co., 1972).

Zeff, Stephen A.: *Forging Accounting Principles in Australia* (Melbourne: Australian Society of Accountants, 1973).

Moonitz, Maurice: *Obtaining Agreement on Standards in the Accounting Profession,* Studies in Accounting Research #8 (Sarasota, FL: American Accounting Association, 1974).

Chatov, Robert: *Corporate Financial Reporting: Public or Private Control?* (New York: The Free Press, 1975).

Zeff, Stephen A.: *Forging Accounting Principles in New Zealand* (Wellington: Victoria University Press, 1979).

Previts, Gary John and Barbara Dubis Merino: *A History of Accounting in America* (New York: Ronald Press-Wiley, 1979), esp. Chaps. 5–7.

A contemporary comparison of the American and British financial disclosure systems may be found in:

Benston, George J.: *Corporate Financial Disclosure in the UK and the USA* (Westmead, England and Lexington, MA: Saxon House/Lexington Books, 1976).

A work in which the author undertakes a study of the standard–setting process along sociological lines is:

Kelly-Newton, Lauren: *Accounting Policy Formulation: The Role of Corporate Management* (Reading, MA: Addison-Wesley Publishing Company, 1980).

The FASB after Ten Years:
History and Emerging Trends

Paul A. Pacter
Executive Assistant to the Chairman
Financial Accounting Standards Board
Currently Commissioner of Finance
City of Stamford, Connecticut

Marshall S. Armstrong, the first chairman of the FASB, likes to tell the story about two meetings that took place in the autumn of 1972. Both meetings involved Ralph Kent, president of the then newly organized Financial Accounting Foundation, which was incorporated in June 1972 to launch and oversee the FASB. At that time, of course, the FASB existed only on paper. The Foundation's sole assets were commitments of support from the American Institute of Certified Public Accountants, the Financial Executives Institute, the Financial Analysts Federation, the American Accounting Association, the National Association of Accountants, and other organizations concerned with improving corporate financial reporting.

During this period, Kent met with a Stamford, CT real estate developer. Handing the developer two documents, Kent explained, "here is a report from the 'Wheat Committee,' an AICPA study group, recommending creation of an independent and self-supporting Board that will establish accounting standards in the United States, and a certificate of incorporation of the Foundation. We would like a long-term lease on 30,000 square feet in one of your new corporate office parks."

"May I have a copy of your balance sheet?" the developer asked.

"We don't have any financial statements," Kent confessed. "We don't have a staff or even a Board. In fact, all we do have is a desk at the AICPA's offices."

A few days later, Kent showed up for a second meeting, at the offices of a major New York bank, where he presented a loan officer with the same two documents …and the same story. His request this time: a $1 million credit line.

Skeptics would suggest that Kent was shooting for the moon. The fact is, however, that Kent walked away from the two meetings with a 10-year lease and an offer of a $3 million line of credit. An amazing outcome? Not really. It simply speaks of the strong commitment of the American business community to private-sector accounting standards setting. And the fact that the Foundation has never drawn down even a nickel of the line of credit says even more.

From FASB Viewpoints (April 7, 1983) 8 pp. Reprinted by permission of the Financial Accounting Standards Board. Copyright © 1983, Warren, Gorham and Lamont, Inc. All rights reserved.

Editor's note: Expressions of individual views by members of the FASB and its staff are encouraged. Official positions of the FASB are determined only after extensive due process. The views expressed here are those of Mr. Pacter.

TWO "ERAS"

The Standards Board's first 10 years seem to be divisible into two "eras" from a number of perspectives:

- Start-up vs. maturity
- Pre-conceptual framework vs. post-conceptual framework
- Pre-Moss and -Metcalf vs. post-Moss and -Metcalf
- Presunshine vs. postsunshine

Interestingly, the dividing line between the two eras from each of those perspectives seems to be somewhere around the end of 1977.

THE FIRST ERA

During the first era, the Board set out to establish itself both organizationally and institutionally. Its first chairman, Marshall Armstrong, was a recognized statesman of the public accounting profession who had served as a member of the FASB's predecessor, the AICPA's Accounting Principles Board, and as president of the AICPA.

As chairman of a new and unique organization, Armstrong was confronted with innumerable precedent-setting decisions: how to set the technical agenda; to organize and design FASB Statements, Interpretations, discussion memorandums, and exposure drafts; to establish the relationship between the Board and staff; to keep the public informed of Board activities; to solicit and analyze public comments on technical issues; to distribute pronouncements and proposals; to effectively utilize the expertise of task forces and the Advisory Council; and to organize the Board's "back office" (publications production, purchasing, accounting, meeting coordination, and so on). Decisions on these and many other matters, large and small, continue to be part of the Board's modus operandi to this day.

The first Board had four persons from public accounting backgrounds and one each from industry, academe, and government. The public accounting majority on the Board was mandated by the Foundation's By-Laws, and the trustees of the Foundation were appointed by the AICPA's board of directors (though they were nominated by the five sponsoring organizations of the Foundation). These slight deferences to the public accounting profession during the FASB's early days were entirely reasonable when one considers that CPAs alone had been responsible for setting accounting standards for the preceding 40 years.

Two criteria were used by the Board in selecting its initial agenda in April 1973 from a list of approximately 35 potential projects: (1) Is the accounting question an important one for which guidance is urgently needed? (2) Would the resulting accounting standards be pervasive in their application, affecting a broad spectrum of companies? The reason for these criteria seems obvious enough. During the start-up era, the Board had to establish itself by gaining recognition and acceptability, and taking on urgent and pervasive problems was the best way to do that. Relatively narrow issues, questions affecting only a single industry, and interpretations of the old accounting literature could all take a back seat to major projects for a while.

The initial agenda included accounting for leases; reporting information about segments of a business (industries and geographic areas); foreign currency translation; accounting for self-insurance, catastrophe losses, expropriations, and other contingencies; accounting for research and development costs; materiality; and the objectives of financial accounting and reporting.

By July 1, 1973, all seven Board members had arrived, a staff of approximately 40 (including 20 accounting professionals) had been engaged, new quarters were completed, FASB operating procedures were adopted, the AICPA's governing council had recognized FASB standards under the CPA's code of ethics, and the Accounting Principles Board folded up shop. The FASB was off and running. Not long thereafter, the Securities and Exchange Commission recognized the authoritativeness of FASB pronouncements in a statement of policy issued by the Commission.

Each of the seven Board members took one of the initial agenda projects under his direction, task forces were appointed, and research projects were begun. Before the end of the year, the first discussion memorandum (on R&D costs) was published, followed, during the first six months of 1974, by discussion documents on foreign currency translation, contingencies, leases, segment reporting, general price level accounting, and the objectives of financial statements.

During this era, the Board experimented with several internal organization structures. Initially, each Board member had a senior staff person working directly for him. Together they drafted the documents, led the task forces, supervised the research, and generally ran their project. A group of staff professionals, under the research director, provided research support for the various projects as needed.

By mid-1974, public hearings were being held, comments on the first six discussion memorandums were rolling in, and Board deliberations and decision making on technical issues began. Board members no longer had the time to devote to individual projects that they had while the "pipeline" was being filled. Senior staff people who had worked directly for Board members were consolidated with the research staff under a single staff director responsible for overseeing all work on the agenda projects.

Despite the Board's initial intention to address only major pervasive issues, brushfires that required its attention began to break out. As more and more staff time was required for these emerging problems, in late 1975 the Board's technical staff group was divided into two, with one director heading up the emerging problems area and another the major projects.

The start-up era was an era of organizational fluidity, as one would expect in a brand-new and unique enterprise that had to learn by experimentation the most effective way to go about setting standards. In fact, the Board's plan to deal with only broad standards and major projects was sidetracked almost before the paint was dry on the walls of its High Ridge Park headquarters because of an emerging accounting problem that required immediate attention. The United States devalued its dollar in the summer of 1973, and the prevalence of floating rather than fixed foreign exchange rates resulted in large foreign exchange adjustments to be reported in corporate financial statements for 1973. Accounting for those adjustments was being addressed in one of the initial major agenda projects, but the acceptability in practice of numerous accounting alternatives, the absence of specific disclosure requirements in existing pronouncements, and the magnitude of the 1973 adjustments required that the Board act quickly to provide uniform minimum disclosures until the accounting questions could be resolved. By October 1973 an exposure draft had been issued, and before the end of the year final foreign currency disclosure standards were adopted to be effective for calendar-year 1973 financial statements. This was the Board's first Statement.

By the end of 1975, the Board had issued eight Statements, including four that resulted from the initial major agenda projects and four relatively narrow amendments of the existing accounting literature. The four that resulted from the initial agenda projects were Statement 2, on research and development costs; Statement 5, on contingencies; Statement 7, on reporting by development stage companies; and Statement 8, on foreign currency translation.

PORTENTS OF THE CONCEPTUAL FRAMEWORK

I have called the Board's first era the "pre-conceptual framework era" because, despite a great deal of staff and Board effort (including an evaluation of the objectives in the "Trueblood Report," an aborted project on general price level-adjusted disclosures, and a discussion memorandum on elements of financial statements and their measurement), the Board had not yet reached final conclusions on any of the parts of the conceptual framework by the end of 1977. Concepts Statement 1, on the objectives of financial reporting by business enterprises, was not published until December 1978. It was followed in 1980 by Concepts Statement 2, on the qualitative characteristics of accounting information; Concepts Statement 3, on the elements of financial statements; and Concepts Statement 4, on the objectives of financial reporting by nonbusiness organizations. Two other phases of the framework are moving toward completion–reporting income, cash flows, and financial position (on which an exposure draft has been issued) and accounting recognition criteria (on which some tentative decisions have already been reached by the Board and a staff research report has been published).

I have called the second era the "post-conceptual framework era" because it contrasts nicely with "pre-conceptual framework." However, the "post" prefix is not intended to suggest that the framework is finished and in place. While it is not yet that far along, and indeed probably never will be properly described as "finished," the Board has made substantial progress on it in the last five years, and it is well on its way to becoming a useful whole. Although there were no final pronouncements on the conceptual framework during the start-up era, one can discern a number of conceptual threads that were woven into the Board's early pronouncements and reworked into whole cloth during the second era.

One such thread is the concept of an asset as a thing rooted in the real world—a bundle of probable "future benefits" that are expected to manifest themselves in cash flows to the enterprise. The Board's early Statements did not allow for assets that were simply deferred debits awaiting disposition in the earnings statement. Research and development costs, for example, were required to be charged to expense when incurred because the probability of future benefits is not assessable at the time the expenditures are made. A development stage company could no longer defer a cost by looking to a definition of an asset different from that looked to by an established operating company. In the post-conceptual framework era, the Board went on to define assets as probable future benefits to an enterprise resulting from past events and transactions.

Another thread visible in the early pronouncements is the concept that liabilities are probable future sacrifices resulting from past events and transactions, later to become the substance of the liability definition in Concepts Statement 3. In one of its first pronouncements, the Board proscribed accrual of self-insurance "reserves" because there is no obligation until an event giving rise to a loss occurs. Similarly, insurance companies were stopped from accruing reserves for possible future catastrophes and multinational companies from accruing reserves for possible future expropriations by foreign governments.

Still another common conceptual thread in the early pronouncements is rejection of accounting practices whose only rationale is normalization or smoothing of earnings trends: Recognize the effects of events when they occur, the Board implied in Statements 2, 5, 7, and 8, not before and not later. That thread was woven tightly into the concepts Statements issued during the second era.

WATERSHED EVENTS

Another reason for using the end of 1977 as the dividing line between the two eras of the FASB is the remarkable number of watershed events that occurred around that time:

- The Moss subcommittee investigation
- The Metcalf subcommittee investigation
- A comprehensive review of the FASB's structure and operations by the trustees of the Foundation
- A lawsuit by Arthur Andersen & Co. in which Andersen challenged the right of the SEC to rely on accounting standards adopted by the FASB
- Hearings conducted by the SEC (and also by the Department of Energy) on Statement 19, which prescribes accounting standards for oil- and gas-producing companies
- An amendment to the Energy Policy and Conservation Act of 1975, proposed by Senator Haskell in late 1977, that thrust the FASB directly into the congressional lawmaking arena

What makes these events even more remarkable, in my judgment, is that the Board came out the better for each of them.

The Moss subcommittee investigation focused broadly on regulatory reform. As part of that investigation, the subcommittee, in late 1976 and 1977, delved into the relationship of the SEC and the FASB and questioned the SEC's reliance on a private-sector rulemaking body. The subcommittee suggested that the SEC take over responsibility for setting accounting standards. The chairman of the FASB and the president of the Foundation defended private-sector standards setting in submissions to and testimony before the subcommittee. In the course of its hearings, the subcommittee made some suggestions for greater oversight of the Board by the SEC, and legislation was drafted—though not enacted—that would have involved the federal government to a much greater extent in setting corporate accounting standards.

The Metcalf subcommittee's investigation of the accounting profession began in January 1977 with a staff report contending, among other things, that the FASB was dominated by and served the special interests of big business—not the needs of financial statement users or the public interest. Again, accounting standards setting by the federal government was suggested. The Board and the Foundation provided extensive (not to mention costly) submissions to the Senate subcommittee documenting its independence of thought as evidenced by the pronouncements that had then been issued to date and the safeguards that had been established to ensure independence in fact and in appearance. The investigation ended with a subcommittee report that was basically complimentary to the Board and the trustees of the Foundation.

After five years' experience with a new and unique organization, 1977 was a logical time for a comprehensive review of the FASB's structure by the Foundation's trustees, though there is little doubt that the Moss and Metcalf subcommittees provided added impetus for a review at that time. The review brought about some important structural changes that resulted in more public participation in the standards-setting process, more openness of the Board's operations, and greater efficiency in fulfilling its mission. Board meetings were opened to public observation, as were task force, Advisory Council, and trustee meetings. The Board inaugurated a weekly news bulletin to announce upcoming meetings and inform the public of recent Board decisions on technical issues. The Board's voting requirement was changed from five out of seven to a simple majority. No longer was the FASB required to have a majority of its members come from public accounting backgrounds. The Board began publishing its technical plan quarterly. The Board's technical staff was once again consolidated (remember, it had been divided into emerging problems and major projects groups back in 1975) under a single research director, a position placed on par with that of a Board member, and staff responsibilities were increased substantially. Greater reliance was placed on task forces and "leveraging" the work of others. Comment letters received by the Board were placed on view in a public reference room. Layman's language summaries were added to FASB pronouncements and proposals. The role of the Board's Advisory Council as a sounding board and consultative body representative of the FASB's principal constituencies was enhanced considerably, and an independent FASAC chairman and executive director were engaged. Trustees of the Foundation were now elected by representatives of the sponsoring organizations rather than by the AICPA's board of directors. The board of trustees was expanded to include a representative of the banking community (after earlier having been expanded to include a representative of the Securities Industry Association). A government relations office was opened in Washington, with a staff person to monitor congressional and regulatory agency activities that might concern the FASB. These and other changes that resulted from the 1977 review strengthened the Board as it moved into its second era.

Sunshine (opening Board meetings to public observation) introduced a planning and reporting rigor into the Board's internal processes that had not been necessary in the presunshine era. With sunshine, meeting agendas had to be set and announced well in advance of the meeting. Therefore, materials for the meetings had to be ready by certain deadlines and procedures had to be developed for quickly summarizing the decisions reached so that they could be reported publicly. At the same time, sunshine heightened the public's awareness of progress on the Board's technical agenda projects. In the presunshine days, the Board and its staff were especially careful to maintain confidentiality about the direction in which a project was heading prior to publication of an exposure draft or final pronouncement to ensure impartiality to all of its constituencies. With sunshine, anyone could be a cognoscente.

The Andersen challenge to the SEC's reliance on the FASB was rejected by a federal court. The Haskell amendment, which was lobbied for strongly by certain oil and gas companies seeking to preserve the full cost accounting method, was defeated.

The Board's encounter with the SEC over Statement 19 has turned out, with four years' hindsight and from the somewhat biased viewpoint of an FASB staff member, to be probably as much of a beauty mark on the Board's face as it may be a blemish. The Commission's rejection of the FASB's standards on reporting by oil- and gas-producing companies was a special situation in which Congress (in the Energy Policy and Conservation Act of 1975) had directed the SEC to develop a reporting system for oil and gas producers and had explicitly permitted the Commission to rely on the FASB for accounting and reporting standards. The FASB issued those standards in 1977, within the time frame specified in the Act.

After extensive consideration, including its own public hearings and those conducted by the Department of Energy, the SEC concluded in 1978 that existing historical cost based accounting practices, including the one favored by the FASB, were inadequate. The Commission set out to develop a new system of "reserve recognition accounting," but subsequently, in 1981, it announced that it no longer considered RRA to be a potential method of accounting in the primary financial statements and that it would support an FASB effort to develop disclosure requirements for oil and gas producers. A final Statement was issued in November 1982.

RECENT TRENDS

The Board chairmanship changed hands at the start of the second era. As the Board's second chairman, Donald J. Kirk took on responsibility for implementing many of the structural changes recommended by the trustees in 1977, developing an organizational and management approach appropriate for a mature and firmly established enterprise and broadening the Board's horizons into new areas that required financial reporting standards.

During this era, the pace of FASB activity heightened. Considerable progress was made toward developing the conceptual framework. Pronouncements were issued on the disclosure of the effects of changing prices, interest capitalization, reporting by pension plans, compensated absences, disclosure of long-term obligations, and a host of specialized industry accounting matters, among other subjects. Major projects were undertaken on reporting by rate-regulated companies, accounting for income taxes, and consolidation and the equity method. The Board's early Statement on foreign currency translation was substantially revised. A series of amendments and interpretations of Statement 13 on lease accounting was issued, leading to an integrated volume reflecting all of the changes to the original leases pronouncement. New vehicles for communicating with constituents were developed—public conferences, press symposiums, "Viewpoints," "Highlights," "Action Alert," a computerized data base of selected accounting information, and a current text loose-leaf service.

A number of trends that emerged during the Board's second era are worth examining. They may help suggest some directions for the decade ahead. These include:

- Reliance on concepts
- Focus on the whole of financial reporting, not just financial statements
- Recognition of the reporting problems of small business
- Involvement in the nonbusiness area
- Concern about specialized industry accounting questions
- Willingness to reexamine established standards
- Evolving staff responsibilities

RELIANCE ON CONCEPTS

Perhaps the biggest challenge confronting the FASB as it moves into its second decade is developing and using the conceptual framework for financial accounting and reporting. Sound concepts will guide the Board in setting accounting standards that measure and report real-world phenomena as faithfully and as factually as possible. The concepts will also provide a frame of reference for resolving accounting questions in the absence of a specific standard, as well as a common frame of reference for user understanding of the information presented.

The first concepts Statement issued by the Board dealt with the objectives of financial reporting by business enterprises. Those objectives identify investors, creditors, and other outsiders as the principal users of a company's financial report, recognize their need for information helpful in assessing the amounts, timing, and uncertainties of a company's cash flows, and describe the types of information that fulfill that need.

In Concepts Statement 2, the Board identified and described the qualities that make accounting information useful—understandability, relevance to users' decisions, and reliability.

Concepts Statement 3 defined the basic elements of financial statements—assets, liabilities, owners' equity, revenues, expenses, gains, losses, and comprehensive income. As noted earlier, assets and liabilities are defined in terms of probable future benefits and probable future sacrifices, thereby excluding deferred charges and deferred credits whose *sole* justification is avoidance of distortion or smoothing of earnings trends.

Perhaps a word about "comprehensive income" is appropriate at this point. Some who have read "Concepts Statement 3" have concluded—with trepidation— that comprehensive income necessarily involves measurements on a current cost basis or some other "current value" basis and abandonment of the traditional asset and income recognition practices. Not so, in my judgment.

As defined in Concepts Statement 3, comprehensive income is the effect of all recognizable events and transactions that change owners' equity during a period other than transactions with the owners themselves. That definition does not presume any particular method of measuring the events and transactions that enter into determining comprehensive income. Nor does it establish criteria for deciding which events and transactions are recognizable in determining comprehensive income. (Recognition and measurement criteria are part of a separate conceptual framework project currently under way.)

Even if certain value changes were to be deemed recognizable events, the definition of comprehensive income does not preclude subtotals of components of comprehensive income, including a historical cost "net income" figure as we know it today. In fact, Concepts Statement 3 and the Board's exposure draft on reporting income, cash flows, and financial position strongly suggest the appropriateness of segregating various components of comprehensive income to aid the user of a financial report in assessing an enterprise's performance. Finally, neither Concepts Statement 3 nor any of the other FASB pronouncements or proposals relating to the conceptual framework suggests that comprehensive income would necessarily be reported in a single financial statement that would replace the present income statement. If certain unrealized changes in the values of net assets were to be deemed a component of comprehensive income, those changes could be reported in a separate financial statement or as supplementary information (much like the supplementary constant dollar and current cost information that large companies are now required to present in conformity with Statement 33).

Value changes are real-world events that accountants have selectively recognized (for example, in reporting accounts receivable, inventories, and certain marketable securities) and selectively ignored (for example, most fixed assets and long-term debt). In its conceptual framework projects, the Board is attempting to develop concepts that will guide in selecting the events to be recognized, how they should be measured, and how they should be reported. In a recent address, the chairman of the FASB commented about the value of a conceptual framework to accounting standards setting:

> Even with such a framework in place, the standards-setting process will be evolutionary, not revolutionary. There are cost/benefit trade-offs and practical limitations that will constrain the standards setter even if the course charted by the concepts may seem clear. With a framework, standards setting will have direction. Without a framework, progress may well be slower than with one; and certainly the lack of a framework will result in criticism that the standards-setting process has no direction or theme that guides it.

The results of the conceptual framework project to date are already proving helpful to the Board in dealing with specific standards issues. The definition of a liability (a future obligation resulting from a past event) has helped the Board in its thinking on pension accounting, for example. Key questions in that project are whether current employee service creates a liability prior to (or regardless of) funding and whether the initiation or amendment of a pension plan that gives rise to prior service credit creates an obligation that meets the definition of a liability. (The Board's deliberations to date have answered those questions in the affirmative.) As another example, the definitions of assets and liabilities surely will be looked to as the Board studies the area of accounting for income taxes, a project added to the Board's agenda in 1982.

FOCUS ON THE WHOLE OF FINANCIAL REPORTING

During the FASB's early years, it, like its predecessors, focused primarily on financial statements and the footnotes thereto. Gradually, it has come to recognize the need for standards for some financial information that meets the tests of usefulness, understandability, relevance, and cost/benefit but that may not have the degree of reliability that warrants presenting that information in the basic financial statements themselves. The supplementary changing prices disclosures required by Statement 33 are a good example. Another is the Board's disclosures for oil- and gas-producing companies, disclosures that include the discounted cash flows associated with proved reserves. Though disclosures of that type were considered by the Board when it was developing Statement 19, they were rejected as not sufficiently reliable for inclusion in financial statements. Inasmuch as the SEC's subsequent rejection of Statement 19 and embarkation on the development of reserve recognition accounting were based on stated inadequacies of all historical cost based methods of accounting in the oil and gas industry, one can only speculate on what the SEC's actions might have been if, back in 1977, the Board has taken the broader financial reporting focus and mandated some sort of "value based" disclosures.

RECOGNITION OF SMALL-BUSINESS REPORTING PROBLEMS

Some managers and auditors of small businesses allege that not all GAAP requirements are relevant to small-business financial reporting needs, and even when relevant, some GAAP requirements cost more than they are worth to a small business. The FASB has been urged to recognize small-business reporting problems in setting accounting and reporting standards. Among the proposals for doing so are:

  • *Differential disclosures.* Certain GAAP disclosure requirements should apply to only larger companies.
  • *Differential measurement.* Small businesses should be exempted from certain GAAP measurement standards (possibly by having a larger materiality threshold for small businesses, thereby screening out some applications of measurement standards without changing the principles, or a cost/benefit test that would screen out some measurements for small businesses because of their relatively higher cost).
  • *Comprehensive basis of accounting other than GAAP.* Small businesses should be permitted to prepare their financial statements on a basis other than GAAP.

To date, the Board has selectively taken a differential disclosure approach, with smaller or nonpublic companies exempted from requirements relating to earnings per share; industry, geographic, and major customer information; current cost and constant dollar data; and oil and gas industry disclosures.

But those were ad hoc decisions, and the Board has recognized a need to address the small-business reporting question more comprehensively. In particular, the Board needs to gain a better understanding of the information needs of users of financial statements of small businesses and the costs companies incur in complying with established standards.

With that objective in mind, the Board published an invitation to comment soliciting the views of preparers, auditors, and users of the financial statements of small businesses and is working on several research projects on the subject. A research report summarizing the responses to the invitation to comment was recently published. Out of this effort will come a coordinated approach by the FASB to deal with small-business reporting problems.

ACTIVITY IN THE NONBUSINESS AREA

The FASB, like its predecessors, has focused principally on financial reporting by business enterprises, though much of the official GAAP accounting literature is looked to by non-business organizations (governmental units and nonprofit organizations) as well. In the past few years, the Board has begun to become involved more directly in the nonbusiness area.

That involvement began with a conceptual framework project on the objectives of financial reporting by nonbusiness organizations, a project that culminated in late 1980 with the publication of Concepts Statement 4. That Statement, together with the Board's concepts Statement on business reporting objectives, will serve as the foundation of an integrated conceptual framework for financial accounting and reporting that has relevance to all reporting entities while allowing for different reporting objectives and concepts that may apply to only certain types of entities.

The Board is now proceeding in the nonbusiness area mainly at the conceptual level, considering the applicability of the qualitative characteristics and elements definitions in Concepts Statements 2 and 3 in a nonbusiness context and the concepts underlying five pervasive nonbusiness accounting standards issues: (1) accounting for contributions and grants (do these fit the definition of revenue in Concepts Statement 3?); (2) depreciation; (3) definition of the reporting entity (this is part of the overall consolidation/equity method agenda project); (4) displaying financial position and results of operations; and (5) accounting for investments, particularly income on restricted investments. Although the Board has considered one nonbusiness standards project (on accounting for fund-raising costs) and stands ready to deal with others as needed, it believes that its initial efforts in the nonbusiness area should be concentrated at the concepts level because of the significant number of inconsistencies in current accounting practices of different types of nonbusiness organizations.

The Board has deferred activity in one aspect of the nonbusiness area—financial reporting by state and local governmental units—in light of discussions that currently are under way regarding the appropriate structure for setting governmental accounting standards. There is a need for better financial reporting by governments. Groups representing state and local government have expressed a willingness to look to the private sector for leadership in implementing a new standards-setting structure, though they have expressed a preference for a governmental accounting standards board apart from the FASB. The Financial Accounting Foundation is working with key groups—including representatives of the federal, state, county, and local levels of government, the Municipal Finance Officers Association, the AICPA, and others—to organize a GASB.

INDUSTRY ACCOUNTING PRINCIPLES

Traditionally, the FASB and its predecessors have tended to address accounting issues that affected a broad spectrum of companies. Specialized industry accounting principles were specified by others, most notably industry committees of the AICPA. By the mid-1970s, the AICPA had published over 40 industry accounting guides, industry audit guides, and statements of position that dealt with specialized industry accounting matters. As the FASB got into more and more projects, some of its conclusions necessarily conflicted with some of the AICPA guides and statements, but because those publications were not part of the FASB's official accounting literature, the FASB could not act to amend them. Also, practice questions relating to those guides were brought to the FASB for resolution, but again the pronouncements were not the FASB's to amend or interpret. Furthermore, the specialized industry principles in the AICPA guides and statements had a lesser degree of authority than did FASB standards, and in some cases the principles were not being complied with.

Because of those problems, and with the concurrence of the AICPA, the FASB began a series of projects to extract the specialized industry accounting principles from the AICPA documents, expose them for public comment as FASB exposure drafts, and adopt them as FASB standards. Thereafter, the FASB will be in a position to amend or interpret those standards as needed.

Most of the extraction projects have been completed. FASB standards now prevail in the franchise, record and music, cable television, motion picture, insurance, broadcasting, mortgage banking, and real estate industries. The long-term benefit of these projects will be a more coordinated, up-to-date, retrievable, and enforceable body of generally accepted accounting principles.

WILLINGNESS TO REEXAMINE ESTABLISHED STANDARDS

The FASB stands ready to interpret, amend, or replace any established standards when questions or problems are called to the Board's attention. Statement 52 on foreign currency translation (superseding Statement 8), the series of amendments to Statement 13 on lease accounting, and the Board's current projects on pension accounting, income tax accounting, and consolidations and the equity method are among the examples of the Board's willingness to take another look at a question.

Few, if any, standards have or ever will receive the unanimous endorsement of the Board's large and diverse constituencies, and some pressure to reconsider any established standard is almost inevitable. But it is reasonable to expect that the pressure will be reduced after the principal parts of the conceptual framework are in place and the Board has begun to rely on the framework in setting standards, because the concepts will tend to lessen some of the political and personal factors that influence the outcome of the standards-setting process.

EVOLVING STAFF RESPONSIBILITIES

During the Board's second era, the size of the technical staff doubled to around 40 professionals—a level that seems to be an optimal equilibrium for the next several years at least. In the second era, also, the staff have been given increased responsibilities in the standards-setting process. Staff members, rather than Board members, direct the work of task forces and are responsible for developing discussion memorandums and invitations to comment. The staff are responsible for preparing recommendations for the Board to consider on all technical issues and for leading Board discussion at open meetings. The FASB's program for providing implementation guidance through issuance of technical bulletins is a staff responsibility (subject to negative clearance by the Board). And the staff have taken an increased role in the public communications aspects of Board agenda projects.

This approach has worked well, allowing Board members to concentrate more on decision making, and there is no reason why this trend will not continue in the Board's second decade.

A FINAL OBSERVATION

The FASB is a joint effort of diverse private-sector groups, sometimes with conflicting points of view. Although the Board is often labeled by some as an arm of the AICPA or as a governmental agency, it is neither of those. It is independent and broadly supported. Its success during its first 10 years is due in no small measure to the confidence of its constituencies in private-sector standards setting and in their willingness to abide by FASB standards even if they do not always agree with them. A recent review of the FASB by the structure committee of the Foundation concluded that the FASB's operations are running efficiently and effectively, that the due process mechanisms are well designed and followed conscientiously, that the views of all parties at interest are carefully considered, and that the Board is dealing with the right issues.

No pronouncement of the FASB or any other standards setter can satisfy all of the people all of the time. But if they are satisfied with the standards-setting *process*—and by all indications the great majority of the FASB's constituents believe in the soundness and fairness of the process—the Board is on solid ground as it moves into its second decade.

The Rise of "Economic Consequences"

Stephen A. Zeff
Rice University

In the late 1960s, a literature began to build on the two related subjects of (a) the growing interest by third parties in the establishment of accounting standards, and (b) the impact of accounting standards, and especially changes in those standards, on the behavior of affected parties. In 1968, Moonitz wrote that

> The stake of nonprofessionals in the consequences of any given set of [accounting] principles is too great for them to accept the decisions of a body of technical experts on a voluntary basis, no matter how eminent those experts or how persuasive the research support for their findings [1968, p. 631].

He later urged the standard-setting bodies to cultivate allies, such as the Securities and Exchange Commission (SEC), in order to secure the enforcement of their pronouncements in the face of political action by "nonprofessionals" [1974, Chap. 7]. In 1969, Hawkins argued that "the time has come . . . to pay greater attention to the possible impact of accounting practices on people's actions" [1969, p. 21]. He referred not only to the possible dysfunctional effect of reported accounting figures on the behavior of managers, but also to the creation of an illusion of managerial performance when none exists [1969, p. 13].

By the mid-1970s, the literature on the politics of the standard-setting process, once a neglected subject, was growing apace [see, e.g., Stamp and Marley, 1970; Gerboth, 1973; Horngren, 1973; Moonitz, 1974; and Chatov, 1975], and the number of articles dealing with various phases of the social and economic consequences of accounting standards was also very much on the rise. Such terms as "feedback effects" [Prakash and Rappaport, 1976], "information inductance" [Prakash and Rappaport, 1977], "economic impact" [Buckley, 1976; Horngren, 1976; Rappaport, 1977; and FAF, 1977], and finally "economic consequences" [FASB, 1977a and FASB, 1978] began to populate the literature. At the same time, and not entirely by coincidence, articles began to appear on the

> fundamental questions of resource allocation and social choice [which] appear to underlie the question of choice among financial reporting alternatives [Demski, 1974, p. 232].

As suggested above, these two developing strains in the literature—the increasing involvement of "nonprofessionals" in the standard-setting process, and the economic (and social) consequences of the accounting standards themselves—are inextricably related. The very intervention by outside parties in the setting of standards appears to be due, in large measure, to their belief in the fact of economic consequences. The

From *Stanford Lectures in Accounting 1978*, pp. 11–19. Reprinted by permission of Stephen A. Zeff.

Editor's note: I gratefully acknowledge the suggestions of Alfred Rappaport, Lawrence Revsine, George J. Staubus, and Joseph G. San Miguel during the planning stage of writing this paper. Responsibility for what has emerged , however, is mine.

two themes were novel in the accounting literature, and it would not be an exaggeration to label the suggestion that standard-setting bodies take account of economic consequences as nothing less than revolutionary. Judging from accounting textbooks, treatises, articles, and earlier statements emitted from standard-setting bodies and committees of the American Accounting Association, one would have fairly concluded that conventional accounting wisdom supported a resolution of accounting controversies exclusively by reference to some combination of accounting theory, "accounting principles," and "fair presentation." To suggest that accounting policy makers should seriously consider the impact of proposed accounting standards on the micro- and macro-economic welfare of affected parties would have been, only a few years ago, a heresy. Until recently accounting policy making was either assumed to be neutral in its effects or, if not neutral, it was not responsible for those effects. Today neither assumption is unquestioningly accepted as valid, and the subject of social and economic consequences "has become *the* central contemporary issue in accounting" [AAA, 1977b, p. 4]. That the Financial Accounting Standards Board (FASB) has commissioned research papers on the economic consequences of selected standards [see, e.g., FASB, 1977b and c] and has held a conference devoted entirely to the subject [FASB, 1978] underscores the current importance of this mode of inquiry.

In these discussions, the terms "professional" and "nonprofessional" are troublesome. The phrase "accounting profession" is used in a variety of senses. In the United States, it is confined in the strictest sense to independent certified public accountants. But some might include controllers, internal auditors, management accountants, and government accountants. In Great Britain, the term typically refers to a broader array of qualified accountants than in the United States. In the Institute of Chartered Accountants in England and Wales, nonpracticing accountants played leadership roles in the development of accounting principles as long ago as the early 1940s, nonpracticing members have been members of the Council since 1943, and the first nonpracticing president was elected in 1968 [Zeff, 1972, pp. 7–9], while it was not until 1978 that the American Institute of Certified Public Accountants (AICPA) changed its by-laws to permit nonpractitioners to become officers. It is not my intention to endeavor to resolve this problem of definition, but only to suggest that the terms are open to ambiguity. In the ensuing discussion, I will use "third party" or "outside party" in place of "nonprofessional."

Accounting policy makers have been aware since at least the 1960s of the third-party intervention issue,[1] while the issue of economic consequences has surfaced only in the 1970s. Indeed, much of the history of the Accounting Principles Board (APB) during the 1960s was one of endeavoring to understand and cope with the third-party forces which were intervening in the standard-setting process. In the end, the inability of the APB to deal effectively with these forces led to its demise and the establishment in 1973 of the FASB.

---

[1] In this paper, I am chiefly concerned with third-party intervention in the standard setting for unregulated industries. Accounting policy makers in this country have been alive for several decades to the accounting implications of the rules and regulations of rate-making agencies in the energy, transportation, and communication industries. See, e.g., May [1943, Chaps. 7–8], Paton [1944], and Davidson [1952].

The true preoccupations of the intervening third parties have not always been made clear. When endeavoring to understand the third-party arguments, one must remember that prior to the 1970s the accounting model employed by the Committee on Accounting Procedure (CAP) and the APB was, formally at least, confined to technical accounting considerations (sometimes called "accounting principles" or "conceptual questions"), such as the measurement of assets, liabilities, and income, and the "fair presentation" of financial position and operations. The policy makers' sole concern was with the communication of financial information to actual and potential investors, for, indeed, their charter had been "granted" by the SEC, which itself had been charged by Congress to assure "full and fair disclosure" in reports to investors. Third-party interveners, therefore, would have had an obvious incentive to appeal to the accounting model being used by the policy makers, rather than implicitly suggest that the policy makers should adopt an economic consequences model preferred by the third parties.

When management intervened in the standard-setting process, therefore, its true position may well have been disguised. The following three-part classification of management arguments suggests the range of tactical rhetoric employed over the years:

1 Arguments couched in terms of the traditional accounting model, where management is genuinely concerned about unbiased and "theoretically sound" accounting measurements.

2 Arguments couched in terms of the traditional accounting model, where management is really seeking to advance its self-interest in the economic consequences of the contents of published reports.

3 Arguments couched in terms of the economic consequences in which management is self-interested.

If one accepts Johnson's dictum that it requires a "lively imagination" to believe that management is genuinely concerned with fair presentation when choosing between accounting alternatives [1966, p. 91; also see Moonitz, 1968, pp. 628–30], it could be concluded that Argument 1 has seldom been employed in third-party interventions. In recent years, particularly since the early 1970s, management appears to have become increasingly more candid, by electing Argument 3 in discussions with accounting policy makers. That the economic consequences issue was not scrutinized earlier than the 1970s was probably due, at least in part, to the habit of the APB to resolve, and to be seen to resolve, each controversy in the context of the traditional accounting model. Another possible explanation is the predominance of instances of Argument 2, which would have encouraged the Board to confine itself to the traditional model.

THE U.S. HISTORY OF THIRD-PARTY INTERVENTIONS OF THE "ECONOMIC CONSEQUENCES" VARIETY (CAP, APB, FASB)

It may be believed by some that third-party intervention coupled with the intrusion into accounting policy debates of economic-consequences considerations are of recent origin. Indeed, if one overlooks the unwitting support which a committee of the American Institute of [Certified Public] Accountants (AIA) gave to Congress as a pretext to impose LIFO inventory accounting on financial reporting [AIA, 1936, p. 465], the first evidence of economic-consequences reasoning in the pronouncements of American policy makers occurred as long ago as 1941. In Accounting Research Bulletin No. 11, "Corporate Accounting for Ordinary Stock Dividends," the CAP, in accordance with "proper accounting and corporate policy," required that fair market value be used to record the issuance of stock dividends where such market value was substantially in excess of book value [AIA, 1941, pp. 102–03]. George O. May, the *de facto* chairman of the CAP at that time, later wrote:

> The phrase 'proper accounting and corporate policy' indicates that the committee went beyond consideration of purely accounting questions. In the early stage of discussion such a step was not contemplated but as the study progressed, the committee came to feel strongly that it had an opportunity, in conjunction with the [New York] Stock Exchange, to take a step in the interest of *financial morality* and to safeguard against recurrence of abuses such as took place in and immediately prior to 1929 in connection with the issue of periodical stock dividends [May, 1952, p. 1; emphasis mine].

Evidently, both the New York Stock Exchange and a majority of the Committee on Accounting Procedure regarded periodic stock dividends as "objectionable" [May, 1941, p. 1], and the CAP acted to make it more difficult for corporations to sustain a series of such stock dividends out of their accumulated earnings. As far as I know, the United States is still the only country in which an accounting pronouncement requires that stock dividends be capitalized at the fair market value of the issued shares [see, e.g., *Price Waterhouse International,* 1975, Table 145], and this position was originally adopted in this country, at least in part, in order to produce an impact on the stock dividend policies of corporations.

A second evidence of economic consequences entering into the debates surrounding the establishment of accounting standards, this time involving management representations, occurred in 1947–48. It was the height of the postwar inflation, and several corporations had adopted replacement cost depreciation in their published financial statements [*Depreciation Policy When Price Levels Change,* 1948, Chap. 14]. Among the arguments employed in the debate involving the CAP were the possible implications for tax reform, the possible impact on wage bargaining, and the need to counteract criticisms of profiteering by big business [see, e.g., "Dual Accounting System Suggested for Depreciation," 1948; "Institute Committee Holds to Depreciation on Cost," 1948; *Changing Concepts of Business Income,* 1952, p. 64; *Depreciation Policy When Price Levels Change,* 1948, Chap. 13; Storey, 1964, pp. 34–38; and Paton, 1948].[2] Notwithstanding the pressures for accounting reform, the CAP reaffirmed its support of historical cost accounting for depreciation in Accounting Research Bulletin No. 33 and in a letter issued in October, 1948.

---

[2] In a survey conducted by the American Institute of [Certified Public] Accountants in 1948, the business executives who replied divided 31-22 in favor of reporting net income after subtracting cost of goods sold and depreciation expense on a current-cost basis *if that were accepted for tax purposes.* The executives divided 31-22 *against* such financial reporting if it were not accepted for tax purposes [AIA, 1948, pp. 1, 10].

A clear use of economic consequences occurred in 1958, when three subsidiaries of American Electric Power Company sued in the Federal courts to enjoin the AICPA from allowing the CAP to issue a letter saying that the Deferred Tax Credit account, as employed in the recently issued Accounting Research Bulletin No. 44 (Revised), should be classified as a liability [see *The AICPA Injunction Case,* 1960]. The three public utility companies were concerned that the SEC, under authority granted by the Public Utility Holding Company Act, would not permit them to issue debt securities in view of the unfavorable debt-to-equity ratios which the proposed reclassification would produce. The case reached the Supreme Court, where *certiorari* was denied. In the end, the clarifying letter was issued. Nonetheless, the SEC accommodated the public utility companies by consenting to exclude the Deferred Tax Credit from both liabilities and stockholders' equity for purposes of decisions taken under the Public Utility Holding Company Act [*SEC Administrative Policy...,* 1961, pp. 35–39].

Shortly after the creation of the APB, the accounting treatment of the investment tax credit exploded upon the scene. The three confrontations between the APB and the combined forces of industry and the administrations of Presidents Kennedy, Johnson, and Nixon have already been amply discussed in the literature [see Moonitz, 1966; Carey, 1970, pp. 98–104; and Zeff, 1972, pp. 178–80, 201–02, 219–21, and 326–27]. The Government's argument was not that the accounting deferral of the investment tax credit was bad accounting, but that it diluted the incentive effect of an instrument of fiscal policy.

In 1965, the subject of segmental reporting emerged from a hearing of the Senate Subcommittee on Antitrust and Monopoly on the economic effects of conglomerate mergers. The aim of the Senatorial inquiry was not to promote better accounting practices for investor use, but to provide the Subcommittee and other government policy makers with accounting data that would facilitate their assessment of the economic efficacy of conglomerate mergers. Company managements naturally looked upon such disclosures as potentially detrimental to their merger ambitions. Pressure applied by this powerful Subcommittee eventually forced the hand of the SEC to call for product-line disclosures in published financial reports. The repercussions of this initiative which had its origin in a Senate hearing room are still being felt [see, e.g., Plum and Collins, 1976].

In 1967–69, the APB responded to an anguished objection by the startled Investment Bankers Association of America (IBA) (known today as the Securities Industry Association) to a provision, once thought to be innocuous, in APB Opinion No. 10 which imputed a debt discount to convertible debt and debt issued with stock warrants. The IBA was concerned about the impact of the accounting procedure on the market for such securities. In APB Opinion No. 14, the Board rescinded its action in regard to convertible debt, while retaining the rest [see Zeff, 1972, pp. 202, 211].

During 1968–71, the banking industry opposed the inclusion of bad-debt provisions and losses on the sales of securities in the net income of commercial banks. Bankers believed that the new measure would reflect unfavorably on the performance of banks. Eventually, through a concerted effort by the APB, SEC, and the bank regulatory agencies, generally accepted accounting principles were made applicable to banks [see Carey, 1970, p. 134; Moonitz, 1974, p. 38–39; and Zeff, 1972, pp. 210–11].

In 1968–70, the APB struggled with the accounting for business combinations. It was flanked on the one side by the Federal Trade Commission and the Department of Justice, who favored the elimination of "pooling of interests" accounting in order to produce a slowing effect on the merger movement, and on the other side by merger-minded corporations who were fervent supporters of "pooling of interests" accounting. The APB, appearing to behave as if it were a pawn in a game of political chess, disenchanted many of its supporters, as it abandoned positions of principle in favor of an embarrassing series of pressure-induced compromises [see Chatov, 1975, pp. 212–22; and Zeff, 1972, pp. 212–16].

In 1971, the APB held public hearings on accounting for marketable equity securities, leases, and the exploration and drilling costs of companies in the petroleum industry. In all three areas, powerful industry pressures thwarted the Board from acting. The insurance industry was intensely concerned about the possible effects on its companies' stock prices of including the unrealized gains and losses on portfolio holdings in their income statements [see Horngren, 1973, pp. 63–64]. The leasing question was squelched after senators, representatives, and even the secretary of transportation responded to a letter-writing campaign by making pointed inquiries of the SEC and APB. The letter-writers raised the specter of injury which the Board's proposed action would cause to consumers and to the viability of companies in several key industries [see Savoie, 1974, p. 326].[3] The petroleum industry was unable to unite on a solution to the controversy over full costing v. successful-efforts costing, as it was alleged that a general imposition of the latter would adversely affect the fortunes of the small, independent exploration companies [see the testimony and submissions in *APB Public Hearing on Accounting and Reporting Practices in the Petroleum Industry,* 1972]. Using its considerable political might, the industry succeeded in persuading the Board to postpone consideration of the sensitive subject [see Savoie, 1974, p. 326].

On each of the occasions enumerated above, outside parties intervened in the standard-setting process by an appeal to criteria which transcended the traditional questions of accounting measurement and fair presentation. They were concerned instead with the economic consequences of the accounting pronouncements.

---

[3]Several of the letters sent to congressmen and senators were in all material respects identical, and although the addresses of those whose names appeared at the bottom of the letters were in different states, the secretary's initials (kh) and the type face used were all the same. These letter-writers uniformly claimed the following economic consequences of requiring lessees to capitalize leases:

1. Raise the cost of electric power to the public by an estimated $550 million yearly towards the end of the decade.
2. Raise the cost of freight transportation to industry and the public.
3. Reduce the inventory of railroad cars and locomotives.
4. Increase the costs of air fares to the public.
5. Damage the aerospace industry.
6. Raise the costs of all goods and services to the public.
7. Prevent many small and growing businesses from acquiring modern cost-cutting machinery and equipment.
8. Negatively affect our present adverse international balance of trade.

Economic consequences have been invoked with even greater intensity in the short life of the FASB. Such questions as accounting for research and development costs, self-insurance and catastrophe reserves, development stage companies, foreign currency fluctuations, leases, the restructuring of troubled debt,[4] domestic inflation and relative price changes, and the exploration and drilling costs of companies in the petroleum industry have provoked widespread interest in their economic consequences [see, e.g., Burns, 1976; AAA, 1977b, pp. 9–12; Rappaport, 1977, pp. 90, 92; FASB, 1978; U.S. Department of Energy, 1978].[5] The list is both extensive and impressive, and accounting academics are busily investigating the validity of claims that these and other accounting standards are empirically linked with the specified economic consequences.

RESPONSE OF STANDARD-SETTING BODIES TO THIRD-PARTY INTERVENTION AND "ECONOMIC CONSEQUENCES"

What have been the reactions of standard-setting bodies to (a) the intervention by outside parties, and (b) the claim that accounting standards should or should not be changed in order to avoid unhealthy economic consequences? The reactions have been of three kinds: procedural alone, procedural with apparent substantive effects, and explicitly substantive. The first two kinds of reactions predominated until the early 1970s [Zeff, 1972, pp. 167–208]:

1940s The CAP improved liaison with outside parties and expanded the circulation of early drafts and subcommittee reports.

1950s The CAP greatly enlarged the list of individuals and organizations to whom exposure drafts were sent.

1957–58 The AICPA appointed a prominent member of the Controllers Institute of America (now known as the Financial Executives Institute (FEI)) to the AICPA's

---

[4] At the Board's public hearing, some bankers warned of the dire economic consequences of requiring banks to write down their receivables following restructuring. Walter B. Wriston, chairman of Citicorp, said:

> If the banks that held the New York City obligations had been required to record an immediate write-off of say, 25 percent of principal as a result of restructuring, that restructuring just might not have happened. Several of the banks whose cooperation was essential might not have been able to afford it, not from an economic point of view, but in terms of the way that readers of financial statements would interpret such charged earnings. Some New York banks were at that time under severe earning pressure and the prospect of a significant additional charge with a corresponding reduction in capital would have been totally unacceptable [Wriston, 1977, pp. 69–70].

Yet the FASB, in its lengthy "Basis for Conclusions" in Statement No. 15 (in which the feared write-downs were not required), did not refer to bankers' claims about the economic consequences of requiring significant write-downs. Does that omission imply that the Board paid no attention to those assertions? Did the Board conduct any empirical research (as it did concerning the economic consequences claims raised in connection with Statement No. 7, on development stage enterprises) to determine whether there was adequate ground to sustain such claims?

[5] Evidence attesting to the attention given by the FASB to economic consequences issues may be found in the "Basis of Conclusions" sections of the applicable statements. In addition to companies and industry groups, government departments (such as the Department of Commerce, in Statement No. 7, and the Departments of Energy and Justice, in Statement No. 19) were actively involved in the discussion of economic consequences.

Special Committee on Research Program. (The Controllers Institute had complained about its small role in the standard-setting process, and the appointment of a controller to this important AICPA committee was perhaps the first instance in which an individual who was not a practitioner or academic was named to a policy-level AICPA committee.)

1959 The AICPA appointed two financial executives to the first APB. (This was evidently the first appointment of accountants in industry to an AICPA policy-making committee.)

1959–60 The APB began to appoint to the project advisory committees of its research studies some persons who were not members of the Board.

1964–65 For the first time, the APB employed subject-area committees to prepare drafts of proposed pronouncements, and non-Board members began to be appointed to the committees.

1964–65 The Board chairman and AICPA president urged interested organizations to collaborate more intensively with the Board, and several important bodies reorganized their liaison activities.

1960s The Board intensified the exposure process, increasing the number of organizations and individuals to whom exposure drafts were routinely sent. During one period it published exposure drafts in *The Journal of Accountancy*, and later sent drafts to all members of the Institute by separate mail. In the deliberations leading up to Opinions 16 and 17, the Board sent some 20,000 exposure drafts to a wide range of interested organizations and individuals, in addition to sending copies to all AICPA members.

mid-1960s The Board began to issue "mini-exposure" drafts to interested organizations in order to obtain their views before publishing its formal exposure drafts.

1965-66 The Board's subject-area committees began to hold informal meetings with the representatives of interested organizations.

1966–67 The AICPA created the position of executive vice president who was to be a spokesman to the press and at meetings of interested organizations.

1968 At the initiative of the AICPA, a two-day symposium was held to exchange ideas between the preparers and users of accounting information; representatives attended from the four co-sponsors: AICPA, FEI, Financial Analysts Federation, and Robert Morris Associates.

1969 In order to fortify the liaison with interested organizations, the Board began to hold symposia on the drafts of proposed pronouncements; attendance was by invitation and the proceedings were closed.

1971 In an effort to meet criticisms of its symposia (e.g., not all interested groups were invited), the Board began to hold public hearings, for which the subject-area committees prepared brief discussion memoranda.

It is evident from the series of steps taken by the AICPA and the APB that they endeavored to bring interested organizations more closely into the standard-setting process, hoping, one supposes, that these organizations would be satisfied that their opinions were given full consideration before the final issuance of opinions. These accommodations were, however, of a procedural sort, although it is possible that these outside opinions did have an impact on the substantive content of some of the resulting opinions. It would appear that the APB was at least somewhat influenced by economic consequences in its prolonged deliberations leading to the issuance of Opinions 16 and 17 [Wyatt, 1977, pp. 92–93]. Yet it is interesting that during the public hearings in 1971 on marketable equity securities and the accounting practices of companies in the petroleum industry, in which management representatives on several occasions asserted economic consequences as relevant considerations, none of the members of the Board's subject-area committees asked questions about the empirical basis for those assertions or, indeed, inquired about their relevance to the setting of accounting standards [see *Proceedings,* 1971; and *A PB Public Hearing...,* 1972].

In view of the fact that it was the APB's inability to cope with the pressures brought by outside organizations which led to its demise, it is noteworthy that the FASB includes the Financial Executives Institute among its co-sponsors. In my opinion, the incorporation of the FEI in the formal structure of the FASB is one of the most significant advantages which the FASB possesses in relation to its predecessor.[6] Horngren, an APB member in its final years, has said,

> The FEI as an institutional body representing management, by and large, was opposed to the Board, particularly in the latter years, on almost every issue....[T]he FEI seemed in favor of scrapping the APB; to the extent that it could be an institutional force it helped in its termination. They felt...that they should have more of a direct voice in the formation of accounting principles [Horngren, 1974, p. 95].

The procedural machinery established for the FASB is even more elaborate than that which existed in the final years of the APB. The object of these additional procedures has been to expand and intensify the interaction between the Board and interested outside parties, notably companies, industry associations, and government departments and agencies. Task forces drawn from a broad spectrum of interested groups are appointed prior to the preparation of each discussion memorandum. The memorandum itself is much bulkier than the modest document which the APB had issued prior to its public hearings; it contains a neutral discussion of the entire gamut of policy issues which bear on the resolution of the controversy before the Board. A Financial Accounting Standards Advisory Council (FASAC), composed of representatives of a wide array of interested groups, was appointed to be a sounding board for the FASB. The Board itself has been composed of members drawn from accounting practice, the universities, companies, and government— again, so that it would be responsive—and would appear to be responsive—to the concerns of those "constituencies." In an effort to persuade skeptics of the merit of its recommendations, the Board includes in its statements a lengthy explanation of the criteria, arguments, and empirical considerations which it used to fashion the recommended standards.

Following criticism from within the profession of the Board's operations and procedures, the Financial Accounting Foundation (FAF), the Board's parent, conducted a study in 1977 of the entire Board operation. Among its many recom-

---

[6] The inclusion of the FEI could conceivably become the undoing of the Board. If the FEI were to lose confidence in the Board, it is possible that many of the companies which now contribute to the Financial Accounting Foundation might decline to continue doing so, provoking a financial crisis that could threaten the Board's viability.

mendations were proposals that the Board expand its formal and informal contacts with interested groups and that it include an economic impact analysis in important exposure drafts [FAF, 1977, pp. 51, 52]. On this latter point, the FAF's Structure Committee concluded:

> The Board need not be unduly influenced by the possibility of an economic impact, but it should consider both the possible costs and the expected benefits of a proposal [FAF, 1977, p. 51].

In addition, the Structure Committee recommended actions that would strengthen the roles of the task forces and FASAC [FAF, 1977, pp. 23–25]. In 1978, under pressure from Congress, the Board began to conduct virtually all of its formal meetings (including those of the FASAC) "in the sunshine."

The history of the APB and FASB is one of a succession of procedural steps taken to bring the Board's deliberations into closer proximity to the opinions and concerns of interested third parties. As in the case of the APB, it is possible that an effect of these more elaborate procedures has been a change in the substance of the FASB's conclusions and recommendations.

By the middle 1970s, however, it was decided that the FASB should add economic (and social) consequences to the substantive issues which it normally addresses. The inclusion of "Probable Economic or Social Impact" among the "other qualities of useful information" in the Board's Conceptual Framework discussion memorandum [FASB, 1976, paras. 367–71], coupled with the Board's announcement of its interest in empirical studies of economic consequences [FASB, 1977a] and the recommendation of the FAF Structure Committee that the Board inform itself adequately on the "various impacts its pronouncements might have" [FAF, 1977, p. 31] collectively confirm this new direction. The issue of economic consequences has, therefore, changed from one having only procedural implications for the standard-setting process to one which is now firmly a part of the standard setters' substantive policy framework.

WHAT FACTORS HAVE CONTRIBUTED TO THE EMERGENCE OF "ECONOMIC CONSEQUENCES" AS A SUBSTANTIVE ISSUE?

Economic consequences has finally become accepted as a valid substantive policy issue for a number of reasons:

• The tenor of the times. The decade of the 1970s is clearly one in which American society is holding its institutions responsible for the social, environmental, and economic consequences of their actions, and the crystallized public opinion on this subject eventually became evident (and relevant) to those interested in the accounting standard-setting activity.

• The sheer intractability of the accounting problems being addressed. Since the mid-1960s, the APB and FASB have been taking up difficult accounting questions on which industry positions have been well entrenched. To some degree, companies which are sensitive to the way their performance is evaluated through the medium of reported earnings, have permitted their decision-making behavior to be influenced by their perceptions of how such behavior will be seen through the prism of accounting earnings. Still other such companies have tailored their accounting practices to reflect their economic performance in the best light—and the managers are evidently loathe to change their decision-making behavior in order to accommodate newly imposed accounting standards. This would also be a concern to managers who are being paid under incentive compensation plans [see Rappaport, 1978].

• The enormity of the impact. Several of the issues which have been facing the APB and FASB in recent years have portended such a high degree of impact on either the volatility or level of earnings and other key financial figures and ratios that the Board can no longer discuss the proposed accounting treatments without encountering incessant arguments over the probable economic consequences. Particularly apt examples are accounting for foreign exchange fluctuations, domestic inflation and relative price changes, and the explorations and drilling costs of companies in the petroleum industry.

• The growth in the information economics/social choice, behavioral, income smoothing, and decision usefulness literatures in accounting. Recent writings in the information economics/social choice literature have provided a broad analytical framework within which the problems or economic consequences may be conceptualized. Beginning with Stedry [1959], the literature on the behavioral implications of accounting numbers has grown significantly, drawing the attention of researchers and policy makers to the importance of considering the effects of accounting information. The literature on income smoothing has suggested the presence of a managerial motive for influencing the measurement of earnings trends. Finally, the decision usefulness literature, although it is confined to the direct users of accounting information, has served to lessen the inclination of accountants to argue over the inherent "truth" of different accounting incomes, and instead to focus on the use of information by those who receive accounting reports [AAA, 1977a, pp. 5–29].

• The insufficiency of the procedural reforms adopted by the APB and FASB. Notwithstanding the succession of procedural steps which both Boards have taken to provide outside parties with a forum for expressing their views, the claims of economic consequences—and the resulting criticisms of the Boards' pronouncements—continue unabated. The conclusion has evidently been reached that procedural remedies alone will not meet the problem.

• The Moss and Metcalf investigations. By the middle of 1976, it was known that Rep. John E. Moss and Senator Lee Metcalf were conducting investigations of the performance of the accounting profession, including their standard-setting activities, and it could have reasonably been inferred that the responsiveness of the standard-setting bodies to the economic and social effects of their decisions would be an issue.

• The increasing importance to corporate managers of the earnings figure in capital-market transactions. Especially in the 1960s, when capital markets were intensely competitive and the merger movement was fast-paced, the earnings figure came to be viewed as an important element of managerial strategy and tactics.

• Accounting figures came to be viewed as an instrument of social control. The social control of American enterprise has been well known in the rate-regulated energy, transportation, and communications fields, but in recent years the earnings figure has, to an increasing degree, been employed as a control device on a broader scale.[7] Examples are fiscal incentives (such as the investment tax credit and redefinitions of taxable income which diverge from accounting income) which have an influence on debates surrounding financial reporting,[8] the price-control mechanism of Phase II [Lanzillotti et al., 1975, pp. 73–77; and Grayson and Neeb, 1974, pp. 71–76], and the data base which is contemplated by the Energy Policy and Conservation Act of 1975.

• The realization that outsiders could influence the outcome of accounting debates. Prior to the 1960s, accounting controversies were rarely reported in the financial press, and it was widely believed that accounting was a constant, if not a parameter, in the management of business operations. With the publicity given to the accounting for the investment credit in 1962–63, to the fractious dialogue within the AICPA in 1963–64 over the authority of the APB, and to other accounting disagreements involving the APB, managers and other outside parties came to realize that accounting may be a variable after all—that the rules of accounting were not unyielding or even unbending.

• The growing use of Argument 3 (see above) in accounting debates. Mostly for the reasons enumerated above, outside parties began to discard the pretense that their objections to proposed changes in accounting standards were solely, or even primarily, a function of differences over the proper interpretation of accounting principles. True reasons came out into the open, and accounting policy makers could no longer ignore their implications.

It is interesting that economic consequences have become an important issue at a time when accounting and finance academics have been arguing that the American capital markets are efficient with respect to publicly available information and, moreover, that the market cannot be "fooled" by the use of different accounting methods to reflect the same economic reality [see, e.g., Beaver, 1973].

IMPLICATIONS FOR THE FASB

What are the implications of the "economic consequences" movement for the FASB? It has become clear that political agencies (such as government departments and congressional committees) expect accounting standard setters to take explicitly into consideration the possible adverse consequences of proposed accounting standards. This expectation appears to be strongest where the consequences are thought to be significant and widespread—and especially where they might impinge on economic and social policies being pursued by the government. In these instances, the FASB must show that it has studied the possible consequences and that its recommended standards either are innocent of such consequences or that the benefits from implementing the standards outweigh the possible adverse consequences. Where the claimed consequences have implications for economic or social policies of national importance, the FASB should not be surprised if a political resolution is imposed by outside forces.

---

[7]D R Scott, though writing in a different context, nonetheless was prophetic in his prediction that accounting would increasingly be used as a means of social control [1931, esp. Chap. 14].

[8]The "required tax conformity" issue of the early 1970s [see Zeff, 1972, pp. 218–19] is another instance.

But to say that any significant economic consequences should be studied by the Board does not imply that the accounting model—accounting principles and fair presentation—should be dismissed as the principal guiding factor in the Board's determination. The FASB is respected as a body of accounting experts, and it should focus its attention primarily on matters on which its expertise will be acknowledged. While some may suggest that accounting standards should be determined only with regard to their consequences for economic and social welfare, the FASB would assure the termination of its existence if it were to begin to make decisions primarily on other than accounting grounds.

The Board is thus faced with a dilemma which requires a delicate balancing of accounting and nonaccounting variables. Although its decisions should rest—and be seen to rest—chiefly on accounting considerations, it must also study—and be seen to study—the possible adverse economic and social consequences of its proposed actions. As in all micro- and macro-economic policy making, the identification and measurement of possible economic and social repercussions will be exceedingly difficult tasks.[9] In order to deal adequately with the consequences issue, the Board would be wise to develop a staff of competent analysts from allied disciplines, notably economics.

Economic consequences bid fair to be the most challenging accounting issue of the 1970s. We have entered an era in which economic and social consequences may no longer by ignored as a substantive issue in the setting of accounting standards.

[9]For a discussion of some of these problems of implementation, see Swieringa [1976, pp. 31–35].

REFERENCES

The AICPA Injunction Case: Re: ARB No. 44 (Revised), Cases in Public Accounting Practice No. 1 (Chicago: Arthur Andersen & Co., 1960).

APB Public Hearing on Accounting and Reporting Practices in the Petroleum Industry, Cases in Public Accounting Practice No. 10 (Chicago: Arthur Andersen & Co., 1972).

American Accounting Association, Committee on Concepts and Standards for External Financial Reports, *Statement on Accounting Theory and Theory Acceptance* (Sarasota, Florida: AAA, 1977a).

American Accounting Association, *Report of the Committee on the Social Consequences of Accounting Information* (Sarasota, Florida: AAA, 1977b).

American Institute of Accountants, *1936 Year Book of the American Institute of Accountants* (New York: AIA, 1937).

American Institute of Accountants, *Accounting Research Bulletins,* No. 11, "Corporate Accounting for Ordinary Stock Dividends" (New York: AIA, 1941), pp. 99–106.

American Institute of Accountants, "Accounting and Changing Price Levels," unpublished preliminary report, September 1, 1948, 48 pages.

Beaver, William H., "What Should Be the FASB's Objectives?" *Journal of Accountancy,* August 1973, pp. 49–56.

Buckley, John W., "The FASB and Impact Analysis," *Management Accounting* (U.S.), April 1976, pp. 13–17.

Burns, Joseph M. *Accounting Standards and International Finance, with Special Reference to Multinationals* (Washington, D.C.: American Enterprise Institute for Public Policy Research, 1976).

Carey, John L., *The Rise of the Accounting Profession: To Responsibility and Authority,
1937–1969* (New York: American Institute of Certified Public Accountants, 1970).

Changing Concepts of Business Income, Report of Study Group on Business Income (New
York: The Macmillan Company, 1952).

Chatov, Robert, *Corporate Financial Reporting: Public or Private Control?* (New York: The
Free Press, 1975).

Davidson, Sidney, *The Plant Accounting Regulations of the Federal Power Commission*
(Ann Arbor: University of Michigan Press, 1952).

Demski, Joel S., "Choice among Financial Reporting Alternatives," *The Accounting Review,*
April 1974, pp. 221–32.

Depreciation Policy When Price Levels Change (New York: Controllership Foundation,
Inc., 1948).

"Dual Accounting System Suggested for Depreciation," *The Journal of Accountancy,*
February 1948, p. 103.

Financial Accounting Foundation, Structure Committee, *The Structure of Establishing
Financial Accounting Standards* (1977).

Financial Accounting Standards Board, *Conceptual Framework for Financial Accounting
and Reporting: Elements of Financial Statements and Their Measurement,* Discussion
Memorandum (Stamford, Connecticut: FASB, 1976).

———*Status Report,* No. 45 (February 7, 1977a).

———*Status Report,* No. 47 (April 19, 1977b).

———*Status Report,* No. 50 (July 7, 1977c).

———*Conference on the Economic Consequences of Financial Accounting Standards*
(Stamford, Connecticut: FASB, 1978).

Gerboth, Dale L., "Research, Intuition, and Politics in Accounting Inquiry," *The Accounting
Review,* July 1973, pp. 475–82.

Grayson, C. Jackson, Jr., and Louis Neeb, *Confessions of a Price Controller* (Homewood,
Illinois: Dow Jones-Irwin, Inc., 1974).

Hawkins, David F., "Behavioral Implications of Generally Accepted Accounting Principles,"
California Management Review, Winter 1969, pp. 13–21.

Horngren, Charles T., "The Marketing of Accounting Standards," *Journal of Accountancy,*
October 1973, pp. 61–66.

———,edited dialogue, in Thomas J. Burns (ed.), *Accounting in Transition: Oral Histories
of Recent U.S. Experience* (Columbus: College of Administrative Science, The Ohio
State University, 1974), pp. 82–100.

———,"Will the FASB Be Here in the 1980s?," *Journal of Accountancy,* November 1976, pp.
90–96.

"Institute Committee Holds to Depreciation on Cost," Editorial, *The Journal of Accountancy,*
November 1948, pp. 353–54.

Johnson, Charles E., "Management's Role in External Accounting Measurements," in
Robert K. Jaedicke, Yuji Ijiri, and Oswald Nielsen (eds.), *Research in Accounting
Measurement* (American Accounting Association, 1966), pp. 88–100.

Lanzillotti, Robert F., Mary T. Hamilton, and R. Blaine Roberts, *Phase II in Review: The
Price Commission Experience* (Washington, D.C.: The Brookings Institution, 1975).

May, George O., letter to J.S. Seidman, July 14, 1941 (Deposited in National Office Library,
Price Waterhouse & Co., New York), 2 pages.

———,*Financial Accounting: A Distillation of Experience* (New York: The Macmillan
Company, 1943).

———,letter to John B. Inglis, August 5, 1952 (Deposited in the National Office Library,
Price Waterhouse & Co., New York), 2 pages.

Moonitz, Maurice, "Some Reflections on the Investment Credit Experience," *Journal of Accounting Research,* Spring 1966, pp. 47–61.

———,"Why Is It So Difficult to Agree upon a Set of Accounting Principles?," *The Australian Accountant,* November 1968, pp. 621–31.

———,*Obtaining Agreement on Standards in the Accounting Profession,* Studies in Accounting Research No. 8 (Sarasota, Florida: American Accounting Association, 1974).

Paton, William A., "Accounting Policies of the Federal Power Commission—A Critique," *Journal of Accountancy,* June 1944, pp. 432–60.

———,"Accounting Procedures and Private Enterprise," *The Journal of Accountancy,* April 1948, p. 278–91.

Plum, Charles W., and Daniel W. Collins, "Business Segment Reporting," in James Don Edwards and Homer A. Black (eds.), *The Modern Accountant's Handbook* (Homewood, Illinois: Dow Jones-Irwin, Inc., 1976), pp. 469–511.

Prakash, Prem, and Alfred Rappaport, "The Feedback Effects of Accounting," *Business Week,* January 12, 1976, p. 12.

———,"Information Inductance and Its Significance for Accounting," *Accounting, Organizations and Society* (1977, No. 1), pp. 29–38.

Price Waterhouse International, A Survey in 46 Countries: Accounting Principles and Reporting Practices ([n.p.], PWI, 1975).

Proceedings of Hearing on Accounting for Equity Securities, Accounting Principles Board (New York: American Institute of Certified Public Accountants, 1971), Section A—Transcript.

Rappaport, Alfred, "Economic Impact of Accounting Standards—Implications for the FASB," *The Journal of Accountancy,* May 1977, pp. 89–98.

———,"Executive Incentives vs. Corporate Growth," *Harvard Business Review,* July-August 1978, pp.81–88.

SEC Administrative Policy Re: Balance-Sheet Treatment of Deferred Income-Tax Credits, Cases in Public Accounting Practice Nos. 5 and 6 (Chicago: Arthur Andersen & Co., 1961), 2 vols.

Savoie, Leonard M., "Accounting Attitudes," in Robert R. Sterling (ed.), *Institutional Issues in Public Accounting* (Lawrence, Kansas: Scholars Book Co., 1974), pp. 317–27.

Scott, D R, *The Cultural Significance of Accounts* (New York: Henry Holt & Company, 1931).

Stamp, Edward, and Christopher Marley, *Accounting Principles and the City Code* (London: Butterworths, 1970).

Stedry, Andrew C., *Budget Control and Cost Behavior* (Englewood Cliffs, New Jersey: Prentice-Hall, Inc., 1959).

Storey, Reed K., *The Search for Accounting Principles* (New York: American Institute of Certified Public Accountants, 1964).

Swieringa, Robert J., "Consequences of Financial Accounting Standards," *The Accounting Forum,* May 1976, p. 25–39.

U.S. Department of Energy, Comments before the Securities and Exchange Commission, "Accounting Practices—Oil and Gas Producers—Financial Accounting Standards," unpublished memorandum, April 3, 1978, 53 pages.

Wriston, Walter B., Transcript of Public Hearing on FASB Discussion Memorandum on Accounting by Debtors and Creditors When Debt Is Restructured (1977, Volume 1, Part 2), pp. 57–76.

Wyatt, Arthur R , "The Economic Impact of Financial Accounting Standards," *Journal of Accountancy,* October 1977, pp. 92–94.

Zeff, Stephen A., *Forging Accounting Principles in Five Countries: A History and an Analysis of Trends* (Champaign, Illinois: Stipes Publishing Company, 1972).

The Politicization of Accounting

David Solomons
University of Pennsylvania

There was once a time, not so many years ago, when accounting could be thought of as an essentially nonpolitical subject. If it was not as far removed from politics as was mathematics or astronomy, it was at least no more political than psychology or surveying or computer technology or statistics. Even in areas of accounting such as taxation, which might be thought to be most relevant to questions of public policy, practitioners were generally content to confine themselves to technical issues without getting involved as accountants in the discussion of tax policy.

Today, to judge from current discussions of the standard-setting process, accounting can no longer be thought of as nonpolitical. The numbers that accountants report have, or at least are widely thought to have, a significant impact on economic behavior. Accounting rules therefore affect human behavior. Hence, the process by which they are made is said to be political. It is then only a short step to the assertion that such rules are properly to be made in the political arena, by counting heads and deciding accounting issues by some voting mechanism.

There are several articulate spokesmen for this point of view. Dale Gerboth writes that "a politicization of accounting rule-making [is] not only inevitable, but just. In a society committed to democratic legitimization of authority, only politically responsive institutions have the right to command others to obey their rules."[1] And, in another passage from the same article, Gerboth says, "When a decision-making process depends for its success on public confidence, the critical issues are not technical; they are political.... In the face of conflict between competing interests, rationality as well as prudence lies not in seeking final answers, but rather in compromise—essentially a political process."[2]

In the same vein, Charles Horngren writes that

> the setting of accounting standards is as much a product of political action as of flawless logic or empirical findings. Why? Because the setting of standards is a social decision. Standards place restrictions on behavior; therefore, they must be accepted by the affected parties. Acceptance may be forced or voluntary or some of both. In a democratic society, getting acceptance is an exceedingly complicated process that requires skillful marketing in a political arena.[3]

Robert May and Gary Sundem take a similar position:

> In practice as well as in theory, the social welfare impact of accounting reports apparently is recognized. Therefore it is no surprise that the [Financial Accounting Standards Board] is a political body and, consequently, that the process of selecting an acceptable accounting

From *The Journal of Accountancy,* (November 1978), pp. 65–72. Reprinted by permission of The American Institute of Certified Public Accountants. Copyright © 1978 by David Solomons.
    [1]Dale L. Gerboth, "Research, Intuition, and Politics in Accounting Inquiry," *Accounting Review,* July 1973, p. 481.
    [2]Ibid. p. 479.
    [3]Charles T. Horngren, "The Marketing of Accounting Standards," JofA, Oct. 73, p. 61.

alternative is a political process. If the social welfare impact of accounting policy decisions were ignored, the basis for the existence of a regulatory body would disappear. Therefore, the FASB must consider explicitly political (i.e., social welfare) aspects as well as accounting theory and research in its decisions.[4]

Other voices that call for an explicit recognition of the probable economic and social impact of a new accounting standard are not always easily distinguished from those asserting that political considerations should determine what the standard should be.[5] However, these two views should not be confused.

The structure committee of the Financial Accounting Foundation grappled with the question of the political nature of the standard-setting task in *The Structure of Establishing Financial Accounting Standards.* On the nature of the standard-setting process, it says:

> The process of setting accounting standards can be described as democratic because like all rule-making bodies the Board's right to make rules depends ultimately on the consent of the ruled. But because standard setting requires some perspective it would not be appropriate to establish a standard based solely on a canvass of the constituents. Similarly, the process can be described as legislative because it must be deliberative and because all views must be heard. But the standard setters are expected to represent the entire constituency as a whole and not be representatives of a specific constituent group. The process can be described as political because there is an educational effort involved in getting a new standard accepted. But it is not political in the sense that an accommodation is required to get a statement issued.[6]

There is something here to please everyone. Yet the committee does finally come out on the side of the angels: "We have used the word constituency to indicate that the FASB is accountable to everyone who has an interest. We are not suggesting that the Board members are in place to represent them or that the standards must necessarily be based on a numerical consensus."[7]

That accounting influences human behavior, if only because it conveys information, is obvious enough, though research into the workings of "the efficient market" has cast doubt on some of the supposed results of accounting choices. There are, without question, political aspects of accounting. There are similarly political aspects of physics, which result in enormous expenditures on research into nuclear energy and weaponry. Geology, in its concern with the world's reserves of fossil fuels, obviously has political implications. Research into sickle cell anemia became a political question when the heavy incidence of this disease among black Americans came to light. There are very few areas of human knowledge which are devoid of political significance. But that does not mean that the processes by which knowledge is advanced or by which new applications are found for old knowledge are themselves

[4] Robert G. May and Gary L. Sundem, "Research for Accounting Policy: An Overview," *Accounting Review,* October 1976, p. 750.

[5] John Buckley (in "FASB and Impact Analysis," *Management Accounting,* April 1976, p. 13) straddles this line most uncomfortably. His article has been thought to support politically slanted standards although he nowhere explicitly says that he does.

[6] Structure committee, *The Structure of Establishing Financial Accounting Standards* (Stamford, Conn.: FAF, April 1977), p. 19.

[7] Ibid.

political processes in the sense in which that term is usually understood. Political motives for asking a question may be entirely appropriate. A politically motivated answer may or may not be appropriate. It obviously depends on the nature of the question.

It may be useful to look more carefully at the part which politics should and should not play in accounting standard setting. The future of the FASB may depend on a better understanding of that issue. Indeed, the very credibility of accounting itself may be at stake.

ACCOUNTING AND NATIONAL GOALS

The most extreme expression, so far as I am aware, of the view that political considerations should enter into the formulation of accounting standards—not merely into the choice of accounting questions to be studied but also into the formulation of the standards themselves—is to be found in a lecture given in New York in November 1973 by Professor David Hawkins. He noted that Congress and the executive branch of the federal government were

> becoming more and more aware of the behavioral aspects of corporate reporting and its macro economic implications. Increasingly, I believe, these policy makers will demand ...that the decisions of those charged with determining what constitutes approved corporate reporting standards result in corporate reporting standards that will lead to individual economic behavior that is consistent with the nation's macro economic objectives.... This awareness on the part of economic planners brings accounting standards setting into the realm of political economics.[8]

Events since 1973 have not shown any diminution in this awareness. The question is whether this is to be regarded as a threat to the integrity of accounting or as an opportunity, perhaps even an obligation, on the part of accountants to cooperate with government in furthering its economic policy. Hawkins left us in no doubt where he stood in this matter:

> The [FASB's] objectives must be responsive to many more considerations than accounting theory or our notions of economically useful data....Corporate reporting standards should result in data that are useful for economic decisions *provided that the standard is consistent with the national macro economic objectives and the economic programs designed to reach these goals.*[9]

And, as if that were not enough, he added that "because the [FASB] has the power to influence economic behavior it has an obligation to support the government's economic plans."[10]

In that last passage, the word "because" is noteworthy, implying as it does that the power to influence economic behavior always carries with it an obligation to support the government's plans. Even if the matter under discussion were, say,

---

[8] David F. Hawkins, "Financial Accounting, the Standards Board and Economic Development," one of the 1973–74 Emanuel Saxe Distinguished Lectures in Accounting, published by the Bernard M. Baruch College, City University of New York, April 1975, pp. 7–8.
[9] Ibid. pp. 17, 9–10.
[10] Ibid. p. 11.

pricing policy or wage policy or some aspect of environmental protection, the assertion would be open to argument. In relation to accounting, where the end product is a system of measurement, the position which Hawkins urges on the FASB could, I believe, threaten the integrity of financial reporting and deprive it of whatever credibility it now has.

There is no question as to the sensitivity of some, indeed most, of the issues that have been or are now on the agenda of the FASB or its predecessors, and of course this sensitivity stems from the fact that standards dealing with those issues have influenced or will influence behavior. This can only mean that there is widespread skepticism about the "efficient market" hypothesis. The financial community is not indifferent to the accounting rules imposed on it by the FASB. It is not the purpose of this article to explore the nature of this concern.[11] It will be enough to recognize that the FASB's constituents think it matters whether leases are capitalized or not, whether foreign currency transactions are accounted for by one method or another, whether contingencies are provided for by charges against income or by allowing retained earnings to accumulate. These questions do not affect the amount of information that is disclosed but simply the way in which these economic phenomena are reported; yet this fact does not desensitize them. Perhaps investors *are* naive. Only on the basis of such an assumption (and on the assumption that no new information will be disclosed by a politically motivated standard) is the impact of politics on accounting standards worth discussing at all.

THE ECONOMIC IMPACT OF ACCOUNTING STANDARDS

Few if any accounting standards are without some economic impact. The requirement that U.S. companies write off purchased goodwill is said to give an advantage to foreign companies in bidding for American businesses because, not being subject to the same accounting requirement, they can afford to offer a higher price. FASB Statement no. 2, *Accounting for Research and Development Costs,* which requires that R&D be expensed as incurred, has been said to constitute a threat to technological progress, especially by smaller companies that may be contemplating seeking access to the capital market and will therefore want to show good profits before doing so.[12] FASB Statement no. 5, *Accounting for Contingencies,* by greatly restricting the circumstances in which an estimated loss from a loss contingency can be accrued by a charge to income, is said to have caused U.S. insurance companies to reinsure risks for which previously they would have relied on self-insurance.

---

[11] Yet one cannot ignore the troublesome paradox posed by the numerous empirical studies which have shown "that the capital market does distinguish between [accounting] changes that appear to be reporting changes of no economic importance and those that appear to have substantive economic implications." (Nicholas J. Gonedes and Nicholas Dopuch, "Capital Market Equilibrium, Information Production, and Selecting Accounting Techniques: Theoretical Framework and Review of Empirical Work," *Studies on Financial Accounting Objectives: 1974,* supplement to vol. 12 of the *Journal of Accounting Research.*) If the market can "see through" accounting changes that result from changes in standards, why do they generate so much heat?

[12] This argument, when the treatment of R&D was still on the FASB's agenda, led Hawkins to say, in his 1973 Emanuel Saxe Lecture (p. 14), "I do not believe the Board can eliminate the alternative capitalization." Events proved him wrong.

One of the most sensitive standards has been that dealing with foreign currency translation (Statement no. 8, *Accounting for the Translation of Foreign Currency Transactions and Foreign Currency Financial Statements*). Under the so-called temporal method mandated by the board, monetary assets and liabilities of a foreign subsidiary of a U.S. corporation have to be translated, for consolidation purposes, at the rate of exchange current at the balance sheet date. Assets which, in accordance with generally accepted accounting principles, are carried at cost or cost less depreciation have to be translated at the rate current at the time they were acquired. Exchange gains and losses, realized and unrealized, have to be brought into the income statement. For companies that formerly used a current/noncurrent classification, the important changes lie in the treatment of inventories and of long-term debt. Inventories, as current assets, were formerly carried at the current rate and are now carried at the historical rate; long-term debt, as a noncurrent liability, was formerly carried at the historical rate and now, as a monetary item, is carried at the current rate. Moreover, unrealized translation gains, formerly kept out of the income statement, now have to be brought in. The result has been greatly to increase the volatility of the reported earnings of companies with important foreign operations. Criticism of Statement no. 8 has focused on this increased volatility rather than on whether the new rules result in a better or worse representation of financial performance.

Whatever one may think about the merits of FASB Statement no. 19, *Financial Accounting and Reporting by Oil and Gas Producing Companies,* there can be little doubt that the Securities and Exchange Commission would not have acted as it did at the end of August to overrule this standard if there had not been political pressure from certain oil and gas companies which felt that they would be injured by the mandatory use of the "successful efforts" method of costing. It will be some time before the full effect of this action on the standard-setting process can be seen in its true light.

Numerous other politically sensitive accounting issues could be cited, but none has received as much attention as accounting for inflation, for none has such widespread potential repercussions throughout the business world. Each method which has been proposed to replace or to modify traditional methods would affect different companies differently, making some look more prosperous than they are under present methods and others less prosperous. For example, current purchasing power adjustments to historical cost accounting (general price level accounting) tend to make utilities with heavy debt capital look better off; replacement cost accounting tends to make companies with a large investment in depreciable assets, such as steel companies, look relatively less profitable. A system using exit values (e.g., continuously contemporary accounting, or COCOA) would make firms using assets that are not readily salable look bad. Though the protracted arguments about the relative merits of these and other rival systems have not generally overtly recognized the vested interests that stand to gain or lose by the way the argument goes, the political implications of inflation accounting have probably had as much responsibility for the difficulty in reaching agreement on the direction in which to move as have the technical problems involved.

In some of these instances, notably those concerning contingency reserves and foreign currency translations, critics of the FASB are asserting that economic behavior, such as reinsurance or hedging, which would not have been rational under the old accounting rules becomes rational under the new ones. Such an assertion is difficult to defend because the new rules have not changed the underlying cash flows or the risks attached to them. Only if significance is attached exclusively to "the bottom line," rather than to the present value of the enterprise, can the change in behavior be defended.

MEASUREMENT AND POLITICS

The above examples will serve to illustrate some of the points of contact between accounting and politics. Many more could be cited. Indeed, because standards need to be set mainly in areas where there is controversy, it is highly probable that in every case someone will find the new treatment less favorable than the status quo and there is constantly a temptation for such people to rush off to their legislative representatives to get the government to interfere.[13] That sort of initiative represents the gravest threat on the horizon to the private control of standard setting.

If we are looking for ways to achieve political ends by tinkering with methods of measurement, there is plenty of scope outside the accounting field. Indeed, the danger has already been observed in other areas. For instance, the index of retail prices has a powerful effect on wage settlements in many industries. There is nothing absolute about a price index. The number obtained depends on the choice of base year, the items chosen for inclusion in the market basket and the weights attached to the items in constructing the index. A statistician who agreed with Hawkins about the responsibilities of those concerned with measurement could easily construct an index which would damp down price changes and could take credit for aiding in the fight against inflation.[14]

I have suggested elsewhere[15] that one way of reducing the traffic accident rate would be for highway authorities to lower the average speed by arranging to have all speedometers consistently overstate speeds so that drivers would think they were driving faster than they actually were. Speedometers influence behavior. Why not influence it in a beneficent direction?

This last example will serve to lay bare the profound threat to accounting implicit in the propositions of Hawkins and of the others referred to above. If it ever became accepted that accounting might be used to achieve other than purely measurement

---

[13]The letter dated October 6, 1977, addressed to the FASB chairman-designate by Senator William Proxmire (D-Wisconsin) and four Wisconsin congressmen and reported in the FASB *Status Report* no. 55, "Persons Opposing the FASB Exposure Draft on Oil and Gas Accounting Apparently Seek Support in Congress for Retention of Alternatives," October 14, 1977, is a case in point.

[14]There is nothing farfetched about this. In *The Final Days* (New York: Avon Books, 1977, p. 177), Bob Woodward and Carl Bernstein state that "late in 1971, Nixon had summoned the White House personnel chief, Fred Malek, to his office to discuss a 'Jewish cabal' in the Bureau of Labor Statistics. The 'cabal,' Nixon said, was tilting economic figures to make his administration look bad." Another example came to my notice when I was in Singapore in 1976. There the administration was accused of keeping the price index down by changing the grade of rice included in the collection of food items going into the index.

[15]In my Price Waterhouse lecture at Stanford University in 1972 entitled "Financial Accounting Standards: Regulation or Self-Regulation?"

ends, faith in it would be destroyed[16] just as faith in speedometers would be destroyed once it was realized that they were subject to falsification for the purpose of influencing driving habits.

Hawkins's view that "because the [FASB] has the power to influence economic behavior, it has an obligation to support the government's economic plans" is, I believe, not only destructive of accounting but it is also infeasible. Governments have a habit of changing their plans from year to year, and even from month to month. Are accounting standards to be changed with every change in the political climate? One has only to recall President Nixon's turnabout from a "no wage and price controls" stance to an espousal of rigorous controls in 1971–72—or President Ford's switch from proposals for tax increases to "whip inflation now" to an acceptance of tax cuts to stimulate employment in 1974—to see how futile it is to talk about supporting the government's economic plans or how impossible it would be for a standards board to keep up with the government.

THE IMPORTANCE OF NEUTRALITY

Simply because information has an effect on human behavior does not mean that it should not seek to be neutral as between different desired modes of behavior. Unless it is as neutral as the accountant can make it, it is difficult to see how it can be relied on to guide behavior. As Chambers observes, "If the form of accounting is permitted to change with changes in policy, any attempt to scrutinize and to evaluate specific policies will be thwarted."[17]

Neutrality in accounting implies representational accuracy. Curiously, it has been little discussed, though other terms related to it have received more attention. The American Accounting Association's 1977 committee on concepts and standards for external financial reports gets near the heart of the matter when it says:

> Users of financial information prefer that it have a high degree of reliability. Reliability is that quality which permits users of data to depend upon it with confidence as representative of what it purports to represent. But reliable information is not necessarily useful. It could, for example, be reliable but unrelated to the use at hand. Several relatively general terms are often used as synonyms for, or to cover parts of, the concept of reliability. Thus, verifiability, objectivity, lack of bias, neutrality, and accuracy all are related to reliability. Like relevance, reliability (above some minimal level) is a necessary but not a sufficient condition for usefulness of data.[18]

---

[16]Support for this view is to be found in Arthur R. Wyatt's article, "The Economic Impact of Financial Accounting Standards," *Arthur Andersen Chronicle,* September 1977, p. 49. Somewhat ironically in the circumstances, the same view has been espoused more recently by the chairman of the SEC. In his Statement of August 29 on accounting practices for oil and gas producers, setting aside FASB Statement No. 19, Harold M. Williams said: "If it becomes accepted or expected that accounting principles are determined or modified in order to secure purposes other than economic measurement—even such virtuous purposes as energy production—we assume a grave risk that confidence in the credibility of our financial information system will be undermined."

[17]Raymond J. Chambers, *Accounting, Evaluation and Economic Behavior* (Englewood Cliffs, N.J.: Prentice-Hall, Inc., 1966), p. 326.

[18]Committee on concepts and standards for external financial reports, *Statement on Accounting Theory and Theory Acceptance* (Sarasota, Fla.: American Accounting Association, 1977), p. 16.

If the preceding sentence is true, these two qualities (relevance and reliability) together go far toward ensuring usefulness. Relevance comprehends subsidiary characteristics of information one might list such as timeliness. And the essential element in the reliability of information (at least for our present purpose) is that it shall as accurately as possible represent what it purports to represent.[19] This implies neutrality.

Neutrality, in the sense in which the term is used here, does not imply that no one gets hurt. It is true, as the AAA 1977 committee on the social consequences of accounting information says,

> Every policy choice represents a trade-off among differing individual preferences, and possibly among alternative consequences, regardless of whether the policy-makers see it that way or not. In this sense, accounting policy choices can never be neutral. There is someone who is granted his preference, and someone who is not.[20]

The same thing could be said of the draft, when draft numbers were drawn by lot. Some people were chosen to serve while others escaped. It was still, by and large, neutral in the sense that all males of draft age were equally likely to be selected.

ACCOUNTING AS FINANCIAL CARTOGRAPHY

Information cannot be neutral—it cannot therefore be reliable—if it is selected or presented for the purpose of producing some chosen effect on human behavior. It is this quality of neutrality which makes a map reliable; and the essential nature of accounting, I believe, is cartographic. Accounting is financial mapmaking. The better the map, the more completely it represents the complex phenomena that are being mapped. We do not judge a map by the behavioral effects it produces. The distribution of natural wealth or rainfall shown on a map may lead to population shifts or changes in industrial location, which the government may like or dislike. That should be no concern of the cartographer. We judge his map by how well it represents the facts. People can then react to it as they will.

Cartographers represent different facts in different ways and match the scale of their maps to their purpose. Every map represents a selection of a small portion of available data, for no map could show physical, political, demographic, climatological, geological, vegetational and numerous other kinds of data and still be intelligible. The need to be selective in the data that one represents does not normally rob the map of its neutrality, although it could.

As with the geographic features that cartographer's map, different financial facts need to be represented in different ways, and different facts are needed for different purposes. It is perfectly proper for measurements to be selected with particular

---

[19]This is close to Yuji Ijiri's statement that "in general, a system is said to be reliable if it works the way it is supposed to" (*The Foundations of Accounting Measurement: A Mathematical, Economic, and Behavioral Inquiry* [Englewood Cliffs, N.J.: Prentice-Hall, Inc., 1967], p. 137). But his more formal definition of reliability is couched more in terms of the predictive value of information, an aspect of the matter with which I am not here concerned.

[20]Committee on the social consequences of accounting information, *Report of the Committee on the Social Consequences of Accounting Information* (Sarasota, Fla.: AAA, 1978), p. 24.

political ends in mind or to be adapted to a political end if it is made clear to users of the measurement what is being done. For example, the government is entitled, for taxation purposes, to define taxable income in whatever way suits it. It would be quite another matter for it to tell accountants that they were to use this definition for all purposes to which an income number might be put.

SOME CONTRARY VIEWS

There have recently been some expressions of a different view of accounting from mine that deserve comment here. Sometimes the difference in the weight to be given to economic impact in standard setting is merely one of emphasis. Sometimes it is more fundamental in nature. Sometimes neutrality is dismissed on other grounds.

Probably no one argues that those who formulate accounting standards should do so with total unconcern for their economic consequences. Indeed, without some concern for such consequences, the selection of problem areas that call for standards could not be made. It was the economic consequences of not having a standard to deal with some particular problem which presumably directed attention in that direction in the first place. To require the FASB to report on the probable economic impact of a proposed standard when an exposure draft is issued[21]—if it can be done, for the impact will often not be clear or unambiguous—is not at all objectionable, so long as the standard is designed to bring about a better representation of the facts of a situation, with whatever behavioral results flow from that, and not to promote some preselected economic objective or mode of behavior.

Some of those who would play down the value of neutrality in accounting standards do so because, they argue, the financial phenomena which accountants must report are not independent of the reporting methods selected. This view is expressed by the AAA 1977 committee on the social consequences of accounting information in the following passage from its report:

> The view that measurement merely involves representing or describing stocks and flows is a static view. It assumes that stocks and flows are history, fixed forever, no matter how you measure them. But what about tomorrow's stocks and flows? They are governed by the business decisions of enterprises—decisions which might change depending upon how you choose to measure the stocks and flows. The traditional framework fails to take this interdependence of measurement and decisional behavior into consideration.[22]

It is true that, where human beings are the subjects of measurement, behavior and measurements are not independent of each other. But this does not make neutrality a less desirable quality of measurement in such cases. If one substitutes speedometers for accounting and driving behavior for stocks and flows in the AAA committee's statement above, one can see that as an argument against neutrality it is quite unconvincing. There is nothing static about the relationship between the speed of a vehicle and the reading on the speedometer, and there is unquestionably

---

[21] As recommended by Prem Prakash and Alfred Rappaport in "The Feedback Effects of Accounting," *Business Week,* January 12, 1976, p. 12.

[22] Social consequences committee, p. 23.

feedback. The behavior of the driver is reflected on the dial, and what is on the dial affects the behavior of the driver. Speedometers still should register speed accurately and neutrally. The decision about how to react to the reading must be left to the driver.

A different criterion for the selection of approved accounting methods is put forward by William Beaver and Roland Dukes in a discussion of interperiod tax allocation:

> The method which produces earnings numbers having the highest association with security prices is the most consistent with the information that results in an efficient determination of security prices. Subject to [certain] qualifications..., it is the method that ought to be reported.[23]

And, having found that "deferral earnings are most consistent with the information set used in setting security prices," they conclude that "if one accepts market efficiency, the results suggest that the [Accounting Principles Board] made the 'correct' policy decision...in the sense that it requires a method which is most consistent with the information impounded in an efficient determination of security prices."[24]

Beaver and Dukes themselves point out that any inferences to be drawn from their evidence are "conditional upon the prediction models used to test the accounting measures.... Any findings are the joint result of prediction models and accounting methods, and only appropriately specified joint statements are warranted."[25] In other words, the identification of the accounting method found to generate earnings numbers or cash flow numbers most closely associated with security prices depends on the way that "unexpected returns" are defined. The results of this analysis do not point unambiguously, therefore, toward a particular accounting method.

This could explain why, left to themselves, companies do not all choose the same accounting methods. They do not all use the same prediction models, and therefore the accounting method that has the most information content for one company is not the one with the most for another company. One moral that might be drawn from this is that we do not need accounting standards at all but, rather, that in an efficient market laissez-faire should prevail. A different conclusion about the Beaver and Dukes study is reached by Gonedes and Dopuch when they say that "under the contemporary institutional setting, capital market efficiency—taken by itself—does not imply that the prices of firms' ownership shares can be used in assessing the desirability of alternative information-production decisions."[26] In any case, whichever way the efficient market points us, it does not point us toward politically motivated accounting standards.

---

[23] William H. Beaver and Roland E. Dukes, "Interperiod Tax Allocation, Earnings Expectations, and the Behavior of Security Prices," *Accounting Review,* April 1972, p. 321. They add, in a footnote, that "the criterion suggested above provides a simplified method for preference ordering of alternative measurement methods."

[24] Ibid. p. 331.

[25] Ibid. p. 332.

[26] Gonedes and Dopuch, p. 92.

LIMITATIONS OF THE ANALOGY WITH CARTOGRAPHY

There is a danger, with any analogy, of pushing it too far, and the analogy between accounting and cartography is no exception. Most maps represent external phenomena that have an independent existence of their own. The accountant is on safe ground only when he is doing the same thing—representing external phenomena such as cash flows, contractual rights, market values, etc. Of course, cartographers have sometimes amused themselves by drawing maps of fictitious countries, like Erewhon or Atlantis, an activity which, too, has had its accounting counterparts.

Whatever limitations representational accuracy may have in pointing us toward right accounting answers, it will at least sometimes enable us to detect a wrong answer. For instance, FASB Statement no. 2, which requires all R&D expenditures to be expensed as incurred, is bad cartography because to represent the value of the continuing benefits of past research expenditures as zero will usually not be in accord with the facts of the situation, however expedient the treatment may be. Off-balance-sheet financing requires that certain unattractive features of the landscape be left off the map, so that again the map is defective. The criterion by which rules are to be judged is not the effect which they may or may not have on business behavior. It is the accuracy with which they reflect the facts of the situation.

CONCLUSION

It is not at all palatable for accountants to be confronted by a choice between appearing to be indifferent to national objectives or endangering the integrity of their measurement techniques. But if the long-run well-being of our discipline is what matters, the right choice should be easy to make. It is our job—as accountants—to make the best maps we can. It is for others, or for accountants acting in some other capacity, to use those maps to steer the economy in the right direction. If the distinction between these two tasks is lost sight of, we shall greatly diminish our capacity to serve society, and in the long run everybody loses.

The Marketing of Accounting Standards

Charles T. Horngren
Stanford University

"A prerequisite to the solution of a problem is the recognition of the existence of the problem.... Most of the literature that I read is in the nature of a fairy tale.... Specifically, the problem is that the accountant has been given a responsibility without concomitant authority."[1]

These words by Robert R. Sterling reinforce my previous description of a problem about the responsibility of the Accounting Principles Board in relation to the Board's place within an institutional structure. My hypothesis is that the setting of accounting standards is as much a product of political action as of flawless logic or empirical findings. Why? Because the setting of standards is a social decision. Standards place restrictions on behavior; therefore, they must be accepted by the affected parties. Acceptance may be forced or voluntary or some of both. In a democratic society, getting acceptance is an exceedingly complicated process that requires skillful marketing in a political arena.

The history of the APB provides evidence for the above perceptions. The focus of this article is a description of a problem of accounting power. My conclusions do not include magic solutions, but they do include a plea to the Financial Accounting Standards Board to get equipped now for its marketing as well as its production responsibilities.

The terms "marketing," "selling" and "lobbying" will be used occasionally in this article. These terms should not be narrowly interpreted as representing carnival hawking or shady dealings in smoke-filled rooms. Instead, they should be viewed in their broadest, most elevated light—the art of getting packages of ideas accepted by all affected parties in a professional manner.

THE INSTITUTIONAL STRUCTURE THAT CONFRONTED THE APB

Decentralized Management

The APB has taken its final breath. Its demise was largely caused by institutional forces rather than by internal disintegration. Let's examine these forces to see what the FASB might learn so that its life can extend indefinitely (or at least 40 years).

My description of the institutional structure was published in May 1972.[2] Although I want to minimize repetition, that description is my framework for discussion. In sum, the institutional setup has been as shown in Figure 1, p.46. Although most

From *The Journal of Accountancy,* (October 1973), pp. 61–66. Reprinted by permission of the American Institute of Certified Public Accountants. Copyright © 1973 by the American Institute of Certified Public Accountants, Inc.

[1] Robert R. Sterling, "Accounting Power," JofA, Jan. 73, p. 63.

[2] Charles T. Horngren, "Accounting Principles: Private or Public Sector?" JofA, May 72, pp. 37–41.

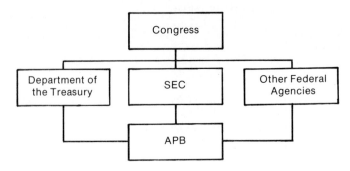

FIGURE 1
Accounting information, principles and objectives preferred by various parties.

accountants have claimed that the responsibility for the setting of standards has been kept within the private sector, this view is oversimplified and misleading.

The (informal) organizational relationship is similar to decentralized management in industry. Figure 1 shows a single organization whose products are accounting standards. The key idea is a *decentralized* structure. A crude parallel can be drawn as you descend the chart. Congress has ultimate power but, with rare exceptions, has delegated this power to the SEC (and other federal agencies). In turn, the SEC has delegated much of this power to the APB.

Decentralization is frequently defined as the relative freedom to make decisions. Top management adopts decentralization when it believes that lower management has more information and ability to make decisions that obtain the overall goals of the organization. In industry, the extent of decentralization varies from company to company. The heavier the decentralization, the greater the latitude of the lower-level managers to make a host of decisions, including acquisition of materials and equipment and sales of products and services. Decentralization lies along a continuum and is subject to recentralization, either selectively or totally, whenever higher-level management so decides.

The implications of this informal decentralized organizational structure are far-reaching. Both the SEC and the APB are subjected to constraints exerted by superior management, Congress, and the entire organizational unit is subjected to the influence exerted by the customers, the parties affected by the standards (reporting companies, practitioners and users of the reports).

The key to a successful enterprise is to generate a product that is *acceptable* to customers. The decentralized manager may develop what he perceives as a superior product, but his perceptions must overlap with those of his customers (see Figure 2, p. 47).

If new standards are proposed that seem unacceptable, the customers must be persuaded otherwise. If the standards are sufficiently unappealing, the customer may complain to higher management (the SEC or Congress).

Of course, regarding particular standards, in the short run the customers have no alternative if the pinnacle of management (Congress) decides that lower manage-

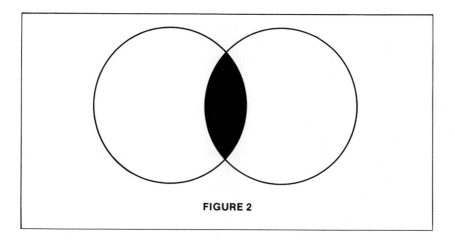

FIGURE 2

ment's product is desirable for society as a whole. But the product is complex, and top management may decide not to support innovation (because in an ultimate sense the customers in a collective, indirect way via their votes can replace top management itself).

Is the Description Accurate?

The foregoing description is not faultless, but I persist in defending its essential accuracy. Shortly after it was published, an APB member expressed his displeasure about my referring to the Board as lower management. The thrust of his objection was that the APB was not the obsequious lackey of the SEC. Of course, my article was not aimed at conveying the impression that the APB was the machine shop foreman in a factory run by a despotic plant manager. After all, the article stressed the *decentralized* nature of the structure. So I attributed his reaction to his failure to read with sufficient care.

But the January 1973 issue of *The Journal of Accountancy* reinforced the shortcomings of my May 1972 article. Apparently, the crucial idea of decentralization was overlooked by John Burton, who became Chief Accountant of the SEC during mid-1972. When he was asked whether he agreed with my top management-lower management description, Burton replied:

> No,...I feel that, as Chairman Casey said, we are in partnership....I do not believe that we are top management with veto power, although such power does legally exist. As a practical matter the strength of the private sector would dry up if Professor Horngren's article were a reflection of reality. No person of quality would want to serve on a principles board.[3]

[3] News feature, "Paper Shuffling and Economic Reality," an interview with John C. Burton, JofA, Jan. 73, p. 26. William J. Casey addressed the annual meeting of the American Institute of Certified Public Accountants on October 2, 1972. His speech was entitled, "The Partnership Between the Accounting Profession and the SEC."

When asked whether Casey's "partnership" description of APB-SEC relations is correct, one practitioner reacted, "Well, in my firm there are partners and then there are partners! "The partnership description in its classic sense that implies an equal distribution of power may be handy public relations, but it is misleading. Moreover, does the assertion that "no person of quality would want to serve on a principles board" imply that no person of quality would want to be a junior partner in a public accounting firm or be the head of a division in a decentralized organization? Do all persons of quality have to be managing partners and presidents?

Although my analogy of decentralized management may be imperfect, it is used here to stress the existence and interrelationships of forces that affect the setting of accounting standards. Alternatively, these forces may be likened to line-staff relationships, executive-legislative-judicial relationships or partnership relations. No matter what the analogy, power has been wielded by more than the APB alone. We need to study how the exercise of power affects the acceptability of accounting standards.

Working as Decentralized Management

The APB has been given great leeway to make many delicate decisions because it has been judged adequately objective and competent. However, the Board's freedom has definitely been constrained on several occasions. The scenario of the investment tax credit is well known, so it will not be repeated here. In that case, the APB and the SEC were united in their stand and they went down in flames together. The scenario of marketable securities is not well known, but it offers several lessons about how the APB contended with its environment.

The heart of the issue concerning marketable securities deals with when portfolio gains and losses should be recognized. There is a variety of views ranging from predominant present practice (whereby only realized gains and losses are included in income) to some version of spreading (whereby all gains and losses from changes in market prices are included in income but on some three- to ten-year moving-average, long-term yield basis) to a flow-through approach (whereby all gains and losses are included in income as the prices of marketable securities fluctuate from quarter to quarter).

Another set of issues concerns whether portfolio losses or gains belong in an income statement in the first place. Instead, some accountants believe that a two-statement approach is needed. If adopted, a separate statement of realized and unrealized gains would be used.

An even more fundamental issue is whether the controversy is much ado about nothing. That is, a growing body of academicians would maintain that if market values are disclosed in the balance sheet (as they are in the insurance industry) it makes no difference whether the related losses and gains are reported in the income statement as realized, on some spreading basis, or on a flow-through basis. Why? Because the essential data, market values, are already disclosed. Therefore, the aggregate investors are not fooled by how or when the related gains and losses affect reported income, if at all.[4]

---

[4]T.R. Archibald, "Stock Market Reaction to Depreciation Switch-Back," *The Accounting Review* (January 1972), pp. 22–30. Robert Kaplan and Richard Roll, "Investor Evaluation of Accounting

The relative merits of the theoretical arguments are not germane here, but the history of the Board's deliberations is enlightening. An intensive study of this topic was begun in September 1968. Heavy interaction persisted between the APB and all interested parties, particularly representatives of the insurance industry, whose income statements would be dramatically affected by any new accounting standards. In May 1971, there was a two-day public hearing on the issues.[5]

After about three years of spasmodic deliberations, the APB was ready to issue an exposure draft of an Opinion. The Board had narrowed its preferences to two methods using one income statement: either flow-through or spreading. In September 1971, the Board approved a draft favoring flow-through. The draft was to be "mini-exposed" to the SEC, the insurance industry and others who had been actively involved. The intention of the Board was to have full public exposure of the Opinion after the October APB meeting.

The insurance companies were bitterly opposed to flow-through. They blitzkrieged Washington. The SEC, armed with its own preferences and buttressed by industry reactions, informed the APB that it could not support flow-through. At this point, flow-through was a dead duck because higher management (the SEC) had, in effect, overruled the APB.

At its October meeting, the APB again discussed the topic. Because flow-through was no longer an acceptable alternative, the Board changed its preferences to either spreading or a two-statement approach. The Board voted in favor of a two-statement approach, although strong voices were raised in support of spreading. In November, these alternatives were explored with the SEC and the insurance industry. At its December meeting, the Board was informed that the fire and casualty companies had also strongly objected to the spreading method. One potent spokesman for the SEC found some merit in the spreading method, but he informed the Board that the SEC would not impose it or any solution on an industry that was adamantly opposed to it. So spreading was dead.

The Board then discussed two alternatives: (1) some version of a two-statement method and (2) a modification of predominant current practice whereby all companies in all industries would show marketable securities at market value in the balance sheet, unrealized gains and losses in stockholders' equity, and only realized gains and losses in the income statement. However, the fire and casualty companies also vigorously opposed the two-statement method.

Note how the feasible alternatives changed in response to the likelihood of acceptability. The constraints became more binding as the months wore on:

1 September—flow-through or spreading
2 October—spreading or two-statement
3 December—two-statement or slight modification of status quo

Discussions of various versions of the December alternatives were renewed in

Information: Some Empirical Evidence," *Journal of Business* (April 1972), pp. 225–257. William H. Beaver and Roland E. Dukes, "Interperiod Tax Allocation and Depreciation Methods: Some Analytical and Empirical Results," *The Accounting Review*, forthcoming. July 1973—Eds.

[5] *APB Public Hearing on Accounting for Investments in Equity Securities Not Qualifying for the Equity Method*, Cases in Public Accounting Practice, Volume 8 (Chicago: Arthur Andersen & Co., 1971).

early 1972. But the Board could not resolve the issues and the SEC was noncommittal on anything except "no flow-through." During the course of the discussions, the top managements of 15 or 20 large insurance companies met together about the issue more than once and also with the SEC commissioners at least once.

An observer of a visit of Institute representatives to the SEC wrote to me that an SEC commissioner

> asked the APB for a summary of the alternative methods together with the pros and cons of each. He also said that, once the SEC received this report, the SEC would tell the APB the parameters in which the APB could consider the subject. Presumably any method selected by the APB within these parameters would be acceptable to the SEC.... This event is perhaps the clearest demonstration of an SEC order to the APB that I can recall.

The marketable securities scenario was concluded by an APB report to the SEC in March 1972 that summarized the APB deliberations and the alternatives. However, the report offered no preferred solution.

Among the many inferences that can be made from this APB experience, three are notable here. First, this series of events is evidence that, in relation to the SEC, the APB is not a "partner" but is a subordinate. Second, widespread industry hostility can constrict the feasible alternatives for setting standards. Third, the outlook for so-called fair value accounting is gloomy.

The failure of the APB to reach even an exposure draft stage for so obvious a candidate for fair value as marketable securities reinforces my pessimism about fair value as a goal over the next 10 to 20 or more years. After all, if the fair market value idea cannot be implemented for that category of assets, there is little practical hope for more radical schemes.

Obtaining Acceptance of Standards

How does a standards board attempt to market its product when it faces the constraints that are imposed directly by senior management and indirectly by customers? There are many general strategies, but consider the implications of three: (1) abdication, (2) confrontation and (3) incrementalism.

Complete abdication is an extreme alternative that is perceived as repugnant by most accountants. What would occur if the accounting profession gave up its decentralized management status and assumed a submissive role to some governmental group similar to the Cost Accounting Standards Board? Who knows? Some have cited the possibility of enlightened governance[6] that would be more clear-cut and less costly to the profession as a whole and to society in general. But most accountants evidently fear that unenlightened governance would result.[7] They predict detailed, ponderous rules that would reduce the professional challenge of accounting, undermine the status of the profession and fail to attract bright recruits to both practice and the universities.

[6]Sterling, *op. cit.*, p. 66. Also see Maurice Moonitz, "The Accounting Principles Board Revisited," *The New York Certified Public Accountant,* May 1971, pp. 344–345.
[7]For an example of such a prediction, see John C. Burton (ed.), *Corporate Financial Reporting: Conflicts and Challenges* (New York: AICPA, 1969), pp. 76–83.

At the other extreme, the profession could take radical action to force confrontation on how accounting principles should be set. For example, suppose the Board had voted to issue its Opinion on the investment tax credit that requires the deferral method, despite the recent Congressional legislation permitting latitude on accounting for the credit. Then, under the rules of the AICPA, public accounting firms would have to qualify their professional opinions for all clients using the flow-through method. Some idealists maintain that until accountants are ready to be that courageous, their independence will be tainted and their prestige will be limited. By being bold defenders of principle, accountants will force Congress and the Treasury to see the wisdom of letting the professionals set the accounting standards.

Most accountants probably favor a middle stance, which might be called incrementalism:

> Under the incremental approach, a policy-maker does not attempt to consider the whole range of hypothetical alternatives but limits his choice to a few that represent relatively small changes from the present state . . . because at most times "radically different" changes are not politically feasible.[8]

Despite existing constraints, these accountants believe that more progress can be made by some version of the current decentralized setup. To them, abdication is unthinkable. Similarly, confrontation is infeasible because of the high risk that any existing power will be recentralized. First, there is not enough unity within the profession itself to support bold moves. Second, outcries from industry will spur legislative action that will completely shut the private sector out from the throttles of power. Therefore, the profession should persist in pushing the constraints to see how binding they really are. Sometimes decentralized management will win a battle (for example, requiring the allocation of income taxes), but frequently it will lose. However, the most progress will be made when the Board judiciously uses its active role as a decentralized manager.

The informality of this decentralized setup and the uncertainty regarding acceptability often mean that constraints are unknown until some definite action occurs. On several occasions, the APB has attempted to discover the nature of the constraints by making early, venturesome moves. The marketable securities scenario is an example; so is the full costing controversy in the petroleum industry. Another example is the Board's early approach to the issue of business combinations. A preliminary draft of an Opinion was prepared that abolished pooling completely.[9] Its reception by industry and by many practitioners was unequivocally negative, and the SEC's attitude at best was neutral or lukewarm. So the Board retreated and was described by many critics as "weak-willed." However, at least the Board tried to pinpoint the constraints by taking an activist stand with the hope that such would survive. Perhaps the APB could have avoided much criticism from practitioners and industry by being less brave from the start. At least the APB would not have

---

[8] Dale L. Gerboth, "'Muddling Through' with the APB," JofA, May 72, p. 45. Gerboth offers many references on the theory and practice of incrementalism.

[9] *The Wall Street Journal,* September 24, 1969, p. 10.

appeared so vacillatory. But that posture would have engendered the criticism of excessive meekness from many parties. Of course, harsh words would be aimed at the Board from some important sources no matter what strategy it adopted.

PROBLEMS FACING THE FASB

My portrayal of behavioral patterns and authoritative structures for making accounting laws is a description, not a criticism. For example, within some limits I believe that industry and public accounting firms should have the freedom to state their cases to governmental authorities. After all, as one SEC commissioner said: "Public officials must talk with people." Perhaps the present institutional structure is close to optimality. However, if the APB or FASB wants to win its points, it must contend with these imposing forces. More of us should see things as they are, not as we may wish them to be.

The euphoria surrounding the Financial Accounting Standards Board will be short-lived. The FASB will face intricate issues. Inherent complexity and great expectations are almost always conflicting terms. The same institutional and environmental problems that confronted the APB will still exist. Congress, the Treasury, the SEC, industry and the public accounting profession are still there. If you picture the environment in a global sense, the APB has been replaced—but little else has changed.

Consider the comments of Leonard Savoie, who, as executive vice president of the AICPA, was directly involved in APB experiences:

> Can it be that the APB has been replaced not because of structural deficiencies but because of prevailing attitudes—attitudes within the public accounting professions and the attitude of business?
>
> Is it possible that too many accountants and businessmen have been so determined to have their own way on matters of accounting principle that they preferred to bring down the structure rather than submit to an APB Opinion that impinged on their prerogatives?
>
> Although the APB's procedures for hearing all sides of controversial issues were substantially equivalent to the procedures recommended for the new FASB, is it possible that APB watchers have not been satisfied merely by communicating with the APB?
>
> Let us look at some of the events of the last few years.
>
> In the case of certain proposed APB Opinions, opponents have issued press releases denouncing the APB, published briefs, circulated white papers, threatened to sue the APB, petitioned the SEC, asked the FPC for a ruling, sought Treasury Department intervention, asked Congress to put financial reporting flexibility into law.
>
> Will this happen to FASB?[10]

How can the new structure better insure the general acceptability of FASB pronouncements? Many new provisions will help. Surely, the wider base of membership, the high-salaried full-time members, the independence of members from all other organizations and the broad-based Advisory Council are features that should increase the likelihood of acceptability. On the other hand, the large accounting firms will no longer have a direct voice or vote. When the issues become torrid, will

---

[10]From a speech by Leonard M. Savoie, "Financial Accounting Standards: Regulation or Self Regulation?" (Stanford, Calif.: Stanford Business School, May 1972), p. 1.

these firms be as inclined to accept the FASB pronouncements as well as they did the APB pronouncements?

Obviously, the pressures will not wither away. Gaining acceptance is a task of marketing or lobbying. The FASB is no more supreme in its stranglehold on power than the APB. The FASB needs strong voices in Washington. The tactics in 1971–72 regarding the investment tax credit and marketable securities will indeed continue. (Leases got similar attention.) The sources of ultimate power such as Congress, the SEC and the Treasury Department will be buffeted by industry and practitioners. Therefore, some provision should be made at the outset for getting a stable of able spokesmen for FASB positions, individuals who will be listened to by commissioners, legislators and cabinet members. Some of these individuals will be on the FASB, but some will not.

The FASB cannot depend solely on the impeccable logic of its standards to sway these ultimate sources of power. It must be equipped by the convincing credentials of its members and by their ability to sell their wares to the decision-makers in Washington. They must be articulate and persuasive as individuals and, in my view, they need professional help to represent their positions. The job, then, of the FASB is a twofold one of production and marketing: (1) to develop the best possible accounting standards *and* (2) to see that such standards are accepted. The latter task is more formidable than the former. The ad hoc supplications that dotted the history of the APB are not enough.[11]

The new FASB structure has been created because its supporters perceive it as the best available means for setting accounting standards to benefit society as a whole. The lobbying effort probably should be a continuing one that stresses the principle of noninterference. The aim of such a strategy would be to convince Congress, the SEC and other powerful forces that the FASB is the premier group of experts on accounting standards. Furthermore, the reasoning would stress that, to benefit society at large, it is generally desirable to allow the experts to make the decisions without harassment. Lobbying may also have to be conducted on an issue-by-issue basis, but the long-run effort would be to persuade all affected parties that noninterference is the least costly way to benefit society as a whole.

The affected parties are not only the SEC and Congress. They include practicing accountants and financial executives. The FASB has been repeatedly cited as being the private sector's last chance for maintaining a direct role in setting accounting standards. The new Board should play this theme for all it's worth. All interested parties should have an ample chance to voice their views as issues arise, but they should also be willing to accept the outcomes without divisive lament. These parties may maximize their immediate private good by undermining the work of the Board. Still, these short-run gains may come at the expense of society's collective good and may result in the eventual tearing down of the entire structure for setting standards. Therefore, in the long run, the affected parties may find it too costly not to accept the FASB decisions.

---

[11] For example, Steven S. Anreder, "Called to Account," *Barron's,* October 2, 1972, p. 10, reports, "...the Congressmen have taken an even more direct approach with the investment tax credit, despite efforts to head it off by the SEC and the Institute (which never got farther than a staff assistant to Representative Wilbur Mills in presenting its case)."

Of course, when specific issues reach a white heat, it is easy to ignore these long-run implications.[12] These issues are nearly always complicated; for example, each of two opposing views may be based on a plausible chain of reasoning.

CONCLUSION

This article has described the marketing problems of the setting of accounting standards. The problems may be obvious, but they are not trivial. I have not raised these issues to voice a cynical or pessimistic view. On the contrary, I have focused upon them because I truly desire the successful implementation and operation of the new FASB. There is no visible alternative to keeping the function of setting accounting standards in private hands to the greatest extent possible. To be successful, we must recognize the political role of the new Board, the need to deal with pressures that will exist no matter what structure for setting standards is used— whether that structure be private, public or some combination thereof.

In the 1960s and early 1970s researchers in accounting borrowed heavily from quantitative methods and the behavioral sciences. I hope that the 1970s sees some concentration on the optimal methods for wielding accounting power in a democratic society. The literature of organizations, political action, social change and social choice may be more closely related to the development of accounting standards than we have been willing to admit.[13] As Arrow states: "The notion of a 'democratic paralysis,' a failure to act due not to a desire for inaction but an inability to agree on the proper action, seems to me to deserve much further empirical, as well as theoretical, study."[14]

More consideration might be given to the cost and value of information model[15] and its implications for accounting standards, not only with respect to data-gathering costs but also with respect to the costs of education of accountants, managers and users regarding any suggested innovations. In addition, what can we learn from social scientists about the theory and practice of policy-making?[16]

---

[12] See the letter by R.E. Pfenning, formerly chief financial officer of General Electric, which criticizes the tactics of those who opposed the APB proposed Opinion on the investment tax credit, *Financial Executive* (June 1972), pp. 12–13.

[13] See Dorwin Cartwright, "Influence, Leadership, Control," in James G. March, ed., *Handbook of Organizations* (Chicago: Rand McNally & Company, 1965), pp. 1–48. In particular, see his section on bases of power, pp. 28–39. See also Richard M. Cyert and James G. March, *A Behavioral Theory of the Firm* (Englewood Cliffs, N.J.: Prentice-Hall, Inc., 1963), Chapter 6; Amitai Etzioni, *Modern Organizations* (Englewood Cliffs, N.J.: Prentice-Hall, Inc., 1964), Chapter 8; Peter M. Blau and W. Richard Scott, *Formal Organizations* (San Francisco: Chandler Publishing Company, 1962), pp. 59–86 and 244–47; Timothy W. Costello, "Psychological Aspects: The Soft Side of Policy Formulation," *Policy Sciences* 1, 1970, pp. 161–168.

[14] Kenneth H. Arrow, *Social Choice and Individual Values* (2nd ed., New Haven and London: Yale University Press, 1963).

[15] Gerald A. Feltham and Joel S. Demski, "The Use of Models in Information Evaluation," *The Accounting Review* (October 1970), and Joel S. Demski, "Choice Among Financial Accounting Alternatives," unpublished, December 1972. Published in the April 1974 issue of *The Accounting Review*—Eds.

[16] Charles A. Tritschler, "A Sociological Perspective on Accounting Innovation," *The International Journal of Accounting*, Vol. 5, No. 2 (Spring 1970), pp. 39–67, explores the problem of gaining acceptance of complex accounting innovations. Also see the references in Gerboth, *op. cit.*

In the tradition of articles by academicians, I end with a plea for more research. Given the FASB, are there better ways to obtain acceptability than accountants have used in the past? The political difficulties of setting accounting standards are not subordinate problems. How they are handled will affect the useful life of the FASB and, consequently, the useful life of the private sector's direct influence on accounting standards.

The SEC and Financial Reporting: The Sand in the Oyster

John C. Burton
Columbia University

The pearl is one of nature's most beautiful creations. It is formed by the reaction of certain oysters to an irritant, usually a grain of sand, that becomes embedded inside the shell. The oyster coats this grain with layers of nacre, and ultimately a pearl is formed. The pearl is the joint result of the irritant and oyster; without both, it cannot be created.

Professional accounting standards and practices may not achieve the luster of the pearl, but the process of their development has many similarities. Both currently and historically, the accounting profession has exhibited a comfortable, conservative commitment to the status quo in the absence of an external stimulus for change.

The process of innovation in accounting, therefore, has required the cooperative efforts of a creative irritant that provides the stimulus for change and of a responsive body to build on it. Since its inception in 1934, the Securities and Exchange Commission has been a principal source of creative irritation in accounting, and the practicing public accounting profession has generally served as the host which builds on it. This combination of SEC stimulation and professional reaction emerges logically from the historical and economic forces at work and results generally in a satisfactory balancing of diverse interests and objectives. In today's financial reporting environment, substantial change will not occur without SEC stimulation. If there is to be innovation, the commission must be a principal source. At the same time, the commission must operate within the limits of a consensus that the various parties involved in financial reporting help to define.

It is only fair to report that many do not see this process in particularly pearly terms. Some suggest that the SEC has been neither creative nor a force for improvement but, rather, that it has hampered the development of financial reporting by its omnipresence and its disregard of market factors and that it has not offered

From *Journal of Accountancy,* (June 1982), pp. 34, 36, 38, 40, 42, 44, 46, 48. Originally published in *Government Regulation of Accounting and Information* edited by A. Rashad Abdel-khalik © 1980 by the Board of Regents of Florida. Reprinted by permission—also by permission of the American Institute of Certified Public Accountants.

concomitant benefit to the investors. At the other end of the spectrum are those who suggest that the SEC has been captured by the accounting profession, that it has not accomplished its mission because of its inaction.

There are also wide differences in the perception of the results of the process. Some view financial reporting in the U.S. today as a model to be emulated; others see primarily its deficiencies and shortcomings.

It is difficult for many to accept the view that a governmental agency should be the catalyst for change while the private sector and the marketplace seem to stand as defenders of the status quo. They suggest that leadership and dynamism should come from creative individuals responding to the incentives of the marketplace.

While this is an appealing model, it does not reflect current realities. If government were a neutral force, the marketplace could be the source of risk-taking innovation in financial reporting. In fact, however, securities regulation in the U.S. is legislatively designed to protect against perceived abuse by raising the cost of error in auditing and financial reporting through the imposition of substantial liabilities on both registrants and professionals involved.

In addition, the courts and the SEC have liberally interpreted congressional intent in this regard, and the plaintiff's bar has been creative in its litigation thrusts. The commission's increased enforcement activity, aimed at professionals who fail to maintain professional standards, also has added to the pressure. Even though a number of recent Supreme Court decisions limit liability to some degree, the aggregate result of securities legislation and its judicial and regulatory interpretation has been to impose on registrants and experts the onus of avoiding any presentation that might be deemed misleading.

The economic forces brought to bear by this regulatory structure have resulted in substantial pressure to find means of reducing risk of liability. Accountants have been urged to define standards with greater precision, and the commission has been asked to specify its requirements with ever-increasing detail. Auditors have expanded their work and their quality controls to decrease the likelihood of undiscovered error.

At the same time, companies have been very hesitant to experiment with new and untried accounting and disclosure techniques, particularly those requiring uncertain estimates that may later turn out to be incorrect. The possible benefits of such estimates to investors are far outweighed by the potential costs to the corporation and, more specifically, to the decision makers involved. A strong tendency to value objectivity above relevance has developed in financial reporting. For many years, the SEC's policy was also a force in this direction.

In preregulatory days, it was not unusual for an enterprise to perceive market advantage in presenting data in an innovative way. A presentation might then be emulated by others and ultimately become common practice; other innovations might prove to be without value and would gradually disappear. In this environment, standards were developed from practice. Although abuses existed, and commonality among presentations was lacking, the system was a dynamic one. It resulted in substantial development in accounting and reporting during the early decades of this century, even though this development was selective and uneven across companies.

PROTECTION RATHER THAN INNOVATION

As the environment changed and greater emphasis was placed on uniformity and the avoidance of abuse, the economic incentives changed to favor protection rather than innovation. This was not necessarily a bad social result—the abuses of the 1920s had high social costs—but it did change the behavior of those reporting financial results. They sought certainty and the avoidance of liability, which had the effect of changing the standard-setting process as well.

Originally, standards were developed from what was seen as the best practice, and they evolved as practice developed. Increasingly, however, standards came to be viewed as authoritative pronouncements, imposed on all enterprises and enforced. This approach provided protection but made evolution more difficult, and the standards themselves tended to emphasize objectivity and conservatism.

Since private sector standard setting is largely in the hands of those who are exposed to the costs of disclosure, it is not surprising that standards seem to enshrine the status quo and to minimize uncertainty and risk. Only under external pressure have standard setting bodies demonstrated significant innovative spirit.

Thus, standards have become the only source of "safe" new methods of accounting, with changes in practice resulting from changes in standards rather than the other way around. At the same time, the market incentives for standard setters to avoid change and endorse the most conservative practices have increased.

Abuses have not been avoided entirely by this approach, since circumstances still exist in which the potential benefits of "creative" accounting outweigh possible costs, such as in new and high-risk businesses. It was in such businesses that the application of principles designed for other circumstances provided much material for the accounting critics of the 1960s. Computer leasing and franchise operations are two principal examples. Unfortunately, economic incentives only become substantial enough to outweigh possible costs when the potential for abuse is particularly high.

Another reason why the SEC's regulatory mandate has provided countervailing incentives to the development of an efficient information market as an alternative to authoritative prescription is the underlying commitment of the securities laws to fairness in the disclosure process. To make the capital markets fair, and perceived as fair, the commission prohibits the disclosure of significant information to one investor in preference to another. Insider trading rules have been carefully developed, and the use of inside information to obtain economic gain in securities transactions has been made illegal. The commission has been largely successful in making information a public good, and thus the incentive for investors to seek and pay for new kinds of disclosure is substantially diluted. Incentives for change have, therefore, been reduced, on both the supply and the demand sides of the market for information.

While some may assert that, in the absence of regulation, suppliers of information would have an incentive to produce the optimum amount of information based on their own economic self-interests, this is neither analytically nor empirically demonstrable. The incentives and the timing of those incentives are not always consistent with the interests of an informed investor. For example, an enterprise under economic stress and seeking capital may have powerful shortrun incentives to hide the state of its affairs from potential investors. In addition, the fragmentation of the market of capital suppliers doesn't make it clear that the necessary cost-saving and power-centralizing coalitions would form and then make the bargain for information an effective one, in the light of existing frictions. Even if market forces worked well in a historically unregulated market, they would be unlikely to be as effective in a world where behavior patterns have been shaped by 45 years of regulation.

The regulator in this setting must be able to provide additional incentives for necessary change when market forces fail to do so. In a sense, the regulator must replace the very market its own activities have biased in favor of the status quo. Its regulatory objectives of a fair and efficient capital market require a dynamic system of information exchange to reflect an everchanging world.

To do this, the commission must take the role of advocate for investors to offset the preparer bias that institutionally exists in the standard-setting process. Subjective judgments about the needs and interests of investors are required. In reaching such judgments, the commission relies on the representations of analysts and investor organizations, expressed in letters of comment, appearances at hearings and informal contacts, plus a continuing survey of the literature of security analysts, such as the *Financial Analysts Journal.* In addition, the experience of members of the commission and its staff plays a significant role.

In making these judgments, the commission's objective is to achieve a level of public disclosure at least the equivalent of the disclosure likely to be sought by a provider of capital who negotiates on an arm's-length basis and who has equivalent power with a capital user. If the commission errs in this objective, it seeks to do so on the side of providing more information rather than less, since an underlying premise of its regulatory purpose is to assure the existence of adequate information so that the capital-allocating mechanism of the marketplace will work effectively. The potential benefits of such a mechanism are substantial, although they are difficult to demonstrate empirically. Compared to these benefits, the costs of providing additional information are likely to be small. The commission does not, however, disregard cost factors in reaching its judgments. It regularly requests comments on the costs of its proposals from information preparers, including both out-of-pocket costs and possible costs arising from competitive disadvantage. The SEC staff also does research on these matters.

This representation of the investor viewpoint offsets the fact that the investment community is made up of many investors. The benefit to any one investor of devoting substantial resources to gathering information would not be economically justified, perhaps even without the constraint of insider information rules. Thus, the commission acts as a countervailing force to offset the economic weakness of investors in their pursuit of adequate information.

The commission inserts itself into the negotiations for investor information in a number of ways. In part, it offers suggestions through the speeches of its chairman, its commissioners and its senior staff. Although each speech carries the traditional disclaimer that the speaker is presenting individual views and not those of the commission, major policy addresses serve as a significant means of communication. In addition to speeches, the commission exercises the rule-making powers granted to it by Congress under the Securities Act of 1933 and the Securities Exchange Act of 1934. In the accounting area, it has chosen to use these powers with considerable discretion; it has consistently recognized the difficulty of taking over the standard-setting mechanism, and it also has realized the importance of leveraging its resources by using the private sector. Governmental rule making has inflexibilities that do not exist in the private sector, and, in addition, the human and financial resources of the SEC have historically been less than those of the private sector. The securities acts give the commission permissive rather than mandatory standard-setting authority, and they leave the audit role explicitly to independent public accountants.

The importance of the permissive nature of the commission's power under the securities laws is great. If the commission had been directed to establish standards, it would have done so and the results would probably have been quite different. To cite one recent example, the commission was mandated by law to deal with the oil and gas accounting issue. Results were demonstrably different, in both process and outcome, from the commission's normal dealings with accounting standard-setting bodies.

THE SEC AS RULE MAKER

In a number of cases in which no mandate existed, however, the commission exercised its discretion and concluded that it was necessary to enter the rule-making forum. There are a number of reasons for this, varying in degrees for different rules. Most significantly, the commission acts when it concludes that important data are not being made available to investors on a voluntary basis. Without such a conclusion, rules are not adopted. A rule also may be adopted primarily to provide protection to registrants who would otherwise fear liability from certain disclosures. By creating a disclosure requirement, the commission provides assurance that particular classes of disclosure may not be deemed by a court to be misleading per se. When a new kind of disclosure is required, this may be important. Replacement costs, the capital value of leased assets and forecasts are examples.

More recently, the commission moved to reduce risk by adopting safe-harbor rules, which attempt to offer additional legal protection by recognizing the uncertain nature of some disclosures, and by providing that good-faith errors in estimation will not be viewed as violations of certain sections of the securities laws.

Besides reducing legal risk, rule making provides protection against comparative competitive disadvantage. Companies often hesitate to make disclosures because they believe that making certain disclosures, which their competitors do not, will put them at a disadvantage. If everyone must make the disclosures, there is less concern, although the impact of disclosure requirements may still fall with unequal weight on competitors. Line-of-business profit disclosure is an example of an area in which voluntary efforts were not making much progress until the commisson's rule-making authority was brought to bear.

Legal risk and competitive disadvantage are two of the most common factors that deter disclosure initiatives in the absence of rule making or of clear economic incentives. Other fears of a less specific nature also are significant. The law of anticipatory multiplication, which provides that both the probability and the potential cost of unpleasant possible outcomes are multiplied whenever change is being considered, suggests that the estimation of the expected value of change is likely to be biased in favor of the status quo. Thus the commission, by rule making, often plays the role of one who pushes a reluctant swimmer into the water to demonstrate that the experience will really not be as bad as it may appear from the dock. In this way, corporations can observe the lack of the frequently predicted disastrous impact from disclosure initiatives.

While disclosure requirements serve an end in themselves, they also may create an environment that is more sympathetic to the development of basic reporting standards by private sector entities. In addition to forcing a trial of new methods, such rules also may provide standard setters with a data base to support subsequent actions. This was the case, for example, in lease accounting, in which the commission mandated the use of present value techniques to compute a lease liability figure, and in the area of replacement cost accounting, in which a rule was adopted requiring certain companies to provide replacement cost information. In both cases, the Financial Accounting Standards Board was provided with information and was able to adopt or propose more extensive rules that brought these disclosures into a more systematic framework.

Rule-making powers also have been used to prevent the erosion of current accounting standards and practices. Anecdotal evidence suggests that, in the application of accounting principles, techniques develop and become commonly used that accelerate the recognition of income or create other effects desired by management. These effects may not be consistent either with economic reality or with the conventional application of the accounting models, and they are widely perceived as abuses. They raise questions about the validity of accounting measurement in general. Some of these cases arise when the interpretation of an established standard makes possible results that were not anticipated by the standard setters.

Beyond its rule-making powers, the commission extensively uses its review and comment process, together with the power not to accelerate the effectiveness of a registration statement, to discourage accounting applications its staff believes inappropriate.

In addition to adopting formal rules, the commission sometimes uses accounting series releases as a vehicle for identifying general problems, which it then urges registrants and public accountants to address in financial reporting. These releases may deal with limited topical problems, or they may identify problems of great breadth and very general application, such as disclosure of inventory profits and disclosure of unusual risks and uncertainties in financial reporting. Such exhortation is frequently a means of calling attention to a problem that the commission believes ultimately should be dealt with by a private standard-setting body.

CONTACT WITH STANDARD SETTERS

While speeches, rule making and public releases are effective techniques in the commission's stimulation of standard setting, direct formal and informal contact with standard-setting bodies in the private sector also is essential in the exercise of its oversight role. The commission and its staff spend a great deal of time monitoring professional standard-setting bodies, and they frequently see representatives of such bodies who are seeking communication, counsel and sometimes approval of proposed actions. The commission's chief accountant frequently discusses current problems from his vantage point, urging actions of various sorts. In a few cases, the standard-setting body has been asked to take action on specific problems, presenting the clear alternative of formal SEC action if no professional standard is promulgated. These cases are the exception and, in most circumstances, the informal communications between the bodies are simply part of a cooperative effort to achieve the best solutions to difficult problems.

In the case of accounting standards, the commission does not make formal responses to FASB proposals, because the commission's statutory authority is such that it can't express an official view on a standard and then accept a significantly different result. In the case of auditing and other kinds of standards, however, the chief accountant, with the authorization of the commission, does sometimes offer specific comments and, from time to time, these comments may forcefully express concern. Such expressions are normally given considerable weight by the bodies involved.

Beyond its impact on standard setting, the commission has exercised significant influence on financial reporting by overseeing the audit function and the activities of the public accounting profession. It has devoted substantial resources to the assurance of audit quality and independence, and it has encouraged expansion of the auditor's role. This has been done in part through enforcement activities the staff has investigated in which it has sought to correct shortcomings by developing remedial sanctions and through extensive reports of the commission's view on audit deficiencies.

The commission also has steadily supported the formation of corporate audit committees through a series of exhortative releases and proxy disclosure rules. It has encouraged the accounting profession to develop improved concepts of auditor independence, and it has led the profession in a number of respects by imposing its own guidelines. The commission also has moved to develop the concept of continuous auditing and the more regular involvement of auditors with corporate reports.

CONCLUSIONS

In summary, the SEC's role has been an extremely active one, one in which its encouragement of innovation and change has contributed to the development of financial reporting. Looking to the future, it seems likely that the importance of the commission's role will continue. The basic economic forces that impinge on standard setters seem to point in this direction.

To suggest this, however, is not to suggest a dominant position for the SEC. The commission's role is to contribute to an environment in which standard-setting bodies can work with greater imagination and creativity than they otherwise could. Traditionally, the more active the commission, the more active the private sector in developing accounting methodology and disclosure approaches. The dynamism of accounting in the 1980s, therefore, is likely to depend on the joint action of the private sector accounting institutions and of their creative irritant, the SEC.

I: Accounting: What Does It all Mean?
The Commission's Biggest Failure

Homer Kripke
Chester Rohrlich Professor of Law Emeritus
New York University
Distinguished Professor of Law
San Diego State University

Accounting was Congress' most important charge to the Commission and represented the Commission's greatest opportunity to be of use to the investor.[1] There is little in mandated disclosure of use to the investor other than financial data presented principally in accounting terms. The description of the business is usually too brief and general; it suffers both from the SEC's desire to keep its mandated documents short and from the relics of its notion that it is prescribing disclosure for the layman, the person in the street. For anyone making a serious analysis of a company, information about a company's market position, technology, and the other sophisticated factors related to its business has to come from sources outside mandated disclosure. Anyone who has read a good brokerage or analytic write-up of a company knows how much better it describes the company's operations than the mandated disclosure does.

Similarly, the mandated documents are of little use in appraising the competitive position or the quality of the management of a company. A company cannot reasonably be expected to be able or willing to disclose meaningfully either its competitive position or the strengths or weaknesses of its management. A useful appraisal of these facts for the serious investor must come through the opinions of management's peers, not from mandated disclosure.

This leaves the financial data. There is nothing as important, yet as baffling and as difficult, as the translation of the events of the real world into numerical abstraction. The accounting system has the potentiality to abstract concepts such as annual income or net worth so that a meaningful comparison can be made between companies and of the performance of the same company from year to year. Which system of abstraction is meaningful and useful? This is *the* key problem of mandated securities disclosure, and it is the one problem which the SEC chose to turn over to the technicians while it sat on its own hands for 40 years. While Dr. John C. Burton, the SEC's recent Chief Accountant, was an innovator whose tenure marked the high point in the SEC's contact with accounting principle and the needs of investors, he too was born into and accepted the tradition and leadership of the accounting profession.

From *The SEC and Corporate Disclosure: Regulation in Search of a Purpose,* pp. 142–158. Reprinted by permission of Homer Kripke and Law and Business, Inc. Copyright © 1979 by Law and Business, Inc.

[1]In this part "accounting" includes financial reporting unless the context indicates otherwise.

Dr. Burton has said that the Commission could never have had the manpower and the resources to establish accounting principles. But one thinks of the enormous financial and human resources the SEC has devoted to exposing alleged impairment of the *"integrity of the books"* by pursuing "questionable payments" all over the world which may not even have been illegal when made and which are reflected on the books as sales expense. Wouldn't these resources have been better devoted to consideration of the *meaning of the books,* the optimum usefulness of accounting, instead of passing on this fundamental responsibility of the SEC to the practitioners?

Accounting is an art and technique by which the real world of economic events is abstracted into numbers that can be grouped by periods through arithmetical addition and subtraction, and compared with the numbers of the same economic entity for different periods and with the numbers of other entities for the same and different periods.

Accounting is not *discovered* but instead is an *agreed-on* set of techniques whose selection *legislates* its meaning and prima facie determines how we are permitted to see the world. Its correctness and its usefulness depend on what one wants to achieve. The present structure of double-entry bookkeeping began in Renaissance Italy and its technical history and structure can be accurately traced by accounting historians from that time (Yamey and Littleton, 1956, particularly the essay by Edey and Panitpakdi; Edey, 1965). The question of what accounting *means* is the ultimate issue of securities regulation and securities disclosure. It is a question which the SEC should have made its special concern, but which it never formulated or even grasped until recently.

When securities disclosure requirements were adopted in the 1933 and 1934 Acts, accounting disclosure was made a key feature, but no consistent theory of accounting existed nor was it understood that accounting had developed without any specific relation to the needs of investors.

Its origins in a primitive trading economy and its later use for the reports of stewards to landowners caused accounting to be thought of primarily as a report of stewardship. With the growth of large-scale enterprise in the corporate form, the inadequacy of this concept should have been obvious, but it was not.

Until the early 1970s many persons asserted that the function of accounting was primarily a stewardship of the funds entrusted to management by the owners of the business. This was the view expressed in 1968 by Thomas Murphy, then controller, now chairman, of General Motors Corporation (Burton, 1968, p. 229). This stewardship concept was the description which best fitted accounting practice in the view of Herbert Knortz, Senior Vice-President and Controller of I.T.&T. (although he did not agree with this narrow view) (Knortz, 1971; see also Rosenfield, 1972).

But in the modern corporate era, accounting's responsibilities have outgrown its simple techniques. Its fundamental structure, the accrual system of double-entry bookkeeping, arose to fit the needs of simple mercantile companies. Under the rules for realization of income, it serves the useful purpose of postponing the recognition of expenditures as expenses until the income to which they are related is permitted to enter the income account. It serves to prevent meaningless fluctuations of income by reason of the timing of payment of bills or collection of receivables. The double-entry system is beautiful in its conception and execution, with an infinitely expansible technique that is flexible enough to record any data supplied to it. But our question here is whether the data are useful—whether the abstraction of the economic world fits the needs of investors.

The twentieth century explosion in the size and complexity of financial transactions has outrun the conceptual basis for the simple concepts of accrual and deferral. Here is a list of some of the complexities of modern corporations:

—Fixed assets and depreciation to spread their cost over several accounting periods
—The treatment of initial losses and startup costs
—The treatment of research and development (R&D)
—Long-term debt, fluctuating interest rates and discounts
—Failure to recognize the time value of money and the total burden of a debt contract, including interest
—Currency conversion
—The investment tax credit and its result in the use of leasing instead of purchase with ordinary debt arrangements
—Complex capital structures, convertibles, "funny money" and potential dilution of earnings per share
—The heavy load of taxation, divergence of tax accounting and financial accounting, and the problem of deferred taxes

With its new responsibilities, accounting needed a new conception of its function.

I argued in 1971 that the purpose of accounting was to serve the needs of the serious investor (Kripke, 1972). This was also essentially the view expressed by Dr. Robert T. Sprouse and Mr. David Norr in opposition to Mr. Murphy's stewardship view (Burton, 1968, pp. 48, 201). It was also the view that Mr. Burton expressed in his many lectures as chief accountant of the SEC.

But accounting and financial reporting were not developing to fill the needs. As stated by Prof. A. D. Barton, Head of Accounting at the Australian National University (1977, pp. 467, 489):

> The most fundamental defect of current accounting practice is that it is not designed as a financial information system for the purposes of decision-making and evaluation, and as a consequence it lacks direction....
>
> The final problem in providing useful information occurs because all *decision-making* by creditors, investors and management *of necessity requires information about the future as well as about the present. Yet ex post accounting provides only information about the past and current periods, i.e., it provides only one half the information required*[2] [emphasis added].

Financial reporting as controlled by the SEC thus became less and less adequate to the needs of investors. One study reported that only one of eight points deemed important in an analysis of Xerox Corporation was an accounting point (Ross, 1970, p. 108). Given a choice of additional information, other analysts chose

---

[2]See also *Financial Executives Research Foundation,* 1973 (pp. 16, 19), emphasizing that future earnings are pivotal for evaluation, but cannot come from financial statements.

economic and industry information in preference to accounting information (Pankoff and Virgil, 1970, p. 7).

The accountants, to their credit, responded to the need by breaking the shackles of the stewardship concept. Some rejected it altogether. The simple truth was effectively stated by Mr. Graham Corbett (1972, p. 7), a British member of one of the largest international firms of accountants:

> As far as stewardship is concerned, I think it is time we all recognized that balance sheets and profit and loss accounts are not in fact used, and perhaps never were used, by shareholders or by anyone else to ascertain whether proper standards of stewardship have been observed. They look to the auditors to tell them this and—without prejudice—I believe they are entitled to do so.

Others, including the FASB, reinterpreted stewardship to mean a flexible concern for the information needs of investors, present and prospective (Rosenfield, 1972). The first papers of the FASB's Conceptual Framework present a picture of accounting and financial information which emphasizes the information needs of investors (1976a, ¶¶1–10; 1976b, ¶¶8–20; 1978, ¶¶22, 34–44).

Where was the SEC, which had the statutory responsibility for accounting, during this period? Nowhere at all, prior to the advent of John C. Burton as Chief Accountant. It is true that it had always spoken of the needs of investors, but it never examined how accounting fitted their needs. The SEC was wrong in its rigidity, wrong in arbitrarily excluding values, wrong in excluding computations of cash flow, wrong in excluding projections of the future.

The present structure of accounting is in part a matter of history and in part a matter of technique forced on accountants, issuers, and users by the SEC. Except for its still tentative venture into requiring replacement cost data (but even then as supplemental information outside the formal financial statements), the SEC seemingly has never recognized that accounting is a matter that can be shaped to meet the needs of investors. Far from working at the job itself or from pressing the accounting agencies to do so, the Commission originally obstructed the effort or did nothing. In 1952, Earle C. King, then Chief Accountant of the SEC, objected to suggestions that price level accounting be explored (Study Group on Business Income, 1952, at 122). SEC spokesmen criticized the first integrated efforts toward a conceptual framework, Accounting Research Studies Nos. 1 and 3 by Professors Moonitz and Sprouse, which came very close to current modern thinking about fair value accounting. Its then Chief Accountant, Andrew Barr, took a negative view (ASR No. 3, p. 60) and William W. Werntz, its former Chief Accountant, while more thoughtful, was essentially more conservative (id., p. 79). In the 1960s the SEC opposed the presentation of price level adjusted data in registration statements and discouraged the AICPA from taking action in the area (Arthur Andersen & Co., 1969, p. 10–11). In 1965 the SEC refused to permit a public utility company to file a registration statement in which it supplemented its financial statements based on historical cost with statements based on current cost to reflect the effect of inflation on utility plant balances and depreciation (id.). The commission apparently had no input into the next integrated effort, APB Statement No. 4 (1970), and no visible input into the AICPA's decision to go ahead with the study which led to Objectives of Financial Statements (1973) (the Trueblood Report).

The Commission's failure to consider the purposes and nature of financial accounting led to forty years' stagnation of accounting thought within the practicing profession. The SEC had professional discussion primarily with the AICPA, which would necessarily accommodate the Commission's views. It essentially ignored the academic accountants and their organization, the American Accounting Association, which over this period were moving steadily toward accounting based on value (Fiflis and Kripke, 1977, pp. 194–96, 431–36).

The Advisory Committee suggested that accounting should be shaped to provide information as to the amounts, certainty, and timing of future cash flows (Report, pp. D–29, 499–505), but the Commission, awaiting movement by the FASB on the Conceptual Framework (Williams, 1978b), has taken no action in this respect.

Even now, as the SEC belatedly realizes the importance of a conceptual framework of accounting, the Commission remains outside the effort, offering peripheral advice to the FASB in speeches while encouraging others like the Financial Executives Institute to support a new approach to accounting (Williams, 1978b).

Viewing the structure of accounting as something existing independently in the world, the SEC has considered the structure to be one best discovered and perfected by accounting specialists and thus has primarily left the matter to "self-regulation" by the profession.

II: "Self Regulation" by Accountants

Homer Kripke
Chester Rohrlich Professor of Law Emeritus
New York University
Distinguished Professor of Law
San Diego State University

The SEC's delegation of its statutory responsibility for the control of accounting has been challenged by the Moss Committee and Metcalf Committee.[1] The subject matter is referred to as "self-regulation" by the accounting profession, or as "formation of accounting principles in the private sector," as distinguished from government control. These terms are misnomers and they obscure the real issues.

The term "self-regulation" appropriately concerns discipline of members of the profession. Discipline has been a responsibility of the Ethics Committee of the AICPA and the Committee has failed. Professor Briloff has pointed out that the Ethics Committee boldly names names and punishes local accountants for minor infractions like advertising, while it lacks either the will or the courage to address the

Source: From *The SEC and Corporate Disclosure: Regulation in Search of a Purpose,* pp. 149–158. Reprinted by permission of Homer Kripke and Law and Business, Inc. Copyright © 1979 by Law and Business, Inc.

[1] Succeeded after Senator Metcalf's death by a subcommittee headed by Senator Eagleton.

problems presented by the serious auditing failures of major firms. He points to the careful anonymity surrounding expulsion of members of a major firm even after criminal conviction (Briloff, 1976, pp. 350–353). I am not aware of any serious attempt to rebut Briloff's comments. The result of this failure at self-regulation has been that the real task of disciplining the major firms has been taken over by the SEC through proceedings which consider the firms' right to practice before it. However, the punishments have usually been slaps on the wrist such as short-term suspensions timed to do the firms the least possible harm, or requirements for continuing education.

That self-regulation has been a failure is in effect conceded by the SEC in its 1978 Report to Congress, pp. 4–7, 15. The AICPA, in response to the pressures of the Congressional committees, has acted to change its organizational structure by creating a Division of CPA Firms with an SEC Practice Section wielding disciplinary powers, and with a Public Oversight Board studded with distinguished names, including two former chairmen of the SEC.

Apart from discipline, I submit that the term "self-regulation" obscures the nature of the functions that have actually been performed by the accountants' agencies. These agencies were the Committee on Accounting Procedure of the AICPA, which was followed by the Accounting Principles Board of the AICPA. While the AICPA includes in its membership certified public accountants who are officers or employees of issuers, academics, and others, these two AICPA agencies were principally composed of, were chaired by, and were dominated by representatives of the auditing, or public accounting, profession. The present Financial Accounting Standards Board (FASB), which succeeded the APB, was purposely structured originally to preserve the dominance of the AICPA. Although its constitutional structure has recently been changed to reduce this dominance, the FASB in all likelihood will continue primarily to reflect the point of view of the public accounting profession.

Should such a private agency, under the rubric of self-regulation, be allowed to determine the scope of certified financial statements—that is, determine how much work its primary constituents, the public accountants, will perform at the expense of issuers? This power of the public accountants, delegated and rubber-stamped by the SEC, calls to mind ancient analogies—the farming out of tax collection and the franchising of toll collection on roads and rivers to private individuals. Since by statute publicly traded corporations must supply certified financial statements, should not the public agency charged with control of accounting mediate between the issuers, which must pay the cost, and the monopolistic profession which "certifies" the statements? Should government which mandates public protection through the certification process let the protector determine how much "protection" he shall furnish, and charge fees accordingly?[2] By requiring segmented disclosures the FASB recently expanded public accountants' work and fees at the expense of

[2] While my use of the term "protection" and the analogy it suggests is no accident, I do not mean to disparage the FASB or the public accounting profession, for both of which I have the highest respect. But the mere fact that such a suggestive analogy is possible illustrates to me that the present structural situation and the passivity of the SEC are wrong.

issuers, without their consent. The SEC obligingly acquiesced because this was a determination of " generally accepted accounting principles," and it failed either to hold a hearing on this delegated rulemaking, or to consider the costs involved, the relationship of the costs to the benefits, and the vital question of who reaps the benefits for this tax which the FASB imposes on issuers.

Seemingly, the FASB and its predecessor failed to recognize that they were mediating between their primary constituency, the public accountants, and issuers. Wherever certified financial statements were desired, they imposed with total insensitivity significant costs and wasteful effort on private corporations (and on public corporations in nonpublic situations), who were required to make the same full computations and presentations of earnings per share and of segmented information required of public corporations in public situations (APB Opinion No. 15; FASB Statement No. 14). Only public protest by small issuers forced FASB to suspend these requirements (FASB Statement No. 21).

More fundamental than the foregoing problems is that "self-regulation" permits private parties with no public mandate to adjudicate important private rights under the rubric of "accounting principles." Accounting principles have (or may have) important substantive effects. Professor Rappaport has said (1977):

> There is a growing recognition that the setting of financial accounting standards which govern what business corporations report (i.e., disclosure issues) and how they must describe their economic operations (i.e., measurement issues) needs to be viewed more broadly than simply from a technical accounting perspective....
>
>   The expanded view of standard setting comes from an increasing recognition that the legislation of accounting standards involves a potential redistribution of wealth, i.e., it imposes restrictions or costs on some while conferring benefits to others. This phenomenon places a particularly heavy burden on the FASB as a private sector body, because in the final analysis the responsibility of mediating conflicting values in our society rests with Congress rather than with any private sector organization. Congress...has, in fact, delegated standard setting to the SEC and other federal agencies.

Rappaport adds, "The SEC, in turn, has delegated some of its power to the FASB"; but I ask what authority it has to do so.

Rappaport repeats: "...it can be concluded that financial accounting standards existing at a particular time have an economic impact by their influence on securities prices and thereby on the wealth of market participants."

A debate rages over how much the FASB should take these effects into consideration (Rappaport, 1977, and authorities cited; Wyatt, 1977). The FASB has responded by appointing several study panels to consider the economic impact of its decisions. But the FASB's recognition of the problem merely highlights the SEC's untenable position of passivity, and its enforcement of private legislation of rights under the guise of recognizing generally accepted accounting principles.

Banks and bank regulatory agencies recently brought heavy pressure on the FASB concerning the rules it was considering on restructuring of debt in troubled situations (which became FASB Statement No. 15). All of these persons believed that the rules to be adopted would have important substantive effect—in Rappaport's words, they would transfer wealth from some persons to others. Regardless of the merits of the controversy, by what right did a private agency undertake to legislate these private rights (after it complied with its own invented "due process") and by what authority did SEC franchise its own statutory responsibility to FASB to make these decisions after compliance with the Administrative Procedures Act?

I have questioned this kind of delegation for many years, beginning before the FASB was created. While the Wheat and Trueblood Committees were still working on the studies which led to the establishment of the FASB, a meeting was called at Northwestern University to discuss how the new agency would develop accounting principles. I there said (1972, p. 393):

> ... The spectacle of the SEC submitting position papers to the APB as to what accounting principles should be, in order that the APB can make a determination which the SEC will then enforce (presumably whether or not the Board has agreed with the SEC's submission) reverses the appropriate state of affairs. This reversal of role happened only recently on a question of cost and value intimately related to our present problem, as reported in the *New York Times* of May 25, 1971, p. 53, when the APB held a hearing on the valuation of marketable securities by insurance companies. The SEC submitted that the continuing weight of authority for adherence to historical cost should not be disregarded.
>
> A more proper allocation of responsibility would have the Accounting Principles Board and other accountants submitting their views to the SEC before the SEC announced the rules governing accounting measurements that would be enforced on the public....

Similarly, I think that it is simply wrong that the Chairman of the SEC should have to be out on the hustings (1977a, 1977b, 1978c) trying to marshal public support to persuade the FASB that financial disclosure should show the erosion of capital through inflation. The content of financial disclosure is a matter the SEC should *decide,* not lobby for.

The determination of what accounting should mean is the SEC's most important job—too important to be left to others. I do not say that accountants' organizations and other private groups should not be consulted. Determining what accounting means is the responsibility not only of accountants but, also, of such users of accounting data as financial analysts and other securities professionals, as well as the representatives of the issuers. The analogy to the legal aspects of securities regulation is a close one, and should have been followed by the SEC: on these legal aspects, when SEC proposes new rules the SEC does not enfranchise a lawyers' organization like the American Bar Association to take over, but invites comments to aid its own decisional process. The ABA, other lawyers' groups, and all other professional groups are free to respond and do respond, and the SEC carries through the rule-making procedures prescribed by the Administrative Procedures Act. Only in the field that is considered to be accounting (an expanding field, as will be seen below) does the SEC enfranchise representatives of the technicians involved to decide the issue, with other interested parties having to make their points to the technicians while the SEC remains passive.

There was no reason for the SEC to abdicate in this fashion. It could have worked out a relationship with the accountants like the one it has with the Bar, which has always been cooperative in making its experience available on draftsmanship, frequently challenging the SEC's proposals on principle or usefulness, but never challenging the SEC's right to make the decisions within the framework of the statutes. Only the accountants succeeded, in the SEC's formative days, in forcing delegation to them by, in effect, threatening not to cooperate with the SEC. (This long story is well told in Chatov, 1975, Chapters 6 and 8).

The SEC's permitting and encouraging the accountants' organizations to take the lead in formulating accounting principles might have been appropriate if the Commission had regularly (and not merely in the isolated instances to which it now points) viewed their determinations as proposals for Commission rules affecting private rights rather than rubber-stamping them as "generally accepted accounting principles."

Professor Horngren's paper (1972) rightly observed that the Commission is potentially a supreme court with the power to reverse the determinations of the accounting agencies. This reality makes it ineffective for the Commission to maintain its usual "hands-off" stance toward accounting determinations and then sometimes to wage guerilla warfare to influence them. Fiflis and Kripke, 1977, pp. 562–564 and 568, recounts the Commission's disapproval of APB actions and interventions to achieve the capitalization of leases in accordance with its views. The SEC's hasty adoption of ASR 190, requiring replacement cost disclosure in order to forestall the FASB's "purchasing power" accounting proposal, constitutes another example of guerilla warfare. The SEC's requirement of valuation of oil and gas reserves (Rels. 33–5878 and 5966 CCH $_\pi$ 81356 and 72275), which the FASB had just rejected in its statement No. 19, is a further example. (The fact that I agree with the Commission's substantive positions in these matters does not nullify my distaste for these spasmodic recaptures of a jurisdiction unwisely abandoned.)

The SEC's abdication was never complete—in a few isolated instances the SEC forced the issue on a point of accounting (Kripke, 1970, p. 1178). Ironically, in ASR 150, after the SEC reaffirmed its delegation of leadership in accounting to the newly formed FASB, the SEC assumed a slightly more activist role in 1972–1976 while Dr. John C. Burton was Chief Accountant. He drew a distinction between measurement principles, which the SEC had delegated to the FASB, and issues of financial disclosure, which it had reserved for itself (Burton, 1974, pp. 151–153). However, the distinction was tenuous: the FASB and the accountants did not accept the distinction between measurement and disclosure, and bemoaned the SEC's encroachment on the "private sector."

It has frequently been said publicly that the accounting profession, despite its original deprecation of emphasis on annual earnings per share, was finally pushed into treating this computation as an accounting matter (Fiflis and Kripke, 1977, pp. 473–475, quoting Mr. J. S. Seidman, who was then a member of the APB and a former president of the AICPA). While no one has quite said publicly that it was the SEC that did the pushing, I take this for granted.[3]

---

[3] The accounting rules which stemmed from these events (APB Opinion No. 9, ¶¶30–51) had to be revised within three years (APB Opinion No. 15) and have since had to be interpreted endlessly. The total result, including the unfortunate emphasis on earnings per share for one year, has not commended itself to many and has resulted in a bewildering proliferation of "bottom lines" on income statements. Such computations should have been left to the individual security analyst or security buyer, because they involve judgments as to the appropriate treatment of convertibles, warrants, and so forth. However, the expression of such a view, which might have come from the security analysts, was precluded by jurisdiction being taken by the accounting profession under the secret pushing of someone, presumably the SEC.

Should not a public agency's input be open to public view rather than being visible only in the context of guerilla warfare? Should not its input be open to review under the Administrative Procedures Act, in contrast to the determination of the accountants' private organizations which cannot be reviewed? (See the Appalachian Power case, cited in note 4, below.)

With Dr. Burton gone, the SEC has not pressed the distinction between measurement and disclosure. But the APB's and FASB's blunders in requiring inappropriate expenditures of effort by small and private companies in disclosing earnings per share and in segmented disclosure occurred precisely because these requirements are concerned with disclosure, not measurement. Measurement principles should not change on the basis of whether the economic events are reported by a small or a large company or for private or public use. But disclosure requirements are frequently affected by these different circumstances, as in the examples mentioned. FASB Statements have increasingly become detailed "cookbook" prescriptions on disclosure. See, for example, Nos. 5, 8, 12, and 13.

Indeed, the accounting profession now seeks to take over from the SEC all responsibility for financial reporting and the SEC shows a disposition to acquiesce. The FASB's *Statement of Financial Concepts No. 1* (1978) defines its topic as "Objectives of Financial Reporting," and its subject matter is "not restricted to information communicated by financial statements" (¶16). SEC Chairman Williams (1978a, 1978b) believes that this extension of FASB scope is wise, but in my opinion this additional sloughing off of SEC's statutory jurisdiction presents serious problems.

A proper approach to the relationship of the public and private sectors was taken by Congress in the Energy Policy and Conservation Act of 1975. It there permitted the FASB to formulate rules for the treatment of exploration expenses for oil and gas (the successful efforts versus full costing problem), but it required the SEC to reach an independent judgment, which it did, disagreeing with the FASB (ASR 253). This procedure should be the model for development of all accounting principles and SEC's finally granting them official status. When this sytem is adopted, an FASB rule will not exist in a twilight zone, not subject to judicial consideration, but will result in a public agency determination which has clear procedures for adoption and review under the Administrative Procedures Act.[4]

This model was used by the Interstate Commerce Commission, which provided that it will formally notice the FASB determinations and after a response period and consideration of objections, these determinations will become agency determinations with a clear status in our legal system.

Since it is apparent throughout this book that I have no overwhelming admiration for the SEC's overall performance in the field of disclosure in recent years, one may wonder why I advocate that the SEC have a strong role in determining accounting principles. Apart from the reasons of principle enumerated above, I have a reason of policy. I hope that by taking the technicians out of control of securities disclosure the SEC can, in the light of present knowledge of the operations of the securities market, take a fresh approach to the meaning and purpose of disclosure. See Part V.

Why has the SEC so long played this game? Why has it delegated authority to the

---

[4]See *Appalachian Power Co. v. AICPA,* discussed in Fiflis and Kripke, 1977, pp. 533–34.

accountants' agencies, sometimes expressly or implicitly threatening the accountants with withdrawal of the delegation if they did not move a little faster (Chatov, 1975, pp. 223, 227, 240, 250), but always closing ranks with the accountants against Congressional committees and other outside criticism (SEC Report to Congress, 1978). Why does the SEC insist on this delegation of its authority?

We are told that the Commission does not have the manpower to take over the job.[5] That may be true, but it is the result of the decision to delegate, taken over forty years ago. That decision is reflected in budgets and in the Commission's failure to acquire a reputation as a good training ground for young accountants in contrast to its excellent reputation as a training ground for lawyers.

This excuse is inconsistent with the SEC's refusal to allow a transfer of its jurisdiction under the Public Utility Holding Company Act. It fought unsuccessfully to retain in the Bankruptcy Act of 1978 its role under Chapter X of the Bankruptcy Act of 1898, although it kept the staff allotted to the function at a minimum, and few observers found its role useful. In addition, the SEC wants control of disclosure in the municipal bond field, although the Municipal Finance Officers Association is pressing for a new type of "control in the private sector." Again, why does the SEC delegate authority in accounting while reaching for authority in other areas?

My answer is that the Commission concerns itself with surface problems that can be forced into the mold of morality. It has not developed a capacity to probe beneath the surface to the hard problems—in the case of accounting, the nature of the financial reality to be abstracted and the kind of reporting that will be useful for the investor.

It is so much easier to submerge these hard problems under the rubric of leaving accounting principles to the private sector while crusading on moralistic issues like "questionable payments" and "perks."

---

[5]The Commission's former Chief Accountant, Dr. Burton, has said: "The SEC is not in a position to establish accounting principles, even though we have the statutory authority to do so. The [accounting profession] can devote more hours and financial resources to this area than can the Commission." (Burton, 1973, p. 57.)

BIBLIOGRAPHY & STATUTES, ETC.
(Extracts)

Advisory Committee Report. (See SEC: Report of the Advisory Committee on Corporate Disclosure.)

American Institute of Certified Public Accountants, 1952. Study Group on Business Income, *Changing Concepts of Business Income.*

American Institute of Certified Public Accountants, 1973b. "Objectives of Financial State-ments" in *Report of the Study Group on the Objectives of Financial Statements*—the "Trueblood Report."

American Institute of Certified Public Accountants, 1974. *Objectives of Financial Statements, Volume 2, Selected Papers.*

Barton, A. D., 1977. *The Anatomy of Accounting* (2d ed.).

Briloff, A., 1976. *More Debits than Credits.*

Burton, J. C. (ed.), 1968. "Corporate Financial Reporting: Conflicts and Challenges"(Report on the First Seaview Conference).

Burton, J. C., 1973. "The SEC and the Changing World of Accounting," *J. Contemporary Business* (Spring 1973).

Burton, J. C., 1974. "Elephants, Flexibility and the Financial Accounting Standards Board," 29 *Bus. Lawyer* 151 (special issue, March 1974).

Chatov, R., 1975. *Corporate Financial Reporting.*

Corbett, G., 1972. "Accounting Principles and Reports," in "Facing the Future," Eight Papers Presented at a Conference on "The Changing World of the Accountant," organized by the London District Society of Chartered Accountants.

Edey, H., 1965. "Company Accounting in the 19th and 20th Centuries," 48 *The Accountants J.,* April 1965 at 65, May 1965 at 127.

Edey, H. and Panitpakdi, P., 1956. "British Company Accounting and the Law, 1844–1900," in B. S. Yamey and A. C. Littleton (eds.), *Studies in the History of Accounting,* p. 356.

Fiflis, T. J. and Kripke, H., 1977. *Accounting for Business Lawyers* (2d ed.).

Financial Accounting Standards Board. 1976a. Discussion Memorandum: *Conceptual Framework for Financial Accounting and Reporting: Elements of Financial Statements and Their Measurement.*

Financial Accounting Standards Board, 1976b. *Tentative Conclusions on Objectives of Financial Statements of Business Enterprises.*

Financial Accounting Standards Board, 1978. *Statement of Financial Accounting Concepts No. 1: Objectives of Financial Reporting by Business Enterprises.*

Horngren, C. T., 1972. "Accounting Principles: Private or Public Sector," 133 *J. Accountancy* 37 (May 1972).

Knortz, H. C., 1971. "The Credibility of Accounting Principles," *The Conference Board Record* 33 (April 1971).

Kripke, H., 1970. "The SEC, the Accountants, Some Myths and Some Realities," 45 *N.Y.U.L. Rev.* 1151.

Kripke, H., 1972. "The Objective of Financial Statements Should Be to Provide Information for the Serious Investor," in A. Rappaport and L. Revsine (eds.), 1972, reprinted in 42 *CPA J.* 389 (1972) and cited to that source; also reprinted in Zeff and Keller, 1973.

Pankoff, L. and Virgil, R., 1970. "Some Preliminary Findings from a Laboratory Experiment on the Usefulness of Financial Accounting Information to Security Analysts," in *Empirical Research in Accounting: Selected Studies,* 1970, p. 1.

Rappaport, A., 1977. "Economic Impact of Accounting Standards—Implications for the FASB," *J. Accountancy* 89 (May 1977).

Rosenfield, P., 1972. "Stewardship," in *AICPA, 1974,* p. 123.

Ross, H., 1970. "The Wonderful World of Accounting," in *Empirical Research in Accounting—Selected Studies,* p. 108 (Supplement to Vol. 8, *J. Accounting Research*).

Williams, H., 1977a. Lecture on Gerald Loeb Awards, Oct. 18, 1977.

Williams, H., 1977b. "Inflation, Corporate Financial Reporting and Economic Reality," address before the Conference Board, New York, Dec. 13, 1977.

Williams, H., 1978a. Address to AICPA, Jan. 4, 1978.

Williams, H., 1978b. "Current Problems in Financial Reporting and Controls," address to Financial Executives Institute, Los Angeles, Oct. 9, 1978.

Wyatt, A., 1977. "The Economic Impact of Financial Accounting Standards," 37 *The Arthur Andersen Chronicle* 49 (Sept. 1977).

Yamey, B. S. and Littleton, A. C. (eds.), 1956. *Studies in the History of Accounting.*

STATUTES, AGENCY REPORTS, AND LEGISLATIVE
HEARINGS AND REPORTS
(Extracts)

HOUSE OF REPRESENTATIVES, UNITED STATES CONGRESS, 1976. "The Moss Committee Report,"COMMITTEE ON INTERSTATE AND FOREIGN COMMERCE, SUBCOMM. ON OVERSIGHT AND INVESTIGATIONS, Report: Federal Regulation and Regulatory Reform, 94th Cong., 2d Sess., Ch. 2 (Subcommittee Print).

METCALF COMMITTEE REPORT. See Senate Committee on Government Operations.

MOSS COMMITTEE REPORT. See House of Representatives, Committee on Interstate and Foreign Commerce.

Securities and Exchange Commission, 1977. "Advisory Committee Report." Report of the Advisory Committee on Corporate Disclosure to the Securities and Exchange Commission, printed as House Committee Print 95–29 and 95–30, 95th Cong., 1st Sess. (1977) for the use of the House Committee on Interstate and Foreign Commerce.

SENATE, UNITED STATES CONGRESS, 1977. "The Metcalf Committee Report": The Accounting Establishment, A Staff Study Prepared by the Subcommittee on Reports, Accounting and Management, of Senate Committee on Government Operations, Senate Doc., No. 95–34, 95th Cong., 1st Sess.

THE PLACE OF OBJECTIVES AND A CONCEPTUAL FRAMEWORK

Since the early years of the century, accounting academics and professionals have sought to develop a general theory of accounting. Such works as Charles E. Sprague's *The Philosophy of Accounts* (Sprague, 1908), William A. Paton's *Accounting Theory—With Special Reference to the Corporate Enterprise* (Ronald, 1922), and John B. Canning's *The Economics of Accountancy* (Ronald, 1929) were early efforts by American educators to understand and develop general theories of accounting. An attempt by a professional accountant was Kenneth MacNeal's *Truth in Accounting* (University of Pennsylvania Press, 1939), and in the same year Stephen Gilman, an accounting educator, sought to discover harmonies in a discordant theory literature in *Accounting Concepts of Profit* (Ronald, 1939). In 1940, Paton combined with A. C. Littleton to produce *An Introduction to Corporate Accounting Standards*, which was published by the American Accounting Association. The Paton and Littleton monograph, as it came to be known, has had a profound effect on the American accounting literature.

This is not to suggest that only Americans were concerned with accounting theory. Such writers as Edwards and Bray in Great Britain; Schmalenbach, Schmidt, and Walb in Germany; Limperg in the Netherlands; Zappa in Italy; and Fitzgerald in Australia were foremost among the pioneers who made major contributions to accounting theory during the first half century.

In the second half of the century, the number of contributors to the theory literature multiplied several times. Beyond the very substantial writings of academics and professionals, working on their own, there have been significant attempts by accounting bodies to fashion an accounting theory. It is these institutional initiatives that are of primary interest here, as the very utterances by accounting bodies have been intended to lead to a direct improvement in the quality of companies' financial reporting.

Probably the earliest attempt by an accounting body to formulate a coherent statement of theory occurred in 1936, when the fledgling American Accounting Association published a five-page "tentative statement" of the "bases upon which accounting standards rest."[1] The leaders of the association, mostly academics, had hoped to crystallize opinion on accounting principles within the profession, lest the task of establishing accounting principles and practices be left, by default, to the recently created Securities and Exchange Commission. The Paton and Littleton monograph, issued four years later, was proposed as an elaboration of the bases set forth in the 1936 AAA principles statement. In 1941 and later years, the association issued revisions of its 1936 statement.

An organization composed chiefly of academics seldom can compete with a practitioner body for influence on professional practice. Yet, prior to 1938 there was nowhere in the world a practitioner body that had undertaken, on a continuing, programmatic basis, to issue pronouncements in order to guide the course of accounting practice. It was therefore an event of considerable significance when in 1938 the American Institute of Accountants (as the AICPA was then known) empowered its Committee on Accounting Procedure to issue a series of Accounting Research Bulletins for the edification of practicing accountants and their client companies. The Institute was reacting to pressure from the SEC to provide "substantial authoritative support" for assistance in limiting the range of "generally accepted accounting principles."[2] From that time forward, the initiative for promoting changes in American accounting practice has been in the hands of the accounting profession, although the public sector (chiefly the SEC) has closely monitored its progress and has occasionally intervened in the profession's decision-making process.

While the Committee on Accounting Procedure had, on several occasions in the late 1930s and 1940s, considered expressing itself on fundamental accounting principles, in order to guide its thinking on particular practice issues, it always retreated from the task. In the 1950s, however, it became clear to the committee and to Institute leaders that little progess could be made on the really difficult issues until agreement was reached on fundamental concepts. Such issues as tax allocation, price-level accounting, the all-inclusive versus current-operating-performance concept of the income statement, and accounting for business combinations had either divided the committee or driven a wedge between the committee and the SEC. Underlying these confrontations was a deep philosophical difference over whether a committee which was unable to unite on a single recommended practice could, by the political expediency of a two-thirds majority, impose its will on accounting firms and companies who agreed with the minority. Institute leaders concluded that these differences could best be addressed by a major investment of resources in fundamental research. If agreement could be reached on fundamentals, it was believed, the accounting principles and rules implied by those fundamentals would become evident to all. In 1959, the Institute dramatized the new emphasis on research by terminating the Committee on Accounting Procedure in favor of an

---

[1] "A Tentative Statement of Accounting Principles Affecting Corporate Reports," *The Accounting Review* (June 1936), p. 187.

[2] See Stephen A. Zeff, *Forging Accounting Principles in Five Countries: A History and an Analysis of Trends* (Champaign, IL: Stipes, 1972), pp. 134–139.

impressive-sounding Accounting Principles Board. The new Board was equipped with an accounting research division, and both were charged with divining the "basic postulates" and "broad principles" of accounting.

In 1961–1962, two research studies were published under APB auspices: *The Basic Postulates of Accounting* by Maurice Moonitz and *A Tentative Set of Broad Accounting Principles for Business Enterprises* by Robert T. Sprouse and Moonitz. But the Board found itself unable to accept the "radical" recommendations for accounting reform contained in the two studies, and the first phase of its optimistic search for fundamentals died aborning. Since the APB had to develop opinions on particular issues coming before it, the Board proceeded to face each issue on an ad hoc basis, without a body of fundamental theory to guide it, just as its predecessor, the Committee on Accounting Procedure, had done. This was the first inkling that the task of obtaining agreement on a basic accounting theory—one that would underlie the principles to be applied to the particular problems of accounting practice—was a very difficult one indeed.

The APB made two other stabs at providing a basis for accounting theory development, but both were primarily descriptive rather than normative. In 1965, the Institute published Paul Grady's survey of existing practice and pronouncements, entitled *Inventory of Generally Accepted Accounting Principles for Business Enterprises*, which had been commissioned by the Board. Five years later in 1970, the Board issued Statement No. 4, "Basic Concepts and Accounting Principles Underlying Financial Statements of Business Enterprises," which was, in the main, an enumeration of the concepts and principles reflected in existing practice. (Furthermore, as a statement, not an opinion, the pronouncement was only advisory and not mandatory.)

As the accounting profession entered the 1970s, there was a growing and persistent belief that progress on accounting standards could not be achieved without the development of a conceptual framework (as it came to be called). The APB had been issuing opinions in even more controversial areas than had the Committee on Accounting Procedure, and the rising chorus of criticism of the APB's work served to rededicate leaders of the Institute to a search for fundamental principles. In 1971, the Institute, amid criticism from all sides, appointed a special study to inquire into the objectives of financial statements. Membership in the study group was broadly based: three partners of Big Eight firms, two accounting professors, two financial executives, an investment analyst, and an economist. Robert M. Trueblood, a distinguished practitioner and former Institute president, was named chairman. In its 67-page report entitled *The Objectives of Financial Statements* (AICPA, 1973), the study group broke with the traditional orientation of financial statements toward reporting on stewardship and instead emphasized their usefulness in providing investors and creditors with information "for predicting, comparing, and evaluating potential cash flows to them in terms of amount, timing, and related uncertainty."[3]

---

[3] *Objectives of Financial Statements* (AICPA, 1973), p. 20. For a summary of the main conclusions of the Trueblood Study, written by the study's research director, see George H. Sorter, "Objectives of Financial Statements—An Inside View," *CAmagazine* (November 1973), pp. 30–33. A set of critiques of the study's conclusions, written by Ross M. Skinner, Edward Stamp, Robert K. Mautz, and R.J. Chambers, may be found in "The Trueblood Report: Promise or Progress?," *CAmagazine* (December 1973), pp. 12–20. A lengthier criticism may be found in K. V. Peasnell, *Accounting Objectives: A*

(In a path-breaking principles statement published in 1966, a committee of the American Accounting Association had foreshadowed the Trueblood Study report by focusing on the usefulness of accounting information for economic decisions, rather than on stewardship.[4])

In 1973, as in 1959, the standard-setting deck was swept clean, and the Financial Accounting Standards Board replaced the much-criticized Accounting Principles Board. In addition to issuing Statements of Financial Accounting Standards (SFASs), which constituted substantial authoritative support of "generally accepted accounting principles," the FASB began a series of Statements of Financial Accounting Concepts (SFACs). The SFACs were intended to be the building blocks of the Board's conceptual framework. SFAC No. 1, issued in 1978, entitled "Objectives of Financial Reporting by Business Enterprises," largely endorsed the recommendations of the Trueblood Study group, although the Board expanded its concern from financial statements alone to all forms of financial reporting by a company's management, including quantitative and qualitative disclosures.

SFAC Nos. 2 and 3, both issued in 1980, dealt with the "qualitative characteristics of accounting information" and the "elements of financial statements," respectively. But once these SFACs were published, the Board came to the realization that the really hard decisions on "recognition" and "measurement" defied an easy consensus. Recognition refers to the criteria for determining when changes in assets, liabilities, and owners' equities (including revenues, expenses, and losses) are to be recorded in the accounts. "Measurement" concerns the dollar numbers to be assigned to these changes, once they are "recognized." These are the fundamental questions of asset and liability valuation and income determination—questions which bedeviled both the Committee on Accounting Procedure and the Accounting Principles Board. Apart from an SFAC dealing with nonbusiness organizations, no further SFACs have since been issued by the FASB.

Institutionally sponsored research has been conducted in other countries on both objectives and a conceptual framework.[5]

Studies on objectives have appeared in Australia and the United Kingdom. In 1972, Australia's Accountancy Research Foundation published a study, entitled *Objectives and Concepts of Financial Statements*, by W. J. Kenley and G. J. Staubus, which was preceded by a 1970 study, *A Statement of Australian Principles*, written by W. John Kenley and patterned on Paul Grady's 1965 *Inventory* done for the APB. The Australian standard-setting bodies (there were then two) failed to take any action on the two studies. A second Australian study, sponsored by the same foundation, was published in 1982: Allan D. Barton, *Objectives and Basic Concepts of Accounting*. An even more ambitious project was undertaken in the United Kingdom in 1974–75, when an eleven-member working party of the Accounting Standards Steering Committee produced an 81-page discussion paper

Critique of the Trueblood Report, ICRA Occasional Paper No. 5 (Lancaster, England: International Centre for Research in Accounting, University of Lancaster, 1974).

[4] *A Statement of Basic Accounting Theory* (Sarasota, FL: American Accounting Association, 1966).

[5] An interesting review of the efforts in several countries appears in K. V. Peasnell, "The Function of a Conceptual Framework for Corporate Financial Reporting," *Accounting and Business Research* (Autumn 1982), pp. 243–246.

on the "scope and aims of published financial reports in the light of modern needs and conditions."[6] Entitled *The Corporate Report*, the discussion paper contained some daring recommendations, including proposals that management publish a value added statement and a statement of future prospects, and a suggestion that companies' financial reports incorporate multiple valuation bases (i.e., some combination of historical cost restated for inflation, replacement cost, net realizable value, net present value, and value to the firm). Even though the members of the working party, who represented a wide spectrum of interests and occupations in the accounting profession and the financial community, approved the report unanimously, the parent Accounting Standards Steering Committee never formally addressed its recommendations.

In 1980, the Canadian Institute of Chartered Accountants published a major study dealing with both the substance of a conceptual framework and the process by which it might be implemented by a standard-setting body. Entitled *Corporate Reporting: Its Future Evolution*, the study was written at the request of the CICA by Edward Stamp, who is both a U.K. academic and a Canadian chartered accountant. Stamp proposes a number of criteria (the FASB earlier had used a different term, "qualitative characteristics," to describe its own criteria) to be used by preparers, users, standard setters, and others for assessing the quality of financial reporting to users. In regard to the manner of implementing a conceptual framework, Stamp writes, "It is an integral part of the philosophy of this Study that the development of accounting standards should be evolutionary, and that it is not right to adopt a deterministic, authoritarian, or normative approach."[7] He recognizes that user needs are not homogeneous and unchanging, and he rejects the view that a conceptual framework may not provide for alternative permissible accounting treatments and even different valuation bases. (Stamp was an influential member of the U.K. working party which gave favorable consideration to multicolumn reporting in 1974–75, using different valuation bases.) He believes that the FASB's approach to developing a conceptual framework and setting accounting standards may be likened to the codification mentality found in civil law jurisdictions. Stamp favors a common law approach in which the CICA's Accounting Standards Committee would use the knowledge and experience of its members to develop standards based on objectives and qualitative criteria such as those proposed in his study. He also provides for an appeals board to hear problems raised by auditors in the course of their engagements. Stamp's view of the standard-setting process is essentially judicial, while it would seem that the FASB sees itself more as a legislative body.[8]

Institutional differences make comparisons between Canadian and American

---

[6] *The Corporate Report* (London: Accounting Standards Steering Committee, 1975), p. 1.

[7] Edward Stamp, *Corporate Reporting: Its Future Evolution* (Toronto: Canadian Institute of Chartered Accountants, 1980), p. 95.

[8] For a criticism of the Stamp Report, see John Boersma, "Corporate Reporting in Canada and the US," *CAmagazine* (July 1981), pp. 30–35, and Stamp's reply, Letters, *CAmagazine* (October 1981), pp. 13, 15. Also see the papers by T. Ross Archibald, John F. Dewhirst, and Gordon C. Fowler in *Research to Support Standard Setting in Financial Accounting: A Canadian Perspective*, edited by Sanjoy Basu and J. Alex Milburn (Toronto: The Clarkson Gordon Foundation, 1981), pp. 218–253. An article in which Stamp summarizes his approach is "Accounting Standards and the Conceptual Framework: A Plan for Their Evolution," *The Accountant's Magazine* (July 1981), pp. 216–222.

solutions difficult. In Canada, provincial securities commissions and federal and provincial legislative authorities have, in the main, vested substantial autonomy in the CICA; with few exceptions, the CICA's Accounting Standards Committee is unfettered by the continuing surveillance of an aggressive government agency. In the United States, by contrast, the SEC monitors the FASB closely, and it imposes highly specific reporting requirements on companies subject to its jurisdiction. The SEC's thirst for detailed reporting and its bureaucratic aversion to flexible treatments serve as constraints on the FASB's professional liberty.

Notwithstanding the worldwide research that has been conducted both by individuals and institutions, in no country has the standard-setting body published any definitive judgments on the most difficult issues of substance and process that form part of a conceptual framework. The Americans have taken the longest strides, but the hardest ground—veritably a minefield of problems—is yet to be traversed. In his article, "The Conceptual Framework: Make No Mystique About It," Paul A. Pacter contributes the assessment of an FASB staff member. He reviews the efforts of the APB and discusses the work done to date by the FASB. Pacter reports that "there are significant differences of opinion among board members about the concepts that should guide recognition in financial statements." And the Board has concluded, he adds, that measurement questions are inseparable from recognition questions. At the close of his article, Pacter suggests some implications of SFAC Nos. 1–3 for some of the Board's recent and current standards projects.

Nicholas Dopuch and Shyam Sunder, in a widely cited article, "FASB's Statements on Objectives and Elements of Financial Accounting: A Review," argue first, that there is little reason to be optimistic that a conceptual framework will point toward a resolution of controversial accounting issues, and, second, that the meaningfulness of a conceptual framework is open to serious question when accounting is seen in its social context. They believe that reporting issues cannot be viewed only through the eyes of external users of information. As they write, "A user-primary notion in the selection of objectives of financial accounting which ignores how firm managers are likely to adjust their behavior to the new information system (and how this adjustment in management behavior will affect the interests of the so-called users) represents a very short-sighted view of the problem. As such, solutions derived from this simplified approach will not work." Managers also have needs, and they will make cost-benefit calculations when advocating preferred standards before the FASB and when selecting alternative standards or methods in the preparation of their companies' financial statements. When, in 1966, Dudley E. Browne, a senior financial officer of Lockheed Aircraft Corporation and past president of the Financial Executives Institute, defended the use of "accounting as a competitive tool," he shocked the profession.[9] More than a decade later, academics and leading professionals came to realize that managers as well as financial statement users have needs and unless both sets of needs are accommodated, the standard-setting process may not be politically viable.[10]

---

[9] Dudley E. Browne, "Cost of Imposing Uniform Accounting Practices," *Financial Executive* (March 1966), p. 44.

[10] For development of the thesis that managers' interests should be understood and accommodated, see Lauren Kelly-Newton, *Accounting Policy Formulation: The Role of Corporate Management* (Reading, MA: Addison-Wesley Publishing Company, 1980).

In "Uses and Limitations of a Conceptual Framework," Charles T. Horngren, an accounting academic who served on the Accounting Principles Board, accepts the view that accounting policy-making is a social-choice problem, and he counsels the FASB on what this view implies for the conceptual framework. Each Board member and each interested party, Horngren maintains, will have his or her own individual "technical framework." An official conceptual framework "may help if it structures the arguments and provides a common language when dealing with a complicated issue," but the final decision necessarily will be a reflection of the compatibility of the collective individual frameworks of those who cast the votes. Horngren contends that it is futile for the Board to attempt to develop a conceptual framework in highly concrete terms, since such a framework is likely to lose the Board a considerable amount of constituent support. It is important that the Board secure acceptance for its policy decisions, and a framework at a fairly high level of generalization (i.e., without seeming to tread on the perceived interests of a great many parties) is most likely to gain that acceptance. Once such a framework is in place, Horngren believes it will be helpful in leading to the resolution of some controversies, but perhaps not in others.

In "Economic Impact of Accounting Standards—Implications for the FASB," Alfred Rappaport examines the issue of economic consequences in relation to a conceptual framework. He suggests that the Board may choose from three possible strategies: pure conceptual framework, pure economic impact, or a mixture of conceptual framework and economic impact. Rappaport prefers the last of the three. A pure conceptual framework strategy, he maintains, would be seen as unresponsive to the interests of affected parties. A pure economic impact strategy raises both the question of the social legitimacy of the FASB as well as "serious reservations about whether the accountant's education and training are particularly suited toward assessing the impact of accounting choice and then making the social choice implied by the measurement or disclosure standard adopted." The most feasible strategy, Rappaport claims, is a mixture of the two, which he illustrates in the context of the controversy over the restructuring of troubled debt (FASB Statement No. 15).

BIBLIOGRAPHICAL NOTES

A number of important studies (other than those cited above) have proposed general accounting theories, of which the following are among the most prominent:

Edwards, Edgar O. and Philip W. Bell: *The Theory and Measurement of Business Income* (Berkeley, CA: University of California Press, 1961).

Staubus, George J.: *A Theory of Accounting to Investors* (Berkeley, CA: University of California Press, 1961). (Reprinted in 1971 by Scholars Book Co.)

Hansen, Palle: *The Accounting Concept of Profit* (Amsterdam: Einar Harks, 1962). (Second edition was published in 1972 by North-Holland Publishing Company, Amsterdam.)

Mattessich, Richard: *Accounting and Analytical Methods* (Homewood, IL: Richard D. Irwin, Inc., 1964). (Reprinted in 1978 by Scholars Book Co.)

Bedford, Norton M.: *Income Determination Theory: An Accounting Framework* (Reading, MA: Addison-Wesley, 1965).

Chambers, Raymond J.: *Accounting, Evaluation and Economic Behavior* (Englewood Cliffs, NJ: Prentice-Hall, Inc., 1966). (Reprinted in 1974 by Scholars Book Co.)

Ijiri, Yuji: *The Foundations of Accounting Measurement* (Englewood Cliffs, NJ: Prentice-Hall, Inc., 1967).

Sterling, Robert R.: *Theory of the Measurement of Enterprise Income* (Lawrence, KS: The University Press of Kansas, 1970). (Reprinted in 1979 by Scholars Book Co.)

Revsine, Lawrence: *Replacement Cost Accounting* (Englewood Cliffs, NJ: Prentice-Hall, Inc., 1973).

Baxter, William T.: *Accounting Values and Inflation* (London: McGraw-Hill Book Company (UK) Limited, 1975).

Anthony, Robert N.: *Tell It Like It Was* (Homewood, IL: Richard D. Irwin, Inc., 1983).

The AICPA's 1961 study on "basic postulates" by Moonitz and 1962 study on "broad accounting principles" by Sprouse and Moonitz, no longer available from the Institute, have been reprinted, together with other articles of the day and some previously unpublished papers, in the following volume:

Zeff, Stephen A. (ed.): *The Accounting Postulates and Principles Controversy of the 1960s* (New York: Garland Publishing, Inc., 1982).

A volume containing many of the papers considered by the Trueblood Study Group during the course of its deliberations is:

Cramer, Joe J., Jr. and George H. Sorter (eds.): *Objectives of Financial Statements—Volume 2, Selected Papers* (New York: AICPA, 1974).

A study that was undertaken at the request of the U.K. Accounting Standards Committee and which concludes that "A 'conceptual framework' for accounting should be regarded rather as a common basis for identifying issues, for asking questions and for carrying out research than as a package of solutions," is:

Macve, Richard: *A Conceptual Framework for Financial Accounting and Reporting: The Possibilities for An Agreed Structure* (London: The Institute of Chartered Accountants in England and Wales, 1981).

A comprehensive study of Canadian standard setting is:

Skinner, Ross M.: *Accounting Principles: A Canadian Viewpoint* (Toronto: Canadian Institute of Chartered Accountants, 1972).

A wide-ranging critique of traditional accounting practice and promulgated standards, which makes a case for an improved set of standards with particular reference to Australia, is:

Company Accounting Standards, Report of the Accounting Standards Review Committee, chaired by R. J. Chambers (Sydney, Australia: Government Printer, New South Wales, 1978).

In the 1960s and 1970s, four Seaview Symposiums were held to discuss the views of preparers and users of financial statements. The proceedings from three of the Symposiums were published in the following volumes:

Burton, John C. (ed.): *Corporate Financial Reporting: Conflicts and Challenges* (New York: AICPA, 1969).
Burton, John C. (ed.): *Corporate Financial Reporting: Ethical and Other Problems* (New York: AICPA, 1972).
Carmichael, D. R. and Ben Makela (eds.): *Corporate Financial Reporting: The Benefits and Problems of Disclosure* (New York: AICPA, 1976).

Several conferences have been held to discuss standard setting and the fashioning of a conceptual framework, five of the proceedings from which are as follows:

Berkeley Symposium on the Foundations of Financial Accounting (Berkeley, CA: Schools of Business Administration, University of California, 1967).
Rappaport, Alfred and Lawrence Revsine (eds.): *Corporate Financial Reporting: The Issues, The Objectives and Some New Proposals* (Chicago, IL: Commerce Clearing House, Inc., 1972).
The Conceptual Framework of Accounting (Philadelphia, PA: The Wharton School, University of Pennsylvania, 1977).
Economic Consequences of Financial Accounting Standards: Selected Papers (Stamford, CT: FASB, 1978).
Basu, Sanjoy and J. Alex Milburn (eds.): *Research to Support Standard Setting in Financial Accounting: A Canadian Perspective* (Toronto: The Clarkson Gordon Foundation, 1982).

The FASB has sponsored two research studies on the "recognition" problem:

Ijiri, Yuji: *Recognition of Contractual Rights and Obligations* (Stamford, CT: FASB, 1980).
Johnson, L. Todd and Reed K. Storey: *Recognition in Financial Statements: Underlying Concepts and Practical Conventions* (Stamford, CT: FASB, 1982).

The Conceptual Framework: Make No Mystique about It

Paul A. Pacter*
Executive Assistant to the Chairman
Financial Accounting Standards Board
Currently Commissioner of Finance, City of Stamford, Connecticut

Goethe said it a century and a half ago: "All theory is gray."[1] And the Financial Accounting Standards Board's conceptual framework project is probably no exception. While you can get your hands around a good old-fashioned "black-and-white" accounting practice question, concepts are often intangible. There is a mystique about them.

The FASB's project is much more down to earth, however, than the mystical image that the phrase *conceptual framework* may conjure up. Board deliberations in developing the framework are punctuated repeatedly by pragmatic discussion of how proposed concepts would apply to real case situations. The concepts pronouncements that have been issued to date include illustrative examples. (There is a whole section of these in FASB Concepts Statement no. 3, *Elements of Financial Statements of Business Enterprises*.[2]) And the board and its staff now routinely assess the implications of the established concepts in each standards project addressed by the FASB.

This article has two purposes. One is to describe the FASB's progress up to now in developing a conceptual framework for financial accounting and reporting and to summarize the board's plans in this area for the remainder of this year and beyond. The second is to illustrate some implications of the concepts to specific accounting questions. The FASB's conceptual framework eventually will encompass reporting by nonbusiness organizations as well as business enterprises; however, the focus throughout this article will be on concepts applicable to financial reporting by businesses.

THE APB AND THE CONCEPTUAL FRAMEWORK

Although the FASB's predecessor—the Accounting Principles Board—didn't reach agreement on a set of concepts designed to point a direction for setting accounting standards, it wasn't for lack of trying. The American Institute of CPAs' special committee whose 1958 report led to the creation of the APB a year later had urged

---

From *Journal of Accountancy* (July 1983), pp. 76–78, 86–88. Reprinted by permission of the American Institute of Certified Public Accountants. Copyright © 1983 by the American Institute of Certified Public Accountants, Inc.

*Ed. note: The views expressed in this article are those of Mr. Pacter. Official positions of the Financial Accounting Standards Board on accounting matters are determined only after extensive due process and deliberations.

[1] Johann Wolfgang von Goethe, *Faust*, "Mephistopheles and the Student," line 2038.

[2] Financial Accounting Standards Board Concepts Statement no. 3, *Elements of Financial Statements of Business Enterprises* (Stamford: FASB, 1980).

the APB to work on concepts as well as specific standards. Such concepts, that committee said, would "provide a meaningful foundation for the formulation of principles and the development of rules or other guides for the application of principles in specific situations."[3]

Two of the early research reports that were published under the APB's auspices dealt with the "postulates" and "broad principles" of accounting.[4] But neither of those studies began with a statement of what the objectives of corporate accounting were—or ought to be. And the second study contained a number of specific broad principles that were quite different from accounting practice then or now. For example, one of the principles was that most inventories should be reported at replacement cost, whether greater than or less than historical cost, thus recognizing a holding gain or loss before the sale. Another principle involved measuring plant and equipment at current replacement costs and another restating the basic financial statements for changes in the general purchasing power of the dollar.

The APB, after reviewing the two studies, concluded that they "contain inferences and recommendations in part of a speculative and tentative nature."[5] In its very first public utterance in 1962—even before its first opinion was published—the APB stated that "they are too radically different from present generally accepted accounting principles for acceptance at this time."[6]

Just a few months after the public statement, the APB issued its first two opinions. While Opinion no. 1, *New Depreciation Guidelines and Rules*,[7] was relatively noncontroversial, Opinion no. 2, *Accounting for the "Investment Credit,"*[8] was anything but. It called for the deferral method of accounting for the newly enacted investment tax credit. As a result, during 1963 and 1964 the APB's efforts were turned away from accounting concepts and toward a struggle for its credibility and perhaps even its survival.

Because of the problems that developed with the APB's investment credit opinion, the AICPA council, in the spring of 1964, appointed a special committee on opinions of the Accounting Principles Board to reexamine the AICPA's program for establishing accounting principles. That committee reported to council a year later.[9] Among its major recommendations were

> At the earliest possible time, the [APB] should:
>
> **1** "Set forth its views as to the purposes and limitations of published financial statements...."

---

[3]Special Committee on Research Program, "Report to Council of the Special Committee on Research Program," JofA, Dec. 58, p. 63.

[4]Maurice Moonitz, Accounting Research Study no. 1, *The Basic Postulates of Accounting* (New York: AICPA, 1961); and Robert T. Sprouse and Maurice Moonitz, Accounting Research Study no. 3, *A Tentative Set of Broad Accounting Principles for Business Enterprises* (New York: AICPA, 1962).

[5]Accounting Principles Board Statement no. 1, *Statement by the Accounting Principles Board* (New York: AICPA, 1962), par. 2.

[6]Ibid., par. 3.

[7]APB Opinion no. 1, *New Depreciation Guidelines and Rules* (New York: AICPA, 1962).

[8]APB Opinion no. 2, *Accounting for the "Investment Credit"* (New York: AICPA, 1962).

[9]Special Committee on Opinions of the Accounting Principles Board, *Report of the Special Committee on Opinions of the Accounting Principles Board* (New York: AICPA, 1965).

2 "Enumerate and describe the basic concepts to which accounting principles should be oriented."

3 "State the accounting principles to which practices and procedures should conform."

4 "Define the words of art employed by the profession, such as 'substantial authoritative support,' 'concepts,' 'principles,' 'practices,' 'procedures,' 'assets,' 'liabilities,' 'income,' and 'materiality.' "[10]

In short, the APB was again charged with developing a conceptual framework.

In response to this charge, the APB began a project that led, in October 1970, to the publication of APB Statement no. 4, *Basic Concepts and Accounting Principles Underlying Financial Statements of Business Enterprises*.[11] APB Statement no. 4 described the environment and objectives of financial accounting and catalogued all of the then-current broad accounting principles the APB could identify as having some degree of general acceptance.

In its own words, APB Statement no. 4 was "primarily descriptive, not prescriptive."[12] Thus, the objectives discussed in that statement were the goals toward which corporate financial reporting was then being directed, not necessarily the objectives toward which it ought to be directed. This was particularly true for the principles of financial statement measurement and presentation in APB Statement no. 4.

This approach led one APB member, in his dissent to Statement no. 4, to write that "guidelines for the future are urgently required, but the [APB] is looking backward to what has occurred rather than forward to what is needed.... This Statement—by providing a conceptual basis for, and by giving authoritative status to, current accounting practices—will represent an unfortunate deterrent to the achievement of improvements in practice."[13]

APB Statement no. 4 was issued at a time when abuses of accounting principles—most notoriously in the areas of accounting for business combinations and goodwill—were much discussed in the business and popular press. The unfavorable publicity caused the AICPA's board of directors, in January 1971, to call a meeting of 35 prominent CPAs representing 21 major accounting firms, with AICPA President Marshall S. Armstrong presiding, to discuss accounting standard setting. After extended discussion, the conference adopted a resolution strongly urging the AICPA president to appoint two study groups, which would act independently of one another, one to review the operations of the APB and the other to define the objectives of financial statements.[14] With the approval of the AICPA board of directors, Armstrong appointed a study group on the establishment of accounting principles headed by Francis M. Wheat and a study group on the objectives of financial statements headed by Robert M. Trueblood.[15]

The result of the Wheat study group, whose report was published in March 1972,

---

[10]"Summary of the Report of the Special Committee on Opinions of the Accounting Principles Board," JofA, June 65, p. 12.

[11]APB Statement no. 4, *Basic Concepts and Accounting Principles Underlying Financial Statements of Business Enterprises* (New York: AICPA, 1970).

[12]Ibid., par. 3.

[13]Ibid., George R. Catlett's dissent.

[14]"Conference Recommends Study of Efforts to Establish Accounting Principles," JofA, Feb. 71, pp. 11–14.

[15]"Wheat, Trueblood Head Studies on Financial Reporting," JofA, May 71, pp. 10–12.

was the creation of the FASB.[16] The Trueblood study group continued its work until October 1973, when its report, *Objectives of Financial Statements*, was published by the AICPA and transmitted to the FASB.[17]

FASB INITIATIVES

The new FASB met in March and April 1973 to plan its initial technical agenda. Needless to say, members and staff of the FASB were mindful that its predecessor was criticized for not having made adequate progress toward developing a normative set of objectives and concepts for corporate financial reporting. And so, among the seven projects on the FASB's initial technical agenda was one that encompassed the objectives of financial reporting (though it was originally titled "broad qualitative characteristics") and another on the concept of materiality.

Work on the FASB's objectives project began with consideration of the Trueblood study group's report. An FASB discussion memorandum (DM) entitled *The Objectives of Financial Statements and the Qualitative Characteristics of Financial Reporting*[18] inviting comment on the objectives in the Trueblood report was issued in June 1974, and a public hearing was held in September.

But then two years went by before the FASB published its tentative conclusions on the objectives of financial reporting. A period of extraordinarily high rates of inflation had begun in 1973 and continued for almost the rest of that decade. As a result, in 1974 the board's conceptual discussions turned away from objectives and toward measurement. Late that year, the board proposed to require supplemental financial statement disclosure of historical data restated to dollars of constant purchasing power. Several months later, though, that proposal itself was sidetracked as a result of a 1975 proposal by the Securities and Exchange Commission, adopted in 1976 as Accounting Series Release no. 190, to require supplemental disclosure of certain replacement cost data.[19] In light of ASR no. 190, the FASB deferred action on its constant dollar proposal and turned its efforts to a broader look at accounting measurement questions as part of the conceptual framework project.

In December 1976 the board published both a DM, *Elements of Financial Statements and Their Measurement*,[20] and Preliminary Views, *Tentative Conclusions on Objectives of Financial Statements of Business Enterprises*[21]—the latter a preexposure draft of the board's thinking on objectives.

The board held a public hearing on objectives and elements in August 1977 and a

[16]Study on Establishment of Accounting Principles, *Establishing Financial Accounting Standards* (New York: AICPA, 1972).

[17]Study Group on the Objectives of Financial Statements, *Objectives of Financial Statements* (New York: AICPA, 1973).

[18]FASB Discussion Memorandum, *The Objectives of Financial Statements and the Qualitative Characteristics of Financial Reporting* (Stamford: FASB, June 1974).

[19]Securities and Exchange Commission Accounting Series Release no. 190, *Notice of Adoption of Amendments to Regulation S-X Requiring Disclosure of Certain Replacement Cost Data*, March 23, 1976.

[20]FASB DM, *Elements of Financial Statements and Their Measurement* (Stamford: FASB, December 1976).

[21]FASB Preliminary Views, *Tentative Conclusions on Objectives of Financial Statements of Business Enterprises* (Stamford: FASB, December 1976).

second hearing, principally on measurement issues, early in 1978. In December 1977, the board published a two-part Exposure Draft (ED), *Objectives of Financial Reporting and Elements of Financial Statements of Business Enterprises.*[22] After reviewing the comments on that ED, the board voted unanimously to issue Concepts Statement no. 1, *Objectives of Financial Reporting by Business Enterprises*, in November 1978.[23] The board deferred for separate consideration its tentative conclusions on the elements of financial statements. The December 1977 ED also had included a section on the qualitative characteristics of accounting information; tentative conclusions on that area also were deferred for separate consideration by the board.

Meanwhile, during this period, the board also was working on standards for reporting the effects of changing prices. Late in 1978 the board issued an ED, *Financial Reporting and Changing Prices*,[24] which was finalized in September 1979 as FASB Statement no. 33, *Financial Reporting and Changing Prices*.[25]

The board continued its work on the conceptual framework in 1979 and 1980, completing Concepts Statement no. 2, *Qualitative Characteristics of Accounting Information*,[26] in May 1980 and Concepts Statement no. 3 in December 1980.

With this historical perspective in mind, we can turn now to the substance of the board's conclusions on accounting and reporting concepts to date and then to the probable direction of events for the next year or two.

CONCEPTS STATEMENT NO. 1—OBJECTIVES

Concepts Statement no. 1 identifies investors, creditors and other outsiders as the primary users of the general purpose external financial reports of business enterprises. These individuals generally lack the authority to prescribe the information they want and must rely on the information managements communicate to them in reports designed to meet their common information needs.

The overriding objective of financial reports is to provide information useful in making investment, credit and similar decisions. It is worth noting that this objective relates to the whole of financial reporting, not just to financial statements. The objective will be met in part by information contained in financial statements and in part by supplementary information.

Building on this overall objective, Concepts Statement no. 1 recognizes the users' primary need for information helpful in assessing the amounts, timing and uncertainties of an enterprise's cash flows, and it describes the types of information that fulfill that need. This includes information concerning the enterprise's resources, obligations and owners' equity; information about enterprise performance; infor-

---

[22] FASB Exposure Draft, *Objectives of Financial Reporting and Elements of Financial Statements of Business Enterprises* (Stamford: FASB, December 1977).

[23] FASB Concepts Statement no. 1, *Objectives of Financial Reporting by Business Enterprises* (Stamford: FASB, 1978).

[24] FASB ED, *Financial Reporting and Changing Prices* (Stamford: FASB, December 1978).

[25] FASB Statement no. 33, *Financial Reporting and Changing Prices* (Stamford: FASB, 1979).

[26] FASB Concepts Statement no. 2, *Qualitative Characteristics of Accounting Information* (Stamford: FASB, 1980).

mation about liquidity, solvency and funds flows; and information about management stewardship and performance.[27]

These objectives are the foundation of the conceptual framework. That foundation is supporting two groups of projects. Projects in the first group deal with (1) defining, (2) recognizing and (3) measuring the basic elements of financial statements. In other words, they deal primarily with the concepts underlying the items and dollar amounts included in the financial statements in an enterprise's financial report.

The second group of projects is concerned with concepts for the display and disclosure of the elements of financial statements and other information that is useful in fulfilling the objectives of financial reporting. In short, these projects are concerned with presentation. Concepts being developed in this group, for example, will deal with the reporting of income, cash flows and financial position and with criteria for differentiating among financial statement disclosures, supplementary disclosures and information that is not part of financial reporting at all.

CONCEPTS STATEMENT NO. 2—QUALITATIVE CHARACTERISTICS

The project on qualitative characteristics, which led to Concepts Statement no. 2, links both groups of projects. In that statement, the board identified the characteristics or qualities that make accounting information useful. The key user-specific quality is understandability. Information can't be useful if it isn't understandable by those for whom it is intended. Understandability is partly within the control of the standard setter, but it also depends in part on the knowledge level of the user.

Relevance and reliability are the two primary qualities that make accounting information useful for decision making. Because these qualities are decision-specific, they are the principal concern of the standard setter.

To be relevant, information must have predictive value or feedback value, or both, and it must be timely. To be reliable, information must faithfully represent what it purports to represent, it must be verifiable and it must be neutral in the sense that it doesn't purposefully try to influence the decision maker toward or away from any specific decision. Comparability among companies and consistency from period to period in the information reported by a given company are secondary qualities that interact with relevance and reliability to contribute to the usefulness of information.

The qualities identified by the board in Concepts Statement no. 2 are tempered by several constraints. First of all, the board recognized that while the choice of an accounting alternative should ideally produce information that is more relevant and more reliable than other alternatives, there are trade-offs between relevance and reliability, and it may be necessary to sacrifice some of one quality for a gain in

[27]FASB Concepts Statement no. 1 doesn't include FASB conclusions on several of the objectives in the Trueblood report—for example, reporting current value and changes in current value, providing a statement of financial activities, providing financial forecasts, determining the objectives of financial statements for nonbusiness organizations and reporting enterprise activities affecting society. Some of those issues are dealt with in other current aspects of the FASB's conceptual framework project.

another. Also, information can be useful and yet be too costly to justify providing it; thus there is a cost-benefit constraint. Finally, all of the qualities of information are subject to a materiality threshold derived from the probable impact on a user's decision.

I might mention that the board's original materiality project was folded into this qualitative characteristics project when the board concluded that no general standards of materiality can be formulated to take into account all the considerations that enter into an experienced human judgment. Quantitative materiality criteria may be established in specific standards in the future, as they have been in some cases in the past.

CONCEPTS STATEMENT NO. 3—ELEMENTS

Concepts Statement no. 3 defines the elements of financial statements of business enterprises. The elements are the basic building blocks with which financial statements are constructed—namely, assets, liabilities, owners' equity, revenues, expenses, gains, losses and comprehensive income.

Assets are defined as probable future benefits that have arisen from past transactions or events. *Liabilities* are defined as current obligations for probable future sacrifices. *Owners' equity* is the difference between the two.

By defining assets and liabilities in terms of probable future benefits and sacrifices, the board has excluded from assets and liabilities those deferred charges and deferred credits whose sole justification is normalization or smoothing of earnings trends. To illustrate, in the past year or two some regulators of banks and thrift institutions have permitted their institutions, for regulatory reporting purposes, to defer losses on the sale of low-yielding mortgage portfolios and to amortize those losses over the term of new higher-yielding investments purchased with the proceeds from the sale. Such deferred losses are not assets under Concepts Statement no. 3.

Similarly, the old "reserves" for self-insurance, expropriations or catastrophes that some companies had systematically accrued in advance of a loss event wouldn't meet the board's definition of liabilities because, until the loss event occurs, nothing is owed to anyone.

Contrast the FASB's definition of an asset with the APB's definition in APB Statement no. 4:

> Assets—economic resources of an enterprise that are recognized and measured in conformity with generally accepted accounting principles. Assets also include certain deferred charges that are not resources but that are recognized and measured in conformity with generally accepted accounting principles.[28]

The APB had a parallel definition for liabilities. As a description of accounting practice in 1970, and to a somewhat lesser extent today, the APB's definition was appropriate. An asset was whatever GAAP chose to report as an asset, whether or not it represented a resource to the enterprise. And whatever GAAP chose to report as a liability was a liability, whether or not there is an obligation for future sacrifice

---

[28] APB Statement no. 4, par. 132.

involved. Those definitions don't provide a great deal of guidance for resolving an accounting question such as whether a bank should defer losses on sales of investments.

COMPREHENSIVE INCOME[29]

In FASB Concepts Statement no. 3, the board defined *comprehensive income* as the net effect of all recognizable events and transactions that change owners' equity during a period other than transactions with the owners. Thus, except for transactions with owners, under Concepts Statement no. 3 each and every change in owners' equity also is either a revenue or a gain or an expense or a loss, and the net effect of all of these is comprehensive income. Comprehensive income can be likened to the "all-inclusive" concept of income that most accountants have been familiar with for years and to which the APB gave support in its Opinion no. 9, *Reporting the Results of Operations.*[30]

Unfortunately, the board's concept of comprehensive income has sometimes been misinterpreted. The most serious misunderstanding, in my judgment, is the contention that comprehensive income requires that measurements be made on a current cost basis or on some other current value basis and that traditional asset and income recognition practices be abandoned. I do not believe that was the board's intent at all.

For one thing, the definition of comprehensive income does not presume any particular basis for measuring the events and transactions that enter into determining comprehensive income. And for another, the definition does not include criteria for selecting those events and transactions that should be recognized in determining comprehensive income. Recognition and measurement criteria are part of a separate conceptual framework project currently under way (discussed later in this article).

Current values are already the basis for certain measurements under the so-called historical cost GAAP accounting model today—for example, for accounts receivable, inventories, marketable equity securities and warranty obligations. Even if more value changes were ultimately to be deemed recognizable events, the board's definition of comprehensive income allows for subtotals of components of comprehensive income, such as the conventional historical cost net income figure. Indeed, the board has strongly suggested, in both Concepts Statement no. 3 and its 1981 ED, *Reporting Income, Cash Flows, and Financial Position of Business Enterprises,*[31] that the various components of comprehensive income may well need to be segregated to help the user of a financial report assess an enterprise's performance. Examples of segregating components of comprehensive income would include operating vs. nonoperating, recurring vs. nonrecurring and realized vs. unrealized.

Furthermore, the board hasn't yet reached any conclusion on whether comprehensive income would be reported in a single financial statement that would replace

---

[29] Also discussed by Paul A. Pacter in "The FASB at Ten: A View from Within," *Corporate Accounting,* Winter 1983, p. 30.

[30] APB Opinion no. 9, *Reporting the Results of Operations* (New York: AICPA, 1966).

[31] FASB ED, *Reporting Income, Cash Flows, and Financial Position of Business Enterprises* (Stamford: FASB, November 1981).

the current income statement. Unrealized changes in the values of net assets, if recognized at all in measuring comprehensive income, could be reported in a separate financial statement, or in a statement of changes in owners' equity or as supplementary information.

I might add that Concepts Statement no. 3 purposely doesn't define the term *earnings*, which is reserved for possible use to designate a significant intermediate component of comprehensive income, such as the traditional historical cost net income number or income from continuing operations.

RECOGNITION CONCEPTS[32]

As mentioned earlier, recognition and measurement concepts are being addressed as part of a separate conceptual framework project currently under way. Another current project addresses presentation concepts.

The recognition project got started even before the elements definitions were finalized. Two commissioned research studies were published by the board late in 1980—one surveying current practices in recognizing revenues, expenses, gains and losses and the other the recognition of contractual rights and obligations as assets and liabilities.[33] In addition, the board's staff undertook a research project, the results of which were published in mid-1982, describing basic recognition concepts and practical conventions.[34]

During 1981 and more extensively during 1982, the board spent considerable time deliberating accounting recognition issues. Several things became clear during those deliberations. First, there are significant differences of opinion among board members about the concepts that should guide recognition in financial statements. Second, recognition concepts are often inseparable from measurement considerations. And third, board members' views on financial statement presentation concepts are often related to views concerning recognition criteria. I would like to elaborate on each of these three points.

The differences of opinion within the board with regard to accounting recognition, which became apparent during the first half of last year, relate to concepts for recognizing changes in assets and liabilities while they are held. The focal point of the division was whether more current price changes should be recognized than are now recognized under GAAP. Some board members believe that changes in current prices are relevant and should be recognized—if they can be reliably measured. Other board members believe that historical costs evidenced by completed transactions and, in certain circumstances, recoverable costs are more relevant; they would therefore tend to prohibit expanded recognition of current prices.

However, board members are not split into two well-defined camps; rather, there

---

[32]Some of the discussion in this and the three following sections is based on a report, "Status of Conceptual Framework Projects," published in the FASB's *Status Report*, March 2, 1983.

[33]Henry R. Jaenicke, FASB Research Report, *Survey of Present Practices in Recognizing Revenues, Expenses, Gains, and Losses* (Stamford: FASB, 1981); and Yuji Ijiri, FASB Research Report, *Recognition of Contractual Rights and Obligations* (Stamford: FASB, 1980).

[34]L. Todd Johnson and Reed K. Storey, *Recognition in Financial Statements: Underlying Concepts and Practical Conventions* (Stamford: FASB, 1982).

is a range of views within the board. To my knowledge, no member of the board or its staff advocates reporting historical costs in all circumstances or current prices in all circumstances.

Moreover, board members who are inclined to lean conceptually toward greater recognition of current price changes than at present also acknowledge that the need for reliable measurements may well dictate a different answer at the accounting standards level. And all board members agree on one major point: if any significant change is ultimately concluded to be necessary, the change must be accomplished through a gradual, evolutionary process.

The nature of the differences among board members' views has led to the decision to use two separate staff teams, along with an outside consultant, to develop materials that will serve as a basis for discussions with the goal of developing a single set of recognition concepts that can be supported by a majority of the board. Those concepts will then be exposed for comment in a preliminary discussion document. If a significant minority view remains, it, too, will be exposed for comment. Any dissent to a majority view also will be included in that preliminary discussion document.

MEASUREMENT CONCEPTS

During its deliberations, the board has come to conclude that recognition decisions can't be separated from measurement decisions. For example, if a decision is made to recognize changes in the price of a marketable security while it is owned, a measurement decision has been made as well. The same is true for a decision to recognize a decline in the replacement cost or recoverable amount of inventory while it is held or a decision to recognize precious metals and agricultural commodities at their selling prices when they are mined or harvested. Furthermore, these aren't only balance sheet recognition and measurement decisions; each one has an effect on comprehensive income as well.

The inseparability of measurement and recognition issues caused the board to decide that the recognition project should incorporate the question of the attribute to be measured—such as historical cost, recoverable cost, current cost and current value. In deciding on the appropriate attribute to be measured, the board will have to look to the objectives of financial reporting and to the qualities that make accounting information useful for decisions, principally relevance and reliability.

PRESENTATION CONCEPTS

Concurrent with its consideration of recognition issues, the board also worked on three projects dealing with presentation concepts—one on reporting income, a second on reporting funds flows and liquidity and a third on financial statements and other means of financial reporting. Separate discussion documents on each of those areas were issued, with a combined ED on reporting income, cash flows and financial position published in November 1981.

While that ED was deliberately neutral on recognition issues, discussion within the board about the comments received on the ED revealed that board members' views on concepts of reporting income closely parallel their views on recognition. For example, adopting the conventional realization test for recognition of revenues and gains would preclude any need for a presentation concept dealing with reporting unrealized gains.

Because the concepts for determining what is to be recognized are interrelated with the concepts for reporting the resulting amount of income, the board has decided to defer further consideration of the issues related to reporting income until it has made basic decisions about recognition and measurement. The board hasn't decided whether the concepts of reporting income will be included in the recognition-measurement discussion document or addressed in a separate document.

REPORTING CASH FLOWS

The ED on reporting income, cash flows and financial position included concepts that suggested expanded reporting of cash flows—as opposed to working capital flows—in the statement of changes in financial position. This suggestion received substantial support in the comment letters. At about the time the ED was issued, the Financial Executives Institute took the initiative to encourage companies to report cash flows in their 1982 statements of changes in financial position. In light of the FEI initiative, the board has decided not to take action to amend APB Opinion no. 19, *Reporting Changes in Financial Position*,[35] at this time. The board's staff will be reviewing the funds flow reporting in 1982 corporate annual reports, and an FASB decision about whether to add a project to the board's agenda to amend APB Opinion no. 19 will be made after that review is completed. The staff also is currently conducting preliminary research on the appropriateness of funds flow reporting by banks and other financial institutions.

IMPACT OF ASSET AND LIABILITY DEFINITIONS

Like all other board discussion of technical issues, the debate over recognition of current price changes has been conducted "in the sunshine" and has received considerable publicity. Quite understandably, the debate on this issue has attracted the attention of the board's constituents. Regardless of the ultimate outcome of that debate, though, its impact on accounting practice is likely to be long-term rather than immediate.

Less attention has probably been paid to what might be regarded as a more immediate recognition issue—recognition, within the context of cost-based deferral and accrual accounting, of assets and liabilities as defined by the FASB in Concepts Statement no. 3. Those definitions have already begun to influence the board's thinking on any number of accounting standards issues.

For example, a company's obligation for compensated absences, such as vested vacation days or sick days that haven't yet been taken, is a present obligation for a probable future sacrifice and therefore meets the definition of a liability. That is the conclusion the board reached in Statement no. 43, *Accounting for Compensated*

---

[35] APB Opinion no. 19, *Reporting Changes in Financial Position* (New York: AICPA, 1971).

Absences.[36] Likewise, an employer's obligation for special incentive benefits granted to a limited group of employees over a short period of time as an inducement to terminate employment appears to satisfy the liability definition. And so does a company's obligation for the unfunded accumulated pension benefits earned to date by its employees.

Without an agreed-on definition of a liability, equally convincing arguments can be made for and against recognition of these obligations in the balance sheet in a historical-cost, accrual-accounting framework. Furthermore, a concept of income that is based on a loosely defined principle of matching costs and revenues does little to provide guidance on whether these liabilities—and their related income effects—should be recognized.

By having defined assets and liabilities, and having defined income in terms of changes in assets and liabilities, Concepts Statement no. 3 provides a frame of reference within which the FASB can question recognition or nonrecognition practices. The asset and liability definitions themselves are likely to have a direct and ongoing impact on accounting practice.

Other examples can be cited. The board looked to its definition of an asset in developing Statement no. 71, *Accounting for the Effects of Certain Types of Regulation.*[37] In that statement, the board concluded that a cost whose future recovery is assured by the rate-making process should be capitalized as an asset, even if the nature of the cost is such that companies in other industries would charge it to expense.

As another example, the board recently relied on its definition of a liability in addressing the question of whether a debt obligation is extinguished when cash or securities are deposited with a trustee for the purpose of repaying the obligation at some future date. The board concluded that a liability exists until the obligation to the creditor is fully satisfied.

Both the liability and asset definitions were relevant to the board's consideration of accounting for early retirement incentives. The board concluded that an employer incurs a present obligation to transfer assets as a result of the decision by an employee to accept the company's offer of early retirement and that the liability for termination benefits doesn't result in a probable future benefit that should be recognized as an asset.

Other examples of current standards projects in which accounting recognition issues have arisen include the projects on sales of receivables with recourse and, of course, the pension accounting project. Without a doubt, the definitions of assets and liabilities will be looked to in the board's reconsideration, recently begun, of accounting for income taxes; deferred income tax debits and credits, under the method of accounting prescribed by APB Opinion no. 11, *Accounting for Income Taxes,*[38] are not assets or liabilities as defined in FASB Concepts Statement no. 3, though the FASB's definitions do not rule out (or for that matter require) other methods of interperiod income tax allocation. These and other FASB projects

---

[36] FASB Statement no. 43, *Accounting for Compensated Absences* (Stamford: FASB, 1980).

[37] FASB Statement no. 71, *Accounting for the Effects of Certain Types of Regulation* (Stamford: FASB, 1982).

[38] APB Opinion no. 11, *Accounting for Income Taxes* (New York: AICPA, 1967).

highlight the need for sound and workable recognition concepts in an accrual, cost-based accounting context.

BENEFITS OF THE CONCEPTUAL FRAMEWORK

The foregoing examples illustrate, I believe, that the most apparent beneficiary of the conceptual framework, at least initially, is the board itself. The board has already begun to look to the concepts in developing standards; and the board's staff, in presenting its recommendations to the board, is required to demonstrate the consistency of the staff's recommendations with the agreed-on concepts.

The benefits of the framework to others are equally real, though perhaps less apparent. Over time, the objectives and concepts will help produce a body of standards that is more internally consistent and less ad hoc than at present, enhancing the credibility of corporate accounting information. Also, the concepts will provide a frame of reference to financial statement preparers and auditors in resolving accounting questions in the absence of established standards. And ultimately the conceptual framework may well reduce the need for some specific standards.

The framework also should help those who use accounting information to understand better the purposes, content, characteristics and limitations of the information in a financial report.

Because the effects of the concepts are long-range and pervasive, FASB concepts statements are published in a series separate from FASB statements. Concepts statements, when issued, do not require or even justify any changes in current accounting practices; they do not amend any established standards, nor do they require disclosure of an accounting practice that appears to be at variance with an agreed-on concept. The FASB recognizes that in some respects current GAAP may be inconsistent with the concepts. The board will deal with those inconsistencies as it addresses individual accounting standards issues.

The conceptual framework won't provide all the answers to accounting questions. Because the concepts themselves are subject to interpretation, environmental influences may at times affect specific accounting standards, and the concepts themselves might change. But a coherent set of objectives and concepts will provide a direction for setting standards and for resolving accounting practice questions, and it should reduce the influence of personal biases and political pressures in making accounting judgments. Those will probably prove to be the principal long-run benefits of the board's effort.

FASB's Statements on Objectives and Elements of Financial Accounting: A Review

Nicholas Dopuch
Washington University

Shyam Sunder
University of Minnesota

We thus have cause to feel grateful to the drafters of recommendations; and this review should on no account be construed as an attack on them. Obviously, they have devoted much time and care to their task, and have been prompted by a high sense of public service. If harm should in the end come from their work, the blame should attach more to disciples who have accepted their teaching too eagerly, and have invested it with an ex cathedra *quality that could not perhaps have been foreseen [Baxter, 1962, pp. 419–20].*

The Financial Accounting Standards Board (FASB) issued an exposure draft of the proposed statement on Objectives of Financial Reporting and Elements of Financial Statements of Business Enterprises on December 29, 1977. The first part of the Exposure Draft, dealing with the objectives of financial reporting, was issued in revised form a year later as the Statement of Financial Accounting Concepts No. 1 (SFAC 1) [FASB, 1978]. A final statement on the elements of financial statements has not yet been issued. In this paper we review the FASB's statement on objectives (as contained in SFAC 1) and on elements (as contained in the Exposure Draft). Though many of our comments could also be applied to other aspects of the project on the conceptual framework undertaken by the FASB, we shall limit our discussion to the two documents mentioned above.[1]

Few general criteria, other than internal consistency, have been proposed for evaluating conceptual frameworks. The approach taken in the reviews by Littleton [1962; 1963] of the Moonitz [1961] and the Sprouse and Moonitz [1962] monographs; by Ijiri [1971] of the *APB Statement No. 4* [AICPA, 1970]; by a subcommittee of the American Accounting Association (AAA) to respond to the FASB's Discussion Memorandum of the Conceptual Framework [AAA, 1977b]; by Sterling [1967] of the AAA's *A Statement of Basic Accounting Theory* [1966]; by Vatter [1963], Hanson [1940], and Kester [1940] of Paton and Littleton [1940]; and by Deinzer [1964] of various statements sponsored by the AAA [1936; 1941; 1948; 1957; 1964a; 1964b] seem too diverse to provide common criteria for evaluating a conceptual framework. We decided, therefore, to use two criteria in our review: (1) To what

From *The Accounting Review* (January 1980), pp. 1–21. Reprinted by permission of the American Accounting Association.

We have benefited from many helpful comments in particular those by Professors Raymond J. Chambers, William W. Cooper, Sidney Davidson, Rashad Abdel-khalik, William R. Scott, Stephen A. Zeff, and the anonymous reviewers.

[1] These documents were preceded by two Discussion Memoranda [FASB, 1974; 1976a]; the latter was accompanied by a statement of tentative conclusions on objectives of financial statements [FASB, 1976b].

extent do these statements differ from previous attempts of this nature; and, regardless of the answer to (1), (2) to what extent will these statements, if adopted, yield the benefits expected by the FASB? Since we arrive at pessimistic answers to both questions, we are led to consider two further questions: (a) What are the fundamental difficulties in developing a set of objectives of financial accounting, and (b) Why do authoritative bodies persist in trying to develop a conceptual framework? The final section of the paper contains the summary and concluding remarks.

1. COMPARISON WITH PREVIOUS ATTEMPTS TO DEVELOP A FRAMEWORK

Objectives

The SFAC 1 is divided into two parts: Introduction and Background, followed by Objectives of Financial Reporting. The introductory section includes subsections on: (a) financial statements and financial reporting, (b) the environmental context of objectives, (c) the characteristics and limitations of information provided, (d) potential users and their interests, and (e) general-purpose external financial reporting. Financial statements are defined to be a subset of financial reporting, but no limits are provided on the number of elements of financial reporting that one may include in financial statements. The discussion of the environmental context of accounting bears a resemblance to the discussion by Moonitz [1961, Chapter 2] and by the Accounting Principles Board in Statement No. 4 (APBS 4) [AICPA, 1970, Chapter 3]. A discussion of the major characteristics of the U.S. economy in the statement of objectives would be justified if it were accompanied by a theory which linked the characteristics of various economies to alternative financial accounting systems. Since no such theory is provided, it is not clear how a vague description of the U.S. economy is useful for determining or understanding objectives.[2]

In the sections on potential users and general-purpose financial reporting it is stated that the specific objectives here refer to the general-purpose financial reports that serve the informational needs of external users who lack the authority to prescribe the financial information they want from an enterprise, a statement very similar to Objective No. 2 of the Trueblood Report [AICPA, 1973]. The FASB relies considerably on the Trueblood Report when it states that financial reporting "should provide information to help present and potential investors and creditors, and other users in assessing the amounts, timing, and uncertainty of prospective net cash receipts...." [FASB, 1978, para. 37]. The need for information on cash flows leads to the need for information on "the economic resources of an enterprise, the claims to those resources (obligations of the enterprise to transfer resources to other entities and owners' equity), and the effects of transactions, events, and circumstances

---

[2] For example, paragraph 13 refers to efficient allocations of resources within a market economy, but there are several definitions of allocation efficiency which might be employed. In the absence of an agreed-upon definition, inefficiencies cannot be identified.

that change resources and claims to those resources" (para. 40). After more discussion, the Board arrives at the conclusion that the

> primary focus of financial reporting is information about an enterprise's performance provided by measures of earnings and its components.... Information about enterprise earnings and its components measured by accrual accounting generally provides a better indication of enterprise performance than information about current cash receipts and payments [FASB, 1978, para. 43–44].

This last statement is not an objective, but a means to an objective.

Although these paragraphs encompass many of the specific objectives of the Trueblood Report, the emphasis and order of presentation are different. Other departures from the Report are an omission of any reference to providing financial forecasts and to non-profit and social accounting (Objectives 10, 11, and 12, respectively, of the Trueblood Report).

In wording and substance, little is new or different in SFAC 1. Had the FASB pointed out the parts of the existing reports,[3] such as APBS 4 and the Trueblood Report, that it agreed with and emphasized its disagreements, its contribution would have been easier to discern. Without such aid, we are hard-pressed to discern the FASB's net contribution to these earlier efforts. Given that previous authoritative efforts to write objectives are generally considered inadequate in helping to resolve accounting issues, a basic test of the FASB's contribution is the extent to which SFAC 1 may succeed where others have failed. We shall apply such a test after discussing the elements of financial statements and characteristics of financial information as provided in the FASB's Exposure Draft [FASB, 1977].

Elements of Financial Statements

The second major section of the Exposure Draft [FASB, 1977], paragraphs 36 through 66, deals mainly with definitions of the main categories of accounts appearing in financial statements: assets, liabilities, owners' equity, revenues, expenses, gains, and losses. Supplementing these definitions are subsections containing discussions of the bases for definitions, the matching of efforts and accomplishments, and the need to provide financial statements which articulate with one another. The elements of financial statements are integrated—revenues and gains result in, or from, increases in assets, decreases in liabilities or combinations of the two; expenses and losses result in, or from, decreases in assets, increases in liabilities, *etc.*

A noteworthy feature of the FASB's definitions is their dependence on unspecified "accounting rules and conventions" [FASB, 1977, p. 19], again in the tradition of the definitions provided by two previous authoritative bodies, the American Institute

---

[3]Most and Winters [1977] analyzed the objectives promulgated by the Trueblood Study Group, APBS 4, several of the Big Eight firms, the AAA, the National Association of Accountants, *etc.* They found that of the ten main objectives issued by the Trueblood Study Group (Objectives 3 on cash flows, and 11 on non-profit accounting, were omitted), eight similar objectives could be found in APBS 4. Similarly, Objectives 1,2,4,5,6,7, and 8 in the Trueblood Report had antecedents in from five to as many as eight other statements of objectives.

of [Certified Public] Accountants' Committee on Terminology and Accounting Principles Board.[4] This qualification appears to be inconsistent with the claim that conceptual frameworks can lead to the selection of appropriate principles and rules of measurement and recognition. How can a conceptual framework guide choices from among alternative principles and rules if the elements of the framework are defined in these very same terms?

The dependence of the FASB's definitions on unspecified rules and conventions leaves little basis on which to evaluate them, since a specific evaluation of these definitions would be speculative as long as we do not know what conventions will be adopted by the FASB at the subsequent stages of its project.

A second feature of the FASB's definitions is that they provide only the necessary conditions for a resource or obligation to be included in the asset or liability categories, respectively, rather than both the necessary and sufficient conditions. For example, a resource other than cash needs to have three characteristics to qualify as an asset:

> (a) the resource must...contribute directly or indirectly to future cash inflows (or to obviating future cash outflows), (b) the enterprise must be able to obtain the benefit from it, and (c) the transaction or event giving rise to the enterprise's right to or interest in the benefit must already have occurred [FASB, 1977; para. 47].

Similarly, three characteristics are also necessary for an obligation to qualify as a liability:

> (a) the obligation must involve future sacrifice of resources—a future transfer (or a foregoing of a future receipt) of cash, goods, or services, (b) it must be an obligation of the enterprise, and (c) the transaction or event giving rise to the enterprise's obligation must already have occurred [FASB, 1977, para. 49].

Since these are only necessary characteristics, their presence does not imply that an obligation will qualify as a liability or that a resource will qualify as an asset. All of these conditions may be satisfied and an obligation still may not qualify as an asset or, alternatively, as a liability. In the absence of sufficient conditions, these definitions will be of limited use to accountants.

The definitions of revenues and expenses given by the FASB follow the traditional practice of defining these as increases and decreases in assets or decreases and increases in liabilities, respectively, provided that the changes in assets and liabilities relate to the earning activities of the enterprise (broadly defined). Gains and losses are defined as increases and decreases in net assets, *other* than revenues and expenses or investments and withdrawals by owners.

---

[4]For example, the Committee on Terminology defined assets in Accounting Terminology Bulletin No. 1 [AICPA, 1953] as follows:

"Something represented by a debit balance that is or would be properly carried forward upon a closing of books of account according to the *rules or principles of accounting*...on the basis that it represents either a property right...or is properly applicable to the future" (para. 26, emphasis added).

The APB in its Statement No. 4 defined assets as: "economic resources of an enterprise that are recognized and measured *in conformity with generally accepted accounting principles*..." [AICPA, 1970, para. 132] (emphasis added).

The definitions of revenue and expense in APB Statement No. 4 [AICPA, 1970] are similar to the above except that the definitions there do not explicitly distinguish between revenues and gains nor between expenses and losses. A distinction between revenues and gains is also made by Sprouse and Moonitz [1962, p. 50] and by Paton and Littleton [1940, p. 60]. But while a distinction between expense and loss is made by Sprouse and Moonitz, Paton and Littleton do not do so. Indeed, they do not even provide an explicit definition of expense, which is consistent with their emphasis on *cost* rather than on the asset-expense distinction. It is not until their discussion of income that Paton and Littleton stress a distinction between costs matched against revenues (expenses) and those deferred to future periods (assets) [1940, Chap. V].

On the whole, the differences between the FASB and the APB definitions are small and seem unimportant. An explicit discussion of the main sources of disagreement would have been more fruitful than a "new" set of definitions. Circular as they are, the conflict on definitions seems to us to be only a proxy debate whose principal, to which we return later, is the debate about the accounting rules themselves.

Characteristics and Limitations of Financial Information

A part of the last major section of the Exposure Draft has been included in the introductory section of SFAC 1. There we find statements about: (a) the reliance of accounting on monetary transactions, (b) the emphasis of financial reports on individual enterprises and not on individual consumers or on society as a whole, (c) the role of estimation in accounting, (d) the fact that much of financial information reflects past events, (e) the coexistence of other sources of financial information, and (f) the costs of financial reporting.

The more well-known desirable "qualities" of accounting information, such as relevance, freedom from bias, comparability, consistency, understandability, verifiability, *etc.*, are also referenced in the Exposure Draft, but are excluded from SFAC 1. The FASB acknowledges that trade-offs among these qualities are not easily accomplished in practice. The objectives and definitions of the elements of financial statements are expected to guide the Board in future phases of the conceptual framework project when these trade-off issues arise in more concrete form.

The characteristics and desirable "qualities" of accounting information discussed in the Exposure Draft are familiar to accountants and appear as "qualitative" objectives in APB Statement No. 4 and as components of accounting concepts or as postulates in other conceptual frameworks.

The above review of SFAC 1 and of certain parts of the Exposure Draft reveals little that is new on the objectives of financial reporting and definitions of the elements of financial statements. Lack of novelty, of course, does not imply worthlessness. It is quite possible that the FASB's effort may yet have the potential to yield some benefits. The FASB has suggested that the following benefits may manifest themselves as a result of achieving agreement on the conceptual framework [1976c, pp. 5–6]:

1 Guide the body responsible for establishing standards,
2 Provide a frame of reference for resolving accounting questions in the absence of a specific promulgated standard,
3 Determine bounds for judgment in preparing financial statements,
4 Increase financial statement users' understanding of and confidence in financial statements, and
5 Enhance comparability.

In reviewing this early part of the conceptual framework, it is probably fair to ask how reasonable it is to expect that the above-mentioned benefits will actually be realized. Of course, this evaluation may have to be changed when all of the pieces of the conceptual project are in place. However, the evaluation of this part of the project, tentative as it is, should not await completion of the project.

In the following section we examine the degree to which the first two benefits stated by the FASB, *viz.*, guidance for establishing standards and resolution of accounting questions in the absence of standards, are likely to be attained on the basis of the given objectives and definitions. The effect of the project on users' understanding of, and confidence in, the financial statements is an empirical question and is beyond the scope of this review paper.[5] We are not sure what precisely is meant by (3), determination of the bounds of judgment in preparation of financial statements and by (5), enhancement of comparability. Since the empirical or analytical contents of these benefits are not clear, it is difficult to evaluate, beyond purely subjective opinion, whether and to what extent these benefits will be derived from the FASB's objectives and definitions. We shall, therefore, confine ourselves to an evaluation of the first two benefits stated by the FASB.

2. RESOLUTION OF THREE ACCOUNTING ISSUES

As a means of evaluating the potential benefits the FASB's objectives and definitions may provide in resolving accounting issues, we selected three which have been debated for some time and which have received much attention from accountants and others. The issues are: (1) deferred credits, (2) treatment of costs of exploration in the oil and gas industry, and (3) reports on current values of assets and liabilities.

Deferred Credits

The FASB defines liabilities as "financial representations of obligations of a particular enterprise to transfer economic resources to other entities in the future as a result of a past transaction or event affecting the enterprise" [FASB, 1977, para. 49]. No specific reference to deferred credits appears in this section, although reference is made to liabilities arising from the collection of cash or other resources *before* providing goods or services, or from selling products subject to warranty. It is also stated that "legal enforceability of a claim is not a prerequisite to representing it as a liability" if future transfer is probable.

[5]The FASB may wish to commission such a study now, so that a preconceptual framework measure of confidence and understandability can be taken before this opportunity is lost.

The APB, in Statement No. 4, is more direct:

> Liabilities—economic obligations of an enterprise that are recognized and measured in conformity with generally accepted accounting principles. Liabilities also include certain deferred credits *that are not obligations* but that are recognized and measured in conformity with generally accepted accounting principles [AICPA, 1970, para. 132, emphasis added].

A footnote to the last sentence specifically singles out deferred taxes as an example of liabilities which are not obligations!

Neither Paton and Littleton [1940] nor Sprouse and Moonitz [1962] refer to deferred credits arising from differences between financial and tax reporting, with both concentrating on the obligations of enterprises to convey assets or to perform services in the future.[6]

The FASB's definition of liabilities is so general that at this stage we cannot predict the Board's position on deferred taxes. However, those who favor the recognition of deferred taxes can adopt a somewhat broad interpretation of the FASB's definition of liabilities to justify the inclusion of deferred taxes as an element of financial statements, particularly at the individual asset level. In contrast, those who do not could take the FASB's statements literally and just as easily argue against the inclusion of deferred taxes. Hence, these broad definitions will not help resolve the issue.

Accounting for Oil and Gas Exploration Costs

Bitter controversy still surrounds the issue of how to account for petroleum exploration costs. The issue surfaced in the petroleum industry some two decades ago when the full-cost method was introduced. But the essence of the issue has an earlier precedent.

Hatfield [1927, Chap. 2] considers the problem of whether the acquisition costs of successful experiments should be limited to the costs of the successful experiments themselves or whether they should also include the costs of unsuccessful experiments. Hence, the full-cost versus successful-efforts debate is part of a more general issue of what constitutes the costs of assets when the acquisition process is risky.

The issue reflects a difference of opinion regarding the level of aggregation at which the historical acquisition cost principle is applied to record assets for subsequent amortization. But there is no reference in the Exposure Draft to alternative levels of aggregation for asset recognition and measurement. The only explicit statement bearing on this problem is that "[i]nformation about enterprise earnings and its components measured by accrual accounting generally provides a better indication of enterprise performance than information about current cash receipts and payments" [FASB, 1978, para. 44]. However, both full-cost and successful-efforts accounting are forms of accrual accounting, so that proponents of the former (*e.g.*, the Federal Trade Commission) have the same support for their position as do proponents of the latter (*e.g.*, the FASB). The fact that the framework supports two

---

[6] The issue of deferred taxes did not appear in the accounting literature until about 1942. See AICPA [1942].

opposing principles of accounting is preliminary evidence that the framework is unlikely to be a useful guide in resolving this issue.

Selecting the Valuation Basis for Assets and Liabilities

Alternative theories of valuation and income were discussed in accounting texts published 50 years ago. For example, Hatfield [1927] states:

> Having accepted the principle that the original valuation of assets is normally their cost price, and having noticed the practical and theoretical difficulty in determining the exact cost price, there remains the more important question as to subsequent revaluations of assets....Shall the accountant base revaluation on (1) the original cost...(2) on the estimated present cost of acquiring a similar asset...or (3) on what the asset might be expected to bring if thrown upon the market in the process of liquidation? [p. 73]

Similar discussions appear even earlier in Paton [1922], in Hatfield [1909], and in a much more detailed fashion in Canning [1929].

Liquidation values were generally ruled out in such discussions because they seemed inconsistent with the going-concern notion, and since discounted values had not yet achieved popularity then, the choice between alternative valuation bases was usually limited to historical or replacement costs.

With respect to these alternatives, it might be informative to quote some statements from Paton and Littleton [1940], who, some accountants believe, had no tolerance for valuation bases other than historical cost accounting. On pages 122–123, they state:

> With the passing of time, however, the value of the particular productive factor—as reflected in the current cost or market price of like units—is subject to change in either direction, and when a change occurs it becomes clear that the actual cost of the unit still in service or still attaching to operating activity is not fully acceptable as a measure of immediate economic significance.

Later, on page 123, they ask the question:

> [W]ould accounting meet more adequately the proper needs of the various parties concerned if, in the process of separating the charges to revenue from the unexpired balances, the estimated replacement costs or other evidence of current values were regularly substituted for recorded costs incurred? There seem to be no convincing reasons for an affirmative answer. Recorded costs are objectively determined data; estimated current values are largely matters of opinion and for some types of cost factors are conspicuously unreliable.

In the section on "Limitations of Estimated Replacement Cost," they comment: "In the first place continuous appraisals at the best are costly, and can be used only if the benefits to be derived clearly justify the additional cost incurred" (p. 132). They then suggest that in periods of price stability and situations involving complex enterprises, such benefits are unlikely to exceed the costs of implementation. Finally,

> The fair conclusion is that the cost standard of plant accounting holds up well, as compared with any alternative plan, when faced with typical business needs and condi-

tions.... At the same time it would be going too far to hold that under no circumstances can any useful purpose be served by introducing into the accounts and reports, by appropriate methods, data designed to supplement the figures of actual cost [Paton and Littleton, p. 134].

The latter statement led them to recommend that alternative valuations be limited to supplementary schedules.

The above are practical, not theoretical, arguments and are probably representative of the views of many accountants who have expressed a reluctance to accept current costs in published financial statements. No conceptual framework, however logically conceived, can counter practical issues regarding the reliability of *estimates* of, say, replacement costs. The "true" replacement costs of assets are not observed until those assets are actually replaced (nor are "true" exit prices observed unless the assets are sold). So the issue is not whether current costs are useful "in making economic decisions;" rather, the issue is what criteria may be used to evaluate alternative estimates of unknown parameters. Unfortunately, neither SFAC 1 nor the Exposure Draft addresses this problem of estimation.

On the basis of the above analysis, we conclude that the results of the FASB's effort to write objectives and definitions are hardly different from previous attempts of this nature and, as such, are unlikely to help resolve major accounting issues or to set standards of financial reporting as the FASB had expected. Pessimistic as our conclusions are, they should not surprise those familiar with the standard-setting process during the past 30 years. The charge of the Trueblood Study Group was very similar to the first two benefits expected by the FASB:

> The main purpose of the [Trueblood] study is to refine the objectives of financial statements. Refined objectives should facilitate establishment of guidelines and criteria for improving accounting and financial reporting [AICPA, 1973, p. 67].

Both the supporters and the critics expressed doubts that this purpose of the study would be met. Bedford [1974, p. 16], while largely supporting the report, said, "I refer to the extremely difficult task of logically deriving accounting standards from objectives—not that I think it can be done but because I fear some will think it is appropriate." Miller [1974, p. 20], a critic of the report, stated, "The greatest shortcoming of the Trueblood Report is, it seems to me, that the accept/reject criteria are not sufficiently precise. I wish Professor Sorter and his associates had been less subtle." Sprouse stated, "I have no illusions about the use of such a document to prove that a particular accounting standard is 'right'" [1974, p. 28]. These doubts about the accomplishments of the Trueblood Report are very similar to our reservations about the fruits of the FASB's labors.

Since our conclusion about the potential value and effect of the FASB's objectives and definitions is pessimistic, we are led to inquire into the very nature of objectives of financial accounting and the fundamental difficulty of defining them in a social setting. The inability of different authoritative drafts of objectives produced in the last decade to achieve general acceptance on a conceptual framework is hardly due to the lack of diligence on the part of their authors; it may stem from addressing the wrong problem.

3. THE NATURE OF OBJECTIVES
OF FINANCIAL ACCOUNTING

> An objective is something toward which effort is directed, an aim or end of action, a goal [FASB, 1974, p. 13].

Financial accounting is a social or multiperson activity. Members of society engage in financial accounting or in other social activities when they are motivated by their individual goals and objectives. We shall assume that the meaning of the terms "goal" and "objective," as they apply to individuals or homogeneous groups of individuals, is self-evident for the purpose of the present discussion. Given a clear definition of the objectives that motivate each individual to engage in an aspect of a social activity, what meaning can we assign to the term "objective" when it is applied not to individuals or groups, but to the activity itself? In what sense can a social activity be said to have an objective?

We suggest three different interpretations of the meaning of the objectives of a social activity: functional objectives, common objectives, and dominant group objectives. In this section we shall first explain the meaning and implications of each interpretation and then examine the nature of the objectives of financial accounting in light of these interpretations.

Functional Objectives

The union of individual objectives could be referred to as the objective of the social activity in a *functional sense*. A functional explanation of social phenomena assumes that the consequences of a social arrangement or behavior are essential elements of the *causes* of that behavior (see Stinchcombe [1968], esp. pp. 80–100). Objectives that motivate individuals to engage in an activity on a continuing basis must also be the consequences of the activity; otherwise the individuals will not continue to engage in it. Thus, the functional explanation implies that the union of individual objectives can be identified without probing into the motivations of individuals by simply observing the set of consequences of the social activity. These consequences themselves therefore can be regarded as the objectives of the social activity. Since the consequences are observable phenomena, they can be objectively determined. However, the set of consequences may be so large that a complex and lengthy description may be the result. Nevertheless, a statement of consequences is one possible interpretation of the objective of a social activity.

Common Objectives

A second possibility is to define the intersection of individual objectives, *i.e.*, the subset of objectives common to all individuals, as the objective of the social activity. By definition, common objectives are equal to or fewer in number than the functional objectives. If all individuals are motivated by an identical set of objectives, common objectives are the same as the functional objectives; if each individual is motivated by different objectives, the intersection is null and there are no common objectives.

DOMINANT GROUP OBJECTIVES

A third possible interpretation of the objectives of a social activity is the objectives of an individual or subset of all individuals in the society who are able, through whatever mechanism, to impose their will on all others involved in the activity. In the presence of such a dominant group, the objectives of individuals not included in the group become irrelevant, since the dominant group objectives become the objectives of the social activity. Obviously, this interpretation cannot be used if the dominant group does not have the power to impose its will on the society.

Accounting as a Social Activity

Accounting is a social activity engaged in by (1) corporate managers who perform in activities that are recorded by the accounting system; (2) corporate accountants who gather the data and compile the reports; (3) auditors who scrutinize and attest to the fairness of the reports; (4) outside government and private agencies, investors, employees, customers, *etc.*, who read these reports; and (5) college and university personnel who train their students in accounting. Each group of individuals engaged in financial accounting possesses its own private motives or objectives leading to this involvement. In the light of the three possible interpretations of the objectives of a social activity discussed above, what meaning can we assign to the objectives of financial accounting?

Functional Interpretation of Accounting Objectives

Since all consequences of accounting are included in the functional interpretation of objectives, consider the following sample of objectives that would qualify under this interpretation:

1 Increase employment of accountants, auditors, and teachers of accounting;
2 Help companies market their securities to creditors and investors;
3 Help outsiders monitor the performance of management;
4 Maximize the wealth of the present owners of the company;
5 Minimize income tax burdens of companies;
6 Aid in controlling inflation;
7 Disclose the impact of enterprise operations on the quality of the environment;
8 Help management avoid hostile takeover attempts;
9 Systematically record, classify, and report data on the business transactions of the enterprise;
10 Aid in enforcing anti-trust laws.

Each of the objectives listed above could be viewed as legitimate by one or more sets of individuals involved in financial accounting. Note that a complete description of the consequences of financial accounting will include not only "facts" but what is regarded as "fiction" by specific individuals. For example, a manager may regard the avoidance of hostile takeover attempts as a valid objective of financial statements while a shareholder may believe that the effect of financial accounting practices on avoidance of hostile takeovers is non-existent. In order to be included in the set, it is sufficient that someone involved in financial accounting believe in that consequence or use it as a personal objective. Note also that this set includes contradictory objectives and consequences. For example, management may believe that one accounting method for inventory accounting will help market the firm's securities, whereas shareholders may believe that an alternative inventory method is more revealing of management's competence. Similarly, the objective of accountants to increase the demand for their services may be in conflict with the objective of corporate managers to maximize their own or the shareholders' wealth.

Although probably not intended as such, the objectives stated by the FASB may be viewed as functional objectives. For example, the first objective given by the FASB is:

> Financial reporting should provide information that is useful to present and potential investors and creditors and other users in making rational investment, credit, and similar decisions. The information should be comprehensible to those who have a reasonable understanding of business and economic activities and are willing to study the information with reasonable diligence [FASB, 1978, para. 34].

If "should" is removed from each sentence, this objective is reduced to a mere statement of an empirically verified and a widely accepted consequence of financial accounting. Financial accounting does, indeed, provide information useful to investors and creditors, and it is comprehensible to those willing to study the reports with reasonable diligence. But, being purely descriptive, functional objectives themselves cannot serve as normative goals to guide policy making. Nevertheless, if they are reasonably complete, they can serve to improve the understanding of the role of financial accounting in society.

There is reason to believe that the FASB did not intend to offer its statement as one of functional objectives. First, the statement is far from complete, concentrating on a few facts and a few unverified theories about the consequences of financial accounting, without any effort to present, for example, the motivations behind the supply side of financial accounting services. And the normative tone of the statement precludes the possibility that the FASB has attempted to provide a statement of the union of individual objectives of all persons involved in financial accounting.

Common-Objectives Interpretation of Accounting Objectives

A second possible interpretation of the objectives of accounting is the subset of individual objectives which are common to all individuals involved in accounting. Cyert and Ijiri's [1974] model of heterogeneous interests can be modified to apply to the objectives. Cyert and Ijiri use a Venn diagram to illustrate their point. The elements of the sets considered by them are *pieces of information* which various interest groups—users, managers, and auditors—may be willing to use, provide, or attest, and the intersection of the three sets is the actual information provided by the financial statements. The choice problem posed by Cyert and Ijiri could be moved to a higher level of abstraction by considering the sets of *accounting principles* that each group would prefer to be used in the preparation of financial statements. A still higher level of abstraction would involve specific sets of *objectives* that each group would seek to fulfill through its involvement in financial accounting.

It is conceivable that the intersection of the three sets will become progressively smaller as we move to higher levels of abstraction from pieces of information to accounting principles to objectives, in which case the Venn diagrams at the three levels of abstraction might appear as in Figure 1.

We do not know whether the intersection of the sets grows larger or smaller as we move from items of information to principles to objectives and vice versa.[7] Generally, agreement on principles and objectives will be easier to obtain if such statements are sufficiently vague so as to allow room for various interest groups to adopt their own interpretations. But vagueness, while necessary to obtain initial agreement, will reduce the usefulness of a statement of objectives in setting accounting standards. The proposition is borne out by the statements of objectives we have seen thus far. The vagueness of statements of this nature is consistent with the level of generality at which agreement is sought. It allows enough room for each interested party to maneuver to protect its own interest when actual accounting standards and rules are written.

Some empirical evidence is available on the non-overlapping nature of accounting objectives. In 1976, when the FASB carried out a survey to determine how many people involved in various aspects of financial accounting agreed with the Trueblood objectives, the Board was surprised to learn that only 37 percent of the respondents believed that providing information useful for making economic decisions was an objective of financial accounting:

> Let me point this up for you. In our first discussion memorandum on the conceptual framework of accounting,...we sought an expression of opinion from respondents on the following as a basic objective of financial statements; it is taken directly from the Trueblood Report:

> The basic objective of financial statements is to provide information useful for making economic decisions.

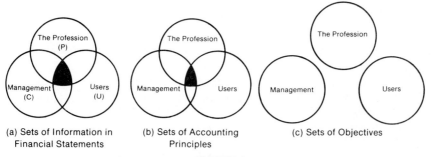

(a) Sets of Information in Financial Statements

(b) Sets of Accounting Principles

(c) Sets of Objectives

FIGURE 1

[7]The question is subject to debate; see, for example, the analysis of responses of various parties to the FASB's pronouncements by Coe and Sorter [1977–78] and Watts and Zimmerman [1978].

Could there be disagreement with a statement such as this? I am sure you will be astounded to learn that only 37 percent of our respondents were able to recommend the adoption of this objective. Twenty-two percent recommended that it be rejected out of hand; and 10 percent insisted that it needed further study. It is difficult to believe that only 37 percent can agree that the basic objective of financial statements is to provide information useful for making economic decisions. I think this suggests the problem quite clearly [Armstrong, 1977, p. 77].

We are puzzled at the Board's puzzlement. Why should we believe all groups of interested parties would adopt the provision of information useful for making economic decisions as their motivation for being involved in the financial reporting process? For example, we should not be surprised if auditors, like everyone else, seek to maximize their own wealth through participation in the accounting process. If the provision of economically useful information implies greater exposure to the risk of being sued without corresponding benefits of higher compensation, they will not see the provision of economically useful information (however defined) as *their* objective of the financial accounting process. Similar arguments could be made about any other interested party who might have been surveyed by the FASB. The members of each group probably stated what they believed were their objectives for being involved in the process.

At present, we do not have data to determine which, if any, objectives are actually common to all participants in accounting. Consequently we cannot yet determine whether the common-objectives approach is a feasible interpretation of the objectives of accounting.

Dominant Group Interpretation of Accounting Objectives

Unlike the Trueblood Study Group, the FASB has not stated explicitly how it selected its subset of objectives from a much larger set of potential objectives. But from the objectives which the FASB did select, we can infer that it has followed the Trueblood Study Group in relying on the notion of user-primacy in financial accounting.[8] This notion represents the dominant-group approach to defining the objective of a social activity that we identified above.

Most of the discussion appearing in the literature on the objectives of financial accounting during the past ten years tends to rely on the notion of user-primacy. Beaver and Demski[1974], for example, concentrated their attention on the problems generated by the heterogeneity of tastes among the users of financial statements, on the assumption that this group would be the primary group whose interests would be reflected in the objectives of financial statements officially adopted by the authoritative agencies:

There seems to be a consensus that the primary purpose of financial reporting is to provide

---

[8]"While mindful of the importance of the audit function, the Study Group has been primarily concerned with the nature of information and not its attestability."[AICPA, 1973, p. 10.] The Trueblood Study Group left the problem of attestation and the interests of the management to "implementation" and did not consider these interests worthy of consideration within the set of objectives of financial reporting.

information to financial statement users. Yet, the basic, fundamental role of objectives within this utilitarian, user-primacy framework remains obscure—largely we speculate because the problem of heterogeneous users has not been forcefully addressed.... A basic purpose of this summary and synthesis, then, is to offer a view of the nature and role of financial accounting objectives that explicitly rests on heterogeneous users [p. 170].

Cyert and Ijiri [1974] considered the heterogeneity of preferences for *information sets* among three diverse groups (assuming that the intragroup heterogeneity is unimportant) and analyzed the problem of determining accounting standards under the assumption that the user interest is primary. Referring to 1(a) of our Figure 1, they stated:

This is a logical, if not a unique approach since in many user-corporate relationships the corporation is *accountable* to the users for its activities. If the users are in a position to demand information from the corporation based on a contractual or statutory relationship between them, it makes sense to define what Circle U is and then attempt to move Circle C toward it. Furthermore, in the interaction of the three groups, the profession's purpose is to help keep a smooth flow of information from the corporation to the users. Hence, Circle P is clearly subordinate to Circles C and U. Thus, it is perhaps the most practical way to state as objectives the need to move Circles C and P toward the goal of a newly defined Circle U [p. 32].

If the user group had the power to enforce its preferences at no cost to itself, the objectives of this group could be called the objectives of financial accounting. This would simplify the problem of setting objectives. Indeed, if the user group were homogeneous, the problem would be trivial. However, there is little evidence that the user group has the power to impose its preferences on financial accounting.

A considerable amount of confusion about the objectives of financial accounting has been generated by comparing them to the objectives of the firm. For example, Bedford [1974] notes, "'The basic objective of financial statements is to provide information useful for making economic decisions.' This statement is as direct as the statement that 'the basic objective of private enterprise is to make a profit' *and it is equally operational*" [p. 15; emphasis is added]. Few would dispute that, as stated, the profit-maximizing objective of the firm is merely a shorthand way of stating the objectives of the *shareholders* of the firm under the assumption of homogeneous shareholder preferences; it does not represent the specific objectives of the managers, employees, creditors or of any other parties inside or outside the firm. Besides, profit is a net concept in the sense that it is the difference between revenues and expenses, and its use as an objective implies that additional revenue should not be generated beyond the point at which the additional cost exceeds it. Provision of information for decision making, unlike profit, is a gross concept and cannot provide guidelines as to how far the firm should go in providing information for economic decisions.

The analogy to the theory of the firm is more apparent than real. In that theory, if the objective is to maximize the owners' wealth, production-investment variables can be chosen in view of the cost and revenue functions which serve as the environmental variables. What is the FASB (or any other agency entrusted with the task of writing accounting standards) supposed to maximize or optimize? When the

FASB recommends that the objective of financial statements is to provide information useful for making rational credit and investment decisions, should we understand that the provision of such information should be maximized without regard to the cost and other consequences of making such information available? What are the variables over which to optimize, and what is the trade-off among these variables? Unless these trade-offs are defined, a statement of objectives that will be useful in arriving at the most satisfying accounting standards cannot be said to have been laid down, nor can there be a way of determining if the recommended objectives have been achieved by a given accounting standard.

The extraordinary emphasis of the recent pronouncements regarding objectives of financial accounting on user primacy can probably be traced to inappropriate applications of single-person decision theory in a multi-person context. In single-person decision theory, the generation of information is regarded as a more-or-less mechanical process which remains unaffected by its ultimate uses. The person making the choice of an information system out of the available alternatives calculates the expected present value of the benefits to be derived from the use of information produced by each system and makes the choice on the basis of the excess of these benefits over the respective costs. The same underlying event-generating mechanism is assumed to be common to all information systems, and it remains unaffected by the choice of information system made. This model, developed by the physical scientists and engineers for the control of mechanical or inanimate systems, is inappropriate for social systems, where the object of control is not an unchanging chemical process but a human being with learning capabilities. In control systems where human beings stand at both the sending and receiving end of the information channel, the flow of information affects behavior at both ends. We cannot choose an information system which is best suited to the needs of persons at one end of the information line on the assumption of a constant behavior pattern of the persons at the other end. Indeed, the two-way effect of the information makes the designation of one party as user and the other as sender somewhat ambiguous. A user-primacy notion in the selection of objectives of financial accounting which ignores how firm managers are likely to adjust their behavior to the new information system (and how this adjustment in managment behavior will affect the interests of the so-called users) represents a very short-sighted view of the whole problem. As such, solutions derived from this simplified approach will not work. A similar argument could be offered regarding the exclusion of the auditors from the "primary" groups whose interests must be explicitly considered in any realistic set of objectives of financial accounting.

To summarize, we have examined three possible interpretations of objectives of social activities in general and financial accounting in particular. We have concluded that the union of individual objectives, being too diverse and contradictory, cannot serve to guide policy; intersection of individual objectives may be null; the dominant-group objectives, assuming user primacy, do not reflect the economic reality of the power of suppliers in the accounting marketplace and are, therefore, unworkable. Fundamental to an understanding of the nature of financial accounting as they are, these difficulties in interpreting the objectives of financial accounting have received little attention in the literature. This lack of attention stands in sharp contrast to the repeated efforts to prepare a statement of objectives and definitions and leads us to examine the possible reasons that may stand behind the efforts to prepare an authoritative statement of objectives and definitions.

4. WHY SEARCH FOR A CONCEPTUAL FRAMEWORK?

In the first section of the paper, we compared the SFAC 1 and the Exposure Draft to the previous attempts of this nature and found little substantive difference. In the second section, we examined whether the first two of the five benefits claimed by the FASB may reasonably be expected to flow from these statements and reached a negative conclusion. Then we probed the very meaning of the term "objectives" as applied to financial accounting and found that term too ill-defined. These conclusions led us to inquire into reasons why authoritative bodies have continued to search for objectives and a conceptual framework of accounting. We consider several of these.

The first reason could be that our negative conclusions in Section 2 regarding the usefulness of these statements in resolving accounting issues and standard-setting problems are wrong. If so, it should be easy for someone to illustrate, possibly using issues other than the three we selected, that these objectives and definitions will indeed help resolve the accounting issues. We are not aware of any such illustrations.

A second reason for the search for conceptual frameworks could be provided in terms of the three potential benefits claimed by the FASB and not examined in this paper. It may turn out that the issuance of the conceptual framework increases the users' confidence in, and understanding of, financial statements. Someone may also give workable definitions of "bounds for judgment" and comparability and show that the issuance of conceptual frameworks may have desirable consequences in these respects. Again, neither the theoretical arguments nor the empirical evidence that bears on these issues is available.

Two further reasons are possible: One lies in the form in which accounting problems are brought to the authoritative bodies, while the second lies in the attempts of the accounting profession to keep the rule-making power in its own hands.

Repeated efforts of authoritative bodies to define the conceptual framework of accounting in general and the elements of financial statements in particular may arise from the genuine belief that a determination of precise definitions of certain terms will somehow help resolve accounting controversies.[9] Such belief is reinforced each time an accounting controversy surfaces and the proponents of alternative methods present their arguments in the established terminology of accounting so as to convince the policy makers that the weight of tradition, so highly prized in accounting, is on their side. Given a strong motivation to have an accounting standard accepted which is favorable to one's interests, it is not difficult to devise an argument as to why a given transaction should be recorded in a certain way under the currently accepted definitions of accounting terms.[10] Since the views of various parties are presented to the policy-making bodies not in the form of conflicting

---

[9]See Zeff [1978, pp. 57–58] for a typology of the arguments offered in accounting controversies.
[10]See Kitchen [1954] for a stimulating discussion of the problems of definition in accounting.

private interests, but in the form of conflicting interpretations of accounting definitions, it may appear that a clearer definition of each accounting term will solve the
problem. A frank discussion of the private interests of various contending groups
may be tactically disadvantageous in open public discourse.[11] Hence, the overblown
emphasis on authoritative definitions. However, definitions, no matter how carefully
worded, cannot bear the burden of the struggle for economic advantage between
various interest groups. Legal definitions survive in a similar environment only
because their interpretations by the courts are backed by the power of the state to
enforce them, a power not available to the FASB.

The conceptual framework-seeker behavior of the FASB and its predecessors
can also be explained in terms of a self-interest perceived by the public accounting
profession. The profession has long argued that its interests are best served if it can
maintain control over prescription of accounting standards. This is revealed in its
protests against any hint that the control of the profession over the standard-setting
process may be weakened. Fear of governmental intervention has long been, and
continues to be, the major reason for calls for action in the profession.[12] Consider,
for example, the following:

> If the practitioners, after sufficient time has elapsed, have not come to some substantial
> agreement as to what are or should be considered accepted accounting principles and
> practices, we may well expect the Commission's [SEC's] staff accountants to prepare, and
> the Commission to publish what it shall demand in the way of such practices...[Smith,
> 1935, p. 327].

Appropriate as it is today, note that the above statement appeared in an article
published almost 45 years ago. Disagreements centering on diverse accounting
standards continue to attract much of the criticism leveled at the accounting
profession and are the source of the greatest threat to the profession's control over
the standard-setting process. The presence of diverse accounting practices hurts the
credibility of the standard-setting bodies in two ways. First, the existence of
alternative accounting methods is taken as *prima facie* evidence that the accounting
standard-setting body is not doing its work properly and is simply allowing firms to
record transactions in an arbitrary fashion. Second, whenever the standard-setting
body proscribes the use of all but one of the alternative accounting methods, the
advocates of the methods were no longer permitted to criticize the agency for being
arbitrary in not protecting their interests. No matter what it does, a body like the
FASB can expect to find itself criticized by powerful interest groups. A good
example is provided by the debate on accounting for oil and gas exploration costs.
The FASB was instructed to develop a uniform accounting standard for the oil and

---

[11]Since everybody is assumed to be serving the interests of the information user, proponents of all
accounting methods argue their case because it will benefit such user. Recall that in the heyday of the
LIFO controversy, a major argument for LIFO was that it yields a better measure of income. Watts and
Zimmerman [1979] have attempted to explain the existence of some normative theories in financial
accounting, using a parallel argument.

[12]Of course, the auditors' fear of government intervention is asymmetric. Consistent with their
self-interests, they do want the government to continue to require an audit of certain business firms to
ensure demand for their services but want to keep the standard-setting process free of government
control.

gas industry or face the threat of having such a standard written by a government agency. When the FASB chose the successful-efforts over the full-cost method, it found, aligned against it, a powerful industry group as well as some government departments and agencies. Being largely an offspring of the accounting profession, the FASB has (as did the APB) little defense against the criticism that it does not have legitimate authority to make decisions which affect wealth transfers among members of society.

Thus, a body like the FASB needs a conceptual framework simply to boost its public standing.[13] A conceptual framework provides the basis for arguing that: (1) the objective of its activities is to serve the users of the financial statements (it is easier to use the public-interest argument for the user group than for any other group), and (2) it selects among accounting alternatives on the basis of broadly accepted objectives and not because of pressures applied by various interest groups seeking a favorable ruling from the Board. The ability, intelligence, ethical character, and past services, *etc.*, of the members of the FASB are not sufficient to convince the parties adversely affected by its rulings that it makes social choices through an impartial consideration of conflicting interests in society. Rather, a conceptual framework is needed to provide the rationalization for its choices.

If a more representative body were to take over the function of setting accounting standards, perhaps there would be less of a need for a conceptual framework. Indeed, the demand to develop a conceptual framework may be inversely related to the power of enforcement which the standard-setting agency can command. For example, the Securities and Exchange Commission, which has the legal power to enforce its Accounting Series Releases, has not been hampered by the fact that it has not yet enunciated a conceptual framework of accounting.

5. CONCLUDING REMARKS

There is little evidence that official statements of objectives of financial accounting have had any direct effect on the determination of financial accounting standards. Whenever the APB or the FASB has had to consider a financial accounting standard, various interest groups presented arguments to support the methods that each perceived to be in its own best interests. The standards issued had to be compromises among the contending interests.[14] Whether the standard-setting process stays in the private sector or is transferred to some public agency, this feature is unlikely to change. What, then, will likely be the effect of the FASB's Conceptual Framework Project on the development of financial accounting standards in the future?

Our initial guess is that the objectives selected by the Board will be ignored in future rule-making activities, just as were those from previous authoritative attempts. Following the publication of these objectives, the Board will probably feel obliged to pay lip service to them in its future pronouncements, but these pronouncements

---

[13]A discussion of this public-interest argument appears in AAA[1977b].

[14]See, for example, Horngren[1973, p. 61], "My hypothesis is that the setting of accounting standards is as much a product of political action as of flawless logic or empirical findings."

will not be affected in any substantive way by what is contained in the present documents.

It might have been a more fruitful exercise for the FASB to develop a set of objectives for itself and not for the entire social activity called financial reporting. A few examples of such objectives are provided for consideration:

First, the Board could explicitly recognize the nature of financial accounting as a social activity which affects a varied set of interests, both of those who actively participate and those who do not.[15] As the interests of each group are affected by the actions of the Board, it must expect to hear arguments in support of, and against, its decisions. The representations made by these parties could be viewed in the context of their own private interests. In the past, accountants in public practice (*i.e.*, auditors) have tended to be more vocal in their reactions to the Board's actions than have other parties. But perhaps accountants in public practice should have less direct influence on the rule-making process in the future. In its statement of objectives, the Board could define mechanisms for arriving at a compromise ruling after a hearing has been given to all affected groups in society. The Board's primary objective would simply be to arrive at a compromise ruling after considering various points of view on each issue.

A second objective for the FASB might be to limit the detail and specificity of its accounting standards. The pressure to write increasingly detailed and specific accounting standards is great and, in recent years, the resistance of the Board to such pressures seems to be weakening. In this connection, we might note that one of the three conditions laid down by the Council of the Institute of Chartered Accountants in England and Wales for approving recommendations on accounting principles to its members was simply that the document be reasonably concise in form (see Zeff [1972, p. 11]).[16] Judging from the length and detail of some of its recent pronouncements (*e.g.*, those dealing with leases and oil and gas exploration costs), the FASB seems to have abandoned an attempt to keep its Statements of Financial Accounting Standards concise.

A third objective of the Board could be to abstain from issuing an accounting standard unless the pronouncement could command a substantial majority. The recent move to lower the minimum voting requirement for issuing an FASB recommendation to a simple majority of seven members will probably increase the frequency of FASB pronouncements which are widely opposed by large segments of interested parties and therefore undermine the basis of its support.

In short, the FASB could assume that various functions of financial statements are well established and known generally by those who produce, audit, and use accounting information. Its task would be essentially one of trying to appease conflicting interests in the presence of disagreements over accounting rules, measurements, disclosures, *etc*. But once this role were recognized, what would be the advantages and disadvantages of allowing a private board like the FASB to make

[15] An explicit objective along these lines was also proposed in AAA [1977b, pp. 10–11].

[16] Of course, there is no government agency in the UK which serves an enforcement role like that of the SEC in this country. This factor may allow broader statements in the UK.

compromise decisions? Is this not a function essentially similar to that performed by the courts, and, if so, are we now back to the proposal for an accounting court?[17]

These questions appear to offer fruitful areas of research, more so than trying to deduce *the* objectives of financial accounting. Perhaps we can achieve more progress by developing and testing theories regarding why a major part of the responsibility for standard setting continues to lie with a private agency, and why members of the profession and corporate managers continue to contribute time and money to the process of developing a conceptual framework. It is unlikely that a general fear of government regulation alone can account for the latter. And, finally, to conclude with Baxter [1962, p. 427]:

> Recommendations by authority on matters of accounting theory may in the short run seem unmixed blessings. In the end, however, they will probably do harm. They are likely to yield little fresh knowledge.... They are likely to weaken the education of accountants; the conversion of the subject into cut-and-dried rules, approved by authority and not to be lightly questioned, threatens to reduce its value as a subject of liberal education almost to *nil*. They are likely to narrow the scope for individual thought and judgment; and a group of men who resign their hard problems to others must eventually give up all claim to be a learned profession.

[17] First proposed by Littleton [1935].

REFERENCES

American Accounting Association (1936), Executive Committee, "A Tentative Statement of Accounting Principles Affecting Corporate Reports," *The Accounting Review* (June 1936), pp. 187–91.

———, Executive Committee, "Accounting Principles Underlying Corporate Financial Statements," *The Accounting Review* (June 1941), pp. 133–39.

———, Executive Committee, "Accounting Concepts and Standards Underlying Corporate Financial Statements, 1948 Revision," *The Accounting Review* (October 1948), pp. 339–44.

———, Committee on Concepts and Standards Underlying Corporate Financial Statements, "Accounting and Reporting Standards for Corporate Financial Statements, 1957 Revision," *The Accounting Review* (October 1957), pp. 536–46.

———, Committee on Concepts and Standards—Long-Lived Assets, "Accounting for Land, Buildings and Equipment," Supplementary Statement No. 1, *The Accounting Review* (July 1964a), pp. 693–99.

———, Committee on Concepts and Standards—Inventory Measurement, "A Discussion of Various Approaches to Inventory Measurement," Supplementary Statement No. 2, *The Accounting Review* (July 1964b), pp. 700–14.

———, Committee to Prepare a Statement of Basic Accounting Theory, *A Statement of Basic Accounting Theory* (AAA, 1966).

———, Committee on Concepts and Standards for External Financial Reports, *Statement on Accounting Theory and Theory Acceptance* (AAA, 1977a).

———, Subcommittee on Conceptual Framework for Financial Accounting and Reporting, *Elements of Financial Statements and Their Measurement. Report to the Financial Accounting Standards Board* (AAA, June 1977b).

American Institute of [Certified Public] Accountants (1942), Committee on Accounting Procedure, *Unamortized Discount and Redemption Premium on Bonds Refunded (Supplement)*, Accounting Research Bulletin No. 18, (AICPA, 1942).

———, Committee on Accounting Terminology, *Accounting Terminology Bulletin*, No. 1 (AIA, 1953). Reprinted in FASB [1977b].

American Institute of Certified Public Accountants (1970), Accounting Principles Board, *Basic Concepts and Accounting Principles Underlying Financial Statements of Business Enterprises*, Statement No. 4 of the APB (AICPA, 1970).

———, Study Group on the Objectives of Financial Statements, *Objectives of Financial Statements* (AICPA, 1973).

Armstrong, M. S., "The Politics of Establishing Accounting Standards," *Journal of Accountancy* (February 1977), pp. 76–79.

Baxter and S. Davidson, eds., *Studies in Accounting Theory* (Sweet & Maxwell, 1962), pp. 414–27.

Beaver, W. H. and J. S. Demski, "The Nature of Financial Accounting Objectives: A Survey and Synthesis," *Studies on Financial Accounting Objectives, 1974*, supplement to the *Journal of Accounting Research* (1974), pp. 13–17.

Bedford, N. M., "Discussion of Opportunities and Implications of the Report on Objectives of Financial Statements," *Studies on Financial Accounting Objectives, 1974*, supplement to the *Journal of Accounting Research* 12 (1974), p. 15.

Canning, J. B., *The Economics of Accountancy* (The Ronald Press, 1929).

Coe, T. L., and G. H. Sorter, "The FASB Has Been Using an Implicit Conceptual Framework," *The Accounting Journal* (Winter 1977–78), pp. 152–69.

Cyert, R. M. and Y. Ijiri, "Problems of Implementing the Trueblood Objectives Report," *Studies on Financial Accounting Objectives: 1974*, supplement to the *Journal of Accounting Research* 12 (1974).

Deinzer, H. T., *The American Accounting Association-Sponsored Statements of Standards for Corporate Financial Reports: A Perspective* (Accounting Department, University of Florida, 1964).

Financial Accounting Standards Board, FASB Discussion Memorandum, *Conceptual Framework for Accounting and Reporting: Consideration of the Report of the Study Group on the Objectives of Financial Statements* (FASB, 1974).

———, FASB Discussion Memorandum, *Conceptual Framework for Financial Accounting and Reporting: Elements of Financial Statements and Their Measurement* (FASB, 1976a).

———, *Tentative Conclusions on Objectives of Financial Statements of Business Enterprises* (FASB, 1976b).

———, *Scope and Implications of the Conceptual Framework Project* (FASB, 1976c).

———, *Objectives of Financial Reporting and Elements of Financial Statements of Business Enterprises*, Exposure Draft of Proposed Statement of Financial Accounting Concepts (FASB, 1977).

———, *Objectives of Financial Reporting by Business Enterprises*, Statement of Financial Accounting Concepts No. 1 (FASB, 1978).

Hanson, A. W., "Comments on 'An Introduction to Corporate Accounting Standards,'" *Journal of Accountancy* (June 1940), pp. 440–42.

Hatfield, H. R., *Modern Accounting* (D. Appleton and Company, 1909).

———, *Accounting: Its Principles and Problems* (D. Appleton-Century Company, 1927).

Horngren, C. T., "The Marketing of Accounting Standards," *Journal of Accountancy* (October 1973), pp. 61–66.

Ijiri, Y., "Critique of the APB Fundamentals Statement," *Journal of Accountancy* (November 1971), pp. 43–50.

Kester, R. B., "Comments on 'An Introduction to Corporate Accounting Standards,'" *Journal of Accountancy* (June 1940), pp. 442–45.

Kitchen, J., "Costing Terminology," *Accounting Research* (February 1954). Reprinted in W. T. Baxter and S. Davidson, eds., *Studies in Accounting Theory* (Sweet & Maxwell, 1962), pp. 399–413.

Littleton, A. C., "Auditor Independence," *Journal of Accountancy* (April 1935), pp. 283–94.

———, Review of Moonitz, *The Basic Postulates of Accounting*, *The Accounting Review* (July 1962), pp. 602–05.

———, Review of R. T. Sprouse and M. Moonitz, *A Tentative Set of Broad Accounting Principles for Business Enterprises*, *The Accounting Review* (January 1963), pp. 220–22.

Miller, H. E., "Discussion of Opportunities and Implications of the Report on Objectives of Financial Statements," *Studies on Financial Accounting Objectives, 1974*, supplement to *Journal of Accounting Research* 12 (1974).

Moonitz, M., *The Basic Postulates of Accounting*, Accounting Research Study No. 1 (AICPA, 1961).

Most, K. S. and A. L. Winters, "Focus on Standard Setting: From Trueblood to the FASB," *Journal of Accountancy* (February 1977), pp. 67–75.

Paton, W. A., *Accounting Theory* (The Ronald Press, 1922).

Paton, W. A. and A. C. Littleton, *An Introduction to Corporate Accounting Standards*, Monograph No. 3 (AAA, 1940).

Smith, C. A., "Accounting Practice under the Securities and Exchange Commission," *The Accounting Review* (December 1935), pp. 325–332.

Sprouse, R. T., "Discussion of Opportunities and Implications of the Report on Objectives of Financial Statements," *Studies on Financial Accounting Objectives, 1974*, supplement to the *Journal of Accounting Research* 12 (1974).

Sprouse, R. T. and M. Moonitz, *A Tentative Set of Broad Accounting Principles for Business Enterprises*, Accounting Research Study No. 3 (AICPA, 1962).

Sterling, R. R., "A Statement of Basic Accounting Theory: A Review Article," *Journal of Accounting Research* (Spring 1967), pp. 95–112.

Stinchcombe, A. L., *Constructing Social Theories* (Harcourt, Brace, and World, 1968).

Vatter, W.J., " $\sum_{i=1}^{i=22} (M_3)_i$ —An Evaluation," *The Accounting Review* (July 1963), pp.47–77.

Watts, R. L., and J. L. Zimmerman, "Towards a Positive Theory of Determination of Accounting Standards," *The Accounting Review* 53 (January 1978), pp. 112–34.

———, "The Demand for and Supply of Accounting Theories: The Market for Excuses," *The Accounting Review* (April 1979), pp. 273–305.

Zeff, S. A., *Forging Accounting Principles in Five Countries* (Stipes Publishing Co., 1972).

———, "The Rise of 'Economic Consequences,'" *Journal of Accountancy* (December 1978), pp. 56–63.

Uses and Limitations of a Conceptual Framework

Charles T. Horngren
Stanford University

My perceptions of the role of a conceptual framework in accounting policymaking are heavily affected by the following definitions:

1 The Financial Accounting Standards Board engages in policymaking, which may be defined as the process by which individuals or groups in power choose general rules for action that may affect others within an organization or perhaps affect an entire society. Raymond Chambers states: "Policy-making is 'choosing which' when the choice is a matter of opinion or taste or some other personal or organizational criterion, and not simply a matter of technology."[1]

2 According to the FASB, its conceptual framework is "a coherent system of interrelated objectives and fundamentals that is expected to lead to consistent standards and that prescribes the nature, function, and limits of financial accounting and reporting."[2]

Why is the board building what I will refer to as a technical framework? Several academicians have recently speculated about why. The why is very important to obtaining overall perspective about this multimillion dollar, multiyear effort. In many people's minds, the framework is responsive to an axiomatic belief—that is, if we only had a foundation, deductive logic would lead us to the correct answer.

Although technology is important, accounting policymaking embraces other considerations too, including the political or educational problems of obtaining general acceptance. So policymaking is enormously complicated. As Albert Einstein once remarked, "Mathematics is hard enough, but political science is far too difficult for me."

A PROBLEM OF SOCIAL CHOICE

The policymaking process has been called a social choice problem by several academicians. That term avoids some of the unfortunate connotations associated with calling it a political process. As an example of the latter, my dictionary has five definitions of politics, including one that says "activities characterized by artful and often dishonest practices."

From *Journal of Accountancy* (April 1981), pp. 86, 88, 90, 92, 94–95. Reprinted by permission of the American Institute of Certified Public Accountants. Copyright © 1981 by the American Institute of Certified Public Accountants, Inc.

Author's note: My colleagues at Stanford University, William H. Beaver, CPA, Joel S. Demski and Paul A. Griffin, provided helpful comments on an earlier draft.

[1] Raymond J. Chambers, "Accounting Principles or Accounting Policies," JofA. May 73, p. 52.

[2] Financial Accounting Concepts Statement no. 2, *Qualitative Characteristics of Accounting Information* (Stamford, Conn.: Financial Accounting Standards Board, 1980). p. 11.

Viewing the policymaking process as a social choice problem entails

"**1** An assessment of the consequences of FASB decisions on various constituencies (e.g., analysts, management, auditors, bankers, bondholders, diversified shareholders, undiversified shareholders and the SEC [Securities and Exchange Commission])."

"**2** A decision as to which configuration of consequences is most desirable, which involves tradeoffs among the interests of various groups affected (for example, whose ox will get gored?)."[3]

The focus is on power and preference. Joel Demski says: "More precisely, in this view we define one financial reporting system as more valuable than another when some group (1) unanimously regards the one as more valuable than the other in terms of individual value and (2) has the *power*—socially speaking—to guarantee this choice. For example, returning to APB [Accounting Principles Board] days, if the insurance industry prefers historical to current valuation of marketable securities and if they have sufficient power to enforce this desire, we then regard the former as more valuable than the latter."[4]

The key element is the set of individuals or coalitions with sufficient power to force a choice. We should list those who have power. If we know the list, we can often predict how the choices are made.

The FASB's scope and implications document characterizes the conceptual framework as a constitution,[5] which to me clearly implies a social choice perspective. A constitution defines the powers of various groups (that is, constituencies). When a difference of preferences arises, the constitution specifies who will win. For example, under certain circumstances, the president can veto a bill. Under other specified conditions, Congress can override the veto.[6] For a second example closer to policymaking by the FASB, the existing, implied constitution is less clear as to who will win if one of the constituents is the SEC. You can draw your own conclusions.

The FASB has understandably retreated from the social choice perspective in the sense that its conceptual framework emphasizes the technology of accounting. That is, the board is concerned with measuring the financial impact of events in an evenhanded manner. Nevertheless, the ultimate generality or specificity of its technical framework will be heavily affected by the relative importance the FASB attaches to its various constituencies.

Survival is mankind's primary motivation. Standard-setting bodies in the private sector have had various useful lives. The committee on accounting procedure lasted about 22 years; the APB, 13 years. I hope the FASB has a long useful life—at least 40 years. The useful life of the FASB is not going to rest on issues of technical competence. The pivotal issue will be the ability of the board to resolve conflicts

[3] William H. Beaver, "One Academic's View of the Conceptual Framework Project" (Paper delivered at the Conference of California Society of CPAs. September 1977), pp. 9–10.

[4] Joel S. Demski, "The Value of Financial Accounting," (Work paper, Stanford University, 1980) p. 89.

[5] *Scope and Implications of the Conceptual Framework Project* (Stamford, Conn.: FASB, December 1976), p. 2.

[6] Beaver, p. 10.

among the various constituencies in a manner perceived to be acceptable to the ultimate constituent, the 800-pound gorilla in the form of the federal government, particularly the SEC. (Of course, the federal gorilla is also subject to pressure from its constituents.) This ability will be manifested in the FASB's decisions, appointments and conceptual framework. So the conceptual framework is desirable if the survival of the FASB is considered to be desirable.[7] That is, the framework is likely to help provide power to the board. After all, the board has no coercive power. Instead, the board must really rely on power by persuasion.

I wish the conceptual framework could be extended in the form of a constitution, but I can also understand why the development of the more modest technical framework is a more feasible goal for the next two or three or four years. (But no more than four, please.)

Consider another illustration of why the technical framework is the tip of the iceberg. With social choice being conducted in a multiperiod setting, the agenda is important. Note that the present framework is silent about how the agenda is set or what items should be placed on the agenda. Yet the power to control the agenda may be far more critical to the status and life of the FASB than the nature of the technical framework.

At an FASB symposium on the conceptual framework held in New York City last June, FASB Chairman Donald Kirk said he agreed with the views of Louis Harris: "Ultimate achievement rests on the capability of the FASB to set real, workable and sound standards, but at the same time to convince its constituents to accept its work as the reality they must be prepared to live with."

Above all, we should recognize that the process of setting accounting standards includes the gaining of general acceptance and support. A major role of the conceptual framework is ultimately to enhance the likelihood of acceptability of specific statements to be proposed or already in place. The more plausible the assumptions and the more compelling the analysis of the facts, the greater the chance of winning the support of diverse interests—and retaining and enhancing the board's power.

MOVEMENT FROM INDIVIDUAL MEMBERS' VALUES
TO BOARD VALUES

Precisely what are the implications of the theory of social choice for accounting policymakers? An essential feature is the movement from individual values and choices to social values and choices. Unfortunately, little research has been conducted in this area. Nevertheless, at least some serious thought is being given to describing the problem less naively now than in 1970. Let's concentrate on some difficulties concerning the frameworks of individuals.

Individual Conceptual Frameworks

Most often, the news stories in the business press refer to the FASB as some sort of monolith. But the board is a collection of individuals, just as the accounting

[7]Ibid., p. 12.

departments in universities are collections of individuals. As our professional careers unfold, each of us develops a technical conceptual framework. Some individual frameworks are sharply defined and firmly held; others are vague and weakly held; still others are vague and firmly held.

For example, I suspect that the board's current proposals regarding Statement no. 8, *Accounting for the Translation of Foreign Currency Transactions and Foreign Currency Financial Statements,*[8] reflect changes in some members' conceptual frameworks, in the membership of the board and in the pressures from constituents. I wonder if the board's decisions would have been different regarding foreign currency (or oil or gas) if its conceptual framework had been in place early in the game.

Of course, in a group setting, frameworks are very helpful when they overlap and not so helpful when they clash. At one time or another, most of us have felt the discomfort of listening to somebody attempting to buttress a preconceived conclusion by building a convoluted chain of shaky reasoning. Indeed, perhaps on occasion we have voiced such thinking ourselves. Examples of tortuous reasoning are some vivid justifications of accounting for poolings of interest that frequently involve rivers coming together and then wending onward. (My personal conceptual framework may be showing here.) In my opinion the likening of business combinations to streams of water may be poetic, but it is not a demonstration of applying a technical conceptual framework.

My experience as a member of the APB taught me many lessons. A major one was that most of us have a natural tendency and an incredible talent for processing new facts in such a way that our prior conclusions remain intact.[9] Therefore, no matter what conceptual framework is developed, its success will be heavily affected by individual interpretations.

The role of the framework becomes further complicated by the periodic introduction of new board members. Therefore, the generally accepted framework of the 1974 board may not be the generally accepted framework of the 1980 or 1986 board. Some major difficulties may arise as the conceptual framework moves into the area of earnings recognition and as the board membership changes.

Each person has characteristics that limit the usefulness of a conceptual framework. Receptivity to new ideas and change differs markedly. Given a set of circumstances, most of us can predict the behavior of people we know well. Thus, various board members' attitudes toward seeing a changing accounting world anew will ultimately determine the degree of influence of the framework. Perhaps we should be as much concerned with developing attitudes toward the use of a common framework as with developing knowledge. However, this is easier said than done.

From time to time, the board pleads with its constituents to swallow hard and defer their judgments to the FASB. Why? Because such behavior will further their constituents' private interests in the long run. Similarly, from time to time, the individual board members may have to swallow hard and defer their judgments to

---

[8]FASB Statement no. 8, *Accounting for the Translation of Foreign Currency Transactions and Foreign Currency Financial Statements* (Stamford, Conn.: FASB, 1975).

[9]John Jeuck, "Remarks on the Occasion of the McKinsey Award Dinner," *Issues & Ideas* (Chicago, Ill.: University of Chicago, Winter 1980), p. 11.

the board as a whole. Why? Again, to further their private interests in the long run in the sense of extending the useful life of the board.

General acceptance among the board's members is the first key to the usefulness of the framework. In itself, this is not a trivial task. The second key is the SEC. As FASB members, SEC commissioners and SEC chief accountants come and go, their attitudes and perceptions will help or hinder the role of the framework.

The fragility of any framework is illustrated by the moves of the regulators regarding FASB Statement no. 19, *Financial Accounting and Reporting by Oil and Gas Producing Companies,*[10] and the remarkable six-year old Ping-Pong℗ game between the SEC and the board regarding the role of current costs and constant dollar accounting. That is, the board may be nearly unanimously in favor of constant dollar accounting, serve it softly to the SEC and get a return smash from the SEC consisting of current cost accounting. The theory of social choice tells us that we should not be surprised by such interactions during the multi-play game of continuous policymaking.

Almost everyone says he or she wants a conceptual framework, but his or her conceptual framework may not be yours. For example, four general methods of measuring income and capital are discussed in FASB Statement no. 33, *Financial Reporting and Changing Prices.*[11] Each method has strong advocates, and each method has its variations. Given the historical setting and the diverse interest groups that have real or imagined stakes in the policy decisions and strong preferences for flexibility rather than uniformity, agreement on too concrete a conceptual framework will be hard to achieve. Even the issuance of a statement on a conceptual framework cannot escape political dimensions.[12]

The Varying Influence of a Framework

A conceptual framework can help policymakers. There is no doubt that the use of a generally accepted conceptual framework would make standard setting more efficient and effective, producing faster, more consistent and more defensible answers. The framework definitely can help if it provides a common language, methods of analysis and constraints. However, the degree of help will vary from situation to situation.

Consider this illustration of how a technical framework can help.

APB Opinion no. 21, *Interest on Receivables and Payables,*[13] was adopted by the unanimous vote of the 18 members of the board. The opinion requires the imputation of interest in specified circumstances. One of its introductory paragraphs says that "the primary objective of this Opinion is to refine the manner of applying existing accounting principles in this circumstance. Thus it is not intended to create a new

---

[10]FASB Statement no. 19, *Financial Accounting and Reporting by Oil and Gas Producing Companies* (Stamford, Conn.: FASB, 1977).
[11]FASB Statement no. 33, *Financial Reporting and Changing Prices* (Stamford, Conn.: FASB, 1979).
[12]Charles T. Horngren, "Will the FASB Be Here in the 1980s?" JofA, Nov. 76, p. 96.
[13]Accounting Principles Board Opinion no. 21, *Interest on Receivables and Payables* (New York: AICPA, 1971).

accounting principle." The members applied some widely held, general concepts such as exchange and present value.

Opinion no. 21 was not preceded by an APB research study. Still, each of the 18 members possessed his own conceptual framework, no matter how ill-defined. My point here is that there was sufficient overlap among the 18 frameworks to lead to a unanimous opinion. Moreover, technology played a dominant role in obtaining an accounting standard. Evidence was gathered, logic was applied and a pronouncement was issued. The job of getting general acceptance by the various constituencies was relatively easy, perhaps because the constituents perceived no major economic impact.

Consider an illustration where a framework did not help much.

APB Opinions no. 16, *Business Combinations*,[14] and no. 17, *Intangible Assets*,[15] were preceded by two research studies. Discussions began and continued intermittently at a highly conceptual level worthy of a first-rate doctoral seminar, but the overlap of individual conceptual frameworks was barely great enough to generate the required support by two-thirds of the APB. Moreover, many of the final votes were not influenced solely by conceptual frameworks, as ordinarily conceived. Therefore, a conceptual framework may help if it structures the arguments and provides a common language when dealing with a complicated issue. Still, the framework may become relatively unimportant in the ultimate deliberations when the votes are counted.

My hypothesis is that many final votes are influenced by individual technical frameworks that are favored over any commonly held framework. Moreover, just as in politics, individuals may cast a positive or negative vote as only one in a series of moves to establish, maintain or enhance power. The thinking may be: "I'll vote for something that is technically unacceptable this time because in the longer run I have to live with my fellow members. I'll give in a little now, but I'll win later on more important policy matters." A favorite rationale is: "I'll vote for this defective standard because at least it is an improvement over existing practice."

Does such kind of thinking exist? Undoubtedly! It is vital to the useful life of the board, but it is not captured in any technical framework.

My point in citing these illustrations is that a conceptual framework that deals with the "technology" of accounting may be very helpful in most situations and may be of limited help in other situations. Furthermore, the credibility of the FASB can be hurt by the purported use of a conceptual framework where it does not fit. Arthur Wyatt expressed the situation well: "Research (in this context, a conceptual framework) disregards politics and other compromises necessary in making decisions. Decision makers should acknowledge the political and other required compromises when deviating from the proper research answer, explain their decisions on pragmatic grounds, and not try to justify the answer that they come up with as being the one that is most sound, the best conceptually."[16]

---

[14] APB Opinion no. 16, *Business Combinations* (New York: AICPA, 1970).
[15] APB Opinion no. 17, *Intangible Assets* (New York: AICPA, 1970).
[16] Arthur R. Wyatt, "Research and the APB," Thomas J. Burns, ed., *Accounting in Transition* (Columbus, Ohio: Ohio State University, College of Administrative Science, 1974), p. 128.

SOME REFLECTIONS AND PREDICTIONS

All regulatory bodies have been flayed because they have used piecemeal approaches, solving one accounting issue at a time. Observers have alleged that not enough tidy rationality has been used in the process of accounting policymaking. Again and again, critics have cited a need for a conceptual framework.

I heartily applaud the FASB's efforts to construct a conceptual framework. Its constituents demand it. Let's get the framework built.

There are two major schools of thought regarding the FASB's pace in the construction of the framework.

The first, which is apparently favored by most board members, is patience and plenty of due process. Like the Egyptian-Israeli peace talks, it may be better for all concerned simply to continue the dialogue without necessarily obtaining complete agreement on both sides. It is not hard for me to see why this point of view has merit. Note that the more complete the closure, the greater the restrictions placed on future plays in the game. Moreover, constituents and present and future board members may be unwilling to restrict freedom of choice.

The second school of thought, which I tend to favor, is to proceed more rapidly. Let's not get bogged down in trying to get too concrete a structure. No matter what effort is expended, the structure will be fragile. Let's not carry due process to an extreme, having too many symposiums and too lengthy exposure periods.

Given the experiences of the APB, the FASB and the nature of policymaking, I predict

- Production of a general framework and acceptance by the board.
- Highly successful application in some cases but not in others.
- Varying interpretations of the framework by individual board members.

As individual accounting standards are issued, the board will be accused of not properly applying the framework in a consistent way and using a piecemeal approach to standard setting. Nevertheless, I have high hopes (a) that the lack of a conceptual framework will not be cited as often as in the past as a reason for postponing action on accounting standards and (b) that the long-standing clamor for a conceptual framework will diminish because proponents will finally realize that such a framework is only a part of the policymaking process, a part whose prominence fluctuates from standard to standard.

SUMMARY

Many who ardently favor a conceptual framework imply that "if we had a framework, we would know what to do." But there are doubters, including me. A framework that is supposed to provide guidelines for the policymakers may differ, depending on the eyes of the beholder.

Accounting policymaking is obviously complex. Progress will continue to come in fits and starts. It will always be considered as too fast by some critics and too slow by other critics. Most people favor "improvements" in accounting—the quicker the better, but one person's improvement is often another person's impairment. These trade-offs are the nucleus of policymaking.[17]

I hope the framework proceeds and gets in place. There is no doubt that it will help, but let's not expect too much from it. Great expectations and inherent complexity are almost always conflicting terms. A technical conceptual framework is only part of the policymaking process. A framework is desirable, but it is not sufficient.

[17]Horngren, p. 96.

Economic Impact of Accounting Standards— Implications for the FASB

Alfred Rappaport
Northwestern University

There is a growing recognition that the setting of financial accounting standards which govern what business corporations must report (i.e., disclosure issues) and how they must describe their economic operations (i.e., measurement issues) needs to be viewed more broadly than simply from a technical accounting perspective. Horngren[1] exhorts the Financial Accounting Standards Board to equip itself for its marketing as well as its production responsibilities. Mautz[2] suggests that

> accounting legislators have to learn to develop and maintain a broad point of view. It is not enough just to be an expert accountant. They must be expert accountants with an appreciation of the environment in which accounting functions and of the impact that accounting decisions have on that environment.

Moonitz[3] calls for the FASB to conduct an active campaign for "allies" such as the stock exchanges, the Securities and Exchange Commission, regulatory agencies and major accounting organizations.

The expanded view of standard setting comes from an increasing recognition that the legislation of accounting standards involves a potential redistribution of wealth, i.e., it imposes restrictions or costs on some while conferring benefits to others. This phenomenon places a particularly heavy burden on the FASB as a private sector body, because in the final analysis the responsibility of mediating

From *The Journal of Accountancy* (May 1977), pp. 89–90, 92, 94, 96–98. Reprinted by permission of the American Institute of Certified Public Accountants. Copyright © 1977 by the American Institute of Certified Public Accountants, Inc.

[1]Charles T. Horngren, "The Marketing of Accounting Standards," JofA, Oct. 73, pp. 61–66.
[2]Robert K. Mautz, "Problems in the Development of Accounting Standards," unpublished mimeograph dated April 26, 1975.
[3]Maurice Moonitz, Studies in Accounting Research No. 8, *Obtaining Agreement on Standards* (Sarasota, Fla.: American Accounting Association, 1974).

conflicting values in our society rests with Congress rather than with any private sector organization. Congress, on the other hand, is not presently equipped to deal effectively with the complex disclosure and measurement issues in contemporary corporate reporting. It has, in fact, delegated accounting standard setting to the SEC and other federal agencies. The SEC, in turn, has delegated some of its power to the FASB. In brief, no single organization has both the technical competence to deal with the complex measurement and disclosure issues and the social legitimacy to assess and resolve conflicts among competing interests. Indeed, as one moves down the Congress-SEC-FASB hierarchy, one observes increasing technical competence and decreasing social legitimacy.

What then can the FASB do in light of its organizational position and of the increasing belief that accounting standards can induce far-reaching economic consequences? In the first section of this article, the process by which financial accounting standards can affect resource allocation and the redistribution of wealth in the economy is briefly presented. The strategic options currently available to the FASB are then enumerated and discussed in the second section. In the final section, a recommended standard setting process that might be advantageously adopted by the FASB for dealing with the potential economic impact of financial accounting standards is outlined.

ECONOMIC IMPACT OF ACCOUNTING STANDARDS[4]

Financial accounting standards can affect behavior in the economy and therefore wealth distribution in essentially three different ways:

1 By their effect on the behavior of intended recipients of corporate reports, e.g., shareholders and other investors.

2 By their effect on the behavior of "free riders," i.e., those for whom corporate reports are not directly intended but who can gain access because the reports are publicly available, e.g., competitors, labor, suppliers, customers, government agencies and special interest groups.

3 By their effect on the behavior of the reporting company which, in anticipation of potentially adverse feedback arising from its reporting according to required measurement and disclosure standards, might choose to alter its economic behavior. (Prakash and Rappaport use the term "information inductance" or simply "inductance" to refer to the complex process through which the behavior of an information sender is influenced by the information he is required to communicate).

Intended Recipients

Much of the empirical research in financial accounting during the past 10 years has been dedicated toward testing the relationship between accounting numbers and security prices. The evidence confirms that accounting information such as changes

---

[4]This section is adapted from Prem Prakash and Alfred Rappaport, "Information Inductance and Its Significance for Accounting," *Accounting, Organizations and Society*, vol. 2, no. 1 (Oxford, England: Pergamon Press, 1977).

in earnings per share are associated with changes in security prices. Indeed, there is some evidence that security prices anticipate reported earnings numbers several months before the announcement date. It must be added, however, that the market does not accept the earnings number in an uncritical fashion. There is evidence to support the idea that the market looks beyond accounting numbers and adjusts for the accounting method employed to generate those numbers.

In brief, accounting numbers can affect the investment decisions of shareholders and other investors, the intended recipients of corporate financial reports. The collective evaluation of the company by the market based on accounting information as well as other sources of information is reflected in the company's security price. Since accounting standards govern both what is to be disclosed and the basis for measurement, insofar as security prices impound accounting information, it can be concluded that financial accounting standards existing at a particular time have an economic impact by their influence on security prices and thereby on the wealth of market participants. Security price changes affect not only the present wealth of investors, but they also can have an impact on the company's resource allocation decisions because of their influence on the company's cost of capital. The results of such decisions, in turn, manifest once again in the company's financial reports.

Free Riders

Not only can financial accounting reports affect the behavior of intended recipients, but such publicly available reports also affect the behavior of free riders, who can use them for their own decision making purposes. For example, unions might use financial accounting reports as a basis for labor negotiations; regulatory bodies might use the reports as a basis for antitrust regulation, rate regulation and environmental protection regulation; and competitors, suppliers and customers may each adapt their respective strategies on the basis of financial accounting disclosures. In addition, the company's financial accounting numbers serve as an essential data base for the aggregate statistics that describe the state of the economy and, in turn, form an important basis for macro-economic policymaking.

Information that is deemed to be relevant to a specified shareholders' investment decision model would not necessarily be favored by shareholders because sharing this information with free riders might well affect shareholders adversely. Thus, when the free riders are explicitly considered, the relevance of information (i.e., the benefits) to intended recipients must be compared to the potential adverse consequences (i.e. the costs) of sharing this information with free riders. Thus, it is possible that the measurement and disclosure alternative that would be most relevant to the intended user might also be the one he would prefer the company not to disclose publicly.

The Reporting Company

While attention to date has focused primarily on the impact of financial accounting standards on the securities market and only secondarily on the behavior of free riders, the effect of accounting standards on the behavior of the reporting company has received relatively little attention in the literature. It is important to observe that economic factors are influenced not only by the type of information they are provided but also by the type of information they are required to report. Corporate management, in anticipation of the potential feedback from the behavior of intended recipients and free riders, might choose to alter its own economic behavior. Whether the conjectured feedback effects of the company's external reports are, in fact, reasonable or not is not at issue here. What needs to be emphasized is that management's anticipations of the feedback effects, whether reasonable or not, will manifest in changes in resource allocation decisions within the company and, hence, collectively in real changes at the industry and the economy levels. For example, management's concern with the company's security price, together with a belief that earnings per share is instrumental in stock price determination, may lead management to make its capital investment decisions differently in the face of a new accounting standard that affects earnings per share.

A review of some of the more controversial issues facing the FASB suggests that many of the economic-impact-of-financial-accounting-standards arguments are essentially based on conjectures about the expected pattern of information inductance, that is, conjectures about how the economic behavior of the reporting company is likely to be influenced by a proposed change in a measurement or disclosure standard. Consider the following examples of "claimed" changes in the behavior of the reporting company and resultant economic consequences:

- If banks as creditors were forced to reflect losses as a result of restructuring debt

1 Borrowing by higher risk customers (for example, small businesses) would be restricted, thereby limiting economic growth.

2 Banks would hesitate to change or restructure debt terms, with the possibility that this might lead to a higher rate of business failure.

3 To avoid restructuring, bank lending policies might be biased in favor of short term arrangements, thus having an adverse effect on long term markets.

- The recent passage of FASB Statement No. 8, "Accounting for Foreign Currency Translations," was coupled with predictions that the new Standard, which requires that translation gains and losses be immediately reflected in earnings, would induce firms to minimize their accounting exposure via hedging even at the risk of incurring economic exposure. Evidence that some companies did, in fact, increase their hedging activities is offered by the following excerpt from the Philip Morris report to shareholders for the quarter ended March 31, 1976:

> Under these new accounting rules, the company's exposure to foreign currency movements is increased, so the scope and nature of appropriate hedging activities is now substantially enlarged from those appropriate under former rules. Retroactive restatement of prior earnings for a quarter, without a hypothetical adjustment for the effects of an expanded hedging program, would be misleading.

Additional information inductance examples dealing with business combination accounting, price level accounting, full cost accounting in the oil industry, self-insurance accounting and early extinguishment of debt are enumerated by Prakash and Rappaport.[5]

FASB STRATEGIC OPTIONS

Given its position in the Congress-SEC-FASB hierarchy and the political pressures it faces, what strategic options are currently open to the FASB? There appear to be essentially three. The first strategy involves continuing basically along present lines with the hope that the "conceptual framework" project will provide a persuasive justification for present standards and an operational guideline for the setting of future standards. The second strategy would incorporate consideration of potential economic impact into the FASB's formal deliberation process. While these strategies should not be viewed as being mutually exclusive, they each call for a different emphasis and both contain substantial risks for the FASB. The third strategy is a mixed one in that it calls for the simultaneous employment of both the "conceptual framework" and the "economic impact" strategies.

The Conceptual Framework Strategy

A well-founded framework can make a significant contribution to the development of a field of study, for it serves to organize and integrate knowledge into a systematic whole. Because a framework facilitates efficient communication among researchers and practitioners within a field of study, the development of frameworks has consistently engaged the attention of scholars in accounting and in other fields. To contend that a particular framework will provide definitive "solutions" to the setting of financial accounting standards is, however, at best unrealistic and at worst damaging to progress in financial reporting since it promotes expectations that are bound to be frustrated. The much publicized conceptual framework project of the FASB is the third major attempt by the accounting profession during the past 15 years to develop a blueprint for accounting standards. The earlier efforts were Accounting Research Studies Nos. 1 and 3, *The Basic Postulates of Accounting*[6] and *A Tentative Set of Broad Accounting Principles for Business Enterprises*,[7] and, more recently, the Report of the Study Group on the Objectives of Financial Statements, *Objectives of Financial Statements*.[8]

Why is the sole reliance on a conceptual framework strategy likely to prove disappointing? What are risks to the FASB? The adoption of a conceptual framework that serves as the logical point of departure for an authoritative derivation of financial accounting standards is implicitly based on the anachronistic view that

[5]Ibid.

[6]Maurice Moonitz, Accounting Research Study No. 1, *The Basic Postulates of Accounting* (New York: AICPA, 1961).

[7]Maurice Moonitz and Robert T. Sprouse, Accounting Research Study No. 3, *A Tentative Set of Broad Accounting Principles for Business Enterprises* (New York: AICPA, 1962).

[8]Report of the Study Group on the Objectives of Financial Statements, *Objectives of Financial Statements* (New York: AICPA, October 1973).

accounting is essentially a field dedicated to the search for "true" income and "true" wealth, and, once discovered, the truth will become compellingly apparent to all but the unenlightened. An alternative view is that the very act of choosing one framework rather than another is of itself a value judgement.[9] Thus, "the derived concepts of income and wealth are not descriptive, but normative; not objective, but subjective; and not unique, but manifold."[10]

With the growing recognition that no one accounting alternative has an exclusive franchise on truth and each involves potential wealth redistribution, the acceptance of standards will most likely in part be governed by anticipated economic consequences rather than simply the logical appeal of a chosen framework. If this observation proves to be accurate, then the promotion of the conceptual framework as "the answer" imposes serious and unnecessary risks for the viability of the FASB. The adoption by the FASB of a framework from which all standards will naturally evolve may well cause corporate executives, investors and other interested parties to view the FASB as being unresponsive to their concerns. Should these groups look increasingly toward the SEC and Congress to redress their grievances, this could ultimately lead to the demise of meaningful private sector involvement in establishing accounting standards.* Because aggregate corporate performance is a significant component in the evaluation of government performance, if financial accounting standards were formulated in the public sector they might well be even more susceptible to political pressure, particularly to the short run preferences of the administration in power which wishes to report good performance. The current political controversy over the appropriate measures of unemployment and inflation provide excellent examples of what could materialize if corporate income and wealth measures were arbitrated in the public sector.

The Economic Impact Strategy

A second strategy that might be employed by the FASB would incorporate considerations of potential economic impact into its formal deliberation process. This strategy is based on the premise that while there will always be some disagreement on the reasonableness of a proposed standard, the FASB will remain viable only if the process by which it reaches decisions is seen to be both comprehensive and equitable by the various groups affected.

The economic impact strategy also involves potential risks. The formal consideration of the potential consequences of measurement and disclosure choices may call into question the "social legitimacy" of the FASB. Specifically, some might argue that if the consequences of accounting are in fact pervasive, perhaps accounting

---

[9]Committee on Concepts and Standards for External Financial Reports, *Statement on Accounting Theory and Theory Acceptance* (Sarasota, Fla.: American Accounting Association, scheduled for 1977 publication).

[10]Dale L. Gerboth, "Research, Intuition, and Politics in Accounting Inquiry," *Accounting Review*, July 1973, p. 478.

Ed. note: The staff study prepared by the Subcommittee on Reports, Accounting and Management, chaired by Senator Lee Metcalf (D-Mont.), has recommended that the federal government establish accounting and auditing standards for publicly owned corporations (see JofA, Feb.77, p.3, and Mar.77, p.10).

standards should be legislated by elected officials of our representative government instead of a private sector organization. Furthermore, even if the FASB adopts an economic impact strategy, there is always the possibility that those who believe they will be adversely affected by FASB standards might still look to government intervention.

The foregoing risks notwithstanding, as long as there is a public recognition that accounting standards are not absolutes but are necessarily based on value judgments and involve social tradeoffs, the FASB's survival is necessarily conditioned by the confidence inspired by its decision making process. Only a process that carefully evaluates the potential costs and benefits of proposed disclosures and measurements to affected groups is likely to generate such confidence.

The Mixed Strategy

The mixed strategy represents a blend of the conceptual framework and economic impact approaches. This strategy appears to be the FASB's most promising alternative. In brief, it calls for the continual development of a coherent framework that will provide guidelines for measurement and disclosure policy while at the same time assessing the economic impact of such policy. While a mixed strategy is by no means riskless, it does tend to reduce the risks associated with conducting accounting policy on the basis of either one of the component strategies alone.

As stated earlier, a strategy based exclusively on a conceptual framework would undoubtedly be viewed as a strategy that is insensitive to the environment of corporate financial reporting. An exclusive emphasis on an economic impact strategy raises the social legitimacy of the FASB question as well as serious reservations about whether the accountant's education and training are particularly suited toward assessing the impact of accounting choice and then making the social choice implied by the measurement or disclosure standard adopted.

The mixed strategy recognizes the current limitations of accounting theory to contribute to unambiguous policy choices. It further recognizes that policy bodies such as the FASB cannot afford the luxury of waiting for a compelling theory to emerge and thus they must necessarily adopt a set of guidelines or a framework that provides coherence and consistency to legislated standards. The mixed strategy, on the other hand, also recognizes that no conceptual framework is likely to provide unassailable answers to every detailed measurement and disclosure problem that may materialize. Further, it recognizes that a solution derived from the conceptual framework may still prove to be controversial. The controversy might arise because individuals project different economic consequences due to the introduction of the accounting standard, or there may be essential agreement of consequences but conflict over the equity of the projected wealth redistribution. It is important to emphasize that the origins of the controversy cited above are "positive" and normative in nature, respectively. As suggested by Jensen,[11] the former calls for "the development of a positive theory of accounting which will explain why accounting is what it is,

---

[11] Michael C. Jensen, "Reflections on the State of Accounting Research and the Regulation of Accounting," a paper presented at the Stanford Lectures in Accounting, May 21, 1976, p.7.

why accountants do what they do and what effects these phenomena have on people and resource allocation." With respect to the normative or redistributional issue, the mixed strategy approach suggests that the FASB take no measurement or disclosure initiative whose consequences are likely to be contrary to the apparent social and economic policies being pursued by the government. In other words, as a private sector organization the FASB should not engage in social or economic initiatives and, indeed, must exercise great care that its decisions are not inconsistent with those of representative government.

A PROPOSED FASB PROCESS

The essential steps of a proposed FASB standard setting process should include (1) environmental monitoring, (2) preliminary assessment, (3) discussion memorandum preparation and public feedback and (4) exposure draft and issuance of Standard. While the steps essentially parallel the overall current FASB sequence, the proposed process does differ by its advocacy of a formal, explicit consideration of the economic impact of financial accounting standards.[12]

Environmental Monitoring

The primary purpose of environmental monitoring is to anticipate changes in the environment that might give rise to new measurement and disclosure problems. By anticipating problems the FASB might, in some situations, be able to "buy more time" for its deliberations and reduce the crisis atmosphere created by a need for a "yearend solution." The Board already has an organizational unit to do this job—the Task Force on Emerging Practice Problems. This group is composed of about 15 members, all of whom also serve either on the FASB's Advisory Council or on the accounting standards executive committee of the AICPA.

At present, the task force is asked to review requests made of the FASB to have an item placed on its agenda. The task force's response to the Board ordinarily includes recommendations on the following questions:

- Should this issue be dealt with by the FASB or could it be better addressed by the accounting standards executive committee or perhaps some other body?
- If the issue should be addressed by the FASB, does it require an Interpretation of an existing Standard, an amendment of an existing Standard or a new Standard?
- When, at the latest, must a response be issued?

While individual task force members, just like anyone else, may ask that an emerging problem be taken under consideration by the Board, the principal activity of the task force at present appears to be one of reacting to the emerging problems proposed by others. While the task force's screening activity is undoubtedly an invaluable help to the Board, the effective performance of environmental monitoring

---

[12]For earlier pleas for consideration of economic impact, see Prem Prakash and Alfred Rappaport, "The Feedback Effects of Accounting," *Business Week*, January 12, 1976, p. 12, and John W. Buckley, "The FASB and Impact Analysis," *Management Accounting*, April 1976, pp. 13–17.

would call for either an expansion of the task force's responsibilities or, perhaps, organizing a separate group.

Specifically, environmental monitoring should encompass an active and continual monitoring of new developments in business practice, changes in government tax policy, changes in general economic conditions, shifts in social values that may have significant disclosure implications, technological change and other developments that could give rise to new measurement and disclosure issues. Whatever the organizational vehicle for such an environmental monitoring activity should be, the members of the monitoring group ideally should be sensitive to the potential origins of future accounting issues as well as have technical accounting expertise.

Preliminary Assessment

Before a specific issue is placed on the Board's formal agenda, a preliminary assessment that addresses the following questions should be performed:

• What are the fundamental accounting questions governing this issue and are these the same questions involved in either controversial existing Standards or other currently unresolved issues?

• What might be some of the economic consequences of issuing a new Standard, taking into account the measurement and disclosure alternatives that might be imposed? Are the claimed consequences reasonable?

• What industries or other groups are either likely to be affected or will likely claim that adverse consequences will result from new reporting requirements?

The proposed preliminary assessment step offers the following important advantages to the Board:

• It would enable the Board to see whether a given issue ought to be considered jointly with other issues facing the Board.

• By examining some of the claimed consequences that might arise from a new Standard, the Board could conduct preliminary research that anticipates and assesses the merit of the criticism it will likely encounter.

• By examining some of the claimed consequences that might arise from a new Standard, the Board could identify, at a very early stage, the interest groups likely to be most concerned about the Standard and could include representatives in the makeup of the task force that will prepare the discussion memorandum.

• By anticipating the level of concern over economic consequences, the Board could better judge whether placing the issue on its agenda now or deferring its consideration would seem more appropriate.

For purposes of illustration, consider again the recent controversy resulting from the Board's publication of its discussion memorandum on "Accounting by Debtors and Creditors When Debt Is Restructured."* If banks were forced to reflect losses as a result of restructuring debt, the following are some of the consequences claimed by the banking community:

*Ed. note: The FASB issued an exposure draft of its proposed Statement on restructured debt earlier this year (JofA, Feb.77, p.7).

1 Borrowings of high risk customers (for example, small business) would be restricted, thereby possibly limiting economic growth.

2 Banks would hesitate to change or restructure debt terms, with the possibility that this may lead to a higher rate of business failure.

3 To avoid restructuring, lending policies might be biased in favor of short term arrangements, thus having an adverse impact on long term markets.

4 Losses would be charged against the loan-loss reserve, thus reducing profits and, ultimately, retained earnings, part of a bank's capital account. And, because banks limit their lending to a multiple of their capital, lower capital would mean a much lower level of lending activity.

5 The volatility of bank earnings would increase, because restructurings of "problem loans" normally occur when the economy is already depressed in economic downturns and conversely increase in upturns. Wide fluctuations in earnings may translate into a severe impact on equity capital, and in some cases the ability to raise capital may be severely impaired.

6 The market for state municipal long term debt would be adversely affected. Also, states and municipalities in troubled financial condition may find investors reluctant to help stretch out or otherwise restructure debt.

The reasonableness of each of the foregoing claimed consequences needs to be examined using one or more of the following research approaches:

By economic reasoning

• Wouldn't competitive forces meet any temporary vacuum in the long term debt market? (See claimed consequence 3.)

• If bank regulators insist on linking bank lending limits to an accounting measure, such as the bank's capital account, when the accounting measure changes (but the underlying economics does not), would it not be reasonable to simply change the lending limit multiple? (See claimed consequence 4.)

By empirical testing

• The question of whether the volatility of bank earnings would increase can be empirically tested. (See claimed consequence 5.)

By in-depth inquiry about intentions

• Would bankers really hesitate to restructure debt terms at the risk of forcing the debtor company into bankruptcy? (See claimed consequence 2.)

By analogy to some accounting Standard introduced at some earlier date

• To what extent, if at all, has the FASB Standard dealing with contingencies (which, like the debt restructuring issue, deals with the question of whether and when to recognize an economic loss) affected management decisions?

A preliminary assessment that would, at minimum, conduct an initial inquiry into the three questions posed on page 96 (under "Preliminary assessment") would certainly minimize unnecessary public confrontations between the FASB and its various constituencies and would contribute to the preservation of the FASB's most precious commodity—goodwill.

Discussion Memorandum and Public Feedback

If, based on the preliminary assessment, the Board decides to place an issue on its formal agenda, the next step would be the selection of a task force to prepare the discussion memorandum (DM). The DM should address not only the technical accounting aspects of the issue under consideration but also the anticipated economic consequences for each measurement and disclosure alternative under consideration. To accomplish this broadened scope of the DM, representatives of groups likely to be affected by a new Standard should be appointed to the task force.

The expanded DM could then serve to promote three types of responses via written comments to the Board, position papers and public hearing presentations:

1 Technical accounting arguments.
2 Discussion of consequences not considered in the DM.
3 Discussion of "errors" in the DM assessment of potential economic effects.

Expanding the DM to include considerations of economic impact would offer several important advantages for the Board. First, it would force critics to put their arguments into sharper focus. Second, it would enable the Board to use the improved feedback as a better basis for formulating standards. Third, it would minimize the probability of the Board's issuing an exposure draft of a new Standard that would become so controversial as to threaten the continuing viability of the FASB.

Exposure Draft and Issuance of Standard

Taking into account the feedback resulting from the issuance of the DM, the Board would issue an exposure draft of the proposed Standard. The draft should include a brief summary of the technical accounting considerations, the anticipated economic consequences involved for each alternative considered and the Board's recommendation, coupled with a "cost-benefit statement" that presents the rationale for the recommendation.

Unlike the feedback from the DM (which is a "neutral" document), comments on the exposure draft should ordinarily be responsive to the chosen measurement and disclosure Standard. Moreover, the feedback should certainly not be limited to technical accounting arguments and potential economic consequences but should also address the question of whether such projected consequences are clearly inconsistent with national economic and social policy. This latter analysis is critical if the FASB is to achieve its stated purpose of working "within the framework of public policy and social needs."[13]

[13] Financial Accounting Standards Board, *Rules of Procedure* (Stamford, Conn,: FASB, March 29, 1973).

CONCLUSION

There are some who undoubtedly will react with great distress to any suggestion that the FASB expand its considerations beyond technical measurement and disclosure matters to include considerations of likely consequences that might arise from the Board's pronouncements. Some might make an urgent plea that the FASB's responsibility rests with developing accounting standards that will require companies "to tell it like it is." Others with more tolerance for the complexity of economic phenomena quantified by accounting measurements might suggest that, even at the risk of being arbitrary in certain situations, the Board should move in the direction of "reducing the diversity in accounting."

To those who want "to tell it like it is," it must be pointed out that "though one may plead for 'economic reality' in accounting, every accounting description is nonetheless a description of some facet of economic reality."[14] Thus, in valuing an asset (for example. historical cost, replacement cost, exit value and current value), each measures some facet of economic reality. To those who propose to reduce the diversity in accounting, it must be recognized that this, too, constitutes an accounting choice and thus involves a potential redistribution of wealth. In brief, while accounting policymakers can claim to be value free in their standard setting activity by choosing to ignore the consequences of their information choices, the consequences themselves will nonetheless take place. A responsible position of accountability calls for the explicit consideration of economic impact of financial accounting standards by all accounting policymaking bodies. In the particular case of the FASB, such analysis should enable it to remain a major force in shaping financial reporting practices.

[14] Prakash and Rappaport, *Business Week*, p.12.

BIBLIOGRAPHICAL NOTES

Armstrong, Marshall S. "The Politics of Establishing Accounting Standards." *Government Accountants Journal*, Summer 1976, pp.8–13, reprinted in *Journal of Accountancy*, February 1977, pp.76–79.

Arnold, Jerry L. and Keller, Earl C. "The Influence of External Reporting Methods Upon the Internal Decision-Making Process: An Empirical Analysis." UCLA Accounting-Information Systems Research Program, Working Paper No. 76–5, March 1976.

Beaver, William H. "What Should Be the FASB's Objectives?" *Journal of Accountancy*, August 1973, pp.49–56.

Beaver, William H. and Demski, Joel S. "The Nature of Financial Accounting Objectives: A Summary and Synthesis." *Journal of Accounting Research*, Supplement to Vol. 12, *Studies on Financial Accounting Objectives: 1974*, p.170–187.

Campbell, Donald T. "Assessing the Impact of Planned Social Change." *Social Research and Public Policies*. Edited by Gene M. Lyons. Hanover, New Hampshire: University Press of New England, 1975, pp.3–43.

Chambers, Raymond J. "Accounting Principles or Accounting Policies?" *Journal of Accountancy*, May 1973, pp.48–53.

Demski, Joel S. "The General Impossibility of Normative Accounting Standards." *Accounting Review*, October 1973, pp.718–23.

Demski, Joel S. "The Choice Among Financial Reporting Alternatives." *Accounting Review*, April 1974, pp.221–32.

Gerboth, Dale L. "'Muddling Through' With the APB." *Journal of Accountancy*, May 1972, pp.42–49.

Gonedes, Nicholas J. and Dopuch, Nicholas. "Capital Market Equilibrium, Information Production, and Selecting Accounting Techniques: Theoretical Framework and Review of Empirical Work." *Journal of Accounting Research*, Supplement to Vol. 12, *Studies on Financial Accounting Objectives: 1974*, pp.48–129.

Horngren, Charles T. "Accounting Principles: Private or Public Sector?" *Journal of Accountancy*, May 1972, pp.37–41.

Horngren, Charles T. "Will the FASB Be Here in the 1980s?" *Journal of Accountancy*, November 1976, pp.90–96.

Mautz, Robert K. "The Other Accounting Standards Board." *Journal of Accountancy*, February 1974, pp.56–60.

May, Robert G. and Sundem, Gary L. "Research for Accounting Policy: An Overview." *Accounting Review*, October 1976, pp.747–63.

Prakash, Prem and Rappaport, Alfred. "Informational Interdependencies: System Structure Induced By Accounting Information." *Accounting Review*, October 1975, pp.723–34.

Rappaport, Alfred. "Establishing Objectives for Published Corporate Accounting Reports." *Accounting Review*, October 1964, pp.951–62.

Smith, E. Daniel. "The Effect of the Separation of Ownership From Control on Accounting Policy Decisions." *Accounting Review*, October 1976, pp.707–23.

Watts, Ross L. and Zimmerman, Jerold L. "Toward a Positive Theory of the Determination of Accounting Standards." Graduate School of Management, University of Rochester, Working Paper Series No. 7628, July 1976.

ISSUES IN ACCOUNTING CHOICE

In recent years, management's decision-making process in the selection of alternatively permissible accounting treatments has been subjected to intense study by accounting researchers. It is now widely recognized that management looks after its own interests both in making these selections and in lobbying for or against accounting standards with the FASB and the SEC.

In earlier years, researchers knew or suspected that managements probably served their "ulterior motives" when deciding on accounting issues. In the inflationary post-World War II period, large corporations such as U.S. Steel, du Pont, Sears Roebuck, Libbey-Owens-Ford, and Allied Chemical and Dye recorded depreciation based on mounting replacement costs in their 1947 reports to stockholders, resulting in much lower reported profits. Their motivations were, one supposes, several:

1 To disabuse stockholders that dividend payment levels could be increased at time of rising replacement costs

2 To discourage labor unions from pressing for higher wages

3 To counter public criticism that the companies were charging exhorbitant prices for their products, leading to excessive profits

4 To persuade Congress to allow corporate taxpayers to deduct depreciation based on replacement costs so that companies could avoid being taxed on capital

All of these motivations may have been compatible with a "fair presentation" of the companies' financial position and results of operations, but they were also consistent with influencing the behavior of parties whose actions would be important to the corporate managements. In the end, the SEC disallowed the use of replacement-cost depreciation in annual and quarterly reports, but some companies, such as U.S. Steel, simply switched to accelerated historical-cost depreciation (as opposed to straight-line, replacement-cost depreciation), yielding roughly similar results.

In 1953, Hepworth suggested a number of benefits that companies could enjoy by "smoothing" their periodic income, including a boost in the confidence that owners, creditors, and workers would have in a management that could report stable earnings. Hepworth proceeded to illustrate accounting methods that were particularly susceptible to attempts at smoothing.[1]

In the 1960s, the Accounting Principles Board, through its elaborate procedures for securing reactions to exposure drafts, made it possible for observers to note the significant efforts of companies, investment houses, banks, and government departments to lobby for or against particular accounting principles. By the end of the decade, the controversy over business combinations demonstrated convincingly that corporations would fight to retain the right to use favored accounting practices. If merger-minded corporations could mount a campaign to perpetuate the use of "pooling of interests" accounting in order to avoid depressing their postmerger earnings per share—just as the Federal Trade Commission could try to influence the APB to eliminate "pooling of interests" accounting as a means of decelerating the pace of the 1960s conglomerate merger movement—what might have been the *true* motivations of lobbyists when other accounting principles were being debated by the APB and FASB? In the debate over the investment tax credit during the 1960s and early 1970s, the federal government conceded that its advocacy of the flow-through method of accounting for the credit was for the purpose of inducing taxpayer corporations, by reporting larger accounting profits, to make even greater use of the tax incentive to expand and modernize their plant facilities.[2] In these and other areas of controversy, researchers became fascinated by the political nature of corporate and governmental lobbying for (or against) accounting standards. As accounting researchers, especially those at the University of Chicago, intensified their use of empirical research methods in the 1960s, studies were conducted of corporate decisions to adopt, or switch, accounting methods. One team of researchers sought to construct a "corporate personality" for companies on the basis of their preferences for accounting methods and an analysis of their financial statements.[3] In another early study, the researcher found that a high proportion of companies switching from an accelerated method of depreciation to straight-line depreciation for accounting purposes showed a lower reported profit in the year of the change than in the immediately preceding year.[4] The reported profits of several other companies showed an increase only because of the change in depreciation method. The smoothing hypothesis would suggest that companies anticipating a drop in

[1] Samuel R. Hepworth, "Smoothing Periodic Income," *The Accounting Review* (January 1953), pp. 32–39.

[2] See the letter dated November 7, 1967 from Stanley S. Surrey, assistant secretary of the treasury (Tax Policy), to the AICPA concerning the investment tax credit. The letter is reproduced in Thomas F. Keller and Stephen A. Zeff (editors), *Financial Accounting Theory: Issues and Controversies,* Volume II (McGraw-Hill Book Company, 1969), pp. 447–449.

[3] George H. Sorter, Selwyn W. Becker, T. Ross Archibald, and William H. Beaver, "Accounting and Financial Measures as Indicators of Corporate Personality—Some Empirical Findings," in Robert K. Jaedicke, Yuji Ijiri, and Oswald Nielsen (editors), *Research in Accounting Measurement* (American Accounting Association, 1966), pp. 200–210.

[4] T. Ross Archibald, "The Return to Straight-Line Depreciation: An Analysis of a Change in Accounting Method," Empirical Research in Accounting: Selected Studies 1967, supplement to the *Journal of Accounting Research,* pp. 164–180.

reported profit would look for ways of cushioning the decline. A change to an accounting method that would have this effect, or which might even increase reported profit slightly, would be just one such way.

In recent years, a number of accounting researchers have conducted studies of the apparent reasons why companies and accounting firms lobby for or against accounting standards before the FASB. Much of this research has been spurred by theories developed at the University of Rochester and, in particular, by the research reported in the first article reproduced in this section. In most of this recent work, the researchers have adopted the premise that managers, like other economic actors, are motivated by self-interests rather than by lofty public-interest declarations such as "fair presentation" and "full disclosure."

In "Towards a Positive Theory of the Determination of Accounting Standards," Ross L. Watts and Jerold L. Zimmerman test the self-interest hypothesis. They believe that a consideration of several possible consequences will affect management's assessment of a proposed change in accounting standards: (1) the probable tax consequences, (2) the likelihood of a greater degree of government intervention, (3) the bookkeeping costs of making the change, and (4) the cost of amending any executive compensation plan based on profit if the accounting change were to alter reported profit. If the proposed accounting change were to portend a reduction in reported profit, it is argued that, for large corporations—those in the public eye—the combined effect of the first two considerations would outweigh the second two. A big factor would be the desire of such enterprises to avoid the public scrutiny that is associated with reporting large profits.[5] Smaller companies—not being in the public eye—would not share this concern and would be likely to oppose accounting standards that would reduce their reported profits. Watts and Zimmerman examined the written submissions of major corporations in response to the FASB's 1974 proposal to require General Price Level Accounting (GPLA). The authors concluded that

> The larger firms, *ceteris paribus,* are more likely to favor GPLA (if earnings decline). This finding is consistent with our government intervention argument since the larger firms are more likely to be subjected to governmental interference and, hence, have more to lose than smaller corporations.

Dan S. Dhaliwal, in "The Effect of the Firm's Capital Structure on the Choice of Accounting Methods," uses the Watts and Zimmerman framework to analyze the influence of a company's financial leverage on its management's preference for accounting methods. Dhaliwal proposes that companies having higher debt-equity ratios would be less inclined to favor accounting methods that result in lower earnings, as the consequence may be to violate the terms of a restrictive covenant in a loan agreement. Using a sample of 113 oil- and gas-producing companies—of which 72 were using the full costing method and 41 were following the successful efforts method—Dhaliwal found that "firms using the full costing method have

---

[5]Many would contend that the principal factor that drove Congress to impose the Windfall Profits Tax on the oil and gas industry in 1980 was the reporting of enormous increases in quarterly and annual profits by major oil and gas companies in 1979.

significantly higher long-term debt than firms which use the successful efforts method." (The full costing method would be consistent with higher earnings.) Therefore, the conclusion is that a company's capital structure may have a bearing on its preference for accounting practices.

In the final article in this section, "Managing Earnings Using An Insurance Subsidiary: A Case of Restraint by Sears/Allstate," Roman L. Weil describes how Sears Roebuck and Co., the largest U.S. retailer, could manipulate its consolidated profit merely by instructing its 100 percent owned insurance subsidiary, Allstate, to sell securities on which either unrealized gains or unrealized losses had accumulated. This opportunity to "manage earnings" is freely available under U.S. "generally accepted accounting principles" to companies having insurance subsidiaries. In the case of Sears Roebuck and Allstate, Weil was "impressed at the absence of apparent attempts to smooth Sears' income by using realized gains and losses in Allstate's investment portfolio."

BIBLIOGRAPHICAL NOTES

An extensive study of the income-smoothing phenomenon, including a critical review of a sampling of smoothing studies, may be found in:

Ronen, Joshua and Simcha Sadan: *Smoothing Income Numbers: Objectives, Means, and Implications* (Reading, MA: Addison-Wesley Publishing Company, 1981).

An article that reveals the "secrets" behind how managers massage their reported profits is the following:

Ford S. Worthy, "Manipulating Profits: How It's Done," *Fortune* (June 25, 1984), pp. 50–54.

Fireman's Fund, an American Express insurance subsidiary, apparently used "special items" to create the appearance that its profits were on the rise. Such was *Fortune*'s conclusion in a recent article (which was not the first article in which *Fortune* has drawn attention to the skill displayed by Fireman's Fund in "managing" its earnings):

Carol J. Loomis, "The Earnings Magic at American Express," *Fortune* (June 25, 1984), pp. 58–61.

Towards a Positive Theory of the Determination of Accounting Standards

Ross L. Watts
University of Rochester

Jerold L. Zimmerman
University of Rochester

Accounting standards in the United States have resulted from a complex interaction among numerous parties including agencies of the Federal government (notably the Securities and Exchange Commission and Treasury Department), state regulatory commissions, public accountants, quasi-public accounting standard-setting boards (the Committee on Accounting Procedures (CAP), the Accounting Principles Board (APB), and the Financial Accounting Standards Board (FASB)), and corporate managements. These parties have, in the past, and continue to expend resources to influence the setting of accounting standards. Moonitz [1974], Horngren [1973] and [1976], Armstrong [1976] and Zeff [1972] document the sometimes intense pressure exerted on the "private" accounting standard-setting bodies (i.e., CAP, APB, FASB). These pressures have led to several reorganizations of the standard-setting boards.

Ultimately, we seek to develop a positive theory of the determination of accounting standards.[1] Such a theory will help us to understand better the source of the pressures driving the accounting standard-setting process, the effects of various accounting standards on different groups of individuals and the allocation of resources, and why various groups are willing to expend resources trying to affect the standard-setting process. This understanding is necessary to determine if prescriptions from normative theories (e.g., current cash equivalents) are feasible.

Watts [1974] and [1977] has started to develop such a theory. This paper expands on this initial work by focusing on the costs and benefits generated by accounting standards which accrue to managements, thereby contributing to our understanding of the incentives of management to oppose or support various standards. Management, we believe, plays a central role in the determination of standards. Moonitz supports this view:

> Management is central to any discussion of financial reporting, whether at the statutory or regulatory level, or at the level of official pronouncements of accounting bodies. [Moonitz. 1974. p. 64]

From *The Accounting Review* (January 1978), pp. 112–134. Reprinted by permission of the American Accounting Association.

Author's note:—We wish to thank members of the Finance Workshop at the University of Rochester, members of the Accounting Seminar at the University of Michigan and, in particular, George Benston, Ken Gaver, Nicholas Gonedes, Michael Jensen, Keith Leffler, Martin Geisel, Cliff Smith and an anonymous referee for their helpful suggestions.

[1] See Jensen [1976] and Horngren [1976]

Hence, it seems appropriate that a precondition of a positive theory of standard-setting is understanding management's incentives.

The next section introduces those factors (e.g., tax, regulatory, political considerations) which economic theory leads us to believe are the underlying determinants affecting managements' welfare and, thereby, their decision to consume resources trying to affect the standard-setting process. Next, a model is presented incorporating these factors. The predictions of this model are then tested using the positions taken by corporations regarding the FASB's Discussion Memorandum on General Price Level Adjustments (GPLA). The last section contains the conclusions of the study.

FACTORS INFLUENCING MANAGEMENT ATTITUDES
TOWARDS FINANCIAL ACCOUNTING STANDARDS

In this paper, we assume that individuals act to maximize their own utility. In doing so, they are resourceful and innovative.[2] The obvious implication of this assumption is that management lobbies on accounting standards based on its own self-interest. For simplicity, (since this is an early attempt to provide a positive theory) it could be argued that we should assume that management's self-interest on accounting standards is congruent with that of the shareholders. After all, that assumption has provided hypotheses consistent with the evidence in finance (e.g., the risk/return relationship of the various capital asset pricing models). However, one function of financial reporting is to constrain management to act in the shareholders' interest. (For example, see Benston [1975], Watts [1974], and Jensen and Meckling [1976a].) Consequently, assuming congruence of management and shareholder interests without further investigation may cause us to omit from our lobbying model important predictive variables. To reduce this possibility, we will examine next the effects of accounting standards on management's self-interest without the congruence assumption. The purpose of the examination is to identify factors which are likely to be important predictors of lobbying behavior so that we can include them in our formal model.

The assumption that management selects accounting procedures to maximize its own utility is used by Gordon [1964, p. 261] in an early attempt to derive a positive theory of accounting. There have been several attempts to test empirically Gordon's model, or variants of it, which we call the "smoothing" literature.[3] Problems in the specification of the empirical tests in the smoothing literature leave the Gordon model essentially unconfirmed.[4] Also, certain aspects of the Gordon model contribute to the model's lack of confirmation. Essentially, Gordon [1964] assumed that shareholder satisfaction (and, presumably, wealth) is solely a positive function of

---

[2] Many economic models assume a rather limited version of economic man. In particular, they assume that man maximizes his own welfare when he is constrained to play by certain rules and in certain institutional settings, ignoring his incentives to avoid or change the rules, setting, etc. Meckling [1976] analyzes this issue.

[3] Ball and Watts [1972]; Barefield and Comiskey [1972]; Barnea, Ronen and Sadan [1975]; Beidleman [1973]; Copeland [1968]; Cushing [1969]; Dasher and Malcom [1970]; Gordon [1964]; Gordon, Horwitz and Meyers [1966].

[4] For these defects see Ball and Watts [1972], Gonedes [1972] and Gonedes and Dopuch [1974].

accounting income. This assumption avoids the conflict between shareholders and management by implying that increases in stock prices always accompany increases in accounting income. However, recent research casts serious doubt on the ability of management to manipulate directly share prices via changes in accounting procedures.[5]

We assume that management's utility is a positive function of the expected compensation in future periods (or wealth) and a negative function of the dispersion of future compensation (or wealth). The question is how do accounting standards affect management's wealth?[6] Management's total compensation from the firm consists of wages, incentive compensation (cash bonuses and stock or stock options), and nonpecuniary income. including perquisites (discussed in Jensen-Meckling, 1976a). Since it is unclear what role accounting standards play in the level of nonpecuniary income, we exclude it and focus on the first two forms of compensation. To the extent that management can increase either the level of incentive compensation or the firm's share price via its choice of accounting standards, they are made better off.

This analysis distinguishes between mechanisms which increase management's wealth: 1) via increases in share price (i.e., stock and stock options are more valuable) and 2) via increases in incentive cash bonuses. The choice of accounting standards can affect both of these forms of compensation indirectly through i)taxes, ii)regulatory procedures if the firm is regulated, iii)political costs, iv)information production costs, and directly via v)management compensation plans. The first four factors increase managerial wealth by increasing the cashflows and, hence, share price. The last factor can increase managerial wealth by altering the terms of the incentive compensation. Each of these five factors is discussed in turn.

Factors Affecting Management Wealth[7]

Taxes.   Tax laws are not directly tied to financial accounting standards except in a few cases (e.g., the last-in-first-out inventory valuation method). However, the indirect relationship is well documented (Zeff [1972] and Moonitz [1974]). The

---

[5]Fama [1970] and Gonedes and Dopuch [1974]. Further, the results of studies by Kaplan and Roll [1972], Ball [1972] and Sunder [1975] which address the specific issue support the hypothesis that the stock market can discriminate between real events and changes in accounting procedures. Given that the market can on average discriminate, then it must be concluded that managers (on average) expect the market to discriminate. Obviously, managers do and will attempt to influence their share price by direct accounting manipulation, but if these attempts consume resources, then incentives exist to eliminate these inefficient allocations.

[6]For earlier discussions of this question see Watts [1974] and Gonedes [1976].

[7]We have purposefully excluded from the set of factors being examined the information content effect of an accounting standard on stock prices. We have done this because at present the economic theories of information and capital market equilibrium are not sufficiently developed to allow predictions to be made regarding the influence of an accounting standard on the capital market's assessment of the distributions of returns (see Gonedes and Dopuch, 1974). We believe that a theory of the determination of accounting standards can be developed and tested ignoring the information content factor. If at some future date, the information content factor can be specified and included in the theory, then the predictions and our understanding of the process will be improved. But we see no reason to delay the development of a theory until information content is specified.

adoption of a given procedure for financial accounting does not decrease the likelihood of that procedure's being adopted in future Internal Revenue codes, and more likely, will increase the chance of adoption. To the extent that management expects a proposed financial accounting procedure to influence future tax laws, their lobbying behavior is affected by the future tax law effects.

Regulation.[8]   Most public utility commissions base their rate-setting formulas on accounting determined costs. A new accounting standard which reduces a utility's reported income may provide its management with an "excuse" to argue for increased rates. Whether the utility commission grants the increase depends on whether groups opposed to the rate increase (e.g., consumer groups) are able to exert political pressure on the commission.[9] This depends on such factors as information costs (to be discussed later). However, to the extent that there is some probability of a rate (and hence cashflow) increase (either temporary or permanent) as the result of an accounting standards change, utilities have an incentive to favor that change. Similarly, they have an incentive to oppose changes in accounting standards which might lead to a rate decrease.

Political Costs.   The political sector has the power to effect wealth transfers between various groups. The corporate sector is especially vulnerable to these wealth redistributions. Certain groups of voters have an incentive to lobby for the nationalization, expropriation, break-up or regulation of an industry or corporation.[10] This in turn provides an incentive for elected officials to propose such actions. To counter these potential government intrusions, corporations employ a number of devices, such as social responsibility campaigns in the media, government lobbying and selection of accounting procedures to minimize reported earnings.[11] By avoiding the attention that "high" profits draw because of the public's association of high reported profits and monopoly rents, management can reduce the likelihood of adverse political actions and, thereby, reduce its expected costs (including the legal costs the firm would incur opposing the political actions). Included in political costs are the costs labor unions impose through increased demands generated by large reported profits.

The magnitude of the political costs is highly dependent on firm size.[12] Even as a percentage of total assets or sales, we would not expect a firm with sales of $100

---

[8] We deal in this paper with public utility regulation and the forms of rate regulation employed. Other industries (e.g., banking and insurance) are regulated differently and these industries are ignored in this paper to simplify the analysis.

[9] For the economic theory of regulation upon which this discussion is based see Stigler [1971], Posner [1974], and Peltzman [1975]. Also, Horngren [1976].

[10] Stigler [1971], Peltzman [1975], and Jensen and Meckling [1976b]. An example of an industry facing such action is the oil industry.

[11] For an alleged example of this, see Jack Anderson, Syndicated Column, United Features (New York, April 10, 1976).

[12] Several studies document the association between size and anti-trust [Siegfried 1975]. In proposed anti-trust legislation, size *per se* has been mentioned specifically as a criterion for action against corporations. See the "Curse of Bigness." *Barron's,* June 30, 1969, pp. 1 and 8. Also see a bill introduced into the Senate by Senator Bayh (U.S. Congress, Senate, Subcommittee on Anti-trust and Monopoly

million to generate the same political costs (as a percentage of sales) as a firm with $10 billion of sales. Casual empiricism suggests that Superior Oil Company (1974 sales of $333 million) incurs considerably less costs from anti-trust, "corporate responsibility," affirmative action, etc., than Exxon with sales of $42 billion.

Information Production (i.e., bookkeeping) Costs.   Changes in accounting procedures are not costless to firms. Accounting standard changes which either increase disclosure or require corporations to change accounting methods increase the firms' bookkeeping costs (including any necessary increases in accountants' salaries to compensate for additional training).[13]

Management Compensation Plans.   A major component of management compensation is incentive (bonus) plan income (Conference Board [1974]), and these plans are based on accounting income. Our survey of 52 firms in our sample indicates that the majority of the companies formally incorporate accounting income into the compensation plan.[14] Hence, a change in accounting standards which increases the firm's reported earnings would, *ceteris paribus*, lead to greater incentive income. But this would reduce the firm's cashflows and share prices would fall. As long as the per manager present value of the after tax incentive income is greater than the decline in each manager's portfolio, we would expect management to favor such an accounting change.[15] But this assumes that the shareholders and nonmanager directors do not oppose such an accounting change or do not adjust the compensation plans for the change in earnings.[16] In fact, the increased cashflows resulting from the political costs, regulatory process and tax effects of an accounting change assumes that various politicians/bureaucrats (i.e., the electorate) do not fully adjust for the change. A crucial assumption of our analysis is that the shareholders and nonmanaging directors have more incentive to adjust for and control increases in reported earnings due to changes in accounting standards than do politicians and bureaucrats.

(1975), pp. 5–13) would require divesture for oil firms with annual production and/or sales above certain absolute numbers. In the hearings on that bill, Professor Mancke of Tufts University argued that absolute and not relative accounting profits are the relevant variable for explaining political action against corporations.

Mancke said, "Nevertheless, precisely because the actions of large firms are so visible, the American public has always equated absolute size with monopoly power. The major oil companies are among the very largest and most visible companies doing business in the United States.

"Huge accounting profits, but not high profit rates, are an inevitable corollary of large absolute firm size. This makes these companies obvious targets for public criticism." (U.S. Congress, Senate, Subcommittee on Anti-trust and Monopoly (1976), p. 1893).

[13] We are assuming that any change in accounting standards does not reduce the firm's information production costs. Although there may be cases where a firm is using a costly procedure which is eliminated by a simpler, cheaper procedure, information production costs in this case may decline, but we expect these situations to be rare.

[14] The frequency is 69 percent.

[15] At this early stage in the development of the theory, we assume that management of the firm is composed of homogeneous (i.e., identical) individuals to simplify the problem.

[16] Our examination of the description of 16 management compensation plans indicated that all the plans were administered by the nonmanaging directors.

Incentives for Various Groups to Adjust for a Change in Accounting Standards

An individual (whether a shareholder, nonmanaging director, or politician) will adjust a firm's accounting numbers for a change in accounting standards up to the point that the marginal cost of making the adjustment equals the marginal benefits. Consider the incentives of the outside directors to adjust bonus compensation plans due to a change in accounting standards. If these directors do not adjust the plans, management compensation rises and share price falls by the full discounted present value of the additional compensation.[17] Each outside director's wealth declines to the extent of his ownership in the firm and there is a greater chance of his removal from the board.[18]

If nonmanaging directors did not control management (including adjusting the compensation plans for changes in accounting standards), the decline in firm value offers incentives for an outsider or group to tender for control of the firm and install outside directors who will eliminate those managerial activities which are not in the best interest of the shareholders.[19] This group would then gain a proportionate share of the full capitalized value of the eliminated abuses (e.g., the present value of the incremental compensation resulting from the change in accounting standards). Therefore, the benefits for shareholders and nonmanaging directors to adjust compensation plans for changes in accounting standards are immediate and direct, if there is an efficient capital market for equity claims.

However, for the politicians and bureaucrats, our analysis suggests that the lack of a capital market which capitalizes the effects on the voters' future cashflows reduces the benefits accruing to the politicians of monitoring accounting standards, and the result is that they will perform less adjustments for changes in accounting standards.[20] For example, what are the benefits accruing to a utility regulator for adjusting a utility's accounting numbers for a change in standards? In the previous case of an outside director, the share price will fall by the discounted presented value of the increased compensation resulting for an incomplete (or inaccurate) adjustment of the compensation plan. But if the regulator does not completely adjust for a change in accounting standards and allows the utility's rates to increase (resulting in a wealth transfer from consumers to the utility's owners), then the only cost the regulator is likely to incur is removal from office due to his incomplete adjustment.

---

[17]Likewise, we would expect the outside directors to adjust the incentive compensation targets in those circumstances when it is in the shareholders' interest to report lower earnings (e.g., LIFO), thereby not reducing the managers' incentive via bonus earnings to adopt LIFO.

[18]Our analysis indicates that outside (nonmanaging) directors are "efficient" monitors of management, Watts [1977]. If this were not the case, the capital market would quickly discount the presence of outside directors. As far as we can determine, firms are not required by the New York Stock Exchange listing requirements or Federal regulations to have outside directors. Paragraph 2495G of Commerce Clearing House, Volume 2, New York Stock Exchange encourages listed firms to appoint outside directors. "Full disclosure of corporate affairs for the information of the investing public is, of course, normal and usual procedure for listed companies. Many companies have found this procedure has been greatly aided by having at least two outside directors whose functions on the board would include particular attention to such matters." This listing statement is consistent with our observation that outside directors provide monitoring benefits.

[19]This assumes, of course, that such takeovers earn a fair rate of return net of transactions costs.

[20]See Zimmerman [1977] and Watts [1977] for further discussion of this issue.

He incurs no direct wealth change. For small rate increases, the *per capita* coalition costs each consumer (or some group of consumers) would bear lobbying for the regulator's removal would vastly outweigh the small *per capita* benefits they would receive via lower regulated rates. Hence, rational consumers would not incur large monitoring costs of their regulators and other politicians (Downs [1957]; Alchian [1969]; and Alchian and Demsetz [1972]). Knowing this, it is not in the regulators' and politicians' interests to adjust changes in accounting standards as fully as if they were confronted with the same change in accounting standards in the role of outside directors or shareholders in the firm. The benefits of adjusting for changes in accounting standards are lower in the political sector than in the private sector.[21] Hence, there is a greater likelihood that a given accounting standard change will result in increased tax, regulatory, and political benefits than will the same change result in increased management compensation. For a given accounting standard change, managers should expect their own shareholders and outside directors to make a more complete adjustment than politicians.

Given this analysis, we predict that managers have greater incentives to choose accounting standards which report lower earnings (thereby increasing cashflows, firm value, and their welfare) due to tax, political, and regulatory considerations than to choose accounting standards which report higher earnings and, thereby, increase their incentive compensation. However, this prediction is conditional upon the firm being regulated or subject to political pressure. In small, (i.e., low political costs) unregulated firms, we would expect that managers do have incentives to select accounting standards which report higher earnings, if the expected gain in incentive compensation is greater than the foregone expected tax consequences. Finally, we expect management also to consider the accounting standard's impact on the firm's bookkeeping costs (and hence their own welfare).

The next section combines these five factors into a model of corporate lobbying standards.

A POSITIVE THEORY OF MANAGEMENT LOBBYING ON ACCOUNTING STANDARDS

Given a proposed accounting standard, management's position depends on the size of the firm (which affects the magnitude of the political costs) and whether the proposed standard increases or decreases the firm's reported earnings.[22] Figure 1 separates the standard's impact on earnings into decreases (1A) and increases (1B). The curve GB in Figure 1A (earnings decrease) denotes the proposed accounting standard's present value to management including the tax, regulatory, political, and

---

[21] It could also be argued that politicians and regulators have a higher marginal cost of adjusting than do shareholders, nonmanaging directors, and other capital market participants since the former group does not necessarily have a comparative advantage of adjusting financial statements, whereas, existing capital market participants probably have a comparative advantage at such activities.

[22] The expected effect of an accounting standard could vary over time (i.e., it could increase current reported income and decrease some future reported income). In that case, the analysis is slightly more complex, but the criterion is still the same (i.e., the effect on the manager's wealth). However, for simplicity, the remainder of the paper refers to standards increasing or decreasing reported income as though the whole time series of future income shifts up or down.

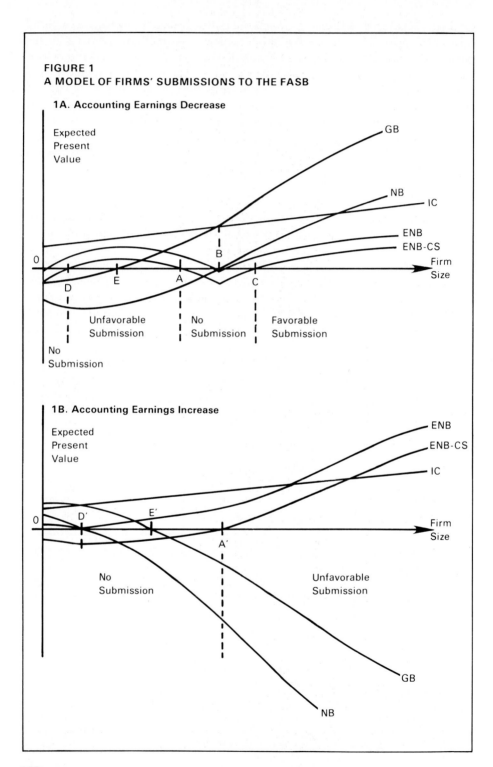

FIGURE 1
A MODEL OF FIRMS' SUBMISSIONS TO THE FASB

1A. Accounting Earnings Decrease

Expected Present Value

GB

NB
IC
ENB
ENB-CS

0

Firm Size

D

E

A

B

C

No Submission

Unfavorable Submission

No Submission

Favorable Submission

1B. Accounting Earnings Increase

Expected Present Value

ENB
ENB-CS
IC

0

D'

E'

A'

Firm Size

No Submission

Unfavorable Submission

GB

NB

compensation effects as a function of firm size. For small firms (below size E), not subject to much political pressure, these managers have an incentive to oppose the standard since their bonus compensation plans will have to be adjusted (a costly process), if their incomes are to remain unchanged by the new standard. Above size E, the political, regulatory, and tax benefits of reporting lower earnings due to the new standard are assumed to dominate the incentive compensation factor.

The benefits (costs) of a proposed accounting standard are expected to vary with the firm's size. This relationship can exist for two reasons: (1) the magnitude of the reported income change may be larger for larger firms and (2) for an income change of a given magnitude, the benefits (costs) vary with firm size.[23] Hence, the present value of the stream of benefits (or costs) to the firm, GB, are an increasing function of firm size.[24]

Information production costs, curve IC, are also expected to vary to some extent with firm size due to the increased complexity and volume of the larger firm's accounting system. The difference between the gross benefits, GB, and the additional information costs, IC, yields the net benefits curve, NB.

If the firm size is in the region OB, the net benefits curve, NB, is negative, and the firm will consider making an unfavorable submission to the FASB. Before the firm makes a submission, management holds beliefs regarding the likelihood the FASB will adopt the standard and the likelihood the FASB will adopt the standard if the firm makes an opposing submission.[25] The difference between these beliefs is the change in the adoption likelihood if management makes a negative submission. The product of this difference and the negative net benefits, NB, (i.e., the present value[26] of the cashflows arising from the five factors) is the expected present value of the net benefits curve, ENB. For example, a firm will incur negative net present value benefits of $100,000 if the standard is adopted. They believe the likelihood of adoption is .60. By making a negative submission to the FASB the likelihood falls to .59. The expected net present value of the benefits of the submission is then +$1000.

Firms larger than size B face positive net benefits if the standard is adopted. They

---

[23] Whether the magnitude of the income change does vary with firm size depends on the particular accounting standard in question. For certain accounting standards (e.g., requiring all firms to report depreciation based on current replacement costs) it is apparent *a priori* that there will be a correlation between the income change and firm size. For other standards (e.g., general price level accounting) *a priori*, it is not obvious that a relationship will exist (e.g., net monetary gains may offset depreciation in larger firms). However, since political costs depend on firm size then we expect the benefits (costs) of standard changes to vary with firm size. For example, if all firms' earnings decline by $1 million (due to a standards change) then we would expect larger firms to incur larger benefits since the likelihood of anti-trust actions are expected to be associated with firm size.

[24] We would expect firms in different industries to be subject to different political pressures, tax structures, and regulation. Hence, Figure 1 is developed for firms in the same industry that only differ by size.

[25] In this situation, it is possible that management will lobby on an accounting standard because of secondary (or gaming) effects (i.e., vote trading thereby influencing subsequent FASB pronouncements). We chose not to introduce gaming because it complicates the model and such complication is only justified if it improves or is likely to improve the empirical results. We are able to predict corporate behavior without considering gaming, and we do not consider it likely to improve these results.

[26] The firm is discounting the future cashflows with the appropriate, risk-adjusted discount rate. Furthermore, we are assuming that this discount rate is not increasing in firm size which is consistent with the available evidence.

will consider supporting the standard to the FASB, thereby increasing the standard's likelihood of adoption.[27] Hence, the expected net benefits curve is also positive beyond point B since it is the product of a positive net benefit and a positive change in the FASB's likelihood of adoption given a favorable submission.

If the cost of the submission is $ CS, consisting primarily of the opportunity cost of the manager's time, then the total expected net benefits of a submission given the submission cost is a vertical downward shift in the ENB curve by the amount CS, ENB⁻CS. A firm will make a submission if ENB⁻CS is positive. This occurs in the regions DA, where opposing submissions occur, and beyond C, where favorable submissions are made. Between O and D and between A and C no submissions are made.

In Figure 1B, the proposed standard increases reported income. This case is similar to the previous one except the gross benefits are only positive for small firms where the management compensation plans are expected to dominate the tax, political, and regulatory factors. Beyond size E' gross benefits are negative since, for those firms, the income increases are expected to increase governmental interference (political costs), raise future tax payments, and lead the public utility commission to reduce the firm's revenues (if the firm is regulated). The net benefits curve is again the algebraic sum of GB (gross benefits) and IC (information costs) and the submission's expected net benefits less submission costs, ENB—CS, cuts the axis at A'. Accordingly, firms with asset sizes in the interval OA' make no submissions and firms of sizes beyond A' make unfavorable submissions.

When we consider the implications of both figures, we see that larger firms (firms larger than size C in Figure 1) will make favorable submissions if their incomes are decreased by the accounting standard, and unfavorable submissions if their incomes are increased. Smaller firms (firms smaller than size C in Figure 1) will either not submit or make unfavorable submissions.

While Figures 1A and 1B reflect the general tendency of costs and benefits of an accounting standard to vary with firm size, there will be exceptions to this relationship. We have omitted variables, some of which we recognize. In particular, regulation costs borne by utilities depend not only on net income but also on operating earnings.[28] The effect of an accounting standard on operating earnings may vary with firm size.

The increment to a regulated firm's value of an accounting change which reduces operating earnings is increasing in firm size. Most public utility commissions set revenues according to the following type of equation:

$$\text{Revenues} = \text{Operating Expenses} + \text{Depreciation} + \text{Taxes} + r \cdot \text{Base} \tag{1}$$

[27] We are assuming that the likelihood of the FASB adopting the standard, if the firm makes a submission, is independent of firm size. This is unrealistic since large firms, we expect, would have more influence with the Board. However, inclusion of this additional dependency does not change the results; in fact, it strengthens the predictions.

[28] Operating earnings, although explicitly defined by each public utility commission, are generally, utility revenues less operating expenses, including depreciation but excluding interest and taxes. We assume that the adoption of GPLA would mean that price-adjusted depreciation would affect operating earnings while the gain or loss on monetary assets would be treated like interest and would only affect net income.

where r is the accepted rate of return allowance on the investment base (usually the historic cost of net plant and working capital) [Haskins and Sells 1974.] Interest is not directly included in the rate-setting formula. The approach is to work on a return to total assets. Since all the terms on the right-hand side of equation (1) are highly correlated with firm size, any accounting standard that increases reported operating expenses, depreciation, or the recorded value of the asset base proportionally will, in general, result in an increase in the utility's revenues. And these increments to the utility's cashflows will, in general, be increasing in firm size.

When an accounting standard increases net income and decreases operating earnings of utilities, as do price-level adjustments [See Davidson and Weil, 1975b], we would not necessarily expect the relationship between management's attitude to the standard and firm size to be as we specified above (i.e., larger firms favoring or opposing the standard depending upon the effect on net income and smaller firms opposing the standard). As a consequence, we concentrate on testing that relationship for unregulated firms.

Another omitted variable is the political sensitivity of the firm's industry which clearly affects the political cost of an accounting standard change. We do not have a political theory which predicts which industries Congress singles out for wealth transfers (For example, why was the oil industry subject to intensive Congressional pressure in early 1974 and not the steel industry?[29] Consequently, we do not consider it formally in our model. As we shall see, political sensitivity has an impact on our results (only one steel company submitted on price-level accounting compared to seven oil companies submitting), but it does not eliminate the general relationship between firm size and management's accounting lobbying behavior.

EMPIRICAL TESTS

Data

On February 15, 1974, the FASB issued the discussion memorandum "Reporting the Effects of General Price-Level Changes in Financial Statements" and scheduled a public hearing on the topic for April 25, 1974. Public comments and position papers were solicited. One hundred thirty-three accounting firms, public corporations, industry organizations, and government agencies filed written comments.

We assume the submission indicates the position of corporate management. Clearly, this assumption could introduce some error into our tests. For example, some controllers of corporations may submit not because of corporate effects, but because they receive nonpecuniary income from the submission (e.g., if they are officers in their local chapter of the National Association of Accountants). However, we expect the error to be random. Ignoring this error biases our tests of management's attitudes on accounting standards towards rejecting the theory.

Almost all the corporations making submissions (49 out of 53) were New York

---

[29]This does not mean we do not have any ideas as to which variables are important. For example, in the case of consumer goods industries, we suspect that the relative price change of the product is important.

Stock Exchange firms. Of the remaining four firms, one was listed on the American Stock Exchange, one was traded over the counter, and the other two were not traded. Of the 53 firms, 18 submitted opinions expressing favorable views on general price level adjustments whereas 34 expressed opinions ranging from strong objection to discussions of the merits of current costing to skepticism and feelings that GPLA was premature. These 34 were classified as opposing GPLA. For one firm, Transunion, an opinion could not be ascertained, and this firm was subsequently dropped from the sample. The firms making submissions and their position on the issue are listed in Table 1.

Once the sample of firms was identified from their submissions to the FASB, 1972 and 1973 financial data was obtained from the COMPUSTAT tape and the 1974 Moody Manuals. In addition, data on the existence of management incentive compensation plans was obtained by a questionnaire mailed to the chief financial officer of each firm. Missing data on the nonresponses (30 percent of the firms) was obtained from the firms' proxy statements and annual reports. If no mention of an incentive plan was found, we assumed the firm did not have one. Firms classified as having management incentive compensation plans based on accounting earnings[30] are denoted by an (M) in Table 1.

The precise impact of reported earnings on executive incentive compensation is difficult to estimate simply because the firm has such a plan. The most common procedure companies use is to take some fraction of reported earnings after deducting a return on invested capital as a pool out of which incentive compensation is paid. However, most companies do not pay out all of this pool each year. The important point, though, is that managers in firms with management compensation plans which report higher adjusted earnings will not suffer a decline in their incentive compensation and it may actually increase their compensation (depending on the monitoring by the outside directors).

Methodology

The FASB's General Price Level Adjustment (GPLA) standard would require supplementary price adjusted statements. Even though the supplementary statements will not replace conventional reports, users of the information will obviously make comparisons [See Ijiri, 1976] and if adjusted income is above (below) unadjusted income, we expect our previous reasoning to hold, and we assume the effect is the same as an increase (decrease) in reported income.

A price-level adjusted income figure does not exist for all firms in our sample. Since only a few firms voluntarily published GPLA statements, income proxies must be constructed. Fortunately, a previous series of studies by Davidson and Weil [1975a and 1975b] and Davidson, Stickney, and Weil [1976] developed an adjusting procedure which relies solely on published financial statements and GNP deflators. Using either their published figures for 1973 financial statements or using their

---

[30] If the firm had an incentive plan, but it was not tied to reported earnings then this firm was coded as not having an incentive plan (Gillette).

TABLE 1

Firms Making Submissions to the FASB on
General Price Level Adjustments*

Firms advocating GPLA	Firms opposing GPLA
Regulated Firms	
AT&T	Aetna Life & Casualty (M)
Consumer Power (M)	Commerce Bank of Kansas City
Commonwealth Edison	Liberty Corporation (M)
Detroit Edison	Northeast Utilities
Duke Power	People's Gas
Indiana Telephone	Southern Natural Resources (M)
Iowa Illinois Gas & Electric	Pennzoil
Northwestern Telephone	Texas Eastern Transmission (M)
Southern Company	Texas Gas Transmission
Unregulated Firms	
Exxon (M)	Continental Oil (M)
Gulf Oil (M)	Standard Oil of Indiana (M)
Shell Oil (M)	Texaco (M)
Standard Oil of California (M)	Rockwell International (M)
Caterpillar Tractor	United Aircraft (M)
Dupont E. I. DeNemours (M)	Automated Building Components
General Motors (M)	Copeland Corporation (M)
Ford Motor Company (M)	General Electric (M)
Marcor (M)	General Mills (M)
	Gillette
	W. R. Grace (M)
	Harsco (M)
	Inland Steel (M)
	International Harvester (M)
	American Cyanamid (M)
	IT&T (M)
	Eli Lilly & Co. (M)
	Masonite (M)
	Merck (M)
	Owens-Illinois, Inc. (M)
	Reliance Electric (M)
	Seagrams Sons, Inc. (M)
	Sears Roebuck (M)
	Texas Instruments (M)
	Union Carbide (M)

*Transunion Corporation made a submission, but they did not state a position on GPLA. It made two technical comments.

M denotes the firm has a management compensation plan.

procedures, we were able to obtain estimates of the direction of change in reported price-level income.[31]

In addition to using the Davidson and Weil results or procedures, we constructed proxy variables based on unadjusted depreciation and net monetary assets. Both of these variables have a direct negative impact on GPLA earnings (i.e., the larger depreciation or net monetary assets, the lower the adjusted income and the smaller or more negative the difference between GPLA adjusted income and unadjusted income). If we assume that our sample of firms has the same age distribution of depreciable property, then (cross-sectionally) depreciation and net monetary assets can serve as a surrogate for the effect of GPLA earnings.[32] Those numbers are readily available for our sample.

Davidson and Weil [1975c] also estimate the effect of GPLA on income for 1974 (which was in the future at the time of the submissions). Even though the adjustment procedure was slightly different, only two of our 19 firms in the combined samples reverse the direction of the income effect between 1973 and 1974. Similarly, all of the utilities, (24), and 35 of the 50 other companies in their sample have income effects of the same sign in both years. Since the effects of income changes in the immediate future are less heavily discounted, these results suggest that the error introduced by our assumption of stationary income changes is not likely to be severe.

Tests of the Theory

In the reported tests, we use asset size as the surrogate for firm size.[33] Based on our model, we can make predictions about the relationship between asset size and firm submissions. We predict that firms whose earnings are increased by GPLA will oppose GPLA regardless of their size (i.e., there will be no association between size

---

[31] 1973 was a period of high inflation. If firms based their FASB lobbying position on the price adjustments produced by high unexpected inflation without considering more "typical" years, then this would introduce errors into the data and finding a statistically significant result becomes more difficult. If these errors are systematic with respect to firm size, then our results could be biased. We do not expect this to be the case. To control partially for this, statistical tests are performed which are independent of the magnitude of the price change. Net monetary assets in 1973 may still be abnormally small (large) due to the high rate of inflation, but these preliminary tests suggest that our results are not dependent upon 1973 being atypical.

[32] The assumption that the age distribution of depreciable property is the same across our firms is reasonable. The firms who submitted to the FASB on the GPLA issue, generally, were large, capital-intensive and long-established firms. Moreover, the results using these surrogates are consistent with the results using Davidson and Weil's estimates.

[33] In this case, firm size is measured by the firm's *Fortune* 500 rank in assets. The results are identical when rank in sales is used. Furthermore, the intent of government intervention depends on the metric used by the courts, legislators, and regulators. Market share, concentration and size are among the commonly used indicators. Absolute size is important in explaining government regulation for both theoretical and empirical reasons. An implication of Peltzman's (1975, p. 30) theory of regulation is that the amount of wealth redistributed from firms by government intervention is a positive function of economies of scale. Since we expect large firm size to indicate the presence of economies of scale, implication of Peltzman's theory is that government intervention will be greater for larger firms. Empirically, we observe numerous cases of politicians and regulators echoing the conventional wisdom of certain segments in society, that big business is inherently bad. (See, "Curse of Big Business," *Barron's* June 16, 1969 and footnote 12).

and submission). However, for firms whose earnings are decreased by GPLA, we predict that they will either support GPLA or will not make a submission depending on where asset size C (Figure 1) occurs in their industry. Since we cannot determine the asset size corresponding to point C, we are in a position analogous to being able to predict the sign of a regression coefficient but not its magnitude. Consequently, our test of the model does not include asset size C (analogous to the magnitude of the coefficient). The test is only of the prediction that there is a positive relationship between asset size and submission for firms with income decreases.

Firms making submissions were classified according to the direction of change in their net income and ranked by their asset size (Table 2). Of the 26 firms with income decreases, eight voted yes and 18 no.[34] The eight yes votes came from the larger firms, thus supporting our prediction. To test the null hypothesis that the eight firms which voted yes are drawn from the same population of firms (with respect to size) as the 18 that voted no, we performed a Mann-Whitney U test. Our tables indicate that we can reject the null hypothesis at the .001 level.[35]

Of the eight firms with income increases or no changes in net income, seven voted no. Thus, the general tendency of these firms is to vote no as predicted by our model.

The results in Table 2 are consistent with the implications of our model including our assumption that the management compensation factor is dominated by political and tax considerations. Of the 31 unregulated firms with management compensation plans, eight had increases or no change in income and 23 had decreases in income as a result of price-level adjustments. If management compensation dominates tax and political factors, then firms with increases in income would be more likely to support price-level adjustments than firms with decreases. In fact, the reverse is true. The frequency of firms with income decreases which support price-level adjustment is seven out of 23 (30 percent) while the frequency of firms with income increases that support price-level adjustments is one out of eight (12.5 percent).

The above results support the relationship between management's attitudes on GPLA and firm size for the 23 unregulated firms. However, if we assume that firm size and the direction of the income change are independent (Table 2 supports this assumption), then (if there is no size effect) the average size of firms supporting GPLA should be the same as the average size of firms opposing. Thus we can use the voting behavior of all 52 firms in our sample to test the size relationship.

Table 3 presents the median rank on asset size for both regulated and unregulated firms favoring and opposing GPLA. The median rank in the *Fortune* 500 of the nine

---

[34] We use the term "vote" to mean responding to a discussion memorandum by issuing a corporate opinion.

[35] Siegel [1956], p. 274. Even after any reasonable adjustment for the degrees of freedom lost due to previous statistical analysis, this result is still significant.

An intuitive idea of the strength of the relationship between management's attitude and firm size can be obtained by considering an analogy. Suppose we put 26 balls in an urn representing the firms with earnings decreases; eight red balls representing the firms that voted yes; and 18 black balls, representing the firms that voted no. Now, we randomly draw 13 balls out of the urn without replacement representing the largest 13 firms (out of the 26). The probability that we draw eight red balls (analogous to the probability of the eight firms voting yes being the "large" firms if the null hypothesis of no association between votes and size is correct) is .001. If the votes of firms are not independent, as in the case of gaming, this analogy is inappropriate. But we do not have any evidence of vote dependence (via gaming or otherwise).

TABLE 2

Asset Size, Direction of Earnings Effect and Corporate Position on GPLA

Rank on asset size	Firm	Rank in Fortune 500 (1973)	Corporate position, classified by earnings change†	
			Increase or no change	Decrease
1	Exxon	1		Yes
2	General Motors	2		Yes
3	Texaco	3	No	
4	Ford	4		Yes
5	Sears Roebuck (Rank 1 in retail sales)	7		No
6	IT&T	8	No	
7	Gulf Oil	9		Yes
8	Standard Oil of California	10		Yes
9	General Electric	11	No	
10	Standard Oil of Indiana	12		No
11	Shell Oil	16		Yes
12	Dupont E.I. Nemours	18		Yes
Point C*				
13	Union Carbide	22		No
14	Continental Oil	26		No
15	Marcor (Rank 2 in retail firms)	33	Yes	
16	International Harvester	34		No
17	Caterpillar Tractor	47		Yes
18	Rockwell International	54	No	
19	W. R. Grace	55	No	
20	Owens-Illinois	80	No	
21	Inland Steel	85		No
22	American Cyanamid	92		No
23	United Aircraft	107		No
24	Seagrams Sons, Inc.	108		No
25	Eli Lilly & Co.	135		No
26	Merck	143		No
27	General Mills	156	No	
28	Texas Instruments	164		No
29	Gillette	167		No
30	Reliance Electric	332		No
31	Harsco	368		No
32	Masonite	386		No
33	Automated Building Components	Not Ranked		No
34	Copeland Corporation	Not Ranked		No

*Point C in Figure 1 is determined by minimizing the number of misclassifications.
†Yes= Favored GPLA
 No= Opposed GPLA

unregulated firms supporting GPLA is 10. The median rank of the 25 unregulated firms opposing GPLA is 92.

TABLE 3

Median Ranks of Firm Size by Regulation and Position on GPLA*

	Regulated (N=18)		Unregulated (N=34)	
	In favor (9)	Against (9)	In favor (9)	Against (25)
Median Rank	13	38	10	92

*Fortune [May and July, 1974].

For regulated firms, there also appears to be a relationship between size and management attitudes. The net incomes for all the utilties investigated by Davidson and Weil [1975b] are increased by GPLA suggesting none of the utilities should favor GPLA. However, as noted in the preceding section, operating earnings are relevant to rate determination. Those earnings fall for all the utilities investigated by Davidson and Weil [1975b] and this could explain why relatively larger regulated firms favor GPLA.

If we assume our model is correct and that asset size C is the same for all industries, we can estimate C by minimizing the number of prediction errors (analogous to estimating a regression coefficient by minimizing the sum of squared errors). This estimate provides information on the relative importance of political and/or tax costs for different size firms. Given the data, C is between the 18th and 22nd largest firms in the *Fortune* 500 in 1973 (see Table 2). This suggests that reduced political and/or tax costs outweigh information production and/or management compensation factors in determining management's position on GPLA only for very large firms. For most other firms, information production costs dominate.

Are the major benefits of reporting lower adjusted incomes derived from tax or political considerations? It is very difficult to differentiate between these two factors, but one possible way is the following. Is the change in adjusted income proportional to firm size? If it is, then both the tax and political factors may be operating. But if there is no association between firm size and the magnitude of the income change, then the tax effect cannot explain why larger firms favor GPLA. Therefore, this result could only be due to political costs. We can obtain estimates of the income effect of GPLA for 11 of the firms whose incomes would be reduced by GPLA (six supporting, five opposing).[36] The average reduction in income for the six firms which supported GPLA is $177.7 million, while the average reduction for the five which opposed GPLA is $38.5 million. Thus, it appears that the income change does vary with size and the preceding results are consistent with both the tax and political costs affecting management's attitudes.

[36] This test was performed on 11 firms with income decreases which Davidson and Weil reported 1973 adjusted earnings. Firms which were manually adjusted by us for Table 2 were excluded from this test since only the sign of the earnings change was calculated.

The preceding results test only whether the size effect exists for firms which did submit to the FASB. It is interesting to examine the effect of GPLA on firms which did not submit. In particular, the firms of asset size above our estimated C which did not submit are of interest since our model predicts they would submit on the basis of the income effect. Dupont is the last firm above asset size C in Table 2 to vote. It is ranked 18th in the *Fortune* 500 in 1973. There are seven firms ranked higher than 18th which did not make a submission to the FASB. They are IBM (ranked 5th), General Telephone (6th), Mobil Oil (7th), U.S. Steel (13th), Chrysler (14th), Tenneco (15th), and Atlantic Richfield (17th).

The size of the income change is crucial to determining why these seven firms did not submit. If changes are not associated with firm size, the expected benefits of a submission could be very small and may not exceed the submission costs. Unfortunately, Davidson and Weil only estimated the change in earnings in 1973 for three of these seven firms: IBM, U.S. Steel, and Chrysler. All three have income reductions with GPLA and their average reduction is $88 million. This is less than the average reduction for the six firms with income reductions which did submit ($177 million), but it is not trivial. Further, the reductions for two of the three nonsubmissions (IBM and General Telephone) exceed the reductions for four of the six submissions. Consequently, it is difficult to attribute the fact that the three firms did not submit to the lack of an income effect.[37]

In summary, these tests confirm the relationship between size and management attitudes on GPLA. Political costs and, perhaps, tax effects influence management's attitudes on accounting standards. Although we are not able to explain some of the notable nonsubmitting firms' decisions, we would point out that most of the firms submitting are large, and the likelihood of submission increases with asset size (12 of the 18 firms ranked 1–18 in the *Fortune* 500 submitted, four of the 18 firms ranked 19–36 submitted, two of the 18 firms ranked 37–54 submitted, one of the 18 firms ranked 55–72 submitted, etc.).

Discriminant Analysis

The preceding tests were based on the direction of the earnings change, not the magnitude of the change. A discriminant analysis is conducted including management compensation, depreciation, and net monetary assets as independent variables, and using data on 49 of the 53 firms making submissions to ensure consistency of the Davidson and Weil procedures.

---

[37] A more likely explanation of U.S. Steel's failure to submit is the fact that the steel industry was not as politically sensitive as the oil industry (for example) at the time. In other words, a given earnings effect has less political cost or benefit. This possibility is not included in our model. This could also explain Chrysler's failure to submit. As number three after General Motors and Ford they may be subject to less political pressure (and hence cost). In addition, the "free rider" effect may explain some of these nonsubmissions.

While we can only expect a positive theory to hold on average, the failure of IBM to submit is puzzling. That firm has anti-trust suits outstanding and some economists allege that it earns monopoly profits. For a discussion of one of these suits and statements by economists that IBM earns monopoly profits, see "The Breakup of IBM" *Datamation,* October 1975, pp. 95–99.

The change in price-adjusted income is correlated with the magnitudes of depreciation and net monetary assets. The larger both of these variables in unadjusted terms, the larger will be the decline (in absolute dollars) in adjusted net income. We do not perform an actual price-level adjustment, but rely on the unadjusted magnitudes of depreciation and net monetary assets.

The general form of the discriminant function we estimate is[38]

$$p_i = \alpha_1 + \alpha_2 \frac{DEP_i}{MKTVL_i} + \alpha_2 \frac{NMA_i}{MKTVL_i} + \alpha_3(SALES_i)CHG_i$$

$$+ \alpha_4\left(\frac{SALES_i}{TSALES_i}\right)CHG_i + \alpha_5 MCOMP_i + \alpha_6 REG_i$$

where

$$p_i = \begin{cases} \dfrac{\text{Number of opposing firms}}{\text{Total firms in sample}} & \text{If the } i^{th} \text{ firm favored GLPA} \\[2ex] \dfrac{\text{Number of supporting firms}}{\text{Total firms in sample}} & \text{if the } i^{th} \text{ firm opposed GPLA} \end{cases}$$

$MKTVL_i =$ the market value of the firm's equity (number of common shares outstanding x average share price)

$REG_i = \begin{cases} 1 & \text{if the } i^{th} \text{ firm was regulated} \\ 0 & \text{otherwise} \end{cases}$

$MCOMP_i = \begin{cases} 1 & \text{if the } i^{th} \text{ firm had a management incentive scheme} \\ 0 & \text{otherwise} \end{cases}$

$DEP_i =$ unadjusted depreciation expense in 1973 for the ith firm

$NMA_i =$ net monetary asset position in 1973 for the ith firm

$CHG_i = \begin{cases} +1 & \text{if price-level adjusted income is below unadjusted} \\ & \text{income or if the firm is regulated} \\ -1 & \text{if price-level adjusted income is above unadjusted income} \\ 0 & \text{otherwise} \end{cases}$

$SALES_i =$ Sales of the ith firm

$TSALES_i =$ Total sales of the Compustat firm with the same SIC code as firm i.

$\dfrac{SALES_i}{TSALES_i} =$ a proxy variable for market share

---

[38] Northwestern Telephone, Commerce Bank of Kansas City, and Indiana Telephone were dropped from the sample due to a lack of data.

TABLE 4
DISCRIMINANT ANALYSIS
Coefficients (t-statistics)

Model number	N	Sample	Constant	DEP/ MKTVL	NMA/ MKTVL	SALES × CHG	SALES — × TSALES CHG	MCOMP	REG	R^2	Yates Adjusted Chi Square*
1	49	total sample	-.0241 (-.12)	122.6 (.60)	-38.9 (-1.62)	.000044 (3.67)	-.4131 (-1.11)	-.2355 (-1.42)	-.3443 (-1.29)	.358	9.25
2	49	total sample	-.0855 (-.44)	160.4 (.79)	-14.2 (-.98)	.000043 (3.53)	-.4381 (-1.17)	-.1619 (-1.03)		.332	9.25
3	49	total sample	-.0973 (-.50)	143.0 (.70)	-15.6 (-1.07)	.000034 (3.58)		-.1601 (-1.02)		.311	9.25
4	34	unregulated firms	.0431 (.19)	74.0 (.27)	-36.5 (-1.06)	.000044 (3.58)	-.3271 (-.89)	-.2186 (-.89)		.366	19.96
5	34	unregulated firms	.0412 (.18)	86.2 (.32)	-35.3 (-1.03)	.000038 (3.73)		-.2335 (-.96)		.347	13.16
6	49	total sample	-.0079 (-.04)	215.3 (1.09)		.000033 (3.44)		-.2365 (-1.39)	.0077 (.05)	.293	11.74
7	49	total sample	-.0662 (-1.03)			.000033 (3.44)				.201	5.98

*The Yates correction for continuity is useful in establishing a lower bound on the χ^2 statistic.

164

Table 4 presents the results of various functional forms of equation (2) fitted over various subsets of the data.[39] The first two terms,

$$\frac{NMA}{MKTVL} \text{ and } \frac{DEP}{MKTVL},$$

normalize the unadjusted figures by the market value of the equity[40] and the estimated coefficients measure the extent to which an increase in relative depreciation or net monetary assets affect voting behavior. These coefficients, which should capture the tax effects, are predicted to be positive under that hypothesis (the larger the depreciation and net monetary assets the greater the decline in adjusted income and the greater the tax benefits).

The sign on normalized depreciation is as predicted, but normalized net monetary assets is of the wrong sign. One of the following three hypotheses explains this result: the tax effect is only operating via depreciation;[41] depreciation and net monetary assets, being inversely related (correlation coefficient ranging from −.41 to −.55), are entering the regression with opposite signs; or the tax effect is not an explanatory factor. Since our sample is very small, it is not possible to use a holdout subset to distinguish between these hypotheses.

The next two variables,

$$(SALES)CHG \text{ and } \left(\frac{SALES}{TSALES}\right)CHG,$$

are proxies for political costs. These two variables, assume that political costs are symmetric for both earnings increases and decreases. The multiplicative dummy, CHG, is positive if earnings decline (based on the Davidson-Weil [1975a] results) or if the firm is regulated.[42]

The sign on SALES x CHG is as predicted, positive, and in addition has the highest t-statistic of all the independent variables. In addition, the coefficient on SALES x CHG is the most stable coefficient across various realizations and subsamples which leads us to conclude that firm size is the most important variable.

---

[39] The discriminant function is estimated using ordinary least squares. t-statistics on the coefficients are reported. The usual t-tests cannot be performed since the dependent variable is not normally distributed nor can asymptotic properties of large samples be used. However, the t-statistic is still useful as an index of the relative importance of the independent variable.

[40] Normalizing by the market value of the common stock introduces some error since we are not including the market value of the debt or preferred stock. However, since the market value of the common is highly correlated with total market value of the firm, we do not expect serious problems except that there may be some systematic, negative understatement of normalized net monetary assets.

[41] That is, this sample of firms does not expect the tax laws to be changed to include in taxable income gains/losses on net monetary assets.

[42] Since the regulatory commission bases rates on depreciation, net monetary assets are not expected to be an important consideration, hence operating earnings decline for regulated firms.

The sign of the coefficient on the variable

$$\frac{SALES}{TSALES} \times CHG$$

is of the wrong sign. But this is probably due to the crude metric of market share,

$$\frac{SALES}{TSALES},$$

which this variable is attempting to measure.[43] When the market share proxy is eliminated, the model's predictive ability is not impaired.

MCOMP, a dummy variable for management compensation schemes is expected to have a negative sign regardless of the change in earnings. Prior research indicates that executive compensation is more highly associated with operating income (which includes depreciation) than net income (which includes gains/losses on monetary assets).[44] Therefore, MCOMP is not multiplied by CHG. The sign of MCOMP being negative is consistent with our predictions.

If the firm is regulated, the dummy variable, REG, is one. Regulated firms' price-level adjusted operating incomes decline, unambiguously, and therefore these firms should tend to favor GPLA if the regulatory factor is operating. Yet, the sign of the coefficient of REG is negative in Model 1. This sign is negative because REG is inversely related to

$$MCOMP \text{ and } \frac{NMA}{MKTVL}$$

(correlation coefficients of −.60 and −.86 respectively). When

$$\frac{NMA}{MKTVL}$$

is deleted from the model (Model 6), the sign of REG reverses, the importance of

---

[43] Our measure of industry sales does not include firms in the industry not on the COMPUSTAT tape and furthermore all the firm's sales are assumed to be in the firm's dominant SIC category.

[44] Our examination of management compensation plans indicates that although the minimum and maximum amounts transferred to the bonus pool depend on the final net income number, we find that the actual bonus paid is most highly associated with operating or current income (depreciation is included, but extraordinary gains and losses are excluded). We correlated the change in management incentive compensation expense for 271 COMPUSTAT firms with changes in operating income and changes in net income after extraordinary items. The correlation coefficient for changes in operating income exceeded that for changes in net income after extraordinary items for over two-thirds of the firms. Gains or losses on monetary assets are not included in operating income. Consequently, only adjusted depreciation (ignoring inventory adjustments) are expected to affect management compensation and the effect is to reduce management pay.

$$\frac{DEP}{MKTVL}$$

increases, and the discriminatory power of the model improves from a Chi-Square of 9.25 to 11.74. However, the multicolinearity between

$$REG, MCOMP, \text{ and } \frac{NMA}{MKTVL}$$

precludes our drawing any conclusions regarding the impact of management compensation or regulation on lobbying behavior.

Models 4 and 5 are fitted using only the unregulated firms (N=34). REG and then

$$\frac{SALES}{TSALES} \text{ x } CHG$$

have been deleted. The R^2 statistic still remains high and the Yates adjusted Chi Square is significant at the 1 percent level. In fact, Model 4 correctly classifies the voting behavior for 32 out of the 34 firms.

The constant should be capturing the partial effect of information production costs after controlling for the other factors. When the total sample is used in the estimation, the constant is negative as expected. When the regulated firms are excluded, the constant is positive. But in all models the constant is close to zero.

The estimated discriminant functions are consistent with the tests of the theory. All of the discriminant functions are statistically significant and the intervening variable driving these findings is firm size. In fact, firm size explains over half the explained variance in voting behavior (Model 7).

These results are consistent with those using the Davidson and Weil findings. The discriminant functions indicate that the political cost factor is more important than the tax factor in affecting management's attitudes.

The major empirical problem in the discriminant analysis is the rather small sample size which precludes using a hold-out sample and, furthermore, does not allow more sophisticated econometric techniques to control for the multicolinearity. Hence, it is difficult to control for the interaction between the underlying factors. However, these preliminary results are encouraging and suggest that additional research in this area is warranted.

SUMMARY AND CONCLUSIONS

We have focused in this paper on the question of why firms would expend resources trying to influence the determination of accounting standards. The histories of the Committee on Accounting Procedure, the Accounting Principles Board, and FASB are replete with examples of managements and industries exerting political pressure on the standard-setting bodies.

A possible answer to this question is provided by the government intervention argument, namely, that firms having contact (actual or potential) with governments, directly through regulation (public utility commissions, Interstate Commerce Commission, Civil Aeronautics Board, etc.) or procurement, or indirectly through possible governmental intervention (antitrust, price controls, etc.), can affect their future cashflows by discouraging government action through the reporting of lower net incomes. The empirical evidence with respect to the position 52 firms took before the FASB on price level restatements is consistent with respect to this hypothesis.

The single most important factor explaining managerial voting behavior on General Price Level Accounting is firm size (after controlling for the direction of change in earnings). The larger firms, *ceteris paribus,* are more likely to favor GPLA (if earnings decline). This finding is consistent with our government intervention argument since the larger firms are more likely to be subjected to governmental interference and, hence, have more to lose than smaller corporations.

The existence of costs generated by government intervention may have more fundamental and important effects on the firm's decisions than just its lobbying behavior on financial accounting standards. Not only would we expect the firm to manage its reported earnings, but also to alter its investment-production decisions if the potential costs of government interference become large. For example, government intervention costs may lead the firm to select less risky investments in order to eliminate the chance of high returns which then increase the likelihood of government intervention. If the total risk of these less risky investments tends to be positively correlated with the systematic risk of the firm, then we would expect the beta (the estimate of the covariance between the return on the stock and the market return normalized by the variance of the market) on the common stock to be significantly below one (average risk) for those firms facing large government intervention costs. The evidence from the sample of firms making submissions to the FASB on GPLA is consistent with this hypothesis. The average β is .67. Furthermore, firms favoring GPLA tend to have lower betas than the firms in opposition.[45]

Our findings, in a preliminary extension of these results, tend to confirm the decline in systematic risk as firm size increases and as government intervention costs rise. These tentative findings are suggestive of fertile research possibilities of examining the effects of politically motivated factors on the maximizing behavior of firms' managements and shareholders.

We believe that the general findings in this paper, if confirmed by other studies, have important implications for the setting of financial accounting standards in a

---

[45] The average betas of various subclasses are:

	Regulated	Unregulated	Combined
Firms opposing GPLA	.67	.72	.71
Firms favoring GPLA	.50	.65	.59
Combined	.59	.70	.67

Note that as a firm grows via diversification its beta should tend to one.

mixed economy. As long as financial accounting standards have potential effects on the firm's future cashflows, standard setting by bodies such as the Accounting Principles Board, the Financial Accounting Standards Board, or the Securities and Exchange Commission will be met by corporate lobbying. The Committee on Accounting Procedure and the Accounting Principles Board could not withstand the pressure. The former Chairman of the FASB also has complained of the political lobbying, and the FASB has been forced to defer the controversial GPLA topic. The SEC has, until recently, avoided direct involvement in the setting of accounting standards. One could hypothesize that this was in their own interest. By letting the American Institute of Certified Public Accountants be the scapegoat, the Securities and Exchange Commission could maintain their "credibility" with Capitol Hill and the public.

REFERENCES

Alchian, A.A., "Corporate Management and Property Rights," in *Economic Policy and the Regulation of Corporate Securities* (H. Manne, ed.), (American Enterprise Institute, 1969).

—— and H. Demsetz, "Production, Information Costs and Economic Organization," *American Economic Review* (December 1972), pp. 777–95.

Armstrong, Marshall S., "The Politics of Establishing Accounting Standards." A speech before the Third Annual Securities Regulation Institute in San Diego, California, January 16, 1976, as reported in Arthur Andersen & Co., *Executive News Briefs,* (February 1976), p. 1.

Ball, R., "Changes in Accounting Techniques and Stock Prices," *Empirical Research in Accounting: Selected Studies, 1972,* Supplement to *Journal of Accounting Research* (1972). pp. 1–38.

—— and Ross Watts, "Some Time Series Properties of Accounting Income," *Journal of Finance* (June 1972), pp. 663–82.

Barefield, R.M., and E.E. Comiskey, "The Smoothing Hypothesis: An Alternative Test," *The Accounting Review* (April 1972), pp. 291–98.

Barnea, A., J. Ronen, and S. Sadan, "The Implementation of Accounting Objectives—An Application to Extraordinary Items," *The Accounting Review* (January 1975), pp. 58–68.

Beidleman, C.R., "Income Smoothing: The Role of Management," *The Accounting Review* (October 1973), pp. 653–67.

Benston, George J., "Accountants, Integrity and Financial Reporting," *Financial Executive* (August 1975), pp. 10–14.

The Conference Board, *Top Executive Compensation* (Conference Board, 1974).

Copeland, Ronald M., "Income Smoothing," *Empirical Research in Accounting: Selected Studies.* Supplement to *Journal of Accounting Research* 1968, pp. 101–16.

Cushing, B.E., "An Empirical Study of Changes in Accounting Policy," *Journal of Accounting Research* (Autumn 1969), pp. 196–203.

Dascher, B.E. and R.E. Malcom, "A Note on Income Smoothing in the Chemical Industry," *Journal of Accounting Research* (Autumn 1970), pp. 253–59.

Davidson, Sidney, Clyde P. Stickney and Roman L. Weil, *Inflation Accounting* (McGraw-Hill, 1976).

—— and Roman L. Weil, "Inflation Accounting: What Will General Price Level Adjusted

Income Statements Show?" *Financial Analysts Journal,* (January–February 1975a) pp. 27–31; 70–81.

——— and Roman L. Weil, "Inflation Accounting: Public Utilities," *Financial Analysts Journal,* (May–June 1975b), pp. 30–34; 62.

——— and Roman L. Weil, "Inflation Accounting: Some 1974 Income Measures," *Financial Analysts Journal,* (September–October 1975c), pp. 42–54.

Downs, A., *"An Economic Theory of Democracy,"* (Harper and Row, 1957).

Fama, Eugene F., "Efficient Capital Markets: A Review of Theory and Empirical Work," *Journal of Finance,* (May 1970), pp. 383–417.

Gonedes, N., "Income-smoothing Behavior Under Selected Stochastic Processes," *Journal of Business* (October 1972), pp. 570–84.

———, "Class Discussion Notes: Section 8," unpublished manuscript, University of Chicago (January 1976).

——— and N. Dopuch, "Capital Market Equilibrium, Information Production, and Selecting Accounting Techniques: Theoretical Framework and Review of Empirical Work," *Studies on Financial Accounting Objectives: 1974.* Supplement to *Journal of Accounting Research* (1974).

Gordon, M. J., "Postulates, Principles and Research in Accounting," *The Accounting Review* (April 1964), pp. 251–63.

———, B. N. Horwitz, and P. T. Meyers, "Accounting Measurements and Normal Growth of the Firm," *Research in Accounting Measurement,* eds. Jaedicke, Ijiri and Nielsen (American Accounting Association, 1966), pp. 221–31.

Haskins and Sells. *Public Utilities Manual* (New York, 1974).

Horngren, Charles T., "The Marketing of Accounting Standards," *Journal of Accountancy* (October 1973), pp. 61–66.

———, "Setting Accounting Standards in 1980," unpublished speech before the Arthur Young Professors Roundtable (March 30–31, 1976).

Ijiri, Yuji, "The Price-Level Restatement and its Dual Interpretation," *The Accounting Review,* (April 1976), pp. 227–43.

Jensen, Michael C., "Reflections on the State of Accounting Research and the Regulation of Accounting," Presented at the Stanford Lectures in Accounting, May 21, 1976.

———, and William H. Meckling, "Theory of the Firm: Managerial Behavior, Agency Costs and Ownership Structure," *Journal of Financial Economics* (October 1976a), pp. 305–60.

———, and William H. Meckling, "Can the Corporation Survive?" Public Policy Working Paper Series, PPS76–4, Graduate School of Management, University of Rochester, (April, 1976b).

Kaplan, R. S., and R. Roll, "Investor Evaluation of Accounting Information: Some Empirical Evidence," *Journal of Business* (April 1972), pp. 225–57.

Meckling, William H., "Values and the Choice of the Model of the Individual in Social Sciences," *Revue Suisse d' Economie Politique et de Statistique* (December 1976).

Moonitz, Maurice, *Obtaining Agreement on Standards.* Studies in Accounting Research No. 8 (Sarasota, Florida: American Accounting Association, 1974).

Peltzman, S., "Toward a More General Theory of Regulation," *Journal of Law and Economics,* (August 1976), pp. 221–40.

Posner, Richard A., "Theories of Economic Regulation," *The Bell Journal of Economics and Management Science,* (Autumn 1974), pp. 335–58.

Siegel, Sidney, *Nonparametric Statistics* (McGraw-Hill, 1956).

Siegfried, John, "Determinants of Antitrust Activity," *Journal of Law and Economics* (October 1975), pp. 559–81.

Stigler, G. J., "The Theory of Economic Regulation," *The Bell Journal of Economics and Management Science,* (Spring 1971), pp. 3–21.

Sunder, S., "Empirical Analysis of Stock Price and Risk as They Relate to Accounting Changes in Inventory Valuation," *The Accounting Review* (April 1975), pp. 305–15.

U.S. Congress, Senate, Subcommittee on Antitrust and Monopoly of the Committee on the Judiciary, *Hearings, The Petroleum Industry,* Part I, 94th Congress, 1st Session, 1975.

U.S. Congress, Senate, Subcommittee on Antitrust and Monopoly of the Committee on the Judiciary, *Hearings, The Petroleum Industry,* Part III, 94th Congress, 1st Session, 1976.

Watts, Ross, "Accounting Objectives," Working Paper Series No. 7408, Graduate School of Management, University of Rochester, (April 1974).

Watts, Ross, "Corporate Financial Statements: Product of the Market and Political Processes," *Australian Journal of Management* (April 1977), pp. 53–75.

Zeff, Stephen, *Forging Accounting Principles in Five Countries: A History and an Analysis of Trends,* Arthur Andersen Lecture Series (Stipes Publishing Company, 1972), pp. 110–268.

Zimmerman, Jerold, "The Municipal Accounting Maze: An Analysis of Political Incentives," Supplement to the *Journal of Accounting Research* (1977).

The Effect of the Firm's Capital Structure on the Choice of Accounting Methods

Dan S. Dhaliwal
University of Arizona

Watts and Zimmerman [1978] have examined the effect of taxes, regulation, political costs, information production costs, and management compensation plans on management's attitude towards accounting standards. In this paper, I examine the effect of another variable—the capital structure of the firm—on management's attitude towards accounting standards. In particular, empirical evidence is presented which supports the hypothesis that managers of highly leveraged firms will oppose accounting standards which decrease reported earnings or increase the variability of reported earnings.

An overview of Watts and Zimmerman's theory is given in the next section. Next, the relationship between the firm's capital structure and management's attitude

From *The Accounting Review* (January 1980), pp. 78–84. Reprinted by permission of the American Accounting Association.

Editor's Note: The author would like to acknowledge the capable research assistance of William Salatka and the helpful comments of Daniel Collins, William R. Kinney, Jr., and Gerald L. Salamon. Russ Barefield, Michael Rozeff, and Jerold Zimmerman provided helpful suggestions on an earlier version of this paper. This article represents the views of the author, and not of any organization.

towards accounting standards is discussed. The formulation of the research hypothesis and the results of testing it are discussed in the final section.

AN OVERVIEW OF THE WATTS AND ZIMMERMAN THEORY

Watts and Zimmerman [1978] argue that management's support or opposition to a proposed accounting standard depends upon the size of the firm and whether the proposed standard increases or decreases the firm's reported earnings. Among other things, they argue that large firms will support an accounting standard that would reduce reported earnings. They would do so because lower reported earnings will result in benefits in the form of tax, political, and regulatory considerations which exceed the additional costs to be incurred in the form of adjustment for bonus compensation plans, information production costs, and lobbying costs. They argue that for small firms, however, the benefits provided by lower reported earnings due to tax, political, and regulatory considerations will be smaller than the additional cost of adjusting bonus compensation plans. Therefore, smaller firms will oppose an accounting standard which reduces their reported earnings. The above hypothesis was tested empirically by examining corporate responses to the solicitation by the Financial Accounting Standards Board (FASB) for comments and positions on its discussion memorandum, "Reporting the Effects of General Price-Level Changes in Financial Statements" [FASB, 1974]. Their results indicate that:

> The single most important factor explaining managerial voting behavior on General Price Level accounting is firm size (after controlling for the direction of change in earnings). The larger firms, *ceteris paribus,* are more likely to favor GPLA (if earnings decline). [Watts and Zimmerman, 1978, p. 131].

These results were consistent with the theory developed by Watts and Zimmerman [1978]. However, it is possible that the size variable was acting as a surrogate for variables omitted by Watts and Zimmerman as well as the variables that Watts and Zimmerman had discussed earlier (tax, political, and regulatory considerations, *etc.*). The purpose of this paper is to extend the work of Watts and Zimmerman [1978] by examining the effect of one omitted variable—the capital structure of the firm—on management's attitude towards accounting standards. In the next section, theoretical arguments are presented which link management's attitude towards proposed accounting standards with the capital structure of their firms.

EFFECT OF THE FIRM'S CAPITAL STRUCTURE ON MANAGEMENT'S ATTITUDES TOWARDS FINANCIAL ACCOUNTING STANDARDS

Management's attitude towards accounting standards is related to the capital structure of the firm because of the existence of restrictive covenants in credit agreements and indentures. Most publicly and privately placed debt issues contain restrictive covenants designed to prevent the debtor from unilaterally altering the creditor's risk. The nature of some of these covenants is described by Fogelson [1978, p. 769] as follows:

An institutional loan agreement may require the borrower to maintain a specified excess of current assets over current liabilities, a specified current ratio and a specified amount of net tangible assets ("NTA"). In addition, the borrower may be prohibited from incurring (or permitting to have outstanding) current or funded indebtedness in excess of a specified percentage of NTA. The borrower may also be prohibited from incurring lease liabilities in excess of a specified percentage of NTA and may be permitted to pay dividends or repurchase its securities only out of net income earned subsequent to a "peg" date (usually the end of the fiscal year immediately preceding the date of the loan) plus an agreed amount.

A typical public debt issue will have a dividend restriction tied to net income and may have a senior debt restriction tied to NTA as well as a secured debt and sale and lease back provision tied to NTA.

NTA, net income, current assets and current and funded indebtedness are normally defined with reference to generally accepted accounting principles ("GAAP").

The nature of restrictive covenants is such that firms which have large amounts of debt relative to equity will oppose a proposed accounting standard which would cause a reduction in reported earnings or net tangible assets. Such an accounting standard would result in a firm's having less earnings available for dividends or stock repurchases and less net tangible assets. Accordingly, a leveraged firm may be put into technical default in the year that a standard becomes effective. For example, adoption of Statement of Financial Accounting Standards (SFAS) No. 12, "Accounting for Certain Marketable Securities," caused an immediate technical default by Aristar, Inc., under its loan agreements, since it was required to charge net worth by $3,400,000 to appropriately adjust its investments. A note to its financial statements for the year ended June 30, 1976 states:

> During the nine months ended March 31, 1976, the Company was in technical default under several of its long-term debt agreements. The default occurred because the Financial Accounting Standards Board adopted on December 27, 1975, a statement of financial accounting standards..., which required a reduction of stockholders' equity for unrealized losses on marketable equity securities. This required change in accounting caused stockholders' equity to be reduced below an amount necessary to maintain defined debt ratios in such agreements. The agreements have been amended to allow computation of such ratios without regard to unrealized losses on marketable equity securities [Aristar, 1976, p. 25].

Thus, the adoption of an income-reducing or net worth-reducing accounting standard may put a leveraged firm into the position of having to obtain amendments to its credit agreements. The probability of a firm getting into this situation increases as its leverage increases. A private debt covenant can be re-written easily, but a lender who is earning a rate of interest currently less than market may use the situation as an opportunity to renegotiate the loan. Public issues which require amendments may be even more costly to effect, however. Difficulties encountered in obtaining these amendments are summed up by Fogelson [1978, p. 778] as follows:

> ...it is a more difficult task to amend a public debt instrument since such action requires a

meeting of the public debt holders and normally the approval of the holders of two-thirds of the outstanding debt. Consideration also must be given to whether the amendment of a restrictive financial covenant represents the sale of a new security subject to registration under the Securities Act of 1933 (the "1933 Act") in the absence of exemption, such as the recapitalization exemption of section 3(a)(9) of the 1933 Act. Moreover, if a purchase or sale of a security is involved, such transaction would be subject to the antifraud provisions of section 17(a) of the 1933 Act and Section 10(b) of the Securities Exchange Act of 1934 and rule 10b–5 thereunder.

In summary, then, an accounting standard which would cause a reduction in reported earnings or net worth may put highly leveraged firms into the position of having to obtain costly amendments to their credit agreements. Thus, firms with high debt-to-equity ratios are hypothesized to oppose such an accounting standard.

Similarly, an accounting method which increases fluctuations in reported earnings and leaves the average (over time) of reported earnings unchanged would increase the probability of a firm's getting into technical default on its credit agreements. Thus, according to earlier discussion, firms with high debt-to-equity ratios would be expected to oppose such an accounting standard.

In the next section I present empirical evidence which is consistent with the hypothesis that firms with high debt-to-equity ratios are more likely to oppose an accounting standard which decreases reported earnings and/or increases volatility of reported earnings than are firms with low debt-to-equity ratios.

FORMULATION OF RESEARCH HYPOTHESIS, SAMPLE SELECTION, AND TEST OF HYPOTHESIS

Research Hypothesis

In December, 1977, FASB issued SFAS No. 19, "Financial Accounting and Reporting by Oil and Gas Producing Companies." Basically, this statement specifies that exploration costs must be accounted for under the successful efforts method. Prior to SFAS No. 19, two methods of accounting for exploration expenses were available: (1) full cost method, and (2) successful efforts method. Under successful efforts costing, only those prediscovery costs which are directly identifiable with the discovery of a commercial reserve may be capitalized. All other costs are treated as operating expenses under this method. On the other hand, all prediscovery costs are capitalized irrespective of their result under the full costing method. The mandated switch from full cost to successful efforts method by oil and gas producing companies is likely to reduce their reported earnings and equity and increase the variability of their reported earnings. For example, Collins *et al.* [forthcoming] state:

> ... while successful efforts accounting is presently used by most of the large "integrated" oil companies, the new FASB statement will force many of the smaller oil and gas "producing" companies to change from the "full cost" method to the successful efforts method, thereby substantially reducing reported equity and earnings in most cases.

Similarly, John Chalsty, Managing Director of Donaldson, Lufkin & Jenrette

Securities Corporation, in testimony at the Department of Energy (DOE) hearings, stated:

> "[successful]" efforts accounting will bring about a significant reduction in the reported earnings of most full cost exploration oriented companies and a significant increase in the volatility of such earnings.

Furthermore, Arthur Andersen & Co. [1978] presents empirical evidence which indicates that a change to the successful efforts method will result in reductions in reported net income and equity. Thus, if my theory concerning the effect of capital structure on management's attitude towards accounting standards is correct, firms which opposed the successful efforts method would be expected to have a higher debt-to-equity ratio than the firms which supported this method. Firms which were using the full cost method prior to SFAS No. 19 strongly opposed the adoption of this Statement through position papers submitted to the FASB and the Securities and Exchange Commission (SEC). Alternatively, it can be argued that these firms did not support the successful efforts method because they voluntarily chose the full cost method. Similarly, firms using the successful efforts method prior to SFAS No. 19 can be viewed as supporting this method. Therefore, the following hypothesis was tested:

> Null: There is no difference in the average debt-to-equity ratios of firms using the full cost method and firms of similar size using the successful efforts method.

> Alternative: The average debt-to-equity ratio of firms using the full cost method is greater than that of firms of similar size using the successful efforts method.

Sample Selection

Two samples of oil- and gas-producing firms, once consisting of 72 firms which were using the full cost method and the other consisting of 41 firms which were using the successful efforts method prior to SFAS No. 19 were obtained from Dyckman [1977]. As mentioned earlier, Watts and Zimmerman's [1978] results indicate that the size of a firm is the major determinant of its management's attitude toward accounting standards. Since the purpose of this paper is to examine the effect of a firm's capital structure on management's attitude towards accounting standards, the samples were matched on sales revenues in order to control for the effect of firm size.[1] For a pair of firms to be admitted to the sample, the sales revenue of the smaller pair member had to be greater than or equal to 90 percent of the sales revenue of the larger pair member. This process resulted in 33 matched pairs. For each of these 66 firms, the debt-to-equity ratio for the year 1976 was obtained from Moody's *Industrial Manual.*[2]

---

[1] The samples were matched on sales revenue instead of asset size because the asset size of a firm is affected by whether it uses the full cost method or successful efforts method.

[2] The year 1976 was the most recent year for which the data on all firms were available to me.

TABLE 1
Accounting Method and the Debt-to-Equity Ratio
Matched-Pairs *t*-Test Results

	Mean	Degrees of freedom	Observed t	Level of significance for Level A one-tailed test
Full Cost	.82			
Successful Efforts	.54	32	1.35	0.09

Test of Hypothesis

The null hypothesis that there is no difference in the average debt-to-equity ratio of firms using the full cost method and firms using the successful efforts method was tested by using the matched-pairs *t*-test. The result of the test of this hypothesis (summarized in Table 1) is that the average debt-to-equity ratio of firms using the full cost method is significantly greater than that of firms using the successful efforts method.[3][4] This finding is consistent with the hypothesis that firms with a high debt-to-equity ratio are more likely than firms with low debt-to-equity ratio to oppose an accounting standard which reduces reported earnings or equity and/or increases fluctuations in reported earnings. Because the experimental design used in this study allowed me to control for the effect of firm size, these results support the hypothesis that the capital structure of the firm is an additional determinant of management's attitude towards accounting standards. In determining the practical importance of the observed significance level of this test, one should consider that the debt-to-equity ratios of full costing firms are understated (relative to those of successful efforts costing firms) because of the capitalization of dry hole costs. The observed differences in the debt-to-equity ratios of the two groups would have been more pronounced if these ratios had been computed for both groups using the same accounting method. Consequently, the finding of statistically significant differences between full costing and successful efforts costing firms of nine percent appears to provide empirical evidence of practical importance in support of the hypothesized effect of financial leverage on management's attitude towards accounting standards.

In order to avoid the effect of the method of accounting for exploration expenses on the debt-to-equity ratios, the differences in the average total amounts of long-term debt between the two groups were examined as an alternative to the previous test. Because the samples have been matched on sales revenue, it is logical to argue that

---

[3] In order to avoid the distributional assumptions of the matched-pairs *t*-test, non-parametric Wilcoxon matched-pairs signed-ranks test was also employed. The results obtained were almost identical.
[4] Debt-to-equity ratio was calculated by dividing long-term debt by total equity.

the size based on assets would be approximately the same for each group if the same accounting method were employed by both of them. This implies that the sum of debt and equity would be approximately the same for each group. Therefore, if the two groups were to have equal debt-to-equity ratios, their total debt must be equal. Assuming that the ratio of long-term debt to total debt is the same for both groups, their long-term debt would be equal. Accordingly, the following hypothesis was tested.

Null Hypothesis:	There is no difference in the average total long-term debt between firms which use the full costing method and those firms which use the successful efforts method.
Alternative Hypothesis:	Firms which use the full costing method have, on the average, higher total long-term debt than those firms which use the succesful efforts method.

The result of the test of this hypothesis is that firms using the full costing method have significantly higher long-term debt than firms which use the successful efforts method. As expected, the significance level observed in this test ($\alpha=.025$) is lower than that observed in the previous test ($\alpha=.09$). Thus, these results confirm my prior results that firms which use a relatively large amount of long-term debt relative to equity tend to oppose accounting standards which reduce the reported earnings or equity and/or increase the variability of reported earnings.

A crucial assumption in this study is that the control on sales revenues is an effective control of size. If the operating characteristics of firms in each sample differ systematically, then the sales/assets ratios of firms in one sample might differ systematically from the same ratios of firms in the other sample. That is, two samples may have different asset sizes.[5] This possibility was examined as described below. In their 1977 annual reports, 19 of the 33 full costing firms reported the approximate reduction in the book value of their respective equities which would have resulted if they were required to change from the full costing method to the successful efforts method of accounting for exploration costs.[6] The reduction reported by each firm was subtracted from its asset size to obtain an approximation of what the asset size of the firm would be under the successful efforts method of accounting. The average of the size measures thus obtained for these full costing firms was compared with the average asset size of the corresponding 19 successful efforts firms, using matched-pair t-test. The result of this test is that firms using the full costing method have a significantly ($\alpha=0.10$) larger asset size than firms using the successful efforts method. The difference between the asset size of the two groups, however, does not diminish the significance of the results of this study. In fact, it strengthens my results. As described previously, prior research shows that, *ceteris paribus,* larger firms tend to support income-reducing accounting standards. The fact that larger firms (*i.e.,* full costing firms) with high financial leverage

---

[5] This possibility was pointed out by one of the reviewers of this paper.

[6] Disclosure of this information was prompted by the issuance of Staff Accounting Bulletin No. 16 by the SEC in September 1977.

opposed an income-reducing accounting standard (SFAS No. 19) is consistent with the hypothesized effect of the capital structure of a firm on management's attitude towards accounting standards.

CONCLUSIONS

The objective of this paper was to examine the impact of the firm's capital structure on management's attitude towards accounting standards. It was argued that an accounting standard which causes a reduction in reported earnings or equity and/or increases volatility of reported earnings may put a firm into technical default under its loan agreements. Therefore, it was hypothesized that highly leveraged firms would be expected to oppose such an accounting standard. The results of this study are consistent with this hypothesis.

REFERENCES

Aristar, Inc., 10-K Report for the Year Ended June 30, 1976.

Arthur Andersen & Co., Report of Arthur Andersen & Co. to the Committee to Permit Producers to Compete in Energy Exploration (March 1978).

Collins, D. W. and W. T. Dent, "An Empirical Assessment of the Stock Market Effects of the Proposed Elimination of Full Cost Accounting in the Extractive Petroleum Industry," *Journal of Accounting and Economics* (Spring, 1979).

Collins, D. W., W. T. Dent, and M. C. O'Connor, "Market Effects of the Elimination of Full Cost Accounting in the Oil and Gas Industries: A Review of Empirical Studies," *Financial Analysts Journal* (forthcoming).

Dyckman, T. R. (1977) with the cooperation of A. J. Smith, "Financial Accounting and Reporting by Oil and Gas Producing Companies: Report on the Effect of the Exposure Draft on the Returns of Oil and Gas Company Securities" (Financial Accounting Standards Board).

Financial Accounting Standards Board (1974), *Reporting the Effects of General Price-Level Changes in Financial Statements,* Discussion Memorandum (February 15, 1974).

Fogelson, J. H., "The Impact of Change in Accounting Principles on Restrictive Covenants in Credit Agreements and Indentures," *The Business Lawyer* (January 1978), pp. 769–87.

Watts, R. L. and J. L. Zimmerman, "Towards a Positive Theory of the Determination of Accounting Standards," *The Accounting Review* (January 1978), pp. 112–34.

Managing Earnings Using an Insurance Subsidiary:
A Case of Restraint by Sears/Allstate*

Roman L. Weil
University of Chicago

Insurance companies report holdings of marketable equity securities at market value on the balance sheet, but only realized gains and losses are shown in the income statement. Unrealized gains (losses) are credited (debited) directly to a balance-sheet owners' equity account. (The treatment of both gains and losses on all of an insurance company's equity holdings is like that required by FASB *Statement No. 12* for losses on long-term investments in equity securities by non-insurance companies).

For example, assume that a portfolio of securities first acquired during Period 0 for $1,000 has a market value of $800 at the end of Period 0. Journal entries for Period 0 are:

Equity securities held as investments 1,000
   Cash 1,000
To record acquisition.
Unrealized loss on investments (owner's equity) 200
Equity securities held as investments 200
To record decline in market value during Period 0. The account debited appears on the
balance sheet as a subtraction from owners' equity. It does not enter reported income for
the year.

Assume that securities originally costing $100 in Period 0 had a market value of $110 at the end of Period 0 and were sold for $150 during Period 1. Assume that the securities remaining in the portfolio at the end of Period 1 originally cost $900 and had market value then of $960. The journal entries for Period 1 are:

Cash 150
   Equity securities held as investments 100
   Realized gain on disposition of investments 50
To recognize realized gain; reported income is
increased by $50 for the year.

Equity securities held as investments 260
   Unrealized loss on investments (owners' equity) 200
   Unrealized gain on investments (owners' equity) 60
To adjust book value of remaining portfolio to market value, to remove the unrealized
loss from owners' equity and to add the unrealized gain to owners' equity. Neither of the
accounts credited appears on the income statement.

The gain reported for the year is the difference between selling price and original cost of the security sold. The adjusting entry at period-end changes the book value

From *The Accounting Review* (October 1980), pp. 680–684. Reprinted by permission of the American Accounting Association.
   *The impetus for writing this note was provided by the author's discussions over several years with the co-author Sidney Davidson and a question by George Getschow of *The Wall Street Journal*.

of the remaining portfolio to its period-end market value. In the example, income for Period 1 was increased by $50 but owners' equity increased by $310 (=$50+$260).

MANAGING EARNINGS OF INSURANCE COMPANIES

Assume that an insurance company has been in business long enough to hold a portfolio of equity securities, some of which have unrealized holding gains (market price increases since acquisition), while others have unrealized losses (market price decreases since acquisition). Its income can be manipulated as follows: if more income is wanted, sell securities with unrealized gains; if less income is wanted, sell securities with unrealized losses. Over long time spans, income can be smoothed, even if it cannot be managed arbitrarily. Limits to income management are imposed by the overall portfolio performance.

A company with an insurance subsidiary accounted for on the equity method (as in the case of Sears and Allstate) can similarly smooth income by timing realizations of gains and losses.

The possibility for managing earnings is removed if all gains and losses, whether realized or not, are treated identically, either all reported in income (as now for realized gains and losses) or all excluded from income (as now for unrealized gains and losses).

ILLUSTRATION FOR SEARS/ALLSTATE

Sears Roebuck and Co. owns 100 percent of Allstate Insurance Company and accounts for its investment using the equity method.[1] Thus, Sears' income includes only the realized gains and losses on Allstate's investments. Sears' assets at the end of 1979 totaled $16.4 billion. These assets included its equity in Allstate of $2.4 billion, while Allstate's assets totaled $8.1 billion.

Figure 1 shows data since 1973, when Allstate changed its disclosures for some investments. Column (4) shows Sears' income as reported, and Column (5) shows the percentage change from year to year in that income. Column (3) shows Allstate's realized gains and losses, after taxes, on its investments in equity securities. Column (1), derived by subtracting Column (3) from Column (4), reports Sears' consolidated income excluding Allstate's realized gains and losses. Column (2) shows the percentage change in Column (1). Column (1) is "unmanageable" operating income, unmanageable at least with respect to the methods discussed here. Column (3) is "manageable."

Column (6) shows the change in market value of the portfolio for the year (unrealized gain or loss), and Column (7) shows the sum of realized, reported income from Column (4) plus the unrealized gain (or less the unrealized loss) from Column (6). Column (7) shows the total economic impact of operations for a year

[1] Using the taxonomy of Burnett *et al.*, [1970, p. 816], Sears' equity method for Allstate is Type B: Equity in the net income (after taxes) of the subsidiary is separately reported as "other income" above tax expense in the consolidated income statement.

FIGURE 1.
Reported and Unreported (but disclosed) Income of Sears Roebuck and Co. and Allstate Insurance Company
(Dollar Amounts in Millions)

Year[a]	Income and (loss) items as reported					Unreported income and loss			Size of manageable income pool at year-end (pretax)		
	Sears' income plus Allstate's operating income		Allstate's aftertax realized investment gains (losses)[b] (3)	Reported total[b]		Allstate's unrealized gains (losses) (6)	Sears' total increase (decrease) in wealth		Unrealized gains on securities with gains (9)	Unrealized (losses) on securities with losses (10)	Net unrealized pretax gains (losses) (11)
	Dollars (1)	% Change (2)		Dollars (4)	% Change (5)		Dollars (7)	% Change (8)			
1973	$653.8	−23.4%	$26.1	$679.9	−24.8%	$(258.7)	$421.2	−78.8%	NR	NR	$ (63.2)
1974	500.6	2.1	10.8	511.4	2.2	(422.1)	89.3	789.6	NR	NR	(498.8)
1975	510.8	34.4	11.8	522.6	32.9	271.8	794.4	3.7	$104.3	$(304.6)	(200.3)
1976	686.5	21.8	8.0	694.5	20.7	129.6	824.1	4.9	140.2	(211.0)	(70.8)
1977	836.3	1.7	1.7	838.0	10.0	26.2	864.2	10.9	128.4	(172.2)	(43.8)
1978	905.5	8.3	16.0	921.5	10.0	36.5	958.0	10.9	156.2	(162.0)	(5.8)
1979	785.2	−13.3	24.9	810.1	−12.1	79.4	889.5	−7.2	234.6	(121.1)	113.5

[a]Year ends on December 31 of this year for Allstate and on January 31 of the next year for Sears.

[b]As originally reported, not as restated in subsequent reports for accounting changes.

NR: Not reported or disclosed.

Column (4): Taken from Sears' income statements.

Columns (3), (6), (9), and (10): Taken from Allstate's financial statements and notes thereto in the Sears' annual reports.

Column (1) = Column (4) − Column (3).

Column (7) = Column (4) + Column (6).

Columns (2), (5), and (8): Computed from preceding column.

Column (11) = Column (9) + Column (10), if not reported.

181

Presumably, Allstate's income could have been smaller by 30 percent before taxes.[2] Of course, these opportunities for income management implicit in the data in plus holdings of investments (but without income-tax effects of unrealized gains and losses). The income reported in Column (7) is "unmanageable" and fluctuates more than the "unmanageable" operating income in Column (1). That is, holding marketable securities injects fluctuations into the earnings of a combined retailer/-insurance underwriter.

Analysis of Sears/Allstate

The data in Columns (9)–(11) show the magnitude of Sears/Allstate's opportunity for managing earnings. Examine 1976, for example. At the end of 1976, Allstate had $140.0 million of unrealized gains in its portfolio. Presumably, Allstate's and, hence Sears', income could have been larger by up to 20 percent before taxes. Similarly, at the end of 1976, Allstate had $211.8 million of unrealized losses in its portfolio. Columns (9)—(11) are not independent of each other. If, for example, Allstate had realized all of the gains available at the end of 1976, there would have been substantially smaller (perhaps zero) unrealized gains at the end of 1977.

  In the circumstances, I am impressed at the absence of apparent attempts to smooth Sears' income by using realized gains and losses in Allstate's investment portfolio.[3] While the variance in percentage changes reported in Column (5) about its long-run average is less than that for column (2), the difference is small. There does seem to be some attempt to smooth, but the evidence is ambiguous.[4]

  Notice, however, how generally accepted accounting principles mask the economic reality reported in Columns (7) and (8), where total income, realized plus unrealized, is shown to be substantially more variable than is realized income. As a member of the efficient markets school, I am unimpressed by statements such as the following, taken from Sears' 1974 annual report:

> In the absence of operating or investment reasons compelling liquidation, it is inappropriate to reflect in income temporary fluctuations in market values of long-term equity invest-

---

  [2] These percentages are calculated before allowing for the effect of any income tax assessed against the gains and losses, once they are realized. The effective income tax rate on such gains and losses is difficult to estimate prior to realization, and it is possible, by timing the realization of gains and losses judiciously, that the effective rate could be far below the statutory rate.
  [3] It has been pointed out that an insurable company has another opportunity, related to its portfolio, for manipulating earnings that I neither thought of originally nor have investigated after having been informed. Assume a portfolio that originally consisted of low-dividend "growth" stocks. Consider converting that portfolio to one consisting primarily of high-yielding, dividend-paying stocks. The reported income would increase each year because of increased dividends, which are "realized earnings." For a given total return, there is a compensating decline in unrealized gains of the sort reported directly with credits to owners' equity accounts. For a given total return, the total of owners' equity (excluding tax effects) does not change, but the amount of reported income can be increased. The cause of the increase is not so obvious as it is with sales of securities to realize capital gains.
  [4] Others have examined the same evidence and drawn different conclusions, e.g., "Dipping into the Allstate venture capital pool enabled Sears to report only a 3.4% drop in earnings [for the first quarter of 1979] and hold up the price of its stock [sic]. This is not the first time Sears has bolstered company earnings with Allstate's venture capital gains, but it was the largest cash [sic] infusion to date; in the recession years of 1973–75, the nation's largest retailer reportedly siphoned several million venture capital dollars..." (See Elsner, [1980, p. 35].)

ments. Consequently, investment results exclude unrealized market decreases in equity investments....

I do not oppose the non-reporting of short-term temporary fluctuations. I deny that the management of Sears or Allstate (or any other management for that matter) can identify which fluctuations are temporary. Any management that can distinguish temporary from permanent fluctuations in market prices of securities is in the wrong business. They should be buying securities where market prices are temporarily depressed.

REFERENCES

Burnett, T., T. E. King, and V. C. Lembke, (1979), "Equity Method Reporting for Major Finance Company Subsidiaries," *The Accounting Review* (October 1979), pp. 815–23.

Elsner, D. M. (1980), "How Entrepreneurs Fare at Allstate," *Venture* (February 1980), pp. 34–39.

HOW MUCH AND WHAT KIND OF DISCLOSURE?

During the last 15 years, questions relating to the extent of corporate financial disclosures have come under searching review. The Securities and Exchange Commission sponsored two reports during the period:

"Disclosure to Investors: A Reappraisal of Federal Administrative Policies Under the '33 and '34 Acts" (The Wheat Report)—undertaken by a small, internal study group chaired by Commissioner Francis M. Wheat and completed in 1969; and

"Report of the Advisory Committee on Corporate Disclosure"—undertaken by a committee composed of 16 public members and completed in 1977.

Over the years, either the APB/FASB or SEC has mandated footnote disclosures in such areas as stock options, long-term leases, earnings per share, discontinued operations, business segments (both product line and geographical), significant accounting policies, and income taxes. In 1974, the SEC began to require registrants to include a narrative section entitled "Management's Discussion and Analysis of the Results of Operations in Filings with the Commission," and in 1980 the SEC announced that this section must appear in the annual report to shareholders. In 1979 the FASB invented the "unaudited footnote," which contains the inflation accounting disclosures required by SFAS No. 33.

The trend in recent years has been to provide readers of U.S. financial reports with a broader array of interpretive and supporting information that facilitates a deeper understanding of a company's operations and of the repercussions on its future operations of decisions already made. Included in this broader array has been "subjective" information that was forbidden by the SEC prior to the early 1970s. Beginning in the early 1970s, such subjective information as management forecasts and replacement cost disclosures was countenanced and even encouraged by the commission. In other countries, especially in Europe, social responsibility reports and value added statements have come to be seen with greater frequency.

In "Emerging Trends in Financial Reporting," John C. Burton, former SEC chief accountant and a close student of financial reporting developments, reviews the major areas in which changes have been occurring in the contents of U.S. corporate financial reports. In most of the areas covered by Burton, disclosure outside of the basic financial statements has either been mandated or is being contemplated. At the outset of his article, Burton suggests reasons for the "steady erosion of the relative importance of financial statements" in the context of the total financial reporting package.

In "What Should Be the FASB's Objectives?," William H. Beaver, a pioneer in the academic literature on efficient capital markets as it relates to accounting policy making, describes the implications of efficient-markets research for accounting standard setting. The APB, Beaver contends, needlessly consumed time and energy to determine whether to flow-through or defer the investment tax credit. Where there is little cost to the company in reporting either method, and where there is little cost to users in adjusting from one method to the other, the efficient-markets solution is to report either method in the financial statements and provide sufficient footnote information to enable users to adjust to the other method. The choice of *which* method is not important. According to Beaver, the policy-making body should "shift its resources to those controversies where there is nontrivial additional cost to the firms or to investors in order to obtain certain types of information (for example, replacement cost accounting for depreciable assets)."

Jacob G. Birnberg discusses the problem of "information overload" in "Human Information Processing and Financial Disclosure." Policy makers should not unquestioningly accept the dictum that more disclosure is better than less, as the load may be too heavy for all but the most "abstract" information processors. Birnberg proposes several guides for policy makers, including the suggestion that the ultimate test of the benefit of incremental disclosure is its relevance to the decision at hand.

Michael F. Morley, in "The Value Added Statement in Britain," examines the advantages and disadvantages of a financial statement that has, since 1975, come to appear in the annual reports of a significant number of large British companies. The suggestion for such a report was floated in *The Corporate Report,* prepared by a working party of the United Kingdom's Accounting Standards Steering Committee. In 1977, the Labour Government issued "A Consultative Document" in which it asserted that "the added value statement is [in the Government's view] a useful addition to the financial information produced by companies."[1] (The Conservative government of Margaret Thatcher, since taking over in 1979, has not reasserted this view.) As Morley indicates, the existence of a Value Added Tax in Britain "has led to an increased awareness of the meaning of VA." A value added statement has also been said to contribute to better employer-employee relations. The statement is a

---

[1] *The Future of Company Reports,* A Consultative Document, Cmnd. 6888 (London: Her Majesty's Stationery Office, 1977), Par. 13.

novel form of disclosure and constitutes, in the main, a reorganization of the contents of the income statement, by placing emphasis on wealth creation. It is difficult to forecast whether value added statements will take hold in North America. From time to time, U.S. fiscal policy specialists have suggested the enactment of a Value Added Tax, and if the United States does move in this direction, it might be that value added statements would not be far behind.

BIBLIOGRAPHICAL NOTES

Expanded disclosure requirements have been proposed in a number of areas, including the following:

Human Resource Accounting

Flamholtz, Eric: *Human Resource Accounting* (Encino, CA: Dickenson Publishing Company, Inc., 1974).

Social Responsibility Reporting

Committee on Social Measurement: *The Measurement of Social Performance* (New York: AICPA, 1977).

Estes, Ralph W.: *Corporate Social Accounting* (New York: John Wiley & Sons, Inc., 1976).

Schoenfeld, Hanns-Martin (ed.): *The Status of Social Reporting in Selected Countries*, Occasional Paper Number 1, Contemporary Issues in International Accounting (Urbana, IL: Center for International Education and Research in Accounting, University of Illinois at Urbana-Champaign, 1978).

Accounting, Organizations and Society, published by Pergamon Press. (This journal frequently carries articles on social reporting. Issues containing several such articles are Volume 4, Numbers 1/2 [1979] and Volume 6, Number 3 [1981].)

Schreuder, Hein: "Employees and the Corporate Social Report: The Dutch Case," *The Accounting Review* (April 1981), pp. 294–308.

Forecasts

Prakash, Prem and Alfred Rappaport (eds.): *Public Reporting of Corporate Financial Forecasts* (Chicago, IL: Commerce Clearing House, Inc., 1974).

Disclosure of Corporate Forecasts to the Investor (New York: The Financial Analysts Federation, 1973).

Public Disclosure of Business Forecasts (New York: Financial Executives Research Foundation, 1972).

Segment Reporting

Mautz, R. K.: *Financial Reporting by Diversified Companies* (New York: Financial Executives Research Foundation, 1968).

Rappaport, Alfred, Peter A. Firmin, and Stephen A. Zeff (eds.). *Public Reporting by Conglomerates* (Englewood Cliffs, NJ: Prentice-Hall, Inc., 1968).

Rappaport, Alfred and Eugene M. Lerner: *Segment Reporting for Managers and Investors* (New York: National Association of Accountants, 1972).

Backer, Morton and Walter B. McFarland: *External Reporting for Segments of a Business* (New York: National Association of Accountants, 1968).
Analysed Reporting (London: The Institute of Chartered Accountants in England and Wales, 1977).

Value Added

Morley, Michael F.: *The Value Added Statement* (London: Gee & Co. [Publishers] Limited, 1978).
Gray, Sidney J. and Keith T. Maunders: *Value Added Reporting: Uses and Measurement* (London: Association of Certified Accountants, 1980).

(Inflation accounting disclosures are considered in Section 8.)

The following work contains a collection of papers dealing with some of the foregoing topics and others:

Lee, Thomas A. (ed.): *Developments in Financial Reporting* (Deddington, Oxford, England: Philip Allan Publishers, 1981).

A study that explores the institutional, legal, and conceptual considerations that should be taken into account when comparing the financial disclosure frameworks in the United States and the United Kingdom is:

Benston, George J.: *Corporate Financial Disclosure in the UK and the USA* (Westmead, Hants., England: Saxon House, D.C. Heath Ltd. and Lexington, MA: Lexington Books, D.C. Heath & Co., 1976).

For a research study involving a questionnaire survey of financial executives and financial analysts on the relationship between financial disclosure and competitive disadvantage, see:

Mautz, R. K. and William G. May: *Financial Disclosure in a Competitive Economy* (New York: Financial Executives Research Foundation, 1978).

Emerging Trends in Financial Reporting

John C. Burton
Columbia University

For the past decade, the financial reporting environment has been in a state of rapid evolution, and the current activities of the Financial Accounting Standards Board, the Securities and Exchange Commission and governmental accountants suggest that this process is continuing. Under such circumstances, it seems important to step back to try to gain a perspective on the direction of the changes taking place. Understanding the consequences of official pronouncements means not only being aware of their issuance but also recognizing the motivating factors behind them. Furthermore, if the profession is to avoid facing the future with misguided expectations and obsolete skills, the shifts in the financial reporting environment should be closely monitored.

CHANGING ROLE OF FINANCIAL STATEMENTS

One of the most significant changes in financial reporting is the steady erosion of the relative importance of financial statements. At one time, financial statements were the whole of financial reporting. Over the past decade, however, more financial reporting innovation has taken place outside the financial statements. This tendency is partly the result of efforts by the accounting profession and the corporate reporting community to reduce their legal exposure and partly in recognition of the deficiencies of the financial statement format for purposes of communicating uncertain, interpretive and subjective data. In addition, the hesitation of both the FASB and the SEC to try to substantially reduce the major elements of inconsistency now existing among financial statements as a result of alternative accounting treatments of some major items has contributed to the relative decline in the statements' importance in achieving the FASB's articulated objectives of financial reporting.

This fundamental change is evidenced by a number of pronouncements and actions taken in recent years. It is significant, for example, that FASB Financial Accounting Concepts Statement no. 1, *Objectives of Financial Reporting by Business Enterprises,*[1] was directed at the objectives of financial reporting rather than at financial statement objectives, which was the charge of the committee chaired by Robert M. Trueblood a few years earlier whose work served as the basis for most FASB conclusions.[2] In its 1977 report,[3] the SEC Advisory Committee on Corporate

From *The Journal of Accountancy* (July 1981), pp. 54–56, 58, 60–62, 64, 66. Reprinted by permission of the American Institute of Certified Public Accountants. Copyright © 1981 by the American Institute of Certified Public Accountants, Inc.

[1] Financial Accounting Standards Board Financial Accounting Concepts Statement no. 1, *Objectives of Financial Reporting by Business Enterprises* (Stamford, Conn.: FASB, 1978).

[2] Study Group on the Objectives of Financial Statements, *Objectives of Financial Statements* (New York: AICPA, 1973).

[3] "SEC Corporate Disclosure Group Issues Final Report," Journal of Accountancy, Dec. 77, pp. 22, 24.

Disclosure further emphasized the need for interpretation and analysis of results by management in its discussion of operations, and the commission's significant enlargement of the requirements for management's discussion and analysis of operations[4] adopted in fall 1980 continued the process of implementing the advisory committee's recommendations.

The FASB also has issued a number of its important standards dealing with information not required to be included in the basic financial statements. FASB Statement no. 33, *Financial Reporting and Changing Prices*[5] (and three statements which expand it to certain specific industries[6]) requires disclosures only outside the financial statements. Business segment reporting also is not required in the basic statements or notes, although the board does view the separate disclosures required by Statement no. 14, *Financial Reporting for Segments of a Business Enterprise*[7] as "an integral part of the financial statements." Both the FASB and the SEC now seem willing to permit disclosure of oil and gas reserve data outside the financial statements, and both are exercising great restraint in responding to the congressional mandate for a single method of accounting for the historical costs related to oil and gas production.

The result of this trend ultimately seems likely to make the financial statements increasingly a well-defined ritual where objective data are arrayed without great regard for their relevance. The most important and relevant information for investment decision making will be presented supplementally, and management will be assigned a reporting role of greater significance in interpreting results, performing some of the functions previously assigned to the user of financial statements.

The impact of this trend on the role of the FASB and the auditing role of the public accounting profession is still in the process of evolution. The FASB has clearly attempted to expand its turf to consider the broader field of financial reporting although it still spends a large part of its time on issues directly related to the financial statements. The conceptual framework effort deals with issues such as relevance and the use of financial reporting to predict future cash flows, but also with specific issues such as the formatting of the income statement.

I hope the conceptual framework, when finally completed, will help the board sort out the issues and provide a matrix of sorts in which its decision-making process can be set. To date, the board's determination to seek consensus and to avoid threatening its various constituencies has led it to defer some of the hard decisions about the conceptual framework. In the next two years, some of these decisions must be made if the framework is to have any meaning. While no one with reasonable expectations believes that the framework will resolve all specific issues,

---

[4]See "New SEC Rulings on Disclosures Change Annual Reports and Other Forms," p. 84.

[5]FASB Statement no. 33, *Financial Reporting and Changing Prices* (Stamford, Conn.: FASB, 1979).

[6]FASB Statement no. 39, *Financial Reporting and Changing Prices: Specialized Assets—Mining and Oil and Gas* (Stamford, Conn.: FASB, 1980); FASB Statement no. 40, *Financial Reporting and Changing Prices: Specialized Assets—Timberlands and Growing Timber* (Stamford, Conn.: FASB, 1980); and FASB Statement no. 41, *Financial Reporting and Changing Prices: Specialized Assets—Income-Producing Real Estate* (Stamford, Conn.: FASB, 1980).

[7]FASB Statement no. 14, *Financial Reporting for Segments of a Business Enterprise* (Stamford, Conn.: FASB, 1976).

it has the potential for providing decision guidelines to the board that should enhance (but certainly not ensure) the consistency and neutrality of its standard-setting efforts. From this, the role of financial statements and other financial reporting should emerge with greater clarity.

The impact of changing reporting trends on the auditor is more difficult to predict. Auditors are torn between their desire to be an important part of the reporting action and their concern about the potential liabilities they may incur by so doing. To date, the auditing standards board of the American Institute of CPAs has addressed this issue several times with ambivalent results, and it seems likely that, in the absence of a major reconstruction of the auditor's role, this conflict will continue.

FUTURE-ORIENTED REPORTING

Related to the growth in supplemental information is the increasing emphasis on the future-oriented objectives of financial reporting. Over the past decade, there has been substantial movement toward articulating the importance of financial data in the predictive process and decreasing the emphasis on the stewardship role of statements. The FASB, following the lead of the Trueblood committee, described the principal objective of financial reporting as providing information which would assist investors in predicting the amount, timing and uncertainty of future cash flows to the company. While the board emphasized that this objective did not imply explicit forecasts, it clearly suggested an obligation of preparers and auditors to be aware of investors' uses of the statements in their forecasting processes.

During the decade, the SEC has evidenced consistent and continuing interest in the forecasting process and the role of financial statements in it. In 1971, then Chairman William Casey indicated that the commission's historical policy of rejecting forecasts of all kinds in disclosure documents was "not cast in stone," and he initiated hearings on projections in 1972 that led to a statement of policy in 1973 which officially lifted the ban on forecasts and adopted a neutral attitude toward them. In 1974, the commission adopted a requirement for the presentation of a management discussion and analysis of the summary of operations that would, among other things, require management to discuss any "material facts, whether favorable or unfavorable,... which in the opinion of management may make historical operations or earnings as reported... not indicative of current or future operations or earnings."[8] In 1977, the Advisory Committee on Corporate Disclosure recommended that the commission move from a policy of neutrality on forecasts to one of encouragement, and, in 1979, the commission adopted this recommendation.[9] It then adopted a "safe harbor rule," which offered legal protection to those who did

[8]Securities and Exchange Commission Accounting Series Release no. 159, *Notice of Adoption of Amendments to Guide 22 of the Guides for Preparation and Filing of Registration Statements Under the Securities Act of 1933 and Adoption Guide 1 of the Guides for Preparation and Filing of Reports and Registration Statements Under the Securities Exchange Act of 1934 (Textual Analysis of Summary of Earnings or Operations),* August 14, 1979.

[9]SEC Release no. 33–5992, *Guides for Disclosure of Projections of Future Economic Performance,* November 7, 1978.

prepare and disclose forecasts in good faith even if they were not subsequently achieved.

Finally, in the fall of 1980, the SEC adopted a substantial expansion of the requirement for management's discussion and analysis which further emphasized the requirement for a discussion of future-oriented variables. The new requirement, included as item 11 in regulation S-K, calls for a description of "any known trends or uncertainties which have had or which the registrant reasonably expects will have a material favorable or unfavorable impact on net sales or revenues or income from continuing operations."[10] The instructions which accompany this requirement include the following:

> The discussion and analysis should specifically focus on material events and uncertainties known to management which would cause reported financial information not to be necessarily indicative of future operating results or of future financial condition. This would include description and amounts of (a) matters which would have an impact on future operations and have not had an impact in the past, and (b) matters which have had an impact on reported operations and are not expected to have an impact upon future operations.[11]

Perhaps of equal importance to the adoption of rules is the indication of the commission's staff that monitoring compliance with the intent of this requirement will be a major priority of the Division of Corporation Finance in 1981 and 1982. The director of the division has indicated in seminars that his staff will be issuing helpful and constructive comments on disclosures made and on occasion seeking additional information regarding the disclosures. He has suggested that if internal company forecasts show any substantial deviation from the trend line fitted to the past year's sales and income from continuing operations, a disclosure obligation exists, and he has indicated that the division staff will be paying special attention to cases where significant changes in sales and earnings are observed if there is no indication of such changes in the previous year's management discussion and analysis of operations.

These various developments suggest that the trend toward future-oriented disclosure is not likely to abate. It seems likely that the FASB will be testing accounting principles adopted in the future by the degree to which they assist in the predictive process, and the more controversial issue of required explicit forecasting will receive continued attention both from the board and the SEC.

LIQUIDITY DISCLOSURE

The emphasis on future cash flows has also led to increasing attention to liquidity and the problems of reporting funds flows in a business. These areas are currently receiving consideration at both the FASB and the SEC, and this examination is likely to lead to substantial changes in historical reporting patterns.

---

[10]SEC Regulation S-K, *Part 229—Standard Instructions for Filing Forms Under Securities Act of 1933 and Securities Exchange Act of 1934.* December 23, 1977; item 11, par. 3ii, of reg. 229.20, September 2, 1980.

[11]Ibid., par. 3iv, "Instructions," par. 3.

The SEC has had an interest in funds flows for a number of years. In 1973, the commission noted its concern that some companies were using "cash flow" as a proxy for income measurement and prohibited the presentation of cash flow per share data; at the same time the SEC noted the importance of funds flow analysis in reflecting managerial decisions about the use of funds generated and the sources of this capital.[12] Former Chairman Harold M. Williams frequently expressed his view that the analysis of cash inflows and outflows might be of greater use to investors than conventional income measurement.

In its rules adopted in September 1980,[13] the commission specifically mandated new disclosures about liquidity, capital resources and financial position. In its expanded management's discussion requirements, the SEC directed management to discuss the registrant's financial condition and changes in financial condition as well as results of operations. The discussion is to include an analysis of the company's liquidity and capital resources as well as any other information necessary to understand its financial condition. This disclosure should identify any known trends or known demands, commitments, events or uncertainties likely to result in any material increase or decrease in liquidity. If a material deficiency is identified, the registrant is to indicate the course of action management has taken or proposes to take to remedy the deficiency. Also, the SEC has charged management to identify sources of liquidity and briefly describe and discuss any material unused sources of liquid assets. These directives impose comprehensive, tight disclosure requirements on many companies.

The rule also required disclosure of the company's capital resources. The registrant is to describe any material commitments for capital expenditures as of the end of the latest fiscal period. The disclosure is to indicate the general purpose of such commitments and the anticipated source of funds needed to fulfill them. This is to be followed by a description of any new material trends, both favorable and unfavorable, in the company's capital resources. Also to be disclosed are any indications of expected material changes in the mix and the relative costs of resources. The management discussion is to include changes in equity, debt and any off-balance-sheet financial arrangements.

It is important to be aware that the SEC, in adopting these rules on liquidity disclosure, is not designing regulations to force registrants to compute a lot of ratios. It is looking at liquidity in dynamic terms: as funds flows, financial flexibility and the ability of the company to meet commitments and its plans for meeting commitments.

It would have been useful if the SEC had laid out the conceptual underpinnings of its liquidity and capital resource requirements. Item 11 in regulation S-K defines liquidity as "the ability of an enterprise to generate adequate amounts of cash to meet the enterprise's needs for cash" and says that liquidity should be discussed on both a long-term and a short-term basis.[14] Presumably, therefore, the objective is to

[12] SEC ASR no. 142, *Reporting Cash Flow and Other Related Data,* March 15, 1973.
[13] SEC ASR no. 279, *Amendments to Annual Report Form, Related Forms, Rules, Regulations and Guides: Integration of Securities Acts Disclosure Systems,* September 2, 1980.
[14] SEC reg. S-K, item 11, par 3iv, "Instructions," par. 5.

help investors recognize potential constraints on a company's activities. In a sense, the traditional pattern of warning about potential difficulties rather than emphasizing opportunities is still evident. However, it seems likely that the commission is equally interested in the implications of liquidity for future success. If such was the objective, one would have hoped that greater emphasis might have been placed on the characteristics of expected future investments, with some indication whether that level would simply sustain current operating levels or provide for real economic growth. The commission's recent further encouragement of capital expenditure projections,[15] in which the commission expressed its belief that projections of capital expenditures are "extremely meaningful," suggests the direction in which the commission intends liquidity disclosure to move.

In December 1980, the FASB, also working in the area of funds flow and liquidity, produced a discussion memorandum entitled *Reporting Funds Flows, Liquidity, and Financial Flexibility.*[16] In it the FASB lays out some fundamental issues in regard to what a funds statement should show and just what it should be. It raises such basic problems as whether to retain the old definition of funds as working capital or to redefine funds as liquid assets. It questions whether the funds statement should be segmented in more ways than is the current practice. It asks whether more information should be required about capital expenditures. It suggests that perhaps capital expenditures should be broken into those for maintaining current capacity, those for increasing capacity and those for complying with environmental and other regulations. It is likely that one of the results of this discussion will be the adoption of a radically different funds statement, perhaps as early as next year. At a minimum, information will be presented in a different format, and additional information regarding the areas noted above will be included.

As a result of this activity in both Washington, D.C., and Stamford, Connecticut, users of financial reporting are likely to see much more data about cash inflows and outflows. This does not mean, however, that income will be ignored. The FASB has frequently noted that income or some segment of it may be the best measure of future cash flows, and, accordingly, the board is currently working on the reformatting of the income statement. It seems likely that what will emerge from this process is some segmentation of income into separate recurring and non-recurring segments, perhaps with the exclusion of certain items from any income definition. The board's Financial Accounting Concepts Statement no. 3, *Elements of Financial Statements of Business Enterprises,*[17] identifies an all-inclusive concept of comprehensive income, defined as the change in equity resulting from all non-owner sources. Other definitions leave unanswered the question of what items will be identified as the components of comprehensive income, such as earnings, operating results, etc. Many arguments remain to be resolved in this area, despite the fact that most of the research on efficient markets suggests that a lot of effort in reformatting financial reporting is

---

[15]SEC Release no. 33–6293, *Revision of Property, Plant and Equipment Disclosure Requirements,* February 25, 1981.

[16]FASB Discussion Memorandum, *Reporting Funds Flows, Liquidity, and Financial Flexibility* (Stamford, Conn.: FASB, December 15, 1980).

[17]FASB Financial Accounting Concepts Statement no. 3, *Elements of Financial Statements of Business Enterprises* (Stamford, Conn.: FASB, 1980).

not of enormous benefit, since the market seems able to see through format and accounting differences in financial reporting.

INFLATION ACCOUNTING

Issues of funds flow, income measurement and future orientation of reporting all are influenced by the significant changes in the environment caused by rapidly changing prices. Inflation in many respects has dominated accounting issues in recent years, and unfortunately it seems likely to do so in the years to come. With price stability, predictability of results is enhanced, funds flows and income flows tend to come together in the long run and the implicit assumption of accounting that a dollar of cost produces a dollar of value has relative stability over time. Under inflationary conditions, however, the weaknesses of accounting are magnified and the traditional accounting model cannot be applied without distortions appearing in virtually every application where significant time lags occur in recording related events.

Since double digit inflation first appeared in the U.S. in 1974–75, both the FASB and the SEC have been active in trying to ensure that investors obtain information which will enable them to determine the effect of changing prices on business enterprises. The SEC adopted ASR no. 190[18] in 1976 requiring supplemental disclosure of replacement cost data relating to inventories, fixed assets, cost of sales and depreciation. In 1979, the FASB adopted Statement no. 33, which supplanted ASR no. 190 and required supplemental disclosure, either in footnotes or a separate section, of general price level adjusted data (the constant dollar approach) and current cost data (which reflect the current costs of the particular products being manufactured or sold and the current cost of facilities.)

The 1980 annual reports of large companies for the first time include all the data mandated by Statement no. 33. These reports provide required supplemental data in a variety of formats, and researchers are now beginning the process of analyzing the information. The FASB has proposed a research plan that will include the creation of a data bank to assist researchers in appraising the data and testing hypotheses regarding its usefulness.

Users are now developing techniques for the interpretation of the data. Some are most concerned with the asset valuation implications. Statement no. 33 data more accurately reflect the value of assets, which has been gravely distorted in financial statements by the use of historical cost and nominal dollars. Current cost disclosure provides data for at least an approximation of the current cost of inventories and property, plant and equipment. Current cost is not the equivalent of the assets' current market price and is therefore not their liquidation value, but it does offer an approximation of what the assets might be worth in an operating entity. Other analysts are looking for more stable relationships between income statement variables when current costs are used and for better approximations of future cash flows. As experience is gained and research completed, a more systematic picture of the value

---

[18]ASR no. 190, *Notice of Adoption of Amendments to Regulation S-X Requiring Disclosure of Certain Replacement Cost Data,* March 23, 1976

of these data will emerge, and conclusions can then be drawn about the feasibility of revising the basic accounting model.

Up to the present, it is rather strange that more time and effort have been devoted by the accounting profession to developing measurement techniques to reflect inflation's effect on financial statements than seems to have been spent by management in creating techniques for managing in an inflationary environment. Only recently have some managements begun to consider the use of the measurement techniques to provide data for planning and operating decisions. In the next few years, it is likely that greater development will come in this area than in external financial reporting.

Any management can deal with inflation intuitively as long as the rate is both known and predictable, even if the rate is high. The major managerial problems arise when the rate is uncertain and variable. Under such conditions, techniques must be developed to deal with a dynamic environment and minimize the impact of change, and here sophisticated measurement and analytical techniques must be developed. Managers must pay more attention to asset and liability balance relationships as well as budgeting operating fund flows. Controls must factor in diverse inflationary assumptions, and the sensitivity of results to changing prices must be known, particularly when long-run investment decisions are being made.

While the managerial impact is based primarily on the unexpected variability of the inflation rate, the direction taken in inflation accounting for external reporting purposes is probably dependent on the average level of the rate of inflation. If the rate should drop to 5 percent, a lot of today's important issues will recede. If the rate goes up to 30 percent, there will probably be mounting pressure for including inflation-adjusted numbers in basic financial statements. By way of illustration, the United Kingdom, with a higher basic inflation rate, now gives companies the option of presenting current cost data either in the basic financial statements or as supplemental data. Both historical and current cost are required, but the company is allowed to choose the presentation method.

PENSION COST

Since inflation causes the greatest accounting problems when a long time span exists between the point where measurement is required and that where cash is transferred, it is not surprising that the FASB is faced with difficulties in the pension accounting area. To date the board has faced only the problem of how pension plans themselves should account. In the near future, however, it must face the far more significant problem of how pension costs should be accounted for by employers, and it is here where the most controversy will arise. Decisions made by the board in this area will likely have the largest effect on reported results of any faced in the decade of the 1980s, since the proportion of compensation represented by deferrals is growing steadily.

Unfortunately, the board's record in dealing with the lesser problem of pension plan liabilities does not provide much confidence that analysts' interest in the approach leading to the most valid prediction of long-run future cash flows will be well served. In 1980, when the FASB issued Statement no. 35, *Accounting and*

Reporting by Defined Benefit Pension Plans,[19] it had to make a number of significant decisions. First, it decided that in pension fund accounts assets must be carried at market value. When considering how to measure the liability for pensions in the pension fund's accounts (not the corporation's statements), the board then had three choices to make. All three of its decisions served to minimize the liability reported by these funds.

First, the FASB mandated use of an accrued benefit method. This in effect means that instead of charging an equal amount each year to build up the amount that will be paid at retirement, the fund will record an amount the first year which will ultimately accrue, by compounding, into an amount sufficient to pay a proportionate share of the value of the payment needed at retirement under the plan's terms. The board thus says that in earlier years a smaller amount is recorded as an increase to the fund's liability and in later years more must be added than under other methods. The result is that the use of the so-called accrued benefit method tends to make the reported liability small in relation to the liability measured in economic terms based on the most likely payments.

Second, the FASB opted for using current salary levels in making the estimate of future disbursements for pensions. That means that even though a pension plan may say that a pension is based on salaries in the last three years prior to retirement, the estimates do not include any provisions for increased salaries resulting from inflation.

Third, the FASB decided that current rates of return are to be used in computing the discount factor. Since current rates of return take inflation into account, they are certainly higher than a pure monetary rate of return, but the salaries used to figure the benefits—the outflows in this actuarial calculation—don't take inflation into account. Thus, each of the FASB's three choices tended to lower the fund's liability.

As the board proceeds with its re-examination of pension issues from the perspective of the employer, it will face a number of these issues again as it evaluates the problem of pension cost. It has indicated that employer cost and the related question of pension liabilities are not simply mirror images of pension plan accounting by issuing a discussion memorandum which addresses issues without the presumption that employer accounting will follow from the decisions made in Statement no. 35. As this project progresses to its scheduled completion in 1983, the board will be faced with significant decisions. If it adopts a similar liability approach to that in Statement no. 35, it will necessarily adopt a measure of pension costs which is loaded toward the closing years of an employee's service, thus allocating this important element of compensation disproportionately over this period. If, as seems likely, companies conform their accounting and their cash contributions to the plan, this will mean that a significant cash outflow will occur in later periods, perhaps affecting the firm's long-run liquidity and financial flexibility. Even if a company elected to pay out cash in a different pattern, the accounting method based on Statement no. 35 would overstate earning power by failing to reflect a realistic

---

[19]FASB Statement no. 35, *Accounting and Reporting by Defined Benefit Pension Plans* (Stamford, Conn.: FASB, 1980).

pension cost. I hope that the board will listen to the concerns expressed by analysts and others and develop an approach to cost measurement which reflects pension cost at a level at least equal to an equal percentage of pay over working life. The issues are not simple—they are highly technical and warrant serious attention because of the magnitude of these costs in the future.

FOREIGN CURRENCY TRANSLATION

The obvious troubles caused by inflation in measuring financial position and results of operations domestically are compounded when an enterprise is subject to various rates of price change throughout the world fluctuating relatively with each other and then is faced with the necessity of translating these results into a single currency unit for presentation to stockholders and other investors. It is not surprising, therefore, that foreign currency translation has caused no end of difficulty for the FASB and other standard-setting bodies around the world.

There is little question that of all the statements published by the FASB, the one that is most faithful to the historical cost accounting model, and the one that is most rigorously logical, is Statement no. 8, *Accounting for the Translation of Foreign Currency Transactions and Foreign Currency Financial Statements.*[20] Its requirements provide fundamental, theoretical consistency with today's accounting model. There is a general perception, however, that its application does not produce economic information which makes sense. In large part the complaints relate to deficiencies in the accounting model but in this case they reached a crescendo which required board attention. To do something about the statement, the FASB had a range of choices which basically fell into two categories.

One option was to tinker with Statement no. 8 and try to make some changes that would ameliorate some of the perceived problems. The other was to make a very fundamental change in the basic principles of consolidations and foreign currency translation. In its first exposure draft, the FASB opted for the second approach. It made fundamental changes. It moved from the so-called temporal method, where items were reflected on the basis of historical cost and exchange rates when assets were acquired, to a current exchange rate basis. In effect, therefore, current value accounting was introduced, at least as far as foreign currencies were concerned. This was inconsistent with the accounting model, but many found the approach to be more understandable.

This change did not solve the problem of removing large and unstable translation gains and losses from income but simply reflected gains and losses on equity investment rather than on net liquid assets investment. To deal with fluctuations, the FASB made another surprising decision. It offered up the long discredited direct charge to surplus and said in the exposure draft that gains and losses on foreign currency translations (those that arise from the accounting process) may be charged into a separate surplus account and need not appear in the income statement. These were two very fundamental changes. They prejudged a number of issues that the

---

[20]FASB Statement no. 8, *Accounting for the Translation of Foreign Currency Transactions and Foreign Currency Financial Statements* (Stamford, Conn.: FASB, 1975).

conceptual framework was to address, and various people were very critical. After hearings last December, which failed to produce a clear majority of views among commentators or board members, FASB Chairman Donald J. Kirk said that the board may have to withdraw the draft for reconsideration. The board will issue a new exposure draft, and it is unlikely that any statement will be effective until calendar year 1983.[21]

MUNICIPAL ACCOUNTING

A final area of financial reporting which is generating controversy and activity at present and which seems likely to be a place where considerable accounting innovation and change will occur in the 1980s is state and local governmental accounting. There seems to be general agreement that state and local governmental financial reporting is deficient, and that it does not provide a sound basis for economic accountability. What is not clear is how this problem should be dealt with. There are broad disagreements both about accounting and reporting issues and about what entity should take responsibility for standard setting in the area.

The "turf" issue is most active at the present time. The FASB views its franchise as broad and believes that it is an appropriate extension of its authority to set standards for governmental units. The representatives of government view this as dangerous, unsatisfactory and unconstitutional. Accordingly, people in the government have said they will resist standards set by the FASB. Basically they argue that those in government know most about its problems and therefore should be the ones to make determinations regarding standards of accountability. This logic was rejected long ago in the private sector. There was a time when it was argued that it should be companies and financial officers who set accounting standards; since then the consensus has held that the authority is best vested in an independent body.

A recent suggestion by a committee made up of members of the AICPA and governmental organizations that a governmental accounting standards board be created seems to be a grave error. Someone with an independent perspective should make standards decisions and the creation of two standards boards will lead to continuing conflicts and possibly the weakening of the FASB. Although testimony at recent hearings held by the committee on its proposal resulted in diverse views, no one stepped forward to provide financing for the proposed GASB, nor were "turf" issues resolved.

Underlying the controversy is a fundamental substantive issue regarding the differences which exist between governmental and nongovernmental accounting. Views range from extreme positions that see no similarities on the one hand and no differences on the other. Actually, a middle ground seems likely to emerge. It is clear that governmental accounting does not have a qualitative bottom line such as net income and that performance in the public sector requires a balancing of intransitive service efforts and service outputs. At the same time, cost measurement in economic

[21]"FASB Statement no. 8 Replacement May Not Take Effect Till 1983, FASB Official Discloses," JofA, June 81, p. 7.

terms is a legitimate objective of both private and public sectors, and the largest number of "accounting" problems seem to arise in this process.

I hope that over time the FASB will be able to move into this area with adequate recognition of the differences which exist between government and the private sector and with adequate staff resources and industry assistance to do the standard-setting job.

SUMMARY

These various trends in financial reporting promise a decade of continuing evolution in the financial reporting scene. As each of these trends is examined, the impact of an inflationary environment on both business and government is a consistent thread, as is the presence of the FASB. If we see a continuation of changing and unpredictable inflationary movements, it is unlikely that any solutions will provide stability in financial reporting, and the most probable projection is for continuing rapid and evolutionary changes in the reporting environment. Under such conditions, the need for an authoritative standard-setting body with a coherent framework for viewing problems is very great. Such a body must provide intellectual leadership in accounting measurement, with due recognition of the problems of the world. While the comments above indicate some disagreements with specific actions taken by the FASB, that board still seems to have a solid institutional structure and to offer the greatest hope for sound, consistent and rigorous standard setting.

The combination of a private sector standard-setting body with oversight and occasional creative stimulation by the SEC has provided us with a generally sound accounting structure in the past. Under conditions of economic strain which test the underpinnings of the accounting model, any system will be challenged to sustain its viability. The emerging trends noted in this article suggest a dynamism in the development of financial reporting that bodes well for its creative and responsive evolution in the decade ahead.

What Should be the FASB's Objectives?

William H. Beaver
Stanford University

Was the acrimony arising out of the investment tax credit much ado about nothing? Does it matter whether special gains and losses are reported in the ordinary income or in the extraordinary item section? When firms switch from accelerated to straight-line depreciation, what is the effect upon investors? Did the Accounting

From *The Journal of Accountancy* (August 1973), pp. 49–57. Reprinted by permission of the American Institute of Certified Public Accountants. Copyright © 1973 by the American Institute of Certified Public Accountants, Inc.

Author's note: The author wishes to acknowledge financial assistance provided by the Dean Witter Foundation. The conclusions expressed here are those of the author and do not necessarily reflect those of the foundation or any of its members.

Principles Board allocate its resources in an appropriate manner? If its priorities needed reordering, where should the emphasis have been shifted? What objectives should be adopted for financial accounting standards?

To answer such questions, the Financial Accounting Standards Board plans to sponsor a sizable research program.[1] For this reason, now is an appropriate time to take stock of the current body of knowledge and assess its implications for the setting of financial accounting standards. This article summarizes the results of recent research that has explored several facets of the relationship between financial statement data and security prices. The findings have a direct bearing on the questions raised at the outset and suggest that our traditional views of the role of policy-making bodies, such as the APB, SEC and FASB, may have to be substantially altered.

Currently we have far too little evidence on important issues in accounting. However, given this paucity of knowledge, it would be unfortunate if we ignored the evidence that we do have. Aspects of this research have already had a considerable effect on the professional investment community. Yet there has been no awareness of this research in accounting at the practical level or in the setting of past standards, as reflected in the APB Opinions. If the hopes for success of the FASB are to be realized, it is imperative that we lead, not lag, in incorporating the current state of knowledge into the setting of standards. Regulating financial accounting standards in ignorance of this evidence makes the prospects for success dim.

THE EVIDENCE

The behavior of security prices with respect to financial statement data is a widely discussed and hotly debated topic. The financial press is replete with articles of alleged effects of financial statement data on prices. In most cases, such allegations are not supported by any evidence. In a few cases, evidence of an anecdotal nature is offered. For example, the price of the stock of the ABC Company changed dramatically at approximately the same time the firm changed its method of depreciation to straight-line. Therefore, the cause was the change in accounting method. Such stories, while often entertaining, hardly constitute convincing evidence for several reasons. First, such an approach may select only those cases which are favorable to the hypothesis of the author while ignoring those instances that would refute it. For example, an examination of the price changes of only one firm or a few hand-picked firms that changed depreciation methods is insufficient. An examination must be made for all firms that changed depreciation methods or at least a large, randomly selected sample. Second, the analysis explains price changes after-the-fact on the basis of a single factor. There may be many factors that cause a price change. Usually, little or no care is taken to account for these other factors.

Unfortunately, until recently such evidence was the only type available. However, the issue is far too serious to be left to casual empiricism. Security prices are of obvious importance because of their impact upon the wealth, and hence the welfare,

---

[1]"Recommendations of the Study on Establishment of Accounting Principles," JofA, May 72, pp. 66–71.

of investors. This importance is formally recognized in SEC legislation. Recent cases arising out of Section 10b–5 testify to the fact that accounting practices are evaluated in terms of their effect on security prices.[2] Moreover, it is inconceivable that the FASB could set optimal financial accounting standards without assessing the impact of their actions on security prices.

The prevailing opinion in the accounting profession is that the market reacts naïvely to financial statement information. This view is reinforced by the anecdotal data of the sort described earlier, and by the obvious fact that the market is populated with several million uninformed, naïve investors, whose knowledge or concern for the subtleties of accounting matters is nil. However, in spite of this obvious fact, the formal research in this area is remarkably consistent in finding that the market, at least as manifested in the way in which security prices react, is quite sophisticated in dealing with financial statement data. One rationale for the observed sophistication of security prices is that the professional investors "make the market" and competitive bidding among one another for securities effectively makes the prices behave in such a manner that they reflect a considerable amount of sophistication. In any event, regardless of what the actual causal mechanism may be, there is considerable evidence that security prices do in fact behave in a sophisticated fashion. In the terminology of this literature, the securities market is said to be "efficient" with respect to financial statement data.[3]

A market is said to be efficient if security prices act as if they "fully reflect" publicly available information, including financial statement data. In other words, in an efficient market the investor is playing a "fair game" with respect to published information. Specifically, this means no investor can expect to use published information in such a way as to earn abnormal returns on his securities. Each investor can expect to earn a return on a security commensurate with its risk.[4] All securities of the same degree of riskiness will offer the same expected return, regardless of what accounting methods are used and no matter how much time is spent gleaning the secrets of the financial statements hidden in the footnotes. Hence,

[2]For example, litigation is currently under way in the cases of *Memorex* and *Occidental Petroleum Corp.*, pursuant to SEC action under Section 10b–5. Brief summaries of issues appear in the June 25, 1971, and March 5, 1971, issues of *The Wall Street Journal,* respectively. In both cases, measures of damages being discussed are directly related to the effect of the firms' accounting practices on security prices.

[3]Three forms of efficiency have been delineated: (1) the weak form, which deals with efficiency with respect to the past sequence of security prices (e.g., the random-walk hypothesis), (2) the semistrong form, which concerns efficiency with respect to published information, and (3) the strong form, which involves all information including inside information. This article deals with efficiency in the semistrong form. There is also considerable evidence with respect to the weak form of efficiency, but it is beyond the scope of this article. For a summary of this literature, see W. Beaver, "Reporting Rules for Marketable Equity Securities," JofA, Oct. 71, pp. 57–61.

[4]A detailed discussion of security risk and how it relates to expected returns is beyond the scope of this article. However, there has been a substantial amount of research in the portfolio theory and capital asset pricing literature dealing with this relationship. Briefly, the literature suggests that expected return must be commensurate with the risk incurred, in that securities with greater risk must offer higher expected return. Of course, the actual return in a given period may differ from expected return. For a more complete discussion of this issue in a nontechnical manner, see C. Welles, "The Beta Revolution: Learning to Live With Risk," *The Institutional Investor,* September 1971, pp. 21–64; W. Sharpe, "Risk, Market Sensitivity and Diversification," *Financial Analysts Journal,* January–February 1972, pp. 74–79.

no amount of security analysis, based on published financial statement data, will lead to abnormal returns. There are obvious implications for the community of professional investors, among others. However, there are also equally dramatic implications for the accounting profession. For this reason, the evidence, which has examined several aspects of market efficiency with respect to financial statement data, is summarized below.[5]

One aspect of efficiency is the speed with which security prices react to public information when it is announced. Empirical evidence indicates that prices react quickly and in an unbiased fashion to a variety of events, including announcements of stock splits, stock dividends, secondary offerings and rights issues, as well as both annual and interim earnings announcements. This finding is exactly what one would expect in a market where the security prices at any point in time fully reflect the information released. Moreover, the studies of earnings announcements find security prices anticipate earnings for several months prior to the announcement.[6]

Another aspect is this: Does the market look behind accounting numbers or is it fooled by them? Does the market act only on reported accounting numbers or does it adjust for other information, such as the accounting method used to calculate these numbers? In other words, does the market use a broader information set than merely the reported accounting numbers? In this respect, there have been several studies of changes in accounting methods and the subsequent behavior of security prices.[7] All of these studies show essentially the same result. There is no increase in price by changing to an accounting method that reports higher earnings than would have been reported had no change been made. The market, as reflected in price behavior, is not so naïve as many people claim. Instead, it acts as if it looks beyond accounting numbers and takes into account the fact that earnings are being generated by a different method.

---

[5]A more detailed summary of the literature is provided in the article by Eugene Fama, "Efficient Capital Markets: A Review of Theory and Empirical Work," *Journal of Finance*, May 1970, pp. 383–417. The implications of this literature for accounting also have been discussed in the following articles: W. Beaver, "The Behavior of Security Prices and Its Implications for Accounting Research Methods," *The Accounting Review* (Supplement, 1972), pp. 407–37; R. Ball, "Changes in Accounting Techniques and Stock Prices" (unpublished paper, University of Chicago, 1972); and N. Gonedes, "Efficient Capital Markets and External Accounting," *The Accounting Review*, January 1972, pp. 11–21.

[6]The studies referred to here are E. Fama, L. Fisher, M. Jensen and R. Roll, "The Adjustment of Stock Prices to New Information," *International Economic Review*, February 1969, pp. 1–21; M. Scholes, "The Market for Securities: Substitution Versus Price Pressure and the Effects of Information on Share Prices," *Journal of Business*, April 1972, pp. 179–211; R. Ball and P. Brown, "An Empirical Evaluation of Accounting Income Numbers," *Journal of Accounting Research*, Autumn 1968, pp. 159–78; P. Brown and J. Kennelly, "The Informational Content of Quarterly Earnings: An Extension and Some Further Evidence," *Journal of Business*, July 1972, pp. 403–21; G. Benston, "Published Corporate Accounting Data and Stock Prices," *Empirical Research in Accounting: Selected Studies, 1967, Journal of Accounting Research* (Supplement, 1967), pp. 1–54; and W. Beaver, "The Information Content of Annual Earnings Announcements," *Empirical Research in Accounting: Selected Studies, 1968, Journal of Accounting Research* (Supplement, 1968), pp. 67–92.

[7]The empirical studies referred to here include R. Kaplan and R. Roll, "Investor Evaluation of Accounting Information: Some Empirical Evidence," *Journal of Business*, April 1972, pp. 225–57; R. Ball, *op. cit.*; I. R. Archibald, "Stock Market Reaction to Depreciation Switchback," *The Accounting Review*, January 1972, pp. 22–30; and E. Comiskey, "Market Response to Changes in Depreciation Accounting," *The Accounting Review*, April 1971, pp. 279–85.

Further evidence compared the price-earnings ratios of firms that use accelerated methods of depreciation for both tax and reporting purposes (A/A group) with the price-earnings ratios of firms that use accelerated methods for tax purposes but straight-line for reporting purposes (A/S group).[8] The price-earnings ratio for the A/A group was larger than the price-earnings ratio for the A/S group. This finding is consistent with a market which recognizes that firms will report lower earnings under accelerated methods of depreciation than they would have under straight-line methods. Further analysis suggested that risk and growth could not explain the difference in the price-earnings ratios. In fact, the average riskiness and average growth rates were the same for both depreciation groups. However, when the earnings of the A/S group were converted to the earnings that would have been reported had they used an accelerated method for reporting, the price-earnings ratios of the two depreciation groups were essentially equal. In other words, when the firms were placed on a uniform accounting method, the price-earnings differences disappeared. Thus, the market appears to adjust for differences in depreciation methods among firms and, in effect, looks behind reported accounting data. Moreover, further testing found that changes in security prices more closely follow changes in certain nonreported forms of earnings than they do changes in reported earnings. This finding is consistent with a market where a broad information set is used in assessing price changes in contrast to one where there is sole, unquestioning reliance upon reported earnings.

In sum then, the evidence, across a variety of contexts, supports the contention that the market is efficient with respect to published information.

IMPLICATIONS

This evidence, together with the evidence on the performance of mutual funds, has led to changes in the investment community.[9]

Many portfolio managers and their clients have moved away from a "beat-the-market," high-turnover philosophy to one where the emphasis is placed upon risk management and the minimization of operating costs. The Samsonite pension fund contract is but one recent example. Wells Fargo Bank has agreed to manage the Samsonite pension fund where the agreement stipulates the maintenance of a given level of risk within prespecified limits, a lid on the maximum amount of turnover

---

[8]W. Beaver and R. E. Dukes, "δ-Depreciation Methods: Some Empirical Results," *The Accounting Review* (forthcoming).

[9]The empirical evidence finds that mutual fund returns fail to cover even research costs and brokerage commissions (let alone loading charges). After deducting these expenses, the net return to the mutual fund shareholder is below the return that could have been obtained from a simple strategy of buying and holding a portfolio of the same degree of riskiness. In fact, only after all such costs were added back in computing the return is the average mutual fund performance approximately equal to (but not greater than) the return from random portfolios of the same degree of riskiness. Moreover, these results not only apply to the average performance of all mutual funds but additional tests also indicate that no individual funds were able to produce superior returns consistently. For example, past performance by a fund appeared to be of no value in predicting superior performance in the future. See M. Jensen, "Risk, the Pricing of Capital Assets, and the Evaluation of Investment Portfolios," *Journal of Business,* April 1969, pp. 167–247. See also M. Zweig, "Darts, Anyone? As Market Pickers, Market Seers, the Pros Fall Short," *Barron's,* February 19, 1973, pp. 11–25.

that can occur and a restriction on the minimum number of securities comprising the fund.[10]

Given the practical impact that this research has had on the investment community, one might suspect that there are implications for the practice of accounting as well. In fact, there are several important implications for accounting in general and for the FASB in particular. However, there has been virtually no reaction on the part of the accounting profession. One reason is a general lack of awareness of this research, because its dissemination has essentially been restricted to academic journals. Another reason is that the anecdotal form of evidence discussed earlier continues to carry considerable weight among many members of the accounting profession. As a result, many readers may refuse to accept the evidence in support of market efficiency. But what if the mounting evidence in support of an efficient market finally becomes so overwhelming and compelling that it is accepted by all seven members of the FASB, all SEC Commissioners and staff, and all congressmen? What are the implications for the FASB? There are at least four major implications.

First

Many reporting issues are trivial and do not warrant an expenditure of FASB resources. The properties of such issues are twofold: (1) There is essentially no difference in cost to the firm of reporting either method. (2) There is essentially no cost to statement users in adjusting from one method to the other. In such cases, there is a simple solution. Report one method, with sufficient footnote disclosure to permit adjustment to the other, and let the market interpret implications of the data for security prices.

Unfortunately, too much of the resources of the APB and others has been devoted to issues that warrant this straightforward resolution. For example, the investment credit controversy belongs in this category, as do the issues regarding the definition of extraordinary items, interperiod tax allocation, earnings per share computations involving convertible securities, and accounting for marketable equity securities. By contrast, the FASB should shift its resources to those controversies where there is nontrivial additional cost to the firms or to investors in order to obtain certain types of information (for example, replacement cost accounting for depreciable assets). Whether such information should be a required part of reporting standards is a substantive issue.

Second

The role of financial statement data is essentially a preemptive one—that is, to prevent abnormal returns accruing to individuals by trading upon inside information. This purpose leads to the following disclosure policy: If there are no additional costs of disclosure to the firm, there is prima facie evidence that the item in question ought to be disclosed.

This relatively simple policy could greatly enhance the usefulness of financial

[10]C. Welles, *op. cit.*

statements. Many forms of information are currently being generated internally by the firm and could be reported with essentially no additional cost (e.g., the current market value of marketable equity securities). Such information, if not publicly reported, may constitute inside information. Merely because prices reflect publicly available information in no way implies that they also fully reflect inside information. One information cost that investors may be incurring currently is abnormal returns earned by those who have monopolistic access to inside information. Opponents of greater disclosure bear the burden of proof of showing that individuals can be prevented from earning excess returns with the undisclosed information or that the cost of disclosure exceeds the excess returns. Given the private incentives to trade on inside information, such a condition is very difficult to ensure.

Incidentally, efficient securities markets also have some important implications regarding the accountants' growing concern over legal liability. Accountants can be held legitimately responsible for insufficient disclosure. However, they should not be held responsible for using a "wrong" method (e.g., flow-through v. deferral) as long as they disclose the method that was used and sufficient data to permit adjustment to the nonreported method.

Third

The FASB must reconsider the nature of its traditional concern for the naïve investor. If the investor, no matter how naïve, is in effect facing a fair game, can he still get harmed? If so, how? The naïve investor can still get harmed, but not in the ways traditionally thought. For example, the potential harm is not likely to occur because firms use flow-through v. deferral for accounting for the investment credit. Rather, the harm is more likely to occur because firms are following policies of less than full disclosure and insiders are potentially earning monopoly returns from access to inside information. Harm is also likely to occur when investors assume speculative positions with excessive transactions costs, improper diversification and improper risk levels in the erroneous belief that they will be able to "beat the market" with published accounting information.

This implies that the FASB should actively discourage investors' beliefs that accounting data can be used to detect overvalued or undervalued securities. This also implies that the FASB must not attempt to reduce the complex events of multimillion dollar corporations to the level of understanding of the naïve, or, perhaps more appropriately labeled, ignorant investor. We must stop acting as if all—or even most—individual investors are literally involved in the process of interpreting the impact of accounting information upon the security prices of firms.

An argument often advanced against fuller disclosure is that the increased disclosure will befuddle and confuse the naïve investor. A specific manifestation of this argument is that earnings under market value rules are more volatile and hence may lead to more volatile security prices. For example, the insurance industry currently opposes the inclusion of such information on marketable securities in the income statement, even though market values are already reported on the balance sheet. Given that market values on the balance sheet are already part of public information, it is absurd to think that there is going to be any further effect on security prices because of the income statement disclosure. Yet considerable resources of the APB, the insurance industry and others have been wasted on an attempt to resolve this issue. In the more general case where there is no reporting of market values, the efficient market evidence implies that the market is not reacting naïvely to the currently reported numbers but, rather, is forming "unbiased" assessments of the market values and their effects on prices. Since the market is currently being forced to assess the effects of market values indirectly, they are probably estimating the values with error. Hence, if anything, reporting the actual numbers may eliminate the estimation errors which may be one source of volatility in security prices.

Moreover, one message comes through loud and clear from finance theory. The investor is concerned with assessing risk as well as expected return. In this context, one role of financial statement data is to aid the investor in assessing the risk of the security. By presenting less volatile numbers, we may be doing him a disservice by obscuring the underlying riskiness of his investment. Hence, it is impossible to argue that less volatile numbers per se are better than more volatile numbers. Taken together with the evidence in the efficient market, this suggests that the market can decide for itself how it wishes to interpret a given piece of information. The same sort of reasoning should be applied to the currently hot topic of reporting and attesting to forecasts. In an efficient market, a paternalistic attitude is unwarranted; furthermore, operationally, if it is used to rationalize lesser disclosure, it is much more likely to result in the protection of management than in the protection of investors, which is its ostensible purpose.

Fourth

Accountants must stop acting as if they are the only suppliers of information about the firm. Instead, the FASB should strive to minimize the total cost of providing information to investors. In an efficient market, security prices may be essentially the same under a variety of financial accounting standards, because, if an item is not reported in the financial statements, it may be provided by alternative sources. Under this view, which is consistent with the evidence cited earlier, the market uses a broad information set, and the accountant is one—and only one—supplier of information. One objective is to provide the information to investors by the most economical means. In order to accomplish this objective, several questions must be addressed: What are the alternative sources of information to financial statements? What are the costs of providing a given piece of information via the alternative source vis-à-vis the financial statements? Most importantly, do financial statement data have a comparative advantage in providing any portion of the total information used by the market, and, if so, what portion?

The nature of the costs has already been alluded to. One set of costs is the "cost" of abnormal returns' being earned by insiders because of monopolistic access to information. A second set of costs is excessive information costs. They can occur in two situations:

1 When the accountant fails to report an item that must be conveyed to the investing public through some other, more expensive source.

2 When the FASB requires firms to report an item that has a "value" less than its cost or items that could have been reported through other, less expensive sources of information. A third set of costs is incurred when investors erroneously believe that they can "beat the market" using published financial statement information. This set includes excessive transaction costs stemming from churning their accounts, improper diversification because of disproportionately large investment in "under-priced" securities and the selection of improper risk levels.[11]

NATURE OF FUTURE RESEARCH

One of the objectives the FASB must face is the establishment of a research program. Several areas should be explored:

1 Although the evidence in favor of market efficiency with respect to published information is considerable, the issue is by no means closed and further work on the particular types of accounting information items is needed.

2 Much more research is needed regarding market efficiency with respect to inside information. Such research will help to specify what the costs of nondisclosure are.

3 Evidence is needed on how individual investors, as opposed to the aggregate prices, react to information. Specifically, what is the process or mechanism by which information reaches individuals and is subsequently impounded in prices? What evidence is there of excessive transaction costs' being incurred by investors who act on information that already has been impounded in prices? Research into volume activity, as opposed to price activity, may be particularly insightful here. What evidence is there that individuals incur improper selection of risk levels by taking speculative positions based on accounting data? There are currently research methods available in finance that can provide at least a partial answer to these questions. The application of behavioral science also offers promise here.

4 More research is needed regarding the association between certain specific financial statement items and security prices. For example, are there certain items that are now being reported which do not seem to be used by the market as reflected in security prices? Conversely, are there certain types of information which are not currently reported but, in spite of that fact, are reflected in security prices? In the former instance, such items are candidates for being considered for possible exclusion from currently reported items. With respect to the latter, such items are candidates for being considered part of currently reported items.

---

[11]The costs of holding erroneous beliefs regarding market efficiency extend beyond investors. For example, consider the recent decision by Chrysler to change inventory methods because of alleged inefficiencies in the capital markets (both debt and equity markets). Even though Chrysler had reported supplemental statements in its previous annual reports, this was judged to be inadequate to overcome the inability of the capital market to look behind the reported numbers. The initial effect of a switch in inventory methods for both book and tax purposes was an incremental tax bill of approximately $50 million spread over a 20-year period. The efficient market evidence suggests that such a decision was a serious misallocation of resources. In fact, if anything, Chrysler is in worse economic position now because it is paying higher tax bills. For a summary of facts, see "Chrysler Posts $7.6 Million Loss for the Year," *The Wall Street Journal,* February 10, 1971.

5 Further research is needed to examine to what extent financial statement data are helpful to individual investors assessing the risk of a security. In an efficient market, the usefulness of financial statement data to individual investors is not to find mispriced securities, since they are nonexistent. What then is the value, if any? The value lies in the ability of financial statement data to aid in risk prediction. Some recent findings in the area by Beaver, Kettler and Scholes are encouraging, but much more research is needed.[12]

ERRONEOUS INTERPRETATIONS

The implications of market efficiency for accounting are frequently misunderstood. There are at least two common misinterpretations.

The first belief is that, in an efficient market world, there are no reporting issues of substance because of the "all-knowing" efficient market. Taken to its extreme, this error takes the form of asserting that accounting data have no value and hence the certification process is of no value.[13] The efficient market in no way leads to such implications. It may very well be that the publishing of financial statements data is precisely what makes the market as efficient as it is. As I was careful to point out earlier, merely because the market is efficient with respect to published data does not imply that market prices are also efficient with respect to nonpublished information. Disclosure is a substantive issue.

A second erroneous implication is, simply find out what method is most highly associated with security prices and report that method in the financial statements. As it stands, it is incorrect for several reasons. One major reason is that such a simplified decision rule fails to consider the costs of providing information. For example, a nonreported method may be less associated with security prices than the reported method because the cost of obtaining the nonreported via alternative sources is too high. Yet such information may be provided via financial statements at substantially lower costs. In another context, suppose the nonreported method showed the higher association with security prices; does it follow that the nonreported method should be reported? No, not necessarily. Perhaps the market is obtaining the information at lower cost via the alternative sources.[14]

---

[12]W. Beaver, R. Kettler and M. Scholes, "The Association Between Market Determined and Accounting Determined Risk Measures," *The Accounting Review*, October 1970, pp. 654–82.

[13]In this regard it is imperative to distinguish between two important aspects of information: (1) The first is to aid the market in arriving at a given set of security prices. One aspect of this role is to provide a market where the investors are playing a fair game with respect to some given information set (e.g., accounting data). (2) The second is to aid individual investors, who face a given set of prices, to select the optimal portfolio. One aspect of this role is the use of financial statement data in risk prediction. It is entirely possible that future research will discover that financial statement data have no role to play at the individual investor level and that the sole role is a social one. In any event, the social level is of paramount concern to a policy-making body such as the FASB. The distinction is made particularly clear in E. Fama and A. Laffer, "Information and Capital Markets," *Journal of Business*, July 1971, pp. 289–298; and J. Hirshleifer, "The Private and Social Value of Information and the Reward to Inventive Activity," *American Economic Review*, September 1971, pp. 561–74.; see also, W. Beaver, *op. cit*, pp. 424–25.

[14]These issues are discussed at greater length in R. May and G. Sundem, "Cost of Information and Security Prices: Market Association Tests for Accounting Policy Decision," *The Accounting Review*, January 1973, pp. 80–94.

Moreover, the choice among different accounting methods involves choosing among differing consequences, as reflected in the incidence of costs and security prices which affect individuals differently. Hence, some individuals may be better off under one method, while others may be better off under an alternative method. In this situation, how is the optimal method to be selected? The issue is one of social choice, which in general is an unresolvable problem because of the difficulty (impossibility) of making interpersonal welfare comparisons.[15]

There are certain specific issues (e.g., similar to those discussed in this article) which closely suggest a policy decision, if one is willing to accept the mild ethical assumption of Pareto-optimality.[16] However, such situations must meet a fairly specific set of conditions.

Regardless of the final resolution by the policymaker, it is still possible to specify the types of evidence that are relevant to choosing among alternatives. In simplest terms, although evidence cannot indicate what choice to make, it can provide information on the potential consequences of the various choices. Without a knowledge of consequences (e.g., as reflected in security prices), it is inconceivable that a policy-making body such as the FASB will be able to select optimal financial accounting standards. In spite of the importance of a knowledge of consequences, currently too little is known about price behavior and virtually nothing is known about the magnitude of the three types of costs outlined earlier.

CONCLUSION

Financial statement information is inherently a social commodity. However, it is clear that decisions regarding its generation and dissemination are of a much different nature than we have traditionally thought them to be. This change in the way we view the FASB is conditioned upon the assumption of market efficiency. While there is need for further future research in this area, there is sufficient credibility in the evidence to date that we should be prepared to face its implications:

1 Many reporting issues are capable of a simple disclosure solution and do not warrant an expenditure of FASB time and resources in attempting to resolve them.

2 The role of accounting data is to prevent superior returns' accruing from inside information and can be achieved by a policy of much fuller disclosure than is currently required.

3 Financial statements should not be reduced to the level of understanding of the naïve investor.

4 The FASB should strive for policies that will eliminate excessive costs of information.

5 The FASB should sponsor a full-scale research program in the areas indicated, so that it may have some evidence of the consequences of their choices among different sets of financial accounting standards.

[15]K. Arrow, *Social Choice and Individual Values* (Yale University Press, 1968). The issue has been discussed in an accounting context in J. Demski, "Choice Among Financial Accounting Alternatives" (unpublished, Stanford University, 1972).

[16]The concept of Pareto-optimality states that a society prefers one alternative to another, if at least some people are better off and no one is worse off.

Human Information Processing and Financial Disclosure

Jacob G. Birnberg
University of Pittsburgh

It could be helpful to review the human information processing (HIP) literature and examine its implications for accounting, particularly in the area of disclosure. To facilitate the presentation of some conclusions concerning financial reporting, this paper is organized into two broad sections. The first section briefly reviews the literature, primarily concerned with its conclusions and their explication for accounting. Thus, it briefly outlines the theory of human information processing in a nontechnical fashion and discusses its relevance to financial reporting. The more detailed arguments supporting the issues, detailed citation of sources, and other trappings of research papers, are omitted from this section. They are, instead, presented in the second section in a manner similar to the inclusion of a technical appendix in a paper.

This approach suffers from an appearance of a paucity of support for the first section. However, it is hoped that, when balanced against the potential for an information overload present in the alternative, it will turn out to be a successful application of the issues subsequently discussed. The reader should be able to select the portion(s) most akin to his needs.

IMPLICATIONS FOR FINANCIAL DISCLOSURE

The issue of information load and, by implication, information overload, is not new to accountants. Whether by good intuition, keen insight, adaptability, or luck, the accountant has developed a variety of methods for reducing the information load while, hopefully, having minimal effects on the amount of information communicated. Four techniques are used:

1 Organization of information load
2 Aggregation
3 Format
4 Precalculation

Organization of the information load refers to the development of a relevant analytical structure and related set of definitions so that data can be presented in an orderly fashion—a fashion meaningful to the user. *Aggregation* refers to the algebraic summing of elements within a category in a manner consistent with the data needs of the user. The sum rather than the elements are then presented within the organized information set. *Format* relates to the manner in which the data are presented. The format should be as consistent as possible with the processing

Adapted from *Corporate Financial Reporting: The Benefits and Problems of Disclosure* (AICPA, 1976), pp. 251–261. Reprinted by permission of the American Institute of Certified Public Accountants. Copyright © 1976 by the American Institute of Certified Public Accountants, Inc.

capacities of the user and the data needs of his model. *Precalculation* is the process of deriving from the information set those outputs that are assumed to be useful either by normative arguments such as profitability, or requests for disclosure, such as earnings per share.

Each of these techniques is useful and reduces the mass of data that must be communicated. As such they would appear to cope with some elements of information overload on the user of financial data. However, demands from users for new data are being made and suggestions for potentially useful disclosure are being offered by the FASB, governmental agencies, analysts and academics. Thus, at some point, the accounting profession must recognize that more data could hurt rather than help the user. It is that question—How much information load can the user absorb efficiently?—and the related one—How can the accountant best take advantage of the user's abilities to most easily communicate with him?—that are central to this paper.

THE USER

The users or consumers of financial outputs are not a homogeneous class. They differ in their ability to handle abstract concepts, their expertise in the areas of accounting and financial analysis, the data sources open to them and their experience in dealing with the information available for financial decisions. However, for practical purposes we can assume that any user—an analyst or the ubiquitous "man on the street"—

1 Is better able to process inputs in some forms than others.
2 Does become overloaded from the sheer volume of information provided even when he knows what data he wants.
3 Tends toward habitual behavior, at least in the short run and, therefore, may require time to adapt to new information and/or new ways of presenting the old information.
4 Is likely to learn and adapt to new conditions in the long run.
5 Is functioning in an uncertain environment so that (a) he may request more information than he needs in hopes of reducing his uncertainty and (b) show less confidence in preprocessed data than in raw data, even when the former is clearly more valuable to him.

Obviously there are interpersonal differences among users that are quite independent of prior training and experience.

1 The degree of abstractness (or complexity) involved in the user's information processing.
2 The decision style of the individual, which affects the way he uses information and the amount of information he requests.

More abstract information processors will utilize information more effectively than their more concrete counterparts. Moreover, he is better able to handle any given information load. Thus, at any given level of information the abstract user will out-perform the more concrete one, and the abstract user will be able to tolerate

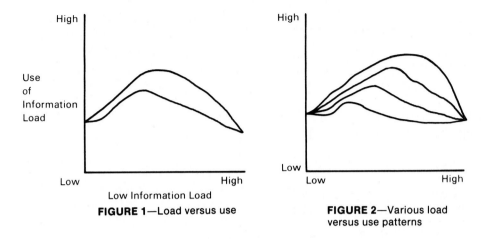

FIGURE 1—Load versus use

FIGURE 2—Various load versus use patterns

(utilize) larger information loads before becoming so overloaded that his level of performance declines. (See Figure 1.) Obviously, there is no reason to believe that people are truly either strictly concrete or abstract. In fact, many degrees of abstract processing ability may exist. If this is assumed to be the case, then Figure 1 would contain a family of curves. Each one would be higher than the next, and with an optimal information load moving progressively toward the right. If the abstract and concrete curves are viewed as the upper and lower limits, the curves would nest between them and their maximums would move from the maximum of the concrete toward that of the abstract. (See Figure 2.)

Decision-makers also vary in the way they approach the decision process. Some are concerned only with ascertaining an ordering of alternatives. For example, is A a better investment than B? Or how should we rank X, Y, and Z as investments? The output of their decision process is simply an ordering of alternatives. Like any ranking scheme, they should require less information than those decision-makers who concern themselves with a complete analysis and rating of all the alternatives. The situation is analogous to two completely different numbering schemes. The latter, a cardinal scale, requires more data and/or processing than the former, which is analogous to a rank order scheme.

THE USER'S ENVIRONMENT

Figure 3 shows the environment within which the ultimate users of financial data function. Most of the items are self-explanatory; the brief statements below, describing each, are intended solely to avoid unnecessary ambiguity.

Nonaccounting Data Stream. All data outside the formal accounting system. Thus, a number such as earnings per share for a *prior* period is part of the financial reporting system while forecast earnings per share is not.

Financial Reporting System. All data reported via the entity's periodic accounting reports. Thus, it would include data from quarterly reports concerning quarterly performance.

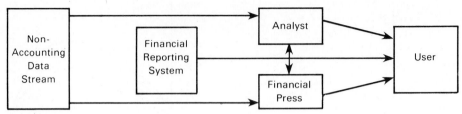

FIGURE 3—Financial reporting environment

Financial Press. All media reporting on business activities.

Analyst. Anyone who processes the information outputs from the three possible sources (nonaccounting data stream, financial press, and financial reporting system) and presents evaluative information derived from that data.

User. Someone who utilizes the available information to make an economic decision. Note that at least two types are available using the Trueblood committee's dichotomy. For practical purposes, the analyst/user who acts upon his assessments (and makes them public as well) is represented in both classes.

Consumer. Used as a shorthand for *both* analysts and users.

SOME RELEVANT QUESTIONS

The interaction of the human information processing model and the environment in which financial disclosure takes place raises several questions. Foremost among these are the following:

1 What effect does the availability of the processed financial data from the analysts have on the extent to which the users utilize the remaining sources of information?
2 Are users able to control the information load by selectively sampling from diverse sources? This would permit them to alleviate information overloading.
3 To what extent is the accounting function servicing the user directly and to what extent only indirectly, via the financial press and the media?
4 Are the more abstract users of financial reports found performing the analyst's function and the more concrete, the user's (in the Trueblood committee's sense of the term)?
5 In the long run, does the highly routine nature of the task performed by user and analyst lead to learning that in turn reduces some of the information load?

PRESENT STATE OF THE FINANCIAL REPORTING SYSTEM

Overload

Information overload occurs when the human information processing system receives so much data that it is not able to accommodate to it. The demands that the information load makes on the processor lead to less than optimal behavior and send the user beyond the level of optimal performance into his area of "negative returns." While it might be interesting to attempt an analysis of current practice to ascertain where we are on the processing curves (that is, the curves illustrated in Figure 1) such a study is likely to be futile and frustrating. Rather, it is probably best to examine those indirect indicators and the anecdotal information that is available.

In general, as far as the remote users of financial statements are concerned, it would appear that the level of information from all possible sources (that is, the financial reports, the financial "press," and the analysts) exceeds the users' needs. For example, most companies who offered their 10-Ks to shareholders failed to elicit shareholder interest. Almost uniformly, only a handful of the shareholders accepted the offer of a copy of the 10-K free of charge when a postcard is returned to the company.[1] Moreover, we have no insight into who did request these copies; some may have been requested by individuals or groups who usually availed themselves of 10-K data from some other sources.

It is tempting to conclude that remote users of financial statements have little interest in raw financial data of the same general type as is already available in a more heavily aggregated form in the "press," in annual reports, and from analysts. If these users were near their point of maximum efficiency they ought to have had some interest in the 10-K data. Given that they did not, we can only suggest that one of two events occurred. The channel (data source) may have been overloaded, causing the users to reject any additional data despite our normative view of its relevance. They may have been so overloaded already that they did not have the ability to use it. Alternatively, they may have felt that the report had no net benefits to them. The cost of postage and processing outweighed anything they could have expected to find in it, even if they had not reached their points of maximum efficiency.

A second, and more anecdotal example, of overload may be present in the Penn Central situation. One study has argued that skilled readers of financial statements should have detected the decline of the Penn Central.[2] History indicates they did not. For some reason, if that study is correct, analysts failed to do their job. The possible answers range from incompetence to massive information overload (that is, too many other companies to worry about) to information overload vis-à-vis available financial data about the Penn Central Company.

Similar arguments have been made concerning the current problems of public utilities. Two analysts, with hindsight, suggested that the Consolidated Edison annual report contained all the data needed to anticipate their (and other utilities') dividend problem(s).[3] While their evaluation of the data may benefit from hindsight, it is clear that the data were present and the bulk of the financial community chose to ignore them, failed to recognize their significance or may even have been unaware of their presence.

The above data are anecdotal and hardly constitute incontrovertible proof that we are already experiencing information overload. However, if they only indicate

[1] For a summary of some firms' experiences see the *Wall Street Journal,* 11 July, 1974, p.1.

[2] S. Davidson, J. Schindler and R. Weil, *Accounting: The Language of Business* (Horton: Glen Ridge, N.J., 1974) pp.50–51.

[3] The original calculations were by I. O'glove and R. Olstein. Summarized in W. Shepherd, ed., "Psychedelic Accounting," *Business Week,* July 27, 1974, p.57.

that we are approaching it, the arguments for more disclosure rather than less *on the basis that more is always better than less* could be improvident. Rather, the data might suggest that the test for disclosure is still *relevance.* They may also question the wisdom of the efficient market theorist who, in an attempt to avoid the pitfalls of private information in his theories, argues for more extensive public disclosure.

At this point one caveat is important. This argument and the research on information overload have assumed that the added information contains relatively small increments of information. By relatively small, we refer to the total amount already available. Clearly, disclosing new information of great relative importance (a potential "bombshell") is a different question; such data should be disclosed even in an overload situation. The relevance of the overload argument in the event of a bombshell is that the human information processing system will make a better decision but not be able to react as quickly (efficiently) as possible.

Coping with Overload

As indicated at the outset of this section, the financial reporting segment of the environment has attempted to use a variety of techniques to cope with the volume of data that it produces. These devices undoubtedly reduce the load on the processing system by making access to the data easier. There is less noise to reduce, and less processing to be performed by the standard user.

The accounting structure as it now exists permits a gradual disaggregation of the data, from the summary data through the financial statements and their related notes. This "unfolding" of the relevant data on a given facet of the entity permits the user to gradually pursue the point, terminating his search when he feels he has "enough." Moreover, by beginning with graphic representations and numerical data and proceeding to text material, the accountant is proceeding from what research has shown is apparently the most easily comprehended information form—graphics and summary statistics—to the least easily understood—text material.

However, any systematic attempt to deal with overload in this fashion does so at the risk that the user will miss valuable data that is present at a point in the process that is beyond his stopping point, for example, in the detailed footnotes. It is probably this fact that causes the lack of confidence in their own decisions exhibited by decision-makers who use only summarized data.

In addition, the user can reduce the information load by being selective in the data sources he utilizes. All users need not utilize all possible sources of information. By being selective, they can reduce their volume of data inputs. Because of the reduced load and redundancy in the sources, the user may move back up the U-shaped curve towards his point of maximum performance because of increases in his decision-making efficiency. The data that are lost (unless they are "bombshells" as we described them earlier) were not being properly utilized anyway.

In this fashion many nonskilled users are able to cope with the problem of overload. They select particular sources and particular elements within reports as relevant and reject others. Usually the sources are secondary sources. Typically, they are analysts' reports or comparable data contained in the financial press. Whether the user is successful or not depends upon the success of his sources (and, in turn, their susceptibility to overloading).

It is only conjecture, but any user of financial statement data experiencing information overload or a welter of data, substantial portions of which are noise, may develop patterns or formulas for examining the data available to him. These rules of thumb permit the user to cope with what he believes to be the essential parts of the available data and reduce the problem to one where the relevant data set is closer in size to the maximum the user can process.

Such rules of thumb do have their limitations. Even when such filtering rules are followed, the volume of data makes the process more difficult than if the set which the decision-maker utilizes was *all* the data available. He must go through the process of sorting until he finds the data he needs.

Rules of thumb may work well in a stable situation where the user has properly evaluated it. So long as the basic decision rule does not change, the decision-maker's approach should serve him well. Significant changes in those properties he examines (for example, earnings per share or the annual rate of growth in sales or profits) will be duly noted by the user and may cause him to reconsider his evaluation. However, should a significant change occur in some aspect of the entity's financial condition that is not included in his rule of thumb, the data are likely to go unnoticed. Even if they are included in the data to be available to the decision-maker, they probably will be ignored since the filtering rule that is used to cope with the volume of data directs attention away from them. This might explain the problems present in recognizing Consolidated Edison's plight.

Who are the Consumers of the Financial Reporting System?

The argument made in the previous section suggests that users select a mix of information channels to suit their needs and capabilities. This is not the only argument that can be made to suggest that all users do not use all channels at all times. Issues of volume aside, users may prefer the reports from analysts because of recasting of data and selectivity. The analysts may serve as a filter for the user to reduce his load and require him to consult the "raw data" of the financial reporting system less frequently. This is convenient for the user if it is successful.

For accountants there are some important implications to the answer of how the user receives the outputs of the financial reporting system—directly or indirectly. If it is indirectly, through analysts, then the accountant is addressing an audience that may be relatively homogeneous. If it is directly, the users may be a heterogeneous group, and the accountant consequently faces more severe problems in determining the optimal possible information load.

Consider the possibility that the analyst is the basic source of user's data. At the present time, we have no knowledge of analysts' information processing capabilities. However, if analysts are generally more abstract information processors than are investors, then there is an increase in the level of complexity possible before the processing system is overloaded. This would mean that attempts to expand the volume of data disclosed could be successful, for they would be addressed to the audience most able to utilize them in an efficient manner. In that sense, it would be the best possible world for accountants, for it would permit maximum detail.

However, it would suggest that the user—as opposed to the analyst—will be overloaded, reducing his ability to utilize the accounting data. Indeed, it suggests that, unless we design two different financial reporting systems, pursuit of the concerns of the user (the philosophy of the Trueblood Report), may reduce our ability to service the analyst, and vice versa.

If the users and the analysts as groups are not distinguishable on the relative abstractness of their information processing, the same question can be posed in a slightly different fashion. Who should be considered in setting the information load present in the outputs of a financial reporting system? In any case, one group will benefit at the expense of the other. And, unlike the previous section, the superior group is not constituted to service the inferior group thereby sharing (selling?) some of their comparative advantage.

In any case, the problem of the optimal level of complexity is likely to be a knotty one for accountants unless all the potential consumers of the outputs of his information system have their point of maximum information load prior to overloading in about the same level of complexity. Only further research can clarify this point.

OTHER INFORMATION PROCESSING CONSIDERATIONS

User Satisfaction

Despite the anecdotal data offered to show that the users of financial data are not as yet gleaning the full benefits from the available data, we witness a constant clamor for more data about various facets of enterprise activities. Some undoubtedly reflect limitations in the current scope of financial disclosure. Others may be less meritorious. The issue, simply, is how can the argument of an overloaded system be rationalized against these demands for expanded disclosure. If the consumer desires more information, is it reasonable to conclude he is overloaded? Why not give it to him?

Unfortunately, while this argument is intuitively appealing, there is ample evidence that people request more data than they need. Indeed, they will pay for more data even if it will increase the overload on the system. The hope, of course, is that the next incremental bit of information is the one that will solve the problem for them.

Moreover, users of aggregated data have been shown to be more efficient decision-makers, when the aggregation is done in a manner consistent with their needs, than individuals receiving raw data. However, they are not as confident in their decisions as their less-effective colleagues. Moreover, they also reveal this lack of confidence by taking longer to make the same decisions than those receiving raw data. All of this is inconsistent with one's intuitive evaluation that if you gave decision-makers what they need they will not only make better decisions but also will (a) take less time, (b) be more confident in their answer, and (c) be more satisfied with the data.

The import of these findings is clear. Dissatisfaction on the part of users cannot be taken as an unequivocal sign of a flawed reporting scheme. Rather, it is likely that financial disclosure will *never* satisfy all of its potential users. It is somehow predestined that there always will be a vocal segment requesting additional information. Thus, a critical examination of the relevance of the data, as practiced by the FASB, is a desirable screening device. In contrast, any expansion of financial disclosure solely because it *might* help would appear self-defeating.

The Effect of Changes in Disclosure Policy

If various studies are correct, one problem in changing the form and/or scope of accounting disclosure is that there must be a lead time for the users and analysts to adjust to the new format and/or technique. Often that time occurs during the period when change is being advocated. The process and explanation that justify the change also educate the consumer. They may even serve to make him a more critical consumer of the currently available data.

Two examples can be offered. Price-level-adjusted statements have been discussed for generations. Their significance is (relatively) well understood. If price-level-adjusted reports were to appear tomorrow, conjecture and research suggests that they could be utilized effectively by the consumers of financial data.[4]

A second proposal of much more recent vintage is that variability in the accounting numbers be reported. That is, critical numbers in the financial reports would be reported as interval rather than point estimates. Supporters of this proposal argue that it would afford the user a more explicit statement of the subjectivity inherent in the reported data.

Aside from the alleged merits of the proposal, studies have not yet shown that consumers receiving such information are able to benefit from it. If its proponents are correct, one obvious reason for the apparent lack of benefit is that the consumer has not been educated to use the new data efficiently. As a result, the reports utilizing interval estimates may be producing added "noise" for the consumer rather than information. If that format were to be adopted, education of the consumer would be necessary to achieve the proposed benefits.[5]

A related problem present in human information processing concerns changes in the format or method of disclosing data as opposed to the expansion of the set of data offered. Individuals exhibit a persistence of set ("fixity") from one period to another. This means that the income statement is viewed as, essentially, the same document summarizing the same categories of events from one period to another. Should a major change occur in those events that are included in the income statement, as was effected by APB Opinion No. 30, there will be a time lag before the consumer of financial data will recognize that the profit figure may have been calculated in a different fashion.

The existence of such functional fixity can delay the benefits from changes in

---

[4]See T. Dyckman, SAR No. 1, Investment Analysis and General Price Level Adjustment (Sarasota, Fla.: American Accounting Association, 1969). See pp. 11–16 and particularly p.17.

[5]This may be an advantage inherent in the process by which changes in financial accounting occur. The period between proposal and adoption serves to educate those who are interested in the process.

financial disclosure unless proper care is taken to publicize the change. In that regard, it is more likely that specialists such as the analyst will adjust more quickly to the change than will the remote user. The amount of "educational material" they receive is significantly greater, not necessarily because they are a preferred group, but because their livelihood depends upon it and so they seek it out.

SUMMARY

In balance there is reason to believe that financial disclosure as it now exists presents a volume of data that to some degree impedes consumers of the output of the financial reporting system. Whether the volume has reached the point where it overloads the routine information processing is a question. However, the filtering of the data by specialists and the use of rules of thumb would appear to make the system susceptible to those situations where the relevant data are outside the set of data usually consulted in decision-making.

Aggregation, precalculation and experimentation with new methods of presenting the data either more simply or in a manner more easily comprehensible have certain limitations. First, many consumers are capable of processing significantly more data than others; thus, all people cannot be satisfied simultaneously. Second, aggregation—even when beneficial to consumers—leads to feelings of apprehension and erodes users' confidence in their own decisions and the data. Third, since we do not know exactly which data are needed—and it is probable that different consumers desire different data—the financial reporting function is likely to produce "noise" as well as information. This noise will also overburden the consumer.

Proposals to expand the information supplied to consumers should be viewed critically. Indeed, some of the data currently supplied may no longer be relevant. In this sense, the injunction of the Trueblood committee's report about relevance is appropriate.[6] However, this should not militate against the inclusion of new information where such information is necessitated by significant changes in the environment.

---

[6] AICPA, Study Group on the Objectives of Financial Statements, *Objectives of Financial Statements,* 3 vols. (New York: AICPA, 1973).

The Value Added Statement in Britain

Michael F. Morley
University of Aberdeen

Since 1975, a new form of accounting statement has been appearing in the corporate reports of some of the larger British companies. It is the Value Added (*VA*) Statement. Already approximately one quarter of the 100 largest companies are voluntarily including a VA Statement in their annual reports, and this proportion is still growing. Further growth seems inevitable, as the government has indicated that it intends to make all substantial British companies include a VA statement in their annual reports [Department of Trade, 1977].

This development of the VA Statement is especially interesting, as it represents a new direction in which financial reporting, in theory and practice, can go. The main thrust of financial accounting development in recent decades has been in the area of *how* we measure income, especially in the face of changing prices. The question of *whose income we measure* has been largely ignored, though Hendriksen's text [1977] is an exception. We accountants ignore the question because we are aware of only one answer. When asked, "whose income?," many accountants reply that net income or profit is the reward of the proprietors, *i.e.,* the shareholders in the case of a company. Proponents of Value Added reply that there are advantages in defining "income" in such a way as to include the rewards of a much wider group than just the shareholders. One can include shareholders and all suppliers of long- and short-term loan capital, together with employees and the government. The "income" of this team is called Value Added, and equals net profit with tax, interest, and wages costs all added back.

The structure of double-entry means that there is another way of arriving at Value Added, which is by deducting from sales revenue the cost of all materials and services which were bought-in from outside suppliers. This will give the same figure for VA, because the reward of our wider team must equal gross team revenues (*i.e.,* sales) less amounts payable to persons outside the team (*i.e.,* bought-in costs). The relationship between VA and profit can be expressed algebraically. We start by defining the retained profit for a given fiscal year as what is left after all costs, dividends, and taxes have been deducted from sales revenue, thus:

$$R = S - B - Dep - W - I - Div - T \qquad (1)$$

where R is retained profit, S is sales revenue, B is the total of bought-in materials and services, Dep is the annual depreciation charge, W is the year's wage cost, I is the interest payable for the year, Div is the total of dividends payable for the year, and T represents corporate taxes.

Re-arranging (1) we have:

From *The Accounting Review* (July 1979), pp. 618–629. Reprinted by permission of the American Accounting Association.

$$S - B - Dep = W + I + Div + T + R \qquad (2)$$

Each side of Equation (2) equals Value Added. As will be seen, there is controversy in theory and divergent practice regarding depreciation in VA Statements, so we call the above *Net* VA, to make clear that it refers to VA after deducting depreciation.

Many accountants would prefer to re-arrange Equation (1) thus:

$$S - B = W + I + Div + T + Dep + R \qquad (3)$$

Each side of Equation (3) then equals *Gross* Value Added, or Value Added before deducting depreciation.

Equations (2) and (3) follow the format of VA Statements prepared in practice. The left-hand side of each equation relates to the upper part of the VA Statement, where bought-in costs are deducted from sales revenue. Having arrived at the figure for the year's VA, the lower part of the VA Statement shows its division among team members, which is symbolically represented in the right-hand sides of Equations (2) and (3).

Table 1 shows the Value Added Statement included in the annual report of BOC International Ltd., (formerly British Oxygen) for 1977. BOC has chosen the net VA form of presentation rather than Gross VA, and so its VA Statement illustrates Equation (2). It can be seen how the company deducts bought-in costs and depreciation from sales to arrive at VA for the year of £259.5 million. The investment income is then added (a complication which has been ignored in Equation 2), and the total available for sharing among team members is £263.7 million. The division of this among the various sub-groups in the team then follows. The heading "to partners in companies not wholly owned by the group" refers to dividends payable by BOC subsidiaries to minority shareholders in subsidiaries not wholly owned by the group. The amounts payable to each team member sum to £238.9 million, leaving £24.8 million as the group's retentions.

It is interesting to consider why so many British companies are, like BOC, deciding to present a VA report. Although the VA Statement is a very recent development, the concept of VA is considerably older. It originated in the U.S. Treasury in the eighteenth century [Cox, 1978], and periodically accountants have discussed whether the concept should be incorporated into financial accounting practice (see Suojanen [1954], for example). However, the VA Statement has taken root only in Britain,[1] and that very recently, and two immediate factors can be suggested as causes. First, Britain introduced a Value Added Tax (VAT) in April, 1973. The administration of this point-of-sale tax does not require production of a VA Statement, and the Statement cannot be used for tax verification due to complicated rules on goods and services which are exempted or zero-rated. However, the tax has led to increased awareness in the business world of the meaning of VA.

---

[1] A few companies in the Netherlands include VA information in their annual reports, but the disclosures often fall short of being a full VA Statement, and the method of arriving at VA is grossly non-standardized. The annual reports of the Dutch companies Akzo N.V., Internatio-Müller, N.V., and SHV Holding N.V. are especially interesting, giving an idea of the variety of VA reporting practice.

TABLE 1

BOC International Ltd. and Subsidiaries Value Added Statement Year to September 30, 1977

	£ million
Sales	670.6
Less	
Bought in materials, services and depreciation	411.1
Value added	259.5
Add	
Investment income	4.2
Available for application	263.7
Applied as follows:	
To employees as pay and Group companies' contributions to pensions and state welfare schemes	180.8
To banks and other lenders as interest	19.6
To government as taxes on profits	25.6
To partners in companies not wholly owned by Group	3.6
To shareholders of BOC International	9.3
	238.9
Profits retained by ourselves and our partners for expansion	24.8
	263.7

Second, the British Accounting Standards Committee, sponsored by the principal U.K. and Irish accounting bodies, published *The Corporate Report* [ASC, 1975], a discussion paper on the purposes of annual reports, and in it the authors suggested that such reports should include a VA Statement.

It is worth mentioning that a frequent synonym for VA is "wealth creation," and this may have encouraged many industrialists to link VA reports on wealth creation with remedial action to halt Britain's relative industrial decline.

ADVANTAGES

The advantages claimed for the VA Statement are considerable. First, it is said that it improves the attitudes of employees toward their employing companies. This effect is alleged to occur because the VA Statement reflects a broader view of the company's objectives and responsibilities. Few workers are said to be enthusiastic about maximizing profit, which is somebody else's reward, and, therefore, a profit statement has little interest or motivational value for employees. However, a company's VA represents the wealth creation available for the company team, in which employees are seen as responsible participants. When fully informed about VA, they should be better motivated to work, be more cooperative and more identified with their company. This hoped-for behavioral change links with ideas on industrial democracy which are popular in some British political circles. (See, for example, the Bullock Report [1977].) Many companies include VA reports in their employee newspapers or other vehicles of communication with their staff, and so the inclusion of a VA Statement in the annual report is said to add credibility to the use of VA elsewhere.

This type of behavioral hypothesis is notoriously difficult to test, as it depends on the sincerity of management, who might merely be producing a VA Statement to follow the herd, with no intention of evolving a more "team-centered" approach to the work force.

A second advantage claimed for the VA Statement is that it makes it easier for the company to introduce a productivity bonus scheme for employees based on VA. A number of British companies, of which Imperial Chemical Industries Ltd. is the best known, have introduced such schemes to enhance productivity. The employees receive bonus payments and/or shares in the company according to a formula based on demonstrated improvements over time in the VA/payroll ratio. If a company wishes to install such a scheme, or wishes to keep open its options to do so, then including a VA Statement in its annual report will be advantageous because it will spread knowledge of and trust in VA. Suspicion of VA should be lessened if VA is reported to shareholders in the annual report as well as forming the basis for productivity schemes.

A third advantage claimed is that VA-based ratios (like the VA/payroll ratio mentioned above) are a useful diagnostic and predictive tool. In many British companies, employees receive 70 percent or thereabouts of VA. Trends in this ratio, comparisons with other companies, and international comparisons may all be useful. This is especially so if the ratio is based on inflation-adjusted VA data. To date, three British companies have presented VA Statements adjusted for inflation: one (Colt International Ltd.) used the single-index, or current purchasing power method, while two (Alcan Aluminium [U.K.] Ltd. and Bowater Corporation Ltd.) used the replacement cost or current cost method. The figures produced by Alcan were especially interesting. Table 2 shows how the payroll costs absorbed 66 percent of VA when measured according to historical cost conventions. However, when the costs of bought-in materials and services and also depreciation were adjusted to current costs, the ratio rose to 110 percent. Naturally, no business could long sustain a figure of over 100 percent for long. The jump from 66 percent to 110 percent is unusually large, but one can see how this ratio draws attention to trends in labor costs and may be helpful in wage bargaining as a means of informing labor representatives. For example, the relationship between this ratio and the level of retained profit (hence investment and longer-term job security) is made clear in the VA Statement.

Another VA-based ratio which is popular is that of taxation to VA. The difficulty with this ratio is that there is a great lack of standardization in the classification of taxes in VA Statements. The recent annual reports of Esso Petroleum Company

TABLE 2

**Alcan Aluminium (U.K.) Ltd. and Subsidiaries Value Added
Information Year to December 31, 1976***

	Current cost £ millions	Historic cost £ millions
Sales	227.3	227.3
Less bought-in costs	175.1	162.0
Gross Value Added	52.2	65.3
Depreciation	17.3	6.7
Net Value Added	34.9	58.6
Payroll costs	38.7	38.7
Payroll/VA ratio	110%	66%

*Extracted from p.16 of Annual Report, December 31, 1976.

Ltd. illustrate this. In the 1976 annual report, the company's VA was £729 million, and central and local government took 74 percent of this in taxes. In the 1977 annual report, VA was down to £301 million, and the government took only 23 percent. This drastic change is surprising, until one reads the detail and sees that the company has changed its accounting policy for treating excise duty and Value Added Tax. In 1976, these were included in VA and in the government's share, but in 1977 they were excluded from both. In brief, Esso has partly fallen into line with prevailing practice in Britain, for most companies report only corporation tax under the government's share. Esso still shows taxes paid to local government and royalties paid to governments under the government's share, neither of which practices is widespread.

Provided taxes are classified consistently and uniformly, this ratio and trends therein are useful for inter-industry and international comparisons.

One other popular ratio is VA/Sales, which measures the degree of vertical integration of a group of companies, and also can be interpreted as an index of vulnerability to disruptive action affecting supplies of materials and services.

Before leaving the topic of VA-based ratios, it is worth mentioning how relevant they are to the testing of rival theories of Britain's relative industrial decline since the end of World War II. Such theories abound, and the VA Statement throws light on most of them. Is the root cause of the problem a disinclination to hard work? The ratios of VA per employee and VA to wages cost are relevant, especially when international comparisons are made. Has the government over-taxed British industry? Ratios of taxes to VA would throw light on this, especially if the ratios for different industries were compared with their growth rates. Is under-investment to blame, or insufficient research and development? Again, the proportions of VA being allocated to these activities will help assess the rival hypotheses.

A fourth advantage of the new Statement is that VA provides a very good measure of the size and importance of a company. To use sales figures as a basis for company rankings can cause distortion, because sales may be inflated by large bought-in expenses which are passed straight on to customers. Capital employed, which is also sometimes used for rankings, can likewise be misleading. For example, a capital-intensive company with few employees may appear to be more important than a labor-intensive company. In a key industry, VA does not have these disadvantages and is, therefore, superior to sales and to capital employed as a ranking basis.

A fifth advantage of the VA Statement is that it links a company's financial accounts to national income. With a number of qualifications, which will be listed later, it is true that a company's VA indicates the company's contribution to national income. Furthermore, the sum of the Values Added by each company will equal national income. VA reports, therefore, start off with an inheritance of credibility, for most users of accounting statements have at least a broad comprehension of, and trust in, national income figures. Hence VA, by providing a link between financial statements and the economists' macroeconomic data, will assist the inter-professional exchanges of data and expertise. For example, the VA Statement is closely related to the economists' input/output analysis of inter-industry relationships. The Statement should, therefore, increase the possibility of companies using input/output methods to improve their internal decision making. Also, there are possibilities for the national income data to be verified and eventually, perhaps, derived from the underlying VA Statements of individual companies, thereby enhancing the accuracy of macroeconomic statistics. This would improve economic forecasts and hence make possible the more timely and accurate use of the instruments of economic policy.

The principal qualifications to the general rule that the sum of the Values Added by all companies equals the economist's national income figure are:

1 National income includes Value Added by government and by other public bodies. For example, the Value Added by defense expenditure is assumed to be equal to its cost.

2 The VA of a company may arise partly in foreign territories. Similarly, Value may be Added in the domestic country by a foreign concern.

3 Economic measures of national income concentrate on production rather than on sales. Differences arise, therefore, in the valuation of increases/decreases in inventories.

4 National income conventions involve several major simplifying assumptions which are not used by financial accountants. For example, the output of durable consumer goods is assumed to have been consumed in the year of manufacture. In effect, the economist depreciates a car by 100 percent in the first year, while the accountant would write off his company's fleet of vehicles at, say, 25 percent of cost in each year.

A final advantage claimed for the VA Statement is that it is built on the basic conceptual foundations which are currently accepted in balance sheets and earnings statements. Concepts such as going concern, matching, consistency, objectivity, and substance-over-form are all just as applicable to the VA Statement as to the earnings statement. Also, the alternative theories of income measurement (based on historical cost, replacement cost, realizable values, deprival values, *etc.*) can all be translated into terms of VA measurement. This point may be expressed in a different form by saying that the VA Statement is identical with a conventional earnings statement except for the matter of whose earnings are included: "earnings" refers to the return accruing to shareholders while VA refers to the return accruing to the whole team of providers of labor and of capital, plus the government.

Having reviewed the advantages which are claimed for the VA Statement, it is natural to consider whether there are any disadvantages in its inclusion in annual reports.

DISADVANTAGES

The first disadvantage of the new Statement is that it implicitly treats a company as a team of cooperating groups, and this attitude may be grossly at variance with the facts. VA is said to be the reward which is earned by the joint and interdependent efforts of employees (who provide labor services), shareholders and lenders (who provide capital), and the government (which provides law and order, defense services, infrastructure, a legal framework for contract-enforcement, *etc.*) It is the government which is the least natural member of the alleged team. The government was not invited to join the team, it plays no part in team decision making, and its share of VA (*i.e.,* corporation tax) is proportional to profits rather than to VA. Another case where team membership seems to be strangely defined is where a supplier of bought-in materials is a specialist supplier to a sole customer. This supplier would be excluded from the team even though he had no other outlet for his production. We have already mentioned the British company BOC, which has a near-monopoly of the supply of industrial gases. Suppose BOC bought all its steel gas cylinders from XYZ Ltd., which makes no other product and has no other market for its cylinders. Under the VA conventions, XYZ would be *excluded* from the BOC team even though its entire commercial future were tied up with BOC. However, a bank which extended temporary credit to BOC would be *included* in the BOC team (as a capital provider) even though it was not committed to or knowledgeable about the industrial gas industry. Common sense here would suggest the exact opposite, *i.e.,* that XYZ Ltd. was part of the team while the bank was not.

The best that can be said to defend the VA Statement from this attack is that for most companies there is already some validity in drawing a line around workers, capital-providers, and government and declaring those included to be a team. And indeed the objection discussed has a certain circularity, for one of the advantages claimed for the VA Statement is that it will lead team-members to regard themselves as part of a team. In short the objector is saying, "I do not find your team-definition to be natural," while the VA proponent is replying, "You will find it natural when all companies adopt it and, moreover, the definition suggested will improve teamwork."

A second disadvantage of the VA Statement is that its inclusion in an annual report can cause confusion with the earnings statement. What would a non-accountant reading the annual report infer if he saw that VA was rising while earnings were falling? Or, indeed, what would he make of the annual report if he saw VA was positive but earnings were negative? This last case would not be all that unusual and can be illustrated by a simple example. Suppose a company's sales for the year were £100, bought-in costs were nil, and it paid £150 in wages. In these circumstances VA for the year would be £100, for that would be the Value placed on the company's efforts by its customers. However, a loss of £50 has been made. What has happened here is that the team has earned £100 of VA but has overdistributed to team members. In effect, shareholders have lost £50 of the company's reserves, as this is the excess of wages over VA. The shareholders can rightly say they have lost Value to the extent of £50, but the VA Statement is not a report on shareholders' welfare. It is a report on the welfare of a more broadly defined team, and that team taken as a whole has benefited by Value Added of £100.

A third disadvantage of the VA Statement is that it raises a new danger of inefficient management, since managers may wrongly seek to maximize their company's VA. One book has already been published which exhorts managers to accept this improper objective [Gilchrist, 1971]. This unsound advice could lead to grossly wasteful decisions in which shareholders' capital would be dissipated in subsidizing uneconomic output. Consider, for example, a company which currently buys a component from a supplier for £100. A manager investigates the possibilities of making the component within the company and finds that to do so would cost £80 in direct materials and £70 in direct labor (overheads are assumed to be nil for simplicity). The foolish VA-maximizer would now decide on internal manufacture, as his bought-in costs would then fall from £100 to £80 and so the VA would rise by £20 for each component. However, this £20 of additional VA would involve an extra £70 of wages, and so shareholders' earnings would fall by £50 per component. The VA-maximizer would, therefore, be dissipating shareholders' capital by manufacturing instead of buying in.

A fourth argument against the VA Statement is that its inclusion in the annual report would involve extra work, therefore extra costs and delay and also a slight loss of confidentiality in view of the additional disclosure involved. In practice the extra work, cost, and delay have proved to be negligible. The only extra disclosure involved for British companies has been their overseas wage cost. This arises because current disclosure requirements cover *U.K.* wage costs, and, therefore, the inclusion of *total* wage cost in the VA Statement implicitly reveals overseas wages. This could be an embarrassing or damaging disclosure if all overseas wage costs arose in one country, *e.g.*, because of considerations of competitiveness with overseas rivals or political sensitivity as in southern Africa.

The final objection to the VA Statement is a very serious one: VA Statements are flagrantly unstandardized. Indeed, an unscrupulous accountant could manipulate the choice of methods of VA calculation to produce almost any VA figure desired. To illustrate the variety and massive effect of VA reporting practices, one can refer back to the accounts of Esso already mentioned. Another example comes from the 1975 and 1976 annual reports of Allied Breweries Ltd. In the former year Allied's VA was £379 million and the government's share was 50 percent. In the latter year VA was £247 million and the government took only 13 percent. Had the beer drinkers *and* the government both become abstemious? In fact, the company had merely decided to re-classify the special excise tax on alcohol as a bought-in cost rather than as part of the government's share of VA.

All the companies mentioned in this article have made clear how they have arrived at the figures used in their VA Statements and so no readers of the

Statements should have been misled. However, it is clear that the VA Statement will not long retain the public's confidence unless it is standardized. The Accounting Standards Committee is already studying the questions of classification and definition in the VA Statement. Depreciation and taxes are the main problems.

It has already been seen that a VA Statement can be framed as a report on Net VA, after deducting depreciation, and Table 1 which showed the Net VA of BOC illustrated this. However, the majority of British companies prefer to set forth their VA Statement as a report on Gross VA, so that depreciation is an application of VA rather than a cost to be deducted in calculating VA. Table 3 shows an example of a report on Gross VA, that of Imperial Chemical Industries Ltd. The VA Statement of ICI shows how depreciation can be added to the retained profit for the year, thereby giving a total which ICI has described as "re-investment in the business." The Gross VA for the year was £1,874 million, and the depreciation charge was £221 million. Had ICI chosen to present a report on Net VA, its VA would have been £1,653 million (*i.e.,* £1,874 million less £221 million). In this case, the choice of Gross or Net VA makes a difference of 13 percent of the Net VA. One can see how the treatment of depreciation has a material effect, especially on the ratios referred to earlier. For example, the reported share of VA going in wages will be higher if we adopt the Net VA definition than if we decide in favor of Gross VA.

The reasons for reporting Gross VA are three. First, Gross VA is a more objective figure than Net VA. This is because depreciation is more prone to subjective judgment than are bought-in costs. Depreciation involves opinions as to likely asset lives, scrap values, straight-line versus percentage of declining balance, and so on. Bought-in costs will involve some subjectivity, for example, regarding closing stock values, but the general run of bought-in costs such as repairs, fuel, telephone costs, and electric power, will be fairly objective. This point has special force if VA is to be used as a basis for some sort of productivity bonus to employees. Workers may suspect the management of manipulating VA to produce lower bonuses if a subjective cost like depreciation is deducted in arriving at VA.

Second, the Gross VA format involves reporting depreciation alongside retained profit. The resultant subtotal usefully shows the portion of the year's VA which has become available for reinvestment. This ratio is less readily calculable from a Net VA Statement where depreciation is separated from retentions.

Third, the practice of reporting Gross VA would lead to a closer correspondence between VA and national income figures, for economists generally prefer gross measures of national income to net ones.

The present writer sees some merit in these arguments but believes that the principal reason why most British companies have reported Gross VA is that they have unthinkingly followed the advice given in *The Corporate Report* [ASC, 1975]. That document did not even mention the possibility of the alternative Net VA format. The following reasons for preferring Net VA are substantial and, in the present writer's opinion, outweigh the earlier points.

ARGUMENTS FOR NET VA

First, it has been explained how "wealth creation" is often used as a synonym for VA. Wealth creation is overstated if no allowance is made for the wearing out or loss

TABLE 3

Imperial Chemical Industries Ltd., and Subsidiaries
Value Added Statement Year to December 31, 1977

Sources of income		£ million
Sales		4,663
Royalties and other trading income		39
Less: Materials and services used		(2,866)
Value added by manufacturing and trading		1,836
Shares of profits of principal associated companies and investment income		96
Exchange loss on net current assets of overseas subsidiaries		(29)
Extraordinary items		(29)
Total value added		1,874
Disposal of total value added		
Employees		
—pay, plus pension and national insurance contributions	1,063	
—profit-sharing bonus	29	1,092
Governments—corporate taxes, less grants		202
Providers of capital		
—interest paid on borrowings	107	
—dividends to shareholders	93	
—minority shareholders in subsidiaries	26	226
Re-investment in the business		
—depreciation set aside	221	
—profit retained	133	354
		1,874

of value of fixed assets which occurs as new assets are created. Another way of putting this is to say that a company theoretically could distribute 100 percent of its *Net* VA in the form of wages, taxes, interest and dividends. But it could not long continue to distribute 100 percent of *Gross* VA, since the company would be consuming its seed corn, and its operations would grind to a halt when the fixed assets were exhausted. If, therefore, Net VA is distributable while Gross VA is not, then Net VA is a better denominator for distribution ratios such as payroll/VA.

Second, Net VA is a firmer base for calculating productivity bonuses than is Gross VA. Several British companies have introduced schemes which pay productivity bonuses based on achieved increases in VA. If these schemes are based on Gross VA, then they make no allowance for capital changes. A company's VA might rise after new capital had been invested in a major plant modernization, and employees might be given "their share" of this increase as a bonus. But if that share is based on VA before depreciation, then no recognition is given to the need for an increased depreciation charge. In short, the wrong people benefit, since the providers of capital deserve the credit for the VA increase. Net VA does not entirely do away with this unfairness, but it lessens it.

Third, the concepts of consistency and matching demand that depreciation be deducted along with bought-in costs to derive Net VA. Bought-in materials are assets bought from outside suppliers, and the cost thereof is matched against sales revenue in the upper part of the VA Statement. Depreciable fixed assets will also have been bought from outside suppliers,[2] and the cost of these should, therefore, also be matched against sales revenue over the assets' useful lives. Net VA treats materials and fixed assets consistently, as both will appear as deductions from VA in accordance with their becoming used up. Gross VA is inconsistent, for costs would be charged under the bought-in heading if the item has a life of under one year. But if the item has a longer life it would be treated as a depreciable fixed asset and its cost would *never* appear as a charge against VA.

Fourth, Net VA involves no double-counting, while Gross VA does involve some double-counting and is misleading. The double-counting arises from the non-deduction of depreciation. Where one company buys a product from another company, the seller's VA will be augmented and the buyer's diminished by the amount of the sale. This elimination of the intermediate transaction reflects the idea that national income arises when a final consumer buys the product but no national income arises merely from inter-company transactions. If company A sells £100 worth of fuel to company B, then no Value is Added, or no wealth is created just by this transaction. The VA will arise when B uses the fuel to generate saleable output which will end up as a consumer product. If B did not deduct the £100 as bought-in cost, then the £100 of VA would be double-counted by A and by B. The VA Statement deals with these transactions satisfactorily so far as materials are concerned. But if the asset which A sold to B had been a depreciable fixed asset, then (a) Net VA would eliminate the double-counting as B would, over the years, deduct the £100 in the form of depreciation alongside other bought-in costs, while (b) Gross VA would not eliminate the double-counting.

Fifth, the team concept behind VA fits Net VA better than Gross VA. If one looks at the Net VA Statement in Table 1, one sees that the team consists of workers, government, and capital providers. The surplus VA which remains after the share-out among team members is retained, and this retained profit is a deferred application of VA to shareholders, who are team members, and may thereby benefit by higher quoted share values and eventually higher dividends. The team concept works. However, if one looks at a Gross VA Statement, as in Table 3, one may justifiably

[2]Some fixed assets may have been made by the company, as where a building contractor builds his own offices. In these cases, the capitalized value of the home-built fixed asset should be added to sales in the VA Statement, the costs (bought-in material, labor, *etc.*) being reported elsewhere. In subsequent years the depreciation on the home-built fixed assets should be merged with depreciation on all other fixed assets in the VA Statement.

ask how depreciation relates to the team concept. One of the ways in which VA has been "disposed" in Table 3 is "depreciation set aside." But depreciation is not an employee, or a capital provider, or the government. In fact the disposal reported as depreciation is a part of wealth which was in the past "distributed" or paid to the company which originally supplied the depreciable fixed asset. In short, suppliers of fixed assets are honorary team-members. This distorts the concept of the company team and introduces inconsistency between classes of supplier.

Accordingly the present writer considers that the VA Statement should be standardized as a report on *Net* VA.

TAXATION

The second major area of non-standardization in current VA practice is taxation. Some companies report only tax levied on profits (which in Britain is corporation tax) under the heading of "VA applied to governments." Other companies report an extensive range of taxes, including withholding taxes deducted at the source from workers' wages, local government charges for sanitation and roads, and taxes levied on the company's outputs. The two examples already referred to (Esso and Allied Breweries) show how large an effect the choice of accounting treatment can have, but these examples are abnormal as they come from industries which attract especially high rates of excise tax (petroleum and alcohol).

Most companies have chosen to include only corporation tax under the government's share of VA. This practice has many advantages. It avoids the need to make subjective judgments as to where to draw the line, for there is a long list of government imposts which could be regarded as part of the government's share. Examples of difficult items include road vehicle taxes, oil royalties, training levies to government-run training schemes for employees, and fines paid. Further, subjectivity arises over how widely "government" is defined—one could include government-sponsored bodies which regulate aviation and broadcasting, or utilities. Related to this danger of a subjective decision on which taxes to include is the simplicity and cheapness of the alternative. Taxes can be left in the accounts into which they have already been analyzed, and the VA Statement will then not require costly additional analysis work. This point is especially applicable where a group of companies with many subsidiaries, some overseas, is preparing a VA Statement. A further advantage for the suggested practice is that the VA Statement is easy to reconcile with the earnings statement if only corporate taxes on profit are included under the government's share of VA. This ease of reconciliation is lost if a wide range of taxes is included.

There are a number of additional minor areas of non-standardization in VA Statements. These include the classification of rents payable (under bought-in costs or under interest payable?) and the way in which the results of associated companies are handled (see Morley [1978]). But it is broadly true that the Accounting Standards Committee could achieve substantial standardization of the VA Statement, thereby defusing the main argument against the Statement, if it prescribed (a) that depreciation should be deducted with bought-in costs, thereby reporting Net VA, and (b) that the government's share of VA should contain only corporation tax.

CONCLUSION

In many ways, the VA Statement is an unsatisfactory innovation to encounter. It is easy enough to understand and to prepare. Much is claimed for it, but the claims are hard to pin down and to verify. The benefits claimed are principally improvement in attitude, motivation, and behavior, and these are remarkably difficult to research. The present status of the VA Statement is that it has achieved sudden popularity in Britain and will probably soon appear in the corporate reports of all major British companies. It is likely that the dangers inherent in the wide selection of accounting treatments will lead the Accounting Standards Committee to issue a standard definition for each major heading in the VA Statement. Standard-setting committees have in the past often operated by discovering the most widespread practice, pronouncing it good, and making it compulsory. This will work well enough for the VA Statement except for the question of depreciation, where, for the reasons given earlier, the prevailing practice should be changed.

REFERENCES

Accounting Standards Committee, *The Corporate Report* (London, 1975).

Alcan Aluminium (U.K.) Ltd., Annual Report (December 31, 1976).

Allied Breweries Ltd., Annual Reports (September 30, 1975 and September 30, 1976).

BOC International Ltd., Annual Report (September 30, 1977).

Bowater Corporation Ltd., Annual Report (December 31, 1977).

Bullock, Lord, *Report of the Committee of Inquiry on Industrial Democracy* (Department of Trade, Cmnd. 6706, H.M.S.O., 1977).

Cox, B., *Value Added—an Appreciation for the Accountant Concerned with Industry* (Institute of Cost and Management Accountants, 1978).

Department of Trade, *The Future of Company Reports* (Cmnd. 6888, H.M.S.O., 1977).

Esso Petroleum Company Ltd., Annual Reports (December 31, 1976 and December 31, 1977).

Gilchrist, R. R., *Managing for Profit: The Added Value Concept* (Allen and Unwin, 1971).

Hendriksen, E. S., *Accounting Theory* (Richard D. Irwin, 1977).

Imperial Chemical Industries Ltd., Annual Report (December 31, 1977).

Morley, M. F., *The Value Added Statement* (published for the Institute of Chartered Accountants of Scotland by Gee & Co., 1978).

Suojanen, W. W., "Accounting Theory and the Large Corporation," *The Accounting Review* (July 1954), pp. 391–398.

CASH & FUNDS: HISTORICAL, CONTEMPORARY & FORECASTED DATA

Financial statements, the end product of the accounting process, are supposed to provide information to users. Who are the users and for what purpose do they use information contained in financial statements? The users are individuals, organizations, governments, and management. The need for information and the kind of information needed varies with the choices with which the user is faced. There are those users who need a score card to determine the results of the past. There are users who need a basis for estimating or predicting the future as a basis for selecting from among competing alternatives.

Financial statements have historically been general purpose statements. The assertion has been made that the information contained in financial statements is useful for any user. The logic is that the balance sheet presents a static view of the firm at a point in time — the end of a year. The income statement and the statement of changes in financial position are representations of the flows occurring during a period of time. The income statement presents the flows resulting from the conduct of normal business operations and the statement of changes presents the sources of capital brought into the business and the uses made of capital during the same period.

Accounting principles have been developed to assist the very difficult process of measuring economic events. The process of quantification of economic phenomena is frequently difficult because the events are complex and result in a multitude of changes. In an effort to achieve some comparability among measures of similar events, accounting principles have been developed at increasing levels of specificity. While this process does enhance the communication of information about specific results, at the same time the result may be the loss of significant information because the specific measurement rules do not take into account the broader aspects of the events.

Historically, accounting principles for the measurement of income have been based on the Hicksian definition of income, i.e., "the maximum value which [a man] can consume during a week, and still expect to be as well off at the end of the week as he was at the beginning."[1] This definition speaks in broad terms about the increase in assets less the increase in liabilities. Recognizing that cash flows measure the fluctuations in one very important asset, cash, but significant increases in other asset values or changes in liabilities may not be reflected in a statement of cash flows, accounting principles have been developed which require the use of accrual concepts. In general, changes in asset values which can be expected to change the amount of cash received in the near future and changes in the amount of cash required to satisfy obligations of the business should be reflected in the statement of operations. Of course, these changes must be measurable with a high level of confidence and the results must be verifiable. Obviously these restrictions limit the changes that may be reflected in financial statements.

As the variety of business transactions has increased and changed over time, the set of accounting rules devised to implement accounting principles has continued to expand. The very complexity of many of the transactions has created significant problems for the accountant who is charged with measuring the impact of each transaction on the business. Since much potentially useful information has not been reported in the standard format of financial statements, increasing criticism has been voiced that the present reporting formats do not meet the needs of many users — particularly those who are making choices among alternatives where more complete financial information is considered to be necessary.

Among the critics are those who argue that the accrual concept of measuring earnings distorts the measure by including factors that will never affect the flow of cash to or from the business. In "Let's Give the Shareholders the Figures They Need," Alfred Rappaport complains that different accounting measures may be used to account for essentially identical transactions with the result that net income is changed not because of a different pattern of events but rather through the choice of different accounting procedures.

There is, of course, an assumption in these arguments that over time aggregate net income should approximate the aggregate increase in cash and/or assets purchased with the cash generated from operations. Rappaport also cites instances where observed phenomena are in conflict with expectations based on published financial data. The argument is then advanced that there must be some other measure of change in wealth which would be more consistent with observed phenomena. He then provides an outline of a proposed reporting format he believes will provide one group of users, investors, with more relevant and therefore more useful information. The details of this proposal were more thoroughly discussed in a report of an American Accounting Association committee in 1969.[2]

There are many who argue that the essence of Rappaport's proposal could be achieved by modifiying the focus of the statement of changes in financial position

---

[1] J. R. Hicks, *Value and Capital* (Oxford, England: Clarendon Press, 1939), 172.
[2] "An Evaluation of External Reporting Practices: a Report of the 1966–68 Committee on External Reporting," *The Accounting Review,* Supplement to Vol XLIV, 1969, pp. 79–123.

from one which measures the change in working capital to one which measures change in cash. The Financial Executives Institute (FEI) commissioned Arthur D. Little, Inc. to study trends in the focus of the statement of changes in financial position. An FEI *Alert,* issued on November 15, 1983, reported that of the more than 750 financial executives, financial analysts, individual investors and commercial bankers responding to a questionnaire, 57% intend to use the cash definition whereas in 1980 only 27 % used this definition. Since 1981 the FEI has been urging members to adopt the cash definition. Such a focus for the statement "better enables users to evaluate a company's operating, financing and/or investing ability and performance."[3] FEI has also been encouraging members "to experiment in developing new, more meaningful formats for the funds statement."

Loyd Heath, in his article, "Let's Scrap the 'Funds' Statement," argues that the present format does not accomplish the objectives of the statement as specified in APB Opinion No. 19:

1 to summarize the financial and investing activities of the entity including the extent to which the enterprise has generated funds from operations during the period
2 to complete the disclosure of changes in financial postion during the period.

Moreover, he does not believe the FEI solution will be adequate. The present format requires too many different types of information to be disclosed in the same statement. He prefers three statements, each one oriented to specific information needs of users:

1 a Statement of Cash Receipts and Payments focused on debt paying ability
2 a Statement of Financing Activities focused on changes in the capital structure of the firm
3 a Statement of Investing Activities focused on changes in long-term investments in plant and securities

The exchange of views following Heath's article is representative of the debates one finds on many issues in accounting, where assertions are made regarding the value of information to users. This exchange enables readers to understand the dynamics that shape the development of accounting principles.

In a companion article, Heath and Paul H. Rosenfield stress the importance of complete reporting. Profitability is not an adequate indicator if, in fact, the requirements of the business demand greater and greater resources to maintain the functioning enterprise. The cry for a broader perspective on financial reporting comes at a time when there has been increasing attention devoted to measures of performance with little attention being given to the development of measurement and reporting standards for reflecting the increased resources required to maintain the enterprise's existing level of activity. The point that Heath and Rosenfield are making is that financial reporting should be seen as more than an accounting for profitability alone. If the level of profits is to be maintained, the resources needed to support the activity and the capital to finance the enterprise must be kept intact.

[3]*Alert,* Volume 10, No. 2 (Morristown, NJ: Financial Executives Institute, November 15, 1983).

In "The Cash Flow Accounting Alternative for Corporate Financial Reporting," Thomas A. Lee argues for adoption of cash flow accounting because of the difficulty, if not the impossibility, of properly allocating cost between accounting periods. Lee appears to be relatively unconcerned about the process of valuing individual assets but is more concerned that users have the information necessary to determine the value of the entity. The discounted cash flow concept as a measure of value is the basis of his thesis that cash flow is more relevant to the user than accrual-based measures of income. The measure of cash flow is also more objective and when combined with a forecast of future performance puts the focus on management accountability. The inclusion of a forecast, he argues, reduces the temptation for management to manipulate profit by timing the cash flows to achieve certain strategic profit objectives.

These articles highlight much of the debate that is raging over what information has decision relevance for users. Throughout this debate, the focus appears to be on the decision maker as user. The rhetoric is often heated, but there has been no hard evidence to demonstrate that one method is clearly preferable to another. There is, of course, the belief by some that once the conceptual framework of accounting is completed, issues such as those raised here can be resolved by reference to the framework. As has been suggested by the readings in Section I, it seems to be a brute fact that the end product of the accounting process is frequently driven by utilitarian forces and seldom by force of accounting logic.

BIBLIOGRAPHICAL NOTES

A research monograph written by one of the authors of an article in this section, and which elaborates upon his views, is:

Heath, Loyd C.: *Financial Reporting and the Evaluation of Solvency* (New York: AICPA, 1978).

The following is a proceedings volume from a conference on cash flow accounting:

Hicks, Barry E. and Pearson Hunt (eds.): *Cash Flow Accounting,* (Sudbury, Ontario, Canada: The International Group for Cash Flow Accounting and the Research and Publication Division, School of Commerce and Administration, Laurentian University, 1981).

A review of most of the British research on cash flow accounting may be found in:

Lee, T. A.: "Cash Flow Accounting and Corporate Financial Reporting," in *Essays in British Accounting Research,* edited by Michael Bromwich and Anthony G. Hopwood (London: Pitman Publishing Limited, 1981).

Several volumes that discuss forecast reporting are cited in the Bibliographical Notes following the introduction to Section Four.

A recent study of the funds statement is the following:

Seed, Allen H. III, *The Funds Statement: Structure and Use* (New York: Financial Executives Research Foundation, 1984).

Let's Give Shareholders the Figures They Need

Alfred Rappaport
Northwestern University

In both corporate reports and the financial press, there is an obsessive fixation on earnings per share as the score card of corporate performance. But earnings per share, or the growth rate in EPS, are an unreliable standard for evaluating a firm's progress in creating economic value for shareholders.

Consider the recent performance of Anheuser-Busch, Avon Products, Clorox, Gillette, Goodyear, Warner Lambert and Xerox. According to the most recent Fortune 500 survey, each of these companies reported compound annual EPS growth rates of 6% to 12% between the end of 1970 and the end of 1980. During the same period, total rate of return (dividends plus capital gains) for each company's shareholders was *negative*.

This experience is not unusual. In an earlier published study of Standard & Poor's 400 industrial companies, I found that 16% of those achieving annual EPS growth of 15% or more from 1974 to 1979 provided negative rates of return to shareholders, while for 35% of the same companies, rates of return were inadequate to compensate shareholders for inflation.

Some of the stock price drops for high EPS growth companies may reflect lower market expectations about a company's investment opportunities. A company's shares are likely to appreciate over time if the market expects management to earn a rate of return on new investments greater than the rate investors can expect to earn by investing in alternative, identically risky securities. But a company can maintain EPS growth even when it is investing below the market discount rate, and thereby decreasing the value of common shares.

There are several important reasons why EPS fails to measure economic value for shareholders. First, earnings figures vary with the use of different accounting methods, for example LIFO vs. FIFO inventory costing. Second, earnings numbers do not reflect differences in business and financial risk faced by various companies or divisions within a single company. Third, earnings do not account for relative rates of investment in working capital and fixed capital needed to support sales growth. Some companies invest as little as 25 cents to produce an incremental dollar of sales, while others require investment rates two or three times as large. Finally, reported earnings do not incorporate changes in a company's cost of capital due to either shifts in inflationary expectations or changes in business or financial risk.

The economic value of an investment is the anticipated cash flow discounted by the cost of capital. Consistent with this economic theory of value, the Financial Accounting Standards Board (FASB) has stated that an essential objective of corporate financial reporting is to provide a basis for assessing the amounts, timing and uncertainty of prospective cash flows. But financial reports are still oriented to earnings with all of its necessarily arbitrary accounting allocations; and most companies give investors little systematically organized information on past cash flows.

The FASB and individual companies via voluntary disclosure have an excellent opportunity to make corporate reporting more meaningful to shareholders. A statement that integrates the cash flow effect of a company's prior five or 10 years' operating, investment, financing and dividend decisions can serve as an essential point of departure for estimating future cash flows. The accompanying table shows a general format for such a statement as follows:

Current funds from operations (CFO) is a measure of operating revenues minus out-of-pocket operating costs and expenses incurred during the period. CFO is based on current revenues and *current* costs and includes no accounting allocations such as depreciation. Therefore, CFO and the CFO/revenue ratio provide an economic basis for evaluating a company's operating trends over time and for making comparisons among companies within an industry.

CFO cannot, however, be viewed in isolation. If economic value is to be created for shareholders, CFO must be sufficient over time to offset needed investments for working capital, fixed capital and research and development, while also compensating shareholders for risk and inflation. For example, a company that needs to invest 50 cents for each additional dollar of sales will require a CFO rate of return on revenue twice that needed for a similar risk company investing only 25 cents per dollar of incremental sales.

To judge the reasonableness of a company's investment growth strategies, the investor also needs to consider its financing and dividend policies. The financing section of the statement shows the relative proportions of capital raised from debt and equity sources which could, in turn, affect the financial risk of the firm and thereby its overall cost of capital. Financing information also provides investors with additional information for estimating future dividends and the possible need to issue additional shares to fund the company's growth.

In the final analysis, the accepted financial performance standard of a publicly held company is the total rate of return realized by its shareholders. Impressive EPS growth statistics offer little comfort to the investor facing a drop in the market value of its equity investment. As accounting earnings become less reliable indicators of changes in economic value, corporate reporting focusing on the cash impact of operating, investment, financing and dividend decisions becomes more essential than ever before.

The financial press, for its part, should redirect its focus from earnings per share to economically more useful measures: current funds from operations, investment requirements, net cash flow and, most important, rate of return earned by share-holders. A shift in the "score card" of American management from accounting numbers to economic returns may well lead to the adoption of a longer-term orientation in corporate planning and decision making. This, in turn, is likely to improve not only the prospects of individual companies but the economy as a whole.

STATEMENT FOR ESTIMATING FUTURE CASH FLOWS

Operating revenues

Costs and expenses:

Current cost of sales (excluding depreciation and other non-cash expenses)
Selling and administrative expenses (excluding non-cash expenses and any
    expensed investments such as R&D)

Current funds from operations before taxes

Income taxes currently payable

Current funds from operations after taxes

Investments for:

Working capital
Capital expenditures
Research and development
Other

Net cash flow

Financing:

Net increase in debt
Net increase in equity
Interest expense—net of taxes

Dividends

Let's Scrap the "Funds" Statement

Loyd C. Heath
University of Washington

Funds statements found in practice today are a hodgepodge of miscellaneous information presented in a confusing and misleading way.

Many accountants see the problem as one of defining "funds." They attribute the confusion over the funds statement to confusion over what is meant by the term "funds." R. A. Rayman, for example, argued:

"The fact that funds analysis has not made more headway may be attributable to the absence of a definition of funds which is generally accepted. There is, in fact, a variety of definitions ranging over the whole spectrum of liquidity, from cash at one extreme to total resources at the other, with compromises like working capital somewhere in between."[1]

In my opinion, the fundamental problem is not a definitional one. Confusion over what is meant by the term funds is merely a symptom of a more basic problem: confusion over the objectives of the funds statement. The solution does not lie in redefining funds; it lies in scrapping the funds statement, identifying the objectives it tries but fails to meet and designing statements that achieve those objectives.[2]

SPECIOUS OBJECTIVES

The stated objectives of funds statements in Accounting Principles Board Opinion No. 19, *Reporting Changes in Financial Position,* are specious. Superficially they appear to be reasonable but when analyzed and applied in practice they are unclear, misleading and unattainable. According to the opinion, the objectives are "(1) to summarize the financing and investing activities of the entity, including the extent to which the enterprise has generated funds from operations during the period, and (2) to complete the disclosure of changes in financial position during the period."

The meaning of the first objective is unclear. It begs the question of what effects of financing and investing activities should be summarized. Financing and investing activities, like all business activities, have many different effects. A single transaction may affect cash, working capital, total assets, capital structure, net assets and so forth. Obviously not all of those effects can be portrayed in a single statement, but the opinion is silent as to which one or ones are the object or objects of attention in the statement. Paragraph 8 says only that the statement "should be based on a broad concept embracing all changes in financial position" without even saying a broad concept of what! The problem reflects more than just poor draftsmanship; it reflects the absence of an underlying concept.

The second objective is unattainable. As noted, business activities have many effects. No statement can possibly "complete the disclosure of changes in financial position" (par. 4) or "disclose all important changes in financial position for the period covered"(par. 11). A meaningful statement must focus on a specific aspect or dimension of financial position such as cash, working capital, net assets, monetary assets and so forth. The possibilities are almost limitless. No statement can portray in an understandable way all effects of all activities on all possible measures of financial position. As Arthur Stone Dewing observed:

> But no representation of anything in this world can be perfect. It must portray one or more aspects or attributes of the thing represented and neglect or throw into insignificance the other aspects or attributes. This observation is conspicuously true when we are dealing with . . . accounting statements. Such statements must select one or at most a very few

---

[1] R. A. Rayman, "Is Conventional Accounting Obsolete?" *Accountancy,* June 1970, p. 423.

[2] The analysis and recommendations that follow are based on my forthcoming research monograph, *Financial Reporting and the Evaluation of Solvency,* to be published by the accounting standards division of the American Institute of Certified Public Accountants.

aspects of the objects represented and neglect all others —as vital statistics consider only the length of years of a man, neglecting every other aspect of his life or characteristics as a human being.[3]

Many of the alleged objectives of funds statements described in accounting literature are even more confusing than those in Opinion no. 19. For example, one widespread belief is that fund statements are somehow supposed to show what "happened" to a company's profits or "where its profits went."[4]

Profits are not a physical "thing" that can be disposed of, retained or paid out. Profit is simply the name given to the change in a company's net assets that results from selected operating, financing and investing activities during a period of time, or, as the APB defined it, "the net increase (net decrease) in owners' equity (assets minus liabilities) of an enterprise for an accounting period from profit-directed activities. . . ."[5] It is a *change* in net assets, not an asset. It is measured in money but it is not money. One could, of course, show what became of a company's *cash* — part of which may have been received as a result of its profit-directed activities. A statement of cash receipts and payments would show that. Similarly, one could also prepare a statement that explains changes in some group of assets, say, its quick assets, part of which may have been received as a result of its profit-directed activities. But to try to show what "happened" to a company's profits is a meaningless objective; no statement can possibly show that.

IMPLICIT OBJECTIVES

Although the APB's stated objectives in Opinion no. 19 are unclear, a careful reading of the opinion suggests that the board was concerned with reporting the effects of *all* business activities (not just financing and investing activities) on at least two and perhaps three different measures of financial position.

The first was to report changes in some measure of the cash or near-cash resources of a company, that is, changes in some measure of its debt-paying ability. A number of specific provisions of the opinion support that view. Paragraph 10

---

[3] Arthur Stone Dewing, *The Financial Policy of Corporations,* 5th ed., vol 1 (New York: The Ronald Press Co., 1953), p. 517.

[4] Perry Mason stated that a funds statement "contributes materially to . . . the answers to such questions as . . . Where did the profits go?" (Perry Mason, *"Cash Flow" Analysis and the Funds Statement,* Accounting Research Study No. 2 [New York: AICPA, 1961], p. 49). Paton and Paton stated that a funds statement "is designed to . . . indicate what disposition has been made of earnings." (William A. Paton and William A. Paton, Jr., *Corporation Accounts and Statements* [New York: Macmillan Co., 1955], p. 440). A. B. Carson maintains that "among other things it supplies an answer to the question: 'What happened to the profit?'" (A. B. Carson, "A Source and Application of Funds' Philosophy of Financial Accounting," *Accounting Review,* April 1949, p. 160). Roy A. Foulke argues that it "gives a clear answer to the question of what has become of the net profits." (Roy A. Foulke, *Practical Financial Statement Analysis,* 6th ed. [New York: McGraw-Hill Book Co., Inc., 1968], p. 474).

For other similar examples, see Donald A. Corbin, "Proposals for Improving Funds Statements," *Accounting Review,* July 1961, p. 398; National Association of Accountants Research Report No. 38, *Cash Flow Analysis for Managerial Control,* (New York: NAA, 1961), p. 58; David F. Hawkins, *Corporate Financial Reporting,* rev. ed. (Homewood, Ill.; Richard D. Irwin, Inc., 1977), p. 125; Donald E. Kieso and Jerry J. Weygandt, *Intermediate Accounting,* 2nd ed. (New York: John Wiley & Sons, 1977), p. 983; and Jay M. Smith, Jr., and K. Fred Skousen, *Intermediate Accounting,* 6th ed. (Cincinnatti: South-Western Publishing Co., 1977), p. 682.

[5] APB Statement no. 4, *Basic Concepts and Accounting Principles* (New York: AICPA, 1971), par. 134.

requires that "the Statement should prominently disclose working capital or cash provided from or used in operations for the period." Paragraph 11 states, "The Statement may be in balanced form or in a form expressing the changes in financial position in terms of cash, or cash and temporary investments combined, of all quick assets, or of working capital." Paragraph 14 further specifically requires that "outlays for purchase of long-term assets... proceeds from sale (or working capital or cash provided by sale) of long-term assets" and "dividends in cash" all be disclosed.

The second type of change that the board appears to have been concerned with having reported was capital structure changes. Capital structure refers to the claims on the resources used to operate a business enterprise, including both debt and equity claims. Changes in the size of a company's capital structure result from activities such as the borrowing and repayment of debt, sale and repurchase of capital stock, profit-directed activities and cash or property dividends. Changes in the composition of a company's capital structure result from activities such as the conversion of convertible securities into common stock and refinancing operations including the "swapping" of one type of financial instrument for another in a financial reorganization.

Many changes in the size and composition of a company's capital structure also affect its cash, its working capital and other measures of debt-paying ability, but some of them do not. Evidence that the board was concerned with having changes in size and composition of a company's capital structure as well as changes in its debt-paying ability reported is found in the requirement in paragraph 14 that "the Statement should clearly disclose" activities such as "conversion of long-term debt or preferred stock to common stock . . . issuance, redemption, or purchase of capital stock . . . for assets other than cash" and "dividends . . . in kind or other distributions to shareholders." Other evidence of the board's concern with changes in a company's capital structure is found in paragraph 6:

> However, a funds statement based on either the cash or the working capital concept of funds sometimes excludes certain financing and investing activities because they do not directly affect cash or working capital during the period. For example, issuing equity securities to acquire a building is both a financing and investing transaction but does not affect either cash or working capital. To meet all of its objectives, a funds statement should disclose separately the financing and investing aspects of all significant transactions that affect financial position during a period. These transactions include acquisition or disposal of property in exchange for debt or equity securities and conversion of long-term debt or preferred stock to common stock.

The third type of change that the board seems to have been concerned with having reported is changes in a company's long-term assets such as plant and equipment and long-term investments. Many of the increases in those assets would, of course, be revealed by a statement that shows only changes in cash or working capital. Some, however, such as those resulting from the issuance of debt or equity securities, would be excluded from that type of statement.

The requirement to show the issuance of securities for consideration other than cash or working capital as sources and uses of funds appears to have been motivated in part by the desire to disclose changes in long-term assets as well as the desire to disclose changes in a company's capital structure. However, the opinion does not contain similar requirements for transactions that increase long-term assets but do not either decrease working capital (or other measure of debt-paying ability) or increase total capital. Such transactions are undoubtedly unusual but do occur. The exchange of a long-term investment in securities for plant and equipment or the exchange of land for securities are examples. The opinion requires that outlays for the purchase of long-term assets be disclosed but whether the term "outlays" embraces or excludes exchanges of the kind mentioned is not clear.

In summary, The APB may have intended to require the disclosure of all increases in long-term assets, but its intentions are not clear. It certainly gave no indication of any desire to show decreases in long-term assets; only the "proceeds from sale (or working capital or cash provided by sale) of long-term assets," not the book value of assets sold, is required to be disclosed.

RELEVANT OBJECTIVES

Changes in all three of the measures of financial position discussed in the last section are clearly of interest to investors, creditors and other external users of financial statements. Changes in debt-paying ability are of such obvious interest to creditors and investors that the matter hardly requires comment; the only real issue is which measure of debt-paying ability is likely to be most useful. Changes in the size and composition of a company's capital structure are also clearly of interest. One of the most widely used financial ratios in credit analysis is the ratio of debt to equity. That ratio would obviously be affected by changes in the composition of a company's capital structure such as the conversion of debentures into common stock and various kinds of refinancing operations. The nature of those activities and a report of how they affect a company's capital structure would, therefore, also be of interest. Changes in the amount or composition of long-term assets are likely to signal changes in a company's future profits and future cash needs so that they, too, are likely to be of interest to investors and creditors.

CONFLICTING OBJECTIVES

The basic problem with Opinion no. 19 is not, therefore, that it requires disclosure of unimportant or irrelevant information but that it requires too many different types of information to be disclosed on the same statement. The result is a confusing statement.

Financial statements are maps of economic territory; they portray the financial characteristic of business enterprises. Different maps are needed for different purposes because only a limited amount of information can be portrayed on a single map. A single geographic map designed to portray changes in annual rainfall, changes in educational level of the population, changes in agricultural crops and changes in unemployment is not likely to portray any of that information clearly. Similarly, a single financial statement designed to portray many different types of changes in the financial position of a business enterprise is not likely to portray any of that information clearly. That, however, is exactly what Opinion no. 19 requires of the funds statement. To achieve the multiple and disparate objectives of that statement, the term funds was defined so broadly that it has become meaningless, and a funds statement based on a meaningless concept of funds does not communicate information effectively. That is the heart of the problem of the confusing funds statements found in practice today.

RECOMMENDATION

Once the basis of the confusion over the funds statement is diagnosed, the general nature of a solution becomes obvious; several different statements are needed to communicate clearly the information now crammed into a single statement. Specifically, three statements are needed to replace the funds statement and achieve its objectives: a statement of cash receipts and payments, a statement of financing activities and a statement of investing activities.

STATEMENT OF CASH RECEIPTS AND PAYMENTS

One of the relevant objectives of funds statements is to report changes in some measure of debt-paying ability. Both historically and currently the measure of debt-paying ability used most frequently in funds statements has been working capital. That measure is rejected here in favor of cash.

The principal reason for recommending a change from working capital as a measure of debt-paying ability to cash is that the approach to evaluation of a company's solvency, or "credit analysis" as it is often called, has changed and the information needs of financial statement users have therefore also changed. During the 1920s when funds statements based on working capital changes were developed, the adequacy of a company's working capital position, particularly as measured by its current ratio, was considered the "alpha and omega" of credit analysis.[6] It was argued that current liabilities are paid with current assets and current assets must therefore exceed current liabilities by an "adequate margin."

During the 1950s there was a searching reappraisal of working capital as a measure of debt-paying ability. Arthur Stone Dewing wrote in 1953 that

> bankers learned by tragic experience that there was no mystical significance in the two-to-one ratio. They observed that in many types of business, under the stress of general disaster, inventories could not be sold, and if such an attempt should be made, not a two-to-one or even a three- or four-to-one ratio would bring them the immediate payment of their debts. If the business failed, the relative amounts of current capital in the days before failure had little significance in the final liquidation of the bankrupt business.[7]

That same year Bion B. Howard and Miller Upton wrote in their classic text that

> it should be clear that the real problem in judging a business' short-term financial position is to ascertain as closely as possible the future cash-generating ability of the business in

---

[6]Foulke, p. 178
[7]Dewing, pp. 708–09.

relation to the claims upon cash that will have to be met within the near future.... It matters not what condition prevails at a given time; the important thing is whether the business in performing its regular operating functions can continue to generate cash in sufficient quantity and in satisfactory time to meet all operating and financial obligations.[8]

More recently, John B. Coughlan observed ironically that "working capital has been thought of as a 'pool' of resources available to satisfy the claims of short-term creditors. But it is unlikely that any banker or creditor will slake his thirst from any part of the pool other than the cash portion. Many a firm has been known to pay its debts with cash, but not one has drawn a check on working capital. Working capital, *per se,* has no bearing on short-term credit standing and it is only useful for whatever implications it may have for cash and cash flow."[9]

Those views are widely accepted by financial analysts today. The emphasis in credit analysis has shifted from analysis of current working capital position to dynamic analysis of future cash receipts and payments in much the same way that the emphasis in security analysis shifted from static analysis of balance sheet values to dynamic analysis of net income some thirty or forty years earlier.[10]

The central question in credit analysis today is not whether a company's working capital is "adequate" but whether the cash expected to be received within a given time period will equal or exceed required cash payments within that same period. Analysis of working capital position does not provide that information. A company's principal sources of cash are from sale of its products or services to its customers, from borrowing and from issuance of stock to investors. Its principal uses are payments to employees, suppliers and governments, repayment of debt and purchase of plant and equipment. Most of the cash a company will receive within the following year is not represented by assets classified as current, and most of the obligations it will have to pay are not represented by liabilities classified as current.

The old concept of current assets as the source from which current liabilities will be paid is meaningless under this framework of analysis. Current liabilities are not paid with current assets; they are paid with cash. Whether a company's current or its noncurrent assets were the source of its cash is an unanswerable question. One can no more determine whether current or noncurrent assets provided the cash generated by a company's operations than he can determine which blade of the scissors cut the cloth, because both were clearly necessary.[11]

The rationale for recommending a statement of cash receipts and payments as one of the statements to replace the funds statement is implicit in the above discussion. If a financial statement user's primary object of attention is the future cash receipts and payments of a company, then it follows that a statement of past

[8]Bion B. Howard and Miller Upton, *Introduction to Business Finance* (New York: McGraw-Hill Book Co., Inc., 1953), p. 135.

[9]John W. Coughlan, "Funds and Income," *NAA Bulletin,* September 1964, p. 25.

[10]For a discussion of this shift in security analysis, see Benjamin Graham, David L. Dodd and Sidney Cottle, *Security Analysis: Principles and Technique,* 4th ed. (New York: McGraw-Hill Book Co., Inc. 1962), p. 214.

[11]The role of current-noncurrent classification of assets and liabilities in the evaluation of a company's solvency is discussed more fully in the monograph referred to in footnote 1. That study concludes that the present practice of identifying certain assets and liabilities as current on a company's balance sheet is misleading and recommends that it be discontinued.

cash receipts and payments would be useful for the same reason that historical income statements are useful in predicting the future income of a company: both provide a basis for predicting future performance.

Reporting cash receipts and payments is widely advocated today by many financial statement users, particularly bankers. For example, Walter B. Wriston, chairman of the board of Citibank, N. A., stated in a recent speech before Peat, Marwick, Mitchell & Co. personnel,

> When I came into the banking business, we were asset-conscious and we loaned money on that basis. Well, assets give you a warm feeling, but they don't generate cash. The first question I would ask any borrower these days is, 'What is your breakeven cash flow?' That's the one thing we can't find out from your audit reports and it's the single most important question we ask. It's important that you figure out a way to present the difference between real cash flow and accrual cash flow.[12]

An example of the form of cash receipts and payments statement recommended, together with a recommended supporting schedule showing details of cash provided by operations, is presented for Example, Inc., in Exhibit 1, page 249.

Only business activities that affected cash are shown on the statement of cash receipts and payments. If financing and investing activities that did not affect cash are shown on statements of cash receipts and payments as if they did, users will become confused over the purpose of the statement and what it shows. Financing transactions that did not affect cash are shown on the recommended statement of financing activities; investing transactions that did not affect cash are shown on the recommended statement of investing activities.

For the purpose of clarity of presentation, details of cash provided by profit-directed activities or what are called operations (to simplify terminology on the statement) are shown on a separate schedule rather than on the face of the statement of cash receipts and payments. Both the absolute magnitude of many of the cash receipts and payments from operations (such as the amount of cash collected from customers and the amount paid for merchandise) as well as the many types of cash payments would tend to overshadow some of the other items on the statement of cash receipts and payments (such as cash borrowed and fixed assets purchased), which may be of greater significance to the financial statement user in estimating future cash receipts and payments.

The schedule of the cash provided by operations illustrates the direct (as opposed to the indirect) method of calculating that amount. When the direct method is used, the schedule shows the actual sources and uses of cash. If the indirect method was used, the schedule would start with net income and adjust that figure for all revenues and expenses that did not affect cash. Those are the two alternative methods of presenting funds provided by operations in statements of changes in financial position that the APB described as acceptable in Opinion no. 19.

The indirect method is basically a set of worksheet adjustments rather than an explanation of how operating activities affected cash. It is analogous to calculating income by subtracting stockholders' equity at the beginning of the year from stockholders' equity at the end of the year and then adjusting the difference for

---

[12] *World* (Peat, Marwick, Mitchell & Co.), Spring 1974, p. 49.

nonincome items, such as dividends and purchases and sales of capital stock. This method, of course, will always "work" if the proper adjustments are made, but if accountants were to prepare income statements in this way, many financial statement users would be confused. They would begin to describe dividends, for example, as a "source" of income in the same way they now describe depreciation as a "source" of funds because they are both "add-backs" when the indirect method of calculation is used. The indirect method of calculating cash provided by operations is pernicious because it is almost certain to continue to confuse financial statement users by reinforcing the incredible belief that profits and depreciation are sources of cash. The direct method, on the other hand, is likely to be useful in dispelling some of the confusion that now exists over the relationship between business activities and cash receipts and payments because it shows clearly that profits are neither cash nor a source of cash, that cash comes from customers, that it is paid for merchandise, administrative and selling expenses, taxes and so forth and that depreciation is neither a source nor a use of cash.

EXHIBIT 1

EXAMPLE, INC.
CASH RECEIPTS AND PAYMENTS STATEMENT
YEAR ENDING DECEMBER 31, 1977

Cash balance December 31, 1976		$15,666
Sources of cash:		
Cash provided by operations (schedule 1)	$27,537	
Sale of marketable securities	3,062	
Sale of land, buildings and equipment	12,793	
Net amount borrowed	31,092	
Received from sale of common stock	7,495	81,979
		97,645
Cash available		
Uses of cash:		
Land, buildings and equipment purchased	62,119	
Dividends paid	13,558	75,677
Cash balance December 31, 1977		$21,968

Schedule 1
Calculation of cash provided by operations

Cash collected from customers		$783,545
Interest and dividends received		1,417
Total cash receipts from operations		784,962
Cash payments:		
For merchandise inventories	$457,681	
For administrative and selling expenses	264,577	
For interest	6,941	
For other expenses	14,953	
For taxes	13,273	757,425
Cash provided by operations		$27,537

STATEMENT OF FINANCING ACTIVITIES

A statement of cash receipts and payments alone would not accomplish all of the objectives of Opinion no. 19. The APB was concerned with the effects of business activities on the size and composition of a company's capital structure and on its long-term assets as well as how those activities affected its debt-paying ability. The second statement recommended in this article, the statement of financing activities, is designed to achieve the second of those objectives: disclosure of the effects of business activities on the capital structure of a firm.

Before describing and discussing the recommended form of the statement of financing activities, it is necessary to clarify what is meant by the term "capital structure." As noted earlier, that term is used to refer to the claims on a company's resources. Typically, however, only equity and long-term debt are considered parts of a company's capital structure; short-term debt is excluded. Some short-term debt, however, such as bank loans and commercial paper, is analogous to long-term debt in the sense that it requires conscious effort or specific negotiation on the part of owners or managers to obtain. Other short-term debt does not require conscious effort or negotiation to obtain; it is "spontaneous" or "self-generating" and grows "out of normal patterns of profitable operations without especial effort or conscious decision on the part of owners or managers."[13] Examples of spontaneous debt include trade accounts payable, wages payable and taxes payable. Debt that requires negotiation, whether short or long term, may be referred to as financing liabilities. Debt that does not require negotiation may be referred to as spontaneous liabilities.[14]

Although both short-term financing liabilities and spontaneous liabilities are usually classified as current, the distinction is useful in preparing a statement of financing activities because different underlying considerations affect the amount of credit available from those two different sources. The amount available from spontaneous sources depends on considerations such as the volume of purchases of inventories and supplies, normal credit terms of a company's suppliers and conventional practices as to frequency of payment of salaries and wages. Credit available from spontaneous sources tends to increase as sales rise and fall when sales decline. Credit available from short-term financing sources, on the other hand, depends on the same basic consideration as credit available from long-term sources, that is, lenders' evaluations of a company's ability to repay a loan when due. Furthermore, financial statement users tend to regard commercial paper and short-term bank loans (which may, in fact, be short term in name only) as financing sources in the same sense that bonds and long-term bank loans are financing sources. Consequently, the term "capital structure" as used in this article refers to both equity capital and

---

[13]Hunt, Pearson, Charles M. Williams and Gordon Donaldson, *Basic Business Finance,* rev. ed, (Homewood, Ill,: Richard D. Irwin, Inc., 1961), p. 116.

[14]R. K. Mautz made a similar distinction. He referred to "primary financing interests" and "incidental financing interests." He argued that incidental financing interests including, for example, trade creditors and employees "provide financing, but this is neither the primary intent of the particular interest nor the basic reason for the transaction." (R. K. Mautz, *An Accounting Technique for Reporting Financial Transactions,* Special Bulletin No. 7 [Urbana, Ill.: University of Illinois, Bureau of Economic and Business Research, 1951], pp. 21–22.)

financing liabilities regardless of whether those financing liabilities are short or long term.[15] A statement such as the current form of funds statement that purports to report financing activities but excludes by definition a class of financing activities that most businessmen regard as major sources of financing is misleading.

A statement of financing activities for Example, Inc., is shown in Exhibit 2, below. This statement is similar in form to the recommended statement of cash receipts and payments. It explains changes in a company's capital structure in much the same way that a statement of cash receipts and payments explains changes in its cash position. However, it includes changes in the composition of a company's capital structure (conversion of securities into common stock) as well as changes in its size. Profits and dividends as well as financing activities more narrowly defined, such as borrowing and repayment of debt and purchase and sale of capital stock, all affect a company's capital structure and should therefore be shown on the statement of financing activities.

EXHIBIT 2

EXAMPLE, INC.
STATEMENT OF FINANCING ACTIVITIES
YEAR ENDING DECEMBER 31, 1977

	Increase or (decrease)
Debt financing	
Notes payable to banks	
Borrowed	$50,000
Repaid	(16,908)
Net amount borrowed	33,092
Mortgage repaid	(2,000)
Net increase in debt financing	31,092
Equity financing	
Convertible preferred	
Conversion of 300 shares $100 par value 5% convertible preferred for 1,500 shares $10 par value common stock	(30,000)
Common stock and capital in excess of par	
Issued 1,500 shares on conversion of 300 shares 5% convertible preferred	30,000
Issued 500 shares for $7,495 cash	7,495
Retained earnings	
Net increase	3,983
Net increase in equity financing	$11,478

---

[15] Other implications of the distinction between financing and spontaneous liabilities are discussed in the monograph referred to in footnote 1. That study recommends that liabilities be classified as financing, operating and tax. Operating and tax liabilities are two types of spontaneous liabilities.

Many business activities that affect a company's capital structure, such as borrowing money, repayment of debt, sale of capital stock and payment of dividends, also affect its cash position and should therefore appear on its statement of cash receipts and payments as receipts and payments of cash as well as on its statement of financing activities. While this might appear to be duplicate reporting of those activities, it really is not. Different effects of them are reported on each of the two statements. The statement of cash receipts and payments reports their effects on cash, whereas the statement of financing activities reports their effects on capital structure. That is necessary to keep both statements clear, simple and understandable. The alternative, of course, is to design a statement that reports both types of effects on a single statement. That is what the APB tried to do in Opinion no. 19. It cannot be done in such a way that both the objectives of the statement as well as the information reported on it are clear and understandable to financial statement users.

Both increases and decreases in each type of debt instrument are shown on the recommended statement of financing activities rather than only net changes. The fact that a company engaged in extensive short-term financing, for example, during the year may be regarded as significant by some financial statement users even though there was little or no net change in that liability. It indicates a dependence on credit that, if jeopardized, could have important implications. Although not illustrated in Exhibit 2, the rate of interest and other significant terms of any new financing might usefully be described briefly either on the face of the statement or in notes to the statement. Other details of financing might also be usefully shown. Divorcing the statement from cash or working capital changes allows both the preparer and user to focus attention on financing activities and may open the door to several additional types of disclosure not illustrated in Exhibit 2.

STATEMENT OF INVESTING ACTIVITIES

A statement of investing activities is the third of the three statements recommended to replace the funds statement. The rationale for such a statement is that long-term investment in plant and in securities acquired for the purpose of control have special significance to financial statement users because they represent relatively inflexible long-term commitments and all changes in those assets should therefore be reported.

A statement of investing activities for Example, Inc., is presented in Exhibit 3, page 253.

The statement of investing activities should disclose all acquisitions of long-term investments (including plant and equipment, investments in other controlled companies and deferred charges of various types) regardless of whether they were acquired for cash, for debt or equity securities or in exchange for other real assets. The statement of cash receipts and payments, of course, would show the cash paid for long-term investments, and the statement of financing activities would show the securities issued, but only the statement of investing activities would disclose all acquisitions. Retirements and other decreases of long-term investments, on the other hand, would appear only on the statement of cash receipts and payments to

EXHIBIT 3

EXAMPLE, INC.
STATEMENT OF INVESTING ACTIVITIES
YEAR ENDING DECEMBER 31, 1977

Plant and equipment

Land, buildings and equipment, December 31, 1976	$319,101
Plus purchases	62,119
	381,220
Less cost of properties disposed of	31,595
Land, buildings and equipment, December 31, 1977	$349,625

the extent they were sold for cash, and they would rarely appear on the statement of financing activities but they would appear on the statement of investing activities.

CONCLUSION

In 1964 John B. Coughlan observed that the funds statement based on working capital changes has "baffled a generation of accounting students" and "it is therefore hardly conceivable that it has enlightened stockholders and other lay readers."[16] In the years since Coughlan wrote, two APB opinions on the subject of funds statements have been issued. They have baffled another generation of accountants by casting the funds statement in the role of a statement with no clear goal or purpose but merely as a dumping ground for reporting heterogeneous transactions not reported elsewhere. The result should have been predictable: these statements do not enlighten either lay or sophisticated users.

The solution to the problem of the enigmatic funds statement does not lie in searching for a new definition of funds that will enable all of the objectives of the statement to be achieved. It lies in identifying clearly the financial reporting objectives that need to be achieved but are not achieved by the balance sheet and income statement and designing new statements that achieve those objectives.

[16]Coughlan, p. 24.

Correspondence Relating to "Let's Scrap the 'Funds' Statement"

James A. Largay III
Lehigh University

Edward P. Swanson
Texas A and M University

Richard Vangermeersch
University of Rhode Island

Max Block
Retired CPA

Loyd C. Heath
University of Washington

THE "FUNDS" STATEMENT: SHOULD IT BE SCRAPPED, RETAINED OR REVITALIZED?

The article by Loyd C. Heath, Ph. D. ("Let's Scrap the 'Funds' Statement," JofA, Oct. 78, p. 94), elicited an unprecedented number of comments from readers, a few of which are reproduced below. The commentators are as follows: James A. Largay III, CPA, Ph.D., Coopers & Lybrand visiting associate professor of accounting, the Amos Tuck School of Business Administration, Dartmouth College, Hanover, New Hampshire; Edward P. Swanson, CPA, Ph.D., assistant professor of accounting, and Richard Vangermeersch, CPA, Ph.D., professor of accounting, both of the University of Rhode Island, Kingston; and Max Block, CPA, White Plains, New York. The replies by Heath, associate professor of accounting at the University of Washington, Seattle, follow each set of comments.

LARGAY'S COMMENTS

Whether by design or oversight, Loyd C. Heath recently performed the extraordinary feat of attacking a primary financial statement in this journal without once mentioning its name. This is unfortunate, for, by internalizing the descriptive title "statement of changes in financial position" (SCFP), the objectives of the statement and its efficiency in achieving them become crystal clear. In the final section of his article, however, Heath adopts the objectives he criticized three pages earlier and recommends the preparation of three separate schedules to accomplish what the SCFP portrayed in a single (but longer), integrated and coherent statement. No, the statement of changes in financial position should not be scrapped. Although it is true that the Financial Accounting Standards Board might well strengthen and elaborate some of the requirements promulgated in Accounting Principles Board Opinion No. 19, *Reporting Changes in Financial Position,*[1] Heath nevertheless sets up a straw man which he is unable to blow down.

In the following remarks, I present a rebuttal of Heath's apparent criticisms of the SCFP and demonstrate that the conventional SCFP provides in one place the information which Heath recommends be disclosed in three places.

Rationale for the Statement of Changes in Financial Position

The statement of changes in financial position was developed to fill a gap previously exisiting in financial reporting. Information about many material transactions that cause the ending balance sheet amounts to differ from beginning balance sheet amounts was not systematically disclosed.[2] In short, the SCFP provides the explanations behind the changes in all balance sheet accounts. It is a complete record of flows which changed the amounts and composition of stocks. Furthermore, Heath's objections to the contrary, the SCFP does facilitate answering such questions as the following:

• What was the effect of operations on financial position or, using the language prescribed by Heath, "what 'happened' to a company's profits...?"
• How were purchases of noncurrent assets financed?
• Why did short-term liquidity, or working capital, decrease although net income was positive?
• What uses were made of the proceeds from a security issue?
• Why must more funds be borrowed for expansion?

It may be that Heath is suggesting that since dollars provided by profit on the one hand and debt on the other are indistinguishable, it is impossible to trace the specific flow of dollars generated by operations into increased stocks of inventories or decreased stocks of debt. But the SCFP was never supposed to provide tracing of this sort. Rather, operations must be considered within the total context of the enterprise's investing and financing activities.

Similarly, the proceeds realized from the issue of securities and the acquisition of plant assets are related and, in the case of a financing transaction, may have a one-to-one relationship. Nevertheless, was it the dollars provided by operations or by the new bond issue that were used to purchase land? Does it matter? So long as the dollars provided by operations are adequate to sustain the firm, it does not matter.

---

[1] Accounting Principles Board Opinion No. 19, *Reporting Changes in Financial Position* (New York: AICPA, 1971), made the SCFP a mandatory primary financial statement, superseding the "funds" statement recommended, but not required, by APB Opinion No. 3, *The Statement of Source and Application of Funds* (New York: AICPA, 1963). See Earl A. Spiller and Robert L. Virgil, "Effectiveness of APB Opinion No. 19 in Improving Funds Reporting," *Journal of Accounting Research,* Spring 1974, pp. 112–42, for an analysis of the requirements of Opinion No. 19 and compliance with those requirements.

[2] Transactions other than operations, dividend declarations and certain changes in stockholders' equity were typically not disclosed. Without the SCFP, a complete reconciliation of the beginning and ending balance sheets generally is not possible.

Finally, computation of working capital (or cash) provided by operations can explain (1) the apparent paradox between positive net income and increased bank loans and (2) the need for further outside financing if growth is to be realized.

After criticizing the APB's stated objectives in requiring the SCFP for being "specious," Heath proceeds to identify three objectives "implicit" in Opinion No. 19.[3] These "implicit" objectives concern disclosing information

> on at least two and perhaps three different measures of financial position. The first was to report changes in some measure of the cash or near-cash resources [cash or current assets and current liabilities]. . . . The second type of change that the board appears to have been concerned with having reported was capital structure changes [noncurrent liabilities and owners' equity]. . . . The third type of change that the board seems to have been concerned with having reported is changes in a company's long-term assets such as plant and equipment and long-term investments [noncurrent assets].[4]

But by accounting for changes in current assets, current liabilities, noncurrent assets, noncurrent liabilities and owners' equity, we account for all changes in financial position! The elements identified as implicit by Heath are, of course, the explicit components of financial position, and the APB was clear in its desire to report all material changes in financial position. It even said that a suitable vehicle for reporting changes in financial position is a statement of changes in financial position.

Heath concludes that these implicit objectives are conflicting. Arguing by analogy, he contrasts financial statements with maps and suggests that maps which emphasize too many different characteristics pertaining to a given geographical area become indecipherable. Two (or three) dimensional space is not adequate to simultaneously report population density, rainfall, elevation, snowfall and average temperature because they are not mutually exlusive. But the three measures of financial position identified by Heath are mutually exclusive. A dollar generated by operations did not increase both current and noncurrent assets.

The APB does distinguish between the most likely effects of operations on financial position (through current assets and current liabilities or working capital) and the most likely effects of nonoperating transactions on financial position (through the noncurrent accounts). The results of operations normally are first reflected in the working capital accounts (or, more narrowly, in cash) and subsequently in the noncurrent accounts. The presently constructed statement of changes in financial position reports all these changes in financial position, without overlap, on one statement. Unlike the map analogy, which may require several sheets depicting the intensity of different characteristics in the same geographical area, the SCFP reports the effects of different transactions on different components of financial position.

---

[3] The stated objectives in mandating the preparation of the SCFP in paragraph 4 of Opinion No. 19 were "(1) to summarize the financing and investing activities of the entity, including the extent to which the enterprise has generated funds from operations during the period, and (2) to complete the disclosure of changes in financial position during the period."

[4] Loyd C. Heath, "Let's Scrap the 'Funds' Statement," JofA, Oct. 78, pp. 95–96.

A Statement of Changes in Financial Position
for Example, Inc.

To demonstrate the emptiness of Heath's case for reform of the SCFP, I now recast the data reported by Heath in his three statements into one conventional statement of changes in financial position (cash basis). This is presented in Exhibit 1, page 258. Since I have no beginning and ending balance sheets to work with, I assume that the company in question has just completed its first year of operations. Entries on the statement are explained in notes where necessary. Note that the conventional SCFP discloses, in one unified statement, the same information shown in Heath's three separate statements. Therefore, I conclude that the case made by Heath in support of statement proliferation is, at best, a weak one.

HEATH'S REPLY

In the accounting research monograph I prepared for the American Institute of CPAs, I discuss the funds statement problem in more depth than in the article that appeared recently in this journal. I state in the monograph that confusion over the role of the funds statement stems in part from "widespread misunderstanding of...the relationship between the activities of a business enterprise and how those activities, particularly the profit directed activities, affect its financial position...".[5]

Much of James A. Largay's criticism of my article, I believe, stems from his misunderstanding and confusion of those relationships.

What is in a Name?

The first evidence of Largay's confusion is his incredible claim that "by internalizing the descriptive title 'statement of changes in financial position' (SCFP), the objectives of the statement and its efficiency in achieving them become crystal clear."

The activities of a business enterprise may be classified as operating, financing and investing. Each of those activities affects a company's financial position in many different ways. There are, therefore, many different types of statements of changes in financial position that can be prepared for a company depending on which activities one wishes to report and which measure of financial position is the focus of attention.

The income statement is one commonly used form of statement of changes in financial position. It shows the effect of what the APB called a company's "profit directed activities" [6] (which includes some operating, some financing and some investing activities) on owners' equity. My article recommends that the statement of changes in financial position required by APB Opinion No. 19 be replaced by three different types of statements of changes in financial position: (1) a statement of cash receipts and payments that shows the effects on cash of all business activities

---

[5]Loyd C. Heath, *Financial Reporting and the Evaluation of Solvency*, Accounting Research Monograph no. 3 (New York: AICPA, 1978), p. 96

[6]APB Statement No. 4, *Basic Concepts of Accounting Principles* (New York: AICPA, 1971), par. 134.

EXHIBIT 1

EXAMPLE, INC.
STATEMENT OF CHANGES IN FINANCIAL POSITION
FOR THE YEAR ENDED DECEMBER 31, 1977 (CASH BASIS)

Sources of cash:

Operations:	
Net income	$17,541 (1)
Plus loss on sale of plant assets not using cash	18,802 (2)
Deduct net debit increase in other working capital	
accounts requiring cash	(8,806) (3)
Cash provided by operations	27,537
Other sources of cash:	
Issue of long-term debt	50,000
Issue of common stock	7,495
Sale of plant assets	12,793
Sale of marketable securities	3,062
Total cash provided	100,887
Financial transactions not affecting cash: common stock	
issued to retire convertible bonds	30,000
	130,887

Uses of cash:

Retirement of long-term debt	16,908
Payment of mortgage	2,000
Payment of dividends	13,558
Purchase of plant assets	62,119
Total cash used	94,585
Financial transaction not affecting cash: convertible	
bonds retired by issuance of common stock	30,000
	124,585
Net increase in cash	$ 6,302

Notes:
[1] Net income = increase in retained earnings ($3,983) + dividends paid ($13,558).
[2] Loss = cost (book value) of plant assets sold ($31,595) − proceeds from sale ($12,793).
[3] This is a plug; normally the individual changes in the working capital accounts, other than cash, would be given here.

(including operating, financing and investing) that affect cash, (2) a statement of financing activities that shows the effects of financing activities (regardless of whether or not cash was affected) on the size and composition of a company's capital structure and (3) a statement of investing activities that shows the effects of investing activities on long-term assets. Other statements of changes in financial position that might be prepared are a statement of changes in monetary assets, a statement of changes in net monetary assets, a statement of changes in owners' equity and so forth.

The types of statements of changes in financial position identified here and in my article by no means exhaust the number of different statements of that type that could be prepared for a company. The possibilities are almost limitless. Which ones should be prepared must, of course, depend on the objectives of financial reporting and on an evaluation of how well those statements achieve those objectives. But contrary to Largay's claim, merely calling a statement a "statement of changes in financial position" (I am not sure how to "internalize" a title) clarifies neither its form nor its objectives and certainly does not help clarify (much less make "crystal clear") how effective a statement is in achieving those unidentified objectives.

Omission of the term "statement of changes in financial position" in my article was both by design and oversight. I intentionally avoided its use because it is unnecessarily long and awkward, because it refers to a broad class of statements rather than to a unique form of statement and because the statement I proposed scrapping is commonly referred to as a "funds" statement by accounting writers and practitioners. Brief mention of the official title of that statement was inadvertently omitted when I shortened the introduction to the article from that used in an earlier version.

A Complete Record of Flows?

Largay further displays his confusion over business activities and how those activities affect financial position when he claims that the form of statement of changes in financial position required by APB Opinion no. 19 "provides the explanations behind the changes in all balance sheet accounts" and that it "is a complete record of flows which changed the amounts and composition of stocks."

It does not and is not.

The conventional form of funds statement found in practice clearly does not provide "the explanations behind the changes" in the cash account. It does not explain where cash came from (e.g., collections from customers) nor how it was used (e.g., payments for merchandise and so forth). Neither does it explain the changes in the retained earnings account (e.g., stock dividends which affect that account are not shown) nor the changes in the plant and equipment account (neither the original cost nor the net book value of plant and equipment sold or retired is shown). It is far from a complete record of flows. The belief that we can show the effects of all business activities on all measures of financial position in a single statement has been one of the main deterrents to progress in developing clear, readily understood statements of financing and investing activities.

What "Happened" to Profits

Largay's claim that funds statements facilitate answering the question "what 'happened' to a company's profits...?" and his later reference to "dollars provided by profit" illustrate his lack of understanding of how profit-directed activities affect a company's financial position.

Dollars are not provided by profit; they are provided by business activities. One effect of those activities is the change in a company's cash. Another effect is the change in its owners' equity. But the change in its owners' equity (the profit) does not provide the cash. Only activities such as collection of receivables, borrowing and issuance of stock provide cash, and those activities provide cash regardless of whether there was any profit.

One could, of course, design a statement of changes in financial position that shows what happened to a company's assets. One could also design such a statement that shows what happened to a company's owners' equity or net assets. But I stand on my original statement in the article that no financial statement can possibly show what "happened" to last year's *change* in net assets. Trying to do that is like trying to explain to a child what "happened" to the two inches he grew last year.

Merely a Matter of Semantics

The differences discussed here are not just quibbling over terminology, or, as it is often called, "merely a matter of semantics." They are matters of semantics all right, but they are important, as are all matters of semantics, because they affect what we report and how we report it.

The cornerstone of the misleading practice advocated by Largay of calculating cash (or working capital) provided by operations by adding depreciation to net income is the belief that profits are a source of cash. However, once profits are shown that way, in order to determine the amount of cash that has actually been provided by operations, depreciation must also be shown as if it, too, were a source of funds—a practice that reinforces the incredible, yet widespread, belief that depreciation provides cash.[7]

Are Financial Statements Maps?

Largay's misunderstanding of the role of financial statements in reporting business activities was probably also the source of his erroneous conclusion that the analogy between maps and financial statements used by me is inappropriate because, according to him, although the geographical attributes referred to in my article are not mutually exclusive, the three measures of financial position identified by me (cash, capital structure and long-term assets) are.

It may be true in some sense that cash, capital structure and long-term assets are mutually exclusive measures of financial position but Largay's criticism misses the point entirely because, as noted above, the role of all types of statements of changes in financial position is to report the effects of business activities, and the business

---

[7]Spiller and Virgil reported that "almost 45 percent of the sample firms conveyed the impression that they had acquired capital assets with depreciation money, financed growth through depreciation, or engaged in similar forms of black magic" (Earl A. Spiller and Robert L. Virgil, "Effectiveness of APB Opinion No. 19 in Improving Funds Reporting," *Journal of Accounting Research,* Spring 1974, p. 131). For specific examples of this confusion in corporate reports, see William J. Vatter, "Operating Confusion in Accounting—Two Reports or One?" *Journal of Business,* July 1963, pp. 290–301, and William A. Paton, "The 'Cash Flow' Illusion," *Accounting Review,* April 1963, pp. 243–251.

activities reported on the three statements illustrated in my article are not mutually exclusive with respect to those measures. Some financing activities, for example, affect both its cash and its capital structure; others affect only its capital structure. Similarly, some investing activities affect both its cash and its long-term assets; others affect only its long-term assets.

Conclusion

The basic reason I advocated that we scrap the form of funds statement found in practice today is that I believe that statement presents information in a confusing and misleading way. Some of the specific features that I find confusing and misleading in the statement prepared by Largay in his effort "to demonstrate the emptiness" of my case for reform are:

• One of the items listed as sources of cash from operations is "loss on sale of plant assets not using cash." It is not clear to me why an item "not using cash" should be included under the caption "sources of cash."

• It is not clear what the unlabeled totals of $130,887 and $124,585 represent. Since one of those apparently has been subtracted from the other to arrive at the "bottom line" of the statement labeled "net increase in cash," the statement has the apparent objective of explaining changes in cash, yet those unlabeled totals include "transactions not affecting cash." If it is not the objective of the statement to explain changes in cash, and it cannot explain changes in all measures of financial position for the reasons already discussed, it is not clear what measure of financial position the statement purports to explain changes in.

• The first objective of a funds statement identified in APB Opinion No. 19 is "to summarize the financing and investing activities ... " (par. 4) and the opinion later states that the statement "should disclose all important aspects of its financing and investing activities" (par. 8). Largay's statement does not appear to focus on either financing or investing activities; at least those terms are not used on the statement and it is not clear which of the activities reported on it are financing activities, which are investing activities and which, if any, are neither.

In summary, the current form of funds statement found in practice today lacks focus: It is "not much more than a miscellaneous collection of plus and minus changes in balance sheet items."[8] It has no clear purpose or objective, and it seems to be generally regarded as a catchall or "third" statement for reporting a number of "important" transactions not reported elsewhere. It is not clear what those transactions have in common or why they are important.

In my opinion, Largay fails to see the problems discussed here and in my article because he does not understand the relationship between business activities and the effects of those activities on a company's financial position. I hope most readers of the *Journal* do not share his confusion. Now that the FASB has decided to put the

---

[8] Duff and Phelps, Inc., *A Management Guide to Better Financial Reporting: Ideas for Strengthening Reports to Shareholders and the Financial Analyst's Perspective on Financial Reporting Practices* (New York: Arthur Andersen & Co., 1976), p. 81.

subject of funds statements on its agenda, I also hope readers will join me in urging the board to identify and state clearly its objectives before designing new statements to achieve those objectives.

SWANSON'S AND VANGERMEERSCH'S COMMENTS

If accountants were to follow Loyd C. Heath's advice in his article, they would be guilty of the age-old maxim of "throwing out the baby with the bath water." Surely Heath makes telling observations that there has been confusion over the objectives of the funds statement, that there is an absence of an underlying concept of the funds statements, that no statement can possibly show what happened to a company's profits and that the funds statement has baffled a generation of accounting students, accountants and stockholders. While all of these criticisms are basically true, Heath has gone too far in suggesting we scrap, rather than revitalize, the funds statement.

Our most important criticisms are directed at the foundation of Heath's proposal, a cash receipts and payments statement. Heath's proposal endorses cash-basis accounting and, as such, represents a giant step backward for accounting. The possibilities for manipulating the cash provided by the operations figure, as well as other sources and uses of cash, are endless. In addition, do we really want an operating figure where the inventory costs deducted are not based on goods sold? In its place, the cash outlay for production and / or purchases is substituted, regardless of whether inventories were being stockpiled or liquidated. Or should a major purchase of equipment be omitted because a check was not mailed by yearend?

Furthermore, even these few examples are sufficient to demonstrate the potentially erratic pattern of actual cash receipts and payments. Consequently, the authors question Heath's crucial assertion that future cash receipts and payments can be predicted better from past cash receipts and payments than from an accrual-based income figure. This surprising assertion is a complete reversal of an argument customarily used to support accrual accounting. For instance, John C. Burton stated in the February 1975 issue of this journal that

> the traditional accounting matching model . . . is essentially an averaging one, designed to report as income for a period the long-run average net cash inflow from operations at the current level of activity in the business. This is what accrual accounting is all about.[9]

The alleged superiority of this new statement in predicting future cash flow is apparently Heath's most important justification for the new statement—clearly Heath is on shaky ground with this assertion.

In addition to overcoming the preceding criticism of cash-basis accounting, the working capital provided by the operations figure overcomes many of the criticisms of accrual-based income, particularly the inclusion of certain arbitrary allocations which have encouraged a greater reliance on cash flow. As a matter of fact, the term "cash flow" is often interpreted by financial analysts to mean an income figure with certain allocations removed, similar to working capital provided by operations (rather than actual cash flow as used by Heath). Specifically, allocations such as depreciation, amortization, extraordinary items and gains or losses from the sale of

---

[9]John C. Burton, "Financial Reporting in an Age of Inflation," JofA, Feb. 75, p. 69.

long-term assets are excluded. Furthermore, two other items affecting income yet not necessarily resulting in an inflow or outflow of working capital are removed. Excluded are income recognized on long-term investments accounted for on the equity method and the change in long-term deferred income taxes (which is ordinarily due primarily to the use of straight-line depreciation for reporting but accelerated for taxes). For these reasons, the authors maintain that the working capital provided by the operations total is not only preferable to the cash from operations figure but it is also usually more useful than net income. In summary, we suggest a statement of working capital flows to replace Heath's statement of cash receipts and payments.

HEATH'S REPLY

In our article entitled "Solvency: the Forgotten Half of Financial Reporting" (JofA, Jan. 79, pp. 48–54), Paul Rosenfield and I criticized the FASB for discussing statements of cash receipts and payments and income statements as if they were alternative and competing statements.

Swanson and Vangermeersch make this same error. They interpret my recommended statement of cash receipts and payments as a challenge to the accrual-based income statement although it is not. Thus, my response to their charge that my proposal "endorses cash-basis accounting and, as such, represents a giant step backward" is that I have not proposed a statement of cash receipts and payments as an alternative to an income statement; I have proposed it as a complementary statement useful in reporting a different type of information. When they rhetorically ask whether we "really want an operating figure where the inventory costs deducted are not based on goods sold," I can only respond yes, we do want an operating figure based on cash receipts and payments but also want an operating figure based on revenue and expenses (including cost of goods sold). When they charge that my argument for a statement of cash receipts and payments "is a complete reversal of an argument customarily used to support accrual accounting," I can only respond that I was not arguing for accrual accounting; I was arguing for a statement that would complement the accrual-based income statement.

Predicting Future Cash Flows

My perception of the roles played by the income statement and the statement of cash receipts and payments in the prediction of future cash flows was apparently not completely understood by Swanson and Vangermeersch as well as several other readers, and I would, therefore, like to comment on that.

I agree with Burton's comment quoted by Swanson and Vangermeersch to the effect that accrual income based on the matching model is a measure of the "long-run average net cash inflow from operations at the current level of activity in the business." Solvency, however, is often a short-run problem. Insolvency often comes as a surprise. Companies that become insolvent sometimes report income right up to the moment they become insolvent. Insolvency results from the fact that creditors demand payment before revenue results in cash receipts. The problem, in other words, is a timing problem, and a measure of long-run cash-generating ability that ignores when revenue will result in cash receipts and when expenses will require cash payments may be too crude a tool to deal with that problem.

Since creditors are interested in future cash receipts and payments, it is not intuitively obvious why statements of past cash receipts and payments would be useful in solvency evaluation. They clearly would not provide a simple solution to the problem of estimating future receipts and payments any more than income statements provide a simple solution to the problem of estimating future income, but I believe that statements of past cash receipts and payments would play an important role in solvency evaluation if they were available. They would provide analysts with insight into how cash provided by operations changes as sales fluctuate, as income fluctuates and so forth. Understanding and knowledge of those relationships would, in turn, undoubtedly be useful in forecasting future short-run cash flows. In other words, if statements of past cash receipts and payments were generally available, I believe analysts would be concerned with the behavior of cash flows in the same way they are now concerned with the behavior of costs.

Working Capital vs. Cash

Swanson's and Vangermeersch's assertion that working capital provided by operations is not only "preferable to the cash from operations figure but it is also usually more useful than net income," and their conclusion that a statement of working capital flows should be used in place of my recommended statement of cash receipts and payments is surprising in view of their earlier defense of accrual-based income.

My reasons for rejecting a statement of working capital changes are summarized in the article they responded to and are explained in more detail in my monograph, *Financial Reporting and the Evaluation of Solvency,* cited in that article. In my opinion, those reasons should be dealt with in the depth at which they are presented and cannot be successfully attacked by the simple assertion that working capital is "preferable" to cash and "more useful" than net income. As I pointed out in the beginning of my article, if we are going to carry on a meaningful dialogue about how to improve the funds statement, the first thing we must do is identify clearly our objectives. Without those, assertions that one measure is more or less useful or preferable to another are meaningless.

BLOCK'S COMMENTS

Loyd C. Heath's article has an additional significance. It supports a position I had advanced that the funds statement be exceptional for nonpublic companies as now are earnings per share and segment data.

A comparative balance sheet with an increase-decrease column is preferable to the present funds statement for the needs of small business managements, and it eliminates a poor financial statement. Should the preparer of the financial statements—usually the independent auditor—deem it advisable to include a statement of financing activities (not a common situation), he could do so on a voluntary basis, in a desire to make the financial report more informative. The same applies to the cash receipts and disbursements statement (for accrual-basis reports) and the statement of investing activities, and any other supporting data.

If Heath's proposal or a variation thereof is adopted, it would make sense to avoid mandatory application to nonpublic companies.

HEATH'S REPLY

I agree with Max Block that the present form of funds statement is a poor statement, but it is a poor statement for public and nonpublic companies alike. The solution, therefore, does not lie in exempting nonpublic companies; it lies in replacing that statement with more useful statements. I see no reason why the statements I have recommended would be less useful to those evaluating nonpublic companies than those evaluating public companies any more than I see why income statements would be less useful to those evaluating nonpublic companies than those evaluating public companies.

Solvency: The Forgotten Half of Financial Reporting

Loyd C. Heath
University of Washington

Paul Rosenfield
Director of Accounting Standards
AICPA

The management of a business enterprise is concerned with two broad objectives: to operate the business profitably and to maintain its solvency. Profitability refers to a company's ability to increase its wealth. Solvency refers to its ability to pay its debts when due.

During the first three decades of this century, issues of solvency evaluation clearly dominated financial reporting. Income statements were not in common use, the balance sheet was referred to as *the* financial statement and short-term creditors, particularly bankers, were assumed to be the primary users of that statement. In 1927, Paul-Joseph Esquerré observed:

> It is undeniable that today almost every business balance sheet proceeds on the assumption that it is going to be used to obtain bank loans; and as the banker is presumed

Authors' note: The authors would like to thank Thomas W. McRae, CPA, a manager in the accounting standards division of the American Institute of CPAs, for his invaluable comments and suggestions during the preparation of this article.

to loan only on the security of liquid assets, all the efforts of the statement of financial status are directed towards the proof of that liquidity.[1]

Beginning around 1930, accountants began to shift their attention from issues of solvency evaluation to those of profitability. By 1952 the pendulum had swung completely:

"...the determination of periodical profit or loss from enterprise operations constitutes the crux of the accounting problem, the central issue around which all other considerations revolve and to which they are unavoidably related."[2]

Since 1952, the focus of financial reporting has remained on profitability. Accounting theorists, accounting educators, groups responsible for promulgating accounting standards, practicing accountants and auditors have been concerned with profitability reporting almost exclusively. With few exceptions, reporting information useful in evaluating the solvency of a company has either been ignored or given a role that is clearly secondary to that of reporting profitability. Financial reporting for solvency evaluation is the forgotten half of financial reporting.[3]

THE RELATIONSHIP BETWEEN SOLVENCY AND PROFITABILITY

Solvency and profitability are clearly related. Long-run solvency depends on long-run profitability. No method of obtaining money to pay debts will be available in the long run to an enterprise that is not profitable. In the short run, however, solvency and profitability do not necessarily go together. An unprofitable enterprise may remain solvent for years because its cash collections continue to exceed its required cash payments. On the other hand, a profitable enterprise in need of cash to finance increasing receivables, inventory and plant may tie itself to an unrealistic debt repayment schedule that could eventually result in its insolvency:

> Though my bottom line is black, I am flat
> upon my back,
> My cash flows out and customers pay slow.
> The growth of my receivables is almost unbelievable;
> The result is certain—unremitting woe!
> And I hear the banker utter an ominous low
> mutter, "Watch cash flow."[4]

---

[1] Paul-Joseph Esquerré, *Accounting* (New York: Ronald Press Company, 1927), p. 41. See also Hector R. Anton, *Accounting for the Flow of Funds* (New York: Houghton Mifflin Co., 1962), p. 5; A. C. Littleton and V. K. Zimmerman, *Accounting Theory: Continuity and Change* (Englewood Cliffs, N.J.: Prentice-Hall, Inc., 1962), pp. 113–17; and Eldon S. Hendriksen, *Accounting Theory*, 3d ed. (Homewood, Ill.: Richard D. Irwin, 1977), pp. 56–59.

[2] Maurice Moonitz and Charles C. Staehling, *Accounting: An Analysis of Its Problems*, vol. 1 (Brooklyn, N.Y.: Foundation Press, Inc., 1952), p. 107.

[3] Some of the material for this article was developed in connection with the preparation of Accounting Research Monograph no. 3, *Financial Reporting and the Evaluation of Solvency*, Loyd C. Heath (New York: AICPA, 1978).

[4] Herbert S. Bailey, Jr., "Quoth the Banker, 'Watch Cash Flow,'" *Publishers Weekly*, Jan. 13, 1975, p. 34.

THE IMPORTANCE OF SOLVENCY

Investors and creditors, the primary users of general purpose financial statements, need to evaluate the solvency as well as the profitability of companies in which they have interest. Creditors are obviously concerned with solvency. In fact, evaluation of solvency is often referred to as credit analysis, although that term should not be taken to mean that creditors are the only parties interested in a company's solvency or even that creditors are more interested in solvency than other financial statement users. If a company becomes insolvent, equity investors are likely to lose even more than creditors because creditors' rights are senior to those of stockholders in bankruptcy and reorganization proceedings.

Even if a company never reaches the point of insolvency, the mere threat or suspicion of insolvency is likely to result in losses to stockholders. The more obvious consequences are that the market value of their shares is likely to decline and that increased credit costs will tend to reduce profits. But less obvious consequences may be just as serious. Even if there is no imminent threat of insolvency, a company that is short of cash will have to pass up profitable investment opportunities and restrict cash payments in ways that are likely to affect long-run profitability.

Other financial statement users are also concerned with a company's solvency. Employees, suppliers and customers are concerned because loss of solvency usually means loss of jobs, loss of customers and disruption of sources of supply. The U.S. government's guarantees of loans to Lockheed Aircraft Corp. several years ago illustrate society's concern over the solvency of at least one major corporation.

EVALUATING SOLVENCY

Solvency is a money or cash phenomenon. A solvent company is one with adequate cash to pay its debts; an insolvent company is one with inadequate cash.[5] Evaluating solvency is basically a problem of evaluating the risk that a company will not be able to raise enough cash before its debts must be paid.

Solvency analysis is not simply a matter of evaluating a company's so-called current assets and liabilities to determine the adequacy of its working capital "cushion." During the last 25 years the emphasis in solvency analysis by sophisticated users of financial statements has shifted from static analysis of working capital position (or "proof of . . . liquidity" as Esquerré called it) to dynamic analysis of cash receipts and payments in much the same way that the emphasis in security analysis shifted from static analysis of balance sheet values to dynamic analysis of net income during the 1930s and 1940s. Today, it is recognized that most of the cash a company will receive within the next year is not represented by assets classified as current (or any other assets now on the balance sheet, for that matter); and most of the obligations it will have to pay during that time are not represented by liabilities classified as current.

---

[5] Liquidity is closely related to solvency but it is a narrower concept. The term "liquidity" is usually used to refer to a company's asset characteristics or to its asset and liability structure. As discussed later in this article, a company's ability to remain solvent depends on more than its present financial position as reflected in its balance sheet.

Any information that provides insight into the amounts, timing and certainty of a company's future cash receipts and payments is useful in evaluating solvency. Statements of past cash receipts and payments are useful for the same basic reason that income statements are useful in evaluating profitability: both provide a basis for predicting future performance.[6] Information about the due dates of receivables and payables is also useful in predicting future cash receipts and payments and, therefore, in evaluating solvency.

Since cash receipts and payments can never be predicted with certainty, solvency evaluation also involves evaluating a company's capacity to control or adjust cash receipts and payments to survive a period of financial adversity, a concept that has been called financial flexibility.[7] Some of the things included under the concept of financial flexibility are a company's unused borrowing capacity and its ability to liquidate assets without adversely affecting the profitability of its remaining assets.

Information about a company's cash receipts and payments is also relevant in evaluating a company's profitability but in a different way. The timing of a company's receipts and payments is irrelevant in the measurement of income except insofar as timing affects the amounts at which assets and liabilities are recorded. The sale of an item for $10,000 cash and the sale of that item for a $10,000 note receivable due in five years with interest at 10 percent are regarded as equivalent transactions in evaluating profitability. They are not equivalent, however, in evaluating solvency because the timing of the cash receipts differs greatly in the two cases. The timing of future cash receipts and payments is the sine qua non of solvency evaluation and the heart of the distinction between issues of solvency reporting and profitability reporting.

EVIDENCE OF NEGLECT

We have neglected solvency. Evidence of that neglect and bias toward the income measurement or profitability point of view can be found in both accounting practice and discussions of accounting problems.

Misleading Balance Sheet Classification.

One of the principal methods now used to report information for use in solvency evaluation is to classify assets and liabilities as current or noncurrent. That practice began shortly after the turn of the century in response to the needs of commercial bankers. The bulletin that governs current-noncurrent classification today, chapter 3A of Accounting Research Bulletin no. 43, *Restatement and Revision of Accounting Research Bulletins,* first appeared in 1947 as ARB no. 30 and has remained virtually unchanged since that time. That bulletin is defective in many ways. It is based on an

---

[6] For a specific proposal that enterprises publish statements of past cash receipts and payments, see Loyd C. Heath, "Let's Scrap the 'Funds' Statement," JofA, Oct. 78, pp. 94–103, and the monograph referred to in footnote 3.

[7] The concept of financial flexibility is discussed more fully in chapter 2 of the monograph referred to in footnote 3.

outmoded, simplistic, static model of solvency evaluation; it contains incomprehensible definitions of current assets and current liabilities together with lists of assets and liabilities that appear to contradict those definitions; it ignores basic principles of classification; and it not only fails to provide information useful in evaluating solvency but it also provides misleading information.[8] The fact that a bulletin that provides guidance on the major device in financial statements intended for solvency evaluation is so defective and has been allowed to remain in effect for over thirty years with no serious effort to change it is a prime example of how little attention has been given to solvency issues by accounting policymakers.

Misdirected "Funds" Statements.

"Where got—where gone" statements, the forerunners of statements of changes in financial position (funds statements), were viewed as tools for use in solvency analysis. William Morse Cole, credited with being the father of funds statements, observed in 1915:

"It is obvious that an important result of constructing such a table . . . is the possibility of seeing from it at a glance the changes in solvency."[9]

During the 1920s when H. A. Finney popularized funds statements that explained changes in working capital, providing information for use in solvency evaluation was still the principal objective of those statements. Working capital was considered to be *the* measure of a company's debt-paying ability, and the funds statement was viewed as a way of explaining changes in that measure.

In spite of the fact that financial statement users have shifted their emphasis from working capital analysis to analysis of a company's cash receipts and payments, nearly all funds statements found in practice today are still based on the outmoded and useless concept of working capital.

To make matters even worse, beginning with APB Opinion No. 3, *The Statement of Source and Application of Funds,* in 1964, companies were required to report "significant" financing and investing activities that did not affect working capital as if they did, so that even changes in working capital are not now reported in an understandable way. Duff and Phelps, Inc., an investment research firm, describes the current form of funds statement as "not much more than a miscellaneous collection of plus and minus changes in balance sheet items" and observes that "the predominant emphasis on working capital serves little purpose since working capital is not an important analytical figure."[10] Earl A. Spiller and Robert L. Virgil note that, under APB Opinion No. 19, *Reporting Changes in Financial Position,* "as long as certain types of transactions are disclosed in the required way, apparently any, all, or no underlying concept of funds is appropriate."[11]

[8] For a discussion of these points, see chapter 4 of the monograph referred to in footnote 3.

[9] William Morse Cole, *Accounts: Their Construction and Interpretation,* rev. and enl. ed. (Boston, Mass.: Houghton Mifflin Co., 1915), p. 102.

[10] Duff and Phelps, Inc., *A Management Guide to Better Financial Reporting* (New York: Arthur Andersen & Co., 1976), pp. 81–82.

[11] Earl A. Spiller and Robert L. Virgil, "Effectiveness of APB Opinion No. 19 in Improving Funds Reporting," *Journal of Accounting Research,* Spring 1974, p. 115.

The important point is that the original objective of funds statements—that of providing information for solvency analysis by explaining changes in some measure of debt-paying ability—has been lost. Funds statements are now viewed as the residual or "third" financial statement whose function is to report any "significant" information not reported elsewhere.[12]

Rejection of Users' Demands.

Some of the strongest evidence of pro-income measurement, anti-solvency bias appears in the accounting profession's response to suggestions by financial statement users that statements of cash receipts and payments would be useful in solvency evaluation because income statements based on accrual accounting conceal the timing of cash movements. Those suggestions have often been interpreted as challenges to the supremacy of the income statement and contemptuously (perhaps fearfully) dismissed. For example, in 1961 J. S. Seidman, a prominent practitioner who was both president of the AICPA and a member of the Accounting Principles Board, stated:

> ...instead of studying various ways and terminology for presenting cash flow statements, I think the profession is called upon to report to companies, to analysts, to stockholders, and the exchanges that cash flow figures are dangerous and misleading and the profession will have no part of them.[13]

More recently, statements of cash receipts and payments were rejected by the Financial Accounting Standards Board in its exposure draft *Objectives of Financial Reporting and Elements of Financial Statements of Business Enterprises.* The board explained in paragraphs 33 and 34:

> Financial statements that show only cash receipts and payments during a short period, such as a year, [cannot] adequately indicate whether or not an enterprise's performance is successful.
>
> Information about enterprise earnings (often called net income or net profit) and its components measured by accrual accounting generally provides a better measure of enterprise performance than information about current cash receipts and payments. That is, financial information provided by accounting that recognizes the financial effects of transactions and other events when they occur rather than only when cash is received or paid is usually considered a better basis than cash receipts and payments for estimating an enterprise's present and continuing ability to bring in the cash it needs.[14]

Ruling out statements of cash receipts and payments on the grounds that they cannot "adequately indicate whether or not an enterprise's performance is successful" indicates the board considered only one aspect of a company's performance to be relevant in measuring success, that is, its earnings performance. Apparently the

---

[12]For suggestions on how to improve disclosure of some of the information now reported in funds statements, see the Heath article referred to in footnote 6.

[13]J. S. Seidman, JofA, June 61, p. 31.

[14]FASB, *Objectives of Financial Reporting and Elements of Financial Statements of Business Enterprises* (Stamford, Conn.: FASB, 1977).

board did not consider a company's success in generating cash and paying off its liabilities to be part of its "performance." Obtaining cash needed to survive and obtaining increased wealth are both necessary parts of an enterprise's performance. Assuring survival and prospering require different kinds of achievement, not simply different amounts of achievement.[15]

The board's argument that enterprise earnings are a "better" indicator of cash-generating ability casts income statements and statements of cash receipts and payments as competing methods of disclosure although they are not. Income statements report the effects of a company's operations on its long-run cash-generating ability; the question of when cash has been or will be received or paid is ignored except as it affects amounts at which receivables and payables are recorded. Statements of cash receipts and payments, on the other hand, report the effects of operations on cash movements during the year; when those movements have affected or will affect income is ignored. Thus, income statements and statements of cash receipts and payments are complementary, not competing forms of disclosure. They report different things for different purposes. The board's rejection of statements of receipts and payments at the objectives level based on the argument that income statements are "better" indicators of cash-generating ability than cash flow statements indicates an insensitivity to the timing of cash movements and, therefore, an insensitivity to solvency issues.

Confusion between Income Effects and Cash Effects of Operations.

Undoubtedly one of the reasons that users' demands for statements of cash receipts and payments have not received more serous consideration is that income measurement so dominates the thinking of many accountants that they do not even distinguish between a company's income and the cash it has generated through operations; they speak of income as if it were synonymous with cash. Thus, they often refer to the retirement of debt and the purchase of plant and equipment "out of profits" when they really mean out of cash generated by operations, and they refer to the income statement as *the* statement of operations even though it shows only one effect of operations. Other effects of operations such as those on cash, on plant and equipment or on capital structure are not, of course, reported in that statement. In fact, before APB Opinion no. 19 became effective in 1971, CPAs routinely stated in their standard reports that a company's financial statements "present fairly . . . the results of its operations" even though only the income effects of operations were reported; no statement was required that even purported to report the effects of operations other than the income effects.

Further evidence of the confusion between the income effects and other effects of operating activities can be found in the common yet confusing and misleading practice of showing income as a "source" of working capital or "funds" on statements

---

[15] For a discussion of this point, see Paul Rosenfield, "Current Replacement Value Accounting—A Dead End," JofA, Sept. 75, p. 72.

of changes in financial position even though this "attempt to tie in these statements with profit and loss misses the major point that these statements are neither segments nor elaborations of income-measuring data, but instead are reports on changes that have occurred in other directions."[16] If accountants are going to provide information useful in solvency evaluation, they must first recognize that net income is not the only effect of operations and that other effects, particularly the cash effect, may be as important as net income.

Effects of Inflation on Solvency.

A period of rising prices creates a cash problem and therefore a solvency problem for many companies, because increased amounts of cash are needed to replace higher priced assets. To meet that need, either cash receipts and payments from operations have to be adjusted or additional outside financing must be obtained. Information useful in evaluating the magnitude of a company's need for additional cash to replace higher priced assets is relevant for evaluating solvency under those conditions. Statements of cash receipts and payments, particularly if they are available for several years in which there have been different rates of inflation, and disclosure of the replacement costs of assets held are two types of information that would be useful in estimating a company's need for additional cash to replace assets.

The problem of financial reporting during a period of rising prices has usually been considered only from the perspective of income measurement rather than from the perspective of solvency. The use of replacement prices has been supported on the grounds that it provides a superior measure of income, not that it provides information for estimating a company's future cash requirements. Even when the solvency dimension of the problem has been recognized, the solution often suggested has been to exclude the excess of the replacement value of an asset over its cost from income to obtain a measure known as "distributable" income—a solution that combines and confuses the income measurement and the solvency dimensions of the problem.[17]

Economic v. Legal Entities.

The distinctions between separate legal entities are ignored when consolidated financial statements are prepared; companies within the consolidated group are treated as one economic entity. Legal distinctions between entities, however, are often necessary to evaluate solvency because creditors' rights attach to the separate entities, not to the consolidated entity. From the solvency perspective, a consolidated balance sheet may be misleading because "the pressing liabilities may be in the

---

[16] Maurice Moonitz and Louis H. Jordan, *Accounting: An Analysis of Its Problems,* rev. ed., vol. 1 (New York: Holt, Rinehart and Winston, Inc., 1963), p. 103.

[17] For discussion of this point, see FASB discussion memorandum, *An Analysis of Issues Related to Conceptual Framework for Financial Accounting and Reporting: Elements of Financial Statements and Their Measurement* (Stamford, Conn.: FASB, 1976), ch. 6. See also Rosenfield, pp. 72–73.

parent company, but the liquid assets which give promise of meeting these liabilities may be in a subsidiary...[where they are] unavailable to the parent...."[18]

Similarly, one subsidiary may have adequate cash available, but the "pressing liabilities" may be those of another subsidiary and legal restrictions may prevent transfer of assets from one subsidiary to another.

Recently the Advisory Committee on Corporate Disclosure to the Securities and Exchange Commission noted this point and made the following suggestion:

> Where there are material blockages to free movements of cash within a consolidated entity (e.g., caused by loan indenture, foreign currency restrictions, or other legal constraints which limit a parent's or a subsidiary's movement of cash to another entity within the consolidated group), separate funds statements might be required for the entity in which the blockage had occurred in order to disclose adequately the significance of this blockage to the ability of the consolidated entity as a whole to meet its dividend, debt service, and other commitments from internally-generated cash.[19]

While separate statements of cash receipts and payments for some or all the companies comprising a consolidated entity probably would be useful in the situation described, they are not a complete solution to the problem described because balance sheets, too, can be misleading under those conditions. The point in raising this issue, however, is not to recommend a solution but to point out that consolidated financial statements raise an important issue in the evaluation of solvency that has received little or no attention from accountants.

Consolidated financial statements are usually justified with the argument that they are intended to portray the economic substance of parent-subsidiary relationships rather than legal form. That argument is specious because a financial statement user concerned with solvency considerations often finds that the legal form of a relationship *determines* its economic substance, and legal form therefore cannot be ignored. The use of consolidated financial statements, like the problem of financial reporting during periods of changing prices, needs to be looked at from the solvency point of view as well as from the income measurement point of view.

Information on Funding Pension Obligations.

A company's obligation to make periodic payments to fund its pension plan often represents a significant cash drain and may be an important consideration in evaluating its solvency. The amount of that obligation cannot be determined by the amount of pension expense reported on its income statement because funding requirements may differ from pension expense reporting requirements.

Current generally accepted accounting principles do not require a company to

---

[18] Ted J. Fiflis and Homer Kripke, *Accounting for Business Lawyers; Teaching Materials,* 2d ed. (St. Paul, Minn.: West Publishing Co., 1977), p. 604. For discussion of a recent example in which this issue is raised, see Abraham J. Briloff, "Whose 'Deep Pocket'?" *Barron's,* July 19, 1976, p. 5.

[19] *Report of the Advisory Committee on Corporate Disclosure to the Securities and Exchange Commission,* printed for the use of the House Committee on Interstate and Foreign Commerce, 95th Congress, 1st sess., Committee Print 95–29, November 3, 1977, p. 505n.

provide any information about its obligation to provide funding for its pension plan over the next several years. They do not even require it to disclose the amount of its contribution to its pension fund for past periods. APB Opinion no. 8, *Accounting for the Cost of Pension Plans,* is, as its title suggests, concerned almost exclusively with the *cost,* that is, the income effect, of pension plans. It ignores their impact on a company's solvency.

LET'S NOT FORGET SOLVENCY

The solvency perspective that dominated U.S. financial reporting for the first three decades of this century was lost when accountants turned their attention to problems of income measurement during the 1930s. For the past 40 or 50 years nearly all financial reporting issues have been considered almost exclusively from the standpoint of income measurement. Reporting practices that have as their objective providing information useful in evaluating solvency, such as classification of assets and liabilities as current and noncurrent and providing a funds statement, are based on an old model of solvency evaluation that has since been rejected by financial statement users as naïve or simplistic.

The solution to the problems discussed here does not lie simply in searching for a new basis of balance sheet classification, in replacing funds statements with statements of cash receipts and payments, in disclosing due dates of receivables and payables, in disclosing replacement costs of assets held, in presenting separate statements of companies comprising a consolidated entity or in disclosing more information about pension obligations—although all those steps would probably help. Those solutions deal only with the current symptoms.

The basic problem is that accountants have forgotten the solvency point of view—not just accounting policymakers but all accountants including management accountants, auditors and accounting educators. The only solution to that basic problem is for them to understand how today's users of financial statements look at solvency issues and to adopt that viewpoint when considering all matters of financial reporting. This does not, of course, mean neglecting the profitability point of view. But unless increased attention is given to providing information useful in solvency evaluation, the accounting profession is likely to find itself subject to increased criticism for failing to provide early warning signals of business failures, of which the Penn Central and W. T. Grant debacles are only two famous examples among thousands that occur every year.

The Cash Flow Accounting Alternative
for Corporate Financial Reporting

Tom A. Lee
University of Edinburgh

1. INTRODUCTION

Financial accounting theory began to take its present form around the turn of the century. It crystalized into what are now the various orthodox rules and ways of perceiving things by the 1930's. Recently, signs of major change have become visible. Perhaps the majority of academic theorists now reject the historical cost rule. And many theorists are attempting far more sweeping changes than this. Many writers, especially the younger theorists, are trying to reconstruct financial accounting on entirely new foundations.[1]

Thomas thus summarizes the present situation in financial accounting and reporting. Winds of change are blowing throughout the accounting world, and reporting accountants are having to cope with a seemingly endless stream of recommendations, requirements, and amendments. It is reasonably clear that the greatest attention is being given to two main areas—that is, the objectives of reporting systems (in particular emphasising the various needs of different user groups); and income and value measurement systems (with specific regard to the problems arising from significant rates of price inflation). In addition, the prevailing debate has made one matter abundantly evident—historic cost accounting has a limited utility for reporting purposes, and the major problem over the next few years will be to find suitable alternatives which meet report users' known needs, adequately reflect economic reality, and can be implemented in practice.

The traditional accounting underlying corporate financial reports is based on accruals—that is, the financial data generated in the accounting system are allocated to the specific reporting periods to which they are judged to relate. The main practice adopted for this purpose is the familiar matching principle whereby revenue outputs are related to allocated inputs when measuring periodic income. Readers will very probably know of no system other than that defined above, and it is understandable that accountants react strongly against any attacks on its adequacy. However, the number of attacks have been few and, consequently, the accrual basis to financial reporting has remained virtually unscathed over the years. Indeed, a review of the history of accounting thought and practice would reveal that accountants have been concerned, almost exclusively, with problems within the accrual accounting context. Unfortunately, most of the problems remain unresolved, despite attempts to standardize practice.

It is therefore my contention that accrual accounting, largely because of its

Adapted from Chapter IV in *Trends in Managerial and Financial Accounting,* Ed. van Dam, Martinus Nijhoff Social Sciences Division (1978), pp. 63–72. Reprinted by permission of Martinus Nijhoff, Social Sciences Division.

[1]A. L. Thomas, "The Allocation Problem in Financial Accounting Theory," *Studies in Accounting Research 3,* American Accounting Association, 1969, p. 105.

dependence on subjective judgments for allocation purposes, has created a stockpile of problems which has diverted accountants' attention away from the more fundamental problem of finding the most suitable financial information to meet the needs of a variety of users of financial reports. For example, they have been far too busy with the problem of how to allocate fixed asset depreciation to bother to investigate whether depreciation is vital to the needs of report users. Even now, when the crucial question of price-level accounting is being debated, the framework for discussion remains the accrual process. The implicit assumption must therefore be that accountants, on the whole, are satisfied with this judgmental allocation system as a proper structure for their financial reports. There is no evidence to suggest otherwise.

2. CHALLENGES TO DATE

The validity of such an assumption deserves to be challenged. It is much too fundamental a point to be left unquestioned for so long. The number of sustainable challenges, however, have been few—the most detailed and direct outside the U.K. being that of Thomas,[2] with Chambers[3] and Sterling[4] also contributing in a somewhat different manner. The U.K. experience is similarly sparse, but will be looked at in detail in the following sections.

Thomas has concluded that the allocation or accrual process is indefensible in terms of attempting to measure information which adequately describes the real world:

> Excepting rare instances where productive processes do not interact, and very high levels of input aggregation, financial accounting's allocation assertions are ambiguous and incorrigible. They may be employed to code the accountant's communication of estimates about the firm, but allocation assertions do not reflect anything that exists in the external world, and do not correspond to any aspects of the firm's economic state or activities.[5]

Thomas' main argument, therefore, is that the arbitrary nature of accounting allocations leads to false descriptions of the reality of economic phenomena in reporting entities. His main solution is the production of allocation-free financial statements—in terms either of exit values or cash flows.

Chambers and Sterling, on the other hand, arrived at their exit value reports when considering the most relevant type of financial information to meet the needs of decision makers, rather than by specifically attempting to resolve the allocation problem. It can therefore be argued that their recommendations avoid the allocation problem whilst remaining within the familiar income and financial position framework. However, their work represents a significantly different approach to financial reporting as compared with other systems depending on accrual accounting.

---

[2]Thomas, *op. cit.*; and "The Allocation Problem: Part Two," *Studies in Accounting Research 9,* American Accounting Association, 1974.

[3]R. J. Chambers, *Accounting, Evaluation and Economic Behavior,* Prentice-Hall, 1966.

[4]R.R. Sterling, *Theory of the Measurement of Enterprise Income,* University Press of Kansas, 1970.

[5]Thomas (Part Two), *op. cit.,* p. 156.

3. THE U.K. EXAMPLE

In the past, several U.K. writers have hinted at the possibility of a cash flow alternative to accruals—that is, a system based on cash transactions. However, to date, only Lawson[6] and myself[7] have investigated the proposal in any depth. As with Thomas, the Lawson-Lee case rests on a fundamental dissatisfaction with accrual accounting and also on doubts about the absolute utility of the income concept. The accountancy profession has remained relatively silent on these matters, but cash flow reporting has achieved a limited support in the recent Sandilands Committee report (although it was felt that it could not easily be accommodated within the present U.K. legal requirements).[8]

There are therefore grounds for hoping that a wider acceptance of cash flow reporting may eventually be forthcoming. With this in mind, the remainder of this paper will be concerned with my own arguments for such a system as they have developed over the years. In no way can they be regarded as entirely original nor, indeed, are they complete. However, at this state, they fall into three groupings— conceptual (being related particularly to the objectives of financial reporting); measurement (being concerned with the validity of accrual accounting, and the relevance of income reporting); and comprehension (being directed at the communications problems facing report users). Each will be discussed in the following sections, and interested readers will find in the appendix to this paper outline cash flow statements, together with exit value statements based on the same data.*

4. THE CONCEPTUAL ARGUMENT   *FoR CASH-FLoW REPORTING*

A conceptual study of accounting for goodwill gave rise to my initial thoughts on cash flow reporting.[9] Typically, such an asset tends either to be ignored or summarily dismissed in financial reports. However, if it is to be accounted for properly, it requires to be continually recognised and valued. But market values do not exist for such a purpose—goodwill cannot be purchased in the market place in the same way as plant or inventory. Its value therefore must depend upon some form of present value calculation involving the discounting of future income benefits to be derived from it. In other words, economic principles of valuation would require to be introduced into the accounting measurement process.

My eventual recommendation was therefore for the reporting of historic and forecast flows for the entity as a whole in order to give decision makers relevant data for purposes of making their own estimates of its economic value (including its

Editors' note: We have reproduced here only the conceptual protion of the paper.

[6]See, for example, G. H. Lawson, "Cash-Flow Accounting," *The Accountant,* 28 October 1971, pp. 586–9, and 4 November 1971, pp. 620–22; 'Distributable Profits and Dividends', *Management International Review,* Vol. 12, No. 2/3, 1972, pp. 113–19; *Memorandum Submitted to the Inflation Accounting Committee,* Manchester Business School, 1974; and "The Rationale of Cash Flow Accounting," *Investment Analyst,* pp. 5–12.

[7]These writings will be referenced in appropriate parts of the remainder of this paper.

[8]"Inflation Accounting," *Report of the Inflation Accounting Committee,* Cmnd. 6225, HMSO, 1975, p. 156.

[9]T. A. Lee, "Goodwill: An Example of Will-O-the-Wisp Accounting," *Accounting and Business Research,* Autumn 1971, pp. 318–28.

goodwill resources). I felt this would prevent the rather dubious exercise of decomposing the total flows in order to value individual assets. The reporting of historic and predicted data, together with explanations of material differences between the two, and disclosures of forecasting assumptions, were also felt to satisfy both the decision making and stewardship objectives of reporting.

These initial proposals were tentatively made but they did contain one firm recommendation—that the reported flows should be measured on a cash rather than an accrual basis, thereby avoiding the inherent problems of the latter. In addition, I believe that forecast cash flows provide a more appropriate basis for discounting purposes than do accrual-based flows. Arbitrary accounting allocations (such as for depreciation, inventory, deferred taxation, etc.) would appear to distort the timing element with which the discounting process is designed to cope in present value calculations.

Initially, therefore, I saw the advantages of a cash flow reporting system as follows:

1 Financial report users would be provided with a data base which could be used by them for purposes of deriving valuations necessary for decisions—for example, for the investor estimating future dividend flows for his share price model.

2 Managerial accountability would be improved by the reporting of actual and forecast data, coupled with explanations of material differences.

3 The major problem of allocation in financial accounting would be largely avoided, although cash flows would require some temporal segregation.

4 The attendant problems of price-level variations could also be largely avoided by using money cash flows, to which a money time preference rate could be applied in discounting by decision makers.

5 All resources (tangible and intangible) of the reporting entity would be represented in its total net cash flow, thereby avoiding incomplete reporting.

6 The classical Hicksian model of income and capital could be applied by decision makers by obtaining opening and closing entity capital from a discounting of forecast cash flows.

In other words, I envisage a system of reporting entity cash flows which avoids the traditional problems of accounting, although introducing new ones—particularly in the area of forecasting. I also see it as a system which distinguishes two separate functions—that of measurement and reporting of relevant data (which I believe to be the domain of the reporting accountant) and that of *overall* valuation (which I believe to be the responsibility of the decision maker when he makes use of reported data). Far too much emphasis has been and still is given to the need to report *individual* values in financial reports. In my view, this has given the impression that the reporting accountant is attempting to give an overall valuation of the entity to decision makers. This is clearly not the case. Whilst I would take issue with the proposition that all forecasting should be left to report users, it is my belief that overall valuations of the entity, or shares in it, should be made by them, and that cash flow data are more relevant than accrual-based data for this purpose. I also believe that they should be provided with entity management's quantifications of future activity as a basis for their personal forecasts.

These conceptual arguments for cash flow reporting have been developed further in two relatively recent papers[10] and, coupled with those contained in my goodwill paper, have been grouped into three main categories—the need for change; the key factor of cash; and the maximising objectivity.

4.1. The Need for Change

The traditional objective of financial reporting is stewardship or managerial accountability but there now appears to be an almost universal acceptance of economic decision making as the major reason for financial reports. Thus, accountants must ensure that reported data adequately meet the latter need, either in terms of historic information with a reasonable predictive ability or in terms of forecast data with a reasonable credibility—or possibly a combination of both.

The predictive ability of historic accounting information is relatively uncertain, either in historic cost or current value terms. Surprisingly, this aspect of accounting has remained inconclusive and unproven,[11] although there is a school of thought which suggests that no form of historic information should be used for predictive purposes.[12] This approach can be summarized as follows:

> The primary goal of financial reporting should be to "feedback" data about values of resources held by the firm as distinct from the shareholders. . . . For present and past measurements to be selected on the basis of their capacity to predict future valuations of the same (distorted) measurements... involves a circularity of reasoning unlikely to be of real use to investors in the end. Investors, after all, want for prediction purposes private information they can trade upon to their exclusive advantage. But accounting messages are public data and, hence, are best used for the verification of expectations.[13]

In other words, there is a very persuasive argument for treating historic information as control information, and for decision makers to use it only within such a context.[14] Additionally, there is evidence (which would apply to historic cost or replacement cost systems, but not to realisable value systems) that the accrual process can introduce variations likely to affect the predictive ability of the resultant data—for example, different accounting techniques and allocations applied to the

[10]T. A. Lee, "The Relevance of Accounting Information Including Cash Flows," *The Accountant's Magazine,* January 1972, pp. 30–34; and "A Case for Cash Flow Reporting," *Journal of Business Finance,* Summer, 1972, pp. 27–36.

[11]The difficulties of assessing predictive ability can be seen in such studies as W. H. Beaver, "Market Prices, Financial Ratios and the Prediction of Failure," *Journal of Accounting Research,* Autumn 1968, pp. 179–92; M. C. O'Connor, "On the Usefulness of Financial Ratios to Investors in Common Stock," *Accounting Review,* April 1973, pp. 339–52. Altogether there have been little more than 20 empirical studies in this area between 1966 and 1975. All have been either restrictive in their coverage or tentative in their conclusions.

[12]For example, M. N. Greenball, "The Predictive-Ability Criterion: Its Relevance in Evaluating Accounting Data," *Abacus,* June 1971, pp. 1–7.

[13]K. V. Peasnell, "The Usefulness of Accounting Information to Investors," *Occasional Paper,* International Centre for Research in Accounting, 1973, p. 20.

[14]There is evidence to suggest that, in relation to annual financial reports, investors use them for purposes of verifying information made public earlier in other sources such as interim reports—see, for example, R. Ball and P. Brown, "An Empirical Evaluation of Accounting Income Numbers," *Journal of Accounting Research,* Autumn 1968, pp. 159–77.

same situation can result in materially different decisions,[15] and fluctuating income series can be smoothed by companies for reporting purposes, thereby masking the true situation.[16] However, due to the limited nature of this evidence, I would be reluctant at this stage to condemn entirely the predictive ability of historic-orientated reporting systems which depend on accrual accounting. But I do believe that the frailties which appear to exist in them are sufficient to warrant investigation of reporting models which appear better suited to meet the needs of decision makers.

In particular, there appears to be merit in the argument for the formal provision of predictive data in financial reports. This recommendation has been made several times in the past and, despite doubts about its credibility, has been used for some years in the U.K. — albeit in the limited context of corporate acquisitions and mergers.[17] My doubts about forecast data concern not so much their inherent subjectiveness (which is unavoidable and can be allowed for by decision makers), but more the additional subjectivity which is created if the accrual basis is adopted as the measurement process. In my opinion, cash flow forecasts are more credible than accrual-based forecasts. They avoid the variability and manipulation which can result from the use of accrual accounting. I also feel that adequate descriptions of the assumptions underlying cash forecasts would be necessary to improve their credibility; as would explanations of material differences between actual and forecast performance (for example, distinguishing between variances due to economic circumstances and variances due to forecasting errors). This would mean the provision of forecast data for predictive purposes and actual data for "feed-back" purposes—all on a cash and, therefore, allocation-free basis.

4.2 The Key Factor of Cash

Whereas the previous section has emphasised certain failures of the traditional reporting system which give rise to the need to examine the cash flow proposal as a suitable alternative, this next section outlines the main reasons why cash flow reporting is of value, *irrespective of the frailties of the accrual system*. My main argument in this connection is that cash is *the* key resource of most reporting enterprises. Irrespective of the vital importance of other resources in business (such as workers and managers), the cash flow of an entity is essential to its very existence. Not to recognise this is to ignore the harsh realities of the business world. Cash is the life blood of a business entity.

In other words, no business entity can survive over the long-term without an

---

[15]See, for example, N. Dopuch and J. Ronen, "The Effects of Alternative Inventory Valuation Methods—An Experimental Study," *Journal of Accounting Research,* Autumn 1973, pp. 191–211, for evidence of effects on individual decisions. At an aggregate level, however, evidence suggests the market is not "fooled" by these variations—see R. Ball, "Changes in Accounting Techniques and Stock Prices," *Empirical Research in Accounting: Selected Studies,* 1972, pp. 1–44. Presumably individual decision variations are compensated at the aggregate level.

[16]For example, R. M. Copeland, "Income Smoothing," *Empirical Research in Accounting: Selected Studies,* 1968, pp. 101–16. These results as with other similar studies, were tentative only, and require replication.

[17]As under the provisions of *The City Code on Take-overs and Mergers,* Issuing Houses Association, revised 1976, p. 19 and pp. 39–41.

adequate and positive net cash flow from its trading operations. Profitability is not enough and reasonable liquidity is required too. However, the traditional financial reporting system, with its considerable emphasis on profitability, is not specifically geared to highlight the key resource of cash. Funds statements are a considerable help in this respect, but they are not universally produced in practice and, in any case, are based on the income-orientated, accrual-based accounting system which does not necessarily identify the stark reality of cash flows. Admittedly, income contributes to liquidity but it is not the only factor to do so, and funds statements are somewhat inadequate for the purpose of isolating pure cash inflows and outflows. Cash is such an essential ingredient in the survival of reporting entities that it is very surprising that reporting accountants have paid so little attention to it. Some emphasis has been given through the use of accrual-based funds statements which are often, and misleadingly, termed cash flow statements (cash flow being defined as reported income after deduction of tax and addition of the depreciation provision). But, as previously mentioned, funds statements are no more than imperfect substitutes for cash flow statements.

It is also equally surprising that the needs of report users in relation to cash data have been virtually ignored. For example, the generally accepted share investment decision model is based on predictions of dividend flows which, in turn, depend to a large extent on the existence of distributable cash in the future. Accrual-based historic information cannot be said to be ideally suited to meet these particular needs. Nor can it be said to meet the needs of creditors anxious to assess a reporting entity's ability to pay its way both in the near-present and future (for example, with regard to interest and capital repayment commitments). Likewise, the employee and his official representatives concerned with wage negotiations, job security, and entity investment performance would find cash flow data more directly relevant to these needs than income-orientated information. In other words, just as a business will collapse through lack of cash, report users would appear to be equally disadvantaged through lack of information relating to cash. This applies whatever the economic climate, although it is most evident in times when cash is in short supply.

4.3. Maximising Objectivity

One of the most fundamental and influential guidelines in traditional financial accounting is that reported information should be as objective as possible. There has been a significant switch of emphasis by accountants in recent years—away from the rather rigid interpretation of this concept in terms of being able to verify independently the fairness of reported information in relation to available evidence, towards the increasingly accepted view of informational neutrality vis-à-vis report users. This change has evolved from a growing awareness on the part of accountants that reported information is in many ways a compromise. In particular, it must be relevant to its users but at the same time it must be credible in their eyes. The problem is therefore one of finding an optimal mixture of the essential features of financial reports. They cannot be completely relevant; nor can they be completely objective. However, they can be reasonably relevant and objective. With this in mind, I have come to the following conclusion in relation to the utility of cash flow data:

> ... If objectivity is accepted as an important criterion of accounting, production of the type of information which appears to present the most reasonable balance of relevance and objectivity should be aimed for at all times—because of its overall utility to the user. Cash flow information appears ... to satisfy these conditions best. Firstly, in its historic form, it is perhaps the most objective information possible, avoiding most of the subjectiveness which enters into the technical adjustments involved in the traditional accrual accounting; it is also the most relevant information for purposes of comparison with forecast information should this be measured on a cash basis. Secondly, forecast cash flows, although involving a great deal of uncertainty (however, no more so than budgeted profits on the accrual basis) clearly avoid the necessary subjectiveness of accrual judgments and opinions. Therefore, they appear to be far less subjective in a *total* sense than profit forecasts.[18]

I would therefore have thought that a cash flow reporting model would be considerably attractive to accountants, in the sense that it appears to increase the relevance of financial reports whilst also increasing the objectivity of historic data and minimising the subjectivity of forecast data. In addition, it tends to switch the burden of responsibility for reporting away from the reporting accountant (by eliminating the absolute necessity for accounting allocations and valuations) towards entity management which, after all, is ultimately responsible for the quality of financial reports. If cash flow reporting were implemented, the onus would be on management to produce credible forecasts and not to manipulate historic flows by accelerating or decelerating cash transactions.

[18] Lee (A Case for), *op. cit.*, p. 30.

DIFFERENCES IN "CIRCUMSTANCES"

Accounting numbers, dollars, are used to describe a great variety of attributes—the value of a building, the amount owed by a customer, the amount owed to a creditor, the selling price of a product or service, the wages paid to employees, the dividends paid to stockholders, etc. The use of this common unit of measure gives the accountant confidence that the quantities so determined can be combined into meaningful measures.

No quantification of any attribute is very significant in itself. The quantity needs to be compared with a standard to determine whether the attribute being quantified is bigger, better, or smaller than the standard to which comparison is made. When comparisons are to be made, the unit of measure and the method of measurement must be consistently applied.

In the case of accounting numbers, there is no standard of comparison. The comparison must be made with similar measures made for other companies. If the comparison is to be a meaningful one—a useful one—then the unit of measure must be the same, the method of measurement must be the same, and the attribute being measured must be comparable. The problem which accountants have is that economic events are seldom identical between two or more entities; there are differences in the circumstances. These circumstantial differences may be sufficiently great to cause discrepancies to arise in the comparison between companies even though the unit of measure is standardized. The question remains: should there be only one permissible method of measuring the economic attribute (e.g., the cost of inventory) or should there be several methods from which the accountant may select the appropriate one given the specific circumstances?

The debate among accountants and users of financial statements has raged for decades. In essence: should there be measurement rules that apply to each situation uniformly or should there be general principles that guide the accountant in measuring economic attributes? There has been a series of committees and boards which have struggled with this question, including the Accounting Principles Board and the Financial Accounting Standards Board. Each has stated that one of its objectives is to narrow the area of difference that exists in current accounting practice. The late Robert M. Trueblood, when he was AICPA president, said, "I think there is a general view that the APB should recommend accounting practices which will make like things look alike, and unlike things look different." [1]

In 1975 the Securities and Exchange Commission adopted Accounting Series Release No. 177 which required an independent accountant, the auditor, to state, in cases where a different method of accounting for a given type of event is adopted, that the new method is preferable to the method previously used. In situations where the existing body of doctrine permits more than one method to be used, the SEC required the accountant to substitute his judgment for that of the profession. In 1957, the SEC had stated flatly of a CPA that "his duty is to safeguard the public interest, not that of his client." [2] Must the adopted principle be preferable so as to safeguard the public interest, make results more comparable, or reflect differences in circumstances?

The editors of a symposium on Uniformity in Financial Accounting, when considering this general question, observed:

> The only factor that makes the accountant's position with respect to his client at all tenable is the objectivity of the standard he is expected to apply in expressing an opinion on financial statements. The prevailing standard is that reflected in the auditor's usual opinion to the effect that the financial statements in question "fairly present" the company's financial position and its operating results for the calendar period "in accordance with generally accepted accounting principles." Under this standard, the legitimacy of a particular treatment of an item to be accounted for is determined by reference to the practices of other firms and other accountants; the accountant's private opinion as to the essential soundness of the method is only incidentally relevant, if indeed it is relevant at all. [3]

Lawrence Revsine, in "The Preferability Dilemma," examines the many facets of the preferability issue. He raises the important question of whether an expressed preference for a method in one situation requires that that same method be used in all similar circumstances. The SEC concluded that there may be different circumstances which would justify the use of an alternative procedure when the circumstances in fact appeared to be similar. Even so, the question of preferable for the client *or* society at large remains an issue. Revsine also raises the inevitable question: If one cannot decide which method selected from several acceptable alternatives is preferable, then what is the meaning of the phrase "these statements present fairly"?

[1] Robert M. Trueblood, "Accounting Principles: The Board and its Problems," in *Empirical Research in Accounting: Selected Studies 1966*, supplement to the *Journal of Accounting Research*, p. 189. This view was echoed in the Trueblood Report, *Objectives of Financial Statements* (New York: AICPA, 1973), p. 59.
[2] Touche, Niven, Bailey & Smart, 37 SEC 629, pp. 670–71 (1957).
[3] "Uniformity in Financial Accounting," *Law and Contemporary Problems*, Vol. XXX, No. 4 (Durham, NC, School of Law, Duke University, Autumn 1965), Foreword.

Can statements that are based on an arbitrary—perhaps even a random—selection of accounting procedures have any economic meaning? This is a very real dilemma when differences in circumstances exist, but principles governing the selection of the appropriate accounting method must be made by the profession or some other authoritative source. Does the solution to this dilemma require the FASB to list the circumstances which must exist in order to justify the use-selected accounting procedures? This question leads to the next. Are accountants expected to communicate to the receivers a message about specific events or are they expected to provide an evaluative statement about the most recent past? An answer to this question would help determine whether specific rules for encoding and transmitting messages are needed.

In "Uniformity in Accounting: An Historical Perspective," Barbara D. Merino and Teddy L. Coe review the continuing debate that has raged since the earliest days of published financial statements. The Holy Grail of uniformity continues to be elusive, and, as the authors suggest, its attainment is likely to continue to be the subject of debate among future generations. Perhaps some attention should be directed at the *nature* of the communication desired between the entity and the users of the information. The role of the auditor as attestor to the verifiability of the measurement seems to be more clearly understood. The role of the accountant as measurer of information appears to be much less understood or accepted.

BIBLIOGRAPHICAL NOTES

For a review of the literature and an empirical study of the views of corporate executives, financial analysts and independent CPAs on the uniformity-flexibility issue, readers should consult the following volume:

Mautz, R.K.: *The Effect of Circumstances on the Application of Accounting Principles* (New York: Financial Executives Research Foundation, 1972).

In countries where a "true and fair view" is the legislative standard for financial reports, the following discussion of the meaning and significance of this elusive term may be of interest:

Flint, David: *The Significance of the Standard 'True and Fair View,'* 1980 Invitation Research Lecture (Wellington: New Zealand Society of Accountants, 1980). A somewhat condensed presentation by the same author appears in *A True and Fair View in Company Accounts* (London: Gee and Co. (Publishers) Limited for the Institute of Chartered Accountants of Scotland, 1982).

The Preferability Dilemma

Lawrence Revsine
Northwestern University

To some observers, generally accepted accounting principles used in reporting financial events possess excessive latitude. In defense of existing practice, this latitude may be justified because of different circumstances. But, clearly, the use of different methods of accounting for the same set of economic events is controversial.

In September 1975, the Securities and Exchange Commission transformed this long-smoldering issue into a major conflagration.[1] In brief, the SEC required an independent accountant to indicate whether a new accounting principle used by his client in certain SEC filings was *preferable* to the old principle. The purpose of this article is to examine the preferability issue and to evaluate the positions that have arisen since the SEC's action.

BACKGROUND

Diversity abounds in accounting. Many alternative techniques for reflecting similar financial events exist. Even in comparatively simple situations like determining ending inventory balances, the accounting options (Lifo, Fifo, weighted average, etc.) are numerous. Theoretically, management selects an accounting principle by examining the underlying circumstances in a specific area. Given these circumstances, the method that is chosen should "present fairly" the financial condition of the firm. In making the choice, management must adhere to two constraints. First, the method selected must be a member of a set of techniques called generally accepted accounting principles. Second, once selected, a technique must be applied consistently from year to year. Unfortunately, it is widely acknowledged that there are no definitive "criteria for relating the choice among some alternative methods, such as inventory methods or depreciation methods, to the circumstances of a particular company."[2] This raises the possibility that virtually identical situations could be accounted for differently by different firms.

The preferability problem is not a new one that arose because of recent SEC action. It has existed all along, but accountants have tended to ignore it. However, when a firm suddenly changes to a new method, the specter of potential statement manipulation is raised. What justification is there for abandoning a method that

From *The Journal of Accountancy* (September 1977), pp. 80–89. Reprinted by permission of the American Institute of Certified Public Accountants. Copyright © 1977 by the American Institute of Certified Public Accountants, Inc.

[1] Securities and Exchange Commission, Accounting Series Release No. 177, *Notice of Adoption of Amendments to Form 10-Q and Regulation S-X Regarding Interim Financial Reporting,* September 10, 1975.

[2] Statement on Auditing Standards No. 5, *The Meaning of "Present Fairly in Conformity With Generally Accepted Accounting Principles" in the Independent Auditor's Report* (New York: AICPA, July 1975), p. 4n.

presumably "presented fairly" in the past? Who bears the burden for justifying the change?

In treating accounting changes, APB Opinion No. 20 clearly indicated that the new principle must be *preferable* to the old. Importantly, however, the burden of proof in establishing and justifying preferability rested with "the entity proposing the change."[3] That is, the ultimate responsibility for accounting choices rested with management and the auditor merely had to determine that the justification provided by management was reasonable. Since definitive criteria for these choices often did not exist, and since the auditor's involvement was indirect (i.e., limited to establishing that a reasonable case could conceivably be made for the principles adopted), diversity was common.

Some critics viewed this diversity with skepticism. They asserted that divergent accounting changes within the same industry could not be justified invariably by differences in circumstances; nor could these differences be used by an auditor to permit one client to shift from principle A to principle B while another was allowed to abandon principle B and move to principle A. However, these criticisms of diversity in current practice are usually based upon informal observations. Critics can assert the existence of abuses, but it is difficult to gather systematic evidence to settle the debate.

In Accounting Series Release No. 177 the SEC altered the auditor's responsibility when a client changes accounting principles. The SEC mandated that when such changes are made "in the first Form 10-Q subsequent to the date of an accounting change, a letter from the registrant's independent accountants shall be filed as an exhibit indicating whether or not the change is to an alternative principle which in his judgment is preferable under the circumstances...."[4]

It was evident that the SEC had shifted to the independent accountant a large portion of the responsibility for determining preferability. Recently, however, Staff Accounting Bulletin No. 14 introduced some ambiguity by suggesting that when making preferability assessments the independent accountant may often "accept the registrant's business judgment and business planning and express reliance thereon in his letter."[5] But SAB No. 14 did reiterate the increased responsibility of the independent accountant for preferability judgments when it stated that "a registrant must furnish a letter from its independent accountant stating that *in the judgment of the independent accountant* the change in method is preferable under the circumstances...."[6] This altered responsibility for preferability judgments was further reinforced in the recent report of the Commission on Auditors' Responsibilities.[7]

Two reasons can be inferred for the SEC's action. First, the SEC was apparently trying to encourage (force?) the accounting profession to delineate explicitly the

[3] Accounting Principles Board Opinion No. 20, *Accounting Changes* (New York: AICPA, July 1971), par. 16.
[4] ASR No. 177, p. 20.
[5] Securities and Exchange Commission Staff Accounting Bulletin No. 14, *Revisions to SAB No. 6 Regarding Reporting Requirements for Accounting Changes,* February 3, 1977.
[6] Ibid. (emphasis supplied).
[7] *Commission on Auditors' Responsibilities: Report of Tentative Conclusions* (New York: AICPA, 1977), p. 20.

criteria used in choosing among divergent accounting principles. Second, the SEC intended to make independent accountants the vehicle for achieving more uniform application of these criteria to specific situations and thereby reduce alternatives.

Auditors have generally reacted unfavorably to the preferability requirement. In a statement urging that the SEC reconsider this issue, the auditing standards executive committee of the AICPA (AudSEC) contended that preferability cannot be determined where diverse alternatives exist and no criteria for choice have been established.[8] In a petition filed before the SEC, Arthur Andersen & Co. added that different auditing firms might reach different judgments on similar issues. They further contended that preferability is not limited to accounting *changes.* Once an auditor expresses a preference for principle A rather than principle B in a change situation, other clients that do not change and continue to use principle B are placed in a difficult position.[9] Other auditors have also expressed the view that the SEC's preferability rule should be rescinded.

Since the release of SAB No. 14, the application of preferability is subject to some interpretation. This article will accept ASR No. 177 at face value and assume that it intends to shift responsibility for preferability judgments to the independent accountant. With this interpretation, the article will analyze whether a basis for these preferability judgments exists. Clearly, the issue is an important one that reaches to the core of the external reporting process and generally accepted accounting principles.

PREFERABILITY JUDGMENTS REQUIRE OBJECTIVES

The Meaning of Preferability

Preferability exists when one situation is considered to be more desirable than another. To establish a preferability relationship between various alternatives, one must determine what the outcomes of each choice would be and then rank these outcomes by reference to some specified objectives or goals. Thus, preferability requires a comparison against a predetermined benchmark.

This same meaning applies in an accounting setting. Alternative accounting principles are frequently available to reflect certain economic events. Each of these alternatives provides a different interpretation of the underlying economic events on the financial statements. That is, different accounting options generate different financial statement outcomes.

But which aspects of the firm's economic events do we prefer to see shown on the statements? Following the general definition of preferability, which outcomes are most consistent with the goals or objectives of the accounting process? It is clear that one cannot make preferability choices unless one also has specified a set of goals or objectives and is able to determine which statement outcomes lead to the desired objectives.

---

[8] Letter from Kenneth P. Johnson, chairman, AudSEC, to George A. Fitzsimmons, secretary, SEC, February 4, 1976, p. 1.

[9] *Petition of Arthur Andersen & Co. Before the Securities and Exchange Commission,* June 15, 1976, p. 8. This point was also made by the Commission on Auditors' Responsibilities, ibid., p. 20n.

Objectives for the accounting process are those outcomes that society wants financial reports to accomplish. Examples include (1) providing information for assessing a firm's prospects of obtaining net cash inflows through its earning and financing activities,[10] (2) generating financial information regarding resources, obligations and earnings that provides comparable data for making comparisons between firms, (3) facilitating efficient resource allocation, or (4) appropriately matching current efforts against current accomplishments.

Pragmatic criteria also play a central role in deciding which objectives are selected for external reports. For example, in order to achieve certain reporting objectives, it may be necessary to use estimates or other subjective data. An independent accountant may reject alternatives of this type because of the legal risk that such imprecise data could precipitate. Thus, the selected objectives will be influenced by the perceived economic consequences for the accountant. In a similar way, accounting goals may be tempered by other types of pragmatic considerations, such as technical feasibility or objectivity. Therefore, the process for choosing objectives is a complex one that incorporates both theoretical preferences and practical constraints.

In theory, the linkage between objectives and preferability judgments is straightforward. To illustrate, assume that the overriding objective of accounting reports is to provide a valid and consistent basis for comparing performance across companies, i.e., comparability is considered to be the primary objective. Now, further assume that an accountant must choose between two reporting alternatives. Principle A provides a valid and consistent basis for comparisons while principle B does not. Since principle A is consistent with the comparabililty objective and principle B isn't, principle A is preferred. Furthermore, a change from principle B to principle A represents a change to a preferable principle. This simple situation illustrates why it is necessary to know the objectives of the accounting process in order to make preferability judgments.

Do We Know Accounting Objectives?

Since preferability judgments require specifying objectives, it is reasonable to ask whether the objectives of the accounting and reporting process are sufficently well-specified to allow individual accountants to make preferability judgments.

At one level, some might contend that the objectives of the accounting process are well-specified. The overriding objective might be to present fairly the financial condition of the enterprise. Unfortunately, this begs the question since the concept "present fairly" has not been precisely defined. For example, in order to present fairly, does one

- Emphasize the effect that *historical-transactions costs* have had on financial condition?
- Reflect the result of *present market prices and circumstances* on existing assets and claims?

---

[10] This is one of the objectives discussed by the FASB in *Tentative Conclusions on Objectives of Financial Statements of Business Enterprises* (Stamford, CT.: FASB, December 2, 1976).

Furthermore, even if all parties involved agreed that we ought to strive to reflect the result of present market circumstances, this is still insufficient. Which present market circumstances are relevant? Do we want to do this for its own sake or as a guide to expected future financial condition? If the latter, with what future elements are we concerned, i.e., the risk of future bankruptcy, the level of future cash-generating potential, anticipated future dividend-paying ability?

Obviously, the accounting profession has not settled these issues. The Financial Accounting Standards Board's conceptual framework project testifies to the importance of and current controversy surrounding appropriate objectives for external accounting reports.[11]

How Do We Establish Objectives?

Objectives are based upon individual beliefs, preferences and values. This means that there are no such things as "correct" or "true" objectives for a process or area of social activity. In the abstract, no objective can be demonstrated to be theoretically superior to any other.

The accounting implications are straightforward. Since objectives arise from subjective beliefs and preferences, no amount of research about accounting or the accounting process will generate a single set of generally appropriate objectives for accounting. There are no underlying true objectives "out there" just waiting to be discovered by accounting researchers.

If that is the case, how do we proceed if we believe it necessary to have well-defined objectives for external reporting? One possibility is to leave it to each individual accountant to develop his own set of objectives. Since various individuals view the world differently and have different value systems, this approach would undoubtedly generate widely divergent objectives among individuals. If the diversity inherent in this approach is unsatisfactory, then the other alternative is to have a policy body like the FASB establish a single set of objectives that would guide the entire profession.

This second alternative has much to recommend it. One of the reasons accountants have not been able to agree on a single set of objectives is that different preferences and values lead to different objectives. Eventually, to win general acceptance, a set of objectives must be in accord with prevailing overall social preferences. That is, there must be some consensus that the chosen objectives lead to socially desirable outcomes.[12]

---

[11] FASB Discussion Memorandum, *Conceptual Framework for Financial Accounting and Reporting: Elements of Financial Statements and Their Measurement* (Stamford, CT.: FASB, December 2, 1976), and FASB, *Tentative Conclusions.*

[12] The way in which this consensus should be reached is one of the classic issues in welfare economics. The fundamental problem is that certain individuals may be better off if one set of objectives is used while other individuals may profit from an alternative set of objectives. Developing a socially preferred objectives framework therefore necessitates interpersonal welfare comparisons and trade-offs. Since some individuals will be harmed and others benefited as these choices are made, the process will always be controversial. Thus the term "consensus" implies some sort of overall social judgment regarding whose preferences will be satisfied. These issues are discussed in Committee on Concepts and Standards for External Financial Reports, *Statement on Accounting Theory and Theory Acceptance* (Sarasota, FL.: American Accounting Association, 1977).

In an accounting setting, the participants in the accounting process are not just accountants. Society as a whole is affected by accounting reports;[13] therefore, overall societal preferences must be taken into account in establishing objectives. To accomplish this, objectives should be formulated by considering the conflicting preferences and values of the various participants in the accounting process. Since others besides accountants are affected, objectives should be set by those with a broad perspective on accounting's impact on society-at-large. Individual accountants may not have the requisite breadth. On the other hand, public bodies that presumably possess broader perspectives on societal goals are unlikely to have the detailed accounting expertise necessary to formulate operational objectives. Weighing these tradeoffs, an FASB-type body (perhaps with a broader representation than it now possesses) could be the appropriate group to develop objectives. Theoretically, its social perspectives would be broader than those of any single accountant and its financial expertise deeper than that of most public bodies. In principle at least, it might have the appropriate balance between breadth and depth that is needed to establish socially acceptable objectives for external reports.

To summarize, in order to make preferability judgments, the objectives of the accounting process must be established. Options that are congruent with these objectives are preferred to options that are inconsistent with these objectives. It was also pointed out that accounting does not have an agreed-upon objectives framework. In the absence of a generally accepted framework, we suggested that individual accountants are each forced to establish their own objectives for the accounting process. Since objectives are derived from personal preferences, it is not a question of right or wrong; different individuals can come up with different objectives. The only way to overcome this diversity is to have some policy-making body impose a set of objectives that they believe to be in the best interests of society.

PREFERABILITY IN THE EXISTING ENVIRONMENT

The preferability judgments required by ASR No. 177 are intended to be applied in the existing accounting environment. Since there are no agreed-upon objectives for the existing accounting process, each individual accountant is forced to establish his own objectives in order to comply with the SEC requirements. The following sections discuss the implications of this individual application of the preferability requirement.

Diverse Objectives

It is virtually certain that individual independent accountants will develop diverse objectives for external reports. As a consequence, one company's accountant might consider a change from principle A to principle B to be a shift to a preferable principle; simultaneously, another company's auditor might deem a shift in the opposite direction to be preferable. Clearly, this situation is troublesome if the two

---

[13]For a summary and illustration of this see Alfred Rappaport, "Economic Impact of Accounting Standards—Implications for the FASB," JofA, May 77, p. 89.

companies are in the same industry or otherwise appear to be subject to a similar set of underlying circumstances.

At the extreme, it is possible that each independent accountant would establish totally different objectives. Instances of inconsistent shifts in what otherwise appear to be identical circumstances would be common. Thus, there would be no tendency for such accounting changes to lead to all enterprises' eventually using similar principles in similar circumstances. In other words, when auditors select diverse objectives, the application of the preferability standard cannot be expected to generate financial statements that will reduce alternatives used by various firms in otherwise identical circumstances.[14] Thus, if the SEC was implicitly using the preferability requirement as a means for eventually reducing the number of available accounting principles alternatives, there is no reason to believe that this will actually happen in an environment of diverse objectives.

Linkage Between Accounting Principles and Objectives

In order to make preferability judgments, it must always be possible to determine which accounting principles will lead to the desired reporting objectives. Consider a hypothetical case of accounting for long-term construction contracts as an illustration. Assume that the independent accountant has selected the prediction of cash flow potential as the overriding objective of financial statement preparation. Specifically, the independent accountant is trying to select accounting principles that generate financial statement numbers about current performance in order to provide users with the best possible basis for predicting future operating cash flows. Assume that a construction client proposes to switch from the completed-contract method to the percentage-of-completion method for recognizing profit on long-term construction projects. In order to determine whether this change is to a preferable principle, the independent accountant must be able to determine whether the financial statements under the percentage-of-completion method provide a better basis for predicting cash flows than do financial statements prepared using the completed-contract method. In other words, he must know the linkage between each of the accounting principles options and his specified objective for the accounting process.

How would this determination be made? One possibility is to evaluate the alternatives using logic and intuition in order to assess whether the new method is more likely to achieve the desired objective. Often this may work. Logical analysis or some formalized evaluation technique may indicate which alternative is more consistent with the specified objective. But often it may not work since the answer may not be apparent without hard empirical evidence. Unless this evidence is available, there is no rigorously supportable basis for the required preferability judgment. Since gathering the required evidence takes time, it will often not be

---

[14] As one major firm describes elements of existing practice: "In many important areas of accounting, alternative principles and practices cannot be justified by differences in circumstances." (*Petition of Arthur Andersen & Co. Before the Securities and Exchange Commission,* p. 8.)

possible to express a preference at the time of the SEC filing. Indeed, the problem may be so complex that sophisticated experimental controls and statistical techniques more within the province of the academic researcher may be necessary. To elicit such studies may take still more time.

Another point to remember is that the principles from which the accountant can choose are limited to those that comprise GAAP. The options, of course, are based upon nominal historical costs. Some critics have questioned whether historical cost principles have any demonstrable relationship to meaningful economic goals or decision-making objectives.[15] In other words, if the independent accountant selects some meaningful objective for the accounting statements, it is possible that none of the restricted GAAP options that are available will conform to the objective that he specified. As an example, consider the objective that financial data ought to reflect the rate of return currently being earned by the firm under existing competitive circumstances, i.e., under existing levels of costs and prices. Notice that this objective necessitates both balance sheet and income statement data.

Now, assume that a preferability choice must be made between Lifo and Fifo. If the objective is to depict the current rate of return, each of these inventory flow assumptions is flawed. In periods of changing prices (that is, virtually always), Fifo generates an income statement number that does not conform to the assumed economic objective, i.e., it does not reflect operating income at existing levels of costs and prices. Lifo generates a balance sheet inventory number (based on old inventory costs) which also does not reflect existing circumstances. Thus, neither option is consistent with the assumed objective.[16]

Accordingly, even if each independent accountant has a clearly defined set of objectives, it may still be difficult to make a preferability judgment. We have seen two reasons for this. First, it may not be clear which alternative accounting principle better achieves the desired objective. Actual evidence may be needed to establish such linkages and this evidence may not be available. Second, it is possible that none of the GAAP options will be wholly consistent with the selected objectives of an

---

[15]For example, Sterling said that he was unable to establish the relevance of historical cost numbers to any meaningful economic decision and challenged the readers to provide an example of how such data would generate meaningful input in a decision situation. No such examples have been reported to my knowledge. See Robert R. Sterling, "Relevant Financial Reporting in an Age of Price Changes," JofA, Feb.75, pp.47–48.

[16]This point may be restated as follows: Ideally, a current rate of return ratio would have the following characteristics:

$$\text{Current \% return} = \frac{\text{Income measured at current costs and prices}}{\text{Assets measured at current costs}}$$

While Fifo generates an asset (inventory) number that is consistent with the objectives of this ratio (i.e., ending inventory is comprised of the most recent inventory costs), the numerator (net income) arises from a matching of the oldest costs against revenues and is thus inconsistent with the *current* return philosophy. By contrast, the Lifo income numerator is measured using the most recent costs and is thus consistent with the current return philosophy. However, the asset denominator (inventory at Lifo cost) represents the oldest costs and thus is inconsistent with the ratio's data requirements. Thus, neither option generates numbers that are consistent with the ratio objectives in both the numerator and denominator.

individual accountant.[17] In this case, there is seemingly no basis for a preferability judgment.

Shopping Around

Consider the case of a firm that wishes to change accounting principles. The firm's independent accountant does not deem the proposed new principle to be preferable to the old principle. That is, the new principle is inconsistent with that accountant's assumed set of objectives. However, in an environment in which objectives for the accounting process are individually derived, it is highly probable that another independent accountant has a different set of objectives. The proposed new principle may be quite consistent with this second accountant's presumed objectives and preferable to the old principle in his view.

The crucial question is whether the prospect of having the accounting change designated as "not preferable" would induce the firm to seek another auditor.[18] Clearly, the potential exists. ASR No. 177 introduces yet another source for friction between companies and their auditors. This switching possibility is clearly detrimental to auditors' self-interests. However, this phenomenon may also be undesirable from an overall social cost-benefit perspective.

In mandating the preferability requirement, the SEC apparently wanted to pressure independent accountants to reduce the alternative principles contained in external reports. The hoped-for simplification represents the intended social benefit that ASR No. 177 was expected to achieve.

But will this benefit, in fact, be realized in an environment characterized by diverse objectives? Not necessarily. Even if a firm's independent accountant considers a principle change to be not preferable, the firm can still effect the change by changing both the accounting principle *and* its auditor. That is, so long as the firm is able to find some auditor who views the prospective principle as preferable to the existing one, the change can be made. Thus, ASR No. 177 has prevented nothing. Alternative principles and "unsupportable" changes would still exist.[19]

Thus, if a firm changes auditors, the intended social benefits of the preferability rule may be subverted. Worse yet, the process of subverting the intended benefits

---

[17]A related problem arises when several options are equally consistent with assumed objectives. If more than one option conforms to the selected objectives, preferability judgments will again be difficult if a firm switches from one of these "conforming" principles to another.

[18]If a change is designated as "not preferable," it appears that the SEC will not accept the resultant financial statements and would require the registrant to consistently apply the original principle. There is no direct statement of this in ASR No. 177, but it can be inferred from the following letter to AudSEC from the SEC: "If in fact there is no professional basis for concluding that one accounting principle is preferable to another... then APB Opinion No. 20 makes it clear that no change can be made which is in conformity with generally accepted accounting principles." (Letter from George A. Fitzsimmons, secretary, SEC, to Kenneth P. Johnson, chairman, AudSEC, April 30, 1976, p. 3).

In other words, if the new principle is not preferable, it is also not acceptable. This means that preferability disputes are precisely equivalent to the types of accounting disagreements that must be disclosed on SEC Form 8-K, if and when a change in auditors is made.

[19]Of course, the change in auditors that arose from an accounting dispute would have to be disclosed on Form 8-K. But the effects of the change would have been reported in any case under existing reporting standards as a consistency exception.

can consume real resources. There may be social costs associated with the change in auditors since the new auditor is not as familiar with the company, its operations, its internal control systems and other characteristics that affect the nature and scope of the audit engagement. In order to compensate the new independent accountant for these start-up costs, it is possible that the initial-year audit fee may be higher than the old fee. Alternatively, the fee may remain the same, but the level of ancillary audit services may be lower in the first year(s) until the new auditor becomes familiar with the firm. In the first alternative, the same level of service is provided but more resources are used; in the second alternative, a lower level of service is provided with no change in resource utilization. But both alternatives lead to a lower level of audit benefit per unit of audit effort. In other words, the real cost of audit services would increase.

To summarize, when a firm is motivated to change auditors in order to subvert the preferability requirement, the intended social benefits implicit in the SEC rule will not be realized. Furthermore, it is possible that costs will be increased, thereby creating an unfavorable social cost-benefit relationship.

Will this happen? The answer is unclear. The key determining factor is the frequency with which firms will be motivated to subvert the requirements by changing auditors. There are also legal liability ramifications. The way in which the SEC enforces the preferability rule and expectations about the private sector's reactions to accounting changes will influence both the willingness of firms to change auditors and the willingness of new auditors to accept such engagements. The possibility of changing auditors is a feasible one since, in all likelihood, different auditors will select different objectives for the accounting process. But whether firms will utilize that escape route is uncertain. Clearly, the possibility exists. If it is used, the social benefit objectives of ASR No. 177 will not be accomplished. Of course, if firms are reluctant to change auditors or if new auditors are unwilling to accept such engagements, then the preferability requirement may indeed accomplish its intended objectives. But since we cannot forecast the behavior of firms or auditors—the key variables—we cannot say with certainty that the favorable social effects envisioned by the SEC will indeed be realized.

Differences in Circumstances

When an independent accountant states that a particular change is to a preferable principle, does this mean that his other clients are precluded from making a change in the opposite direction? Originally, the SEC implied that all such "inconsistent" changes would receive close scrutiny.[20] Subsequently, however, this view was tempered in Staff Accounting Bulletin No. 14: "If registrants in apparently similar

---

[20]"Where the factual circumstances surrounding the accounting changes are similar, the staff would not expect an accounting firm to accept accounting changes in both directions by different clients.... Registrants and accountants may expect the staff to request that it be furnished with the details supporting acceptance of apparently inconsistent positions by the accounting firm." (Securities and Exchange Commission, Staff Accounting Bulletin No. 6, *Interpretation of ASR No. 177*, March 1, 1976).

circumstances make changes in opposite directions, the staff has a responsibility to inquire as to the factors which were considered in arriving at the determination by each registrant and its independent accountant that the change was preferable under the circumstances because it resulted in improved financial reporting. The staff recognized the importance, in many circumstances, of the judgments and plans of management and recognized that such management judgments may, in good faith, differ." [21] Thus, changes in opposite directions by different firms are not precluded. The SEC will apparently permit such changes when they can be justified by differences in underlying circumstances.

But here is the potential danger. Whether differences in underlying circumstances exist depends upon objectives employed by the observer. An environmental aspect that differs between two otherwise identical circumstances may be important to one objectives structure and may cause the independent accountant to differentiate between the two situations; yet that same environmental aspect may be irrelevant to some other objectives structure and may cause some other accountant to view the two situations similarly. Thus, differences in circumstances are not objective, readily discernible phenomena.

In order for it to be meaningful, the SEC staff review of underlying circumstances must employ the same set of objectives that the independent accountant was using. It was from the perspective of those objectives that the independent accountant differentiated between the two situations. It would be chaotic if the SEC employed some alternative set of objectives to determine whether the differences indeed exist. Different objectives could be expected, in some circumstances, to lead to different conclusions regarding underlying circumstances. Thus, if the review suggested in SAB No. 14 is undertaken, it is necessary that the SEC use the same set of objectives that the independent accountant used. This would put the SEC staff in the awkward position of employing several alternative objectives structures in the review process.

RECOMMENDATIONS

Summary

Analysis indicates that the SEC's preferability rule presents serious implementation difficulties. Several causes exist. First, in the absence of an agreed-upon set of objectives for external financial statements, each independent accountant would need to establish his own objectives. These diverse objectives are likely to lead to diverse preferability judgments. Second, even after objectives are specified, it does not automatically follow that preferability judgments will always be possible. One reason is that the linkage between accounting options and specified objectives may be unknown. Another reason is that there may be certain objectives that no GAAP option satisfies. Third, preferability differences among auditors may induce companies to "shop around" rather than forego an accounting change that is resisted by their current auditors. This process is socially costly and may subvert the intended SEC objectives. Finally, in reviewing apparently inconsistent positions, the SEC

[21]SAB No. 14, p.7.

staff would have to employ the same set of objectives that the auditor did. Since different auditors will undoubtedly select different objectives, the SEC review would necessitate a high degree of flexibility.

These characteristics indicate that the SEC's objectives in promulgating the preferability rule are unlikely to be achieved. (That is, many alternative accounting principles will remain and "unsupportable" accounting changes will continue.) Worse yet, social costs may be incurred as firms attempt to circumvent ASR No. 177.

The Dilemma

The accounting profession is in an untenable position. On the one hand, accountants argue that preferability judgments cannot now be made on a defensible basis. On the other hand, when an accountant provides a "clean" audit opinion he asserts that the financial statements present fairly the financial status of a firm.

Unfortunately, these two assertions appear to be somewhat contradictory. The inability to make preferability judgments implies that any one of several different principles will suffice, so long as it is consistent with GAAP; but if numerous options are each equally acceptable, then the one(s) that was (were) chosen must be arbitrary.[22] It is difficult to then argue that a series of such arbitrary choices generates financial statements with unequivocal economic meaning. Rather, if preferences between alternatives cannot be established, external accounting reports appear to be based upon elaborate ritual. In such an environment, audit opinions merely give notice that certain arbitrary accounting traditions have been adhered to.[23] That is, if preferability cannot be established when accounting changes are made, it also cannot be established for those principles currently in use. What does this say about the meaning of present fairly? This is the essence of the preferability dilemma.

Since it has been contended that unequivocal preferability judgments cannot now be made, we have implicitly acknowledged that the factors that cause this also result in arbitrary financial statements.[24] If this is the case, it is not clear that society will be willing, in the long run, to incur significant costs for preparing, auditing and distributing such statements. Clearly, preferability is the visible symptom of a much more serious malady that must be cured and cured quickly.

The malady, of course, is that the accounting profession does not have an

[22] Arbitrary in the sense that they are incapable of being defended against alternatives. This view is developed in Arthur L. Thomas, *The Allocation Problem: Part Two* (Sarasota, FL.: American Accounting Association, 1974).

[23] This does not mean that audits are without value. Even if numerous alternatives exist, the fact that GAAP was utilized limits potential management latitude and manipulative freedom. Furthermore, audits convey information regarding internal controls, custodianship of assets and adherence to prescribed policies.

[24] Under certain circumstances, it is possible to contend that arbitrary statements could conceivably be useful as well. See Arthur L. Thomas, "Useful Arbitrary Allocations (With a Comment on the Neutrality of Financial Accounting Reports)," *Accounting Review*, July 1971, pp. 472–79. However, this may be true only in particular circumstances and it clearly shifts the burden of proof to the accounting community to explain how arbitrary techniques that cannot be defended against alternatives can simultaneously provide useful information.

agreed-upon set of objectives for external financial statements. Again and again in this article, this absence of objectives was seen to be a key factor inhibiting compliance with ASR No. 177. Each of the four implementation difficulties examined in the article and summarized above arises in whole or in part because there is currently no agreed-upon set of objectives of financial reporting. Fortunately, this failing is widely acknowledged and the FASB has recently issued a document in this area. Hopefully, the inconsistencies inherent in the profession's preferability position will induce quick action and culminate in the selection of a broadly based objectives structure.

What Do We Do in the Meantime?

Analysis suggests that the SEC should temporarily suspend the preferability requirements of ASR No. 177.[25] This position does not imply that the SEC was wrong in principle. On the contrary, if financial statements purport to reflect useful information, then those who receive these statements have a right to expect that the statements have been prepared according to principles that are preferable in the circumstances. However, the SEC action was premature since no basis for the required preferability judgment currently exists.

As an alternative, it would be better for the SEC to treat preferability as a long-term objective that can be achieved only after the development of a set of objectives for external accounting reports and a determination of the linkage between alternative principles and the chosen objectives.

This view recognizes that the key to *operational* preferability requirements is action on objectives. We have argued that there are no such things as true or correct objectives since objectives are dependent on individual beliefs and value structures. For this reason, agreement on objectives may not be easy. But the SEC can provide the impetus for quick action—and simultaneously generate substantial improvement in financial reporting—by establishing a deadline for action. For example, after suspending the requirements of ASR No. 177, the SEC could announce the intention of reinstituting these preferability requirements when a set of objectives acceptable to the commission are selected. The FASB and the accounting profession could be given a time frame for accomplishing what must be done. The implication would be clear. Unless suitable objectives were developed by the FASB, the SEC would establish its own objectives and then use the objectives as a basis for reinstituting a preferability requirement.

The proposal to suspend ASR No. 177 for several years pending development of an objectives structure has much to recommend it. First, it is feasible. The FASB document, *Tentative Conclusions on Objectives of Financial Statements of Business Enterprises,* already provides the groundwork for establishing a set of objectives. Since the mechanism is currently in progress, a deadline along the lines suggested above is realistic. Second, this suggested course of action is a practical necessity

---

[25] Perhaps the SEC was attempting to do this in a face-saving way when it issued SAB No. 14. However, this is unclear since SAB No. 14 reiterates the emphasis on preferable "in the judgment of the independent accountant."

since a preferability standard requires some set of objectives in order to be operationally sound. Third, this approach generates an important collateral benefit since
the objectives developed to implement preferability choices are badly needed to
provide a conceptual framework for accounting in general. Pressure induced by the
SEC deadline will certainly hasten progress in achieving consensus on objectives
and thus facilitate improvements in external financial reports.

Uniformity in Accounting: A Historical Perspective

Barbara D. Merino
North Texas State University

Teddy L. Coe
North Texas State University

History can be viewed as an extension of experience fostering greater sophistication
and judgment in addressing contemporary issues. Accountants sometimes fail to
examine issues in historical perspective, thereby ignoring valuable insights that
might enable the profession to respond more forcefully to contemporary demands.
Consider the concept of uniformity in accounting, which has been the subject of
debate for many generations. Historians who have examined the concept of uniformity in relation to political theory have concluded that the "horrible logic of any
policy of uniformity starts with the fear of heterodoxy, becomes regimentation of
opinion, hardens into poisonous orthodoxy, and ends in pathological terror of
contradiction"(Schafer, 1969, p. 11). Accountants, likewise, have rejected uniformity
as a panacea for the development of accounting theory. Since the staff reports of the
late Senator Lee Metcalf (D-Mont.) and Congressman John E. Moss (D-Calif.)
have once again advocated uniformity (although in different forms), it seems
beneficial to highlight the historical evidence with respect to this issue.

This article will discuss briefly the various definitions of uniformity, trace the
evolution of the concept of uniformity as (seemingly) advocated by Metcalf and
Moss and assess the historical validity of accountants' rejection of the concept. The
examples given here should be considered illustrative, since it would require a
voluminous literature to tell the complete story of the history of uniformity.

THE CURRENT CLIMATE TOWARD UNIFORMITY

Accountants today rightfully feel besieged. Congressional committees, the Securities
and Exchange Commission, the courts and the financial community have strongly

From *The Journal of Accountancy* (August 1978), pp. 48–54. Reprinted by permission of the
American Institute of Certified Public Accountants. Copyright © 1978 by the American Institute of
Certified Public Accountants, Inc.

criticized the accounting profession. Such criticisms include lack of uniform financial accounting standards, alleged dominance of the eight largest international CPA firms and the American Institute of CPAs, the lack of auditor independence and the imprecision of the fairness standard. Many critics have resorted to a simplistic solution by advocating uniform accounting principles as the answer to the profession's problems.

The term "uniformity" as applied to accounting has never been satisfactorily defined. However, the following classifications provide a framework of ways in which the work has been used:

- Strong form—no variance in practice allowed; principles and rules are prescribed to indicate a single accounting rule for each type of recognizable accounting event (including rules governing event recognition).
- Moderate–strong form—general uniformity in the application of accounting principles with specific rules of implementation; some variance allowed where it is impractical to gain uniformity.
- Moderate–weak form—general uniformity in the application of accounting principles with a choice of principles resting on the particular industrial and firm economic and technological conditions.
- Weak form—general uniformity to be achieved by limiting the number of accounting choices available, but the choice of a particular accounting principle is left to management.

Metcalf and Moss appear to call for different types of uniformity. Metcalf's staff report advocates the strong form of uniformity: "A comprehensive set of Federal accounting objectives should encompass such goals as uniformity, consistency, clarity, accuracy, simplicity, meaningful presentation, and fairness in application. . . . Congress should establish specific policies abolishing such 'creative accounting' techniques as percentage of completion income recognition, inflation accounting, 'normalized' accounting, and other potentially misleading accounting methods. . . . The Federal Government should directly establish financial accounting standards for publicly-owned corporations" (U.S. Congress, Senate 1976, p.21).

The Moss report appears to recommend the moderate–strong form of uniformity:

> . . . to the maximum extent practicable, the SEC should prescribe by rule a framework of uniform accounting principles. In instances where uniformity is not practicable, the SEC should require the independent auditor to attest that the accounting principles selected by management represent financial data most fairly (U.S. Congress, House 1976, pp.51–52).

The committees appear to assume that uniformity will result in more accurate financial reports. This attempt to gain greater uniformity in accounting is not the first; indeed, interest in the topic predates this century, even though it did not receive widespread attention until the twentieth century. An examination of the historical evidence suggests that the committees' assumption that uniformity would result in better financial reporting may not be warranted.

Uniformity, of course, is not the only issue that has been the subject of recurring debate. Some historians find it ironic that the accounting profession is criticized for the dominance of large firms. A major concern of congressional leaders at the turn of the century was that small accounting firms could not maintain their independence in the face of the enormous powers of investment bankers like J. P. Morgan. The merger movement among accounting firms that began in the first decade of this century was viewed as salutary. Indeed, it was suggested that accountants could not achieve professional status unless the individual firms were large enough to be independent of clients and provide a countervailing power to protect the public interests when auditing corporations like Standard Oil.[1]

HISTORICAL BACKGROUND—INITIAL ATTEMPTS AT UNIFORMITY

The Interstate Commerce Law passed by Congress in 1887 marked an early attempt to regulate industry in the United States. Although the Interstate Commerce Commission was given broad regulatory powers, it is generally agreed that regulation had been ineffective before the turn of the century (U.S. Industrial Commission, 1902, p.353). But the establishment of the ICC secured the idea that government had the right to regulate certain industries.

The Hepburn Act (1906) significantly increased the broad powers of the ICC, including authority over accounting systems of regulated industries. The federal agency established "uniform systems of accounting" making it "unlawful for ... carriers to keep any other accounts, records or memoranda than those prescribed or approved by the Commission" (JofA, Nov.06, p.36).

Accountants responded positively to the ICC requirements that all railroads make annual financial reports public and available to the regulatory agency. The proposal of uniform accounts did not incur the wrath of accountants, simply because they did not believe that the ICC intended to advocate the strong form of uniformity. In response to a somewhat hysterical comment in *Railway Age,* the editor of the *Journal of Accountancy* admitted that uniformity could lead to some undesirable results if one assumed that the ICC would insist on "an inflexible form of accounts." Certainly, he conceded, if "all corporate accounts are to be prescribed by government officials and no others can be kept," then, accounting progress would be checked. But the editorial noted that "all government officials are not so bureaucratically stupid as the pro-railroad people are inclined to make out." Henry C. Adams, the chief statistician of the ICC, was highly respected, and most accountants believed he could be trusted to avoid the pitfalls of "rule-book" uniformity (JofA, Nov.06, pp.36–37).

The American Association of Public Accountants (AAPA, now the AICPA) committee on interstate commerce offered to help the ICC in any way it could and relations between the two, at least initially, were harmonious (JofA, Nov.06, p.77). The criticism of uniform systems came not from American accountants but from

---

[1]Editorial, JofA, Nov 27, pp 366–367, which states that, of 15,000 surveyed companies, only 892 issued audited financial reports. Of the 892 audits, 579 companies were audited by 10 different accounting firms while 199 other accounting firms audited the remaining 313 companies.

their British brethren. An editorial in the *Accountant* (July 20, 1907) condemned the law since it might be designed to reduce rates by requiring railroads to report only minimum operating costs. "The 'reform' is curiously interesting," suggested the editor, "inasmuch as it affords us the rather pathetic spectacle of the United States striving to go back to the low level of British railroad statistics and Great Britain struggling to attain the fullness of perfection exhibited by the now discarded American method."

But the actions of the ICC seemed to suggest that such fears were unwarranted. The ICC's initial concern was not with a rule-book aproach but with such broader issues as whether depreciation was a cost of doing business. Accountants supported the commission's assertion that depreciation was an operating expense and were pleased that the ICC did not attempt to prescribe a specific method of depreciation. Strangely, management, which would benefit since rates would be increased because of lower reported income, became indignant. The explanation was simply that the panic of 1907 had reduced profits to a low level and most firms did not want to be compelled to report additional expenses.[2] CPAs did not oppose ICC regulation because it failed to mandate independent audits as subsequently charged; opposition came when the ICC, in an apparent effort to reduce rates to a bare minimum, began to require that all depreciation be calculated on a straight-line basis. This interpretation of uniformity met with strong criticism, for accountants contended that railroads were being systematically destroyed by the shortsighted policy of regulators. With the low return on investment afforded by the ICC policy, it had become difficult to attract new capital or to maintain existing capital. The accountants' view that profits had been grossly overstated because of inadequate provisions for operating expenses appears to have been justified in the light of the subsequent monumental failure of railroads. The attempts of the ICC to dictate a rule-book approach caused accountants to rebel.

The accountants' response to the ICC reflects a pattern of criticism to such proposals that has been followed by subsequent generations. They said that uncertainty and different environmental conditions made it unfair to treat all business concerns alike and that only incorrect and misleading information results from such treatment.

Ironically, it was the public accounting profession itself that made politicians aware of the benefits of a uniform classification of accounts. At the turn of the century, reformers had demanded greater accountability on the part of public officials. Several CPAs had received national recognition for their work in this area, and the financial press lauded their efforts. By 1901, the *Chronicle* (New York, New York) observed that the "one great advantage in having a uniform or standard system of accounts is that by means of the same it became possible to compare one place with the corresponding results for another" and thus determine the efficiency of political leaders. The AAPA, in response to a Conference on Uniform Municipal

---

[2] For the railroad's view, see M. P. Blauvelt, "Railroad Accounting Under Government Supervision," JofA, June 8, pp.81–92; for an accountant's rebuttal, see J. F. Calvert, "Depreciation in Railway Accounting," JofA, Aug. 8, pp.229–233; for the ICC's view, see Henry C. Adams, "Railway Accounting in Its Relation to the Twentieth Section of the Act to Regulate Commerce," JofA, Oct. 8, pp.381–393.

Accounting called by the U.S. Census Bureau (1904), had appointed a committee "to consider the practical application of true accounting principles in connection with standard schedules for uniform reports on municipal industries and public service corporations." Harvey Chase, chairman of the committee, conducted a highly successful campaign to convince municipalities to adopt the association's uniform system (AAPA, *Report of the Committee on Standard Schedules for Uniform Reports on Municipal Industries and Public Service Corporations, 1906*). CPAs worked closely with the National Municipal League and by 1910 could report that uniform legislation was being adopted in many states (JofA, Apr.10, p.453). Naturally politicians asked why such a simple solution could not be extended to the private sector.

UNIFORM COST SYSTEMS

Edward N. Hurley, chairman of the Federal Trade Commission in 1916, noted that regulated companies were using uniform charts of accounts and that the Harvard Business School had been experimenting with a uniform system of cost accounting for shoe retailers. He asked if such systems would not be advantageous to businessmen. He argued that "intelligent cost accounting lies at the base of efficient management.... Men go into business to make money." In 1916, his major concern was that goods were not being properly priced because costs were not known. He said that "90% of all manufacturers of the United States are pricing their goods arbitrarily" and, therefore, engaging in destructive "cutthroat competition" (Hurley, 1916, pp. 3–14).

Accountants could find no fault with these arguments for they had been trying to convince businessmen of the need for proper cost systems for several generations. But they were uncertain of Hurley's motives, for the FTC was established as a reform agency to administer most of the antitrust legislation and prevent price discrimination and unfair competition.[3] There was some fear that Hurley was attempting to create another ICC, which had resulted not only in temporary displacement of auditors in the railroad industry but in the development of rule-book accounting, and accountants were naturally wary. Hurley, however, asked the AAPA to review the uniform systems developed by the FTC, and relations were cordial. The benefits of such cost systems to businessmen were soon obvious.

UNIFORM FINANCIAL ACCOUNTING

While accountants could accept with equanimity uniform municipal and cost accounting systems—for they were essentially classificatory and involved no profit

[3]The wariness of the association's leadership is clearly shown in the minutes of that group. In 1916, Robert Montgomery characterized Hurley as an "unknown quantity"(minutes, 1916, 110ff.) but by 1917 he was lamenting "the loss of our boy in Washington" (minutes, 1917, 30ff.). The view that Hurley was "pro business" and in favor of "private control" is supported in the historical literature. See Gabriel Kolko, *The Triumph of Conservatism; A Reinterpretation of American History, 1900–1916* (New York: The Free Press of Glencoe, 1963). Even revisionist historians who disagree with Kolko's general thesis that the majority of the FTC commissioners were pro-business concede that Hurley's primary concern was to ensure a "fair return" to business.

calculations—they were caught unaware when Hurley blithely suggested that uniform systems be extended to financial accounting. He proposed that (1) a standard financial statement form for all credit purposes be developed; (2) a set of rules and regulations for the valuation of all assets and the ascertainment of liabilities be developed; and (3) all statements accepted by bankers be verified by an accountant registered with the Federal Reserve Board or with the federal reserve banks (1916, p.175).

The national organization was disconcerted by Hurley's suggestion of federal registration; however, the AAPA attempted to meet Hurley's other demands, and later those of Frank Delano, of the Federal Reserve Board, by at least appearing to acquiesce in their call for a "scientific methodology," for the development of an accounting rule book. *Uniform Accounting* (later reissued under the more appropriate title *Approved Methods for Preparation of Balance Sheet Audits*) neither advocated uniformity nor dealt with accounting principles. *Uniform Accounting* was simply an adaptation of an internal control memorandum prepared by J. Scobie for Price Waterhouse (Demond, 1951, p.140f.).

The demand for uniform financial accounting was a simplistic extension of the concept of uniform cost systems, which was not warranted. Uniform cost systems were designed on an industry-by-industry basis, giving recognition to the different technological and economic environments of various industries; the cost systems for each industry were sufficiently flexible to allow for differences among companies. Indeed, these systems were designed more as uniform charts of accounts rather than as comprehensive accounting systems. In the uniform cost systems, little or no attention was given to such questions as valuation or income-expense recognition. While the cost systems appeared to use the historical cost assumption, the methods of computing depreciation and the valuation of inventories were not specified. Such cost systems were not designed to obtain complete uniformity. However, when demands for uniform financial accounting arose, they appeared to be calls for a strong or moderate–strong form of uniformity.

Uniform Accounting left room for considerable variability in the application of accounting methods, and many matters were simply left to professional judgment. The book's name, however, suggested that there was a uniform accounting methodology accepted by most practitioners. That, of course, was not true. A 1929 editorial in the *Journal of Accountancy* accurately assessed the impact of this document, stating that "prominent members of business at that time were led to extremes by their desire for reform and there was suggestion of a uniform system of accounting and auditing for all sorts of conditions of business." The editorial went on to say that "this excess of zeal [for uniformity] retarded progress" (1929, p.357).

THE SEC—REVIEWING THE DEBATE OVER UNIFORMITY

Accountants were not surprised or unprepared when, in the thirties, political leaders began to advocate the strong form of uniformity. This time they did not avoid the issue but firmly rejected the idea of absolute uniformity. There is overwhelming evidence that if the profession was wary of federal regulation, it had reason to be. The intent of Congress was not clear and, historically, that body had sought unsophisticated remedies for financial reporting problems.

As early as 1906, accountants had noticed the tendency of government officials to resolve all evils by legislative fiat. "For a long time," wrote Joseph Sterrett, "the lazy man's shortcut [has been] pass a law, create a department or bureau...." He added that this has two results: it provides a "modest income" for some employees, but, more important, it lulls the financial community into a "fancied security very far removed from reality" (Sterrett, 1906, p.21). Certainly, the immediate reaction of one legislator to the crash of 1929 indicates that not all political leaders understood the economic system. A U.S. senator is purported to have wired the following message to the New York Stock Exchange:

> Today's activity in your Exchange demonstrates absolute necessity for immediate adoption of a rule limiting amount of loss on any stock during a single session. The country is not prepared to withstand the effect of repetition of what happened today. Unless a rule is adopted and published establishing a reasonable amount of depreciation in any one session, campaign for reform will immediately take shape with possible result either closing Exchange entirely or placing the same under government supervision (*Chronicle,* July 22, 1933, p.581).

One hopes this was an atypical reaction, but it does seem clear that accountants were genuinely concerned that legislation would be enacted which implied that financial reports were merely summations of facts. Accountants claimed that this would be unrealistic and misleading because of the uncertainty of the business environment. This was not a remote threat given the extravagant claims that had been, were and are still made about the "reliability" and "truth" that could be presumed in audited financial statements.

The profession had been genuinely shocked, if not horrified, by Ripley's assertion in the twenties that the "balance sheet is an instantaneous photograph of the condition of a company" (May 1933, p.8). Accountants had warned that such claims were absurd. Robert Montgomery wrote that "our most precious asset is our independence in thought and action. Our method of expressing the use of our asset is by means of opinion and judgment" (JofA, Oct.27, p.253). The Institute showed the direction the profession would take in response to governmental demands for certitude in financial reports when it titled an original draft of its correspondence with the New York Stock Exchange "Value and Limitations of Corporate Accounts and General Principles for Preparation of Reports to Stockholders." [4] While the document established six broad general principles, it stressed the need for professional judgment and the fact that the balance sheet was "merely a reflection of opinion subject to, possibly wide, margins of error" (AIA, 1934, pp.3–4). This emphasis on the limitations of financial reports could be viewed as an adverse reaction to

---

[4]This pamphlet was introduced into evidence at the securities hearings by the New York Stock Exchange and was issued by the American Institute of Accountants under the more familiar title *Audits of Corporate Accounts, Correspondence Between the Committee on Cooperation With Stock Exchanges* and the Committee on Stock List of the New York Stock Exchange (New York, AIA, 1934).

increased responsibility being placed on the profession, but it is probably more accurate to interpret this trend as an effort by accountants to warn investors that financial reports could never attain photographic accuracy.

Initially, it did appear that the desire for certainty, a characteristic of the depression mentality, would lead Congress to demand absolute uniformity. The SEC had the right to dictate accounting principles and several of its leaders had suggested that uniformity should be its goal. George O. May was successful in convincing Judge James M. Landis of the SEC, who had originally favored uniformity, that such a goal was unobtainable (Wiesen, 1978). May agreed that uniformity in classification (such as in treatment of operating expenses of routine transactions) was beneficial, but he warned that income determination involved uncertainty and risk, which, despite wishful thinking, could not be eliminated by legislation or regulation (1937, p.346). The SEC's emphasis on consistency and disclosure rather than on uniformity was considered salutary by the accounting profession.

In 1939, Charles Couchman reviewed the various attempts to establish uniform accounting principles, noting that the ICC, the Federal Power Commission and public service corporations in many states had "experimented with uniform systems." He predicted that "in the ensuing years there may be such growth of bureaucratic control over all forms of industry that accounting will be shackled by it in a manner as to allow us no freedom of discretion or judgment." But, he concluded, if attained, uniformity would not endure since truth must prevail and truth "can't be bound by a rule or a law." Government bureaus, he said, "usually function to protect one class or user group [and] are not fair to all." More important, Couchman believed that politicians would eventually realize that uniformity was an unattainable goal. Writing that CPAs "lacked adequate training, knowledge or prophetic endowment to forsee the future and overcome uncertainty," he added that "administrators are also lacking in this respect" (1939, p.3).

CONCLUSION

While accounting principles have continued to be storm centers of controversy, the profession had established its position with respect to this issue by the late thirties: Namely, that uniformity, when used in the context of absolute rules, was not only impracticable but dangerous. The American Accounting Association's "Tentative Statement of Accounting Principles Affecting Corporate Reports" summarized the position the profession had taken:

> Business enterprises are so different in nature that principles applied to any single corporation must make allowance for its individual characteristics and for the character of the industry as well. In fact, it may be said that any complete statement of fundamental principles must include suitable explanations, extensions and qualifications (1936, p.188).

One finds unusual unanimity on this point within the profession and regulatory bodies. The AIA committee on accounting procedure's stated objective was to limit needless variations by recommending "one or more alternative procedures as being definitely superior in its opinion to other procedures which have received a measure of support..." (AIA minutes, 1939, pp.5ff.). This objective was certainly consistent with the goals of the SEC as expressed by William Werntz, who wrote that the "soundness or correctness of an accounting practice is determinable only by the facts of a particular situation, circumstances alter cases," and, therefore, he thought that consistency, comparability and disclosure should be focal points for financial reporting (Werntz, 1939, pp.17ff.).

An evaluation of previous attempts at uniformity had probably had a significant impact on the rejection of uniformity as a basis for establishing accounting principles. Indeed, the attempts of the ICC to use a rule-book approach to regulate railroads had ended in dismal failure, while the national bank examiners using a similar approach had afforded little protection against the flagrant abuses of the twenties. Thus, the historical evidence with respect to uniformity suggested that even when a regulatory agency, seeking to protect the interests of one specific group, had mandated uniform systems, changes in environmental and political objectives had often necessitated a departure from the rule-book approach or resulted in unfortunate consequences.

The issue became not uniformity but the extent of the profession's responsibility to select appropriate alternatives. Academicians thought that "it should be possible to agree on a foundation which will tend to eliminate random variations in accounting procedures resulting not from the peculiarities of individual enterprises but rather from varying ideas of financiers and corporate executives as to what will be expedient, plausible or persuasive to investors" (AAA, 1936, p.188).

A key but unresolved issue has been whether the accounting profession has the authority commensurate with its responsibility. Much of the subsequent criticism of the AIA committee on accounting procedure and the Accounting Principles Board stemmed from the charge that auditors failed to exercise professional judgment in application of principles once they became "generally accepted."

CONTEMPORARY CRITICISM

If one examines contemporary criticism of the state of accounting principles, there is little to suggest that uniformity should be resurrected as an appropriate response to alleged abuses. The SEC's criticism of the profession has been directed not at the lack of uniformity but, rather, at auditors for placing too much reliance on GAAP. Auditors, it has been alleged, have not assessed risk and uncertainty in various transactions, thereby permitting alternative methods to be used simply because they were in accord with GAAP, even though they were inappropriate and resulted in misleading investors (Accounting Series Release No. 173). Even the vocal academic critic Abraham J. Briloff states that he is "willing to take the framework of GAAP with its alternatives." But an "accountant [should] use those rules or applicable principles that he believes best reflect the situation as he sees it" (*Barron's*, April 26, 1976, p.18). An example of failure to assess alternative procedures with respect to risk and uncertainty can be seen in the continuing debate over the question of percentage-of-completion accounting.

Revenue realization is one area where advocates of strong uniformity would reduce the number of reporting alternatives. Percentage-of-completion revenue realization has come under severe criticism, with some suggesting that it be outlawed.

This technique results in recognizing revenue as the contracted work is performed if there is reasonable assurance that the specified cash payments will be received. The alternate method—completed contract—recognizes revenue only when the contract is fully performed and when there is reasonable assurance that the specified cash payments will be received. The completed contract method is clearly appropriate when there is any considerable uncertainty; it is, however, clearly inappropriate when there is reasonable assurance that the cash will be collected. If revenue realization is made more uniform by outlawing the percentage-of-completion method, the economic performance of some firms will be obscured; circumstances differ, and to ignore these differences in financial reporting results in loss of information, inaccurate information and statements that serve no useful economic purpose.

The basic question that seems to remain unresolved is how the accounting profession with limited power can fulfill its responsibility to exercise professional judgment. The suggestion that uniformity can be substituted for judgment, which seems to be implicit in the Metcalf and Moss reports, is not a realistic remedy. If someone must assess risk and uncertainty to determine the applicability of any given principle, the "rules" simply will not suffice. It is also clear that once a rule is established, with rare exceptions, the administrative process does not facilitate expeditious responses to the dynamic, changing business environment. Uniformity, in its strong form, implies a certainty that does not exist. Accountants have not reacted negatively to such suggestions out of perversity or fear but from a deep-seated conviction that such schemes are not feasible. Despite consistent efforts by the profession to disclaim any suggestion that they are reporting "facts," one consistently finds statements to the contrary made by regulators and politicians. The ultimate goal, everyone seems to agree, is "truth," "fairness," "justice" or perhaps, more simply, that financial statements not be misleading. But these concepts are essentially ethical—and not absolute—terms requiring that someone make a determination of what is fair.

An overriding concern to the Metcalf and Moss committees, as it is to the Financial Accounting Standards Board and to the accounting profession in general, is how to obtain better financial information for economic decisions. Unfortunately, the Metcalf and Moss reports focused on the unworkable but historically popular solution—uniformity. It seems unfortunate for several reasons. First, it ignores the lessons of history, which show that successful attempts to gain absolute uniformity allowed for similar events to be similarly reported and different events to be reported differently. The success of the uniform cost systems is partially attributed to such recognition. Second, the imposition of strong uniformity as in the regulated industries has not resulted in better protection of or in better information for all user groups. Uniformity in financial accounts for the regulated industries was devised to foster some public policy rather than to reflect a firm's financial condition.

The Trueblood report correctly defined the crucial issues of uniformity to be the elimination of *needless* variations by making like things look alike, and unlike things look different (AICPA, 1973, p.59). When uniformity has been proposed, the accounting profession has, in our view, rightly rejected attempts that did not allow for the recognition of the uncertainty inherent in the business world.

Apparently, the search for uniformity by the outside world—outside of the profession, that is—has turned up a will-o'-the-wisp, and it is unlikely that anything more concrete will be found. But history has taught us that the search will undoubtedly be begun again by legislators or others seeking perfection. History, as we know, is condemned to repetition, and it is perhaps with this understanding that the profession can better understand the cyclical nature of demands made on it in the name of the public.

REFERENCES

American Accounting Association (1936) "A Tentative Statement of Accounting Principles Affecting Corporate Reports." *Accounting Review* (March), pp. 187–91.

American Institute of Accountants (1934) *Audits of Corporate Accounts.* New York: AIA.

American Institute of Accountants (1939) Committee on accounting procedure correspondence file regarding Accounting Research Bulletin No. 1. New York: AICPA.

American Institute of Certified Public Accountants (1959) "Organizational Operation of Accounting Research Program and Related Activities." (October) manuscript file. New York: AICPA.

American Institute of Certified Public Accountants (1973) *Objectives of Financial Statements.* New York: AICPA.

Briloff, A. (1976) "No Last Trumpet." "Corporate Pay-Offs." "Accountable Accountants." *Barron's* (April 12, 19, 26).

Couchman, Charles (1939) "The Haunted Balance Sheet." 19 pages, mimeographed, AICPA library, New York.

Demond, C. W. (1951) *Price Waterhouse in America.* New York: Comet Press.

Hurley, Edward N. (1916) *Awakening of American Business.* New York: Doubleday, Page & Co.

May, George O. (1937) "Improvement in Financial Accounts." *Journal of Accountancy* (May), pp. 333–69.

May, George O. (1933) "Transcript of a Speech Before the Illinois State Society." (December 6) AICPA library, New York.

Montgomery, Robert H. (1927) "Accountants' Limitations." *Journal of Accountancy* (October), pp. 245–66.

Schafer, Robert Jones, ed. (1969) *A Guide to Historical Method.* Homewood, Ill.: Dorsey Press.

Sterrett, Joseph E. (1906) "Profession of Accountancy." *Annals of the American Academy of Political and Social Science* (July), pp. 16–27.

"Uniform Accounting" (1971) Washington, DC: Federal Reserve Board.

U.S. Congress, House (1902) *Final Report of the Industrial Commission.* H. Doc. 380, 57th Cong., 2nd sess.

U.S. Congress, House (1976) *Federal Regulation and Regulatory Reform.* Report by the Subcommittee on Oversight and Investigations of the Committee on Interstate and Foreign Commerce. 94th Cong., 2nd sess., October.

U.S. Senate (1976) *The Accounting Establishment.* A staff study prepared by the Subcommittee on Reports, Accounting and Management of the Committee on Government Operations, 94th Cong., 2nd sess., December.

Werntz, William (1939) "What Does the Securities and Exchange Commission Expect of Independent Auditors?" AIA, *Papers on Auditing Procedure and Other Accounting Subjects,* pp. 17–26.

Wiesen, Jeremy (1978) *The Securities Acts and Independent Auditors: What Did Congress Intend?* Commission on Auditors' Responsibilities Research Study No. 2. New York: AICPA.

SEVEN

CONTROVERSIAL ACCOUNTING PROBLEM AREAS

This section is devoted to a series of topics, most of which are encompassed in the standard financial accounting theory course. Our intention is to provide a "different" perspective on a wide variety of issues. The background and the standard accounting treatment in each of these areas is covered in typical intermediate accounting texts. Other topics might have been included here as well as additional perspectives on the topics that have been chosen. We hope this selection will encourage the reader to seek opinions on accounting topics from a wide variety of sources.

The output of the accountant's work—financial statements—has such pervasive influence on so many, in such important ways, that we find opinions—many of which help us to see an old subject in a new light—in letters to editors, case studies of companies, general business publications, and publications written by accountants for accountants. There are almost no areas in accounting on which the definitive word has been written.

There are new forms of old transactions, new insights on old issues, increased awareness of difficulties found in applying existing principles, matters of public policy, and improved understanding of communication links—any one or all of which can create the need to reexamine accepted practice.

ALLOCATION— A PERVASIVE PROBLEM

In many ways, the issue of comparability is the accountant's Achilles' heel. The information about a single enterprise, a single period, a single activity is almost useless unless that information can be compared with similar information of other enterprises, time periods, or activities. Efforts to assign results to compartments, no matter how large, inevitably require that the accountant allocate costs or revenues or assets among the various compartments. To avoid allocation implies that no part of the cost or benefit should be associated with the activity in a particular compartment.

As Arthur L. Thomas so aptly discusses in "The FASB and the Allocation Fallacy," the practice of allocation by whatever means continues to be arbitrary[1]—the question remains: What information is useful to the user of financial statements? What schemes of cost and revenue assignment can be made that will avoid misleading inferences and continue to provide useful information?

As Thomas points out, current value accounting (where depreciation calculations are absent) and funds flow accounting where funds are defined as "net quick assets" are alternatives that are free of allocation problems. In this context, the trend toward the definition of funds as cash or near-cash in American funds statements may lead to the presentation of financial information that is less open to criticism on allocation grounds.[2]

There are a variety of new disclosure requirements included in the Standards of

---

[1] Those who wish to pursue Thomas's logic more fully are encouraged to read his as major works: *The Allocation Problem in Financial Accounting Theory,* Studies in Accounting Research No. 3, (Sarasota, FL: American Accounting Association, 1969) and *The Allocation Problem: Part Two,* Studies in Accounting Research No. 9, (Sarasota, FL: American Accounting Association, 1974).

[2] For a brief discussion of this trend, see the introduction to Section 5.

the FASB. Most of these require a variety of new allocations. The problem that accountants face is one of the increasing complexities of organizations and the need by users for information about each of the parts in order to assess the strengths and weaknesses of the organization as a whole.

BIBLIOGRAPHICAL NOTES

Dialogue involving Thomas and two critics may be of interest:

Sid Himmel, "Financial Allocations Justified," *CAmagazine* (October 1981), pp. 70–73; and "Why Financial Allocations Can't be Justified," by Arthur L. Thomas, *CAmagazine* (April 1982), pp. 28–32.

"Arbritary and Incorrigible Allocations," by Leonard G. Eckel, *The Accounting Review* (October 1976), pp. 764–777; and Arthur L. Thomas, "Arbritary and Incorrigible Allocations: A Comment," *The Accounting Review* (January 1978), pp. 263–269.

The FASB and the Allocation Fallacy

Arthur L. Thomas
University of Kansas

Off to an impressively active start, the Financial Accounting Standards Board has already wrestled with a broad range of accounting issues. Topics on its active agenda or on which it has issued Standards include

1 Accounting for leases.
2 Accounting for research and development costs.
3 Contingencies and future losses.
4 Gains and losses from extinguishment of debt.
5 Interest costs and capitalization.
6 Accounting for pensions.
7 Segment reporting.
8 Business combinations.
9 Interim financial statements.
10 Reporting by development stage entities.
11 Reporting in units of general purchasing power.
12 Translation of foreign currency transactions and financial statements.
13 The recommendations of the Trueblood Report.[1]

From *The Journal of Accountancy* (November 1975), pp. 65–68. Reprinted by permission of the American Institute of Certified Public Accountants. Copyright © 1975 by the American Institute of Certified Public Accountants, Inc.

Author's note: I'm grateful to Paul Rosenfield for his comments on an earlier draft of this article.

[1]"Objectives of Financial Statements," Report of the Study Group on the Objectives of Financial Statements, Robert M. Trueblood, chairman (New York: AICPA, October 1973).

All these topics involve some kind of *allocation*, which is the assignment of a total to one or more locations or categories. A thesaurus gives "division," "partition," "slicing," "splitting" and "apportionment" as synonyms of "allocation." Accounting's allocations include assignment of a lease's costs to the individual years of its life, assignment of R&D costs to the single year of their expenditure and assignment of long term investment interest to successive annual revenues. All the FASB topics listed above fall into one of the following two classes of allocations, with items 7 through 9 falling into both:

1 The first nine topics require deciding when to recognize revenues, expenses, gains or losses—that is, deciding to what periods they should be assigned. For example, the FASB may eventually specify how to allocate pension costs to successive annual pension expenses.

2 The last seven topics involve ways of preparing financial statements composed mainly of allocated data. For example, this is implicit throughout the Trueblood Report and explicit in its position statement and income statement recommendations.

In fact, almost all of our revenue recognition and matching efforts require allocation.

THE ALLOCATION PROBLEM

The foregoing is background to a problem that we accountants acknowledge, but whose severity we usually misjudge. To use a term from formal logic, recent research indicates that, unfortunately, our allocations must almost always be *incorrigible*—that is to say, they can neither be refuted nor verified.[2] Incorrigibility will be a central concept in this discussion, and it is well to give a few examples even if doing so may initially seem to be a detour.

Let's suppose that someone claims that beings live among us who look and act exactly like humans, but who actually are aliens, seeded on this planet by flying saucers. We ask: do they come equipped with authentic looking birth certificates? Yes. Would tests of their internal structure, chromosomes or the like expose them? No. Could psychiatrists unmask them? No. The horrible thing is that they have such good counterfeit memories that even the aliens themselves don't know their real nature—you may be one yourself.

Such claims are incorrigible, for no experiment could prove either that such aliens exist or that they don't. Here are some other incorrigible claims:

• Charles Dickens may not have been a greater author than Shakespeare, but he was more of a person.
• Our bourbon is mellower.
• The official state flower of Unicornia is the marsh mallow.
• Even if the colonists had lost their war of independence, by now America would be independent of Britain.
• Since I've lost weight, I've become more spiritual.

[2]Arthur L. Thomas, Studies in Accounting Research No. 9, *The Allocation Problem: Part Two* (American Accounting Association, 1974), hereafter SAR 9.

Now, if our allocations are incorrigible, practicing accountants should be deeply concerned. We attest that financial statements present fairly the positions of companies and the results of their operations. But if both our revenue recognition and matching are founded upon allocations that we can neither refute nor verify, *we have no way of knowing whether these attestations are true.*

Are they incorrigible? I'll begin with matching and for brevity will disregard extraordinary items (and other nonoperating gains and losses), lower-of-cost-or-market writedowns and the like. Our matchings assign costs of a firm's nonmonetary inputs (inventories, labor, other services, depreciable assets, etc.) to the expenses of one or more accounting periods, temporarily reporting as assets costs assigned to future periods. We're all familiar with the theory behind these matching assignments: each input's purchase price should be allocated to successive periods in proportion to the contribution it makes to each period's revenues. Academics and most practitioners also know that an equivalent matching theory can be developed around contributions to net cash inflows.

The allocation problem has several dimensions, some of which are subtle. But one is easily described: to match costs with revenues, we must know what the contributions of the firm's individual inputs *are*. Unfortunately, as I'll illustrate below, there's no way that we can know this.

Seeing why this is so requires introducing a final concept, *interaction*. Inputs to a process interact whenever they generate an output different from the total of what they would yield separately. For instance, labor and equipment interact whenever people and machines working together produce more goods than the total of what people could make with their bare hands and machines could make untended. As this example suggests, interaction is extremely common. Almost all of a firm's inputs interact with each other—their failure to do so would ordinarily signal their uselessness.

Surprising as it may seem, it can be proved that whenever inputs interact, calculations of how much total revenue or cash flow has been contributed by any individual input are as meaningless as, say, calculations of the proportion of a worker's services due to any one internal organ: heart, liver or lungs. Thus, despite all textbooks and American Institute of CPAs or FASB releases to the contrary— despite what you've been trained to believe—our attempts to match costs with revenues must almost always fail. The next section tries to demonstrate this.

A SIMPLE EXAMPLE

A complete demonstration, meeting all possible counterarguments, is very lengthy.[3] But a simple example reveals the kernel of the matter. What follows is offered in the same spirit as Robert Sterling's recent illustration in these pages that only price-level-adjusted current-value financial statements are fully relevant and interpretable:

> A highly simplified case will be considered in this article. The advantages of simplified cases are that they are easily understood by both the reader and the author and they are

---

[3]See SAR 9, chapters 1–6, for the attempt.

more easily solved. If we cannot solve the simplified cases, then we can be fairly certain that we also cannot solve the complex cases. Thus, if a particular approach fails to provide a solution for simplified cases, then we can avoid wasting effort by trying that approach on complex cases.[4]

However, instead of Sterling's cash, securities, bread and milk trading economy, I'll describe a production process for bread alone and confine the discussion to strictly physical measures (to avoid complications introduced by monetary valuations).[5] If individual contributions are necessarily incorrigible even in the following example, it's hard to imagine how they could be otherwise in the vastly more complex processes by which business enterprises generate their products, services, revenues and cash flows.

A prospector manufactures sourdough bread by a three-stage process:

1 He makes leaven by mixing flour, sugar and water in a crock, then keeps it in a warm place for about a week (until it bubbles).

2 He makes bread by transferring all but a cup of leaven to a large pot, where he mixes it with soda and additional flour, sugar and water, kneads it slightly and then lets it rise. He digs a shallow pit, fills it with coals from his camp fire, covers the pot, places it in the pit, buries it in hot coals and keeps it there until the bread is baked.

3 He replenishes the leaven (for the next baking) by adding enough flour and water to restore the crock to its original level.

Water, airborne yeasts and wood are free goods here. We accountants would be concerned with the following inputs to this process: flour, sugar, soda, labor, the crock, the pot and a shovel. Finally, part of the flour and sugar leaven for one loaf becomes included in the leaven for the next. The output of each baking is one loaf of bread.

Although its manufacture is simple, the moment we try to calculate the contributions of any individual input to this output we face a dilemma. Each input (except, perhaps, the soda and the shovel) is essential. Therefore, we could plausibly assign all of the output to any individual input. For example, we could assign all of the output to the flour, reasoning that were flour withheld from the process there would be no bread. Yet we could equally well assign all of the output to the pot, since without it the loaf would have been incinerated.

Having assigned all output to any one input, we've implicitly assigned zero to each other input. But if either all or zero is appropriate for each input, any intermediate allocation will be equally appropriate—say, half the loaf to the flour and a sixth each to the pot, labor and the crock.

I'm unable to prove which of the infinitely many possible ways of allocating the loaf is correct. Therefore, I can't specify the individual contributions of the inputs; instead, all I'm entitled to say is that they generate the loaf jointly. Research shows that other writers on economics and accounting—even efficient-markets investi-

---

[4]Robert R. Sterling, "Relevant Financial Reporting in an Age of Price Changes," JofA, Feb.75, p.42.

[5]As a technical point, I've also simplified by discussing only incremental contributions of inputs. See SAR 9, especially pp. 32–40, 47–48 and 141–44, for the parallel problems that arise for their marginal contributions.

gators—are equally unable to solve this problem. Perhaps the reader can. But until someone does, any contributions calculated for these inputs must be incorrigible:

1 One can't verify them, because any other calculation is just as good.
2 One can't refute them, because their calculation is just as good as any other.

Therefore, any attempts at matching based on these contributions (say, depreciation of the pot or calculation of a value for the ending leaven inventory) will also be incorrigible. But the sourdough process is so much simpler than the productive processes of business enterprises, that *matching must necessarily be incorrigible for them, too*—unless, again, the reader can show how complications ease the calculations. To generalize, when a company tries to match costs with revenues there's no way either to refute or to verify the results. Instead, all possible ways of matching will be just as good—or bad—as each other.

If it's any consolation, I don't like this conclusion either, and have spent years trying to disprove it. Nor should you accept it without further inquiry. But I urge you at least to suspend disbelief in it (and in what follows) until you've read the detailed research, cited earlier, that backs it up.

And please notice that the difficulty here isn't one of being unable to allocate— there might be some way of getting around that problem. Instead, we're drowned in possible allocations, with no defensible way to choose among them. To be sure, since we must prepare reports, we eventually do pick one set of figures or another. Long before completing our training, we became accustomed to do this with few (if any) pangs. First, we narrow the possibilities by looking to generally accepted accounting principles and then select one of the survivors according to industry custom, apparent advantage to the company, apparent appropriateness of the method to the firm's circumstances or some other plausible rationale. But how can the incorrigible results be useful to decision makers?

Unless you (or someone) can suggest ways in which calculations that can neither be verified nor refuted assist decisions,[6] our allocations of the costs of depreciable assets, inventories, labor and other inputs are irrelevant to investor needs. Indeed, although it's painful to say this, they are mere rituals—solemn nonsense—and our beliefs in them are fallacies. This should trouble all of us, because practitioners spend much time conducting such rituals, and theorists much time elaborating on such fallacies.[7]

The Accounting Principles Board was well aware of this, but, underrating its severity, was satisfied to claim that exact measurements are seldom possible and that allocation often requires informed judgment.[8] With all due respect, acknowledging that few allocations are exact is like replying, "Few animals are ever completely healthy," in response to the statement, "Sir, your cow is dead."

Finally, since what's true of individual inputs also holds for groups of inputs, I'm forced to conclude that our revenue recognition practices are rituals, too. For

[6]Assistance that goes beyond the unsatisfactory, short run utilities is described on pp. 8–9, 40–46, 65–70 and 163–74 of SAR 9.
[7]For examples of the latter, see SAR 9, pp. 94–110, 116–19 and 128–55.
[8]For examples, see APB Statement No. 4, pp. 11, 13–15, 21–22, 46–48, and 102.

revenue recognition allocates the firm's *lifetime* output to the groups of inputs that constitute its resources during the individual years of its life. Once again, the details of this appear in SAR 9.

THE FASB'S RESPONSIBILITY

What, then, of the FASB? We've seen it worry, or propose to worry, about which allocations are most appropriate for various accounting situations. The FASB should stop doing this. Instead, whenever possible, it should *eliminate* allocations. Such incorrigible figures don't do readers of our reports any real good, and they

1 Cost money.

2 Strain relations between auditors and clients (when they disagree about which incorrigible figures to report).

3 Cause much of the nonuniformity problem that plagues us (since allocations are incorrigible, naturally GAAP conflict—there's no way to settle which rules are right).

4 Thereby confuse individual readers, thus violating what the Trueblood Report designates as the basic objective of financial statements.

5 Generally breed distrust in our profession.

When their elimination isn't possible, the FASB should keep allocations unsophisticated (if we must be incorrigible, at least let's be simple), choose allocation rules on expedient, political grounds (ceasing to worry about theory) and be candid about what it's doing. In particular, the FASB should actively

1 Try to convert conventional reporting practices to allocation-free ones. There are two main allocation-free alternatives to conventional accounting: current value reporting and the type of funds statement reporting that defines "funds" as net quick assets.[9] Certainly, Sterling is correct that merely adjusting allocated historical costs for changes in purchasing power serves little purpose: adjusted ritual remains ritual. The same is true of foreign currency translations.

2 Meanwhile, avoid launching any new incorrigible allocations in such areas as interim and segment reports, leases, contingencies, interest and pensions. And eliminate the more flagrantly incorrigible allocations that we now commit. A prime example of the latter (despite its being one of the APB's greatest political triumphs) is tax deferral: we take the difference between an incorrigible book allocation and an incorrigible tax allocation and allocate it, incorrigibly.

In conclusion, I would emphasize that none of these remarks are intended to disparage accounting practitioners. As SAR 9 points out (p. 157), practitioners have honestly believed that allocations are appropriate and have struggled to cope with them, while we academics saddled practitioners with a matching theory that requires such assignments, then failed to provide defensible ways for their calculation. But the hard fact remains that so long as we continue to certify that incorrigible allocations present fairly a firm's financial position and the results of its operations, we're making claims that we just can't back up. Professional responsibility urges that we, and the FASB, cease to tolerate this.

[9]See SAR 9, Chapter 7.

REVENUE RECOGNITION

The timing of the recognition of revenue is an allocation problem—an allocation among time periods. The earning of revenue can be a very complex process involving the manufacture of a product—an activity which may take several years—and the ultimate sale to a customer who eventually pays cash for the product. The process of allocating the increment in asset value that occurs during production and is finally realized with the receipt of cash from a customer is critical in providing information relative to operations.

The guidelines that are followed in the establishment of accounting principles are that the allocation methods should be "reasonable" and "systematic." The results should be conservative in that recognition should be delayed until realization is near certain. The general guidelines are that the earning process is complete when the product is in condition for sale and the sales price has been established by contract with a buyer from whom the receivable is reasonably certain of being collected. In most cases, these guidelines delay the recognition of revenue to the period in which a sales transaction takes place. In short, the revenue earned during manufacture is *conservative* arbitrarily shifted to the period in which sale takes place. There is an exception to this rule in the construction industry where manufacture requires several periods to complete and takes place after receipt of an order from an entity having the ability to pay for the completed product.

The installment method of accounting is another variation on the general principle of allocating revenue between periods. This deviation is, in general, justified when the ultimate realization of the selling price is uncertain. The degree of uncertainty relates, in general, to the practice of customers in preceding periods. The historical experience is assumed to continue into the future. In cases where ultimate collectibility cannot be reliably estimated, the recognition of revenue must be delayed until realized through the collection of cash.

Of course the real question is: Does this arbitrary method of allocating revenue provide statement users with more decision relevant information than the alternatives? Richard A. Scott and Rita K. Scott argue that the installment method does not provide useful information. They conclude that the method is "illogical, internally inconsistent and riddled with flaws."

BIBLIOGRAPHICAL NOTES

Two research studies on the problem of revenue recognition are as follows:

Arthur L. Thomas, *Revenue Recognition* (Ann Arbor, MI: Bureau of Business Research, Graduate School of Business Administration, University of Michigan, 1966).

Robert J. Coombes and Carrick A. Martin, *The Definition and Recognition of Revenue,* Accounting Theory Monograph No. 3 (Melbourne, Australia: Australian Accounting Research Foundation, 1982).

Installment Accounting: Is It Inconsistent?

Richard A. Scott
University of Virginia

Rita K. Scott
Senior Manager
Peat, Marwick, Mitchell & Co.
Richmond, Virginia

The installment method of accounting has been with us for a long time.[1] It is most commonly associated with the retail trade, being an outgrowth of the merchandising tactic, "Buy now-pay later." Just prior to World War II, installment credit to consumers (excluding cash loans and mortgages) was $3.7 billion. By mid-1978 it had exceeded $225 billion.[2] The sheer size and skyrocketing growth of installment selling, in conjunction with the corresponding practice of determining income that was customarily employed by retailers, created an awkward situation for the accounting profession. Recognizing profit piecemeal as cash was collected rather than at the time of sale was a flagrant contravention of the realization principle. In 1932, the American Institute of Accountants (now the American Institute of CPAs) committee on cooperation with stock exchanges stated that

"Profit is deemed to be realized when a sale in the ordinary course of business is

From *The Journal of Accountancy* (November 1979), pp. 52–58. Reprinted by permission of the American Institute of Certified Public Accountants. Copyright © 1979 by the American Institute of Certified Public Accountants.

[1]See, for example, William A. Paton. *Accounting Theory* (Lawrence, Kans.: Scholars Book Co., 1973), pp. 448–49. Originally published in 1922.

[2]United States Department of Commerce, *Survey of Current Business,* July 1978.

effected, unless the circumstances are such that the collection of the sale price is not reasonably assured."[3]

In 1934, the Institute's membership adopted this principle and it remains in force today. By comparison, the installment method of accounting was incongruous. There appeared to be little theoretical justification for permitting some firms to defer profit recognition when the earning process was substantially completed, a legal contract had been executed and customers' accounts were generally beyond reproach or at least within the realm of estimating collectibility. Certainly it might have been argued that collection of the sales price was not reasonably assured in these cases, making them legitimate exceptions to the rule. But then why would sellers consistently engage in many sales transactions where only an unreasonable level of assurance of collection existed? And how would they objectively distinguish them from other reasonable-level-of-assurance sales?

This episode was brought to its inevitable conclusion in 1966. The Accounting Principles Board summarily disposed of installment basis accounting by proclaiming that it was no longer to be considered a member in good standing of generally accepted accounting principles:

> The Board reaffirms this statement [quoted above]; it believes that revenues should ordinarily be accounted for at the time a transaction is completed, with appropriate provision for uncollectible accounts. Accordingly, it concludes that, in the absence of the circumstances referred to above, the installment method of recognizing revenue is not acceptable.[4]

The truth of the matter, however, is that the installment method of accounting is still alive. It is reviving and has been gaining strength. In subsequent parts of this article we trace the rebirth of this aberrant accounting method. In the process we also examine its underlying rationale. By the time our journey is finished we will have been led to the inexorable conclusion that the installment method of accounting is an illogical and contradictory concept that ought to be discarded.

A TINY FOOTNOTE

Installment basis accounting lives on by virtue of an exception contained in microscopic lettering at the bottom of a page. We are told that there will be circumstances requiring the services of an invalid accounting procedure. APB Opinion No. 10, *Omnibus Opinion—1966,* left this possibility open by stating

> The Board recognizes that there are exceptional cases where receivables are collectible over an extended period of time and, because of the terms of the transactions or other conditions, there is no reasonable basis for estimating the degree of collectibility. When such circumstances exist, and as long as they exist, either the installment method or the cost recovery method of accounting may be used.[5]

---

[3]Committee on accounting procedure, Accounting Research Bulletin no. 43, *Restatement and Revision of Accounting Research Bulletins* (New York: American Institute of Accountants, 1953), chap. I, sec. A, par. 1.

[4]Accounting Principles Board Opinion no. 10, *Omnibus Opinion—1966* (New York: AICPA, 1967) par. 12.

[5]Ibid., ftnt. 8 to par. 12.

The issue lay dormant until the early 1970s. It emerged from quiescence, awakened by the crisis in financial reporting for franchising operations and retail land sales. Both cases were characterized by small cash down payments and a protracted transaction period. Often, both buyers and sellers were operating without benefit of a historical backdrop in these sorts of undertakings.

ANSWERING THE CALL

Franchisors would sell not only a franchise but a potpourri of related services and assets as well. For starters they might assist in selecting a site or in conducting a feasibility study of a location. They were ready with financing arrangements and would stand at a franchisee's side in negotiating a lease. In later phases they would provide physical facility designs, supervise construction and be suppliers of furnishings and equipment. Finally, when operations were under way, management training, quality control and advertising programs would be made available. The gamut of commitments made by franchisors was widespread in scope, drawn out in time and steeped in uncertainty—factors that would prove troublesome, as the future soon revealed. Complicating matters a bit more, "many contracts have been written to distinctly favor the franchisor. Typically such contracts [were] specific in detailing obligations of the franchisee, but ambiguous regarding obligations of the franchisor or rights of the franchisee."[6]

In return for the franchise a modest down payment ordinarily was accepted along with a long-term note for the balance. Often these notes either did not bear interest or interest was set at an inordinately low rate. The franchise fee in total would then be recorded as revenue ("front-end loading") without regard for the franchisee's ability to pay or the franchisor's capacity to fulfill its promises to perform. "Little or no provision for collection and cancellation losses were being made."[7] Many franchisees and some franchisors subsequently failed, bringing attention to bear on these industry accounting practices. The situation as it existed in 1971 was summarily described as follows:

"Considerable public brouhaha currently surrounds the subject of franchising.... In addition, some franchise organizations are experiencing serious operational and legal problems within the franchisor-franchisee relationship."[8]

In some SEC fillings, franchisors were required to leave out earnings per share data and to state in a footnote that omission was because income was from only a few franchise sales and therefore future earnings could not be expected to bear any resemblance to past performance.

In an effort to pour oil on the waters of this maelstrom, the AICPA committee on franchise accounting and auditing issued an industry accounting guide[9] in December

[6]P. Ronald Stephenson and Robert G. House, "A Perspective on Franchising," *Business Horizons,* August 1971, p. 38.

[7]Thomas L. Holton and Olden J. Hoover, "The Accountants' Stand on Franchise Reporting," *The New York CPA,* January 1971, p. 50.

[8]Stephenson and House, "Perspective on Franchising," p. 35.

[9]Committee on franchise accounting and auditing, Industry Accounting Guide, *Accounting for Franchise Fee Revenue* (New York: AICPA, 1973).

1972. The effect of the committee's recommendations was to postpone revenue recognition until after the sale when the franchisor had "substantially performed" its obligations and the franchisee's operations had commenced. However, the committee at the same time provided that, when no reasonable estimate of collectibility can be made, the installment method of accounting may be used.

A REPEAT PERFORMANCE

Retail land sales companies followed a well-established game plan. They purchased large tracts of unimproved land and proceeded to subdivide them for sale to widely dispersed customers using intensive marketing programs. During the 1950s and 1960s the retail land sales industry developed a tarnished image. Although its image had improved somewhat as the industry moved into the 1970s, it was still far from pristine. *Business Week,* for example, described member firms as being "notorious for high pressure salesmanship" and characterized their methods as "unsavory."[10] Their efforts were concentrated on persuading customers to commit themselves in writing—usually in the form of a land sales contract—to the purchase of a parcel of land. A minimal down payment of as low as 1 percent of the price was accepted, with the remainder plus interest due to the seller over an extended period. The note receivable was routinely accepted by the land company on the basis of the purchaser's personal credit without a credit check being made. Within a prescribed time the buyer might cancel his purchase contract and demand a refund of the down payment under an escape clause in the Truth in Lending Act.

In the event that contract payments were defaulted, the buyer forfeited both land and accumulated equity but was generally able to free himself from the balance due. Land sales companies could not seek specific performance or deficiency judgments under the law in these cases and, as a practical matter, were usually content to keep the whole affair quiet rather than alarm prospective buyers. Many buyers did in fact default as well as cancel their contracts.

Land development companies offered to do more than simply carve out parcels from large land tracts. They made some improvements (roads, grading) to the land immediately and promised numerous others ("amenities" such as golf courses, swimming pools and recreation centers). Unfortunately, some companies compounded the tenuousness of retail land sales even further by reneging on their promises to make future improvements.

Again an AICPA committee was established in response to a crisis.[11] Revenue had been recognized by land companies under any of a variety of methods, including complete accrual when the contract was signed, despite the risks associated with collection and the substantial costs yet to be incurred. The committee's directive was to defer revenue recognition until several specified conditions were met which indicated that a buyer seemed committed to completing the contract and the seller

---

[10]"Accounting for Premature Profits," *Business Week,* January 23, 1971, p. 87 and "Land-Sales Companies Refigure Their Books," *Business Week,* May 12, 1973, p. 80.

[11]Committee on land development companies, Industry Accounting Guide, *Accounting for Retail Land Sales* (New York: AICPA, 1973).

appeared able to carry out the promised improvements. Until such time the contract was to be treated as a deposit and as such would be a liability until circumstances made revenue recognition appropriate. Another set of criteria was then stipulated which was to be used in deciding whether to apply the accrual method of accounting. If these were not satisfied, the land company was required to use the installment method of accounting. When the criteria were met after installment basis accounting had commenced, the switch to accrual was to be made in that period and treated as a change in estimate.[12] Installment basis accounting by now had entrenched itself in the accountant's repertoire once again and continued its ascendancy.

OTHER APPLICATIONS

Other real estate transactions were being passed off for sales even though they were something else beneath the surface. Financing, leasing and profit-sharing arrangements were being clothed as real estate sales. A transaction that in legal form was a sale might in economic substance be

- A construction contract.
- A contract for services for a fee.
- A lease for use of product or property.
- An agreement to loan or borrow funds.
- An agreement establishing a joint venture.
- An agreement to divide profits in a specified ratio.
- A deposit on or an option to purchase the asset.
- A sale of something (e.g., depreciation deductions) other than the asset that is the object of the sale.

The AICPA committee on accounting for real estate transactions attacked the problem of profit recognition for all kinds of real estate dealings not covered in the industry accounting guide for retail land sales. In the industry accounting guide[13] entitled *Accounting for Profit Recognition on Sales of Real Estate,* it was concluded that a sale was to be recorded as such only when certain circumventing provisions were absent. Furthermore, accrual of revenue at the time of sale was to take place only when a substantial down payment (25 percent of the sales value of the property is usually sufficient, and it may be lower with less risky properties) was received and subsequent annual payments were scheduled by contract to service the balance due (over 20 years in the case of land and, for other types of real estate, the usual term of a first mortgage loan). If the buyer failed to demonstrate a sufficient initial and continuing investment, revenue recognition was to take place according to the timing prescribed by other accounting techniques. The attendant circumstances would dictate the appropriate alternative from among those available: deposit, cost recovery or installment methods.

[12]The AICPA accounting standards division expressed its belief that a switch in methods was not a change in accounting principles. Statement of Position 78-4, *Application of the Deposit, Installment, and Cost Recovery Methods in Accounting for Sales of Real Estate* (New York: AICPA, 1978), p. 10.
[13]Committee on accounting for real estate transactions, Industry Accounting Guide, *Accounting for Profit Recognition on Sales of Real Estate* (New York: AICPA, 1973).

In 1976, the Financial Accounting Standards Board issued its standard on accounting for leases. A portion of that document was devoted to leases that were in substance dealer-manufacturer sales arrangements. When a dealer or manufacturer sells or assigns a lease with recourse to a third party, any profit or loss is to be deferred and recognized over the lease term in a systematic manner.[14] That is, as the lessee-purchaser makes periodic payments, the dealer or manufacturer recognizes a portion of the deferred profit or loss. What we have is installment basis accounting in the midst of a three-party transaction. The same treatment is also accorded direct financing leases where the lessor sells a leased asset, with recourse, to a third party.[15]

Throughout the years when the stature of the installment method of accounting was waning and then rejuvenating, the Internal Revenue Service unabatedly considered it an acceptable reporting technique.[16] Section 453(a) permits dealers in personal property who regularly sell on the installment plan to report profits pro rata over the contract term as cash is received. Sec. 453(b) afforded the same opportunity to sellers of real property as long as payments received in the year of sale did not exceed 30 percent of the sales price. Casual sales of personal property for a price exceeding $1,000 were also included under part (b) of the code section. It is commonplace to apply the installment method of accounting when determining tax liability while at the same time accruing revenue in the year of sale for financial reporting purposes. These disparate treatments cause timing differences which require the interperiod allocation of taxes.[17] The rationale of the IRS is to levy taxes when a taxpayer has the cash to make payment. They are not concerned with the proprieties of income determination. Accountants are concerned, however, and ought to scrutinize accounting methods and question their legitimacy.

Not-for-profit entities employing a cash or modified accrual basis of accounting have somewhat of a tendency to regard an asset's valuation as being equal to the cash paid to acquire it. Several cases have come to the attention of the authors where an asset being purchased on an installment payment plan was capitalized in installments. Only when the asset was completely paid for did its total cost finally emerge.

INQUIRING INTO THE THEORY

An installment sale occurs when a contract is signed calling for the purchaser to make (usually equal) payments in accordance with a plan. A protracted schedule of principal and interest payments is a necessary condition if the installment method of accounting is to be employed. When it is, gross profit on the sale is deferred. Each cash payment made toward the principal, including the initial down payment, is then considered to represent a partial recovery of product cost and an element of profit in the same proportion as these two components held in the original total sales price. For example, an item held for resale cost a dealer $900 and had been

[14]Statement of Financial Accounting Standards, no. 13, *Accounting for Leases* (Stamford, Conn.: FASB, 1976), par. 20.

[15]Ibid.

[16]*Internal Revenue Code* (Chicago: Commerce Clearing House, 1978), sec. 453.

[17]Accounting Principles Board Opinion no. 11, *Accounting for Income Taxes* (New York: AICPA, 1967), par. 15a.

marked to sell for $1,500. It was sold on January 2, 1978, and an installment contract was signed which called for 36 monthly payments, each due on the first of the month. In 1978 cash collections from this contract were $500[18] and realized gross profit, $200. On December 31, 1978, the installment receivable had a balance of $1,000 and deferred gross profit was $400. The total gross profit is 40 percent of the sales price ($600/$1,500). As each dollar unit of the sales price is collected it is seen as returning $.60 of product cost to the seller and $.40 of profit. Therefore, 1978 cash collections, which represent $500 of the original sales price dollars, also represent $300 of product cost recovery ($.60 x 500) and $200 of profit ($.40 x 500). Every dollar of sales price collected from a customer is looked on individually as being composed of two elements: product cost and profit. Both elements are contained in every dollar collected in proportions that remain unchanged throughout the contract's term.

IN DEFENSE OF THE METHOD

As we have already seen, deferral and piecemeal recognition of profit find support in the federal tax code, which makes it possible for a seller to postpone tax payments until cash is received. Another reason offered in support of the installment method is that profit reporting conforms to the timing of cash flows and, consequently, to the availability of funds for dividend distribution. It is also argued that often there are substantial expenses of collection and administration to be incurred after the sale and that installment recognition of profit permits a matching of income with these expenses. Finally, proponents of the installment method point out that the risk and uncertainty associated with these transactions is far greater than with ordinary credit sales. The collectibility of installment receivables is at question by virtue of the protracted pay-out period, and a "contingent loss" may have occurred.[19] If it is probable that receivables have been impaired and the amount of the loss is estimable, an accrual is required.[20] However, if there is significant uncertainty as to collection and an inability to estimate the loss, accrual is precluded and some other method of revenue recognition such as the installment method or cost recovery method ought to be used.[21] Therefore, employing the installment method of accounting necessarily implies both that significant uncertainty as to collection exists and that the loss cannot be measured. Presumably, these circumstances may be present when accounting for franchisors, land development companies, other sellers of real estate and certain lessors since the installment method has been invoked in response to each situation.

---

[18]In this illustration, interest has been omitted for the sake of simplicity. This omission has no effect on the concept in question nor any bearing on the conclusions to which we are led. Including interest would merely alter the pattern of principal amounts included in each equal payment. Instead of being equal in amount as in the illustration above, they would increase gradually as the total debt diminished over time.

[19]Statement of Financial Accounting Standards no. 5, *Accounting for Contingencies* (Stamford, Conn.: FASB, 1975), par. 1.

[20]Ibid., par. 8.

[21]Ibid., par. 23.

ANALYZING THE DEFENSE

Let us analyze each of these arguments supportive of the installment method of accounting.

Tax Code Support

Unquestionably, benefit may be gained by a taxpayer if the installment method is used for determining taxable income. But that benefit can still be enjoyed no matter how income is determined for financial reporting purposes and, consequently, is not germane to the issue.

Profit Timing Conforms to Cash Flows

This proposition supports the idea that income ought to be recognized so as to conform its timing to cash flows and dividend requirements. Carrying this proposal to its logical conclusion, accrual accounting ought to be abandoned in favor of cash accounting. It appears that the concerns expressed in such an idea have more to do with cash management than with the measurement of income.

Post-Sale Matching

The desire to accomplish matching is offered as an explanation by those who would defer income to offset subsequent costs of administration, collection and improvements construction. These post-sale costs can be material amounts to the seller. The deferral process does not, however, result in a proper matching of expenses with revenue. Not only is revenue being deferred when the installment method is applied, but product cost as well, and the latter has nothing to do with subsequent time periods. Moreover, most selling or administrative costs already incurred are not deferred,[22] thereby leaving the logic of this argument incomplete.

Rather than contributing to an improved matching of revenues and expenses, the installment method can seriously distort the income measurement process. Take, for example, land sales made under a seller's promise to substantially improve the property in a later period.

"In many projects, neither purchaser nor seller expects the lot to be used for any purpose until completion of payment, and therefore some or all of the promised improvements are deferred until later in or after the payment period."[23]

If improvements are undertaken after payment by the purchaser is complete, there will be no deferred income left to reflect in those time periods when the final phase of the earnings process is taking place. All of the deferred income will have

---

[22]Certain direct selling costs are to be deferred by land development companies. Indirect selling costs and administrative costs are charged to the period incurred. See: *Accounting for Retail Land Sales,* par. 43b,c.

[23]Committee on land development companies, *Accounting for Retail Land Sales,* par. 6.

been recognized in preceding periods when the cash was collected.[24] It is unlikely that the payment schedule, which in effect establishes the amount of income realized in each time period, is designed with regard for the timing and relative amounts of after-sale expenses that require revenue for matching.

A question arises concerning the proper assignment of revenues to time periods with respect to interest on the note taken on retail land sales. If a sale is recorded by the accrual method, the note receivable is normally discounted to a present value using an imputed interest rate that is higher than the nominal rate. The resulting valuation allowance is thereafter reported as a reduction of the note receivable and systematically amortized to income so that a constant rate of return on the note is experienced. If, on the other hand, the installment method is employed, the nominal rate of the note is accepted as it stands, with the result that interest earned is relatively smaller in amount, both period-by-period and in the aggregate.

Now presumably the land sales company will have certain administrative expenses in subsequent periods when interest is collected, against which the interest revenue will be matched. The implications of different amounts of interest earned that stem from using the two accounting methods are that either there are correspondingly different amounts of administrative expenses or that a smaller profit margin is a natural corollary to use of the installment method. Why either possibility might be so is not clear. However, what is clear is that the installment method, which is enlisted when a more risky transaction is entered into, results in a lower interest rate than the accrual method, which normally characterizes a less risky situation. This incongruous outcome is contrary to the way that lenders ordinarily operate wherein interest rates rise as risk increases.

Another peculiar by-product of the installment method of accounting is how it affects the measure of income over the series of periods when cash is collected. Because of level payments on notes that include a shrinking interest element and an increasing principal component, profit recognition will actually increase as time moves on. A certain portion of each dollar of principal collected is considered realized income. Therefore, as principal amounts of each level payment increase over time, so too will realized income. It is apparent that the proper matching of income to time periods was hardly a consideration when a note's terms were designed.

Unestimable Uncertainty

Finally, let us examine the installment method and its inherent assumptions in light of the conditions under which it is brought into play. We have already observed that the installment method is deemed justified when significant uncertainty as to collectibility exists and losses cannot be measured. This is an indispensable precondition. There is so much doubt and risk surrounding the transaction that accrual accounting is inadequate to deal with it.

Let us return for a moment to the illustration given earlier. In it we witnessed that every dollar of sales price collected from a customer is looked on as being made up of product cost recovery and profit. Each dollar represented $.60 of product cost

---

[24] A provision for future improvements costs is included in determining the deferred income. However, the "Liability for Future Improvements" account is based on estimated cost only.

being recovered by the seller and $.40 of profit. In 1978, $200 of profit was recognized. But this representation is true only under one condition. It is true only if every single dollar of the $1,500 sales price is collected. If a lesser amount is collected, the profit will be correspondingly reduced (offset by the value of repossessed collateral) and, at some point, even wiped out completely. Were $1,200 ultimately collected, profit would be $300, or $.25 on the dollar. If only $900 were recovered, there would be no profit. Only on conclusion of the contract, when all $600 of profit has been collected, can we contend that $.40 of every sales dollar represents profit. When the installment method is used, a representation is made which can only be true if the proposition on which it is founded is false. Only if we are absolutely certain that the total sales price will be collected and the installment receivable is risk-free should the assertion be made that every dollar has a profit component. In other words, the fundamental premise underlying the method contradicts the condition of great risk and uncertainty which justified its use in the first place.

CONCLUSIONS

What must we conclude? If an installment receivable is so shrouded in doubt as to render accrual accounting ineffectual, it would seem that the only reasonable procedure to follow is to view every dollar received as representing product cost until that total is recovered. Thereafter, recognition of profit would be appropriate. This is still a less than satisfactory solution. For one thing, what is the nature of a deferred income account? It certainly isn't a liability although it may be classified as such on the balance sheet. In financial reporting for retail land sales under the installment method, deferred income is to be deducted from the note receivable balance with only the remainder being shown as the asset's valuation. But what exactly does such a remainder represent? The balance that is left after several payments have been received on the notes is even more enigmatic than at the outset. It is not the estimated collectible balance of the notes, their discounted present value or the land's value or cost. What meaning can a banker, for example, attach to these balances? And, in addition, if some form of net asset valuation is the objective, why preclude offsetting the note receivable with a deferred income tax balance that arises when the accrual method is used for financial reporting and the installment method for tax reporting?

It is questionable that accrual accounting must be set aside because accountants are unable to satisfactorily estimate doubtful installment receivables. They have proved themselves able to cope with too many extremely difficult estimation problems in the past to warrant such a conclusion. The installment method of accounting is illogical, internally inconsistent and riddled with flaws. It ought to be abandoned as an acceptable accounting practice; abandoned entirely and unequivocally.

The FASB has now taken the responsibility for dealing with the specialized accounting and reporting principles and practices in current AICPA industry accounting and audit guides and statements of position. It is hoped that the FASB will seriously reconsider any of the authoritative literature that sanctions installment basis accounting, including the currently outstanding industry accounting guides.

INVENTORY

Since the late 1930s, when LIFO became an acceptable method of inventory valuation for federal income tax purposes, many American companies have adopted it for both tax and financial accounting purposes. Section 472 of the U.S. Internal Revenue Code provides that taxpayers may use the LIFO method only if they have used

> no procedure other than [LIFO] to ascertain the income, profit, or loss ... for the purpose of a report or statement covering [the] taxable year
>> (1) To shareholders, partners, or other proprietors, or to beneficiaries or
>> (2) For credit purposes.

Accounting Research Bulletin No. 29, issued in 1947 by the American Institute's Committee on Accounting Procedure, formally endorsed LIFO as being among the "generally accepted accounting principles" for inventory valuation, and in 1953 the same Committee, in ARB No. 43, Chapter 4, reaffirmed that position. In 1972, one-quarter of the 600 companies surveyed by the American Institute in its annual volume entitled *Accounting Trends and Techniques* used LIFO for at least some of their inventories; in 1982, owing chiefly to the spurts of inflation in the middle and late 1970s, two-thirds of the 600 companies reported at least some use of LIFO.

Whether LIFO or FIFO promotes a better measure of inventory value and cost of goods sold is a debatable question. It seems likely that many companies that have adopted LIFO have sought to eliminate most of the "holding gain" from their reported net income (and from taxable income). Although LIFO is nominally a method of historical cost accounting, one can argue that its tendency to exclude most of the "holding gain" from net income, while FIFO would include the "holding gain" in net income, qualifies it as being similar in its effect on net income to current value accounting with a physical-capital-maintenance interpretation (see the introduction to Section 8).

Since, for more than a decade, the SEC has required companies using LIFO to disclose the excess of replacement cost over the LIFO cost of their beginning and ending merchandise inventories (see Regulation S-X, Rule 5–01–6(c)), it is a simple matter for readers to estimate LIFO companies' net income according to FIFO. Even though the capital market can, at little cost, convert LIFO results to FIFO results, many company managements have refused to switch to LIFO and thus reap the tax benefits of showing a lower taxable income during periods of rising merchandise prices.

In his brief article, "Paying FIFO Taxes: Your Favorite Charity?," Gary C. Biddle draws on his prior research to suggest that companies staying on FIFO are wittingly making avoidable contributions to the federal coffers. Why do companies retain FIFO? Is it to bolster the profits on which a management compensation plan is based?

Michael H. Granof and Daniel G. Short, writing 18 months later in a brief article entitled "For Some Companies, FIFO Accounting Makes Sense," report on a questionnaire survey of corporate controllers in which justifications for staying on FIFO inventory accounting are suggested. In a letter commenting on the findings reported by Granof and Short, Biddle professes disbelief.

Selecting inventory valuation methods falls under the general heading of "Issues in Accounting Choice" which was explored in Section 3. The research reported by Watts and Zimmerman in that section would tend to suggest that large companies in the public eye might be disposed to report somewhat lower profits in order to avert the gaze of government regulators and legislators.

BIBLIOGRAPHICAL NOTES

Several empirical studies have been conducted to understand investors' reactions to the impact on earnings of a change in inventory valuation method from FIFO to LIFO:

Sunder, Shyam: "Optimal Choice Between FIFO and LIFO," *Journal of Accounting Research* (Autumn 1976), pp. 277–300.
Abdel-khalik, A. Rashad and James C. McKeown: "Understanding Accounting Changes in an Efficient Market: Evidence of Differential Reaction," *The Accounting Review* (October 1978), pp. 851–868.
Abdel-khalik, A. Rashad and Thomas F. Keller: *Earnings or Cash Flows: An Experiment on Functional Fixation and the Valuation of the Firm,* Studies in Accounting Research #16 (Sarasota, FL: American Accounting Association, 1979).
Ricks, William E.:"The Market's Response to the 1974 LIFO Adoptions," *Journal of Accounting Research* (Autumn 1982—Part 1), pp. 367–387.

A research study conducted by a retired partner of a major public accounting firm deals with the valuation of inventories:

Barden, Horace G.: *The Accounting Basis of Inventories,* Accounting Research Study No. 13 (New York, AICPA, 1973).

A comprehensive study done by three public accounting practitioners is:

Jannis, C. Paul, Carl H. Poedtke, Jr. and Donald R. Ziegler: *Managing and Accounting for Inventories: Control, Income Recognition, and Tax Strategy,* (New York: John Wiley and Sons, 1980). (Previous editions were published by The Ronald Press Company in 1962 and 1970.)

A history of LIFO, including both its use in taxation and in financial statements, is as follows:

Davis, Harry Zvi: "History of LIFO," *The Accounting Historians Journal* (Spring 1982), pp. 1–23. (Reprinted in the *Journal of Accountancy* (May 1983), pp. 96–98, 101–102, 104–106, 108, 110, 112, 114.)

Paying FIFO Taxes: Your Favorite Charity?

Gary C. Biddle
University of Washington

In one of the most puzzling rituals of American business behavior, thousands of U.S. companies are once again preparing their annual reports using FIFO rather than LIFO inventory accounting. By so doing, they will pay as extra taxes funds which could be used for expansion, capital replacement or dividends.

Under FIFO, or the first-in, first-out assumption, inventory costs flow through the firm as if on a conveyor belt. Costs are assigned to units sold in the same order the costs entered inventory. As a result, during periods of rising prices, older and thus *lower* costs are subtracted from revenues when determining reported (and taxable) earnings.

In contrast, under LIFO, or the last-in, first-out assumption, inventory costs are accumulated as if on a coal pile, with the newest costs being removed from the top and assigned to units sold. Unless a cost layer is liquidated by depleting inventories, it can remain in the base of the pile indefinitely. Thus, during periods of rising prices older and lower costs can remain in the balance sheet inventory accounts while the newer and *higher* costs are used to calculate earnings. Compared to FIFO, reported earnings in most cases drop. But so do taxable earnings. The company can keep more cash for itself and for shareholders.

According to their latest annual reports, three long-time LIFO users—Amoco, General Electric and U.S. Steel—have together saved more than $3 billion in taxes compared to what they would have paid using FIFO.

LIFO was deemed acceptable for tax purposes in 1939, and it's been used widely in selected industries, notably steel and petroleum, since the late 1940s. A large number of firms switched to LIFO in 1974, a year of high inflation. And for 1980,

American Hospital Supply, Eli Lilly, Clorox and Williams Cos., among others, have announced they're making the switch.

Yet the vast majority of companies continue to use FIFO. Some managers are perhaps reluctant to incur additional LIFO bookkeeping costs. Some have perhaps dismissed LIFO's tax advantages in light of variable year-end inventory levels or less than galloping prices. Others may believe that since LIFO would result in lower reported earnings, stockholders are content to pay the extra FIFO taxes.

How much extra are stockholders willing to pay? In a forthcoming study in the "Supplement to the Journal of Accounting Research, 1980," I compare the inventory levels and accounts of 106 New York Stock Exchange firms which used FIFO, with those of 106 competitors that adopted LIFO between 1973 and 1975. From 1974 to 1978, by my estimates, the 106 FIFO firms paid an average of nearly $26 million each in additional federal income taxes, thanks to their policy of sticking with FIFO. For 1974 alone, these additional taxes averaged nearly $12 million per firm—more than 1 1/2% of their sales.

Indeed there are good reasons to suspect that the additional taxes paid by FIFO firms put them at a competitive disadvantage. The accompanying table compares estimates of the additional taxes paid by six FIFO firms, with the amounts saved by direct competitors that adopted LIFO or extended its use in 1974.

FIFO firms, of course, do not typically disclose the additional taxes they have paid. I have estimated these amounts, however, using industry specific price indexes and assumptions about procurement to come up with the differences between FIFO and LIFO based earnings. The additional FIFO taxes shown in the table equal these differences multiplied by the corporate income tax rate (then 48%).

	1974-1978	
*FIFO firms LIFO Competitors	Additional FIFO taxes	LIFO tax savings
	(in millions of dollars)	
*Federal Paper Board $8		
Mead Corp		$46
*J.P. Stevens 29		
Burlington Inds..		44
Cone Mill		28
*Jewel Companies 36		
American Stores		18
*Masco Corp. 15		
Wallace-Murray		13
*Minn. Mining & Mfg. 118		
Eastman Kodak		204
*Smith International 32		
Dresser Inds.		125
Hughes Tool Co.		22

The estimates of additional FIFO taxes assume that LIFO is applicable to all of a FIFO firm's inventories. As a result, these amounts may be overstated for firms like Smith International which hold significant portions of their inventories in other countries where LIFO is not permitted. However, the amounts that have been saved by LIFO competitors may understate the potential savings in cases like American Stores where LIFO has been adopted for only a portion of domestic inventories.

The amounts presented suggest that a number of firms have paid millions of dollars each in additional taxes by using FIFO rather than LIFO for domestic inventories. It is unlikely that bookkeeping costs could account for such sums. And fears of negative stockholder reaction appear unfounded in light of the efficient markets research documenting investor preferences for cash flows. While there are some unusual circumstances (like falling prices or inventory levels) in which LIFO could yield smaller cash flows, it is puzzling why so many firms in so many industries have continued to use FIFO.

Perhaps companies sticking to FIFO are showing their support for some worthy federal program. But wouldn't it make more sense to contribute some LIFO tax savings to a favorite tax-deductible charity? Or perhaps I have ignored an important LIFO cost or FIFO benefit. If so, please let me know.

For Some Companies, FIFO Accounting Makes Sense

Michael H. Granof
The University of Texas at Austin

Daniel G. Short
The University of Texas at Austin

The use of FIFO, or the first-in first-out inventory accounting method, may not be so puzzling after all.

It is frequently argued that LIFO, the last-in first-out method, provides companies with substantial tax savings by permitting them to determine their cost of goods sold as if the items purchased last—at presumably higher prices—were in fact the ones sold. Financial analysts and business school professors often wonder why companies using FIFO, or another method called the weighted average, are paying millions of dollars in extra taxes—funds that would otherwise be available for expansion, capital replacement and dividends. The conventional explanation is that companies use FIFO in order to boost their reported earnings, even at the expense of their after-tax cash flow. But we have just concluded a survey that makes clear this interpretation is usually wrong.

From *The Wall Street Journal* (August 30, 1982). Reprinted by permission of *The Wall Street Journal,* © Dow Jones & Company, Inc. 1982. All Rights Reserved.

We asked the controllers of 380 corporations that have not adopted LIFO why they haven't. We received 213 answers. Our survey convinces us that many companies have legitimate reasons for not climbing aboard the LIFO bandwagon.

For one thing, we found that most non-LIFO companies are *not* incurring a tax penalty. On the contrary, in a number of circumstances, the FIFO or weighted-average method can reduce tax payments.

Over 16% of our respondents indicated that the prices of their goods held in inventory have been declining. This was especially true of firms in high technology industries, but was also reported by firms in less glamorous industries such as steel and meat packing. In periods of declining prices, LIFO serves to accelerate recognition of taxable gains and, therefore, results in higher tax payments.

Many controllers—17%—told us that their firms as a whole or various of their subsidiaries are using tax loss or tax credit carryforwards. These carryforwards make it advantageous for the firm to accept the currently higher earnings that go with FIFO in order to have correspondingly lower earnings in the future, when the firm will again be in a tax-paying position.

Some managers explained that adoption of LIFO would prevent them from taking advantage of the "lower of cost or market" rule. This feature of the tax code (which is not available to firms that use LIFO) enables firms that have incurred losses on selected inventory items to give them immediate tax recognition. When LIFO is adopted, inventory must be stated at original cost. Previously recorded losses must be recovered and taxes must be paid on that amount.

Many managers have already taken advantage of a recent relaxation of the LIFO conformity rule. Normally a firm that uses LIFO for tax purposes must do so for financial reporting purposes. As a result of a ruling last year by the Second Circuit Court of Appeals in a case involving Insilco Corp., a parent company may now report the results of a subsidiary in its financial statements based on a method other than LIFO even though its subsidiaries calculate their taxable earnings using LIFO.

In addition, many controllers focused on various drawbacks of LIFO that could outweigh possible tax benefits. If a company's inventory balances fluctuate from year to year, LIFO increases the difficulties of cash planning. This is because LIFO subjects the company to the risk of dipping into its LIFO base—valuing for tax purposes its goods sold at the artificially low prices of past years. The company might then report artificially high profits and have to repay in a single year the accumulated tax savings of several previous years. Other controllers emphasized that the record-keeping requirements of LIFO are burdensome and costly.

While our study uncovered a number of legitimate reasons for not using LIFO, several responses seemed to lack economic support. One company said it did not use LIFO because it is "trying to maintain a record of year-to-year growth in profits, and though the impact of the change would not be material in relation to total profits in the first year, it would be significant in terms of year-to-year profit improvement." Another did not use LIFO because it thought that "such a switch would depress the market price of our stock. Such a switch would reduce the book value of our stock and would depress reported earnings . . . these considerations are more significant to our stock price than cash flow."

These explanations are somewhat surprising in light of the persuasive evidence that the capital markets are able to understand and compensate for differences in earning attributable solely to choices between accounting principles. But only 9% of the controllers gave such explanations.

Our study has convinced us that when it comes to paying taxes, most managers know what they are doing. But managers who have justification for not adopting LIFO need to be careful to explain these reasons to investors. We found that often the justification is not apparent from an analysis of financial statements. Companies that do not use LIFO for sound economic reasons should avoid being confused with companies that do not adopt LIFO for merely cosmetic reasons.

Taking Stock of Inventory Accounting Choices

Gary C. Biddle
University of Washington

Based on their survey of corporate controllers, Granof and Short (*Manager's Journal,* Aug. 30) are convinced "that many companies have legitimate reasons for not climbing aboard the LIFO bandwagon." Their evidence, however, is far from convincing.

A firm facing declining inventory costs would generally pay lower taxes by using FIFO rather than LIFO. Yet only 16% (of the 56% who responded) cited declining costs. Another 17% justified their non-use of LIFO in terms of tax-loss carryforwards and credits. However, this argument applies only when there is some danger that the carryforwards and credits will expire. Otherwise a firm can "lock in" its LIFO tax savings in the form of larger carryforwards in future years. Other controllers explained that the adoption of LIFO would prevent them from taking advantage of "lower of cost or market" writedowns. Yet writedowns below original LIFO costs will be infrequent if inventory costs are rising. Moreover, LIFO can be selectively adopted to avoid inventory items whose costs fluctuate. While it is also noted that previous writedowns must be reversed at the time of a LIFO adoption, the Thor Power Tool Co. decision (which disallowed the writedowns of many FIFO firms) has significantly weakened this LIFO disincentive.

Granof and Short cite other respondents who avoid LIFO because of additional planning and record-keeping costs. For these firms, the value of potential tax savings is apparently small enough to be offset by increased administrative costs. A follow-up questionnaire would provide welcome evidence on this hypothesis (and may reveal some lucrative employment opportunities for cost accountants). Still other respondents were concerned about the impact of LIFO on reported earnings. Surprisingly, Granof and Short are comforted by the fact that "only 9% of the respondents gave such explanations." Recent interest in the Insilco Corp. decision suggests that concern with LIFO's earnings impact is not limited to these few firms.

Granof and Short conclude from their survey that "the use of FIFO may not be so puzzling after all." What is puzzling, however, is how they drew this conclusion from their evidence. Managers undoubtedly have motives for their accounting choices. Yet to judge them as "legitimate" requires both the identification of motives and their reconciliation with optimizing behavior.

COMMITMENTS AND HUMAN RESOURCES

The principal factors traditionally addressed in accounting are the measurement of the economic quantity of a resource and the association of that resource with periods of time and/or functions of the enterprise. There is the related issue of timing the recognition of the existence of an economic resource, which is related to the time at which the resource comes under the control of the entity.

In a variety of instances, economic quantities are excluded from the primary financial statements for a variety of reasons. There may be uncertainty as to whether a contract will ultimately be fulfilled, uncertainty as to its value if it is fulfilled, or uncertainty of the amount of liability that will be incurred in the process of fulfillment. The basic question relates to the likelihood of eventual performance by one or both parties. Under present accounting principles economic quantities are seldom recognized if there exists any substantial uncertainty about future performance and/or benefit. This practice reflects the influence of conservatism and generally refers to the tendency of accounting practice to understate asset values and consequently reduce income.

Yuji Ijiri, in his monograph on the *Theory of Accounting Measurement*, argues that users of financial statements would stand to benefit from an earlier recognition of commitments to receive or deliver future resources. In many instances, accounting entries could be recorded at the time of making a commitment, rather than waiting for half-execution of the contract. He then applies this notion to accounting for human resources.

On the subject of human resource accounting, most managers will attest that the employees are their most valuable asset. Having said this, there is virtually no case where we can find the value of the human resources in the financial statements of a major business. Certainly we find wage and salary expense among the revenue deductions, but there is no balance-sheet recognition of an existing work force which is prepared to contribute to the productive activities of the firm in the years ahead. Ijiri suggests that the present value of future contributions of the employees might be determined and recognized as an asset of the enterprise. This extension of commitment accounting would permit a very important asset of any organization to be reflected in the financial statements. The comparative information among entities could be very valuable to a decision maker considering alternative investments.

Again, the allocation dilemma that Thomas addressed is at the heart of this important accounting issue. The association of effort with revenue generated would be arbitrary. The question is: Is the user better off with imperfect arbitrarily allocated data or no data at all? Or is there an alternative reporting scheme that allows the accountant to avoid the incorrigible allocations?

BIBLIOGRAPHICAL NOTES

A comprehensive work on human resource accounting is:

Flamholtz, Eric: *Human Resource Accounting* (Encino, CA: Dickenson Publishing Company, Inc., 1974).

An article in which the authors question the existence of unrecorded human assets is:

Dittman, David A., Hervey A. Juris, and Lawrence Revsine: "On the Existence of Unrecorded Human Assets: An Economic Perspective," *Journal of Accounting Research* (Spring 1976), pp. 49–65. A further article by the same authors on the subject of unrecorded human assets in Big Eight public accounting firms is "Unrecorded Human Assets: A Survey of Accounting Firms' Training Programs," *The Accounting Review* (October 1980), pp. 640–647.

Accounting for Future Resources

Yuji Ijiri
Carnegie-Mellon University

COMMITMENT ACCOUNTING

Commitment accounting, which we wish to explore here, is an attempt to extend recognition criteria from the present performance basis to what may be called a commitment basis, recognizing changes in resources when parties in the exchange commit themselves to the delivery of resources, even if no such commitments have yet been fulfilled.

A typical example is a lease where two parties make a commitment. The lessor permits the lessee to use the object of the lease for a fixed length of time and the

Adapted from Chapter 8 in *Theory of Accounting Measurement* (American Accounting Association, 1975), pp. 129–140. Reprinted by permission of the American Accounting Association.

lessee agrees to pay a rental fee in each period. Despite firm and sometimes noncancelable commitments enforceable by law, the rights and obligations arising out of such a commitment have not been recognized in present accounting practice except in some special cases.[1]

Another example is materials purchased for future deliveries. The firm agrees to buy certain materials to be delivered in the future for a fixed sum of money to be paid upon receipt of the goods, and the seller agrees to these terms. Even if the contract is noncancelable, the right to receive the materials and the obligation to pay cash are neither recorded nor reported under the present accounting system.

From an economic and financial standpoint, the right to receive materials is equivalent to having materials on hand, except that those goods purchased for future delivery cannot be used until the delivery date. The firm gains or loses depending upon the price change of the materials. For this reason alone, the right to receive materials should be systematically treated in accounting records and financial statements.

On the liability side, the argument is even stronger to have the monetary obligation arising out of a contract recognized immediately, since such liabilities are clearly as important as all the other liabilities currently appearing on the balance sheet.

Construction contracts are still another item which may have an even greater impact than the previous examples on the financial status of a firm, but are nevertheless completely ignored in the balance sheet and accounting records. As soon as a firm signs a construction contract, its financial liquidity is diminished, even if the property constructed is not received nor payments made for several years. The firm is bound to the contract unless it is cancelable without a severe penalty.

Considering the significance of the items which are currently left out of accounting records and reports, we shall suggest an accounting procedure that treats these commitments in a systematic manner instead of trying to remedy present accounting practices by *ad hoc* adjustments. Let us, therefore, construct the recording and reporting framework necessary for accounting on a commitment basis or "commitment accounting."

Assume that a firm engages in buying and selling wheat. The trading results in noncancelable contracts between the firm and its suppliers and customers.

Suppose that the firm makes a deal with a supplier by which the firm receives 1,000 bushels of wheat at the end of each month for 30 months at the price of $6 a bushel. The payment is to be made 30 days after delivery.

As soon as the agreement is reached, a journal entry is made to record the transaction:

Merchandise on order	$180,000		
Commitments payable		$180,000	(1)

---

[1]See APB Opinions Nos. 5, 7, 27, and 31. See also Wojdak [1969] for an attempt to justify the accommodation of leases and other executory contracts under the currently accepted concepts of assets and liabilities. Bedford [1965a] treats this subject as an extension of the accrual concepts. On the need to develop a comprehensive disclosure requirement for all executory contracts, see Birnberg [1965].

The commitments payable account is used to distinguish, whenever necessary, payables for merchandise received from payables for commitments only. Merchandise on order is distinguished from merchandise on hand under the same principle which separates receivables from cash.

Both merchandise on order and commitments payable should be classified further when financial statements are prepared. Merchandise that will be delivered within one year and commitments that will be payable within one year should be distinguished from other merchandise orders and commitments payable.

When at the end of each month 1,000 bushels of wheat are received, the following entry is made.

Merchandise	$6,000		
Merchandise on order		$6,000	(2)
Commitments payable	$6,000		
Accounts payable		$6,000	(3)

These entries generally do not have any impact on the income figure for the current year. However, it is conceivable that in some situations the use of LIFO may be extended to include merchandise on order as the first merchandise to be utilized in calculating the cost of sales under LIFO.[2] Of course, such an extension of LIFO may not be considered proper in some cases. The above example shows the possibility of interaction between price and quantity, since changing the rule that determines quantity can influence the process of determining price.

However, commitment accounting has a more important effect upon the income of the firm, namely, the firm's realization goals may be revised.

Suppose the firm enters into a contract with its customer whereby the customer agrees to buy 2,000 bushels of wheat at the end of each month for 20 months at $7 a bushel. The payment is to be made 30 days after delivery.

When this noncancelable contract is made, the following entry is immediately recorded.

Commitments receivable	$280,000		
Sales orders outstanding		$280,000	(4)

Commitments receivable is separated from accounts receivable to indicate that corresponding commitments on the firm's side have not yet been fulfilled.

Sales orders outstanding is a liability since it indicates the firm's obligation to deliver wheat in the future. However, it is a nonmonetary liability that present accounting does not deal with explicitly. The extension of recognition criteria to cover commitments emphasizes the importance of giving equal recognition to nonmonetary rights and obligations. Sales orders outstanding is a typical nonmonetary liability that must be recognized explicitly under commitment accounting.

---

[2]The difference between acquisition cost and replacement cost is diminished here, but the principle of valuation based on actual (rather than hypothetical) transactions is still maintained.

In the above example, the right to receive wheat is less in quantity than the obligation to deliver wheat (30,000 bushels to be received versus 40,000 bushels to deliver). Even if the inventory balance is added to the amount the firm expects to receive, the sum may still be less than the quantity the firm is obligated to deliver. But this is not an abnormal situation since a firm can be temporarily short of many kinds of resources. For example, sometimes a firm is short of monetary resources, such as when payables exceed receivables and cash.

Now the fundamental question regarding realization principles is how to treat the profit portion of sales orders outstanding. A method consistent with existing practices is to have both the cost and the profit portion of sales orders outstanding included in the liability section of the balance sheet. This can be done either by setting up a single account such as sales orders outstanding, as stated above, or dividing the account into "sales orders outstanding at cost" and "anticipated profit from sales orders outstanding."

It is, however, conceivable that a departure from the conventional realization principle may be desirable for some kinds of performance measurement. When this happens, the anticipated profit may be partially or totally included in the income figure.

Shifting the realization point from the time of delivery to the time the commitment is made is especially suitable in a situation where fulfillment of the firm's obligations is so routine that it is virtually certain.

Generally, the greatest uncertainty reduction occurs when the sales order is received. Once a salesman obtains an order from a customer or once a contract is signed (particularly if it is noncancelable), the goal is considered achieved not only by the salesman, but also by the firm, except when an order cannot be filled due to a material or labor shortage.

The present realization principle, which recognizes profits only after the actual delivery of merchandise to the customer, does permit some exceptions. A typical example is the percentage-of-completion system used in construction industries. Therefore, this same realization principle can be logically extended to include partial recognition for the production of resources covered by sales orders.

The most important issue, however, is whether profit should be recognized only after a commitment has been fulfilled, especially if the fulfillment is reasonably certain. The argument for profit recognition upon commitment is particularly convincing if a normal profit is attributed to the process of fulfilling the commitment and an abnormal profit is recognized at the point of the commitment. This approach is based on the idea that the latter is clearly identified with the effort of getting the sales order, which, in general, is the most severe bottleneck in the firm's cycle of activities.

Profit should be recognized at the time uncertainty is most reduced. Generally there is greatest uncertainty in that part of the firm's activity cycle which creates the most severe bottleneck. In a war economy, procurement or production may be the most uncertain part of the cycle, in which case it may be justifiable to recognize an abnormal profit at the point of procurement or at the time production is completed. An abnormal profit may even be recorded at the time of a breakthrough in research and development. Such a shift in profit recognition may yield more useful performance measures for these situations.

In any event, the idea of recognizing profit upon the receipt of a customer's order is theoretically justified in a situation where uncertainty is greatly reduced by the receipt of the order and no significant degree of uncertainty remains in the process of fulfilling the order.

However, even if we agree to retain the present realization concept, commitment accounting improves the presentation of the firm's financial status on the balance sheet. Among the additional accounts that appear under commitment accounting are:

i Commitments receivable—Including receivables that arise from contracts for the sales of goods or services, the disposal of fixed assets, or bank loans. Accounts should be suitably labeled to indicate the nature of the commitment.

ii Inventories on order—Materials and other merchandise ordered but not yet received.

iii Services contracted for—Utilities, insurance, rentals and other services purchased but not yet received, whether or not cash has been paid (prepaid expenses).

iv Fixed assets contracted for—Buildings, land, machinery, equipment and intangibles which are contracted for but not yet received.

v Commitments payable—Including payables that arise from contracts for purchasing materials and other merchandise, labor, utilities and other services, and fixed assets. A descriptive account name should be used for payables arising from each type of commitment.

vi Sales orders outstanding—Merchandise sold but not yet delivered.

vii Disposals outstanding—Fixed assets disposed of but not yet delivered.

In both (vi) and (vii), the amount is stated at the full sales price if no profit from these contracts is recognized during the period in which the contract is made. The accounts may then be divided into estimated cost and estimated profit or they may be categorized in even more detail indicating such factors as tax accruals. If profit is to be partially or fully recognized in the period of commitment, the amount in these accounts is reduced by the amount of profit recognized, either by a direct deduction or by the use of a contra-account.

On a balance sheet, these accounts are placed close to accounts which represent similar resources. For example, inventories on order is placed directly after inventories, and buildings contracted for is recorded after buildings. However, as stated earlier, if the rights or obligations extend beyond one year from the reporting date, the accounts maturing within one year should be distinguished from the others and each type should be recorded in the appropriate section (current or long-term) on the balance sheet.

EVALUATION OF COMMITMENT ACCOUNTING

Despite the numerous significant commitments an entity makes in its ordinary course of business, commitments alone are not recognized in accounting unless they are half-executed.

This practice of not recognizing rights and obligations created by a contract until one party performs its obligation has a parallel in law dating back to the Middle Ages. Not until the 16th century did English law recognize that promises in a contract were enforceable. Fuller [1947, p. 304ff] states:

Prior to the [16th century]...it may be said that the English law recognized two bases of liability which we would classify as 'contractual.' *First,* a defendant who promised to pay for goods or services became liable to pay the agreed price (which might be in terms of money or goods) *after* he had received the plaintiff's performance...*Secondly,* a defendant who had made a promise under seal was liable in an action of debt or covenant. The principles of liability involved in these two contracts of the early law were (1) that a man ought to pay for what he has bargained for and received, and (2) that a formally-made promise should be binding.

If we compare this early English law of contracts with the modern law we will note that the most important difference lies in the fact that there was no relief for breach of an informal executory bargain. A and B agree on the sale of a horse for £10. When the time comes for delivery, A, the seller, tenders the horse, and B refuses to accept it. Unless B's promise was under seal, the early law granted no remedy to A in this situation. Suit could be brought for the price of goods delivered or services rendered, but not for "damages" for the other party's refusal to carry out the unsealed executory agreement.

Then, in the famous case of 1589 (Strangborough and Warner's Case) an English court declared, "A promise against a promise will maintain an action." As stated in Berman and Greiner, "Not merely the half-executed bargain but the executory bargain—I will do this if you will do that—was now seen to be worth something in and of itself, and to be worth something in secular law and not only in faith." (Berman and Greiner [1972, p. 541]).

This development in English law—from the protection of only half-executed bargains to the protection of executory bargains—has a counterpart in accounting— from the recording and reporting of only full-executed or half-executed transactions to the recording and reporting of executory transactions. However, a gap of almost 400 years exists between the time this principle was recognized in law and now, when this principle is first being acknowledged in accounting.

Today, we cannot think of business activities without contracts and other forms of legal commitments. A firm interacts with other firms, labor unions, government and consumers through a huge network of contracts and other legal relationships. As the society becomes more stable, greater reliance is placed on promises as a way of reducing uncertainty. A promise of execution is considered to be almost as good as the execution itself. The period between commitment and execution becomes longer and longer.

Nevertheless, the present accounting system in effect ignores a large portion of contracts and other legal commitments by demanding that commitments be half-executed before records and reports are initiated. Because this is such an important area in accounting every effort should be made to improve current practices.

The benefits of commitment accounting are twofold. First, both the internal and external users of financial statements would find the data on commitments helpful. Backlogs of sales orders and purchase orders may be very indicative of the future profitability of the firm when compared with prior years' data or competitors' data. If commitments on plant expansion or new construction were given explicit recognition in the balance sheet they would provide valuable data for evaluating the firm's liquidity, profitability, and solvency.

Secondly, commitment accounting would provide stronger control over commitments. Under present accounting practices, a large number of commitments are often not even reported to headquarters, while minor expenses are recorded and reported to the headquarters and to the shareholders.

Clearly, commitments deserve as close control by headquarters as actual expenses. To achieve this, it is essential that all commitments be recorded in the regular accounting system. Such data would provide top management with information for decision making one-step earlier than the present accounting system based on half-execution.

Commitment accounting has an additional advantage in that commitment data are likely to be hard since they are in many cases supported by legal documents. The auditing procedure may be adjusted to make the data even more reliable. For example, sending confirmations of commitments to or from major customers, suppliers and banks, or verifying commitments by checking the actual receipts or deliveries of resources should become a required auditing procedure, just as these methods are used in checking receivables and payables.

A number of problems, however, must be resolved before commitment accounting can be effectively implemented.

The most important item at issue is the cancelability of commitments. In many informal purchase and sales orders, commitments are often canceled by one party without the other party attempting to seek compensation for the breach of contract. In some cases, only one party has the option of canceling. But in other cases which often involve a significant dollar value, a contract is noncancelable unless the canceling party incurs a heavy penalty.

Commitment accounting could first be used for noncancelable contracts and then gradually be extended to apply to other, more flexible commitments.

Furthermore, the contingency of having a contract canceled may not be materially different from the contingency of having merchandise returned by a customer or of having uncollectible receivables. Based on experiences in the past, systematic ways of handling uncollectible receivables have been devised, such as setting aside a reserve for bad debts. There seems to be no reason why the same cannot be done in the case of contract cancellation.

Another problem may occur when a contract does not specify a fixed dollar amount to be paid for resources sold. For example, suppose that A agrees to buy exclusively from B. In addition, B agrees to sell all the wheat A needs for the production of flour during the next n years at x cents above the closing cash price of wheat at the Chicago Commodity Market on the day that B receives a purchase order from A. In this type of open-ended contract, the amount of the contract is indeterminate. Still another example is a cost-plus contract where cost cannot be determined until the project is actually undertaken. If the contract is on the cost-plus-percentage-fee basis, the fee is also indeterminate.

In these cases, entries in the journal cannot be made until the amounts of the contract can be specified. In an open-ended contract, a journal entry is not made when the contract between A and B is originally concluded, but rather when a purchase order is issued by A. In the cost-plus contract, an entry on cost and fee may be made as purchase orders for materials and other inputs to the project are issued.

There certainly are many problems that call for standardized treatment, but these problems must be handled gradually as the use of commitment accounting expands.

However, gradual progress should not be confused with improving upon existing practices by means of *ad hoc* solutions. What differentiates the two is whether or not a modification of the present system is made with a more far-reaching goal in mind. The gradual expansion of commitment accounting proposed above should always be undertaken with the ultimate objective of achieving full-scale commitment accounting. In this way, leases can be treated not as an independent issue, but as a stepping stone toward the full implementation of commitment accounting.

Performance measurements may also be improved in situations where commitments are the key factor in reducing the uncertainty associated with goal achievement. As stated before, however, the issue of profit recognition at the point of commitment can be discussed separately from the other benefits of commitment accounting. Therefore, even when early profit recognition is undesirable in measuring performance, the other benefits of commitment accounting may be enough to justify its implementation.

Finally, from the general standpoint of accountability, commitment accounting is preferable to the current system. Accountability does not have to be limited to half-executed transactions. In fact in many situations, it is more important to emphasize commitments in defining accountability, especially where execution is a routine matter.

For these reasons, commitment accounting is one of the best directions in which present accounting could be extended. Compared with attempts to improve accounting by introducing new valuation bases, commitment accounting is an attempt to change the nature of the objects evaluated. Furthermore, commitment accounting is based on the actions the entity is mostly likely to take (actually, committed to take), whereas the valuation alternatives discussed in Chapter 6 are based on actions the entity is not likely to take (e.g., a firm is not likely to replace or dispose of assets at the present market price). In addition, commitment accounting can readily produce figures hard enough for accountability and performance measurement because it is based on legal actions which are objectively verifiable.

Clearly, we should explore in full detail the prospects of adopting commitment accounting in the future.

HUMAN RESOURCE ACCOUNTING

The shift to commitment accounting would affect the way in which human resources are recorded. Let us first explore the impact of commitment accounting on the treatment of human resources and then suggest various proposals on how to deal with human resources in financial statements and accounting records.[3]

Under present accounting practice, human resources are treated just as any other services purchased from outside the firm. The consumption of labor is treated as an expense just as the consumption of utilities or the expiration of insurance coverage is handled. Accruals and prepayments are used to record the time differential between labor utilization and wage payments. In any event, a record is not initiated

---

[3]The AAA Committee on Human Resource Accounting [1973] provi‹es a good overview of this field and also contains a comprehensive bibliography of human resource accounting. See also Flamholtz [1974], which includes a few case studies.

until the services are performed or payment for the services is made, which is in accord with the general principle of initiating a record with half-executed contracts.

The extent to which commitment accounting necessitates changes in the recording of human resources depends upon many factors. But in particular, it depends upon how cancelable commitments are generally treated in commitment accounting. This is because most labor contracts are cancelable, at least by employees. Therefore, if the practice of commitment accounting is limited to contracts that are not cancelable by either party, commitment accounting may have no impact except in some special cases, for example, when employees are actors or players in professional sports.

However, if the practice of commitment accounting extends to partly cancelable or fully cancelable contracts, then more extensive recognition can be given to human resources as long as there is a high probability that the terms of the contract will be carried out by both sides. Many labor contracts fall into this category. Furthermore, accounting for pension cost becomes a logical application of commitment accounting rather than the *ad hoc* practice of dealing with contingent liabilities.

The extension of human resource accounting to include resources contracted for comes closer to the idea commonly held by economists that human resources should be evaluated by the present value (capitalized value) of discounted future wages and salaries to be paid to employees until their retirement.[4] While the time horizon to retirement may be too long to make a reliable estimate of future wages and salaries, this proposal to capitalize human resources is, like commitment accounting, based on the idea that financial statements should contain more information about the firm's future rights and obligations. Commitment accounting, however, is more conservative in its approach, starting with commitments which are highly objective, verifiable and most indicative of what the firm will do in the future.

There are two other methods by which a firm's human resources may be evaluated. One is the replacement cost system and the other is the economic value system. Both these methods are radically different in principle from the capitalization method and commitment accounting.

The replacement cost approach calls for a valuation of human resources based on their replacement cost, or in other words, the cost the firm would incur if the present employees were to be replaced.[5]

The economic value approach, on the other hand, advocates that human resources be evaluated based on their economic contribution to the firm and be placed on the balance sheet at that economic value.[6] For example, Hekimian and Jones [1967] argue that if a division expects to earn $140,000 a year more profit by hiring 8 additional engineers, the division should be willing to bid up to $1,400,000, at the target return on investment of 10%, in order to obtain the desired 8 engineers from another division. They suggest recording this amount on the balance sheet as part of the investment figure used to calculate the division's actual return on investment.

In determining the replacement cost or the economic value of human resources

[4]See Lev and Schwartz [1971].

[5]See, for example, Brummet [1970] and Flamholtz [1969] for discussions on this approach.

[6]This may also be called the opportunity cost approach since the economic value may be considered the opportunity cost associated with losing the human resources.

we face the same problem that we confront in determining the replacement cost or the economic value of physical resources. Even more difficult questions arise when we are dealing with human resources. With whom shall we replace an employee? What quality of employee should be hired? How soon must the decision be made? Under what conditions should the economic value of an employee be determined? Although there may be situations where specific data on the replacement cost or the economic value of employees would be useful, as in the case where a firm is contemplating firing or transferring employees, it is not necessary to systematically record and report such data.

Curiously, neither the replacement cost approach nor the economic value approach delineates the human resources that are to be evaluated. Both methods are clearly concerned with prices of human resources and not quantities. Therefore, the extent of the future services expected from human resources must be defined before the valuation issue arises. If the extent is limited only to the services performed in the past, the two approaches are simply an application of the valuation alternatives discussed in Chapter 6 to human resources. If the extent goes beyond past services, then the boundary of future services must be established by means of commitments, a planning horizon, or retirement, before we can begin to discuss what prices are to be used.

In other words, the replacement cost approach and the economic value approach are simple applications of the valuation alternatives to human resources. They are not new methods developed because of the peculiarity of human resources. Human resources may at first appear to be different from physical resources from the valuational standpoint because the firm does not own them. However, as observed in the previous chapter, human resources are not the only resources which the firm does not own. Purchases of utilities or insurance, leases and other executory contracts all have elements in common with labor contracts. Therefore, these resources must be treated uniformly rather than giving special, *ad hoc* treatment to human resources. In this sense, the central issue in human resource accounting is determining the extent to which future service flows should be estimated and reported in financial statements, which is precisely the same problem we discussed in commitment accounting.

One might point out here that human resources are treated differently from physical resources because of the need to maintain good relations with employees. But a good relationship with customers, suppliers, banks and governmental agencies is also very important in running a company. Therefore, all these resources must be treated uniformly rather than singling out employees as if they were the only human resource of the firm. Furthermore, from the standpoint of accounting measurement, goodwill is not something that is attributable to human resources in particular; rather it is attributable to the whole composite of human and physical resources.

Considering these points, there is nothing in human resource accounting that has not been covered by the principles governing physical resources. However, one point must be kept in mind when applying different valuation methods to human resources. That is, people are sensitive to the value others place on them. This is why salary data are kept confidential and the replacement cost or the economic value of an employee is rarely measured except in a very limited and informal way. A machine never reacts to an over- or under-valuation of its capacity, but an employee will certainly react if such information is reported. This means that the application of replacement cost or economic value to human resources will have to be severely limited to situations where such data are actually necessary for specific decisions.

In addition to the three approaches discussed above—the capitalization method, the replacement cost method and the economic value method—there is a fourth approach to human resource accounting that covers a much narrower area. This is a method which accepts historical cost as the valuation principle for human resources and advocates a better matching of costs and benefits, particularly in regard to hiring, training and relocation costs. Currently, these costs are expensed in the period in which they accrue, but the proposed change is to capitalize them and amortize them over the expected service life of the employees.

Surprisingly a large number of articles with titles containing human resource accounting are actually devoted to the matching issue.[7] Human resources are not unique in this respect. The capitalization and amortization of research and development costs, intangible drilling costs and deferred charges all have similar characteristics. They are normally expensed because of conservatism or the lack of a reliable estimate for the benefit periods. These items, including human resources, should all be governed by the same accounting principle. Human resources require no special treatment in matching costs and benefits.

In summary, the central problem in human resource accounting is not what kind of resources should be treated, but rather when the resources should be recognized. This timing issue is particularly important because human resources are not owned by the firm, while many physical resources are. However, the firm also uses many services from physical resources which it does not own. The accounting treatment for such services should, therefore, be the same as the treatment used for human resources.

Thus, human resource accounting should be classified as part of the continuing development of what may be called "future resource accounting," which attempts to deal with resources the entity expects to receive or deliver in the future. Present accounting handles future resources only to the extent that they are objects of half-executed contracts. Commitment accounting aims at recording executory agreements where neither party has performed its commitments.[8]

The attempt to extend the object of accounting to future resources need not be limited to executory contracts, if the boundary can be extended without a serious loss in data reliability.[9]

---

[7]See, for example, Brummet, Flamholtz and Pyle [1968].

[8]Undoubtedly, pension accounting is one of the most immediate problems that confronts accountants in developing future resource accounting. APB Opinion No. 8 attempts to lay a foundation for accounting practice. However, numerous issues must be resolved. See, for example, Hicks [1965] and Philips [1968].

[9]For further discussions on commitment accounting as to its theoretical explanation, see Ijiri, *Recognition of Contractual Rights and Obligations: An Exploratory Study of Conceptual Issues,* Financial Accounting Standards Board, 1980.

CAPITALIZATION OF
INTEREST

Economists consider there to be three factors of production—land, labor and capital—and any excess remaining after deducting the cost of these factors from revenue is considered to be rent or profit. Accountants have not followed the same path. Some accountants have determined a company's net income without deducting even the explicitly incurred cost of capital, i.e., interest, preferring instead to regard interest as a distribution of profit.[1] Most accountants, however, reckon net income after subtracting contractually incurred interest, but it is rare indeed to find company financial statements in which a notional charge for the cost of *all* creditor and equity capital is deducted prior to arriving at net income.

Apart from the difficulty of trying to reconcile economic principles with accounting principles, these differences can cause social and political problems. Such problems can arise because in certain industries "accounting profits" are reported which are regarded by some segments of society as being unconscionably large. In some cases high "accounting profits" are necessary to enable the enterprise to attract the necessary capital investment. If interest charges equal to the full cost of capital, regardless of its source, were to be treated as an expense in arriving at net income, the financial statements of companies in some industries would be marked in red.

Robert N. Anthony has long been a proponent of capitalizing interest on both creditor and equity funds, and associating the interest with revenue in the periods in

---

[1]William A. Paton is credited with developing the "entity" viewpoint in accounting. See his *Accounting Theory: With Special Reference to the Corporate Enterprise* (New York: The Ronald Press Company, 1922), especially Chapter XI, where Paton employs the term "net revenue" to signify net income. In 1957, a committee of the American Accounting Association determined "enterprise net income" prior to the subtraction of any interest charges: "Accounting and Reporting Standards for Corporate Financial Statements: 1957 Revision," *The Accounting Review* (October 1957), p. 540.

which the assets acquired with those funds are consumed in operations. American practice in general has been to treat interest on debt as a "period expense," which would affect net income in the fiscal period in which the interest actually accrues on the outstanding debt. In 1979, however, the FASB approved Statement No. 34, which requires that, for certain assets, the interest incurred on debt capital be capitalized. The qualifying assets are, in the main, self-constructed capital assets and assets held "for sale or lease that are constructed or otherwise produced as discrete projects (e.g., ships or real estate developments)."[2] The FASB would not alter the total amount of interest that may be deducted against revenues over the life of the enterprise—as the amount to be capitalized is limited to the interest actually incurred—but it would affect the year-to-year timing of the expense recognition of interest in companies' income statements. The standard does not address the important issues of the treatment of (1) interest associated with routinely produced inventories, standing tracts of timber, aging spirits, and other assets not comprehended by Statement No. 34, and (2) imputed interest on equity capital.

In the article included here Anthony makes the case for recognizing interest on equity as a cost of doing business. In his argument he claims that his proposal would increase the comparability of the income numbers reported by companies with different debt-equity ratios. Anthony recognizes that there may exist some difficulty in determining the cost of equity capital, but he does not believe the problem to be insurmountable.

When evaluating Anthony's argument, one should recall Thomas' discussion of allocation in Section 7 A. At the same time, it is well to invoke the observation (here paraphrased) by Sidney Davidson: Is it better to be vaguely right than to be precisely wrong?

BIBLIOGRAPHICAL NOTES

A fuller statement of Anthony's views may be found in the following volume:

Anthony, Robert N.: *Accounting for the Cost of Interest* (Lexington, MA: Lexington Books, 1975).

An early advocacy of including interest in the cost of production, a practice that was rejected by the American Institute, may be found in:

Scovell, Clinton H.: *Interest as a Cost* (New York: The Ronald Press Company, 1924).

[2]"Capitalization of Interest Cost," *Statement of Financial Accounting Standards No. 34* (Stamford, CT: FASB, October 1979), par. 9(b).

Equity Interest—Its Time Has Come

Robert N. Anthony
Harvard University

Informed readers understand what the numbers on a balance sheet mean—right? Wrong! I shall show that no explanation of the numbers now reported on the right-hand side is consistent with reality. However, with one change in accounting—the explicit recognition of equity interest cost—a meaningful balance sheet can be prepared. This change also would provide more useful information about an entity's performance, its assets and the sources of its funds.

THE PROBLEM

Do the items on the right-hand side of the balance sheet represent obligations, that is, claims against the assets? Some of them do, but others do not. Although most of the liabilities are claims, and the amount reported for preferred stock is sort of a claim, shareholder equity is not. Except by coincidence, shareholders will never claim or receive the amount reported as this equity. In a going concern, they have no claim at all unless the corporation is liquidated, but the balance sheet doesn't purport to state liquidation values.

Does the right-hand side report the sources of the entity's funds? This is closer to reality than the idea of a "claim." The liabilities do report the amount of funds furnished by various parties: lenders, vendors (in the form of accounts payable), employees (in the form of accrued salaries), even the government (in the form of deferred income taxes).

The shareholder equity section, however, doesn't report the amount of funds supplied by shareholders. Although the paid in capital item shows the amount shareholders supplied initially, the retained earnings number doesn't represent a shareholder contribution. "Earnings" were earned by the entity itself, not by the shareholders. The shareholders in a publicly owned corporation have little to say about what fraction of these earnings is retained. (The idea that shareholders "consented" to this retention is true but naïve.)

Moreover, the right-hand side of the balance sheet purports to make a basic distinction between liabilities and shareholder equity, a distinction so basic that the concepts for the measurement of income depend on it. Can an operational distinction be made? I don't think so. Financial Accounting Standards Board Concepts Statement No. 3, *Elements of Financial Statements of Business Enterprises,*[1] defines liabilities as future sacrifices arising from present obligations as a result of past

From *Journal of Accountancy* (December 1982), pp. 76–78, 80, 82, 84, 86, 88, 90, 92–93. Reprinted by permission of the American Institute of Certified Public Accountants. Copyright © 1982 by the American Institute of Certified Public Accountants, Inc.

[1]Financial Accounting Standards Board Concepts Statement No. 3, *Elements of Financial Statements of Business Enterprises* (Stamford, CT: FASB, 1980).

transactions or events. Unfortunately, this definition doesn't distinguish items that properly are included within the defined category from those that are outside it. This is an essential characteristic of any good definition.

Although bonds are classified as liabilities, many convertible bonds don't fit this definition of liabilities because there is no likelihood that the stated amount will ever be "sacrificed"; the bonds will be converted into stock. Conversely, redeemable preferred stock clearly is a liability under this definition, although it isn't treated as such in practice. The amount reported as deferred income taxes doesn't represent a probable future sacrifice of the stated amount.

THE SOLUTION

How can the right-hand side of the balance sheet be described in a meaningful way? The "sources of funds" idea is the most fruitful approach. Liabilities already reflect sources of funds. If the shareholder equity section could be reconstituted so that it also reports sources of funds, the right-hand side would report a conceptually consistent set of facts.

The desired result can be achieved by recognizing that there are three, rather than two, types of sources of funds: (1) liabilities; (2) funds supplied by shareholders, here labeled *shareholder equity*; and (3) funds generated by the entity's own efforts, here labeled *entity equity*.

Shareholder Equity

The amount of funds supplied by shareholders is greater than the amount the entity reports as paid-in capital. In addition to their direct contributions, shareholders also have furnished funds to the extent that the cost associated with the use of these funds hasn't been repaid to them in the form of dividends. I refer to the cost of using shareholder equity funds as equity interest. Unpaid equity interest is a source of funds, just like unpaid debt interest, but it appears nowhere on the balance sheet. The amount reported as shareholder equity should include both paid-in capital and unpaid equity interest.

Entity Equity

Both liabilities and shareholder equity represent funds supplied by outside parties. In addition to these external sources, a profitable entity also generates funds by its own operating activities. However, the amount of these internally generated funds isn't identified on the balance sheet. Retained earnings overstates this amount because the net income that adds to retained earnings overstates the entity's economic profitability; it omits the cost of equity interest. A new category is needed to report the amount of funds that the entity has generated through its own efforts after recovering all the associated costs. This category is entity equity.

Entity equity would report the cumulative amount of net incomes for all years to date.[2] Net income for a year would be the difference between revenues (including gains) and expenses (including losses and equity interest). Each year's net income would be added to entity equity, just as net income is added to retained earnings in current practice, but, because equity interest is recognized as a cost, the amount of entity equity would be much smaller than the amount of retained earnings as currently reported.

Recognition of Interest Cost

Both equity interest and debt interest are costs, and they should be accounted for just like other costs. Since interest is the cost of using funds for specified time periods, interest cost should be charged to cost objects in proportion to the funds used by cost objects. Specifically

1 Interest is an element of the cost of newly acquired plant and equipment (and is now treated as such under FASB Statement No. 34, *Capitalization of Interest Cost*[3]). The cost should include the interest cost of funds tied up during the construction period for self-constructed plant and the interest cost of advance payments or progress payments on purchased plant.

2 The interest cost of funds used during the production process is an element of product cost and should be assigned to products in the same way that depreciation on plant and equipment is assigned.

3 When assets are held in inventory for significant lengths of time, an interest cost is incurred that should be added to the cost of the inventory items. As used here, *inventory* is interpreted broadly to include projects, mineral reserves, timber, nursery stocks and similar assets as well as material, work in process and finished goods. (Interest is now included as a cost of projects under FASB Statement No. 34.)

4 That part of the interest cost of a period that isn't capitalized for one of the above reasons is an expense of the period, just as other non-capitalized overhead costs are expenses.

The mechanics of accounting for these items are described in the appendix, page 363.

The amount reported for inventory would be larger than the amount now reported because of the inclusion of an interest component. (It wouldn't be excessively large because the lower-of-cost-or-market rule limits the reported amount to the realizable value of the inventory.) The amount for plant would be similar to the amount reported under FASB Statement No. 34 except that the amount of interest charged to the plant account would not be limited to the total amount of debt interest. (Under current concepts, this limitation is necessary because, without the explicit recognition of equity interest, any excess of capitalized interest cost over debt interest would end up as an item of income. An entity cannot earn income by dealing with itself.)

---

²Entity equity also will increase by the amount of funds contributed for nonoperating purposes, such as additions to endowment and plant funds in nonprofit organizations. It will increase or decrease by entries such as the change in the valuation allowance of noncurrent equity securities.

³FASB Statement No. 34, *Capitalization of Interest Cost* (Stamford, CT: FASB, 1979).

Revised View of the Balance Sheet

With the proposed changes, each item on the balance sheet gives a meaningful message, as summarized in Exhibit 1, page 356. Each item on the right-hand side represents the amount of funds supplied by the indicated source. Liabilities are amounts supplied principally by creditors but also by the government and other nonowner parties. (The issue of how, if at all, the gross amounts should be discounted is outside the scope of this article.) Shareholder equity represents the amount supplied by equity investors, both directly (as paid-in capital) and indirectly (as that portion of equity interest cost that hasn't been paid them as dividends). Liabilities and shareholder equity together represent the funds supplied by outside parties. The new section, entity equity, represents the amount of funds generated by the entity's own activities.[4]

The items on the left-hand side of the balance sheet report the forms in which the capital acquired with these funds exists as of the balance sheet date. This is, I submit, what the amounts reported as assets actually represent in current practice.

Some have said that the net effect of these changes would be merely to divide the amount now labeled *retained earnings* into two parts. As the appendix demonstrates, this is by no means the case. The change would affect the amount reported as net income and the amounts reported for many asset items. Also, the sum of shareholder equity and entity equity would not correspond to the amount now reported as shareholder equity, nor would any items in these two categories add up to the amount now reported as retained earnings.

The capitalization of interest also would recognize certain economic realities that aren't acknowledged in current practice. Goods that are held for a long time in inventory do incur additional costs as do holding growing timber, mineral reserves or similar assets. These very real costs aren't currently recognized. One reason why the profits of petroleum companies appear to be "obscenely" high is that the costs of holding oil and gas reserves weren't recognized in earlier periods.

Revised View of the Income Statement

Recognition of equity interest as a cost would reduce the amount of net income, as compared with the amount currently reported. More importantly, it would increase the comparability of the income reported by companies with different debt-equity ratios and with assets that are held for different lengths of time. There is no way of taking the effect of these differences into account under current practice except by a laborious and inherently inexact adjustment of income statement amounts.

The proposed income statement also clarifies two concepts that are fuzzy in the current accounting model: (1) the meaning of income, or earnings, and (2) the meaning of financial capital maintenance.

The Income Concept.   FASB Concepts Statement No. 3 defines income as the increase in net assets during a period, with net assets being the difference between

---

[4]In the unusual case in which dividends exceeded the cumulative amount of equity interest cost, the excess would reduce the amount of entity equity.

EXHIBIT 1

SCHEMATIC BALANCE SHEET AS OF DECEMBER 31,19X1
(AS PROPOSED)

Assets*

Items on this side report the forms in which the entity's funds exist and the amount tied up in each form as of December 31, 19X1.

Assets consist of

1   Monetary assets
These are money or claims to specified amounts of money. The amounts are the present value of these claims.

2   Unexpired costs
These are nonmonetary assets to be used in future periods. The amounts are that part of these assets' costs that hasn't yet been charged as expenses.

3   Investments
These are investments in other entities. The amounts are the amounts originally invested plus unpaid debt and equity interest on these amounts.

Sources of funds

Items on this side report the sources of the entity's funds and the amount obtained from each source as of December 31, 19X1.

Fund sources consist of

1   Liabilities
Funds supplied by external parties other than equity investors. These parties include, among others
a   Lenders (amounts supplied directly plus unpaid debt interest).
b   Vendors.
c   Employees (accrued wages and unfunded benefits).
d   Government (deferred income taxes).

2   Shareholder equity
Funds supplied by equity investors (amounts supplied directly plus unpaid equity interest).

3   Entity equity
Funds obtained by the entity's own efforts. The cumulative difference through December 31, 19X1, between revenues (including gains) and expenses (including losses).

*For display, assets may be classified as either current or noncurrent.

---

assets and liabilities. The practical problem with this definition is that it requires a clear distinction between liabilities and shareholder equity. With the proliferation of financial instruments that are almost but not quite debt or almost but not quite equity, this line is almost impossible to draw. Under the proposed arrangement, however, income would be measured directly as the difference between revenues (including gains) and expenses (including losses). The problem of distinguishing between liabilities and equity doesn't arise.

Financial Capital Maintenance.   Viewing the income statement as an explanation of changes in entity equity also leads to a clear way of reflecting the central accounting concept of financial capital maintenance. The conventional income statement implies that an entity has maintained its capital if it earns at least zero net income. This isn't so. With zero income, an entity hasn't provided anything for the cost of using shareholder equity funds. Such an entity is not viable. The use of shareholder equity funds involves a cost, and the entity hasn't maintained its capital unless its revenues are at least equal to all items of cost, including this one.

MEASURING EQUITY INTEREST COST

Shareholders wouldn't furnish funds unless they expected to earn a return, and the expected return is the cost of using these funds. Critics assert that there is no reliable way of measuring this cost. (In most companies, dividends far understate the cost.)

The absence of an accurate measurement method doesn't, however, deter accountants from reporting such items as the cost of employee pension plans. Measuring this cost involves assumptions about the service life and mortality of plan participants, interest rates, inflation rates (and, hence, future benefits) and other factors. Differences in expert judgments can easily result in pension cost estimates for a given company that differ significantly.[5]

Although the shareholder equity interest rate should correspond conceptually to the cost of using shareholder equity funds, an accurate number can be found only in special circumstances, principally in rate-regulated companies whose securities are publicly traded. The capital asset pricing model has been used to estimate the cost of using shareholder equity funds. There are difficult conceptual and practical problems in applying this model to actively traded companies; for any company whose stock isn't actively traded, such an approach isn't possible.

The FASB has at least two practical alternatives, however. It could require either that each company use its own pretax debt interest rate as the rate for both debt and equity or that all companies use a rate obtained from some published source.

The first approach is implicit in FASB Statement No. 34. This standard specifies that the interest cost charged to qualifying assets be calculated by applying the entity's pretax debt interest rate to the funds used in acquiring such assets.

The other approach was used by the Cost Accounting Standards Board in Cost Accounting Standard (CAS) No. 414, *Cost of Money as an Element of the Cost of Facilities Capital.*[6] That standard states that the cost of using facilities capital is to be calculated at a rate specified semiannually by the U.S. Treasury. In contrast to the FASB approach, the CASB standard doesn't link the rate to a particular company's actual interest cost. It has the advantage, however, of being applicable even to companies that have no debt; moreover, no judgment is permitted in arriving at the rate used.

ADEQUACY OF THE APPROXIMATION

The funds used to finance assets are a mixture of debt and equity. The theoretically correct interest rate for measuring the cost of using these funds is an average of the aftertax debt and equity interest rates, weighted by the proportions of each. Using

---

[5]See, for example, Sara A. Lutz, "Pension Plan Disclosures: What They Mean," *Management Accounting,* April 1982, pp. 48–54. As a case in point, Lutz states that General Electric Company reported a pension liability on its balance sheet as of December 31, 1980, of $124 million, which it computed as the actuarial present value of accumulated benefits less net assets available. It disclosed in a note that the liability calculated by the actuarial method actually used by the company was $964 million. Use of the latter amount would have increased its liabilities and decreased its retained earnings by $840 million.

[6]Cost Accounting Standard No. 414, *Cost of Money as an Element of the Cost of Facilities Capital* (Washington, D.C.: Cost Accounting Standards Board, 1976).

the pretax debt rate for both debt and equity, as required in FASB Statement No. 34, results in a satisfactory approximation of this ideal. The pretax debt rate overstates the real cost of the debt component, but it correspondingly understates the cost of the equity component.

These relationships can be illustrated by an example. Assume that a company obtains 40% of its permanent funds from debt and 60% from equity, that the pretax cost of debt is 12% and that the tax rate is 50%. The cost of equity funds is higher than the pretax cost of debt, but by an unknown amount. Assume that the equity cost, if it could be calculated, is 15%. The theoretically correct cost of using funds is then 11.4%, calculated as follows:

	Pretax cost	Aftertax cost	Weight	Weighted amount
Debt	12%	6%	4	2.4%
Equity	15	15	6	9.0
True interest cost				11.4%

In this example the pretax debt cost, 12%, is within six-tenths of a percentage point of the true interest cost of 11.4%. Exhibit 2, page 363, shows how closely the pretax debt rate approximates the theoretically correct rate under a variety of assumptions as to the mix of debt and equity capital and as to the spread between debt and equity interest costs.

In the great majority of companies, the proportion of debt is between 20% and 50% of total permanent funds, and in the great majority the risk premium for shareholder equity over debt is between two and four percentage points. For such companies, the use of a pretax debt rate produces a maximum error of two percentage points. This is less than the probable error (not the maximum error) inherent in the calculation of pension fund expenses.

Studies by J. W. Bartley and L. F. Davidson[7] show that small variations in the interest rate don't have a significant effect on inter-company comparisons in any case. A good approximation is preferable to assuming that equity interest cost is zero, which is the implication of current practice.

PRACTICAL ADVANTAGES

Accounting is supposed to report economic reality, and the basic reason for the proposed change is that it will lead to more realistic and more understandable financial statements. For example, many readers think that "net worth" reports what the company is worth. Many others don't realize that reported income greatly overstates the real profitability of a company. Practical people may regard this as merely a theoretical point, however, and for them several eminently practical consequences are described briefly in this section.

[7]J. W. Bartley and L. F. Davidson, "Accounting for the Cost of Capital: An Empirical Examination" (University of North Carolina Working Paper, March 1980).

EXHIBIT 2

DIFFERENCE BETWEEN TRUE INTEREST COST AND PRETAX DEBT COST OF 12% UNDER VARIOUS ASSUMPTIONS

Assumed percent of debt	Assumed equity cost			
	14%	16%	18%	20%
10%	−1.2	−3.0	−4.8	−6.6
			*	
20	− .4	−2.0	−3.6	−5.2
30	.4	−1.0	−2.4	−3.8
40	1.2	1.0	−1.2	−2.4
50	2.0	1.0	0	−1.0
60	2.8	2.0	1.2	.4
70	3.6	3.0	2.4	1.8
80	4.4	4.0	3.6	3.2
90	5.2	5.0	4.8	4.6

Example

Assume 10% debt (90% equity) and 14% true cost of equity:

	Aftertax cost	Weight	Weighted percentage
Debt	6%	.1	0.6
Equity	14	.9	12.6
Actual cost			13.2
Pretax debt cost			12.0
Understatement of actual cost			1.2

*The capital structure of most companies is within this box.

Comparability

If two companies differ in their debt-equity ratios but otherwise are identical, under current practice the company with more debt will report lower net income than the other company because the amount of debt interest is reported as a cost while the amount of equity interest isn't reported at all. Because interest is not a component of production cost, a company with a large amount of capital tied up in plant understates its inventory and hence overstates its income compared with a company that is less capital-intensive. Similarly, companies with low inventory turnover, or with large mineral reserves, growing timber and other assets that require the use of much capital, understate the real cost of these assets and correspondingly overstate income.

Some financial analysts attempt to adjust the financial statements to allow for these differences, but the process is complicated and the results are crude at best. Recognition of equity interest automatically makes these adjustments and therefore improves the comparability of financial statements. Several studies show that the explicit recognition of equity interest makes a significant difference in reported net income.

D. W. Young reconstructed the financial statements of three timber companies, going back at least 17 years, to recognize the cost of interest tied up in growing timber and to recognize equity interest as a period expense.[8] The effect was to increase the reported ending value of timberland by 83%, 46% and 50% for the three companies and to reduce their reported total income for the period by 60%, 51% and 176%. Analysts could have arrived at a similar conclusion only by repeating this complicated year-by-year analysis.

J. A. Hayes adjusted the 1970 financial statements of 22 integrated oil companies to incorporate interest as a cost.[9] The change in their reported net income ranged from +11% to -292%. A decrease occurred in most cases, but other than that there was no consistent pattern to these changes.

C. J. Casey adjusted the 1974 retained earnings amounts of 189 companies in 16 industries.[10] There was no consistent pattern to the revised numbers, either across industries or within an industry.

Studies such as the above are time-consuming and, in the absence of detailed data, assumptions have to be made about some of the numbers. They are therefore approximations, but they are better approximations than analysts are likely to make, given the constraints on their time. In any event, analysts shouldn't be required to make these adjustments; accountants should report the appropriate numbers in the financial statements.

Correspondence With Investors' Decisions

The studies described above demonstrate that the inclusion of interest as a cost has a significant effect on reported income, assets and retained earnings. They don't by themselves demonstrate that the adjusted numbers are better. Such a conclusion is supported by studies made by J. W. Bartley and by J. W. Bartley and L. F. Davidson.[11] These studies tested whether income as conventionally reported corresponds more closely to the actual behavior of stock market prices than income as adjusted for equity interest. The capital asset pricing model was used, and it was applied to 200 companies in one study and to 210 companies (over a period of 13 years) in the other. The results indicate that, judged by the behavior of stock market prices, investors do tend to allow for the effect of equity interest in the price they pay for stock.

[8] D. W. Young, "Accounting for the Cost of Interest: Implications for the Timber Industry," *Accounting Review*, October 1976, pp. 788–799.

[9] J. A. Hayes and R. N. Anthony, "Accounting for the Cost of Interest" (Harvard Graduate School of Business Administration, Working Paper HBS 75–47, 1975).

[10] C. J. Casey, "Capitalization of Interest Costs: Empirical Evidence of the Effect on Financial Statements" (Harvard Graduate School of Business Administration, Working Paper HBS 78–59, 1978).

[11] J. W. Bartley, "Accounting for the Cost of Capital and the Assessment of Market Risk" (Paper presented at the American Accounting Association Annual Meeting, Boston, Massachusetts, August 1980). Bartley and Davidson, "Accounting for the Cost of Capital: An Empirical Examination."

Income Tax Implications

Debt interest is allowed as a deductible expense on corporate income tax returns, but equity interest is not. The effect is to encourage the use of debt financing and to penalize equity financing. Since companies must maintain a prudent debt-equity ratio, the equity penalty inhibits a company's willingness to raise equity capital, hurts new and growing companies and reduces the total amount of capital formation in the economy. The drying up of equity capital formation is a serious problem.

Furthermore, the different tax treatment of debt interest and equity interest encourages companies to devise securities that are almost like equity but that nevertheless qualify as debt. The Internal Revenue Service has wrestled for years with the problem of drawing a line between these two sources of capital but with no success.

Recognition of equity interest as a deductible expense on the corporate income tax return would solve all these problems. Influential people in Congress recognize this fact, but they are unwilling to advocate the change. They say, "How can you expect us to recognize equity interest for income tax purposes when the accounting profession won't recognize it for financial reporting purposes?" This is a reasonable question.[12]

Consistency With Management Accounting

Many companies recognize equity interest as a cost in measuring the profitability of profit centers. Top management wants profit center managers to understand that no real profit has been earned until equity interest has been recouped.

Moreover, explicit recognition of equity interest cures a serious problem that can arise under conventional accounting. Assume a company accepts capital expenditure projects if the time-adjusted rate of return is at least 15%. If a proposed project requires an investment of $1,000 and is estimated to produce earnings of $300 a year for five years, it should be accepted; the time-adjusted return on such a project is slightly more than 15%. If such an investment is accepted, however, and if straight-line depreciation of $200 a year is charged, reported income in the first year will increase by only $100 ($300–$200), which indicates a return of only 10% ($100 ÷ $1,000).

Conventional accounting always understates the true return in the early years and overstates the true return in the later years. Managers know this, and, if their performances are measured on the conventional basis, they are reluctant to propose an investment that reduces next year's reported profits, even though the investment is worthwhile. Recognition of equity interest, together with annuity depreciation, solves this problem. For the above example, this method reports a profit, after allowing for both interest and depreciation, every year.

Investors focus on reported net income, however, and many companies won't use for internal purposes a practice that gives a different result from that reported on the published income statement.

---

[12]For a discussion of the advantages of allowing equity interest as a tax-deductible expense, compared with other proposals for correcting this inequity, see R. N. Anthony, "Recognizing the Cost of Interest on Equity," *Harvard Business Review,* January-February 1982, pp. 91–95.

Consistency With Nonbusiness Accounting

A nonbusiness organization doesn't ordinarily obtain capital from equity investors, and its revenue therefore needn't provide for the recovery of equity interest. If businesses included equity interest as a cost, their reported net income would be comparable to that of nonbusiness organizations.

Many government-controlled organizations, especially in Europe and including those in the Soviet Union, do have equity capital and do record the interest on that capital as a cost. There are practical advantages in having a single set of accounting principles applying to all organizations—business and nonbusiness, in the U.S. and elsewhere.

Legitimacy of Interest

Until a decade or so ago, the federal government maintained that interest wasn't a cost, except in public utility rate making. Consequently, governmental contractors couldn't recover interest costs, as such, in cost-reimbursement contracts. This attitude is changing. Interest on capital tied up in plant is specifically allowed by CASs No. 414 and No. 417, *Cost of Money as an Element of the Cost of Capital Assets Under Construction.*[13] Office of Management and Budget (OMB) Circular A-21, *Cost Principles for Educational Institutions,* [14] was revised in 1982 to provide for partial recognition of interest as a cost. OMB Circular A-87, *Cost Principles for State and Local Governments,*[15] was revised in 1980 to permit interest as an element of the cost of using buildings. Medicare and Medicaid regulations permit the recovery of debt interest and, in some circumstances, equity interest by health care providers. However, OMB Circular A-122, *Cost Principles for Nonprofit Organizations,*[16] doesn't permit interest as an allowable cost.[17]

Thus, the government is gradually changing its long-standing opposition to the recognition of interest. A financial accounting standard requiring such recognition would give impetus to this movement.

CONCLUSION

Full recognition of equity interest as an element of cost and of entity equity as a source of funds will require major changes in accounting, probably too drastic to be

---

[13]CAS No. 417, *Cost of Money as an Element of the Cost of Capital Assets Under Construction* (Washington, DC: CASB, 1980).

[14]Office of Management and Budget Circular A-21, *Cost Principles for Educational Institutions* (Washington, DC: OMB, 1979).

[15]OMB Circular A-87, *Cost Principles for State and Local Governments* (Washington, DC: OMB, 1981).

[16]OMB Circular A-122, *Cost Principles for Nonprofit Organizations* (Washington, DC: OMB, 1980).

[17]For an excellent description of the historical development and current status of interest recognition in contracts of all types, see the 130-page opinion in the *Pennsylvania Blue Shield* case (ASBCA No. 21113), July 20, 1982. The traditional attitude about interest is in 28 U.S.C. section 2516(a): "Interest on a claim against the United States shall be allowed in a judgment of the Court of Claims only under a contract or Act of Congress expressly providing for payment thereof."

adopted all at once. The FASB's first step in this direction was Statement No. 34. Its next step should be to incorporate interest, on both debt and equity, as an element of cost in long-lived inventories, including growing timber, petroleum and other mineral reserves and nursery stocks.

The final step, which should be salable within a few years, is to recognize equity interest as a cost whenever it is appropriate and to reconstruct the right-hand side of the balance sheet so that unpaid equity interest is reported separately from the equity that the entity has generated through its own efforts. Opposition can be expected from those who believe that (1) the change is of no consequence or (2) there is no satisfactory way of measuring equity interest cost. I have tried to show that neither of these objections is valid.

APPENDIX: Accounting Procedures and Their Effect on the Financial Statements

This appendix describes the mechanics of accounting for the cost of interest and contrasts financial statements prepared on the basis of this accounting with those prepared in accordance with current practice. It is based on Chapter 7 of my book *Accounting for the Cost of Interest* (Lexington, MA: D. C. Heath and Company, 1975), modified to incorporate improvements that have been suggested since the publication of that book.

THE INTEREST POOL

Think of an "interest pool" account that is analogous to the conventional overhead pool. Elements of interest cost are debited to the interest pool account, and the total amount accumulated in it during an accounting period is allocated to various asset and expense accounts. Assume that entries to the interest pool account for 19XI are as follows (omitting $000 or $000,000, as you wish):

Interest pool			
Debits		**Credits**	
Debt		To cost of sales	$32
Interest	$25	To inventory	8
Equity		To plant	4
interest	35	To general expense	16
Total	$60	Total	$60

Debits to the Interest Pool

Debt interest ($25) is the actual amount of debt interest cost incurred during the year.

Equity interest ($35) is the cost of using shareholder equity funds. The amount is calculated by applying a rate to the amount of shareholder equity. The $35 is credited to shareholder equity.

The rate is here assumed to be 10%, the same as the pretax rate for long-term debt. (Alternatively, this rate might be designated by the Financial Accounting Standards Board.)

The amount is here taken as the amount of shareholder equity at the beginning of the year. It would be increased if new shareholder equity funds were obtained during the year. Conceivably, it could be adjusted by the difference between additions (equity interest) and subtractions (dividends) during the year; however, this refinement, which is analogous to compound interest, probably isn't warranted.

An unsettled point is whether this rate should be applied to entity equity funds as well as to shareholder equity funds. Such a treatment assumes that there is a cost of holding entity funds, which some people dispute. On the other hand, it can be argued that there is an opportunity cost of investing entity equity funds in a given project. The counter to this argument is that accounting doesn't recognize opportunity costs.

Interest Chargeout Rate

Interest is charged to cost objects at a rate similar to an overhead rate. The rate is established at the beginning of the year by dividing the estimated interest cost ($60) by the estimated average amount of capital employed during the year. It is assumed here that the average capital employed during 19XI was as follows:

Inventory	$105
Other current assets	168
Plant under construction	44
Other assets (at book value)	350
Total capital employed	$667

These average asset levels are estimated in a manner similar to that used in developing the basis of overhead allocations.

The allocation rate is therefore

$$\frac{\text{Annual interest cost}}{\text{Capital employed}} = \frac{\$\ 60}{\$667} = 9\%$$

This 9% rate is less than the assumed debt and equity interest rate because some funds (such as accounts payable) are obtained at zero explicit interest cost.

A good conceptual case can be made for establishing two allocation rates, one for current assets and a higher rate for noncurrent assets, which have a lower turnover and hence a higher risk exposure. This possible refinement is omitted here.

Charges to Cost Objects

The principal items to which an interest cost is charged are inventory, plant under construction and expense.

Inventory ($40).   Interest is a component of production cost. It is allocated to products in the same way that depreciation is charged. In most circumstances, the best basis of allocation is the sum of annual interest cost and annuity depreciation, which is a level total each year. An interest charge also is added to the cost of products that remain in inventory for a relatively long time. (For items that turn over rapidly, the charge would be immaterial.) *Inventory* is used here in a broad sense to include mineral reserves, growing timber and nursery stock, and projects in process, such as motion picture films and real estate developments.

Plant Under Construction ($4).   Interest is a component of the cost of constructing plant. It is charged to construction in progress in the manner prescribed in FASB Statement No. 34, *Capitalization of Interest Cost.*[1] No interest is added to plant account after the plant goes on stream. The cost of using the funds committed to the plant is an element of the inventory cost (and eventually cost of sales) of products produced in the plant.

Expense ($16).   The balance in the interest pool account, after the above charges have been made, is an expense of the period. The amount of interest associated with the capital used in marketing, administrative and other nonmanufacturing activities could be charged as a cost of these activities, but the effect on net income is the same whether interest expense is shown separately or charged to these cost objects.

FINANCIAL STATEMENTS

Table 1, page 366 shows how financial statements will look when interest is recognized as a cost, compared with those prepared according to current practice. The adjustments assume that this is the first year under the new system. Differences between the two sets of statements and the effect on future years are explained below.

Operating Statement

Cost of sales on the operating statement increases by the amount of the interest component. The total interest cost charged to production was $40, of which $8 remains in inventory, so the additional cost of sales is $32. In subsequent years the amount reported as cost of sales will be higher than under current practice, by the amount of the interest component.

Selling, general and administrative expense decreases by $9. This is the net of two

[1]Financial Accounting Standards Board Statement No. 34, *Capitalization of Interest Cost* (Stamford, CT: FASB, 1979).

TABLE 1

Current and Proposed Financial Statements

	As now reported		As proposed	
Operating statement, 19X1				
Sales revenue		$1,000		$1,000
Cost of sales	$700		$732	
Selling, general and administrative expense	220		211	
Income tax expense	40	960	40	983
Net income		$ 40		$ 17

Balance sheet, December 31, 19X1		
	Assets	Assets
Inventory	$135	$143
Plant and equipment (net)	300	304
Other assets	300	300
Total assets	$735	$747

	Equities	Sources of funds
Current liabilities	$115	$115
Long-term debt	250	250
Shareholder equity	370	365
Entity equity	*	17
Total		
	$735	$747

*No such item on current balance sheet.

items: (1) a decrease of $25 because debt interest, as such, is no longer charged; and (2) an increase of $16 representing the interest cost not charged to asset accounts.

Income tax expense is unchanged. It is assumed that, at least initially, equity interest won't be allowed as a tax deductible item.

Net income decreases by $23, primarily because equity interest is recognized as a cost. The decrease does not correspond to the amount of equity interest because some equity interest ends up in asset accounts. In subsequent years, the reported net income will be lower than is the case under current practice.

Balance Sheet

On the balance sheet, inventory increases by $8—the amount of interest cost charged to products that remain in inventory. In subsequent years the reported inventory amount will be higher than under current practice because of the inclusion of this cost element.

Plant increases by $4, the amount of interest capitalized in plant under construction.

On the present balance sheet, shareholder equity isn't separated from entity equity. In the proposed balance sheet, it is assumed, for simplicity, that entity equity at the beginning of the first year was zero; therefore, shareholder equity was $350. Changes in shareholder equity during the year are as follows:

	Present	Proposed	Difference
Beginning balance	$350	$350	$ 0
Net income	+40	*	–40
Equity interest	*	+35	+35
Dividends	–20	–20	0
Ending balance	$370	$365	$ –5

*Not included in shareholder equity

Since it is assumed that entity equity starts at zero, the balance at the end of the year is equal to the net income, $17. The balance in entity equity will increase in years in which there is a positive net income.

SECTION **SEVEN F**

RESEARCH &
DEVELOPMENT

The problems of accounting for research and development activities have been recognized as among the most complex accounting issues. The situation can be briefly described as one in which an enterprise engages in basic and applied research in order to develop new or improved products to enhance its competitive position in the marketplace. Any benefits to be derived from this activity would not be received until future years. In many cases, there is a high degree of uncertainty surrounding the future benefits. Will the new or improved product be a more effective competitor in the marketplace? Will there be increased profit resulting from the R&D activity? Over what period of time will any improvement in profitability be received? The incorrigible allocation problem is here demonstrated at its zenith.

Looking for a general solution to a problem that requires individual attention leads one to conclude either (1) that all costs associated with R&D should be capitalized and amortized over the future years when the benefits are expected or (2) that all costs associated with R&D should be written off when incurred because there is no defensible way to define the period over which the costs should be systematically and rationally amortized. In Statement of Financial Accounting Standards No. 2, the FASB chose the latter approach.

In "Accounting for Research and Development Costs," Harold Bierman, Jr. and Roland E. Dukes question the rationale of the FASB. They admit that the FASB solution may be the expedient one, but it is hardly defensible as good theory. They recognize the difficulty and arbitrariness of allocating the cost over several periods but find the FASB's alternative in conflict with the general principles of financial reporting. In Statement No. 4, the APB states, "The basic purpose of financial accounting and financial statements is to provide quantitative financial information about a business enterprise that is useful to statement users, particularly owners and

368

creditors, in making economic decisions."[1] Bierman and Dukes question whether this purpose is furthered with the adoption of SFAS No. 2.

Of course, a major issue when any accounting principle is adopted or an existing principle is changed is what the economic consequences of the change or adoption of the new principle are. In essence: What decisions, if any, will be different than they would have been if the change in accounting had not been made? In "The FASB, the SEC, and R&D," Bertrand Horwitz and Richard Kolodny attempt to assess the economic consequences of changing accounting practice with respect to the capitalization and amortization of research and development cost. There were assertions at the time that "affected firms would alter their behavior to 'cushion' the increased earnings volatility and lower earnings" likely to be caused by a requirement to expense all R&D cost. This study supports the prognosis that firms would adjust their behavior to the new standard, an economic consequence that may be in a direction counter to national policy. Specifically, the authors found in a sample of 43 small high technology firms that after the adoption of SFAS No. 2 the level of spending for research and development declined. A survey of key financial officers of similar firms confirms their finding of reduced R&D expenditures. The evidence here seems to indicate that the accounting rules in this case were not neutral, but indeed there were unfavorable consequences.

Additional research needs to be done to ascertain whether the consequences were short-lived or whether they have persisted over time.

BIBLIOGRAPHICAL NOTES

Two research studies undertaken for standard-setting bodies are the following:

Gellein, Oscar S. and Maurice S. Newman: *Accounting for Research and Development Expenditures,* Accounting Research Study No. 14 (New York: AICPA, 1973).

McGregor, Warren J.: *Accounting for Research and Development Costs,* Discussion Paper No. 5 (Melbourne, Australia: Australian Accounting Research Foundation, 1980).

An article in which the authors use an analytical framework from sociology and political science to gauge the degrees of power used by interested parties in the controversy over the U.K./Irish statement on research and development costs is:

Hope, Tony and Rob Gray: "Power and Policy Making: The Development of an R&D Standard," *Journal of Business Finance and Accounting* (Winter 1982), pp. 531–558.

[1]"Basic Concepts and Accounting Principles Underlying Financial Statements of Business Enterprises, *Statement of the Accounting Principles Board No. 4* (New York: AICPA, October 1970), par. 73.

Accounting for Research and Development Costs

Harold Bierman, Jr.
Cornell University

Roland E. Dukes
University of Washington

The accounting profession has four basic choices available as to the method of accounting for assets:

- Use cost of acquisition.
- Use value estimations.
- Use price level adjusted cost.
- Implicitly assume the value is zero and expense the costs associated with the acquisition of the asset.

In its Statement of Financial Accounting Standards No. 2, "Accounting for Research and Development Costs" (October 1974), the Financial Accounting Standards Board concludes that "all research and development costs encompassed by this Statement shall be charged to expense when incurred." This practice implicitly assumes the expected value of R&D is zero. The Board reached its conclusion as a result of a reasoning process in which several preliminary premises were accepted as true. It may be possible to conclude for pragmatic reasons that the expensing decision reached by the Board is a reasonable practice, but we object to the process the Board used in arriving at the conclusion that R&D should be expensed. Specifically, the following five factors that were offered by the Board as support for its conclusion will be considered:

- Uncertainty of future benefits.
- Lack of causal relationship between expenditures and benefits.
- R&D does not meet the accounting concept of an asset.
- Matching of revenues and expenses.
- Relevance of resulting information for investment and credit decisions.

Following are descriptions of these factors and evaluations of their relevance.

UNCERTAINTY OF FUTURE BENEFITS

The primary justification offered by the FASB[1] for expensing the R&D expenditures is the level of uncertainty associated with the benefits. It is argued that R&D expenditures have considerable risk where risk is defined as a large probability of failure for an individual project. In reaching its conclusion to expense R&D costs

From *The Journal of Accountancy* (April 1975), pp. 48–55. Reprinted by permission of the American Institute of Certified Public Accountants. Copyright © 1975 by the American Institute of Certified Public Accountants, Inc.

[1]Financial Accounting Standards Board, Statement of Financial Accounting Standards No. 2, "Accounting for Research and Development Costs" (Stamford, CT: FASB, 1974).

when incurred, the Board states (p. 15) that the "high degree of uncertainty about the future benefits of individual research and development projects" was a significant factor in reaching this conclusion. In elaborating on this conclusion, the Board cites several studies that indicate a high failure rate for research and development projects. Although the Statement is not specific on this point, it appears that because a large proportion of research and development projects are "failures," the Board concludes that all R&D should be treated as failures and expensed. There are several fallacies with this conclusion.

First, it is not clear that the risks and uncertainties of company-sponsored research and development are as formidable as corporate publicists and the references cited by the Board would have us believe. In 1963, Mansfield and Hamburger[2] studied 22 major firms in the chemical and petroleum industries and found that the bulk of the R&D projects carried out by these firms were relatively safe from a technical point of view. Most of the projects were regarded as having better than a 50–50 chance of technical success. In an analysis of 70 projects carried out in the central research and development laboratories of a leading electrical equipment manufacturing company, Mansfield and Brandenburg[3] found that in more than three-fourths of the cases, the ex ante probability of technical success had originally been estimated at .80 or higher, and only two projects had predicted success probabilities of less than .50. After the projects were completed, 44 percent were fully successful technically, and only 16 percent were unsuccessful because of unanticipated technical difficulties.

These findings are consistent with the hypothesis that business firms do not generally begin new product or process development projects until the principal technical uncertainties have been resolved through inexpensive research, conducted either by their own personnel or by outsiders. They are also consistent with the notion that managers are averse to risk and are reluctant to pursue high risk projects when their own reputations and the funds of the company are involved. On the other hand, research and development projects sponsored by the federal government are likely to be more risky than industrial R&D because the federal government bears the financial risk. This point is also made by Scherer.[4]

Second, one has to be careful as to the definition of risk. Because of the historically high profitability of R&D efforts, it may well be that risk defined in terms of expected loss or expected monetary value may be less than many types of plant and equipment expenditures (the different tax treatments afforded the different types of expenditures also affect risk).

Bailey,[5] who computed the rate of return from R&D expenditures in the U.S. pharmaceutical industry, found a rate of return (pretax) of 35 percent in 1954 and 25 percent in 1961. Bailey explains the decrease in rate of return as being the result of

[2]E. Mansfield, "Industrial Research and Development: Characteristics, Costs, and the Diffusion of Results," *American Economic Review,* May 1969, p. 65.

[3]E. Mansfield, *Industrial Research and Technological Innovation* (New York: Norton, 1969).

[4]F. M. Scherer, *Industrial Market Structure and Economic Performance* (Chicago: Rand McNally, 1970), pp. 354–56.

[5]Martin Neil Bailey, "Research and Development Costs and Returns: The U.S. Pharmaceutical Industry," *Journal of Political Economy,* January-February 1972, pp. 70–85.

increased R&D expenditures (170 percent increase between 1954 and 1961) as firms realized the high profitability of R&D in this area. Bailey does forecast decreasing returns in this industry after 1962 as a result of more stringent regulations associated with introducing new products and warns of the difficulty of isolating causal relationships. Also, the measurement of profitability of R&D is difficult because there are many factors affecting earnings. But if Bailey is close to being correct, there may be less risk with R&D expenditures (if a large amount of expenditures are made, spread over a large number of projects) than with plant and equipment.

Bailey's findings are reinforced by studies by Minasian and Mansfield. Mansfield[6] found that "among the petroleum firms, regardless of whether technical change was capital-embodied or organizational, the marginal rates of return average about 40–60 percent." He found other industries also high, but not as high as for the period 1946–62. Minasian,[7] in studying firms in the chemical industry (1948–57), found the gross return on research and development to be 54 percent as compared to 9 percent for the physical capital. While Minasian defines this as a social return and not a private return, it is again evident that R&D has been very profitable. Moreover, the expected profitability affects the risk of the expenditure.

This is inconsistent with the definition of risk apparently used by the FASB, which defines risk only in terms of probability of failure. The Board does not consider the reduction in uncertainty that can be achieved by pursuing a portfolio of research and development projects. A simple example will help to illustrate this point. Suppose a firm is pursuing 100 independent R&D projects. For computational ease, we assume each project costs $10,000, that each has a probability of "success" of .10 and a probability of "failure" of .90. Success results in a $200,000 present value accruing to the firm; failure results in no benefits.

Each individual project has 1 chance in 10 of being successful; this is consistent with the point made by the Board that for any individual project the probability that it will generate future benefits for the firm seems dismally low. However, the more important question is, what is the probability of making a profit from the portfolio of projects? Since each R&D project represents an independent event with two possible outcomes, the number of successes in 100 trials is a random variable whose distribution is the binomial distribution. For this example, the probability that there will be one or more successes is equal to .99997.[8] That is, the firm is virtually assured that it will realize 1 or more successes from a portfolio of 100 R&D projects.[9] This is a substantial reduction in uncertainty when compared to the .10 probability of success attached to individual projects. Moreover, the expected

[6]E. Mansfield, "Rates of Return from Industrial Research and Development," *American Economic Review,* May 1965, pp. 310–22.

[7]Jora R. Minasian, "Research and Development, Production Functions, and Rates of Return," *American Economic Review,* May 1969, pp. 80–85.

[8]The probability that there will be 1 or more successes is equal to 1 minus the probability there will be zero successes. The probability of zero success is given as

$$P \text{ (0 successes)} = \frac{100!}{0! \ 100!} \ [.10]^0 [.90]^{100} = .00003$$

[9]If the probability of success for an individual project is .05, .02, or .01, then the portfolio probabilities of one or more successes are .989, .905, and .633, respectively.

future benefits from the portfolio is $2 million.[10] Thus, while the Board claims a large probability of failure associated with individual projects, it fails to consider the change in the uncertainty (defined in terms of probability of failure) associated with undertaking a portfolio of independent R&D projects.

In the above example, the $20,000 expected future benefit of each project (equal to its probability of success, .10, times the expected future benefit of success, $200,000) is greater than the $10,000 cost of each project. The expected payoff from the portfolio is twice the total cost of $1 million for all 100 research and development projects. To break even, the firm needs 5 or more successes out of 100 projects, and there is .9763 probability of this happening. Thus, rather than .10 probability of success (defined in terms of the individual project), there is .9763 probability of success (defined in terms of the profitability of the portfolio).

Since the firm does not know before it investigates which of the projects will be successful, the appropriate cost of finding the successful projects is the total cost of pursuing the portfolio of projects. Bierman, Dukes and Dyckman[11] discuss this point further with specific reference to accounting for exploration costs in the petroleum industry.

The FASB cites the low probability of success with new products. We argue that this low probability has not been proved. Moreover, it is not a valid measure of risk. The Board needs to define uncertainty and risk more exactly before risk of R&D can be offered as the reason for an accounting treatment. Even if it were agreed that R&D had more risk (a position we do not accept), it is still not clear that this leads to the policy conclusion of expensing the costs of R&D.

There is some uncertainty of future benefits associated with every asset currently recorded on balance sheets. Even the future real benefits that can be realized from holding cash are uncertain, especially during these times of "double-digit" inflation. More analogous to research and development, there is a high degree of uncertainty associated with investments in long-lived plant and equipment, especially in fields where the assets are extremely specialized in nature and where there is rapid technological advance. It is not clear that investments in these kinds of projects are any less uncertain in terms of the probability of making a profit than an investment in a portfolio of R&D projects. If both are uncertain, why should one be recorded differently from the other? It does not appear that using the "degree of uncertainty of future benefits" is an appropriate factor or criterion to employ in helping to resolve this issue. So long as the project has a net positive expected future benefit,

---

[10]The expected present value from the portfolio is the sum of the expected payoffs for the individual projects:

$$\text{Expected present value from portfolio} = \sum_{i=1}^{100} \text{Expected present value of project i}$$

$$= \sum_{i=1}^{100} [(.10)(\$200,000) + (.90)(0)]$$

$$= 100\ (\$20,000) = \$2,000,000$$

[11]Harold Bierman, Jr., Roland E. Dukes and Thomas R. Dyckman, "Financial Reporting in the Petroleum Industry," JofA, Oct. 74, pp. 58–64.

uncertainty should not lead automatically to a conclusion that cost factors should be expensed.

We argue that at the portfolio level there is the possibility of a substantial reduction in uncertainty vis-à-vis the individual project level. Moreover, expected future benefits will in general be equal to or greater than the total cost of pursuing the research and development portfolio. Thus, the existence of a probability of failure cannot be used to justify the expensing of R&D expenditures.[12]

LACK OF CAUSAL RELATION BETWEEN EXPENDITURES AND BENEFITS

In its Statement the FASB cites (p. 16) three empirical research studies that "generally failed to find a significant correlation between research and development expenditures and increased future benefits as measured by subsequent sales, earnings or share of industry sales." The Board does not specify what conclusion is to be drawn regarding the accounting treatment of research and development costs from the above statement, although it appears to consider this lack of evidence of a direct relationship between research and development costs and specific future revenue as an important factor in its conclusions.

Several points can be made regarding this factor. First, even though the studies cited by the Board were unable to detect a significant relationship between costs of research and subsequent benefits, this does not imply that such a relationship does not exist. That is, when logical deductive reasoning leads to a hypothesized relationship that cannot subsequently be empirically observed, the scientist will generally "suspend judgment" regarding the hypothesis rather than embrace the alternative hypothesis that no relationship exists. It is more appropriate to draw conclusions upon the observation of the phenomena under study rather than upon the inability to observe the phenomena.

Second, considerable research in economics does provide support for the hypothesis that research and development efforts do produce benefits for the firm. Scherer[13] reviews much of this literature when he discusses the relationship between market structures and technological innovation. Subsequent to the Scherer review, several additional studies have contributed to the evidence on the relationship between research and development and various measures of benefit to the firm. Bailey[14] found pretax rates of return from investments in research and development in the vicinity of 25 to 35 percent for the pharmaceutical firms included in his study. He also found that "earnings of the companies over time are clearly related to the

---

[12]An irrelevant argument is offered in paragraph 52 of the FASB Statement. It is stated that companies have the philosophy that "research and development expenditures are intended to be recovered by current revenues rather than by revenues from new product." This philosophy (if it does exist) should in no way affect the accounting for R&D. In addition, in evaluating new projects any sensible method of evaluation will consider the revenue (benefits) associated with the new projects. The current product revenues are irrelevant to the decision to go ahead except to the extent that they supply the cash that is used for the financing of the R&D.

[13]Scherer, especially Chapters 15 and 16.

[14]Bailey.

number of patents held by the company." The number of patents held by a firm is an often-used surrogate for research output. In a related study, Angilley[15] found pharmaceutical sales to be significantly related to "innovative output," where innovative output was defined in terms of several measures of new pharmaceutical compounds produced by the company. Equally important, he found that his measures of innovative output were all significantly related to the amount of research and development expenditures incurred by the firm. In a more recent study, Grabowski and Mueller[16] investigated the rates of return on investments in physical capital, in research and development and in advertising. They conclude that their result "indicates that R&D does increase the profitability of the firm over competitive levels." For the 86 firms included in their sample, "additional R&D did increase the rate of return on total capital."

Given this brief review of some of the contrary evidence, the FASB's statement (p. 16) that "a direct relationship between research and development costs and specific revenue generally has not been demonstrated . . . " is confusing and somewhat misleading. Clearly, management expects to generate positive returns from R&D. Moreover, the expected profit from large, expensive research and development portfolios is larger than the expected benefits from smaller, less costly portfolios of research and development. An inexpensive plant may turn out to be more profitable than a much more expensive plant, but this outcome does not "prove" that the plants' costs should have been expensed in both cases.

It is probably true that there is a higher variance of benefits arising from the research and development expenditures. But higher variance does not necessarily imply a higher risk is associated with such expenditures (the capital asset pricing model of Sharpe[17] is of relevance here). Applying the capital asset pricing model, the important measure of risk is the covariability of expected return between the individual project and the overall portfolio of securities. Expenditures on R&D to develop new products or improve old ones are likely to be less correlated with market returns than expenditures for expansion into new markets or expanding market capacity. Thus, it seems likely that many R&D expenditures will have relatively desirable risk characteristics compared to expenditures in physical capital.

In sum, it is incorrect to conclude that, because it has been difficult to observe a significant correlation between expenditures and subsequent benefits, future benefits are not generated by research and development expenditures. Moreover, considerable research does exist in which the findings support the hypothesis that research and development does generate substantive future benefits for the firm. While the Board may still determine that the expensing of research and development expenditures is an appropriate accounting policy, it is not clear that the lack of benefits argument is an appropriate supporting factor in this conclusion.

[15] Alan Angilley, "Returns to Scale in Research in the Ethical Pharmaceutical Industry: Some Further Empirical Evidence," *Journal of Industrial Economics,* December 1973, pp. 81–93.

[16] Henry Grabowski and Dennis Mueller, "Rates of Return on Corporate Investment, Research and Development and Advertising," unpublished working paper, Cornell University, 1974

[17] W. F. Sharpe, "Capital Asset Prices: A Theory of Market Equilibrium Under Conditions of Risk," *Journal of Finance,* September 1964, pp. 425–42.

THE ACCOUNTING CONCEPT OF AN ASSET

The Board appears to be close to requiring the capitalization of research and development when it describes (p. 17) economic resources as those scarce resources for which there is an "expectation of future benefits to the enterprise either through use or sale." While R&D would qualify using this definition, the Board then discusses the criteria of measurability. We argue that the cost of R&D is subject to reasonable measurement. However, the FASB states (p. 17)

> The criterion of measurability would require that a resource not be recognized as an asset for accounting purposes unless at the time it is acquired or developed its future economic benefits can be identified and objectively measured.

Can the economic benefits of an automobile plant be objectively measured at the time it is acquired? This criterion opens the door to the reclassification to expense of many "asset" types of expenditures.

Also, the values of many assets are relatively independent of their costs. A nonregulated pipeline immediately after it has been constructed has value that is independent of its cost. As soon as any cost is incurred, it is a sunk cost and is not price or value determining.

It is probably true that R&D ranks high in variance of relationship between cost and value on specific expenditures. The lack of a one-to-one relationship between benefits and costs tends to argue in favor of a value type of accounting. But if value is excluded from consideration, at least for now, and the choice is between zero (expensing) and cost, lacking other information cost will on the average be a better estimator of value than the zero asset value resulting from the expensing of R&D.[18]

EXPENSE RECOGNITION AND MATCHING

Surprisingly the matching of revenues and expenses of earning those revenues is used as an argument by the Board in favor of expensing R&D (p. 19) because of "the general lack of discernible future benefits at the time such costs are incurred...." The only reason R&D expenditures are made is to benefit future time periods by generating new revenues in those time periods. It is unlikely that R&D will increase the operating revenues of the immediate time period given the time necessary to implement R&D. To argue in favor of immediate expensing is to ignore completely one of the basic principles on which accounting stands—namely, the necessity of matching revenues and expenses. If the Board had chosen to argue that matching was not an important criterion (it wisely did not do so), then its conclusion might be understandable. But to argue that expensing of R&D is consistent with matching is a conclusion that is difficult to comprehend.

RELEVANCE OF RESULTING INFORMATION FOR INVEST- MENT AND CREDIT DECISIONS

In paragraph 50 of the Statement, the Board refers to APB Statement No. 4, which indicates that certain costs are immediately "recognized as expenses because allocating

---

[18] For an expansion on this point, see the article by Bierman, Dukes and Dyckman in the October *Journal of Accountancy.*

them to several accounting periods is considered to serve no useful purpose." Citing evidence of the high degree of uncertainty associated with research and development and the views of security analysts and other professional investors, the Board states that "capitalization of any research and development costs is not useful in assessment of the earnings potential of the enterprise." The Board concludes that "therefore, it is unlikely that the investor's ability to predict the return on his investment and the variability of that return would be enhanced by capitalization."

There are two points to be made regarding the above reasoning and conclusions. First, the usefulness of accounting data regarding the amount of research and development costs to investors is an empirically testable question. In a study related to this issue, Dukes[19] found that the amount of research and development cost incurred and expensed during the period was significantly related to the security price of the firm. All of the firms in the Dukes study followed the accounting policy of expensing research and development costs, yet results were consistent with investors making capitalization adjustments to research and development costs in estimating the future earnings potential of the firm. That is, the "research intensity" of the firm (more precisely, the research intensity of the industry in which a firm found itself) was a significant explanatory variable in explaining the market value of the firm.

The Dukes study suggests that capitalization may serve a useful purpose in aiding the investor to predict the future return of a security. At a minimum, the study provides support to the Board's conclusion that disclosure of the amount of research and development costs is information relevant to the investment decision.

A second significant issue deals with who would be served by the requirement that research and development costs be expensed. If the results of the Dukes study are accepted, then security price behavior is more closely related to earnings computed with research and development capitalized rather than expensed. It is probably reasonable to expect security analysts and other professional investors to be able to make adjusting calculations to the reported earnings numbers, where sufficient information is supplied to adjust the basic accounting data. One is less confident, however, about the ability of nonexpert investors to make the adjustments. For example, consider an investor who takes the accounting measures seriously and does not adjust the information, analyzing two firms both of which have reported earnings of $2 per share. However, one firm has expended (and expensed) $3 per share on R&D and the other firm has spent zero. The R&D firm would have had $5 per share of earnings if it had not purchased any R&D. The expensing of the R&D expenditures results in the two firms having the same earnings per share, thus implying equal value based on this one measure. These earnings are not comparable and the investor who views them as equivalent will be misled. There is another, related problem. Managers are very concerned with earnings per share, and they assume these numbers are used in the investment decision process. The first firm can stabilize its earnings at $2 per share by varying the amount of R&D it purchases.

---

[19]Roland E. Dukes, *Market Evaluation of Accounting Information: A Cross Sectional Test of Investor Response to Expensing Research and Development Expenditures,* unpublished Ph.D. dissertation, Stanford University, 1974.

Thus earnings become a function of decisions to buy or not to buy R&D. It is difficult to see why the decision to buy or not to buy R&D should affect the earnings of the current year. A loss firm can reduce its loss by $1 for $1 of R&D it stops buying. This is a relatively easy way to reduce losses. The result of expensing of R&D may distort corporate decision making and lead to faulty measure of income and changes in income through time.

CONCLUSIONS

The primary purpose of this critique is to question the rationale employed by the FASB in arriving at its conclusion. It may well be that requiring all firms to disclose the amount of their research and development costs and to expense these costs is the best feasible solution. Capitalizing of such costs may not be feasible because of attendant lawsuits when the R&D is found to have less value than the recorded cost. But the resulting practice should not then be justified on the grounds that it is good accounting theory.

Virtually every time an accountant records expenditures he or she runs the risk that a later development might, with the aid of hindsight, show that the recording was "wrong." The asset may turn out to be worth much less than cost. The obvious solution for avoiding this sort of situation and resulting criticisms is to expense all costs associated with the acquisition of assets where there is some significant probability that the asset will turn out to be worth less than the cost of the asset. This "conservative" approach to asset measurement is consistent with the Board's recommendation to expense R&D expenditures. The policy decision to expense R&D costs does not appear to be based on sound accounting theory but, rather, appears to be motivated by a desire to avoid the criticism and problems resulting from situations where, after the fact, an asset is found to be worth less than the amount reported by the accountant. It ignores completely the types of errors that arise from a systematic expense overstatement, income misstatement, asset understatement and stock equity understatement. Unfortunately, criticism and lawsuits may force the adoption of such conservative practices. The way to avoid criticism that past earnings and assets have been overstated is to expense all factors associated with assets whose value is uncertain. Such a solution, however, is really a way of avoiding responsibility and is a too easy solution to an extremely difficult problem. The accountant does exercise judgment; he is an estimator and should be willing to face up to the existence of uncertainty, rather than expensing items because their ultimate value is difficult to forecast at the time the cost is incurred.

Theoretically, the accountant should provide the information most useful to society, considering the costs and benefits of the alternative accounting policies. However, the measurement of these costs and benefits is extremely difficult. Currently, all we can do is offer qualitative evaluations of alternatives rather than explicit measures.

However, Dukes[20] has offered empirical evidence of the importance of the disclosure of R&D expenditures. This evidence supports the Board's recommendation

[20] Ibid.

that more information relative to the magnitude of R&D expenditures be disclosed. Whatever accounting procedure is finally adopted, the disclosure of the amounts of expenditures by year will enable the analyst using the information to make the adjustments that he sees fit. If one accepts the hypothesis that capital markets are efficient in the processing of information, disclosure of the amount of the research and development expenditure is an extremely important first step. Given the basic data regarding the amount of the expenditure, an assumption of efficient capital markets implies market prices will reflect appropriate adjustments to the reported accounting numbers. The Dukes study reports findings consistent with this conclusion. However, we are not suggesting that the ability of the market to digest data should be used as a justification for neglecting accounting practices. In the first place, the adjustment process has a cost. Second, there are many other uses of accounting data besides financial analysis for the evaluation of common stock.

When a firm suffers economic difficulty, it is likely that the accounting (book) value of its assets will exceed their economic value. Technological and social change can cause assets to lose value suddenly. It is virtually impossible for the accountant to anticipate and report these value changes and at the same time use cost-based accounting principles of asset and income measurement in a theoretically correct manner. It would be possible to expense all cost factors whose benefit stream has an element of risk, but this would result in reports that were essentially cash flow statements. The income statement prepared in accordance with theoretically correct accrual concepts is an extremely important report. While it is true that later events may indicate that estimated writeoffs of assets were too rapid or not rapid enough, the accountant has an obligation to attempt to estimate the expenses of earning the revenues of a period rather than reporting as expenses the expenditures made during the period. From the point of view of accounting theory, the expenditures of R&D, which are made in the expectation of benefiting future periods, should not be written off against the revenues of the present period. Justification for such practice must be found elsewhere, if it is to be found.

The FASB, the SEC, and R&D

Bertrand Horwitz
State University of New York at Binghamton

Richard Kolodny
University of Maryland

INTRODUCTION

Until recently, there has been little concern about the possible consequences of mandated changes in the measurement rules used in external financial reporting. In fact, except for discussion of the alleged, but unsupported, consequences of the proposal to mandate use of the deferral method for reporting the investment tax credit in the 1960s, there was not much serious debate about the economic effects of involuntary changes in measurement rules before the public hearings held in 1978 by the Securities and Exchange Commission (SEC). The particular subject of those hearings was the appropriate accounting method for reporting exploration and development costs in the oil and gas industry, but a significant underlying question was whether mandating a uniform reporting rule could produce adverse economic effects.

The subject of this paper is the economic consequences of a rule established by the Financial Accounting Standards Board (FASB) in 1974 for reporting research and development expenditures. The rule, Financial Accounting Standard No. 2, *Accounting for Research and Development Costs,* became effective January 1, 1975. Subsequently, in October, 1975, it was adopted by the SEC in its Accounting Series Release No. 178. The rule required that public and private companies issuing certified financial statements record all outlays of R&D as expenses in the year incurred, regardless of the method voluntarily chosen before the rule. Banned by the rule was the option of capitalizing R&D outlays. Most of the companies previously using the capitalization (deferral) method and, therefore, affected by the rule were small firms whose securities were traded over the counter.

Unlike the R&D rule, the proposals to mandate the deferral method for reporting the tax savings of the investment credit and to mandate a single method (expensing) for reporting exploration and development costs were not enacted because of claimed economic consequences. The adoption of No. 2 permitted a "laboratory experiment" to test whether this rule influenced the R&D investment decisions of affected firms. Aside from the importance of attempting to answer the general question about the economic impact of a mandated rule change, it is important to

From *The Bell Journal of Economics* (Spring 1981), pp. 249–262. Reprinted by permission of *The Bell Journal of Economics.* Copyright © 1981.

This study was partially supported by the National Science Foundation, Grant PRA 78–21782. The findings, opinions, and conclusions are those of the authors and do not necessarily represent the views of the Foundation. The authors acknowledge the helpful comments of the Editorial Board and an anonymous referee.

ascertain what, if any, specific effects a measurement rule change has on company-sponsored R&D expenditures because of the crucial role R&D plays in determining economic growth and productivity.

Evidence, tests, and conclusions related to this issue are presented below. These are based on our empirical research, a summary of which appears in Section 5. Strong doubts are expressed there about the neutrality of the expense-only rule for R&D. Both the background (Section 2) and a discussion of the reasons for possible effects (Section 3) provide preliminary material for the empirical sections.

BACKGROUND

The question of whether any "harm" is likely to result from requiring additional disclosure or fixing single measurement rules has become increasingly important against a background of rising concern with the impact of government regulation on the allocation of resources. Although much of the concern about regulation, and the movement toward requiring agencies to issue economic impact statements, have been directed at environmental, safety, and drug problems, more attention has recently focused on the effects of FASB-SEC type rules for disclosure and measurement.

On June 4, 1975, Congress passed an amendment to the SEC Act of 1934 that reflected concern about impediments to capital formation arising from the high cost of compliance with the SEC's rules, particularly for small business:

> The Commission, in making rules and regulations pursuant to any provisions of this chapter, shall consider among other matters the impact any such rule or regulation would have on competition. The Commission shall not adopt any such rule or regulation which would impose a burden on competition not necessary or appropriate in furtherance of this chapter.[1]

Since passage of this amendment, the SEC has demonstrated a greater recognition of the potential effects of mandated disclosure and measurement rules, particularly on the operations and capital raising ability of small firms. Previously, the SEC had emphasized as its only goal the protection of investors to the extent that, for all practical purposes, compliance costs were not considered. Furthermore, it had been felt that investor protection could be assured, among other ways, if everyone had "equal access" to information. With a few exceptions, the "equal access" doctrine had meant that measurement and disclosure be uniform irrespective of firm size.

Reaction to this type of uniformity coupled with the growth of reporting requirements led to studies which found that the burden of disclosure alone was significantly greater for small companies than for medium and large companies. For example, the SEC found that for filing Form 10-K, small companies (assets less than $100 million) incurred costs that are 60 times greater than large companies (assets over $1 billion) per dollar of sales (U.S. House of Representatives, 1977, Chapter I, p. 28). One result of this finding is that disclosure rules for small business

[1]Amendment to the 1934 SEC Act, 15, USC, Par. w(a)(2), 1975.

have been eased, e.g., S-18, a simplified registration statement for small business, has been introduced.[2] The SEC also has created an Office of Small Business Policy, one of whose tasks is to examine the feasibility of creating a small business class to reduce the burden of the continuous reporting requirements of the Securities Exchange Act of 1934.

The 1975 amendment to the 1934 Securities Exchange Act also was cited as a ground for dropping the proposed oil and gas measurement rule, FASB Statement No. 19 (Financial Accounting Standards Board, 1977). That rule was similar to the R&D rule in that it required use of the expense method; in that case, unsuccessful exploration and drilling costs could not be reported on balance sheets as deferred charges. Testimony at the hearings before the SEC in 1978 raised serious questions about the effect of the rule on companies that had been using the deferral (full cost) method and would have been required to switch methods.

In their research on No. 19, Collins and Dent (1979) not only cited testimony by investment bankers opposing the rule but also presented statistical evidence showing that there was a significant association between the release of the exposure draft on the rule and a negative shift in the level of returns for affected companies relative to the level of returns for unaffected companies (those not required to switch because they already had been expensing). Previous research showing that switches in measurement techniques which did not affect aftertax cash flows, they contended, may not have detected negative returns, because that research had been limited to voluntary changes in financial reporting methods that increased earnings (Collins and Dent, 1979, pp. 7–8). Moreover, they pointed out that much of the previous efficient markets research has been confined to larger companies.[3]

The changes in SEC disclosure requirements for small business as well as the recognition of possible adverse effects of No. 19 for small oil and gas companies reflect the recent concern about the economic effects of the regulation of financial reporting and its implications for concentration. Before presenting our research results pertaining to consequences of the R&D measurement rule, let us consider the mechanism by which that rule may have affected R&D expenditures.

POSSIBLE REASONS FOR FIRMS' REACTIONS TO STATEMENT 2

Efficient market theory suggests that securities markets do not react naïvely to "cosmetic" changes in accounting numbers, but only to real events. Accordingly, measurement changes such as those mandated in Statement 2 would not be expected

---

[2]There have been several other recent amendments based on size. In 1975 the SEC amended its 10-Q requirement for interim reports (ASR 177) stating that "the greatest investor need for these data exists in the case of such companies whose activities are most closely followed by analysts" (i.e., only larger companies). In 1976 the SEC exempted companies with less than $100 million of inventory and gross plant and equipment from reporting on a supplemental replacement cost basis in ASR 190. Also, the FASB's Statement No. 33 on price level accounting exempted companies with less than $1 billion of assets.

[3]As was the case for the firms affected by the R&D rule, the majority of the firms that would have been affected by the oil and gas proposal were small ones.

to alter security price distributions significantly except in instances in which they are accompanied by changes in disclosure or in cash flows.[4]

Accepting the efficient market hypothesis, the Advisory Committee on Corporate Disclosure (Sommer Committee) has emphasized the importance of mandated disclosure rather than measurement rules (U.S. House of Representatives, 1977, Chapter XX). Similarly, others have stressed repeatedly that the FASB should not devote resources to seeking the "best" measurement rule; rather it should concentrate on extending and improving disclosure (Beaver, 1973, p. 53). For example, with respect to the investment tax credit, Beaver argued that:

> Potential harm is not likely to occur because firms use flow-through or deferral for accounting for the investment credit. Rather, the harm is more likely to occur because firms are following policies of less than full disclosure....

Most of the evidence in the finance and accounting literature supports the efficient market hypothesis. Nevertheless, it is important to note that relatively few studies have considered small firms not listed on the major exchanges and such firms comprise the large majority of enterprises affected by Statement 2. Furthermore, as the methodological procedures used in market studies improve, researchers have begun to find a number of inconsistencies that cruder data and techniques missed in the past.[5] Although previous evidence suggests it is unlikely, it is possible that security market participants may have reacted negatively to the lower and more volatile earnings figures and to the higher financial leverage ratios caused by the rule.[6] In an effort to mitigate this type of reaction, management of affected firms may have attempted to offset the changes in reported numbers by reducing R&D expenditures or changing their pattern.

A related explanation for firm reaction to the expense-only rule is not predicated on the securities market's being inefficient, but only on small firms' managers' perceiving it to be so. Spokesmen for the venture capital industry and managers of several small firms testified at the hearings on the R&D issue in March, 1974, that affected firms would alter their behavior to "cushion" the increased earnings volatility and lower earnings level that would otherwise ensue. Implicit in their testimony was the perception that this action was necessary to prevent lower security prices and a higher cost of capital.[7] Whether, in fact, lower security prices

---

[4]Changes in cash flows may occur when measurement methods are mandated for tax reporting as well as for financial reporting. However, this was not the case with respect to the R&D rule. Since 1954, the tax code has allowed companies to expense R&D for tax purposes, even though they deferred for financial reporting purposes.

[5]In reviewing a number of recent efficient market studies, Jensen (1978, p. 95) stated: "We seem to be entering a stage where widely scattered and as yet incohesive evidence is arising which seems to be inconsistent with the [efficient market] theory.... [W]e are beginning to find inconsistencies that our cruder data and techniques missed in the past.... [T]hese pieces of evidence begin to stack up in a manner which makes a much stronger case for the necessity to carefully review both our acceptance of the efficient market theory and our methodological procedures."

[6]As an example of the negative effect on earnings, if the rule had been effective during the 1970–1975 period, it would have resulted in an average earnings decline of 97.2% and a median decline of 15.1% for the firm sample discussed in Section 5.

[7]At the hearings no attempt was made by the quasi regulators (the FASB is a private organization) to provide evidence contrary to these perceptions or to express their views about the neutrality of the mandated rule.

and higher costs of raising funds would have occurred is a separate issue since the expense-only rule may have had an impact on the perceptions and decisions of the preparers of the financial reports (managers) without necessarily directly affecting the users of the information (security market participants).

Two additional possibilities which relate to the contractual arrangements of the firm are suggested as explanations for possible economic effects of the expense-only rule. The first relates to management compensation plans and the market for managers; the second relates to contractual constraints in lending agreements.

Information contained in financial statements such as the level and variability of the firm's earnings stream often is the basis for determining the size of management bonuses, the value of profit-sharing plans, and promotion decisions within the firm. Additionally, accounting results are likely to be used externally in the process of determining a manager's reputation and future wages in the managerial labor market. Therefore, it may be hypothesized that to "protect" his current or future remuneration the manager may alter the firm's financial and/or operating decisions in response to changes in reporting rules which decrease the level or increase the volatility of the firm's earnings stream.

Secondly, because the R&D rule will reduce the reported earnings and equity of the firm, previously existing restrictive covenants contained in the firm's lending agreements may become more binding or possibly even be violated. Most often, restrictive covenants are couched in terms of generally accepted accounting principles in force at the date of calculation and thus changes in accounting methods, such as mandated by No. 2, can effectively change the provisions of these contracts. Consequently, if neither renegotiation nor adjustments are undertaken, debt agreements which contain covenants such as (1) restrictions on dividend payments when net earnings or stockholders' equity falls below a specific level, (2) specifications regarding maximum ratios of debt-to-equity capitalization, and (3) limitations on allowable indebtedness, may force the firm to change its operating and financial decisions.[8] Even if such covenants are not violated, they would tend to become more restrictive and, perhaps, therefore prompt firms to select less risky investments or raise less debt to avoid violating the provisions in the future. A reduction in planned R&D or a change in the pattern of R&D expenditure could have been used as a vehicle to offset the impact of the rule on these financial constraints.

Another reason the R&D rule might affect the firm's behavior concerns security listing requirements. The majority of small companies affected by the rule had securities which were traded over the counter. To facilitate accessibility to the capital markets, such a company would either desire to seek membership in the National Association of Securities Dealers Automated Quotation system (NAS-DAQ), or, if already a member, to remain in the system, or perhaps to qualify for

---

[8]It is important to recognize that renegotiation costs may be significant. These costs include not only transaction costs but possibly the cost of borrowing at a higher interest rate caused either by general changes in interest rate levels or by changes in firm risk since the time that the original contract was arranged. In addition, although lending agreements could be insulated from unanticipated mandatory changes in accounting principles, such agreements would be costly to monitor, since debt is outstanding for long time periods and mandated principles have been frequently imposed or changed.

listing on the American Stock Exchange (AMEX).[9] Both the NASDAQ and the AMEX systems have initial listing and maintenance requirements that would be negatively affected by Rule 2 and thus could prevent listing or cause delisting.[10] There is no automatic waiver because of changes in the measurement of a firm's financial position caused by FASB (SEC) rule changes, and although a hearing can be requested when a firm is delisted, the cost of the hearing, if permitted, is borne by the firm.

Similar to potential problems related to listing requirements, negative changes in accounting numbers and ratios might impair a firm's ability to receive government contracts.[11] In evaluating the financial responsibility of contract bidders, government agencies conduct "preaward surveys," relying extensively on financial reporting ratios which would be negatively affected by Rule 2. Agency policy and training manuals suggest that the government analyst is expected to evaluate such ratios as total liabilities/net worth, net profits/net worth, and net profits/sales where either earnings or net worth appears. As a consequence of Rule 2, ratios with earnings in the numerator were often sharply reduced and leverage ratios were often sharply increased.

To summarize, because of perceived or real market inefficiencies, or because of managerial compensation schemes, restrictions in borrowing arrangements written in terms of generally accepted accounting principles, stock exchange requirements or government contract evaluation procedures, Rule 2 may have affected management's R&D expenditure decisions.

THE DEPARTMENT OF COMMERCE STUDY ON R&D

As noted above, the SEC accepted FASB No. 2 in October, 1975. Although this was about four months after the aforementioned amendment to the 1934 Securities Exchange Act, no research or hearings were conducted on possible adverse consequences of the rule. The SEC may have relied, however, on research done by the Department of Commerce for the FASB. Surprisingly, this research was conducted after the Board published its Statement No. 2 in October 1974.

Because the methodology and results of the Department of Commerce study are so different from those of our research described in the next section and because it is the only known study of its type relevant to the R&D issue, let us examine its approach and conclusions.[12] The motivation for the study was the Department's concern about "a recent drop in R&D investment and the need for incentives to assist technological innovation." Since it was clear that requiring all companies to

[9]Of our sample of 43 affected OTC firms discussed in Section 5, 15 were listed on the NASDAQ system.

[10]Examples of basic requirements for initial inclusion of an issue of domestic stock on the NASDAQ system are total assets of at least $1 million and capital and surplus of at least $500,000. One of the requirements of the AMEX is pretax earnings of $750,000.

[11]More than one third of R&D in the private sector is sponsored by the Federal government.

[12]The study is cited not in FASB No. 2, but in FASB No. 7, *Accounting and Reporting by Development Stage Enterprises,* Par. 50, Financial Accounting Standards Board, Stamford, CT: June 1975.

expense R&D would mainly affect small companies, the study was confined to interviewing suppliers of capital, CPAs, and managers of small, high technology firms.

The conclusion of the study, based entirely on interviews, was that "FASB's Statement Two should not have a significant impact on those firms who have heretofore capitalized R&D" (U.S. Department of Commerce, 1975).[13] Aside from the fact that "significant" in this context is not quantified and is therefore subjective, it is necessary to ask whether any, even insignificant, decline in R&D investment is worth the alleged advantages of uniformity and comparability in financial reporting. Furthermore, we have serious doubts about the validity of the study's conclusion based upon the results of the interviews which were reported.

Only 11 managers of firms were interviewed and no data are presented describing the significance of the R&D outlays for each of these firms. Since the purpose of the study was to determine whether adverse consequences would result from requiring deferral firms to switch to the expense method, the sample of firms should have come from only those firms that had significant expenditures for R&D and had been deferring (capitalizing) R&D before the change mandated by the FASB and the SEC. However, seven of the 11 firms interviewed had been expensing prior to No. 2 and therefore were unaffected. The remaining four firms had been deferring.

The survey revealed that three firms planned to reduce their R&D expenditures, while four firms stated that they expected an adverse effect on their cost of capital, and both types of responses cited Statement No. 2 as the cause. The study did not identify whether the three or four firms which claimed negative effects were from the four deferral firms, but such an inference seems reasonable.

The Commerce study's conclusion rests largely on the remaining interviews with 40 lenders and investors (venture capital firms, SBICs, investment banking houses, commercial banks, and nonfinancial corporations). Only one of the 40 stated that its investment policies might change as a consequence of Statement No. 2; ten of the 40 thought that other sophisticated investors might change their investment policies. More importantly, over 40% of these sophisticated investors thought that the average investor *would* limit his investment in those companies affected by the expense-only rule.[14]

Unfortunately, the study determined neither the importance of unaffiliated sources of funds (sources other than venture capital firms, SBICs, etc.) to the affected firms nor the attitudes of such sources to the rule change. This exclusion may be crucial, because a recent study for the National Bureau of Standards shows

---

[13] It should be noted that the study states that it was not possible to distinguish between small and developing stage companies so both were included. Therefore, FASB No. 7, Par. 50, incorrectly states that "[the study] focused *primarily* on the impact on investment and credit decisions concerning development stage enterprises if they were required to charge research and development costs to expense when incurred" (emphasis added).

[14] FASB No. 7, *Accounting and Reporting by Development Stage Enterprises,* Par. 49, also voiced a concern about the possible adverse effects on the unsophisticated investor. Venture capital enterprises, interviewed for attitudes about the elimination of deferred preoperating costs for development stage enterprises, asserted that a mandated switch would have "little effect" ("little" being undefined) on the amount or terms under which venture capital is provided, but that such a mandated switch "might have an impact on the investment and credit decisions of unsophisticated investors."

that unaffiliated individuals provide about 16% and "unknown" sources about 25% of external sources of funds for small, technology-based firms (National Bureau of Standards, 1976, p. 11).

EMPIRICAL RESULTS

This section reports the results of an investigation designed to: (1) test whether there was an association between (a) the effective date of Rule 2 and (b) changes in R&D expenditure levels among affected firms; and (2) determine the attitudes of the chief financial officers of small, high technology firms regarding the effect of Rule 2 on R&D outlays.

Our analysis of the letters and public testimony on the FASB's Discussion Memorandum and Exposure Draft on R&D reporting led us to confine the study to small companies whose securities were traded over the counter. Only a very small fraction of companies with a sales volume over $1 billion were deferring R&D costs before the new rule. Moreover, public testimony by small companies complained about possible adverse effects.[15]

A sample of treatment companies was selected from the *Disclosure Journal*. Besides limiting the sample to OTC-traded firms, each company was required to have an auditor's qualification in 1974 or 1975 which indicated that a switch from the deferral to the expense method materially reduced profit. Although Rule 2 did not become binding until 1975, firms that made switches in 1974 were also selected, because it was assumed that some companies decided to switch in 1974 after knowledge of the Board's decision was made public in October, 1974. Thus, our reference to "prior" and "post" periods indicates before or after the switch (1974 or 1975 depending on the company) rather than before or after 1975. Also, only companies whose Form 10-Ks were available and whose reports disclosed sufficient data during the 1970–1977 period on R&D outlays and other items necessary to perform the statistical tests described below were selected. The final treatment sample consisted of 43 companies.

A match group of 43 control companies which had been expensing before No. 2 was then selected from a list of approximately 800 companies traded over the counter. An effort was made to select a match for each treatment firm which was similar with respect to several critical variables during the prerule period. In particular, a company-to-company match was made on the basis of the following variables measured over the 1970–1975 period: (1) firm size, as measured by sales, (2) R&D intensity, as measured by the ratio, R&D/sales, (3) R&D growth, and (4) industry, as indicated by SIC code.[16] As in the case of the treatment firms, an additional criterion was that the necessary Form 10-K data be available for the

---

[15] The president of Sperry Rand Corporation said: "I can say quite candidly that Univac would not be here today if we had not had the advantage of the old rule [expense or defer R&D outlays] for so many years," *Business Week,* July 3, 1978, p. 52.

[16] If after matching on the first three variables, a four digit SIC industry match was available, it was selected. Twenty-four pairs were matched on this basis. The industry matches for the remaining nineteen cases were less perfect. Tests on subsets of the paired sample indicate that the results reported below are not sensitive to how closely pairs within the sample were matched by industry.

TABLE 1

TREATMENT AND CONTROL SAMPLES

Treatment	Industry SIC	Control (match)	Industry SIC
Addmaster	(3573)	Anderson Jacobson Inc.	(3573)
AFA Protective Systems	(7393)	Market Facts Inc.	(7399)
Allen Organ	(3931)	IVAC Corp.	(3841)
Andersen 2000	(3881)	Intercontinental Dynam.	(3811)
Andersen Labs Inc.	(3573)	Computer Consoles	(3573)
Aspen Systems	(7372)	Datatab Inc.	(7370)
Buck Engineering	(3825)	Qonaar Corp.	(3820)
Butler National Corp.	(3449) (3662)	Solid State Scientific	(3679)
Cetrol Electronics Corp.	(3673)	Physio Control Corp.	(3699)
Chattem Drug & Chemical	(2830)	Information Internat'l.	(3830)
Coleman American	(6711)	Waters Instrument Inc.	(3699)
Compucorp	(3570)	Hunt Manufacturing	(3570)
Comtech Labs Inc.	(3662)	Communications Industry	(3662)
Cordis Dow Corp.	(3841)	Extracorporeal Medical	(3841)
CPT	(3570)	Computer Products	(3573)
Datascope	(3699)	Nicolet Instruments	(3699)
DBA Systems	(7372)	Nat'l. Data Communicat.	(7370)
Dewey Electronics	(3573)	Advanced Micro Devices	(3670)
Digi-Log Systems	(3573)	Comten Inc.	(3573)
Educational Development	(2731) (3652)	Radiation Dynamics Inc.	(3662)

Electric Regulator	(3622)	Altair Corp.	(3662)
Electro-Catheter	(3841)	U.S. Surgical Corp.	(3846)
Fabri-Tek	(3573)	Universal Instruments	(3550)
General Data Comm.	(3661)	Farinon Corp.	(3661)
Graham Magnetics	(3449) (3679)	Siliconix Inc.	(3679)
Graphic Scanning Corp.	(7399)	Horizons Research	(7399)
Hygain Electronics	(3662)	ESL Inc.	(3573)
Industrial Nucleonics	(7370)	Comshare Inc.	(7370)
Kalvar Corp.	(3861)	Pako Corp.	(3861)
Mor-Flo Industries	(3630)	Rival Manufacturing	(3630)
New Brunswick	(3811)	Gelman Instruments	(3811)
Optical Radiation	(3640)	Aerotron Inc.	(3662)
Fem Metals	(3540)	Scherr-Tumico Inc.	(3540)
Schaevitz Engineering	(3811)	Hach Chemical Co.	(3811)
Sensormatic Electronics	(3662)	Resdel Industries	(3662)
Specialty Composites	(3079)	Eberline Instrument Co.	(3823)
SRC Labs Inc.	(3673) (3499)	United McGill Corp.	(3499)
Staco Inc.	(3612)	Woodhead (Daniel) Inc.	(3699)
T-Bar Inc.	(3679)	Vitramon Inc.	(3679)
Technical Communications	(3573)	Beehive Internat'l.	(3573)
Thetford	(3589)	Acme General Corp.	(3499)
Transidyne General	(3841)	Survival Technology	(3841)
Visual Sciences	(5084)	Analog Devices	(3679)

1970–1977 period. Table I contains a list of company names and SIC codes for treatment and control firms.

The null hypothesis was that there was no change in the level and growth of R&D expenditures by treatment firms relative to control firms after the imposition of the rule mandating use of the expensing method. The alternative hypothesis was that R&D outlays and growth declined for treatment firms. These hypotheses were tested using the Wilcoxon matched-pairs signed-ranks test.[17] The statistical results and definitions of test variables used to measure reductions in R&D are provided in Table 2. Table 3 contains the computed values of the test variables for each of the nine tests conducted.

The first test variable, the mean of the annual percent change in R&D ($\%\ \Delta$ $R\&D$) was computed for each of the treatment (deferral) companies for both prior and post Rule 2 periods. We then used the Wilcoxon test to examine the set of 43 company differences between prior and post observations. The purpose of the test was to ascertain whether there was a systematic reduction in $\%\ \Delta\ R\&D$ across firms subsequent to Rule 2. Next, we performed the necessary computations for a similar test on the control (expense) sample to determine whether there was a systematic reduction in $\%\ \Delta\ R\&D$ for these companies. Finally, we subtracted the difference between each prior and post observation in the control group from the difference between the prior and post observation of its match in the treatment group, and applied the same analysis to these (joint) differences.

Examination of the joint differences for the matched pairs provides a means of partially controlling for other unspecified events that influenced the levels of R&D expenditures during the test period, while simultaneously detecting changes in the location of the $\%\ \Delta\ R\&D$ variable for deferral firms relative to expense firms.[18] More specifically, it may be noted that the Wilcoxon matched-pairs signed-ranks test on differences does not require that the distribution of differences be the same for separate pairs. Also, the test does not preclude the possibility that R&D expenditures for a particular firm are correlated both before and after the rule or that expenditures of treatment and control firms are correlated. This assumption is critical since R&D expenditure levels may have been affected by similar exogenous variables such as credit availability and other regulations.

The results of the three tests described above are presented in the first row of Table 2. Section (a) indicates that there was a significant reduction in $\%\ \Delta\ R\&D$ after No. 2 for the treatment companies. Section (b) indicates that this was not the case for the control companies, and Section (c) indicates that when the treatment and control company results are considered jointly, the reduction for the deferral companies remains significant.

---

[17]The Wilcoxon test has a high power-efficiency relative to other procedures designed specifically for the matched-pair situation. Its asymptotic efficiency as compared with the t-test is 95.5% for large samples in appropriate circumstances (95% for small samples). It is generally regarded as the best of the order tests for two samples and may be superior to the t-test when appropriate assumptions for that test are not met (Hollander and Wolfe, p. 82).

[18]As previously mentioned, the closeness of percentage changes in R&D (R&D growth) between treatment and control companies in the prior period was one of the variables considered in selecting matches.

TABLE 2

RESULTS OF WILCOXON MATCHED-PAIRS SIGNED-RANKS TESTS FOR REDUCTION IN R&D EXPENDITURES.

Test variable	Deferral (a) prior period–post period				Expense (b) prior period–post period				Joint deferral–expense (a)–(b)			
	n	+Ranks (mean)	−Ranks (mean)	z-Score	n	+Ranks (mean)	−Ranks (mean)	z-Score	n	+Ranks (mean)	−Ranks (mean)	z-Score
$\%\Delta R\&D$	43	26 (25.58)	17 (16.53)	2.318***	43	15 (23.33)	28 (21.29)	−1.485	43	26 (24.38)	17 (18.35)	1.944**
$R\&D/Sales$	43	31 (24.65)	12 (15.17)	3.514****	43	19 (22.26)	24 (21.79)	−.604	43	30 (24.80)	13 (15.54)	3.272***
$R\&D/(Y+R\&D)$	43	24 (24.54)	18 (17.44)	1.719**	43	26 (22.15)	17 (21.76)	1.244	43	25 (22.96)	18 (20.67)	1.220
$R\&D_D/R\&D_{D+E}$	43	35 (22.34)	8 (20.50)	3.731****								

Variable definitions:

$\overline{\%\Delta R\&D}$ = Average % change in research and development (R&D)

$\overline{R\&D/Sales}$ = Average ratio of R&D to sales

$\overline{R\&D/(Y+R\&D)}$ = Average ratio of R&D to income before R&D

$\overline{R\&D_D/R\&D_{D+E}}$ = Average ratio of R&D of deferral firm to total R&D of that firm and its match

Note:

One-tail tests

* Significant at the .10 level
** Significant at the .05 level
*** Significant at the .01 level
**** Significant at the .001 level

TABLE 3

TEST VARIABLE OBSERVATIONS

Case	%ΔR&D$_{PRIOR-POST}$ Deferral (D)	Expense (E)	Joint	R&D$_D$/R&D$_{D+E}$ PRIOR-POST	R&D/Sales$_{PRIOR-POST}$ Deferral (D)	Expense (E)	Joint	R&D/(Y+R&D)$_{PRIOR-POST}$ Deferral (D)	Expense (E)	Joint
1	.66699	-.08592	.75292	.16217	-.01096	.02853	-.03949	-.63758	.14979	-.78738
2	-.79823	-.08854	-.70969	.17433	.00687	-.00454	.01141	.23952	-.10198	.34149
3	1.80538	-.33413	2.13951	-.01073	.00542	.03764	-.03222	.11070	.51415	-.40345
4	-.01120	-.03988	.02868	.17620	.12226	-.00406	.12632	.54074	.11621	.42453
5	-.76328	-.29324	-.47004	.20653	-.00791	-.06438	.05647	.24959	-.07825	.32783
6	2.90442	-.05292	2.95734	.02211	.00729	-.00177	.00906	.54827	.01681	.53146
7	.07265	.71444	-.64179	.23619	.00101	-.01926	.02028	-.02710	-.52107	.49398
8	.41209	1.09024	-.67815	.03477	1.31239	-.06061	1.37300	-.07638	-.16487	.08849
9	.40368	.37395	.02973	.04471	.00249	-.00238	.00487	.06726	-.05245	.11971
10	-.61011	-.28324	-.32687	-.05582	-.00622	.16494	-.17116	-.13173	.18430	-.31602
11	2.93343	-.07108	3.00451	-.02607	.05740	.00087	.05653	-.13726	.27335	-.41061
12	-.07204	-.12293	.05089	.10399	-.06201	.00023	-.06224	-.15902	.00455	-.16358
13	4.29438	-.70100	4.99538	-.07445	-.00001	-.00386	.00385	.01810	-.02217	.04027
14	-.15500	.05142	-.20642	.14901	.59304	-.01921	.61225	.51122	-.27712	.78834
15	6.12334	-.07845	6.20179	-.23706	-.02218	-.00483	-.01735	.20966	.11072	.09893
16	.53110	.34396	.18714	-.10573	-.01886	-.00489	-.01398	-.09177	-.05912	-.03265
17	.09632	.14071	-.04439	.05933	.00870	-.12892	.13762	-.11904	.09014	-.20918
18	-4.16335	-.13259	-4.03076	.07604	.03689	-.01225	.04914	-.21861	.05006	-.26866
19	1.29552	-.46108	1.75661	.09463	.24998	.12255	.12742	.58583	.13568	.45015
20	-.14055	.31786	-.45841	.17405	.03690	-.01059	.04750	-.07023	.01043	-.08067

21	-.16909	.73454	-.90363	.01101	.00887	.02669	-.01781	-.19325	.34726	-.54051
22	1.67934	-.31519	1.99453	.09687	-.01254	.00717	-.01970	-.00423	.19224	-.19647
23	.29532	1.16375	-.86843	.35388	.07654	-.00889	.08543	-.17712	-.08806	-.08906
24	.30983	-.99192	1.30175	.17230	.55092	.00019	.55072	.35102	-.30623	.65724
25	.51564	-.12154	.63718	.02496	-.00288	-.00041	-.00247	-.09781	.06604	-.16385
26	7.87496	-.19459	8.06955	-.23918	-.01108	-.00472	-.00636	-.16935	-.26822	.09887
27	-.22869	.07270	-.30139	.00657	.01328	-.00400	.01728	.38455	.00067	.38388
28	.25491	-.32320	.57811	.00149	-.02606	.01695	-.04301	-.43945	.37294	-.81239
29	-.14682	-.49164	.34483	.20977	.07704	-.01065	.08769	.00000	-.09058	.09058
30	.18424	-.16273	.34696	.16217	.00395	.00272	.00123	.06610	.03684	.02926
31	.23988	.16758	.07231	.44224	.03516	-.01321	.04836	.07125	.39067	-.31942
32	1.17363	-.31191	1.48555	.03011	.01681	.00857	.00824	.12124	.23507	-.11384
33	.35334	-.12667	.48000	.00176	.01268	.00244	.01024	-.08589	.17846	-.26434
34	-.07627	-.06103	-.01524	.13505	.02763	.00307	.02456	.34120	-.06598	.40717
35	-.79877	-.14063	-.65814	.13262	.27823	.00196	.27627	.52257	.00139	.52117
36	.17675	.10341	.07334	.08520	.15064	-.01144	.16207	.41812	.20000	.21812
37	.56667	-5.43684	6.00352	.28956	.45184	-.00640	.45824	.51629	-.10757	.62386
38	-.52298	.02370	-.54668	.02946	.00040	.00596	-.00557	.07854	.05866	.01988
39	-.26047	-.65967	.39920	.01378	.01694	-.01065	.02759	.50480	.17375	.33105
40	-.34443	-.17333	-.17111	.22116	.30759	.06267	.24492	.59262	.32652	.26610
41	.26066	-1.53650	1.79716	-.06675	-.00636	-.00594	-.00041	.05536	-.07295	.12832
42	-.16021	.44300	-.60322	.07442	.25876	.14285	.11590	.14264	-.60512	.74776
43	4.97271	.12365	4.84906	.13328	.13040	.00633	.12407	-.10861	-.01073	-.09788

Note: Variable definitions are provided in Table 2.

393

As shown in Table 2, three additional variables were examined by using an approach similar to that described for $\% \Delta R\&D$. These variables were the ratio R&D/sales, the ratio R&D/income before R&D, and the ratio of R&D of the deferral company to the total of R&D of the same company plus the R&D of its match (expense) company.

The results for the deferral companies indicate that the association between the passage of FASB No. 2 (ASR No. 178) and a decline in each of the test variables is significant. The joint results based on the time series of the differences between companies from the two groups are also significant except for one measure.[19] Thus, almost all measures used point to a significant association between a relative decline of R&D outlays for the deferral group and the imposition of the new measurement rule.

That the rule itself was a cause of the relative decline in R&D is supported by the results of a questionnaire distributed to chief financial officers of 380 OTC companies. Each of these companies had ratios of R&D/sales of at least one percent and R&D/income before R&D of at least 5% before the issuance of Rule 2. The response rate to the questionnaire was 34%.

Table 4 presents the responses to five questions which focus on the perceived effects of Rule 2 on the level of R&D and on the companies' access to capital markets. As the table indicates, the responses were classified by deferral and expense firms to test the hypothesis that the responses from the two groups were significantly different. Overall, the results of the survey support the findings presented in Table 2.

Question No. 1 is the only question of the five which related to the behavior of the respondent firm itself. As indicated by the chi-square statistic, there was a significant difference between the deferral and the expense respondents with respect to the change in emphasis placed on R&D, since the adoption of No. 2. Consistent with the empirical findings above, the responses to this question suggest that there was a reduction in emphasis placed on R&D by firms previously deferring relative to expensing firms.

The responses to the remaining questions indicate that a significant number of the officers surveyed believe that the expense-only rule had negative effects. This is true for both deferral and expensing firms, although the belief is more widespread among deferral firms, as expected. Question 2 sought to determine whether managers believed that a reduction in R&D actually occurred, whereas questions 3, 4, and 5 dealt with their beliefs regarding the behavior of capital market participants.

It should be noted that, although for question 3 the chi-square result is not

---

[19]The variable for which the joint test result is insignificant is $R\&D/(Y + R\&D)$. This ratio, unlike $R\&D/sales$, is unstable and has a great variation among companies. *Business Week,* July 3, 1978, reported that the average ratio of R&D to final income was equal to 54% for the computer industry, with one company having a ratio of 10% and another 6,000%.

Because it was difficult to control for all variables in the matching process, joint tests were repeated using the Mann-Whitney test. Like the Wilcoxon test, the Mann-Whitney test is a two-sample test which considers both the order and magnitude of variables, but does not recognize matched pairs. The significance levels for the two joint variables $\% \Delta R\&D$ and $R\&D/sales$ were .015 and .003, respectively. As was the case for the Wilcoxon test, the last variable, $R\&D/(Y + R\&D)$, was insignificant at the 10% level.

TABLE 4

RESPONSES OF SMALL COMPANIES ON EFFECTS OF STATEMENT NO. 2

Question	Deferral firm responses			Expense firm responses			D.F.	Chi* square
1. Since January 1, 1975, has the emphasis placed on R&D within your firm changed relative to the size of your company in any of the indicated ways?	Increase 25.6%	Decrease 28.2%	No change 46.2%	Increase 41.5%	Decrease 11.0%	No change 47.6%	2	6.577 (.0373)
2. Do you think R&D outlays for some small companies would be greater if the deferral option were still available?	Yes 42.1	Possibly 23.7	No 34.2	Yes 18.6	Possibly 35.7	No 45.7	2	6.995 (.0303)
3. Do you believe that the no. 2 standard makes it more difficult and/or more expensive for some small firms to raise capital?	Yes 35.0	Possibly 30.0	No 35.0	Yes 18.3	Possibly 31.7	No 50.0	2	3.915 (.1412)
4. Does the expensing of R&D outlays as incurred create difficulty in evaluating the profit performance of small companies by the unsophisticated investor?	Considerable 65.0	Some 27.5	None 7.5	Considerable 36.2	Some 39.1	None 24.6	2	9.514 (.0086)
5. Do you believe that potential investors are less inclined to invest in developing-stage firms (5 to 10 years old) because of the impact of the no. 2 standard on those firms' financial statements?	Yes 30.6	Possibly 16.7	No 52.8	Yes 12.7	Possibly 23.6	No 63.6	2	4.435 (.1089)

* The number in parentheses is the probability of obtaining the χ^2 value shown if there exists no systematic relationship between groups and responses.

395

significant, there is a tendency for both groups of managers to believe strongly that No. 2 made access to capital more difficult or more costly. Fifty percent of the managers of the control group and 65% of the treatment group believe that No. 2 created problems that affected the ability to raise capital.

Of particular importance is the response to question 4. Almost 93% of the deferral firms expected that the unsophisticated investor had at least some difficulty evaluating the profit performance of small companies because of Standard No. 2. The percent of expensing firms which expressed this belief also was extremely high, 75.3%. As indicated earlier, the unsophisticated investor is an important source of equity funds for small, high-technology firms, and, therefore, his investment behavior is particularly critical to such companies. The Department of Commerce study used by the FASB and cited earlier recognized the importance of this source, but made no further analysis because it claimed that information about the unsophisticated investor group was unavailable.

SUMMARY AND CONCLUSIONS

The FASB (Statement No. 2) and the SEC (ASR No. 178) mandated all companies to expense R&D outlays after January 1, 1975. Implicit in this decision was the assumption that no adverse consequences would ensue for those companies which previously had deferred those outlays.

The results reported here, based on (1) an empirical investigation of changes in R&D expenditure behavior, and (2) a survey of firms heavily engaged in R&D, indicate that the production-investment decisions of affected firms were changed in response to Statement No. 2. In particular, the results suggest that affected companies reduced their expenditures on R&D. These companies were small, high technology firms, a subset of a group that has an important role in the development of innovative processes.

A number of possible reasons for possible adverse consequences of rules such as Statement No. 2 have been hypothesized. These warrant further investigation so that the consequences of FASB-SEC type rules can be fully understood by market participants and regulators. Certainly, in considering proposed changes of financial measurement rules, regulators need to be more explicit about alleged benefits of mandated uniformity and need to devote more resources to the evaluation of possible adverse economic effects.

REFERENCES

Beaver, W. "What Should Be the FASB's Objectives." *Journal of Accountancy* (August 1973), pp. 49–56.

Collins, D. and Dent, W. "The Proposed Elimination of Full Cost Accounting in the Extractive Petroleum Industry: An Empirical Assessment of Market Consequences." *Journal of Accounting and Economics* (March 1979), pp. 3–44.

Financial Accounting Standards Board. "Statement No. 2." *Accounting for Research and Development Costs.* Stamford, CT: FASB, October 1974.

———"Statement No. 19." *Financial Accounting and Reporting by Oil and Gas Producing Companies,* Stamford, Conn.: FASB, December 1977.

Hollander, M. and Wolfe, D. *Nonparametrical Statistical Methods.* New York: John Wiley and Sons, 1973.

Jensen, M. C. "Some Anomalous Evidence Regarding Market Efficiency." *Journal of Financial Economics,* Vol. 6 (1978), pp. 95–101.

National Bureau of Standards. *An Analysis of Venture Capital Market Imperfections.* Cambridge: Charles River Associates, 1976.

U.S. Department of Commerce Domestic Business Policy Analysis Staff, Office of Policy Development. "Impact of FASB's Rule Two on Small and/or Developing Stage Firms." Washington, D.C., January 20, 1975.

U.S. House of Representatives, House Committee on Interstate and Foreign Commerce. *Report of the Advisory Committee on Corporate Disclosure to the Securities and Exchange Commission.* 95th Congress, 1st Session, November 3, 1977.

CORPORATE DIVERSIFICATION AND INTERCORPORATE INVESTMENTS

The variety of arrangements by which one company exercises control over another has grown significantly over the past two decades. In some cases, the terms of a transaction in which control is acquired are designed to meet the specific requirements of the transaction—for example, the acquisition of foreign subsidiaries when the foreign government insists upon a significant degree of local ownership. Indeed, in some instances effective control is secured with less than a 50 percent ownership interest, despite the traditional rule (in U.S. accounting, at least) that no less than majority ownership qualifies for consolidation accounting.

The accounting question is, of course: What is the entity of most relevance to the user of financial statements? For many years, the principal factor was the control over operations, coupled with a similarity of business activity. Frequently, finance and insurance subsidiaries would be excluded from the consolidation because their inclusion would tend to distort the comparability of the consolidated entity with other similar entities. (Another reason, to be sure, is that the admixture of liabilities drawn from the financial statements of industrial and finance or insurance companies would yield an unhelpful gumbo of figures.) Yet, since the 1960s the growth of the conglomerate enterprise has been so pervasive that this argument has lost much of its support. Moreover, the traditional test of majority ownership has been found to lack realism when control can be effectively exercised when the percentage of ownership is significantly less.

EQUITY METHOD/CONSOLIDATIONS

Twenty-five years have passed since the only American accounting standard on consolidations (Accounting Research Bulletin No. 51) was issued, and some 13 years have passed since the Accounting Principles Board published Opinion No. 18 on the equity method of accounting for intercorporate investments. Benjamin S. Neuhausen, in his article, "Consolidation and the Equity Method—Time for an Overhaul," argues that the considerable volume of corporate diversification that has occurred since these standards were established has diluted the quality of useful information provided to the readers of financial statements.

Especially in view of the product-line diversification that occurred during the wave of conglomerate mergers during the 1960s, the continued exclusion of captive finance and insurance subsidiaries from the consolidated statements of industrial parents seems anachronistic. Also, the accounting treatment accorded joint ventures appears to be a function more of the form they take rather than their substance. Finally, Neuhausen proposes that the profession rethink equity method accounting. As an application of accrual accounting, the equity method probably should not, according to Neuhausen, have an arbitrary cutoff such as 20 percent. At the same time, critics who prefer to regard income measures as portents of future cash inflows complain that equity earnings without dividends do not serve this end.

SEGMENT REPORTING

Spurred by the conglomerate merge movement of the 1960s, the reporting of financial information by segment of business activity has become commonplace in the annual reports of diversified American corporations. The encouragement of segment reporting in the U.K. has an even longer history.[1]

In "Segment Reporting: Hindsight After Ten Years," Bertrand Horwitz and Richard Kolodny review the history of the steps taken to mandate segmental disclosures in the annual reports of U.S. companies, examine a number of empirical studies which tend to suggest that segment profit data may not possess high information content, and, in the end, raise questions about the cost which the SEC has imposed on diversified companies. Throughout the article, the competing merits of voluntary versus mandatory disclosures are exposed to analysis and assessment. The authors seem to conclude, albeit in an understated way, that the SEC's requirement that diversified companies disclose their segment profits was a step whose costs exceed the benefits.

BIBLIOGRAPHICAL NOTES

An historical study of consolidation accounting in the U.S. and the U.K., including some discussion of the movement during the early 1970s to adopt the equity method of accounting, is:

Walker, R. G.: *Consolidated Statements* (New York: Arno Press, 1978).

---

[1] For a brief discussion, see "Public Reporting by Conglomerates Recent Developments in the United Kingdom and Australia," in Alfred Rappaport, Peter A. Firmin and Stephen A. Zeff (eds.), *Public Reporting by Conglomerates: The Issues, the Problems, and Some Possible Solutions* (Englewood Cliffs, NJ: Prentice-Hall, Inc., 1968), pp. 143–146.

For a critical analysis of the information content of consolidated statements, see:

Walker, R. G.: "An Evaluation of the Information Conveyed by Consolidated Statements," *Abacus* (December 1976), pp. 77–115.

Two articles on the nonconsolidation of finance subsidiaries in U.S. accounting are:

Benis, Martin: "The Non-Consolidated Finance Company Subsidiary," *The Accounting Review* (October 1979), pp. 808–814.

Burnett, Tom, Thomas E. King, and Valdean C. Lembke: "Equity Method Reporting for Major Financial Company Subsidiaries," *The Accounting Review* (October 1979), pp. 815–823.

In addition to the works cited in the Bibliographical Notes following the introduction to Section 4, the following two discussion papers on segment reporting may be of interest:

An Analysis of Issues Related to Financial Reporting for Segments of a Business Enterprise, Discussion Memorandum (Stamford, CT: FASB, May 22, 1974).

Miller, Malcolm C., and Mark R. Scott: *Financial Reporting by Segments,* Discussion Paper No. 4 (Melbourne, Australia: Australian Accounting Research Foundation, 1980).

Consolidation and the Equity Method— Time for an Overhaul

Benjamin S. Neuhausen
Audit Manager
Arthur Andersen & Co.
New York

The corporate structures of American companies have become increasingly complex in the past 20 years. Companies have diversified into additional lines of business and into foreign markets, frequently establishing new subsidiaries in the process. Activities previously administered directly by parent companies or operating subsidiaries, such as financing sales to customers or obtaining insurance coverage, are now administered by captive finance or insurance subsidiaries. Rising nationalism abroad has forced many companies to sell significant shareholdings in formerly 100-percent-owned subsidiaries to local citizens. Joint ventures have proliferated, encouraged both by the rising costs of new facilities generally and by the high risks of many new ventures. Finally, depressed stock prices have made purchasing other companies' stock an attractive investment opportunity, whether the purchaser is interested in a merger, a purchase of majority interest or a purchase of a substantial minority shareholding.

These complex corporate structures create many questions for accountants—for

From *Journal of Accountancy* (February 1982), pp. 54–56, 59–60, 62, 64, 66. Reprinted by permission of the American Institute of Certified Public Accountants. Copyright © 1982 by the American Institute of Certified Public Accountants, Inc.

example, whether to consolidate a new foreign subsidiary or captive finance subsidiary, how to account for an investment in a partnership or how to eliminate intercompany profit on sales to or purchases from a foreign subsidiary that is now 49 percent owned by local citizens. The accountant who turns to the authoritative literature for guidance, however, often will be disappointed. The American Institute of CPAs pronouncements covering these subjects—primarily Accounting Research Bulletin No. 51, *Consolidated Financial Statements,*[1] issued in 1959, and Accounting Principles Board Opinion No. 18, *The Equity Method of Accounting for Investments in Common Stock,*[2] issued in 1971—provide no guidance in some areas and allow for significant diversity in practice in others. This article discusses some of the more frequent criticisms of existing pronouncements and practices and suggests some issues the Financial Accounting Standards Board should address to eliminate the problems.

EXISTING PRACTICES

A useful starting point is a brief description of existing standards of accounting for investments in subsidiaries, joint ventures and other associated enterprises.

Subsidiaries

ARB No. 51 states:

> There is a presumption that consolidated statements are more meaningful than separate statements and that they are usually necessary for a fair presentation when one of the companies in the group directly or indirectly has a controlling financial interest in the other companies.... The usual condition for a controlling financial interest is ownership of a majority voting interest, and, therefore, as a general rule ownership...of over fifty percent of the outstanding voting shares of another company is a condition pointing toward consolidation.[3]

ARB No. 51 specifies exceptions to that presumption, however, if the majority owner lacks control or exercises control only temporarily or if the subsidiary's activities are substantially different from those of the rest of the group (such as a financial subsidiary of a manufacturing parent).

In the vast majority of cases, the accounts of subsidiary companies are consolidated with the accounts of their parent companies. If a subsidiary is not consolidated, APB Opinion No. 18 requires that the parent account for its investment by the equity method. Under the equity method, the parent's balance sheet includes a single amount for its percentage share of the net assets of the subsidiary, and in each period the parent records its share of the net income reported by the subsidiary.

Joint Ventures

A joint venture is an entity that is owned by a small group of investors, jointly controlled by those investors and operated for their mutual benefit. A joint venture

[1] Accounting Research Bulletin No. 51, *Consolidated Financial Statements* (New York: AICPA, 1959).

[2] Accounting Principles Board Opinion No. 18, *The Equity Method of Accounting for Investments in Common Stock* (New York: AICPA, 1971).

[3] ARB No. 51, par. 1.

may be organized as a corporation (corporate joint venture), a partnership or undivided interests, under which each investor owns an undivided interest in each joint venture asset and is liable for its share of each joint venture liability. Opinion No. 18 requires that investors account for investments in corporate joint ventures by the equity method. It does not address accounting for investments in partnerships and unincorporated joint ventures. Accounting Interpretation No. 2 of Opinion No. 18, *Investments in Partnerships and Ventures,*[4] states that the equity method or, for certain industries, proportionate consolidation would be appropriate to account for many of those investments.

Other Associated Enterprises

APB Opinion No. 18 also requires use of the equity method to account for other investments when the investor's ownership of voting stock gives the investor the "ability to exercise significant influence over operating and financial policies of an investee."[5] If the investor is unable to exercise significant influence over operating and financial policies of an investee, the investment is carried on the investor's balance sheet at cost[6] and the investor recognizes income when it receives dividends from the investee. Opinion No. 18 states

> ...An investment (direct or indirect) of 20% or more of the voting stock of an investee should lead to a presumption that in the absence of evidence to the contrary an investor has the ability to exercise significant influence over an investee. Conversely, an investment of less than 20% of the voting stock of an investee should lead to a presumption that an investor does not have the ability to exercise significant influence unless such ability can be demonstrated.[7]

COMMON CRITICISMS OF EXISTING PRACTICE

Accountants' and financial statement users' criticisms of existing practice usually fall broadly into two categories: diversity in practice and usefulness of financial reporting. Criticisms of diversity in practice arise from flexibility or ambiguity in the pronouncements leading to different accounting by enterprises in similar circumstances. Usefulness of financial reporting can best be assessed by reference to FASB Concepts Statement No. 1, *Objectives of Financial Reporting by Business Enterprises,*[8] which states that financial reporting should provide

- Information useful in making investment and credit decisions.
- Information useful in assessing the amounts, timing and uncertainty of prospective cash flows.

[4] Accounting Interpretation No. 2 of Opinion No. 18, *Investments in Partnerships and Ventures* (New York: AICPA, 1971).
[5] APB Opinion No. 18, par. 17.
[6] Subject to Financial Accounting Standards Board Statement No. 12, *Accounting for Certain Marketable Securities* (Stamford, CT: FASB, 1975), if the investment is marketable.
[7] APB Opinion No. 18, par. 17.
[8] ASB Concepts Statement No. 1, *Objectives of Financial Reporting by Business Enterprises* (Stamford, CT: FASB, 1978).

• Information about the economic resources of an enterprise, claims to those resources and changes in them.

The following sections discuss such criticisms of practices regarding subsidiaries, joint ventures and other associated enterprises.

Subsidiaries

ARB No. 51 is criticized for providing too much flexibility in allowing nonconsolidation of subsidiaries, particularly for reasons of differing lines of business. The criticism is most often directed at nonconsolidation of finance subsidiaries, but unconsolidated insurance, leasing and real estate subsidiaries also are criticized. Under present practice, an enterprise can find support either for consolidating or not consolidating finance subsidiaries, captive insurance subsidiaries, etc., by reference to ARB No. 51. The result is that companies, even direct competitors in some cases, follow different consolidation policies that impair comparability of their financial statements. Those companies that do not consolidate subsidiaries are required by Opinion No. 18 to provide summarized financial information about their unconsolidated subsidiaries in the notes to financial statements, and complete separate financial statements are required in Securities and Exchange Commission filings for unconsolidated subsidiaries meeting certain size tests. Sophisticated analysts can use that information to construct pro forma consolidated financial statements and place different companies on a consistent basis, but the average reader of financial statements may not be able to do so.

The practice of not consolidating subsidiaries in lines of business that are different from the parent, such as finance and insurance subsidiaries, also is criticized for obscuring the resources and obligations of the enterprise. Indeed, obtaining off-balance-sheet financing by removing the subsidiary's debt from the consolidated balance sheet often is a strong factor encouraging nonconsolidation of subsidiaries. Particularly when the subsidiary is captive, doing all or nearly all its business with or for the consolidated group, the practice of omitting its assets and liabilities from the consolidated balance sheet seems questionable. For example, many corporations have established unconsolidated finance subsidiaries to purchase credit card receivables or installment receivables from the parent company. The receivables (economic resources) and associated debt (claims to those resources) disappear from the consolidated balance sheet. The parent company continues to control the receivables through its control of the subsidiary, and the parent usually provides direct or indirect guarantees of the subsidiary's debt that obligate the parent to see that the debt is repaid. As noted earlier, sophisticated analysts can prepare pro forma consolidated financial statements, but the average reader of financial statements may lack that ability.

The flexibility in ARB No. 51 to exclude certain subsidiaries from consolidation was understandable in 1959. Corporate diversification was less common then than it has become in the past 20 years. When most corporations were in only one or two lines of business, it might have seemed more informative to present separate financial information for a subsidiary in a clearly different line of business. When the consolidated group engages in 10 or more lines of business, there is less justification for nonconsolidation of a subsidiary in an eleventh business. Nonconsolidation of certain subsidiaries also may have seemed more appropriate in the absence of required segment information because there was little disaggregation of consolidated financial information for analytic purposes in 1959. Since 1970, however, segment information has been required, first through SEC requirements and subsequently through FASB Statement No. 14, *Financial Reporting for Segments of a Business Enterprise.*[9]

An additional criticism of ARB No. 51 is that its criterion for consolidation— control through ownership of a majority of voting shares—is too restrictive. Among nonbusiness organizations, legal forms may preclude one organization from obtaining a majority voting interest in another, but the first organization might control the second by contract, legal document, or otherwise. AICPA Statement of Position No. 78–10, *Accounting Principles and Reporting Practices for Certain Nonprofit Organizations,* defines control as "the direct or indirect ability to determine the direction of the management and policies" of another organization.[10] ARB No. 51 provides no basis for consolidating an organization controlled by means other than majority voting interest, but consolidation might be appropriate for other means of control. There have been cases among business enterprises, albeit rare, in which one enterprise consolidated another that it controlled through the terms of a 99-year lease rather than through majority voting interest.

Joint Ventures

Two common criticisms have been raised about joint venture accounting, the first of which is diversity in practice. As noted earlier, the authoritative accounting literature is silent about accounting for investments in unincorporated joint ventures. As a result, practice varies with both proportionate consolidation and the equity method being used to account for such investments. Different investors with similar investments in joint ventures use different methods to account for the investments. Some investors with investments in several unincorporated joint ventures use different methods to account for the separate investments or, for a single investment, use a method of accounting on the balance sheet that is different from the method used on the income statement. Observing that diversity in practice, some have advocated establishing either a uniform method of accounting for all investments in unincorporated joint ventures or criteria for using each method.

The difference between a corporate joint venture and an unincorporated joint venture is a difference of legal form. It is a long-standing accounting principle that financial accounting should reflect the economic substance of transactions rather than their legal form. In the case of joint ventures, however, the difference in legal

---

[9]FASB Statement No. 14, *Financial Reporting for Segments of a Business Enterprise* (Stamford, CT: FASB, 1976).
[10]Statement of Position No. 78–10. *Accounting Principles and Reporting Practices for Certain Nonprofit Organizations* (New York: AICPA, 1978), par. 42.

EXHIBIT 1

AN ILLUSTRATION OF HOW A DIFFERENCE IN LEGAL FORM IN JOINT VENTURES MAY ALLOW DIFFERENT ACCOUNTING METHODS

Assume that two oil companies desire to share equally in a new refinery. One option is to establish a corporate joint venture to construct and operate the refinery, with each company owning 50 percent of the stock and entitled to use 50 percent of the refinery's capacity. Another option is to establish a 50/50 partnership to construct and operate the refinery, with each partner entitled to use 50 percent of the refinery's capacity. The investment in the corporate joint venture must be accounted for by the equity method, while the investment in the partnership could be accounted for either by the equity method or by proportionate consolidation. If the refinery costs $500 million, financed by $200 million in cash from the venturers and by $300 million in loans to the joint venture, the balance sheets of the venturers would be affected as follows (000's omitted):

	Venturers' balance sheet*		
	Before joint venture	Equity method	Proportionate consolidation
Current assets	$ 450	$ 350	$ 350
Property, plant and equipment	550	550	800
Investment in joint venture	—	100	—
	$1,000	$1,000	$1,150
Current liabilities	$ 280	$ 280	$ 280
Long-term debt	240	240	390
Stockholders' equity	480	480	480
	$1,000	$1,000	$1,150

*An illustration of the effect on the income statement would require additional assumptions and is, therefore, omitted for simplicity.

The economic substance of the two options is similar—each venturer has use of 50 percent of the new refinery's capacity. The difference in legal form does affect the rights and obligations of the parties: partners bear unlimited liability, while stockholders' liabilities are limited to the amount of their investment. That difference may be more theoretical than real, however, because in arrangements of this type shareholders usually directly or indirectly guarantee debt of a corporate joint venture, and the shareholders might have equitable or moral obligations to satisfy liabilities of their corporate joint venture. The key question is whether the difference in the balance sheet (and income statement) is warranted.

form between corporate joint ventures and unincorporated joint ventures may allow different accounting even though the economic substance of the investment is the same (see Exhibit 1, page 405). If the economic substance of the investors' participations is the same, the method used to account for the investments should be the same.

The second criticism is that the equity method, which is the predominant method of accounting for investments in joint ventures, does not provide useful information about the investor's resources and obligations arising from the investment. That criticism applies particularly when the joint venture is integrated with the investor's operations and is organized as a joint venture to gain efficiencies of scale or to share risks. For example, two companies in an industry might establish a joint venture to construct a plant twice as large as either one needs, with each company committed to use half the capacity and pay half the costs because one large plant is more efficient than two small plants. The two investors are in substantially the same position as if they had each built a smaller plant, but their balance sheets show an investment rather than a plant. If the plant is partially financed with debt, the investors show only a net investment rather than an asset and a liability, making the joint venture a vehicle for off-balance-sheet financing. The suggested remedy is to replace the equity method with proportionate consolidation or with the expanded equity method—under which the investor presents separately in its financial statements its proportionate interest in current and noncurrent assets and liabilities, revenues and expenses of the joint venture rather than just its proportionate interest in net assets and net income of the joint venture.[11]

In addition to those two criticisms, another controversy centers on whether a joint venture represents a separate accounting entity from the investor enterprises. That question has implications for accounting for nonmonetary transactions between investors and joint ventures. If joint ventures are deemed to be separate accounting entities, it would be appropriate, for example, to write up nonmonetary assets contributed to a joint venture to their fair value on the date of contribution. On the other hand, if joint ventures are deemed to be related entities, such write-ups would not be acceptable, just as they are not acceptable for the contribution of assets from a parent to a subsidiary. The authoritative accounting literature does not address the question, and the result has been diversity in practice. Some investors record contributions of appreciated nonmonetary assets to joint ventures at historical cost, some recognize a write-up to the extent of others' interests in the joint venture and some record the assets at fair value at the date of contribution.

Other Associated Enterprises

The accounting requirements of Opinion No. 18, described earlier, have been criticized from two perspectives. On the one hand, many view the equity method of accounting as an application of accrual accounting, since the investor accrues its

---

[11]See, for example, David L. Reklau, "Accounting for Investments in Joint Ventures—A Reexamination," JofA, Sept. 77, pp. 96–103, and Richard Dieter and Arthur R. Wyatt, "The Expanded Equity Method—An Alternative in Accounting for Investments in Joint Ventures," JofA, June 78, pp. 89–94.

share of the earnings or losses of the investee as the investee earns them. By contrast, in this view, the cost method of accounting is more akin to cash basis accounting, because the investor recognizes income only when it receives dividends. As an application of accrual accounting, many believe that the equity method should be extended to all or virtually all long-term investments in associated enterprises, regardless of whether the investor has significant influence over the investee's operating and financial policies. Stated differently, those who hold this view believe that the 20-percent-ownership criterion of Opinion No. 18 is an arbitrary limitation that lacks conceptual support.

Under the other perspective, the equity method is criticized because the increase in an investor's reported earnings often does not result in any cash inflow to the investor. This lack of cash flow supports the notion that equity earnings without dividends are "paper profits" that reduce the quality of reported earnings. Those who hold this view would limit the equity method to those investments for which the investor can demonstrate an ability to influence the investee's dividend policies.

IMPLEMENTATION PROBLEMS

In addition to the criticisms discussed in the previous section, diverse practices have caused a host of implementation problems in both consolidation and the equity method. None of these is crucial, but their resolution would end some longstanding debates and unify practice.

Four questions are commonly raised relating to preparation of consolidated financial statements:

1 ARB No. 51 requires elimination of intercompany profits on sales between two members of a consolidated group. If one of the parties to the transaction is not wholly owned, should practice vary because ARB No. 51 allows, but does not require, allocation of the elimination of intercompany profit between the majority and minority interests?

2 If separate financial statements are prepared for a subsidiary, either as supplemental disclosure to the consolidated financial statements or as a completely separate presentation for creditors, how should transactions with the consolidated group be accounted for and disclosed? In addition, if the subsidiary was acquired in a purchase transaction, should the parent company acquisition adjustments (e.g., valuation of assets at fair value on the date of acquisition) be "pushed down" into the subsidiary's separate financial statements?

3 If a parent wishes to reduce its percentage of ownership of a subsidiary, the objective may be accomplished either by selling a portion of the parent's stockholding to third parties or by having the subsidiary sell newly issued stock to third parties. In the former circumstance, gain or loss is reflected in the consolidated financial statements. In the latter circumstance, the issuance of stock may be accounted for as a capital transaction or as gain or loss in the consolidated financial statements. Both transactions result in the same effect; should the accounting treatment, therefore, be the same in both cases?

4 Should the minority interest in a less-than-100-percent-owned subsidiary be computed on the basis of the separate financial statements of the subsidiary or on the basis of the financial statements of the subsidiary as adjusted by consolidation entries?

In addition to the first three questions above, which also arise in applying the equity method, four other questions are commonly raised about applying that method:

1 Under what circumstances is it appropriate for the investor to adjust the financial statements of an investee accounted for by the equity method?[12]
a To change from one acceptable accounting alternative to another to conform to the investor's accounting policy?
b To change from one acceptable accounting alternative to another if the investor has no transactions affected by the alternatives (for example, investee accounting for long-term contracts)?
c To change subjective evaluations of the investee (for example, bad debt or warranty reserves)?
2 What is the maximum permissible difference between the fiscal periods of an investor and an equity method investee?
3 If parent company financial statements are presented as supplemental information to consolidated financial statements, should the equity method be required for reporting the parent's investments in its subsidiaries?
4 How should an investor account for dividends received from an equity method investee in excess of the investment? Under the equity method, investors credit dividends received against the investment. Some believe that dividends received in excess of the investment should be credited to income. The situation arises frequently with real estate projects that generate cash flows in excess of earnings in their early years.

SUMMARY AND RECOMMENDATIONS

Existing authoritative accounting literature relating to accounting for investments in associated enterprises should be reconsidered. The literature allows an inappropriate degree of diversity in practice without differences in circumstances (for example, nonconsolidation of selected subsidiaries), provides no standards for some common situations (for example, accounting for investments in unincorporated joint ventures), may not be providing the most useful available information to readers of financial statements and needs updating to reflect changes in business and in accounting standards in the past 20 years.

The AICPA accounting standards executive committee views this area of accounting, particularly consolidation practices and joint venture accounting, as one that requires attention now and has sent a series of issues papers (see Exhibit 2, page 409) to the FASB. The FASB has included a project on consolidation and equity method accounting in its discussions of possible future agenda projects and has expressed interest in the topic. Such a project should address the following issues to solve the problems noted in this article:

---

[12]This question also arises for subsidiaries, although it tends to be a lesser problem for subsidiaries because the parent company generally controls the accounting policies of a subsidiary.

EXHIBIT 2

AICPA ACCOUNTING STANDARDS EXECUTIVE COMMITTEE
ISSUES PAPERS RELATED TO CONSOLIDATION
AND EQUITY METHOD ACCOUNTING

1 *Reporting Finance Subsidiaries in Consolidated Financial Statements*, December 27, 1978.

2 *Joint Venture Accounting*, July 17, 1979.

3 *Accounting by Investors for Distributions Received in Excess of Their Investment in a Joint Venture*, October 8, 1979.

4 *"Push Down" Accounting*, October 30, 1979.

5 *Accounting in Consolidation for Issuances of a Subsidiary's Stock*, June 3, 1980.

6 *Certain Issues that Affect Accounting for Minority Interest in Consolidated Financial Statements*, March 17, 1981.

---

1 The circumstances and conditions under which separate financial statements are more useful than consolidated financial statements should be reconsidered. The guidelines for nonconsolidation of subsidiaries should be more objective than those of ARB No. 51 and should result in consolidation of most captive finance, insurance, leasing and real estate subsidiaries.

2 Accounting standards should be established for investments in all joint ventures regardless of legal form. If the FASB believes that different methods of accounting are appropriate for different circumstances or industries, guidelines for use of the different methods should be established to limit diversity in practice.

3 The equity method to account for less-than-50-percent-owned investments, the notion of "significant influence" and the presumptions relating to ownership of less than 20 percent or of 20 percent or more should be reconsidered. The present standards of Opinion No. 18 represent a compromise between two divergent views. Review of the 10 years of experience with Opinion No. 18 might provide a basis for more conceptually sound standards.

4 The implementation problems mentioned in this article should be resolved. In many cases, the diversity in practice is caused by the silence of the existing pronouncements rather than by strongly held divergent views. FASB decisions on the appropriate treatment would unify practice.

As the FASB completes work on some of its current projects, a project on consolidation and the equity method should be added to its agenda.

Segment Reporting: Hindsight After Ten Years

Bertrand Horwitz
State University of New York at Binghamton

Richard Kolodny
University of Maryland

Ten years have passed since the Securities and Exchange Commission (SEC) first required segment profit disclosure for Form 10-K in conformity with the continuing reporting requirements of the 1934 Act. The essential parts of the 1970 rule are still operating, but several additional changes have been made by the SEC in Regulation S-K for segment reports, effective March 15, 1978. These changes are based largely upon the standards set forth by the Financial Accounting Standards Board (FASB) in FASB No. 14, effective December 15, 1976, although, as we shall see, Item 1 of Regulation S-K goes beyond Statement No. 14.

Several interesting and controversial issues related to these SEC and FASB mandates have been raised during the last ten years. As we review the development of segment reporting requirements during this period, the discussion focuses on the following questions: (1) What were the reasons for mandating segment reports for publicly held corporations? (2) What have been the major changes in segment reporting since 1970, and why were they made? (3) Does the research on segment reporting requirements provide evidence that these reporting requirements were justified? and (4) Do the mandate on segment reporting and its amendments provide insight into the balance to be struck between private and governmental regulation of financial disclosure?

THE NEED FOR MANDATED SEGMENT PROFIT

Virtually all groups concerned with financial reporting—preparers, users, and auditors—have taken strong positions on the potential usefulness or harm of segment reporting requirements. Segment reporting, unlike some other issues in external reporting (e.g., restructuring of debt or oil and gas accounting), is not limited to a single industry or to a few, and it encompasses the basic problems of measuring profit and profitability. As the Advisory Committee on Corporate Disclosure to the SEC has said, "Few issues ... have been as enduring or as controversial as that of segment reporting."[1]

Two factors explain the attention that segment reporting has received. First, the growth of certain new types of corporations, the diversified conglomerate and the multinational corporation, controversial themselves as efficient forms of organiza-

From *Journal of Accounting, Auditing and Finance* (Fall 1980), pp. 20–35. Reprinted by permission of the *Journal of Accounting, Auditing and Finance,* Fall 1978, Copyright © 1978, Warren, Gorham & Lamont, Inc., 210 South Street, Boston, Mass. All rights reserved.

[1]Advisory Committee on Corporate Disclosure to the Securities and Exchange Commission, House Committee on Interstate and Foreign Commerce (Washington, DC: 1977), p. 380.

tion, seemed to create demands for different types of financial information for users. Second, an increased emphasis was placed upon the legal notion of fairness, a belief that conditions should be created to eliminate or limit the advantages of inside information thereby increasing the confidence of the public in the securities market. If segment information was useful to insiders and large investors, the fairness doctrine asserted that everyone should have access to it, provided, of course, that required disclosure was timely.

As we would expect, the growth of conglomerates and multinationals resulted in an increase in the voluntary supply of segment financial information, particularly sales revenue data. Thus, although only sixty-nine of the 600 firms surveyed for fiscal 1968 in *Accounting Trends and Techniques* revealed segment profits, 318 of 600 firms did indeed, disclose segment sales revenue in their annual reports [1]. To some extent, this difference can be attributed to a SEC requirement starting in 1949 that required information in Form 10-K on the relative importance of each line of business that contributed at least 15 percent to the enterprise's gross sales [1].

But why was it necessary to mandate segment profit reporting instead of allowing the market to determine the extent of such disclosure? In 1965, an investigation of conglomerates was conducted by the Subcommittee on Anti-Trust and Monopoly of the Senate Committee on the Judiciary, one outcome of which was a perceived, but unmeasured, need by investors for segment profit and profitability data. The SEC, under pressure from the Senate, then began to consider whether the need should be converted into a requirement. The possibility of SEC involvement in establishing rules prompted the Accounting Principles Board of the AICPA to issue Statement (not an Opinion) No. 2, "Disclosure of Supplemental Financial Information by Diversified Companies," in September 1967. The Board expressed an unwillingness to require compliance based upon established guidelines for segmentation at that time, preferring to wait until research showed (1) a need by investors for such data, (2) whether the data were reliable for investment decisions, and (3) whether such data were necessary for a fair presentation of the statements. It, along with the Financial Executives Institute, preferred to rely on voluntary disclosure and urged diversified companies to consider issuing segment profit reports.

Notwithstanding the emphasis initially placed by the APB and the FEI on voluntary segment disclosure, the SEC, following the recommendations of the Wheat Report [2], began requiring comprehensive reports on lines of business in registration statements filed on or after August 14, 1969. The Wheat Report had advocated a requirement by asserting that segment revenue and "to the extent feasible, profits, [were of] crucial importance to security analysis." In October 1970, this requirement was extended to the 10-Ks, and in October 1974, the SEC extended the disclosure requirements to cover corporate annual reports to stockholders.

The SEC's action raised doubts about the seriousness of the Commission when it stated in ASR No. 150 in December 1973: "[T]he Commission intends to continue its policy of looking to the private sector for leadership in establishing and improving accounting principles and standards through the FASB with the expectation that the body's conclusions will promote the interests of investors." It has been contended that in this case the problem was that voluntarism could not work, that compulsion was necessary, and that the APB was incapable of imposing the necessary requirements. Thus, action had to be taken by the SEC [3].

This attitude presumes, of course, that there was no doubt that segment profit reporting was necessary and that the APB was "foot dragging." What is implied is that the private sector's call for further research on the usefulness of segment profit reporting and the additional urging for voluntary reports ("jawboning") were merely screens by the APB based on self-interest. This scenario allegedly offers another example of government regulation's being necessary because voluntary self-regulation was not forthcoming. However, as we shall show later, the SEC and the FASB may have been too precipitate.

More recently, further doubts have been raised about the SEC's contention, expressed in ASR 150, that it looked to the private sector for leadership. These doubts stem from the fact that the SEC, although adopting Statement No. 14 in its S-K requirement effective March 15, 1978, went beyond it in several important respects without even waiting a reasonable period to evaluate the recently mandated requirements of No. 14. The differences are described in ASR No. 236. The important additional requirements were:

1 Regulation S-K requires disclosure of the effect of market prices in intersegment transfers when the basis used for transfer pricing is "substantially higher or lower than those charged to or received from unaffiliated parties . . .[and] is material to an understanding of the segment information."

2 Regulation S-K requires further segmentation of product class within each industry segment.

3 Regulation S-K requires the identity of major customers.

4 Regulation S-K requires five years of retroactive application; No. 14 stated that prospective application was sufficient.

Another significant difference for which, like the others, there was no stated support relates to the auditing area. Statement on Auditing Standards No. 21 states that the objective of auditing procedures relating to segment profit reporting is to provide the auditor with a reasonable basis for concluding whether the information is presented in conformity with No. 14 in relation to the financial statements as a whole. As noted in (1), above, and for other aspects of S-K, the SEC now requires that information be disclosed to the extent that it is material to the segment rather than the company as a whole, an apparent significant expansion of the materiality standard that clearly increases auditing costs without specifying expected benefits. Perhaps the expansion of the auditing task is void in content, however, since no guidelines are provided for defining "material" or "substantial."

Before proceeding to review the results of research on the effects of these segment reporting requirements, let us briefly consider the alternative to regulation, a voluntary system. It is important to point out that just because complete segment disclosure did not seem to be forthcoming under a voluntary system, it cannot be concluded that the existing system was not working.

In a voluntary system of financial reporting, it is to be expected that some companies will not disclose. However, if market participants deem segment reporting important for a particular firm, they will interpret the lack of disclosure by that firm as bad news and will reduce their willingness to buy that firm's shares; therefore, lack of disclosure will lead to a higher cost of equity capital for the nondisclosing firm than for a similar disclosing firm. Presumably, under this system, the costs and benefits as well as the level of disclosure would be determined in the marketplace jointly by corporations and investors.

With respect to segment profit reporting as well as many other areas of financial disclosure, however, there seems to be little inclination to allow market forces to work. One reason that has been given is that the voluntary solution is thought to be too distant. The Advisory Committee has said, "[E]ven if it were true that over the long run the market would penalize issuers which withheld useful information… frequently the 'run' is indeed long."[2] Aside from the fact that there is no empirical evidence to support this assertion, it has a fundamental flaw. It is difficult to understand why the required release of financial information of firms voluntarily withholding it is presumed to have an immediate effect, but the failure to voluntarily release such information is thought to have only a long-run effect. In other words, it is believed that the lack of voluntary disclosure is assumed by the market to be equivalent to "no news" rather than "bad news," even though at the same time some other firms are voluntarily disclosing. Perhaps, in fact, any lack of investor reaction to the nondisclosure of certain information reflects the zero or negative market price of that information.

Another reason for not relying on voluntarism is ethical rather than economic, and hence is difficult to evaluate. Confidence in the securities market has been asserted to rest upon the public's notion of fairness, and fairness is related to the equal access doctrine. Under this doctrine, it is assumed not fair when only some firms voluntarily disclose segment profit, and for those firms not disclosing, only insiders or large investors with sizable resources have access to such information. Thus, a former commissioner of the SEC stated about segment profit reporting: "[T]he fact remains that when some companies were reporting this information and some were not, there was an element of unfairness and possible competitive advantage."[3]

Equal access with respect to disclosure is similar to uniformity with respect to accounting measurement. If their imposition results in a change in allocative efficiency, judgments can be made about their value. If, on the other hand, they result in wealth transfers because processing costs are transferred between affected groups, then judgments are ethical. Both fairness and confidence are difficult to deal with unless they can be directly or indirectly measured. That mandated sameness is fair or increases confidence is, then, merely a matter of opinion. Further, equal access stemming from mandated disclosure assumes that all parties, insiders and outsiders, will have the same quality of information, that is, that timely disclosure can be mandated.

---

[2]*Id.*

[3]A. A. Sommer, "Financial Reporting and the Stock Market: The Other Side of the Issue," *Financial Executive* (May 1974), p. 39.

Related to the equal access argument for increased disclosure is the ascendant attitude about corporate democracy, the auditor as a fiduciary of the public and the special responsibilities of the corporation as a "creature of the state." At a conference on corporate disclosure Professor W. Mueller, formerly chief economist of the Federal Trade Commission, clearly stated the point:

> [T]he formulation of appropriate financial reporting standards for corporations is only one part of the larger issue of the rights and obligations of the large corporation. Indeed, nothing less is at stake than the continued social legitimacy of the modern corporation.... Most Americans seem to have forgotten that business corporations are created by and survive only as a special privilege of the state.... [C]orporate secrecy—not corporate disclosure—is the great enemy of a market economy....[4]

Similarly, those individuals supporting the mandating of federal chartering of corporations have linked it with an SEC requirement for a uniform disclosure rule for segment profitability, the segments to be defined by refining the Standard Industrial Classification Code in conjunction with the Bureau of the Census, the Justice Department's Anti-trust Division, and the FTC.[5] The above suggests the need to examine the research on the value of segment profit data.

RESEARCH ON SEGMENT REPORTING

Recently, the FASB has shown increased concern about assessing the costs and benefits of its standards. This is manifest in its Discussion Memorandum on Reported Earnings, which has been issued as part of the FASB's current review of the form and content of earnings reports, and in its Exposure Draft on Qualitative Characteristics. Both of these documents are part of the Board's work on the development of a conceptual framework.

The Discussion Memorandum associates disclosure requirements generally with the "*likelihood* that users will be able to make improved assessments of future earnings and cash flows and hence make better investment decisions."[6] With respect to segment reporting, in particular, the Memorandum states, "Disclosure of information by segments is . . . *likely* to enable users to make improved assessments of future earnings."[7]

This latter statement is a repetition of the following assertion, which was made earlier in FASB No. 14 and which, as we will show below, has little basis in fact: "The purpose of the information *required to be reported by this Statement* is to assist financial statement users . . . by permitting better assessment of the enterprise's past performance and future prospects."[8]

---

[4]*Corporate Financial Reporting: The Issues, the Objectives and Some New Proposals* (Chicago, IL: CCH, 1972), pp. 67–70.

[5]R. Nader, M. Green, & J. Seligman, *Taming the Giant Corporation* (New York: W. W. Norton, 1976), pp. 175–176.

[6]FASB, Discussion Memorandum, "Reported Earnings" (Stamford, CT: FASB, 1979), p. 27 (emphasis added).

[7]*Id.* at 62 (emphasis added).

[8]FASB, Statement No. 14, *Financial Reporting for Segments of a Business Enterprise* (Stamford, CT: FASB, 1976), par. 5 (emphasis added).

The Exposure Draft on Qualitative Characteristics devotes an entire section to costs and benefits, emphasizing again that the standard-setting authority must "identify and weigh, however subjectively, the probable costs and benefits to preparers and users."[9] It also identifies auditors as a third group whose costs and benefits would be considered.

The research performed on segment reporting has concentrated on examining what benefit, if any, segment reporting is to investors. As noted above, other than benefits associated with equal access, which are difficult to evaluate, proponents of segment reporting argued that required disclosure of profit and identifiable assets would lead to improvements in allocative efficiency due to the ability of investors to assess more accurately the earnings potential and risk of diversified firms. Let us examine the validity of these claims in the light of the research over the last ten years.

Table 1 classifies the relevant research according to a methodological approach. Existing studies have been classified into two general groups: indirect and direct. Many proponents of segment disclosure claimed that disaggregated data on a multiactivity firm permit capital market participants to predict more accurately a firm's future earnings and cash flows than could otherwise be done using only consolidated information. The indirect tests examine this claim by evaluating the ability of investors to make more accurate predictions using segment data. As indicated in Table 1, these indirect studies can be divided into those that report results on: (1) the accuracy of forecast models, (2) the accuracy of analysts' forecasts, and (3) the efficiency of the securities market with respect to segment information. These studies are characterized as "indirect" because they do not assess the impact of segment information on the securities markets directly but assume that if earnings forecasts are altered, security prices will be affected. Central to the indirect studies is the following question: Does the ability of the investor to make earnings forecasts improve when segment profit data are available?

The remaining "direct" studies in which security market effects are evaluated have been divided into (1) those that examine how quickly and accurately future earnings information is impounded in security prices, and (2) those that measure the impact of the release of segment information on security risk and return.

In assessing the results of the various studies, it is important to keep in mind the kind of segment information each author gives attention to (sales, profit, identifiable assets, etc.), where that information has been disclosed (in annual reports, 10-K, etc.), and whether it has been made available voluntarily or involuntarily.

One approach to forecasting the earnings of an n-segment firm is to aggregate the earnings forecasts for each segment where these forecasts have been made on the basis of n time series models, one for each segment. An alternative approach is to predict earnings on the basis of one time series model that uses only consolidated data. Questions have been raised regarding the usefulness of the segment approach to forecasting because of potential data contamination. This contamination is

---

[9] FASB, Exposure Draft, *Qualitative Characteristics: Criteria for Selecting and Evaluating Financial Accounting and Reporting Policies* (Stamford, CT: FASB, 1979), p. 50.

TABLE 1

Empirical Research on the Relevance of Segment Information to Investor Decisions

Indirect studies based on the ability to predict income			Direct studies based on security price adjustments	
Accuracy of forecast models:	Accuracy of analysts' forecasts:	Efficiency of market with respect to segment information	Impounding of future earnings information in security prices	Impact of release of information on security risk and return
Segment-based vs. consolidated-based	Prior vs. post-disclosure	(Prior to disclosure)		
Kinney [4]	Barefield & Comiskey [7]	Collins [9]	Kochanek [10]	Collins & Simonds [12, 13]
Collins [5, 6]	Barefield, Comiskey & Snyir [8]		Griffin & Nichols [11]	Dhaliwal [14]
				Horwitz & Kolodny [15, 16]

perceived to arise because of difficulties in classifying firm activities into segments and the arbitrariness of transfer pricing and joint cost allocation. Because of these problems, it is possible that the use of segment data may lead to invalid forecasts.

The purpose of the indirect research studies by Kinney [4] and Collins [5] was to determine whether market participants are able to make better earnings forecasts employing the segment approach. These studies assumed that if segment-based prediction models yield better forecasts than consolidated-based models, disclosure of this information is useful to investors.

To determine the level of aggregation that provides better forecasts, the following comparisons were made. The *earnings* forecasting accuracy of models that use disaggregated *sales* data was compared with the accuracy of models that use consolidated sales figures. Second, the earnings forecasting accuracy of models that use disaggregated earnings data was compared with the accuracy of models that use consolidated earnings figures. Finally, on the basis of the above analyses, comparisons have been made between the forecasting accuracy of models that use both disaggregated earnings and sales data and the accuracy of models that use disaggregated sales data alone.

In both studies, it was found that models based on segmented *sales* data and a firmwide profit margin permitted better forecasts of earnings than the use of aggregated data. However, with respect to profit data, the authors found that once sales figures are known, little improvement is provided by the knowledge of profit by segment. That is, the predictions produced by segment earnings models were no more accurate than models based on segment sales data and firmwide profit margins.

> Moreover, the main advantage of segment data appears to accrue from segment revenue disclosure, since predictive ability was enhanced only nominally when segment profit margin data were utilized in addition to segment revenue data. This suggests that arbitrary allocations of joint costs may limit the reliability and predictive usefulness of segment profitability data. . . . Investors should avoid placing undue reliance on segment profit figures as presently reported under SEC guidelines.[10]

Before reviewing the results of other studies, it is important to point out a fundamental problem that pertains to this avenue of research: the lack of generalizable results. Although it is possible to conclude that segment data are more useful than nonsegment data for a specific set of models, it cannot be concluded that this relationship holds for other models or that it holds with respect to actual investor experience. As Foster points out, analytical models that indicate the conditions under which disaggregation may improve or impair forecasting ability would be of greater use. "With such models one could then examine the properties of the data available and ex-ante predict the consequences of aggregation on predictive ability."[11]

Rather than relying on results based on hypothetical segment and consolidated earnings models, Barefield and Comiskey [7] and Barefield, Comiskey, and Snyir

---

[10]D. W. Collins, "SEC Line of Business Reporting and Earnings Forecasts," *Journal of Business Research* (May 1976a), p. 126.

[11]G. Foster, *Financial Statement Analysis* (Englewood Cliffs, NJ: Prentice-Hall, 1978).

[8] directly analyzed the effect of segmented profit data on the accuracy of earnings forecasts actually made by security analysts. More specifically, they sought to ascertain whether the enactment of the 1970 SEC requirement mandating disclosure of segment income data (1) had an effect on the average prediction error (bias) made by analysts, and/or (2) whether the requirement changed the level of consensus among analysts. Their results led to a rejection of the hypothesis that the average forecast error was reduced when segment profit data became available in 1971: "[D]ata were examined to see if forecasting performance [of analysts] improved as a result of the implementation of the disclosure requirement. Again, no significant impact was noted on bias [average error] scores."[12] Interestingly, they also found no evidence that analysts were less able to forecast earnings for multisegment companies than for single-product firms prior to 1971.

In the final indirect test of the value of segment data, Collins [9] examined the performance of security trading rules based on segment forecasting models. In particular, if the earnings predicted by the segment models were greater than those elicited from the consolidated models, the trading strategy tested required that the investor purchase the security (take a long position). Conversely, if the segment-based predictions were less than the consolidated-based ones, a short position was taken (the security was sold short).

After testing these trading models, Collins concluded:

> [D]isclosure of segment *revenue* data apparently does make a difference. The results suggest that investors were able to utilize this data to anticipate, to a large extent, changes in earnings which otherwise would have been "unexpected" had they relied totally on consolidated data. Thus, disclosure of segment *revenue* data, as a minimum, is indicated.[13]

In sum, the research conducted on the use of forecasting models indicated that segment sales data can be utilized to improve earnings forecasts and to make better investment decisions, but that the availability of segment profit numbers provides no marginal benefit. Second, when actual analysts' forecasts were examined, it was found that their predictions were no more accurate subsequent to required disclosure of segment profit than before.

The direct studies, that is, those based on security price adjustments to segment reporting, produced mixed results. The first two noted in Table 1, by Kochanek [10] and Griffin and Nichols [11], relate (1) the availability of segment data to (2) the timing of security price adjustments to earnings. The question addressed is, Does the presence of historical segment data permit better forecasts of future earnings, which, in turn, cause security prices to impound future earnings more quickly than if that data were not available? The underlying premise is that if security prices do respond more quickly to future earnings when segment data are disclosed, disclosure is warranted. Investor decisions would benefit, leading to a more efficient allocation of resources in the economy.

---

[12] R. Barefield and E. Comiskey, "The Impact of the SEC's Line of Business Disclosure Requirement on the Accuracy of Analysts' Forecasts of Earnings Per Share," Purdue University Working Paper (March 1975).

[13] D. W. Collins, "SEC Product-Line Reporting and Market Efficiency," *Journal of Financial Economics* (June 1975), p. 156.

Kochanek, and Griffin and Nichols find that the securities of firms that voluntarily disclosed more segment data in their annual reports in the late 1960s generally were subject to less abnormal returns around reporting time, and that earnings information seemed to be impounded in the security prices of these firms earlier than for firms that provided little or no segment data. With respect to the effect of the 1970 SEC disclosure law pertaining to line of business profit reporting, however, the evidence is unclear. Although not consistent across all studies, there is some indication that there was a reduction in perceived risk associated with the requirement [13, 14]. However, an examination of abnormal returns did not indicate that the capital market received any unanticipated information relevant to valuation in the period when line of business profit data were first required by the SEC [15].

The results of all the empirical studies taken together call attention to the fact that it is not sufficient to conclude that segment reporting in general does or does not provide benefits. One must consider the level of segment reporting and the rules pertaining to the measurement of segment data. Even staunch supporters of segment reporting must agree that at some level of detail, both with regard to the number of segments and with regard to information within each segment, no marginal benefit will ensue. Therefore, it is extremely important that further attempts be made to measure benefits and to identify the types, measurement procedures for, and format of segment reporting that are most useful to investors.

Nevertheless, based on the research performed to date and at some cost of generalization, we can conclude that the need and usefulness of segmented revenue data seem clear. However, little if any evidence exists today that supports the usefulness of profit reporting by segment or any of the additional requirements set forth under Statement No. 14 and Regulation S-K.

How then can one explain the initiation of segment profit reporting in 1969 and its subsequent development to S-K? We believe that it is a manifestation of a change in the balance of financial regulation between the FASB and the SEC.

PUBLIC VS. PRIVATE STANDARD SETTING

The SEC, unlike the FASB, is not dependent upon private funds for its survival, and it has manifested less patience with evaluating change before taking additional steps. This was true initially when the APB desired to wait to see how voluntary segment disclosures would work, and it was true recently when the SEC was unwilling to evaluate the results of Statement No. 14 before issuing new rules in Regulation S-K that went beyond No. 14.

It may be that the real issue is not the consequences of increased disclosure, although the language of cost versus benefits is frequently used. As we have summarized in the preceding section, the empirical research cannot be used to support the appropriateness of segment profit reporting. What may be relevant here, as we indicated earlier, is the general movement toward "corporate democracy," and the perception by the SEC that increased disclosure is, like sunshine, the best disinfectant and just as free.

It is not clear whether segment profit reporting helps investors by providing useful information or whether it simply advances government policy generally. One difficulty is that there is no correcting mechanism that will cause the SEC to reduce those disclosure requirements that have little benefit but significant cost associated with their production and dissemination. On the contrary, the SEC has increased the details of segment reporting requirements.

One measure of the trend toward increased disclosure, of which segment profit reporting is only one example, is the secular increase in the size of Form 10-K. In the ten-year period 1968–1978, the 10-K has manifested double-digit growth. For NYSE companies the average number of pages in 1968 was 56, including exhibits, and in 1978 the average number of pages, including exhibits, was 165. This represents an annual growth rate of 12 percent.

Perhaps, like other public agencies, the SEC will usually err on the side of excess. The reason may lie in the nature of a bureaucracy and the functioning of an agency. Public agencies generally avoid risk and do not internalize the costs they impose. As long as it cannot be shown that harmful effects ensue, and that a rule may be neutral, regulatory requirements will generally increase.

The SEC has shown that it is flexible where research indicates possible negative effects of a rule. This was true in the oil and gas decision where the SEC, in spite of its drive toward uniformity in measurement, revoked FASB Statement No. 19 and allowed nonuniform methods. This followed evidence about negative economic effects [17] and lobbying against the successful efforts rule.

Segment profit reporting, however, as indicated earlier, has been tested only for possible benefits. Evaluations have not been made about possible competitive harm. Thus, although the benefits of segment reporting have been found to be questionable, no anticompetitive harm has been found, so the costs have been ignored and disclosure has been mandated. The SEC may believe that for segment profit disclosure the costs will be internalized by all firms to no single firm's disadvantage. In other words, disclosure will be imposed when no external competitive harm can be forecast or determined, regardless of some increase in the reporting costs associated with compliance. When, however, possible harm is forecast or determined, such as in the case of the oil and gas rule, a requirement will not be imposed regardless of the alleged, but unmeasurable, benefits, such as confidence and fairness.

One of the costs associated with segment profit reporting that has not been fully evaluated is the impact in the U.S. capital markets of U.S. companies being required to report segment profits when foreign companies report only segment revenues. At the present time, no foreign law or stock exchange rule mandates public disclosure of profits attributable to industry or geographic segments.

The SEC, considering the need to have foreign issuers conform to U.S. requirements, accepted the contention of foreign companies that segment profit reporting would result in too great a cost burden and would cause them competitive harm. The SEC was thus led to require only segment revenue data on its Form 20-F. It is not clear how the SEC determined that for foreign issuers mandating segment profile was cost-inefficient but for U.S. issuers it was cost-efficient.

More important, if segment profit reporting is so important, as the SEC has argued for the last ten years, doesn't the "secrecy" by foreign firms, which increasingly are raising capital in the U.S. equity market, place those firms in a more favorable

THE HOWARD
MORTGAGE ADMINISTRATION DEPT.
P.O. BOX 1101
NEWARK, NJ 07101

Due to the late receipt of many real estate tax bills, we are unable to analyze New Jersey loans at the present time.

Until we are able to provide you with a new coupon book, it is your responsibility to make your payments when they are due. Please put your loan number on your check or money order, and send it to the address shown above, without a coupon.

Coupons and/or analysis will be mailed to you as soon as possible.

position? If so, does it have economic consequences; that is, is it "anti-competitive," a term used by the SEC in its 1975 amendment to the Securities Act of 1934? Also, and perhaps equally important, does it accord with the Commission's notion of fairness?

In conclusion, many issues associated with segment reporting have been raised. They encompass the basic problems of financial reporting, that is, measurement, disclosure, and auditing. The only regulations that can be compared with segment reporting in terms of their implications and comprehensiveness are the Securities Acts of 1933 and 1934, which first mandated accounting disclosure and assigned responsibility to the SEC for establishing disclosure and measurement rules for financial statements as a whole. The justification for those Acts, besides investor protection, has rested on their contribution to the increase in capital market efficiency.[14] The drive to mandate segment reporting was supported by the same justification—in particular, by arguments that the ability of investors and creditors to evaluate the earnings potential and risk of diversified firms would be enhanced.

With respect to segment profit reporting, which is the focal point of all requirements during the last decade, the research performed thus far indicates that its economic value is questionable. The analysis presented in this article leads us to conclude that the explanation for mandating that profits be reported by segment cannot be sought in economic analysis alone but must also be examined in the light of models that attempt to explain the behavior of public agencies.

REFERENCES

J. Twombly, "Historical Origins of Segment Reporting" (unpublished manuscript, Northwestern University, 1977).

Wheat Report, *Disclosure to Investors* (Chicago: CCH, 1969).

R. Sprouse, "Prospects for Progress in Financial Reporting," *Financial Analysts Journal* (Sept.-Oct. 1979), pp. 56–60.

W. R. Kinney, Jr., "Predicting Earnings: Entity versus Subentity Data," *Journal of Accounting Research* (Spring 1971), pp. 127–136.

D. W. Collins, "Predicting Earnings with Subentity Data: Some Further Evidence," *Journal of Accounting Research* (Spring 1976), pp. 163–177.

D. W. Collins, "SEC Line of Business Reporting and Earnings Forecasts," *Journal of Business Research* (May 1976), pp. 117–130.

R. Barefield and E. Comiskey, "The Impact of the SEC's Line of Business Disclosure Requirement on the Accuracy of Analysts' Forecasts of Earnings Per Share," Purdue University Working Paper (March 1975).

R. Barefield, E. Comiskey, and A. Snyir, "Line of Business Reporting: Its Impact on Analysts' Forecasts of Earnings" (unpublished manuscript).

D. W. Collins, "SEC Product-Line Reporting and Market Efficiency," *Journal of Financial Economics* (June 1975), pp. 125–164.

R. Kochanek, "Segmental Financial Disclosure and Security Prices," *The Accounting Review* (April 1974), pp. 245–258.

P. A. Griffin and G. G. Nichols, "Segmental Disclosure Rules: An Empirical Evaluation" (unpublished manuscript, Stanford University, June 1976).

---

[14]J. Burton, "An Interview with John C. Burton," *Management Accounting* (May 1975), p. 21.

D. W. Collins and R. R. Simonds, "Line of Business Reporting and Security Prices: An Analysis of an SEC Disclosure Rule: Comment," *The Bell Journal of Economics* (Autumn 1978), pp. 646–658.

D. W. Collins and R. R. Simonds, "SEC Line of Business Disclosure and Market Risk Adjustments," *Journal of Accounting Research* (Autumn 1979), pp. 352–383.

D. S. Dhaliwal, "The Impact of Disclosure Regulations on Cost of Capital," in *Economic Consequences of Financial Accounting Standards, Selected Papers* (Stamford, CT: FASB, 1978), pp. 71–100.

B. Horwitz and R. Kolodny, "Line of Business Reporting and Security Prices: An Analysis of an SEC Disclosure Rule," *The Bell Journal of Economics* (Spring 1977), pp. 234–249.

B. Horwitz and R. Kolodny, "Line of Business Reporting: A Rejoinder," *The Bell Journal of Economics* (Autumn 1978), pp. 659–663.

D. Collins and W. Dent, "The Proposed Elimination of Full Cost Accounting in the Extractive Petroleum Industry: An Empirical Assessment of Market Consequences," *Journal of Accounting and Economics* (March 1979), pp. 3–44.

INCOME TAXES

Accounting for corporate income taxes has been a topic of debate which has divided accountants for more than thirty years. The basic issue relates to the critical event in the incurrence of the tax obligation. One group steadfastly holds to the legal position that the obligation arises when the tax calculation is made each year. The other stresses the economic position which is that the obligation to pay arises with the earning of income; by this view it is only the timing of the payment that is determined by the annual calculation of the tax bill.

The APB, perhaps in an effort to compromise the issue and to arrive at a workable solution, adopted the deferred tax concept in APB Opinion No. 11 in 1967. This position requires comprehensive tax allocation and endorses the deferred method in preference to the liability method. The basic difference between these two methods relates to the assumptions made as to future tax rates and the treatment of subsequent changes in tax rates.

The adoption of this position, which was by a bare (two-thirds) majority of the Board, has been followed because the AICPA's Code of Professional Ethics (Rule 203) requires the use of methods consistent with the authoritative pronouncements of the profession. Nonetheless, substantial numbers of accountants and users have criticized the opinion. The topic is again on the agenda of the FASB for reconsideration. The three articles included in this section express several opposing views.

In "Let's Fix Deferred Taxes," R. D. Nair and Jerry J. Weygandt find conceptual problems with the deferred method. They argue for acceptance of the liability method, by which the probability of future tax payments would govern the accounting recognition of income tax expense. The authors point out that the liability method is compatible with the FASB's preference for the asset-liability approach to analyzing accounting problems, while the deferred method is an outgrowth of the traditional

423

emphasis on the matching of costs and revenues (an income statement approach). Acceptance of the liability method would mean, according to Nair and Weygandt, that timing differences relating to depreciation and installment sales would not give rise to income tax allocation entries if a reversal of the effects were not likely to occur in the foreseeable future.

The Canadian Institute of Chartered Accountants adopted comprehensive tax allocation at the same time as the Americans did in 1967, and the Canadians, like the Americans, are currently debating the wisdom of retaining the comprehensive approach or abandoning it in favor of partial tax allocation. Under partial tax allocation, timing differences not likely to reverse in the foreseeable future are not part of interperiod tax allocation. In "Let's Stop Taking Comprehensive Tax Allocation for Granted," Christina S. R. Drummond and Seymour L. Wigle contend that, since the balance in deferred taxes has been growing as a percentage of shareholders' equity for major Canadian companies, it is evident that reversals are not occurring. Therefore, comprehensive tax allocation "results in information that does not reflect the reality of business." The deferred tax credit is, in the authors' view, potentially a contingent liability, but since the government has not yet assessed a claim against the taxpayer, a liability has not been incurred, and an important criterion for recognizing contingent liabilities is not present.

J. Alex Milburn replies to Drummond and Wigle in "Comprehensive Tax Allocation: Let's Stop Taking Some Misconceptions for Granted." He contends that a reversal does occur in the later years of a depreciable asset's life. Merely because the overall balance of deferred taxes rises does not deny the fact that the account has been debited for reversals and credited for newly recognized timing differences for assets acquired during the current fiscal period. Milburn does believe, however, that income tax allocation entries should be based on discounted present values. He does not seem to be opposed in principle to the use of the liability method, but his conception of "reversal" is very different than that of Drummond and Wigle.[1]

BIBLIOGRAPHICAL NOTES

The literature on income tax allocation is fairly extensive. Several studies on the subject are as follows:

Beechy, T. H.: *Corporate Income Taxes: Conceptual Considerations and Empirical Analyses* (Toronto: Canadian Institute of Chartered Accountants, 1983).
Beresford, Dennis R., Lawrence C. Best, Paul W. Craig, and Joseph V. Weber: *Accounting for Income Taxes: A Review of Alternatives* (Stamford, Conn.: FASB, 1983).

---

[1]The proper conception of "reversal" was discussed by Sidney Davidson almost 20 years ago; he would side with Drummond and Wigle. See "Comments by Sidney Davidson," in Homer A. Black, *Interperiod Allocation of Corporate Income Taxes,* Accounting Research Study No. 9 (New York: AICPA, 1966), pp. 117–119. In Opinion No. 10, Par. 6, the APB rejected the discounting approach to accounting for tax allocation; Sidney Davidson and Frank T. Weston dissented. (Interestingly, the accounting firm of which J. Alex Milburn is a partner is affiliated internationally with Arthur Young, of which Weston was a partner.)

Wheeler, James E. and Willard H. Galliart: *An Appraisal of Interperiod Income Tax Allocation* (New York: Financial Executives Research Foundation, 1974).

A review of the circumstances and discussions attending the issuance in the U.K. of two accounting standards on tax allocation accounting within the space of but three years is:

Hope, Tony and John Briggs: "Accounting Policy Making—Some Lessons from the Deferred Taxation Debate," *Accounting and Business Research* (Spring 1982), pp. 83–96.

Let's Fix Deferred Taxes

R.D. Nair
University of Wisconsin-Madison

Jerry J. Weygandt
University of Wisconsin-Madison

Interperiod income tax allocation has been a controversial topic for many years. Accounting Principles Board Opinion No. 11, *Accounting for Income Taxes,*[1] issued 14 years ago, did not still the turmoil but seemed instead to increase it. Now, as the Financial Accounting Standards Board tries to bring greater coherence into financial reporting principles, accounting for income taxes should be reevaluated. In fact, interperiod income tax allocation touches on many of the issues central to the FASB's conceptual framework project, such as the definitions of assets and liabilities, the role of matching in income determination, the prediction of cash flows, the evaluation of an enterprise's liquidity and solvency, the relevance and reliability of financial statement numbers and the costs and benefits of accounting information.

We recommend a change from the current method of accounting for income taxes. This article describes three alternatives and presents our views on which of those would solve the problems associated with the method of interperiod income tax allocation in use at present.

REASONS FOR REEVALUATION

Five reasons why a reevaluation of accounting for income taxes is particularly important at this time follow:

From *Journal of Accountancy* (November 1981), pp. 87, 90, 92–94, 96, 98, 100, 102. Reprinted by permission of the American Institute of Certified Public Accountants. Copyright © 1981 by the American Institute of Certified Public Accountants, Inc.

Authors' note: We are grateful to Ernest Hanson, CPA, Ph.D., and Larry Rittenberg, CPA, Ph.D., who are both professors of accounting and information systems at the University of Wisconsin-Madison, for their comments and to Paul Rosenfield, director of the AICPA accounting standards division, for his extensive editorial suggestions.

[1]Accounting Principles Board Opinion No. 11, *Accounting for Income Taxes* (New York: AICPA, 1967).

1 Recent developments in the U.S. The FASB's issuance of Concepts Statement No. 3, *Elements of Financial Statements of Business Enterprises,*[2] makes imperative a change from the deferred method of comprehensive interperiod income tax allocation, which emphasizes the tax effects of a timing difference on income of the period in which it originates. The discussion in that concepts statement explicitly states that the deferred method does not fit any of the definitions of balance sheet elements adopted by the FASB. It is therefore inevitable that the FASB will reconsider income tax allocation. With the issuance of Concepts Statement No. 3, some businesses have asked the FASB whether they can now depart from the requirements of APB Opinion No. 11. In addition, in 1980 the American Institute of CPAs accounting standards executive committee (AcSEC) unanimously voted to request the FASB to reconsider income tax allocation.

2 Recent developments in the United Kingdom. In October 1978 the U.K.'s Accounting Standards Committee issued Statement of Standard Accounting Practice No. 15 (SSAP 15), *Accounting for Deferred Taxation.*[3] Effective for fiscal years beginning in 1979, SSAP 15 requires tax allocation for short-term timing differences and for other originating timing differences unless it can be demonstrated that the differences will not reverse within three years. If tax allocation is required, partial allocation may be appropriate.

SSAP 15 does not specify the liability method, in which income taxes expected to be paid on pretax accounting income are accrued currently, but allows either the liability or the deferred method. However, alternatives to comprehensive income tax allocation by the deferred method have now become standard practice in the U.K. Practical experience in implementing the partial allocation approach and the liability method in that country should be helpful to the FASB when it reconsiders the issue of accounting for income taxes in the U.S.

3 International standards. International Accounting Standard No. 12, *Accounting for Taxes on Income,*[4] which became effective this year, calls for a type of interperiod income tax allocation that is a combination of the U.S. and U.K. approaches. It permits either the deferred or the liability method and permits either partial or comprehensive allocation; tax allocation is permitted but not required for timing differences that will not reverse for at least three years.

Although the international standard is not binding on U.S. CPAs, it has created an area in accounting in which the international standard is more permissive than the U.S. standard. The increasing attention being given to harmonization of accounting standards across countries is another reason why accounting for income taxes in the U.S. should be reevaluated.

4 Costs to small businesses. Our conversations with practitioners have indicated that the requirements of APB Opinion No. 11 are expensive for companies to implement. The costs of the information being provided seem to exceed its benefits,

[2]Financial Accounting Standards Board Concepts Statement No. 3, *Elements of Financial Statements of Business Enterprises* (Stamford, Conn.: FASB, 1980).

[3]Accounting Standards Committee, Statement of Standard Accounting Practice No. 15, *Accounting for Deferred Taxation* (London, Eng.: ASC, October 1978).

[4]International Accounting Standards Committee, International Accounting Standard No. 12, *Accounting for Taxes on Income* (London, Eng.: IASC, 1979).

especially for small businesses. Evidence from various sources indicates that the requirements of Opinion No. 11 are viewed as burdensome by small businesses and that some small businesses do not fulfill all the disclosure requirements of the opinion.[5] As the FASB tries to reduce the reporting burden of small businesses, income tax allocation is among those areas to which it should direct its attention.

5 Implementation problems. The FASB has recently issued several pronouncements on accounting for deferred income taxes in special situations.[6] Those pronouncements are inconsistent with the concepts underlying the treatment of deferred income taxes in APB Opinion No. 11 and will lead only to confusion and misunderstanding. This is not surprising, as Opinion No. 11 lacks a sound conceptual basis. For example, Raymond Perry states that

> ...the adoption of the deferred method, with its emphasis on mechanical calculations rather than concept, has created numerous interpretation problems over the years... And in the years since APB Opinion [No.] 11 was adopted, differences between reported income and taxable income have proliferated...Applying all of these complications under the with-and-without computation required by the deferred method under APB Opinion [No.] 11 can create a nightmare of computational difficulties and give rise to varying interpretations. In addition to being extremely complex, these interpretations can also have very significant effects on reported income. Accordingly, it will probably be necessary for the patchwork of income tax accounting pronouncements and interpretations that now exist to be reconsidered by the FASB in the early 1980s.[7]

REQUIREMENTS OF APB OPINION NO. 11

APB Opinion No. 11 requires comprehensive income tax allocation to be part of the determination of income tax expense. The tax effects of a transaction that affects both pretax income and taxable income, but in different periods (timing difference), must be recognized in the period in which the transaction first affects either pretax accounting income or taxable income and also must be recognized in the period in which the difference reverses. Income tax expense in the period in which the timing difference originates includes all accruals, deferrals, and estimates necessary to make that expense equal to what it would have been had the pretax income effect and the taxable income effect both occurred in the current period. Under comprehensive tax allocation, the tax effects of a transaction are recognized in the period in which the transaction occurs.

Comprehensive allocation is required even if it is virtually certain that a reversal

---

[5]See, for example, Financial Accounting Standards Advisory Council Small Business Advisory Committee, *Report of Task Force on GAAP Requirement of Concern to Small or Closely Held Businesses* (Stamford, Conn.: Financial Accounting Standards Advisory Council, December 1978); Seymour Eisenman and Steven B. Lilien, "Accounting Deficiencies in Financial Statements," *CPA Journal,* July 1978, pp. 28–34; Robert W. Ingram, Dan M. Guy, Issam J. Merei and Robert T. Justis, "Disclosure Practices in Unaudited Financial Statements of Small Businesses," JofA, Aug. 77, pp. 81–86.

[6]See, for example, FASB Statement No. 31, *Accounting for Tax Benefits Related to U.K. Legislation Concerning Stock Relief* (Stamford, Conn.: FASB, 1979), and FASB Statement No. 37, *Balance Sheet Classification of Deferred Income Taxes* (Stamford, Conn.: FASB, 1980).

[7]Raymond Perry, "Income Taxes," *Handbook of Accounting and Auditing,* John C. Burton, Russell E. Palmer and Robert S. Kay, eds. (Boston, Mass.: Warren, Gorham and Lamont, 1981), ch. 25.

of a timing difference will be offset by another timing difference. Income tax allocation is not used for a transaction that affects either pretax accounting income or taxable income but not both (permanent difference).

In addition to comprehensive allocation, Opinion No. 11 also adopted the deferred method of income tax allocation. Deferred taxes are based on the tax rate in effect in the period the timing difference originates and are not adjusted for subsequent changes in tax rates or to reflect the imposition of new taxes. Opinion No. 11 deals with past tax savings, not future tax payments.

The tax effect of a timing difference that reduces taxes payable before the period in which it reduces pretax income is treated as a deferred credit; the tax effect of a timing difference that increases taxes payable before the period in which it increases pretax income is treated as a deferred charge. The deferred items are positive or negative tax savings and not economic resources or obligations. However, such items were recognized as part of the basic elements of financial accounting by the APB in Statement No. 4, *Basic Concepts and Accounting Principles Underlying Financial Statements of Business Enterprises*:

> Assets also include certain deferred charges that are not resources but that are recognized and measured in conformity with generally accepted accounting principles.... Liabilities also include certain deferred credits that are not obligations but that are recognized and measured in conformity with generally accepted accounting principles.[8]

The APB indicated that deferred income taxes should be classified in two balance sheet categories—one for the net current amount and the other for the net noncurrent amount. The current portion of deferred income taxes relates to assets and liabilities classified as current. For example, deferred income tax credits relating to depreciation of a fixed asset should be classified as a noncurrent item. A deferred income tax charge related to an estimated provision for warranties classified as a current liability should be a current item.

Finally, the APB ruled in Opinion No. 11 that the tax benefit of a realizable loss carryback should be recognized in income of the period of the taxable loss. However, the tax benefit of a loss carryforward should not be recognized until it is used to offset taxable income, except in unusual situations in which realization is assured beyond reasonable doubt.

ANOMALIES INTRODUCED BY THE APB AND THE FASB

In APB Opinion No. 23, *Accounting for Income Taxes—Special Areas*[9] the APB addressed the tax implications of

- Undistributed earnings of subsidiaries.
- General reserves of stock savings and loan associations.
- Amounts designated as policyholders' surplus by stock life insurance companies.
- Undistributed earnings of corporate joint ventures.

---

[8]APB Statement No. 4, *Basic Concepts and Accounting Principles Underlying Financial Statements of Business Enterprises* (New York: AICPA, 1971), par. 132.

[9]APB Opinion No. 23, *Accounting for Income Taxes—Special Areas* (New York: AICPA, 1972).

An enterprise must take specific action for income tax purposes before taxes become payable on timing differences related to those special areas, and the taxes may never become payable unless the enterprise takes those actions. To handle those four special areas, the APB created the indefinite reversal concept by which the tax effect of the initial timing differences need not be recognized if sufficient evidence indicates that the enterprise does not intend to take the action that would reverse the initial timing differences.

The indefinite reversal concept is inconsistent with comprehensive tax allocation.

In FASB Statement No. 31, *Accounting for Tax Benefits Related to U.K. Tax Legislation Concerning Stock Relief,* the FASB clarified the accounting for certain changes in the U.K. tax law on stock relief (in the U.K., inventory is known as stock). Enterprises in the U.K. are permitted to deduct increases in the carrying amount of inventories to determine taxable income. Before Statement No. 31, the tax benefits had been deferred as a timing difference that would reverse, should inventories decrease in future years. That reversal would increase taxable income, causing a clawback (in the U.K., recapture is known as clawback) of the previously granted tax benefits.

In July 1979, the U.K. adopted legislation that provides that the potential for clawback of the stock relief tax benefit in a particular year terminates if it has not been clawed back in the six succeeding years.

The FASB concluded that the tax benefit resulting from stock relief should be deferred unless it is probable the benefit will not be clawed back. The tax benefit should be recognized by a reduction of income tax expense in the period in which it becomes probable the benefit will not be clawed back. Similarly, if the tax benefit had not previously been deferred and circumstances change to make clawback probable, the tax detriment should be deferred by a charge to income tax expense in the period in which clawback becomes probable.

The board said that the treatment of this situation was unique in accounting for income taxes and the treatment should not be used elsewhere. The board nevertheless introduced a probability of reversal criterion into tax allocation. Such a criterion had been rejected in APB Opinion No. 11.

Although APB Opinion No. 11 requires balance sheet classification of deferred tax items to be based on the classification of related assets or liabilities, some timing differences are not tied to an asset or liability. Examples are deferred charges and credits relating to long-term construction contracts, undistributed earnings of subsidiaries and a change in method of accounting for income tax reporting purposes.

The FASB in Statement No. 37, *Balance Sheet Classification of Deferred Income Taxes,* ruled that (1) deferred tax charges and credits not related to assets or liabilities and (2) deferred tax charges and credits related to assets or liabilities whose timing differences do not reverse as a result of reductions of those assets or liabilities should be classified based on the expected reversal dates of the timing differences, applying the criteria used for classifying other assets and liabilities. The board provided several illustrations of how those deferred income tax items should be classified. That ruling is consistent with the view that balance sheet classification should be based on the period of expected turnaround, which implies that the deferred charge or credit is a claim to receive cash or an obligation to pay cash.

Such a classification rule is inconsistent with the deferred method of tax allocation.

The FASB requires deferred income tax charges and credits to be classified as monetary assets and liabilities for constant dollar accounting in FASB Statement No. 33, *Financial Reporting and Changing Prices*.[10]

A monetary asset is money or a claim to receive a fixed or determinable amount of money. A monetary liability is an obligation to pay a fixed or determinable amount of money. Classifying deferred tax items as monetary therefore is inconsistent with the implication in APB Opinion No. 11 that they are not resources or obligations.

Although the FASB justifies its classification on the grounds of practicality, the treatment is symptomatic of problems in the deferred method of comprehensive tax allocation.

DECREASED IMPORTANCE OF MATCHING

APB Opinion No. 11 justified comprehensive tax allocation by contending that it "results in a more thorough and consistent association in the matching of revenues and expenses, one of the basic processes of income determination."[11] However, matching is coming under increasing attack. Robert Sprouse, a current FASB member, says matching is "too often an attractive but empty slogan rather than a meaningful concept one can look to for guidance" and that "what constitutes 'proper matching'...is very much in the eyes of the beholder."[12] In any event, an overzealous attempt at matching leads to deferred amounts that are not resources or obligations, as in Opinion No. 11. In Concepts Statement No. 3, the FASB excludes such deferred items from its definitions of assets and liabilities. The statement also makes clear that the "...deferred method that is prescribed by APB Opinion [No.] 11...does not fit the definitions. Deferred income tax credits are neither liabilities nor reductions of assets in Opinion [No.] 11." The statement also says that only "the liability method and the net-of-tax method are compatible with the definitions in this Statement."[13]

CONFUSING EFFECTS OF TAX ALLOCATION

The erosion of comprehensive income tax allocation by the deferred method after APB Opinion No. 11 points to the need for reevaluation of the concepts in that opinion. The following jumble of effects of tax allocations on income statements also illustrates that need:

- Permanent differences (adjustment to income)—interest received on state or municipal bonds.
- Permanent differences (adjustment to paid-in capital)—tax effect of the difference between stock compensation charged for book and tax purposes is credited to paid-in capital.

---

[10]FASB Statement No. 33, *Financial Reporting and Changing Prices* (Stamford, Conn.: FASB, 1979).

[11]APB Opinion No. 11, par. 31.

[12]Robert T. Sprouse, "The Importance of Earnings in the Conceptual Framework," JofA, Jan. 78, p. 69.

[13]Concepts Statement No. 3; pars. 164 and 163.

• Timing-permanent differences (limited deductibility for tax purposes)— contributions, for example, may be a timing difference for a period but a portion may be lost.

• Timing-permanent differences (interactive)—intangible drilling costs may be expensed or capitalized for tax purposes, but its ultimate benefit is unknown because cost or statutory depletion may interact to magnify the benefit.

• Timing differences (APB Opinion No. 11)—accelerated depreciation for tax purposes versus straight-line depreciation for financial reporting.

• Timing differences (indefinite reversal)—undistributed earnings of a subsidiary.

• Timing differences (probability criterion)—tax benefit from tax relief should be deferred unless it is probable that the benefit will not be recaptured.

Balance sheet classification is also a jumble:

• Current assets—carryback or carryforward of net operating losses; deferred income tax charges.

• Long-term assets—carryforward of net operating losses; deferred income tax charges.

• Current liabilities—deferred income tax credits; income taxes payable.

• Long-term liabilities—deferred income tax credits; income taxes payable.

• Stockholders' equity—paid-in capital from tax effects related to stock compensation awards.

No common thread ties together the various ways to handle timing differences and the various ways to classify the resulting balance sheet amounts. The FASB appears to be moving slowly toward a form of the liability method for deferred income taxes but seems reluctant to acknowledge it. In effect, the FASB appears to be saying that we can ignore APB Opinion No. 11 any time we encounter a problem in this area because the opinion does not help solve the problem.

The board's move toward the liability method is understandable. Recent empirical evidence indicates that deferred tax credits are considerably higher than amounts that will ever have to be paid related to them. Even though such a result is compatible with the deferred method, the FASB seems to be dissatisfied with that result. Examples of the increases in the deferred tax account are given by Sidney Davidson, Lisa Skelton and Roman Weil, who studied 3,108 firms on Compustat tapes for the 19-year period from 1954–55 through 1972–73. They found 18,184 changes in deferred tax credit accounts during the period. Only 3,896 of those were decreases. Also, the decreases totaled $5.9 billion while the increases totaled $39.5 billion. They also point out that deferred tax credits related to depreciation are unlikely to decrease when income taxes are payable and found that, of the 3,896 decreases in deferred tax credits, 688 had a decrease in gross plant and, of those, only 406 had income taxes paid or payable. They conclude that only about 3 percent of the decreases in deferred tax credits related to depreciation occurred in years in which taxes had to be paid. Keith Lantz, Andrew Snyir and John Williams confirm those findings.[14] William Voss found that repayments in his sample occurred less than 2 percent of the time. He concludes that, "With this low frequency, repayment

---

[14]"A Controversy Over the Expected Behavior of Deferred Tax Credits," JofA, Apr. 77, pp. 53–59.

can hardly be called the expected event. Further, the probability of reversal will be lower for firms with a growth in the dollar amount of average investment. As long as the price level is rising, we have such a force working against the expectation of repayment."[15] J.T. Ball points out that, "for many companies, deferred income tax credits have increased considerably more than retained earnings in the past decade."[16]

Both income statement and balance sheet reporting of deferred income taxes are in flux. The movement is away from the deferred method in APB Opinion No. 11 to other bases, especially the liability method, but in a piecemeal fashion without a consistent theme. Credibility in financial reporting is threatened.

A DESCRIPTION OF THREE ALTERNATIVES

Three alternatives to the deferred method of comprehensive income tax allocation have been suggested:[17] (1) the liability method, (2) the net-of-tax method and (3) no interperiod tax allocation.

1 Liability method. Under the liability method of income tax allocation, as mentioned earlier, income taxes expected to be paid on pretax accounting income are accrued currently. The taxes on the components of pretax accounting income may be computed at different rates, depending on when the components were or are expected to be included in taxable income. The difference between income tax expense and income taxes in the period in which the timing differences originate are either liabilities for taxes to be paid in later periods or assets consisting of prepaid taxes. Under the liability method, the initial computations are considered to be estimates and are subject to adjustment if tax rates change, if taxes are repealed or if new taxes are imposed. That treatment contrasts with the deferred method in which deferred taxes are determined on the basis of tax rates in effect when the timing differences originate and are not adjusted; they are allocated to the periods in which the timing differences reverse.

2 Net-of-tax method. The net-of-tax method associates the tax advantage of the ability to deduct the basis of an asset in determining taxable income with the service potential of the asset to provide other benefits. The method allocates the tax advantage over the useful life of the asset.

3 No interperiod tax allocation. Income taxes should not be allocated between years. Income tax expense of a year should be the income taxes paid or payable for the year, that is, the tax on the tax return for the year.

In evaluating the three options given above, we use the conceptual framework being developed by the FASB. Specifically, in Concepts Statement No. 1, *Objectives of Financial Reporting by Business Enterprises,*[18] Concepts Statement No. 2,

[15] William M. Voss, "Accelerated Depreciation and Deferred Tax Allocation," *Journal of Accounting Research,* Autumn, 1968, pp. 262–269.

[16] J. T. Ball, "Accounting for Income Taxes," *Accountants Handbook,* Lee J. Seidler and D. R. Carmichael, eds. (New York: John Wiley & Sons, 1981), ch. 13.

[17] Homer A. Black, Accounting Research Study No. 9, *Interperiod Allocation of Corporate Income Taxes* (New York: AICPA, 1966), and James E. Wheeler and Willard H. Galliart, *An Appraisal of Interperiod Income Tax Allocation* (New York: Financial Executives Research Foundation, 1974).

[18] Concepts Statement No. 1, *Objectives of Financial Reporting by Business Enterprises* (Stamford, Conn.: FASB, 1978).

Qualitative Characteristics of Accounting Information,[19] as well as Concepts Statement No. 3, the FASB has provided guidelines to aid in the choice among accounting alternatives.

Among the objectives in Concepts Statement No. 1 are

- "Financial reporting should provide information about the economic resources of an enterprise, the claims to those resources..., and the effects of transactions, events, and circumstances that change resources and claims to those resources."[20]

- "...financial reporting should provide information...[useful in assessing] the amounts, timing, and uncertainty of prospective net cash inflows to the...enterprise."[21]

- "Financial reporting should provide information about how an enterprise obtains and spends cash...."[22]

- "Financial reporting should provide information...on the [factors that] may affect an enterprise's liquidity and solvency."[23]

In Concepts Statement No. 2, the FASB considers two qualitative characteristics of accounting information, relevance and reliability, to be the most important. Linked to the first characteristic is the concept that information should help users make predictions. Linked to the second characteristic is the concept that a description or measure should represent faithfully what it purports to represent. The benefits of information should exceed its cost in order for it to be useful and worth providing.

The FASB in Concepts Statement No. 3 defines liabilities as "... probable future sacrifices of economic benefits arising from present obligations of a particular entity to transfer assets or provide services to other entities in the future as a result of past transactions or events."[24] The FASB explains that "*probable* is used with its usual general meaning, rather than in a specific accounting or technical sense (such as that in Statement No. 5 [*Accounting for Contingencies*], paragraph 3[25]), and refers to that which can reasonably be expected or believed on the basis of available evidence or logic but is neither certain nor proved."[26] Also, the term "*obligations* in the definition is broader than *legal obligations.* It is used with its usual general meaning to refer to duties imposed legally or socially; to that which one is bound to do by contract, promise, moral responsibility, etc."[27] We shall use the terms *probable* and *obligations* in the same sense as the FASB. The FASB points out that to apply the definition of liabilities "thus commonly requires assessments of probabilities, but degrees of probability are not part of the [definition]. That is, the degree of probability... of a future cash outlay or other sacrifice of future economic benefits ...and the degree to which its amount can be estimated with reasonable reliability

[19]Concepts Statement No. 2, *Qualitative Characteristics of Accounting Information* (Stamford, Conn.: FASB, 1980).

[20]Concepts Statement No. 1, par. 40.

[21]Ibid., par. 37.

[22]Ibid., par. 49.

[23]Ibid., par. 49.

[24]Concepts Statement No. 3, par. 28.

[25]FASB Statement No. 5, *Accounting for Contingencies* (Stamford, Conn.: FASB, 1975), par. 3.

[26]Concepts Statement No. 3, n. 13.

[27]Ibid., n. 14.

that [is] required to recognize an item as a ... liability ... are matters of recognition and measurement that are beyond the scope of this Statement."[28]

THE THREE ALTERNATIVES COMPARED

Our views on the three alternatives for interperiod income tax allocation follow:

1 Liability method. Deferred income taxes calculated by the liability method and partial allocation meet the definition of a liability given in Concepts Statement no. 3. The liability method is not compatible with comprehensive tax allocation. For example, liabilities and related charges to income should not be accrued if it is not probable that taxes in those amounts eventually will be paid. The probability of tax payment should be evaluated on the basis of the company's plans for future growth, investment and sales, impending changes in the tax laws as well as the probability of the company's having positive taxable income in the future. If tax payments are indefinitely postponed, liabilities for them and related expenses should not be reported because the taxes probably will not be paid.

The liability method implies partial allocation, because partial allocation takes account of the fact that the reversal of timing differences will probably be offset by the onset of other timing differences. A traditional objection to the liability method has been that the same is true of accounts payable—that as one payable is settled, it is usually offset by the incurrence of another payable. However, accounts payable are paid, and the cash flows of the company are affected. When reversals are offset, the cash flows of the company are not affected; no money need be paid and therefore no liability exists. Opponents also argue that offsets cannot be relied on to continue, and an offset does not nullify the fact of the reversal. However, even a reversal that is not offset by another timing difference does not automatically create a determinable liability to pay taxes. Payment of taxes would still be contingent on having positive taxable income in the year of reversal, and a liability has been incurred only if that is probable.

The essence of our position is that tax allocation is justified, but only in a few limited instances in which taxes will probably be paid in the future, based on present obligations. It may be argued by those who oppose interperiod tax allocation that a company no more owes future taxes than it owes future wages for work yet to be performed by its employees. The two situations differ. If, for example, a company makes an isolated installment sale of a productive facility and reports the gross profit at the date of sale for financial reporting purposes and as the payments are collected for tax purposes, at the date of sale a liability for future tax payments has been created, because it is probable that a payment will have to be made in the future to satisfy a present obligation arising from a past transaction. The transaction is the sale of the facility. Since it is an isolated installment sale, the reversal of this timing difference will not be offset by the onset of other timing differences. The uncertainty involves whether the company will have positive taxable income in the year of reversal. If that is probable—as we assume in this example—a liability exists. There

---

[28] Ibid., par. 40.

is a present obligation *and* payment is probable. The same reasoning cannot be applied to wages for work to be performed in the next fiscal year by employees. In our view, until the work has been performed, no obligation resulting from a past transaction or event exists.

2 Net-of-tax method. Although the FASB in Concepts Statement No. 3 states that "both the liability method and the net-of-tax method are compatible with the definitions in this Statement,"[29] the net-of-tax method is not compatible with the rest of the framework. Supporters of the net-of-tax method contend that it both results in a helpful allocation and a helpful valuation, because the effects of the net-of-tax method on net income and on net assets are the same as the effects of the deferred method; the only differences are the locations in the balance sheet at which the items are reported and the types of expense charged in the income statement. However, the current accounting framework does not permit the net-of-tax approach. For example, depreciation is a process for allocating costs to periods. The charge for depreciation does not represent the decline in the value of the asset and would equal that decline only by coincidence. In fact, depreciation is now being reported when assets are becoming more valuable. That is a result of the historical cost system. A valuation approach such as the net-of-tax method does not fit that system.

3 No allocation. Not recognizing deferred income taxes as a liability hinders evaluation of prospective cash flows. Application of the definitions in Concepts Statement No. 3 leads to the conclusion that deferred income taxes may, in a few situations, be liabilities and that they should be reported as such.

THE LIABILITY METHOD: ITS TIME HAS COME

Adoption of the liability method with partial tax allocation and related disclosures would solve the problems of interperiod income tax allocation and would eliminate different types of timing differences. The resulting balance sheet amounts would be assets and liabilities that are represented faithfully since they represent economic benefits and sacrifices—amounts that probably will be received from or paid to the government. Those items would be classified like other receivables or payables. The amounts expected to be received or paid during one operating cycle would be classified as current and the remainder would be classified as noncurrent. That classification would help users predict future cash flows of the enterprise and evaluate its liquidity and solvency. The liability approach also has flexibility in that changes in tax rates can be recognized, improving the ability of users to predict future cash flows. The benefits of using the liability method with partial tax allocation would exceed the costs, which may decline, since a smaller number of timing differences would require attention.

A complete and consistent application of the liability method requires discounting of the anticipated tax payments. Discounting would involve two tasks: (1) estimating the time of expected reversal to determine the period over which the payments should be discounted and (2) determining an appropriate interest rate. The first

[29] Ibid., par. 163.

problem is not new. FASB Statement No. 37 requires companies to estimate when certain reversals will occur to classify the related deferred charge or credit. The choice of interest rate is more difficult, and any rate is likely to be arbitrary. The AICPA accounting standards division is at present studying discounting in accounting, including the selection of discount rates. An attractive candidate, in our opinion, is the use of an imputed interest rate in the manner discussed in APB Opinion No. 21, *Interest on Receivables and Payables*.[30] Such a rate would provide an approximate discounted amount of the liability and would help users predict future cash flows and evaluate solvency.

[30]APB Opinion No. 21, *Interest on Receivables and Payables* (New York: AICPA, 1971).

Let's Stop Taking Comprehensive Tax Allocation for Granted

Christina S.R. Drummond
Director of Accounting Research
Price Waterhouse
Toronto

Seymour L. Wigle
Partner
Price Waterhouse
Toronto

The practice of comprehensive tax allocation has been followed in Canada for over 30 years and has been mandatory for almost half that period. The concept is now so well-entrenched that most accountants take it for granted; it is followed simply because "it has always been done that way."

But the amounts set aside in corporate balance sheets as "deferred income taxes" are getting larger and continue to represent a considerable percentage of total assets. Perhaps the time has come to step back and start asking some questions: What, for example, is tax allocation? How did it start? Where is it leading us? Is it really the best method of accounting for income taxes? Have we been going down the wrong road—and for too long?

Income taxes are assessed by the government on the amount of taxable income earned in a period. Accounting income as shown in the financial statements may serve as a starting point for the computation of taxable income; but the two amounts can be—and usually are—very different. Accounting income is calculated in accordance with generally accepted accounting principles; taxable income is subject to strict legislative requirements and to the administrative practices established by Revenue Canada.

From *CAmagazine* (October 1981), pp. 56–61. Reprinted with permission, from *CAmagazine*, October, 1981, published by the Canadian Institute of Chartered Accountants, Toronto, Canada.

Taxation rules and rates are, of course, designed to promote the government's economic policies. Income taxes payable by a corporation are classified as a cost of being in business, and so accountants have invented the concept of comprehensive tax allocation. If income taxes were regarded as a distribution of profit to the government, and not as a business expense, the problems of tax allocation would not arise. The concept is perhaps an attractive one—but it involves considering the purpose and nature of income tax and so is beyond the scope of this article.

WHAT IS TAX ALLOCATION?

According to the tax allocation concept, the charge for income taxes in the financial statements should be based on the accounting income recognized for that period, irrespective of the amount assessed for taxation purposes.

The underlying bases of the concept are straightforward:

• Income tax is a cost of running the business in the same way that wages, salaries and raw materials are costs.
• The matching of costs and revenues is a fundamental accounting concept.
• Income tax is akin to a period cost; therefore, the provision should be based on the accounting income earned in any period.

Very simply, the provision for income taxes is calculated by assuming that accounting income, after adjustment for any non-taxable items, is assessed for taxes at the tax rate in effect that year. This is the amount to be charged in the income statement. The difference between this charge and the amount of taxes actually assessed for the year is transferred to the balance sheet under the caption "Deferred Income Taxes." The concept envisages that deferred tax will be brought back into the income statement in future years when the timing differences reverse and the taxes assessed exceed the charge based on the accounting income of those future years.

Originally, there was considerable controversy over whether deferred tax in the balance sheet represented a liability. Current practice carefully excludes deferred tax from the categories of both liabilities and shareholders' equity. Instead, the amount is described as a "deferred credit" (or, perhaps more aptly, as a dangling credit) and exiled to "no man's land."

HOW DID IT ALL START?

The deferred tax problem dates back to the 1940s and 1950s when the Income Tax Act was altered and claims for capital cost allowances were no longer limited to the amount of depreciation recorded in the accounts. This change eliminated management's dilemma of either charging an excessive amount as depreciation, in order to be in a position to claim maximum capital cost allowances, or making an appropriate depreciation charge and so being unable to claim the full tax allowances. But it raised the spectre of what the appropriate charge for income taxes should be.

In September 1954, the CICA issued Bulletin #10, requiring disclosure of the effect on income taxes of timing differences, and indicating that it was "desirable" to do so by providing for deferred income tax in the financial statements.

By the mid-1960s it was felt that the different methods (providing for deferred income tax as opposed to simply disclosing what it would amount to) were resulting in confusion. In September 1967 the CICA issued Bulletin #26, which made the provision of deferred income tax mandatory (with only isolated exceptions) after 1967—and so "comprehensive tax allocation" came into being. Bulletin #26 was transformed, substantially unchanged, into Section 3470 of the *CICA Handbook.*

A similar situation existed in the US. Comprehensive tax allocation was made mandatory with the issue of APB Opinion #11 in 1967. Since then, the position has remained unchanged in both countries. But, before comprehensive tax allocation was made mandatory, the position in the US had vacillated.

In 1946, the AICPA issued Accounting Research Bulletin #23, which concluded:

"Neither allocation nor disclosure is necessary . . . in the case of differences between the tax return and the income statement where there is a presumption that they will recur regularly over a comparatively long period of time."

In 1958, Accounting Research Bulletin #44 took the opposite view:

"Where material amounts are involved, recognition of deferred income taxes in the general accounts is needed to obtain an equitable matching of costs and revenue and to avoid income distortion, even in those cases where the payment of taxes is deferred for a relatively long period."

In 1966, shortly before making comprehensive tax allocation mandatory, the AICPA published the research study *Interperiod Allocation of Corporate Income Taxes.* This study was based entirely on the premise that income taxes were an expense of doing business and should be allocated between periods. The study concentrated merely on how to allocate, rather than why.

This defect in the study was highlighted in the preface written by the AICPA's director of accounting research, who wrote:

"The study does not answer fundamental questions about the nature of the income tax and the validity of the concept of interperiod income tax allocation. Whether income taxes are conceptually expenses or distributions of income has not really been resolved by the profession. Similarly, whether taxes should be allocated or whether the taxes currently payable should be the income tax expense for a period has never been adequately studied."

It has been suggested that this is a "strange phenomenon of a research study which completely ignores nine-tenths of what should have been its logical subject matter," and that the research study's starting point was "hypothetical tax accounting is here and, therefore, is good."[1]

Terminology for Accountants describes deferred income taxes as: "The accumulated amounts by which income taxes charged in the accounts have been increased or decreased as a result of timing differences."[2]

While this description may be correct from an accounting viewpoint, it is far

[1] *Is Generally Accepted Accounting for Income Taxes Possibly Misleading Investors?* (Price Waterhouse & Co. (US), 1967).

[2] *Terminology for Accountants* (Toronto: CICA, 1976).

from enlightening to the non-accountant. To the average shareholder, the words "deferred income taxes" probably suggests two things—that taxes are payable and that the payment is deferred. This, of course, is not correct. The amounts involved have not been assessed as taxes; they are not payable; consequently, the payment cannot possibly be deferred.

Although the language used for this amount is well established, it is undoubtedly accounting jargon. Jargon may be useful or even necessary in some instances, but not when it risks misleading the shareholders and other users of financial statements.

DEFERRED TAX—SOME CONTRARY ARGUMENTS

Comprehensive tax allocation, as we have said, is designed to uphold the matching concept and to avoid distortions in periodic net income due to the fluctuations in actual taxes payable.

But there are quite a number of reasons that might be put forward to cast doubt on the propriety of comprehensive tax allocation.

• The government assesses income taxes on taxable income computed in accordance with the law of the land. Accounting income as shown in the financial statements is not assessable, and never will be assessable, for income tax. If taxation is not, and never will be, levied on accounting profit, there is no real reason why the tax charge should bear any relationship to the income shown in the financial statements.

• Income tax accrues with the earnings of taxable profits, not with the earnings of accounting profits. Proper matching of costs and revenues should match the tax charge with the taxable income.

• Expenses fluctuate in relation to circumstances, and it is not considered acceptable to apportion them to achieve income smoothing. There is no reason why income smoothing should be applied to income taxes. If one company has a heavy capital investment program, should that company show the same tax charge as a company that has the same accounting income but does not have a capital investment program? Shareholders and other users of financial statements should be aware of the impact of capital investments—not misled, as could happen with income smoothing.

• Many enterprises maintain that their policy on the acquisition of fixed assets indicates the turnaround position will not occur in the foreseeable future; consequently, the deferred tax balances continue to increase.

• Capital cost allowances are designed to encourage capital expenditure, not to recognize the depreciation of assets. Following this argument, there is no need to equate capital cost allowances with the depreciation charge made in financial statements.

• At the end of a financial period, there is no legal liability for payment of taxes other than those assessed on taxable income. The amount of deferred tax that a company may one day have to pay is indefinite and problematical. It is very much of a contingent nature. The *CICA Handbook* has established standards for the recognition of contingencies, but comprehensive tax allocation conflicts with those standards. This point is discussed in more detail later.

• The appropriation of earnings as a provision for deferred tax does not have any impact on cash flow. In the funds statement, deferred tax is shown as an "add-back" and frequently referred to as a source of funds. This is apt to mislead readers of financial statements into thinking that something has been received.

• Dividends are normally considered a distribution of net earnings. When the amount of dividend paid is related to the amount of net earnings—as it generally is—the provision of deferred tax penalizes the current shareholders. On the other hand, it could perhaps be said that the provision for deferred tax represents, in a rough and ready way, some recognition of inflation and a storing of funds that should not be distributed to shareholders.

• Income tax is not a cost of doing business. Rather, it is a special cost imposed by the government and represents a forced distribution of profits to the non-voting shareholder—the government. This viewpoint questions the basic nature of income tax.

HOW HAS COMPREHENSIVE TAX ALLOCATION AFFECTED COMPANIES?

For the past 13 years companies have been required by generally accepted accounting principles to make a charge for deferred tax in their income statement. The amount so charged is accumulated in the balance sheet. This raises two questions: How much has been set aside? Is it necessary to set aside these amounts? In an attempt to answer these questions, we looked at the financial statements of a group of 70 companies.

The companies chosen were the largest public companies in Canada as listed by *The Financial Post*. We chose companies whose financial statements were available for the years 1970, 1975 and 1980. Some large companies had to be excluded because mergers, acquisitions, etc., had made it impossible to compare their 1970 financial statements with those issued for 1980.

The accompanying table illustrates deferred tax accumulated in the balance sheets of companies in eight major industries. Because of the impact of general inflation, it would not be useful to compare absolute amounts expressed in 1970 dollars with absolute amounts expressed in 1980 dollars. The data extracted from the financial statements is, therefore, expressed in percentages that can be compared over time without suffering the distortion caused by inflation.

The table shows deferred tax expressed as a percentage of shareholders' equity and as a percentage of total assets. Statistics for the oil and gas industry were not computed for 1970 because, at that time, many companies in the industry did not provide for deferred tax on all timing differences. While there are variations among industries and, particularly, among individual companies, one overall trend is apparent.

The amount of deferred tax set aside 10 years ago averaged over 12% of the total amount shown in shareholders' equity and over 6% of total assets. By 1980, those amounts had climbed to over 23% and almost 9% respectively. In other words, the

Taxes Accumulated in Balance sheets of Eight Industries

Deferred Taxes as a Percentage

Industry	of Shareholders' equity			of Total assets		
	1980	1975	1970	1980	1975	1970
Food & beverage	17.21	10.71	5.69	7.61	4.91	3.14
Manufacturing	19.32	17.55	14.67	8.66	7.60	6.87
Mining	21.35	19.22	15.36	9.46	8.43	8.95
Oil & gas	24.13	20.83	N/A	12.10	11.32	N/A
Paper & publishing	21.76	24.01	18.61	10.03	10.50	8.91
Real estate	54.49	44.88	22.78	5.63	5.72	4.18
Retail & wholesale	7.27	7.86	5.98	2.72	2.65	2.71
Transportation & communications	35.74	28.76	11.66	10.27	9.01	5.38
Averages						
Excluding oil & gas	23.50	20.19	12.64	8.68	5.71	6.14
Including oil & gas	23.46	20.32	12.64	9.31	8.26	6.14
Increases						
1980 over 1970		85.9%			41.4%	
1980 over 1970 in dollar amounts (excluding oil & gas)			431.79%			

amounts set aside and accumulated as deferred tax, when related to shareholders' equity, have increased by 86% in the 10-year period. When related to total assets, they have increased by 41% in the same 10-year period.

A straight comparison of the dollar amounts set aside as deferred tax in 1970 and 1980 shows an increase of over 400%! This also gives some insight into the cumulative effect of inflation on our dollar over the last 10 years.

WHERE IS COMPREHENSIVE TAX ALLOCATION LEADING US?

These results suggest it is time to pause and reflect why companies are forced to follow this bookkeeping exercise. The question—Where is deferred tax accounting leading us?—can be answered in one word: Nowhere!

Is it really useful to the shareholder, the investment analyst and other users of financial statements to have an amount equivalent to 9% of the total assets and 23% of shareholders' equity set aside on balance sheets as a "nothing" figure? The trend over the past 10 years for this amount to increase presumably will continue. What will the amounts be in 10 years' time? We seriously doubt if there is any benefit in showing such large amounts as deferred tax, especially when they are classed as neither a liability nor an increase in shareholders' equity and may be ignored when calculating balance sheet ratios.

The basic assumption of deferred tax accounting is that corporations will have to pay the amounts accumulated in the deferred tax account to the government at some future time. The income statement is reported as though this were a certainty. This conservative approach may have been justified in the past when it was perhaps unclear whether the deferred tax balances would have to be paid. But the evidence now clearly indicates this is not happening. Even when a business is not expanding, it must still replace its assets to continue in existence. General inflation and specific price changes continue to increase the dollar amounts of replacement costs, generating larger dollar amounts of timing differences and making it less and less likely that deferred tax will ever be repaid. Even in these days of recession and depression, deferred tax balances continue to grow as companies have to replace their assets at higher and higher prices in order to stay in business.

The result of deferred tax accounting is that reported profits and earnings per share are lowered and shareholders' equity is understated, all because of an accounting method that does not reflect the reality of business life.

THE GOING CONCERN CONCEPT

The *Handbook* makes it clear that the going concern concept is a fundamental assumption underlying generally accepted accounting principles. This concept assumes that an enterprise will continue in operational existence for the foreseeable future. Implicit in the financial statements is the absence of any intention or necessity to liquidate or curtail significantly the scale of operations.

It is a fact of life that general inflation exists and is a perpetual phenomenon. It can be taken for granted that an enterprise which is a going concern will continue to replace its assets and that those assets will be replaced at increased dollar amounts. New timing differences will, therefore, continue to arise to offset any reversal of the former timing differences. And because the new timing differences are expressed in larger dollar amounts, they not only offset the reversal of the former timing differences but result in larger amounts being classified as deferred tax. This hypothesis is confirmed by the survey of Canadian companies summarized in this article.

We contend that deferred tax should not be provided on a comprehensive basis because to do so is inconsistent with the going concern concept that is fundamental to the preparation of periodic financial statements.

DEFERRED TAX—A CONTINGENT LIABILITY

We have suggested earlier that deferred tax is very much of a contingent nature. How does the accountant define a contingency or, more specifically, a contingent liability? The CICA's *Terminology for Accountants* offers this definition:

"A legal obligation that may arise in the future out of past and/or present circumstances provided certain developments occur."

This seems a perfectly acceptable definition and one that is as easily understood by the non-accountant as by the accountant. There is an equally good description of a contingency in the *CICA Handbook* itself:

"An existing condition or situation involving uncertainty as to possible gain or loss to an enterprise that will eventually be resolved when one or more future events occur or fail to occur."

Both descriptions convey the same meaning, and both can be said to describe deferred tax: an amount that is not at present a liability, but that may become one in future if certain things happen or do not happen.

The accounting requirements for contingencies are set out in Section 3290 of the *Handbook*. This section is a comparatively recent addition to the *Handbook*, but its underlying principles are not new; it is a section which, when it was issued in 1979, codified what had long been accepted as good accounting practice. The section requires an assessment of the probable outcome of a contingency and a measurement of its uncertainty. Is the chance that some future development will or will not occur high, or slight, or not determinable?

Provisions for a contingent loss should be made in the financial statements only if:

- It is likely a liability has been incurred at the date of the financial statements.

and

- The amount can be reasonably estimated.

If one or both of these conditions are not met at an accounting date, then, according to the *Handbook*, "accrual of an estimated amount would be inappropriate."

This seems to suggest there is a particularly glaring inconsistency between the philosophies underlying two sections of the *Handbook*. Deferred tax, by definition, is not a liability because it has not yet been assessed against the taxpayer. Section 3470 requires that deferred tax be accrued, or provided for against income; Section 3290 stipulates it would be inappropriate to accrue the charge unless a future assessment is likely to result in a liability and the amount can be reasonably estimated.

PARTIAL TAX ALLOCATION—A PARTIAL SOLUTION?

Is there a way out of this dilemma and the apparent contradiction between the two *Handbook* sections?

Partial tax allocation, sometimes referred to as the "probability method" of tax allocation, is not a new concept; it has been suggested in various formats since at least the 1950s. It has reemerged recently as a means of countering the perceived disadvantages of comprehensive tax allocation.

Under partial tax allocation, deferred taxes are set up in respect of only those timing differences that are expected to reverse in the foreseeable future, and to result in income taxes being paid. The foreseeable future is normally interpreted as being at least three years.

The partial tax allocation approach recognizes that, although government incentives and capital cost allowances may be said merely to defer payment of tax, in practice, the continuing availability of such incentives results in permanent non-assessment. The provision of taxes on this basis would also result in the financial statements giving a much clearer and fairer indication of the real impact of taxes on a corporate taxpayer.

A summary of the advantages of partial tax allocation will perhaps best indicate the reasons we believe it should commend itself to further study by the CICA.

• The partial concept recognizes that deferred taxes are not legal liabilities at the accounting date.

• The partial concept recognizes that setting a provision only in the amounts that are likely to reverse within the foreseeable future is in accordance with the accounting treatment of contingent liabilities.

• Partial tax allocation requires the exercise of judgment when assessing the available evidence on the likelihood of circumstances arising that would result in a reversal of the timing difference. But the judgment should be no more difficult to exercise than that necessary for making other estimates entering into the preparation of financial statements.

• Partial tax allocation recognizes fully that financial statements are prepared on the going concern basis.

• The foreseeable future could be interpreted as being at least three years. This is within the period used by most enterprises in their capital budgeting processes.

• Partial tax allocation recognizes that only those timing differences expected to reverse will have an impact on an enterprise's flow of funds.

WHAT SHOULD BE DONE?

We believe that comprehensive tax allocation contravenes both the fundamental going concern concept and the accounting standard on the recognition of contingencies. We do not believe there is much merit in the statement that deferred tax does not constitute a liability but is merely a "deferred credit." The crucial factor is that deferred tax is charged in the income statement as if it were a liability. The fact that accountants describe the balance sheet item as as deferred credit is a play on words with no real substance. There is no doubt, therefore, that Section 3470 and the concept of comprehensive tax allocation is in urgent need of revision.

The reality of business life is that the amount of a corporation's income tax for any one year is based on the income shown in that year's tax return. The fact that this amount is different from what it would have been if the tax were assessed on the income shown on the financial statements may be interesting and relevant information—but it is based on hypothesis. The notional tax charge may perhaps be of some interest to sophisticated investment analysts, but it is not particularly useful unless some estimate of an eventual tax charge in future years can be given. It should not automatically imply that the hypothesis forms part of the basic financial statements, thereby running the risk of misleading the average shareholder who is liable to think it refers to taxes assessable but payable at a later date.

We suggest that tax allocation should not be required when it results in information that does not reflect the reality of business. Instead, there should be a general presumption that the income tax charge reported in any year should be the amount shown on the tax returns as taxes actually payable. The only exceptions are instances where specific differences can reasonably be expected to reverse within the foreseeable future and give rise to a liability. Tax allocation should be applied only when it is reasonably certain that timing differences will affect the flow of funds in the foreseeable future. Therefore, we strongly advocate the adoption of the partial tax allocation method, a method that fully accords with both the requirements on accounting for contingencies and the fundamental going concern concept.

As mentioned earlier, there is a viewpoint that would treat income tax as a distribution of profit to the government and not as a cost of earning income. This suggestion has been put forward by a number of writers and should not be dismissed lightly.

The philosophy would require a complete rethinking on the part of business executives, investment analysts and other users of financial information. The income or earnings before income taxes would have to become the key criterion used to judge an investment or an enterprise's performance. All ratios would have to be computed on a before-tax rather than an after-tax basis.

PLEA FOR A FULL INVESTIGATION

Back in 1966, the preface of the AICPA Research Study indicated that the fundamental questions as to the nature of income taxes had not been adequately studied. Surely, the time has now come to fully investigate this basic question.

Therefore, we urge the CICA to take up the challenge and reappraise the requirements of Section 3470 on comprehensive tax allocation. It is of the utmost urgency that we adopt, in Canada, a method that can be described as a generally accepted accounting principle in the true sense of the term.

Comprehensive Tax Allocation: Let's Stop Taking Some Misconceptions for Granted

J. Alex Milburn
Partner in National Accounting Research
Clarkson Gordon, Toronto

In their recent article "Let's stop taking comprehensive tax allocation for granted" (*CAmagazine,* October 1981, p. 56), Christina S. R. Drummond, CA, and Seymour L. Wigle, FCA, took issue with comprehensive tax allocation. They condemned it as a potentially misleading "bookkeeping exercise," and "an accounting method that does not reflect the reality of business life."

The arguments they raised are not new; they have been discussed and written about over many years.[1] Although the CICA, as well as standard setters in the

From *CAmagazine* (April 1982), pp. 40–46. Reprinted, with permission, from *CAmagazine,* April, 1982, published by the Canadian Institute of Chartered Accountants, Toronto, Canada.

[1] As evidence of this, the reader may wish to refer to the sources included in the list of references at the end of this article.

United States and other countries, has considered and rejected them,[2] Drummond and Wigle are not alone. Of late, a number of articles has appeared expressing similar views. Moreover, fairly recently, the Institute of Chartered Accountants in England and Wales (ICAEW) adopted "partial tax allocation" on the basis of reasoning which paralleled that of Drummond and Wigle.[3]

The case they set may seem persuasive to a casual reader. More than this, their presentation may lead some readers to conclude that the accounting profession and, in particular the CICA Accounting Research Committee, must have been negligent or incompetent in requiring accounting which, if one believes the authors, is so completely without merit.

It is, therefore, most important to thoroughly examine their case. In so doing, I think one should distinguish between the basic principles of tax allocation and the "deferral method" presently required by the *CICA Handbook* Section 3470, "Corporate Income Taxes." One may, of course, agree with the basic principles but find fault with the method by which they are implemented. The purposes of this article are:

• First, to demonstrate that Drummond's and Wigle's case against comprehensive tax allocation is misguided—that it is premised on certain misconceptions. In a positive sense, what follows attempts to demonstrate that the basic principles of comprehensive tax allocation are sound, and follow logically and necessarily from fundamental concepts that are at the basis of our financial accounting model.

• Second, to point out that the "deferral method" of tax allocation fails to recognize an accepted business reality—that a dollar payable in the future is not as onerous as a dollar payable today. In other words, I suggest that more realistic income tax figures would be obtained by an appropriate discounting approach. Moreover, I suggest that the nondiscounting of deferred taxes is the legitimate cause for concern, not the basic principles of tax allocation per se. The second part of this article briefly discusses the deferral method, and what would be involved in considering a discounting alternative.

FRAMEWORK FOR ANALYSIS

The following framework for analysis should help focus the discussion:

• Tax allocation will be evaluated within the "generally accepted" historical cost-matching model. The emphasis here is on its basic concepts—that is, in reasoning forward from accepted concepts of "assets," "liabilities," "income," "expense," and the matching of costs and benefits within the historical cost framework. There are those who have been very critical of this historical cost-matching

---

[2]Note, for example, that *CICA Handbook* Section 3470.09–10 on corporate income taxes lists the main arguments raised by Drummond and Wigle. Unfortunately, however, the *Handbook* section does not contain any discussion of the reasoning underlying the decision to reject these arguments.

[3]"Accounting for Deferred Taxation," Statement of Accounting Practice M15 (London: Institute of Chartered Accountants in England and Wales, October 1978).

model. Thomas, for example, would like to do away with allocations altogether,[4] and others have advocated various forms of current value accounting. But we can only play one game at a time—and the evaluation of tax allocation within other possible systems is beyond the scope of this article.

• The analysis will concentrate on timing differences which result in deferred tax credits and, more specifically, capital cost allowance/depreciation differences. These have resulted in the largest amounts of deferred taxes, and this focus enables the primary issues to be studied without introducing the additional problems of deferred tax debits and other more complex timing difference situations.

• Finally, the claiming of capital cost allowance in excess of depreciation charged will be addressed largely in terms of whether it should result in an increase in current tax expense and a corresponding credit on the liability side of the balance sheet. This is the most common orientation; it is the one Drummond and Wigle took; and it is the perspective adopted by the *CICA Handbook*. An alternative would be to conceive of claiming capital cost allowance as using up some of the tax deductibility value of the particular fixed assets, that is, take a net-of-tax approach. The same fundamental issues can be addressed from a net-of-tax (asset offset) perspective, but it would seem simpler to confine our discussion here to the more traditional "deferred tax credit" approach.

This framework seems consistent with that of Drummond and Wigle.

THE HEART OF THE CASE

There are two very basic, and very old, arguments at the heart of Drummond's and Wigle's claims:

1 Deferred tax credits are not legal liabilities.

2 Deferred tax credits should not be set up where "new timing differences will...continue to arise to offset any reversal of the former timing differences." (I will refer to this as the indefinite deferral argument.) I propose to analyze each of these arguments and then, with these analyses in mind, examine certain statements in the Drummond and Wigle article.

Deferred Taxes and Legal Liabilities

The argument is that deferred income taxes should not be recognized because "there is no legal liability for payment of taxes other than those assessed on taxable income." This implies that "generally accepted accounting principles" recognize costs only to the extent there is a legally binding claim on the entity—which is, of course, false. If this were the basis for accounting, we would recognize no warranty expense in respect of goods sold except where legally enforceable claims had been made at the end of the reporting period; we would recognize no pension expense at

---

[4]A. L. Thomas, *The Allocation Problem in Financial Accounting Theory, Studies in Accounting Research No. 3 and No. 9* (Sarasota: American Accounting Association, 1969 and 1974).

least until benefits had vested; we would recognize no liability for capitalized leases because future lease payments are not legally payable; etc., etc.

In short, our accrual basis of accounting is not tied to legal form, but endeavours to reflect the economic substance of obligations arising from past events and transactions. A Financial Accounting Standards Board Statement of Financial Concepts put it this way:

"...existence of a legally enforceable claim is not a prerequisite for an obligation to qualify as a liability if the future payment of cash or other transfer of assets to settle the obligation is otherwise probable."[5]

The Indefinite Deferral Argument

Drummond and Wigle also argued that a major proportion of deferred income taxes should not be recorded for the more fundamental reason that they may never be paid. This is a much more subtle argument that merits very careful analysis, because it has been the subject of much confusion over many years.

The Institute of Chartered Accountants in England and Wales accepted the argument in its 1978 statement on "Accounting for Deferred Taxation." This statement described the indefinite deferral rationale as follows:

"In many businesses timing differences arising from accelerated capital cost allowances are of a recurring nature, and reversing differences are themselves offset, wholly or partially, or are exceeded, by new originating differences, thereby giving rise to continuing tax reductions or the indefinite postponement of any liability attributable to the tax benefits received."[6]

Having accepted this basic argument, it was a small step for Drummond and Wigle to observe that:

"Even when a business is not expanding, it must still replace its assets to continue in existence. General inflation and specific price changes continue to increase the dollar amounts of replacement costs, generating large amounts of timing differences and making it less and less likely that deferred tax will ever be repaid."

And, to reason from this that: "New timing differences will, therefore, continue to arise to offset any reversal of the former timing difference."

They ultimately concluded that: "...deferred tax should not be provided on a comprehensive basis because to do so is inconsistent with the going concern concept that is fundamental to the preparation of periodic financial statements."

A seductive line of reasoning—but there is a serious flaw in it. This flaw is no mere technicality or petty theoretical point. It goes right to the heart of our financial accounting model and its basic principle of matching costs and benefits.

The indefinite deferral argument erroneously focuses only on the payment of taxes to the tax authority. It fails to take into account what happens when new timing differences are used to offset the reversal of former timing differences.

[5]"Elements of Financial Statements of Business Enterprises," Statement of Financial Accounting Concepts No. 3 (Stamford: Financial Accounting Standards Board, December 1980), par. 29.
[6]ICAEW, "Accounting for Deferred Taxation," par. 9.

Reasoning within generally accepted accounting principles, it can be demonstrated that using the tax deductibility of new assets to offset reversing timing differences is just as real an economic outlay as the payment of taxes. The indefinite deferral approach would result in a fundamental mismatching of benefits and costs. It would reflect a benefit in the period when an originating timing difference reduces income taxes payable, but it would fail to match against that benefit the cost that will be incurred when the timing difference reverses and a portion of the tax deductibility of future assets is used up.

This logic is, perhaps, difficult to appreciate in the abstract, and is best demonstrated by example. Assume this situation:

1 X Co. Ltd. begins operations at the beginning of Year 1 by purchasing one machine for $900. The machine is to be depreciated on a straight-line basis over five years, after which it will be scrapped, with no remaining net cost or scrap value. Assume that, for tax purposes, the company can and will deduct the cost on a five-year sum-of-the digits basis (i.e., $5/15, 4/15, 3/15, 2/15, 1/15$).[7]

2 At the beginning of each year thereafter, the company acquires one machine at $900, with the identical accounting depreciation and tax deduction features.

3 The company generates sufficient income each year to fully use the capital cost allowance deductions for tax purposes.

4 A 45% tax rate is in effect.

The outcome of this situation is set out in Table 1. It illustrates that the company generates timing difference tax deferrals in the first four years until it achieves a "steady state" of five machines (with one machine being replaced each year for $900). Following Drummond's and Wigle's logic, there should be no provision for deferred taxes here because it may be reasoned that there will be no payment of tax in respect of these deferrals for at least as long as the company maintains its "steady state"—which it must do to continue as a going concern at its present level of operation.

Let us first isolate one of these machines to understand how timing differences would behave if there were to be no subsequent machine purchases. Specifically, suppose the machine acquired at the beginning of Year 1 had to stand alone, not to be replaced until its useful life was over (i.e., a replacement machine would not be acquired until the beginning of Year 2). The potential timing difference effects are noted on Table 2.

First, it may be noted from Table 2 that the same amount, $900, is charged against income for both accounting and tax purposes over the five-year period. Only the timing of the charge differs as between accounting and tax. For the single asset standing alone, then, it is arithmetically inescapable that the same total cost will be allocated to accounting and taxable income over a time frame that is limited by the existing asset's life. Periods in which capital cost allowance claims exceed

---

[7]This sum-of-the-digits method (rather than the normal tax declining balance basis) is used here solely to simplify the calculations and, in particular, to leave no residual balance after the five-year period.

TABLE 1

X Co. Ltd.
Calculation of Timing Differences on Machines

	Year 1	Year 2	Year 3	Year 4	Year 5	Each year thereafter to infinity
Purchases at beginning of each year	$900	$900	$900	$900	$900	$900
Number of machines in service	1	2	3	4	5	5
Accounting depreciation	$180	$360	$540	$720	$900	$900
Tax capital cost allowance claim:						
Machine No. 1	300	240	180	120	60	
2		300	240	180	120	60
3			300	240	180	120
4				300	240	180
5					300	240
6						300
	300	540	720	840	900	900
Timing difference:						
—each year	$120	$180	$180	$120	0	0
—cumulative	$120	$300	$480	$600	$600	$600

TABLE 2

X Co. Ltd.
Timing Difference Effects of Machine 1 Standing Alone

	Years					
	1	2	3	4	5	Total
Amount deducted for tax purposes	$300	$240	$180	$120	$60	$900
Depreciation expense	180	180	180	180	180	900
Timing differences	$120	$60	$ 0	$(60)	$(120)	$ 0
Reduction (increase) in taxes payable (at 45%)	$ 54	$ 27	$ —	$(27)	$(54)	$ 0

accounting depreciation charges must inevitably be followed by periods in which they will be less than depreciation charges.[8]

That this is a deferral of tax to later periods can be clearly seen in the offsetting increases in taxes payable in Years 4 and 5. If there were no accounting provision for these timing differences, it would appear as though the tax rate in Years 1 and 2 was less than 45%, and that it increased to more than 45% in Years 4 and 5.

But let us probe a little deeper into the logic of what is happening here. Reasoning within generally accepted accounting principles, what is the accounting depreciation telling us? It should be telling us that the machine is estimated to contribute to earning income in each of the five years in accordance with the depreciation pattern chosen. Forty-five percent of this income after depreciation must ultimately be paid in tax. It may be reasoned, then, that an obligation to pay this tax accrues as income is earned by this asset (in accordance with the depreciation pattern) over the five-year period. But the payment of some of the tax accruing in Years 1 and 2 is deferred to later years by accelerating the deduction of the asset cost for tax purposes. Thus, the claiming of capital cost allowance simply rearranges the timing of the payment of taxes; it does not affect the accrual of income taxes as an obligation of the company as income is earned.

Now let us put this first-year acquisition back into the "steady state" example. Table 3 illustrates how the tax deductibility of subsequently acquired machines offsets the reversals of the originating timing differences on the first machine.

This disaggregated basis demonstrates that the originating timing differences (in Years 1 and 2) in respect of the first machine still do reverse. Rather than resulting in tax payments, however, the reversals in Years 4 and 5 reduce the ability of subsequently acquired machines to produce additional tax payment deferrals. Payment of tax is avoided in Years 4 and 5 by creating new timing differences in those years.

TABLE 3

X Co. Ltd.
Disaggregated Timing Differences—Originating (Reversing)

	Years				
	1	2	3	4	5
Machine 1	$120	$ 60	—	$(60)	$(120)
Machine 2		120	$ 60	—	(60)
Machine 3			120	60	—
Machine 4				120	60
Machine 5					120
etc.					

[8]Note that this situation would not be fundamentally different if we had assumed the normal declining balance tax basis. The originating deferred tax credit would still reverse within the asset's life. It might in later years go into debit balance because some undepreciated capital cost for tax purposes may be left after the asset is fully depreciated for accounting purposes. This debit balance would, of course, either be realized on termination of the asset class or gradually drawn down if it is part of a continuing pool of assets. The tax declining balance method, therefore, just adds a complication; it does not affect the basic argument.

The tax deferral at the end of Year 5 is different from that at the end of Year 4. At the end of Year 5, Machine 1 is gone; its deferral has been "paid for" by claiming capital cost allowances in excess of depreciation on subsequently acquired machines.

The use of the excess tax deductibility of newly acquired machines in Years 4 and 5 results in something of value being given up in those years. This may be demonstrated from two perspectives:

1 A rational company will pay less for an asset if its cost cannot be deducted for tax purposes. This is generally recognized in accounting. For example, in allocating purchase cost to assets in a business combination, the *CICA Handbook* notes that "the value to the acquirer of an asset which is not fully claimable for tax purposes will be less than the value of an identical asset which is fully claimable for tax purposes" (Section 1580.47, "Business Combinations"). Similarly, when a company must apply some of the tax deduction value of a new asset to offset the reversal of timing differences arising from earlier acquisitions, it is clearly giving up something of significance—a part of what it paid for.[9]

2 As an alternative explanation, observe that the excess capital cost allowance claims on the subsequently acquired machines would have resulted in actual tax payment reductions in Years 4 and 5 if they had not had to be applied to offset the reversing timing differences of Machine 1. Look at Year 5 in Table 3, for example. The excess of capital cost allowance claimed over depreciation charged for Machines 4 and 5 was $60 and $120, respectively (which amounts to an $81 reduction of taxes payable, i.e., $180 x 45%). But where is this reduction in taxes payable? It has had to be applied to offset excess taxes that would otherwise have been payable on the reversing timing differences of Machines 1 and 2.

To bring together the analysis to this point, X Co. Ltd. may avoid paying tax in Years 4 and 5 on the reversing timing differences only by giving up some of the tax deductibility of machines to be acquired subsequent to Year 1. This essential question must, therefore, be addressed: Is the consumption of some of the tax deductibility of future capital expenditures, in order to offset the reversal of existing timing differences, equivalent to a tax payment? If it is, then the indefinite deferral argument collapses.

ANALYSIS WITHIN THE GAAP LIABILITY CONCEPT

I think it fruitful to examine this question against the basic concept of a liability in accounting. "Liabilities are *probable future sacrifices of economic benefits* arising from present obligations of a particular entity to transfer assets . . . to other entities in the future *as a result of past transactions or events.*[10] (Emphasis added.)

---

[9] Back in 1959 a frequently cited article observed that: "It has long been recognized that assets which have lost all or a substantial part of their deductibility for tax purposes are not worth the same price as assets which are still eligible for future deduction allowances." See Willard J. Graham, "Allocation of Income Taxes," *The Journal of Accountancy* (January 1959), p. 64.

[10] This definition is borrowed from the FASB's "Elements of Financial Statements of Business Enterprises," par. 28. Unfortunately, there seems to be no useful written authoritative definition in Canada. The CICA's *Terminology for Accountants* (1976) defines "liability" in this circular way: "the

Let us turn first to the simple case (in Table 2) where Machine 1 stands alone for its five-year life (with no replacement expected until Year 6). In this case, the Year 1 timing difference would seem to have the basic attributes of a liability, as defined above. There is a probable future sacrifice of economic benefits (in the form of increased taxes payable in Years 4 and 5) as a result of a past event (the claiming of capital cost allowance for tax purposes in excess of accounting depreciation in Year 1). These taxes will be payable in Years 4 and 5, provided that (1) the company continues to operate the assets in those years to at least break even after deducting accounting depreciation; and (2) taxable income will still be taxable at 45%. Clearly, these would be treated as probable events as at the end of Year 1, unless there was specific evidence to the contrary. (If the operative assumption was that the machine could not break even through Years 4 and 5, then, presumably, the first concern would be to write down its value to an estimated recoverable amount, thus reducing, and perhaps eliminating, the deferred tax credit.)

What happens when we put Machine 1 into the broader "steady state" circumstance (Table 1)? We can still reason that a liability exists at the end of Year 1. There is still a probable future sacrifice (but here it takes the form of the consumption of future assets' tax deductibility) as a result of the same past event (the claiming of excess capital cost allowance to reduce Year 1 taxes payable). But Drummond's and Wigle's logic would hold that there should be no provision for deferred income taxes in Year 1—presumably because they believe that the use of some of the tax value of future assets avoids the payment of taxes in Years 4 and 5 without involving an equivalent economic sacrifice in those years.

Let us consider this use of future tax deductibility in terms of the concept of an asset existing for use in Period 1. The CICA's *Terminology for Accountants* (1976) defines an asset as "the expectation of future benefits arising from events or transactions prior to the accounting date." Clearly, Machines 2, 3, and following are not assets at the end of Year 1, because no past transaction or event has taken place to give rise to them. The cost of Machine 2, and the related outflow of assets, or incurrence of debt, to acquire it is therefore not recorded in Period 1, but is recorded in Period 2, when the transaction occurs.

This seems so obvious as to hardly warrant saying. Yet look what must be done to avoid providing for deferred tax expense in Year 1. One must reach forward into the future to take some of the yet-to-be-acquired (yet-to-be-recorded) value of a future asset, and use it to reduce a current expense. This is clearly contrary to accepted principles of accounting, because this future expenditure is not an asset available for use in Year 1.

Even more fundamental than this, the use of the tax deductibility of future capital expenditures to reduce current tax expense would mismatch costs and benefits. This is so because it would involve bringing back to Period 1 some of the benefits of a future asset, without recording any of the costs necessary to obtain

---

money value of an enforceable obligation that may be included as a credit balance in accordance with generally accepted accounting principles." But the basic concept is clearly the same in Canada as in the United States. See, for example, R. M. Skinner, *Accounting Principles: A Canadian Viewpoint* (Toronto: CICA, 1972), p. 156.

those benefits. In other words, a benefit would be reflected in Period 1 because deferred tax expense would not be provided. But the cost associated with the commensurate loss of tax deductibility to future periods would not be reflected in Period 1. Instead, this cost would fall in the future period when a portion of the tax value of assets acquired then would be unavailable to achieve any reduction of tax expense in that period.

This consumption of future tax deductibility is perhaps not readily recognized as a sacrifice when it occurs, because its reversal is assumed to be covered in turn by subsequent acquisitions. The indefinite deferral argument is, in effect, a lapping operation.

This analysis may be summed up as follows:

• A basic argument of Drummond and Wigle was that deferred taxes should not be set up where new timing differences from future asset acquisitions may be expected to continue to arise to offset the reversal of existing timing differences.

• This argument is invalid within our basic accounting model. The reversals of timing differences on existing assets are, in a sense, obscured by claiming capital cost allowance on subsequent capital acquisitions. The reversals of existing assets' timing differences still occur, however. The actual payment of taxes on these reversals is avoided only by making an economic sacrifice in lieu of payment, that is, by expending resources on new assets and sacrificing a commensurate part of their tax deduction potential.

• There is no rationale in accounting for using the tax deductibility of yet-to-be-acquired assets as the basis for not recording deferred tax expense on existing timing differences. This would contravene the concept of an asset existing for use in the current period, and the result would reflect a benefit without recording the offsetting cost to achieve that benefit.

The flaw in the logic of the indefinite deferral argument is that it focuses too narrowly on the net payment of taxes to the tax authority. It looks at the steady state, or expanding asset, situation and sees net timing differences as stable or increasing through future years. It does not recognize that the obligation is turning over—that it is being paid off by the use of part of the value of later acquisitions.

CLAIMS AND COUNTERCLAIMS

I think it useful to examine some of Drummond's and Wigle's claims in terms of the above analysis. I have selected several statements from their article that I believe to be representative of their case.

• Drummond and Wigle cited *CICA Handbook* Recommendations on "contingencies" (in Section 3290) to argue that deferred tax credits are merely contingent liabilities for which accrual is not appropriate. Their reasoning: (1) a liability is not incurred when a tax timing difference arises and (2) the amount cannot be reasonably estimated (because it may never materialize, being indefinitely deferred by future capital expenditures). These are the "legal liability" and "indefinite deferral" arguments discussed above.

It was demonstrated earlier that a deferred tax credit seems to meet the basic criteria of a liability—that it is a past event that gives rise to a probable future sacrifice of economic benefits, either in the form of a tax payment or by giving up future tax deductibility. (The authors were quite correct, however, in observing that the "deferral method" of tax allocation does not recognize a deferred tax credit as a full-fledged liability, and this is one of the basic problems with the defensibility of that method.)

The amount should normally be estimable within reasonable limits. Existing timing difference credits must reverse within the accounting and tax lives of the existing assets that gave rise to them, so that tax allocation is founded on estimates that should be no more uncertain than those necessary to record and depreciate the assets. In short, the estimates necessary to do deferred tax accounting are well within the range of uncertainty accepted in other areas of accounting.

There is therefore, no "glaring inconsistency" between the contingencies and corporate income taxes sections of the *Handbook,* as Drummond and Wigle contended, because deferred tax credits are not contingencies as defined in Section 3290.

• Drummond and Wigle claimed that "income tax accrues with the earning of taxable profits not with the earning of accounting profits." This claim would seem to assume that there is no relationship between accounting and taxable income—that there is no such thing as timing differences. This claim is sustainable only if one assumes that existing timing differences will not reverse, or that the future sacrifice is a separate event, not linked to the claiming of capital cost allowance in excess of depreciation in past periods. The preceding analysis demonstrates that these are not valid assumptions within our present historical cost/matching accounting model.

• Drummond and Wigle noted that "many enterprises maintain that their policy on the acquisition of fixed assets indicates the turn-around position will not occur in the foreseeable future; consequently, the deferred tax balances continue to increase." They went on to provide evidence as to the very considerable increase in deferred tax credits in recent years. If one rejects the indefinite deferral argument, the fact that fixed assets and deferred taxes have been increasing over time has no relevance to tax allocation accounting. My analysis shows that existing timing differences reverse in the same pattern, regardless of what a company's future asset acquisition policy may be. In other words, it matters not to today's accounting whether existing timing differences will be paid off in future by actual tax payments or by using some of the tax value of future capital expenditures.

• Although they did not pursue it, Drummond and Wigle suggested that "if income taxes were regarded as a distribution of profit to the government, and not as business expense, the problems of tax allocation would not arise." I am not at all sure that this would solve the problem. There must still be an allocation of income between shareholders and the government over time. It would seem incorrect to pay dividends to today's shareholders on the basis of reported income that is not reduced for the effect that existing timing differences will have on future resource outflows. Future shareholders would then have to absorb the cost of paying additional taxes or using up new asset tax deductibility to cover off reversing timing differences from earlier periods.

• Finally, Drummond and Wigle cited as a reason to "doubt the propriety of comprehensive tax allocation" that a provision for deferred taxes does not have any impact on current cash flows. They expressed concern that readers of funds statements may be misled by the "addback." This is no more of a problem than that caused by depreciation provisions, which are not cash flows either. The criticism that deferred taxes are not cash flows has no validity within our accrual-based accounting model. Of course, if we were to adopt an accounting basis that reflected only cash flows, we would not record deferred taxes—but neither would we record depreciation and similar items giving rise to timing differences.

The authors proposed a "partial tax allocation" approach under which only taxes that could reasonably be expected to reverse within "the foreseeable future" (at least three years) would be set up. It should be clear from the above analysis that this is an arbitrary solution, founded on the incorrect premise that a tax timing difference does not give rise to a future sacrifice except if it can be directly traced to additional cash being paid to the tax authority within three years or so.

THE DEFERRAL METHOD

To this point the analysis has concentrated, as did Drummond's and Wigle's arguments, on the basic principles of comprehensive tax allocation. I think it instructive to go one step further—to examine briefly the "deferral method" of tax allocation, which is the method required by the *CICA Handbook* (and by accounting principles in the United States). The method does not rest well within the framework of generally accepted accounting principles. To start with, deferred tax as prescribed by the "deferral method" is treated neither as a liability nor as a reduction in assets. Instead, it is treated, as Drummond and Wigle noted, "'as a deferred credit' (or perhaps more aptly as a dangling credit) and exiled to 'no man's land'." The Financial Accounting Standards Board Statement on "The Elements of Financial Statements of Business Enterprises" concluded that there are two views of deferred tax credits that are compatible with the definitions within its conceptual framework; they may either be liabilities or asset deductions. The statement went on to stress that "the two views...exhaust the possibilities—deferred tax credits cannot be revenues or gains."

This problem of classifying deferred tax credits in the balance sheet results from the way in which they are measured under the "deferral method." Under this method, deferred tax expense is equal to the timing difference originating in the period, multiplied by the current tax rate. This measurement is open to criticism because it shows no benefit from deferring tax in the year of deferral. A company must show as tax expense exactly what it would have paid if deferral had not been achieved. This seems inconsistent with the business reality that tax dollars payable in the future are not as onerous as tax dollars payable today. In other areas, such as pension costs and capitalized leases, accounting is based on discounted values.

I suggest that it is the deferral method and, more specifically, its nondiscounting of deferred taxes, that is the legitimate concern of the accounting profession and the business community—not the fundamental principles of comprehensive tax allocation. The deferral method was an understandable choice some 15 years ago. It was adopted at a time when the concept of discounting and the pervasiveness of its applicability to financial accounting was not as widely recognized as it is today. Also, of course, interest rates were much lower and, as Drummond and Wigle demonstrated, timing differences were not as large. I suggest that the profession should actively consider the conceptual improvements that discounting may provide.

THE DISCOUNTING ALTERNATIVE

The relevant questions relate to how (and perhaps whether) a reasonable discounting approach could be developed. In essence, the deferred tax expense for a particular period would be the present value of the future estimated resource outflows resulting from the timing differences in that year. To calculate this present value we would need to know:

- The discount rate.
- The tax rate.
- When timing differences should be deemed to reverse (be paid).

Each of these gives rise to significant questions that require answers that are not only logical but also capable of reasonable implementation across a wide variety of complex timing differences and industry situations.

Looking briefly at each of these three factors:

- The discount rate should presumably be an after-tax rate, because the discount is not itself deductible in arriving at tax, but simply apportions the total deferred tax expense to accounting periods. But should there be a unique rate for each company? If so, should it be tied to a company's incremental borrowing rate, or to an average rate, or might it more logically relate to the total cost of capital including equity? Some may argue that the rate should be tied to what a company might be expected to earn on the funds that it would otherwise have had to pay the tax authority. Alternatively, might there be a standard discount rate for all companies and, if so, how might it be determined?

There are, therefore, a host of possibilities and, of course, the present value will be very sensitive to the rate selected.

- Tax rate questions include whether, or under what circumstances, a company should attempt to forecast future tax rates or simply use the current rate. Also, should the accumulated deferred tax obligation be restated if there is a change in tax rate?
- Questions relating to the timing and amount of reversing resource outflows are perhaps the most difficult of all, and an adequate discussion of the possibilities is beyond the scope of this article. The preceding analysis has, however, demonstrated that the reversing resource outflow is not indefinitely deferred by future capital expenditures, but must fall within the expected life of the existing asset or liability on which the timing differences arose. But this still leaves a number of possibilities that could yield quite different present values, particularly in respect of long-lived assets. Three possibilities might be mentioned.

TABLE 4

X Co. Ltd.
Originating (Reversing) Timing Differences
On First-In-First-Out Basis

	Year 1	Year 2	Year 3	Year 4	Year 5
Year 1	$120	—	—	$(60)	$(60)
Year 2		60	—	—	(60)
	$120	$ 60	0	$(60)	$(120)

First, looking back at our earlier example, one might project the Machine 1 timing differences through to the end of its estimated life and, perhaps, assume that they will reverse on a first-in-first-out pattern, as set out in Table 4.

The discounted deferred tax expense in Year 1 would, therefore, be the present value of $60 payable three years hence (in Year 4), plus the present value of $60 payable four years hence (in Year 5).

Alternatively, one might assume that the originating timing differences reverse in accordance with the straight-line depreciation method used for accounting purposes, as set out in Table 5.

The approach would reflect the timing difference reversals in accordance with the pattern by which the asset is presumed (by reference to the depreciation pattern) to be contributing to the earning of income. Clearly, it would result in a different pattern from that set out in Table 4 and, therefore, a different discounted deferred tax expense.

Another alternative might be to determine the present value of the future tax deductibility of the asset, and then calculate how much of that tax deductibility has been used in a particular period. This would be most compatible with a net-of-tax approach.[11]

---

[11] This possibility is explained and illustrated in Skinner's *Accounting Principles*, pp. 390–392.

TABLE 5

X Co. Ltd.
Originating (Reversing) Timing Differences
Based on Accounting Depreciation Pattern

	Year 1	Year 2	Year 3	Year 4	Year 5
Year 1	$120	$(30)	$(30)	$(30)	$(30)
Year 2		90	(30)	(30)	(30)
Year 3			60	(30)	(30)
Year 4				30	(30)
	$120	$60	0	$(60)	$(120)

SOUND PRINCIPLES OF TAX ALLOCATION

I suggest that these issues, while difficult, are capable of reasonable and understandable solutions that could result in a tax allocation basis which would better reflect the business reality of deferred income taxes. It must be recognized, however, that an appropriate discounting approach should be constructed upon sound principles of tax allocation accounting. One must be careful not to be misled by misconceived arguments that comprehensive tax allocation per se is unsound.

BIBLIOGRAPHY

Baylis, A. W. "Income Tax Allocation—A Defence." *Abacus,* December 1971, pp. 161–172.

Black, H. A. *Interperiod Allocation of Corporate Income Taxes,* Accounting Research Study No. 9. New York: American Institute of Certified Public Accountants, Inc., 1966.

Carr, G. K. "Accounting for Income Taxes." *The Canadian Chartered Accountant,* October 1963, pp. 238–244.

Dewhirst, J. F. "The Tax Allocation Question Answered." *CAmagazine,* November 1975, pp. 43–50.

Elements of Financial Statements of Business Enterprises. Stamford: FASB, 1980, paras. 163–165.

Graham, W. J. "Allocation of Income Taxes." *Journal of Accountancy,* January 1959, pp. 57–67.

Skinner, R. M. *Accounting Principles: A Canadian Viewpoint.* Toronto: CICA, 1972, pp. 133–145, and 387–392.

Spacek, L. "The Case for Income Tax Deferral." *The New York Certified Public Accountant,* April 1968, pp. 271–276.

CONTINGENCIES AND FORECASTING

Financial statements have always reflected assumptions about the future events and outcomes. Indeed, a going concern is defined as "any enterprise which is expected to continue operating indefinitely in the future."[1] Many allocations in conventional accounting are based on beliefs about the future of the enterprise. All the while, financial statements possess an aura of definiteness and even certainty in the minds of lay readers.

As our whole environment has become more complex and competitive, the fruits of successful analysis go to those who have been sufficiently diligent and perspicacious in obtaining and interpreting information that is not generally available. In many cases, this information relates to possible future occurrences. Obviously, some possible future occurrences have a higher probability of being realized than others. If an astute analyst can gain information about these possibilities and assess the likelihood of occurrence, he or she may be able to use this relatively unknown information for competitive gain.

Managements have come under increasing pressure to disclose more and more information about these contingent events.[2] As more information of this kind has been made available, accountants have come under pressure to reflect its potential impact in the published financial statements. At this point, the questions often raised involve the ability of the users to incorporate into their decision models information about events that have relatively lower probabilities of occurring.

In "The Dilemma in Contingencies and Forecasts Reporting," Yuji Ijiri reviews

---

[1]W. W. Cooper and Yuji Ijiri (editors), *Kohler's Dictionary for Accountants,* 6th Edition (Englewood Cliffs, NJ: Prentice-Hall, Inc., 1983), p. 238.

[2]See the introduction to Section 4.

the principles governing the accounting for contingencies and the reporting of forecasts. He concludes that corporate financial reporting "seems now to be more a system of protecting the corporation from legal liabilities while outsiders try to find in the report something for which they can blame the corporation." He doubts that a system of accountability can survive "under a situation of complete mutual distrust." Ijiri suggests that an improvement in the level of trust must occur if we are to see any real advances in the reporting of less certain outcomes.

The case study of the attempt by Aetna Life & Casualty to include in its 1982 net income the estimated future tax benefits arising from net operating loss carry-forwards, as reported by Carol J. Loomis in "Behind the Profits Glow at Aetna," illustrates Ijiri's allegation of mistrust. In addition, the Aetna case is a vivid example of the problems facing accountants in regard to the possible future outcomes of decisions taken. The question is: Are Aetna's statement users better served by allowing the company's net income to reflect the future tax benefits than they would be without such inclusion? Accounting principles tilt heavily in the direction of conservatism when the possible future consequences to net income are favorable, rather than unfavorable.

Aetna eventually included $203 million of tax benefits relating to net operating loss carry-forwards in its 1982 income statement (the comparable figure for 1981 was $27 million). In the end, however, the SEC rejected the company's accounting, the SEC remaining unconvinced that there was "assurance beyond a reasonable doubt" that the tax benefits would be realized within the 15-year carry-forward period. On July 7, 1983, Aetna issued a Restatement of Financial Statements in which the tax benefits were excluded from its 1982 income statement.

A related scenario is reported by Harold B. Meyers in "A Bit of Rouge for Allis-Chalmers." As this case study concludes, there was some evidence that the contingency would work out, but even then the final outcome was not known. In addition, the Allis-Chalmers case vividly illustrates the concept that a benefit can only be reflected once. If the tax effect of a loss is recognized when the loss arises, then only the tax obligation remains to be recognized when a subsequent profit is earned. The logic of this position cannot be challenged. The unanswered question is: How does the market interpret the reported results? Perhaps a more important question is: Should accountants be concerned about how the market interprets the facts, if the accountant knows the facts and reports them clearly?

BIBLIOGRAPHICAL NOTES

Several references on the subject of management forecasts are given in the Bibliographical Notes at the end of the introduction to Section 4. The following article summarizes the U.K. experience with companies' profit forecasts:

Carmichael, D. R.: "Reporting on Forecasts: A U.K. Perspective," *The Journal of Accountancy* (January 1973), pp. 36–47.

The literature on contingencies is not extensive. The FASB's discussion memorandum on "future losses" is of interest here:

Accounting for Future Losses, Discussion Memorandum (Stamford, CT: FASB, March 1974).

A section of the Cohen Commission Report on Auditors' Responsibilities addresses the question of reporting on uncertainties:

The Commission on Auditors' Responsibilities: *Report, Conclusions, and Recommendations* (New York: AICPA, 1978), pp. 23–30.

The Dilemma in Contingencies and Forecast Reporting

Yuji Ijiri
Carnegie-Mellon University

In spite of the belief of many CPAs that they are not prophets, the current trend has been to call on accountants more and more frequently to become involved with prophetic statements. Contingencies and forecasts reporting is perhaps the most typical example of "forward looking" information. An examination of the problems associated with contingencies and forecasts reporting can bring to light a deeper dilemma—the conflicting forces that are at work in corporate financial reporting today.

THE CURRENT PRACTICES

With respect to contingencies, Financial Accounting Standards Board Statement No. 5, *Accounting for Contingencies,*[1] requires a corporation to accrue an estimated loss from a contingency as a charge to income if the future event (or events) that will confirm the loss is "probable" (defined as likely to occur) and "estimable." A contingency is defined as an existing condition, situation or set of circumstances involving uncertainty as to possible gain or loss to an enterprise that will ultimately be resolved when one or more future events occur or fail to occur. Examples of loss contingencies include uncertain collectibility of major receivables, warranty obligations, risk of catastrophe losses, threat of expropriation of assets, pending or threatened litigation, actual or possible (tax or other) claims and assessments and guarantees of indebtedness of others.

If a loss is not probable but is "reasonably possible" (defined as more than remote but less than likely), the nature of the contingency and an estimate of the possible

---

From *Journal of Accountancy* (November 1980), pp. 38, 40, 42, 44–46. Reprinted by permission of the American Institute of Certified Public Accountants. Copyright © 1980 by the American Institute of Certified Public Accountants, Inc.
    [1] Financial Accounting Standards Board Statement No. 5, *Accounting for Contingencies* (Stamford, Conn.: FASB, 1975).

loss or range of loss (or the fact that such an estimate cannot be made) must be disclosed in the financial statements. In addition, an FASB exposure draft[2] issued in March 1980 will require, if adopted, disclosure of commitments involving certain loss contingencies (e.g., guarantees, take-or-pay contracts, etc.) even though the possibility of loss may be remote.

Gain contingencies, on the other hand, according to paragraph 17 of the statement, are "not reflected in the accounts since to do so might be to recognize revenue prior to its realization," and, while adequate disclosure can be made, "care shall be exercised to avoid misleading implications as to the likelihood of realization."

In September, the FASB issued Statement No. 38, *Accounting for Preacquisition Contingencies of Purchased Enterprises,*[3] which specifies that lawsuits and other preexisting uncertainties that can affect the price of an acquired enterprise are required to be estimated and recorded at the time of acquisition. Subsequent adjustments are to be included in net income when the adjustments are determined, except in specified limited circumstances. The statement is effective for preacquisition contingencies assumed in business combinations initiated after December 15, 1980.

With respect to forecasts reporting, the Securities and Exchange Commission issued on November 7, 1978, *Guides for Disclosure of Projections of Future Economic Performance.*[4] The salient features of this and related SEC releases to date are

• Corporations (the issuers) may voluntarily disclose their projections of their future economic performances in filings with the SEC and are in fact encouraged to do so.

• Assumptions underlying the projections may need to be disclosed concurrently so as not to make the projections misleading.

• Once disclosure is made, the corporation has the responsibility to update previous disclosures if they no longer have a reasonable basis of expectation and to inform investors of management's intentions with respect to furnishing updated projections. Corporations are encouraged not to discontinue or resume projections in SEC filings without a reasonable basis.

• A third party review of projections, such as one by an independent accountant, is permitted but not required in the filings. However, while the SEC decided to allow a third party review of forecasts, it requires that if a third party review is given,

"there should also be disclosure of the qualifications of the reviewer, the extent of the review, the relationship between the reviewer and the registrant and any other material factors concerning the process by which any outside review was sought or obtained."

Furthermore, the rule states that "the reviewer would be deemed an expert and an appropriate consent must be filed with the registration statement."(Recently, the

[2]FASB Exposure Draft, *Disclosure of Guarantees, Project Financing Arrangements, and Other Similar Obligations* (Stamford, Conn.: FASB, 1980).
[3]FASB Statement No. 38, *Accounting for Preacquisition Contingencies of Purchased Enterprises* (Stamford, Conn.: FASB, 1980).
[4]Securities and Exchange Commission, *Guides for Disclosure of Projections of Future Economic Performance* (SAR 5992, EAR 34-15305 and Guide 62). November 7, 1978.

American Institute of CPAs published a guide for a review of a financial forecast.[5])

• According to the "safe harbor" rule adopted in June 1979,[6] a projection would be deemed not to be a fraudulent statement unless it is shown that such statement was made or reaffirmed without a reasonable basis or was disclosed other than in good faith.

RELEVANCE VS. RELIABILITY

It is natural to question why a corporation should disclose loss contingencies and performance forecasts. Those who favor such disclosure base their arguments on the objectives of financial reporting. Paragraph 34 of Financial Accounting Concepts Statement No. 1, *Objectives of Financial Reporting by Business Enterprises,*[7] states that "financial reporting should provide information that is useful to present and potential investors and creditors and other users in making rational investment, credit, and similar decisions." Since contingencies and forecasts information is very useful to investors, it therefore should be reported, proponents argue. Some people go even further and base the disclosure requirement on management's accountability.

There is little doubt that contingencies and forecasts information can be highly relevant to investment decisions. However, it is possible that disclosure of relevant but unreliable information can be harmful to the investor. If a relevance-reliability tradeoff is evaluated and it is determined that the disclosure of particular information is beneficial to investors, the cost-benefit issue should be considered. Namely, the benefits to investors must be weighed against the direct and indirect costs of disclosure.

COSTS OF DISCLOSURE

On the cost side of the cost-benefit equation, a number of direct and indirect costs should be considered. For example, the clerical costs required to compile information for disclosure may not be insignificant, but they may be a relatively minor portion of the potential full costs of disclosure. A major cost to the corporation can come from the negative consequences of disclosure.

Unasserted claims can be a particular problem. In recognition of this problem, paragraph 10 of Statement No. 5 treats disclosure of unasserted claims differently from other contingencies. It states:

> "Disclosure is not required of a loss contingency involving an unasserted claim or assessment when there has been no manifestation by a potential claimant of an awareness of a possible claim or assessment unless it is considered probable that a claim will be asserted and there is a reasonable possibility that the outcome will be unfavorable."

This additional test would certainly reduce the frequency of disclosure of unasserted claims, although, for those that still meet the criteria, a damaging effect on the company can occur.

[5] Financial Forecasts and Projections Task Force, *Guide for a Review of a Financial Forecast* (New York: AICPA, 1980).

[6] Securities Act Rule 175.

[7] FASB Statement of Financial Accounting Concepts No. 1, *Objectives of Financial Reporting by Business Enterprises* (Stamford, Conn.: FASB, 1978).

Another problem area can be the effect of forecasts reporting on internal management. A forecast motivating and improving productivity and real economic performance would of course be a welcoming consequence of disclosure. However, if it results in, for example, a premature sale of properties solely to pick up accounting earnings in order to meet the forecast, the consequence could be highly detrimental. Some fear that forecast disclosure might also stimulate accounting manipulations to bring the actual earnings closer to the forecast.

However, the most important cost of disclosure may be, despite the adoption of the safe harbor rule, the litigation costs that can arise out of a lawsuit when disclosure is challenged as being possibly misleading.

An additional detrimental effect of forecasts, which is quite different in nature from the other disclosure effects discussed, is the possibility that the mere act of forecasting will add credence to the item being forecast.

IMPACT ON EARNINGS

While most of the issues in contingencies and forecasts reporting are on the subject of disclosure, there is one issue that is related to the determination of net income—the accrual of the estimated loss from a loss contingency. Under FASB Statement No. 5, an estimated loss from a loss contingency must be charged against net income as soon as the loss becomes probable and estimable. In addition, now that the use of prior period adjustments has been extremely narrowed by FASB Statement No. 16, *Prior Period Adjustments,*[8] almost all such loss accruals must be charged against current income.

Another impact of FASB Statement No. 5 on earnings is that accrual of contingency losses is prohibited unless it is probable that an asset has been impaired or a liability has been incurred and that the loss is estimable. Thus, companies are prevented from providing reserves for future losses such as fire and the like through annual charges to income. Similarly, reserves for general or unspecified business risks cannot be made. For a number of companies, the volatility of their earnings was increased as a result of this self-insurance proscription, which is the major source of complaints about FASB Statement No. 5.

The lack of symmetry in the treatment of a loss contingency and a gain contingency in present practice also seems to be a source of concern. For example, it is quite possible for a defendant to be required to accrue an estimated loss from litigation while the plaintiff is not allowed to recognize the corresponding gain until the final settlement. Is the doctrine of conservatism stretched too far in this case? It seems that this asymmetry may be another element that creates an uncomfortable feeling with accrual for loss contingencies.

A SYMPOSIUM

Last year I attended a symposium on contingencies and forecasts reporting. It was held by Carnegie-Mellon University's Graduate School of Industrial Administration

---

[8]FASB Statement No. 16, *Prior Period Adjustments* (Stamford, Conn.: FASB, 1977).

under the sponsorship of the Gulf Oil Corporation. Some thirty participants representing diverse constituencies engaged in a round-table discussion from which a number of important and still timely issues arose. Opinions of some of the participants on various aspects of contingencies and forecast disclosure follow:

• *On investors' wants.* "I think the desire demonstrated by the SEC to encourage forecasts is based on the fact that the company is in the best position to make that kind of projection of the future; that's what investors most want to have when they are going to make an investment decision. Although I cannot speak for the commissioners, I think it's as simple as that. They [the investors] believe it's a good thing."—A. Clarence Sampson, chief accountant of the SEC.

• *On management's accountability.* "Forecasts are viewed by at least some as nothing more than an extension of the accountability of management to activities in the future. Therefore, they ought to be subject to some minimal standards of reporting, just as is the case with normal historical cost accounting."—Alfred Rappaport, Leonard Spacek professor of accounting and information at Northwestern University.

• *On relevance.* "To conclude that future-oriented information is relevant is not necessarily to conclude that management forecasts should be reported to the investing public. Considerations of relevance must be weighed against considerations of reliability and cost."—Victor H. Brown, vice-president and controller of Standard Oil Company (Indiana).

• *On the operating budget.* "Budgets [as reliable forecasts of performance] are not necessarily managements' estimates of the most likely results. In many cases budgets reflect managements' desires or philosophies."—Thomas V. Fritz, regional managing partner of Arthur Young & Company.

• *On litigation.* "If you are involved in litigation and have to estimate the magnitude of the loss and disclose it to the public at the very time you are still litigating against having any liability at all, you may well influence the outcome of the litigation."—Robert S. Kaplan, dean of Carnegie-Mellon University's Graduate School of Industrial Administration.

"In order to protect yourself, you may have to make disclosures of underlying assumptions that are harmful to the company and to the existing shareholders."—Robert M. Loeffler, partner in charge of Jones, Day, Reavis & Poque's (Los Angeles).

"I propose that litigation be the disclosure requirement of the legal profession in order to eliminate the existing mishmash of responsibilities and functions, because the financial officer and the auditor do not have the tools to really review these legal judgments."—James L. Murdy, vice-president-finance of Gulf Oil Corporation.

"Financial statements are only a part of financial reporting, and even if an argument can be made for exclusion from financial statements, disclosure of contingencies should nevertheless be within the umbrella of financial reporting."—Robert C. Wilkins, project manager at the FASB.

"Assessment of a loss contingency represented by litigation is essentially a forecast and involves the imperfections of quantification and verification of any forecast.... Even though a contingency, or any other fact, is material to an investment decision, this should not mean that the financial statements are where that fact should be presented to the investor. Financial statements are not intended to be complete prospectuses."—Bruce D. Evans, partner of Reed Smith Shaw & McClay.

• *On the accountant's role.* "The SEC believes that an independent, objective look by a third party has great value and needs to be preserved even though it is different from the usual audit context."—A. Clarence Sampson.

IMPLICATIONS FOR CORPORATE FINANCIAL REPORTING

Any discussion of contingencies and forecasts reporting brings to mind how difficult it is to take a positive stand on corporate financial reporting today. There seems to be something amiss in the current financial reporting system.

When a chief executive officer addresses shareholders at an annual meeting, he or she refers to the company as "your company." This two-word phrase, often praised in foreign countries as being indicative of the fine accountability relationship between management and shareholders in the U.S., seems to have become totally empty. If the management-shareholder relationship is in fact what it should be, would it not be most natural for management to report to shareholders not only the company's past performance but its future plans and prospects as well as impending contingencies?

Yet, such a relationship appears to be a fantasy. The fact of the matter is, there are strong adversary feelings between management and some segments of the investing public. As a result, corporate financial reporting may be fading away as a system of providing useful information to present and potential investors and creditors. It seems now to be more a system of protecting the corporation from legal liabilities while outsiders try to find in the report something for which they can blame the corporation.

While a system of accountability, of which a financial reporting system is an important part, does not assume complete mutual trust, it can never survive under a situation of complete mutual distrust. A doubt begets a doubt, a suspicion begets a suspicion and, eventually, the escalation of distrust destroys any accountability system, no matter how carefully it is constructed.

Many problems and difficulties in contingencies and forecasts reporting seem to stem from this fundamental dilemma—a too-soft ground trying to support a too-heavy burden. Unless this seemingly intensive mutual distrust is gradually eased by efforts toward mutual understanding, any action is likely to be at best a temporary cure.

Behind the Profits Glow at Aetna

Carol J. Loomis
Member
Board of Editors, *Fortune*

Like every other company in the business, giant Aetna Life & Casualty has been swamped by a viciously competitive swing in the property and casualty insurance market. But Aetna's responses to this sea of troubles have been unique.

The dynamics of the business are inexorable. When interest rates are high, the insurance crowd fights for premiums to sink into investments. As the claims from this cut-rate business come due, cash flow needs become compelling. Now, in the depths of an unusually long and low trough, the insurers are writing policies in a spirit of abandon—asking all the while when it will ever end.

Aetna has acted with less abandon than most. In early 1981, like King Canute trying to hold back the waves, it even made a jawboning effort to firm up prices. Canute couldn't do it and neither could Aetna.

The company has meanwhile been an amazingly active diversifier, putting more than $1 billion into four separate ventures in the last year. One move, the acquisition of Geosource, a large oil-field services company, seemed so inappropriate that Wall Street hammered Aetna's stock.

Even so, Aetna is mighty. With more than $40 billion in assets, it is the largest publicly owned U.S. insurer, and its business spread-eagles the field, embracing not only property and casualty but also the life, health, and pension markets. Accordingly, analysts continue to respect the company's earning power. At a round-table discussion staged by the *Wall Street Transcript* last May, five insurance analysts all lamented Aetna's property and casualty troubles, yet went on to predict that the improved first-quarter results already reported would be followed by improved results for the year. One analyst, Donald Franz, then at Smith Barney and now with Donaldson Lufkin & Jenrette, framed his prediction memorably. Recalling that Aetna's chairman, John H. Filer, had recently made some positive statements about 1982, Franz said that earnings would quite likely rise "to ensure that the chairman will not be called a liar."

Some of the statements Franz had in mind appeared in Aetna's first-quarter report, in a letter signed by Filer and William O. Bailey, the company's president. They spoke of "increased balance and stability," of earnings improvements over the last three quarters, and of "our belief that Aetna will maintain reasonable and improving profits this year."

The remarkable thing about that letter, about a second-quarter letter that followed, and about the analysts' forecasts to boot is that none of these declarations about Aetna mentioned the overwhelming and extraordinary reason why its 1982 earnings are up. The reason, made visible only by a terse footnote to Aetna's financial statements, is tax benefits that the company has been plugging into its earnings even though at best it will not realize the benefits until sometime in the future.

TWO SETS OF BOOKS

Like most companies, Aetna prepares one set of accounts for the Internal Revenue Service and another for its shareholders. In its shareholder accounts, Aetna reports large amounts of income from municipal bonds and dividends. In the company's filings with the IRS, most of this income escapes taxation. During the suicidally competitive phase of the property and casualty business, Aetna has been reporting operating profits to its shareholders and large operating losses to the IRS—a legal and not unusual dichotomy.

These tax losses can be carried forward to offset future taxable profits. In Aetna's case, the operating loss carry-forwards, as they are called, came to a huge $736 million at the end of 1981 and apparently topped $1 billion in midyear. If Aetna realizes taxable operating profits within 15 years, which is the time limit on carry-forwards, its tax losses will be available as offsets, and taxes on the profits will be avoided. This potential deliverance from future taxes is what Aetna is recognizing in today's profits.

The effects on the company's 1982 earnings have been dramatic. In the first six months of the year, Aetna took $138 million of these anticipated tax benefits into its earnings, an amount accounting for no less than 62% of reported operating earnings of $222 million. Without this boost, the company's operating earnings would have been 60% lower than in 1981. Had they been reported in this skimpy form, the earnings would not have even covered Aetna's first-half dividends.

And just how unusual are Aetna's tactics? Extremely and undeniably so, to the degree that it is almost impossible to overstate the point. It is not that operating tax-loss carry-forwards are scarce; lots of companies have them and would no doubt be delighted to convert them immediately into current earnings. But generally accepted accounting principles come close to prohibiting the practice. The problem is addressed in Opinion No. 11, a pronouncement issued by a predecessor of the profession's self-regulatory body, the Financial Accounting Standards Board. The opinion declares that realization of the tax benefits ordinarily is not "assured" because a company can't know with absolute certainty that it will have taxable profits in the future against which the loss carry-forwards can be used. Therefore, says the opinion, tax benefits arising from loss carry-forwards should not be recognized in profits until they are realized, except in unusual circumstances when realization is assured "beyond any reasonable doubt."

A company might pass this test, the opinion then says, if three conditions, each and all, are satisfied. The first concerns the character of the loss being carried forward: it must have resulted from "an identifiable, isolated, and nonrecurring cause." The second concerns the character of the company: it must have been continuously profitable over a long period or have suffered occasional losses that were more than offset by taxable income later on. The third concerns the character of the taxable income expected: it must with near certainty be large enough to offset the loss carry-forward and must come along fast enough to deliver the tax benefits within the carry-forward period.

Some accountants, among them Aetna's auditors, Peat Marwick Mitchell, have interpreted this listing of conditions as providing "such as" guidance; that is, if a company can meet tests "such as" the ones stated, it may consider its tax benefits to be realizable beyond a reasonable doubt. The problem with this interpretation is that the accounting office of the Securities and Exchange Commission doesn't agree with it. The SEC regards the conditions as absolute requirements that must be met. That makes the standard of "beyond any reasonable doubt" terribly difficult to satisfy. As an FASB staff member says, "Those are tough words."

So strong are the SEC's feelings about Opinion 11 that it has on occasion forced a company to restate its earnings and remove the offending tax benefits. One such occasion in the mid-1970s involved Rapid-American Corp., a trouble-prone company run by a controversy-prone chairman, Meshulam Riklis.

Instances in which the SEC has allowed future tax benefits to worm their way into earnings are hard to find. Stumped to name examples, a Big Eight partner who often handles questions from the press excused his non-helpfulness by stressing the unacceptability, and therefore rarity, of the accounting practice: "The language in Opinion 11 creates a very strong presumption that one doesn't do that."

THE FRANKLIN HAD THE HABIT

Further digging, however, turned up about a dozen companies that at one time or another have shown future tax benefits in earnings. Some dignify the practice still more poorly than Rapid-American. Two were Detroit's Bank of the Commonwealth, which fell into deep trouble in the early 1970s, and Franklin New York Corp., which with its subsidiary, Franklin National Bank, went bankrupt in 1974.

The dozen specimens, however, also include a few companies of a vastly different and significantly higher financial character, among them none other than Aetna itself. A second example is another big (and, like Aetna, Hartford-based) multi-line insurer, Travelers Corp. Aetna took future tax benefits into its earnings in 1975. Travelers did so in 1975 and 1976, years when the property and casualty business was ensnarled in another traumatic downcycle.

These Hartford-hewn accounting aberrations did not pass the SEC unchallenged. As Robert H. McMillen, a Travelers senior vice president, remembers things, the SEC noticed in a 1975 Travelers quarterly report that the company had begun to book tax benefits related to a tax-loss carry-forward and promptly requested Travelers to justify its action. The SEC wanted to know, first, just how Travelers knew it was going to earn taxable profits sufficient to realize the tax benefits and, second, how cyclical losses could be construed as rising from "isolated and nonrecurring causes."

Travelers gave the matter some deep thought, McMillen says, and then replied. The answer to the first question, the company told the SEC, is that we have experienced depressed conditions in the property and casualty business before and these always come to an end, whereupon we begin to earn profits that exceed our earlier losses; you should assume, therefore, that this pattern will repeat. The answer to the second question, Travelers continued, is harder to substantiate, since we are not fortune-tellers and cannot say definitely that our current variety of tax-loss carry-forwards will not crop up again. But we can tell you we have never before had tax-loss carry-forwards of any kind and that they arose now because of a wicked, two-fisted punch: double-digit inflation rates that ballooned our claim costs and price controls that prevented our raising premiums. We argue, said Travelers, that these causes are "isolated and nonrecurring."

John C. ("Sandy") Burton, then chief accountant of the SEC and now dean of Columbia's Graduate School of Business, says he listened to Travelers' presentation and came reluctantly to the conclusion—"I was sullen but not mutinous"—that the company should be allowed to recognize the future tax benefits it wished to. Aetna says it had similar dealings with Burton and also received permission to proceed.

Only a short time later, however, in mid-1976, the SEC suddenly braced itself in regard to Opinion 11, issuing an accounting bulletin that reminded the corporate and accounting communities of the opinion's "restrictive tests." Edmund Coulson, assistant chief accountant of the SEC, explains the bulletin's origins: "We had noted in some filings with us that there was laxity in applying Opinion 11 and we wanted to make it clear that shouldn't happen." One point in the bulletin concerned losses attributable to "a general economic or industry decline," which would seem to describe the cyclical variety. The bulletin indicated that such losses would not normally justify the recognition of future tax benefits in earnings.

Since that 1976 milestone, the number of instances in which future tax benefits have been recognized seems to have dwindled from few to mini-few. The conclusion arises from a search of annual reports that *Fortune* made through the National Automated Accounting Research Service (NAARS), a computerized data base. NAARS provides access to the financial statements (and accompanying footnotes) of 4,000 public corporations and allows a search for all the companies using a given accounting practice. To query NAARS, a trained searcher feeds key words into a computer. Within seconds the computer identifies all companies using those words in a certain fashion and proclaims itself ready to deliver, via videoscreen and printout, the relevant sections of their annual reports.

A STANDOUT IN THE CROWD

The expert performing this small miracle for *Fortune* was Hortense Goodman, a staff member of the American Institute of Certified Public Accountants. Spending 43 minutes and nine seconds at a computer terminal (cost to *Fortune*: $155.65), Mrs. Goodman interrogated the 1981–82 file of annual reports. She found a good number of companies that said they were *not* recognizing future tax benefits because their realization was open to at least some doubt. She found only one company among the entire 4,000 that *was* recognizing future tax benefits in 1981, and that was Aetna (which began the practice in the fourth quarter). "In the opinion of management," Aetna's footnote said, utilization of the company's loss carry-forwards to offset future taxable income" is assured beyond any reasonable doubt."

One point needs to be made about Aetna's lonely prominence in the NAARS data base: the data are being updated gradually and still contain some 1980 annual reports. So complete 1981 data might show other companies booking future tax benefits.

Donald Conrad, Aetna's executive vice president, says its 1981 decision to begin recognizing future tax benefits was not accompanied by consultation with the SEC—though, he adds, "we would be perfectly willing to talk to the SEC about the issue now." But Conrad also points out that Aetna has filed three registration statements with the SEC during 1982. The fact suggests, he says, that the commission has observed what Aetna is doing and decided it is okay.

In fact, the SEC hasn't decided any such thing. Because of budget constraints, the agency is engaged these days in "selective review" of registration statements. That means some filings get virtually no attention at all, and that's what happened to Aetna's three 1982 registrations. No one at the SEC appears to have known that Aetna was recognizing future tax benefits in current earnings until *Fortune* called to ask whether the registrations were reviewed. Howard P. Hodges, chief accountant of the Division of Corporation Finance, said then that he certainly planned to look at Aetna's financial statements now that he knew of the situation. He may look with a jaundiced eye, since his view of "beyond any reasonable doubt" appears to be hard-line. He says, "We think the test is very difficult to meet."

THE FOCUS OF AETNA

Aetna says nevertheless that it meets the test—absolutely and positively. John Filer, its chairman, sounds patiently impatient about the whole matter: "My view is that that interpretation is correct. My view is that the certainty of using the loss carry-forward over a 15-year time span is absolute." In forming that opinion, he says, Aetna relied on lawyers, accountants, and its own judgment. He goes on: "The numbers are large, but I don't think that's the focus of what's going on at the Aetna."

Why, he is asked, did he not render an explanation of these large numbers—60% of reported earnings—to the shareholders in the quarterly reports? "That's the simple answer I gave you a moment ago. I don't think this is one of the urgent, important issues at the Aetna. This is an accounting issue. I think the important issues are operational issues, strategic issues, changes of markets, acquisitions and divestitures, financings."

The company is equally categorical in discussing a related matter: Aetna's mode of presenting future tax benefits in its balance sheet. When such a benefit is taken into earnings, it must also make an appearance on the balance sheet, since it is an asset realizable down the road. Indeed, Opinion 11 states that in those rare cases when future tax benefits are recognized, an asset shall be set up and amortized as the benefit is realized.

But Aetna has not set up an asset. Instead, a detailed June 30 balance sheet—included in a recent Aetna prospectus though not in the quarterly report to shareholders—copes with $144 million in tax benefits by displaying them in the liability column. They are called deferred federal income taxes and presented as negative numbers—that is, they are enclosed in parentheses. Sorting out all these double negatives is a challenge. Think about it for a moment, however, and you will see that a "negative liability" is an asset.

But since not all readers of the prospectus might make that semantic leap, and since Opinion 11 does not remotely contemplate the presentation of tax benefits on the liability side, *Fortune* asked Aetna why it had handled the matter that way. One of the company's accounting executives, Heath Fitzsimmons, explains that Aetna believed that the expected tax benefit would be more visible as a separately stated item on the liability side than it would be if lumped into miscellaneous assets on the asset side. Well, perhaps—except why could it not be stated as a separate item on the asset side, possibly captioned as "future tax benefits" (a label that other companies have used in the past)? Fitzsimmons said that treatment was not justified because the amount of $144 million was a lower order of magnitude than the other huge asset numbers on the books. But, said *Fortune,* are there not also huge numbers on the liability side, among which you are saying the future tax benefits are nicely visible?

This colloquy, conducted in a telephone conference call, was joined by a Peat Marwick partner, Walter P. Schuetze, vice chairman of the firm's committee on accounting practice. Refreshingly, Schuetze said straight out that putting future tax benefits on the liability side of the balance sheet does not meet the directives of Opinion 11. He said, however, that Peat Marwick believed the treatment permissible.

The overriding question, of course, concerns Aetna's decision to include the tax benefits in its current statements in any form at all. The company's alternative would have been to wait until the tax benefits are actually realized, assuming they are, and then to present them as extraordinary items, which is the procedure directed by Opinion 11. That approach would have clobbered Aetna's earnings in the first half and would continue to clobber them until the moment the tax benefits begin to arise, which could be several years out. Even then the damage would not be entirely redressed, since investors ordinarily do not value extraordinary earnings as highly as they do the consistently delivered variety. These complications help explain why Aetna's executives do not take questions about their tax-benefit policies lightly.

THE ACCOUNTANT FOR THE DEFENSE

If Aetna's accounting is now challenged by the SEC, the point man in the defense may turn out to be Schuetze of Peat Marwick. It is not clear how he felt about Aetna's decision to book the tax benefits, but it is clear that he now has the accounting defenses mustered. He is familiar, he says, with the original intentions of Opinion 11—its legislative history, so to speak—and he says that the criteria the opinion sets forth, such as "isolated and nonrecurring causes," were never meant to be more than examples. "Opinion 11," he says, "prescribes just one test and that is 'beyond any reasonable doubt.'"

Suppose the SEC does not agree with that reading of history or says its policies, in any case, supersede history? On the phone, Schuetze seems to draw in a deep breath: "Then I will convince Clarence"—that's Clarence Sampson, the SEC's chief accountant—"that I am right."

If Aetna is allowed to defend itself on the ground of "beyond any reasonable doubt," it is likely to haul out an arsenal of talking points. Its inside and outside accountants mention two recent changes in the tax law as important. One, by extending the tax-loss carry-forward period from seven years to 15, supplies Aetna with more maneuvering room in which to realize the taxable profits it needs. The other tax change gives a multi-line insurance company increased freedom to consolidate the results of its life insurance subsidiaries, which might be earning operating profits today, with those of property and casualty subsidiaries, which almost certainly are earning operating losses. The problem with this bit of help is that Aetna's life insurance business is itself feeling profit pressures, the result of huge shifts in consumer attitudes toward life products.

Several Aetna executives, accounting and otherwise, also mention the company's ability to boost taxable income by shifting its property and casualty portfolio away from tax-exempt securities toward the taxable variety, whose higher yields would be tax-sheltered by the carry-forwards. This shift, however, cannot be accomplished by a wholesale shedding of tax-exempts, since most holdings in the portfolio could only be disposed of at a loss. Instead the shift must be accomplished gradually, as tax-exempts mature and income from investments and new cash flow is plowed into taxables.

Unfortunately, Aetna may even now be suffering from "negative cash flow." That is, premium revenues may not be supplying the cash needed to meet claims payments and other expenses. In part Aetna's weak cash flow position reflects its 1981 decision to try to stiffen its prices while encouraging the whole industry to do likewise. The effort was premature and, in any case, the industry is too fragmented to accept price leadership. In short, the effort didn't work. It did, however, cost Aetna some market share, a loss it is still feeling.

Still another source of possible taxable profits for Aetna is the flock of non-insurance businesses it has been pursuing. Its U.S. deals include the purchase of Geosource and the formation of a real estate partnership with Twentieth Century-Fox Film; an acquisition in process is Federated Investors, a mutual-fund management company. Aetna has also bought an interest in a British merchant bank, Samuel Montagu, but the taxable U.S. profits it will generate are apt to be minor.

Aetna's Conrad says each venture looks good as an investment and that the taxable income coming along will look "very attractive" also. But the immediate income may be limited: even at their best the acquired businesses do not produce huge profits, and one, Geosource, is right now caught up in the oil-patch slump.

WAITING FOR THE TURN

The strongest hope of Aetna's executives, not surprisingly, is that the property and casualty cycle will turn upward and begin to shower the company with profits, an event that would be signaled by firming prices. The key to that hope is interest rates, which in the four-year-old downward leg of the cycle have encouraged insurers to "buy" business so that they could sink the premiums into high-yielding investments— or at least avoid the necessity of selling holdings at a loss to meet current expenses. If interest rates stay down at their current levels or decline still further, that proposition would begin to seem a whole lot less interesting and prices should begin to firm. But there is no telling when all this is going to happen or what the durability of the upward leg of the cycle will be. To state matters simply, this is a business about which there are "reasonable doubts."

A Bit of Rouge for Allis-Chalmers

Harold B. Meyers
Associate Editor, *Fortune*

The accounting that appears in annual reports sometimes serves a cosmetic purpose—it is there not so much to inform stockholders as to help management keep them happy, or at least quiet, by touching up blemishes and brightening beauty spots. When a company is not doing well, and at the same time is trying to fend off an unwanted merger, the cosmeticians of accountancy can sometimes perform wonders—even when they are limited to shades of red. Quite a number of companies in this year's directory used bookeeping devices of various kinds to brighten their results. But Allis-Chalmers Manufacturing outdid them all at the rouge pot.

As 1968 ended, long-suffering Allis-Chalmers, No. 130 among the 500, found itself with some conflicting needs and desires. It presumably wanted to put the best possible face on 1968 results in order to maintain stockholder support in a bitter battle against a take-over by White Consolidated Industries, No. 143. But the new president of Allis-Chalmers, David C. Scott, who took office September 1, wanted to write off at once the tremendous charges associated with past mistakes and thereby turn the company around. To do that, he had to slap stockholders with some very bad news just when White Consolidated's onslaught was hotting up.

Allis-Chalmers resolved this conflict with some intricate accounting that let it accept Scott's write-off while minimizing the bad news that had to be reported to stockholders. The published results were still pretty dismal: on sales of $767,313,100, the company reported a loss of $54,589,720. That was, however, a whole lot better than the $121,588,931 that the company *actually* lost last year.

TAKING CREDIT FOR A LOSS

To understand how an actual loss of $122 million can become a reported loss of $55 million requires some comprehension of tax accounting. It is well known, of course, that a corporate dollar earned is roughly 50 cents lost to the tax collector. The converse is also true, i.e., *a dollar lost is 50 cents earned.* Allis-Chalmers simply claimed a credit on its profit-and-loss statement for the taxes that it saved by achieving a loss. The company said, in effect: "If Uncle Sam deserves his slice of the profits, he also deserves his slice of the losses. We cannot be said to have lost $122 million when we thereby hung on to something over $60 million in taxes that we otherwise would have had to pay."

This logic is applicable to stockholder reports, but not to a company's tax returns. The tax carry-forward created by a loss can be used only in years succeeding the one in which the loss occurred. For this reason alone, then, Allis-Chalmers' tax return for 1968 can bear only a passing resemblance to its stockholder report. In addition, not all of that $122 million represented operating losses. The figure included $69 million that Scott charged off in 1968 in the form of special reserves for costs that he expected to incur later; i.e., the company provided for losses that had not yet occurred and that can't be claimed on the tax form until they do occur.

The shakiest aspect of tax-benefit accounting arises from the fact that tax credits are worth nothing until there are profits to apply them to. By using credits to cut the same losses that created the credits, a company's accountants must flout an ancient accounting adage: provide for all losses but *anticipate no profits.* To be sure, not all the $60-odd million of tax credits that Allis-Chalmers used were anticipatory. Some $14 million represented a carryback against taxes that were paid on earnings for 1965, 1966, and 1967. No problem there: the past profits were already available to ensure a tax refund. Nor is there a problem with some other substantial credits that Allis-Chalmers made available to itself by various accounting changes and tax adjustments. But included in the total tax credits used to cut down the 1968 loss that the company reported was around $43 million in "estimated future income tax benefits." In fact, Allis-Chalmers will not get the benefit of any such amount until it comes up with some $86 million in pre-tax profits.

WHAT AUDITORS CAN'T AUDIT

Allis-Chalmers argues that it had no real choice about these prospective tax benefits. In his brief tenure, Scott has lopped 3,300 non-production employees off the payroll, with more to go, thereby assuring savings of perhaps $40 million. Since all the company's projections are for continued high sales, Scott's drastic cost cutting seems certain to show up in profits on the bottom line. With profits thus "assured," Allis-Chalmers felt that it would have been misleading *not* to use the tax credits to reduce its reported loss.

Still, for a company that has just lost $122 million in a single year to assume future income of $86 million might appear a bit presumptuous. And, indeed, Allis-Chalmers' insistence on counting so many unhatched chickens while its incubator was out of order seemed to make its auditors rather nervous. Price Waterhouse's certificate in the Allis-Chalmers annual report was half again as long as the usual auditors' statement, and carried less conviction. There was, of course, the conventional observation that the auditors' examination was made "in accordance with generally accepted auditing standards." But Price Waterhouse commented that Allis-Chalmers' substantial amounts of "reserves and anticipated tax benefits reflect the best current judgment of the Company's management," and that this judgment was beyond the auditors' ability to audit.

Reserved as Price Waterhouse's statement was, it apparently satisfied both the Securities and Exchange Commission and the New York Stock Exchange. Neither has raised any objection to Allis-Chalmers' report to its stockholders. One N.Y.S.E. official says that, in general, a company "hates to have a qualified auditors' opinion," but such a statement does not affect the listing of the company's stock. He adds: "When the unknowns are substantial, we have to assume that any national firm of certified public accountants is using its best professional judgment." That is, of course, precisely the assumption that an ordinary stockholder must make about any company and its auditors.

As it happens, President Scott has been making good on his promise of earnings for Allis-Chalmers. The company had pre-tax profits of $11,700,000 in the first quarter of 1969. Because the tax effect of 1968 losses was applied to 1968 results, however, the company must now deduct taxes from any earnings that it reports to stockholders. The net it can report on that profitable first quarter is only $5,100,000. Explains an Allis-Chalmers accountant: "Since we took our cake in 1968, we have to take taxes out of our 1969 profits."

LIABILITIES

The question of uncertainty applies with equal force to liabilities. Prior to the 1960s, liabilities were recognized to the extent that they were legally owing, based on contracts that had been partially or wholly performed by the creditor or based on statutes that imposed an obligation currently to be enforced. But with the rise of long-term financing via leasing arrangements, as well as a host of others enumerated in the article by Richard Dieter and Arthur R. Wyatt, "Get It Off the Balance Sheet!," accounting for liabilities has become a much more subjective undertaking. Perhaps, mainly to improve their debt-equity ratio, especially to distance themselves from the restrictions contained in loan covenants, companies have sought to remove as much debt from the balance sheet as possible.

In a *Wall Street Journal* article, "Loose Ledgers: Many Firms Hide Debt To Give Them an Aura of Financial Strength," Lee Berton continues the theme developed by Dieter and Wyatt. Berton writes, "Reacting to inflationary distortions, accounting loopholes and heavy debt burdens, corporations have concocted so many ways to hide or disguise borrowings that deciphering their true liabilities is often impossible." Is it any wonder that there is a growing mistrust of information developed by management in the audited financial statements?

In "The Curious Accounting Treatment of the Swedish Government Loan to Uddeholm," Stephen A. Zeff and Sven-Erik Johansson describe the successful attempt of the Swedish government to circumvent the normal accounting treatment for a government loan to a major company that found itself perilously close to defaulting on its long-term loans. While the transaction between the government and the company was represented as being a loan, the Swedish Parliament enacted legislation requiring that it be accounted for as if it were a subsidy—i.e., as revenue—hence improving the company's balance-sheet "solidity." The events described here illustrate how the economic consequences of a transaction can dictate its accounting treatment, regardless of how absurd the accounting treatment might turn out to be.

Another means by which corporations may remove long-term debt from their balance sheets without actually paying the debt off is by a practice known as "defeasance." In November 1983, the FASB, in Statement No. 76, approved the early extinguishment of debt by this maneuver, which involves a company's acquiring Treasury bonds that match the terms of its bonds payable, placing them in an irrevocable trust, and using the returns to pay the interest and principal on the company's bonds. Since defeasance implies the debtor's release from legal liability, the term is, strictly speaking, a misnomer here. What actually occurs is that the financial liability is being satisfied by the trusteed asset, but the company continues to be the primary obligor under the debt obligation. It is this point that caused three of the seven FASB members to dissent from Statement No. 76, as they believe that a debt cannot be said to have been extinguished until the issuing company is no longer the primary obligor. In early 1984, it was predicted that a growing number of corporations would probably "defease" their debt during the year.[1] The article by Michael Blumstein, "Pros and Cons of Defeasance," appearing in *The New York Times,* describes the practice of "defeasance" and raises questions concerning the financial wisdom of removing debt from the balance sheet in this manner.

BIBLIOGRAPHICAL NOTES

The following article conveys the thinking of the Vice Chairman of the FASB, who has been a prime advocate within the Board for the asset-liability, as opposed to the revenue-expense, approach to analyzing accounting problems.

Sprouse, Robert T.: "Accounting for What-You-May-Call-Its," *The Journal of Accountancy* (October 1966), pp. 45–53. (Reproduced in *Financial Accounting Theory: Issues and Controversies,* Volume II, Thomas F. Keller and Stephen A. Zeff (eds.) (McGraw-Hill, 1969).)

An Australian contribution to the development of a conceptual framework for liabilities is

Kerr, Jean St.G.: *The Definition and Recognition of Liabilities,* Accounting Theory Monograph No. 4 (Melbourne, Australia: Australian Accounting Research Foundation, 1984).

[1]"How 'Defeasance' Will Help Companies and the Treasury," *Business Week* (February 6, 1984), pp. 12, 16.

Get It Off the Balance Sheet!

Richard Dieter
Partner
Arthur Andersen & Co.
Chicago

Arthur R. Wyatt
Partner
Arthur Andersen & Co.
Chicago
(From January 1, 1985 Wyatt will be a member of the Financial
Accounting Standards Board, having resigned from Arthur Andersen
& Co.)

Get it off the balance sheet! More and more frequently that appears to be the demand of corporate treasurers facing financing alternatives. Finding a way to do the financing, they say, but do it so that resulting obligations do not have to be recorded. Ingenuity in structuring financing arrangements is a quality that they seek. Whereas the coup of the '60s was to pull off a pooling-of-interests business combination in purchase and sale circumstances, the coup of the '70s was to arrange long-term financings that need not be recorded in liability incurrence situations.

METHODS THAT CAN BE USED

A number of vehicles have been developed to enable companies to obtain needed financing without including it in the balance sheet:

Finance Subsidiaries

The accounting literature guiding preparation of consolidated financial statements helps by permitting the nonconsolidation of finance subsidiaries. The American Institute of Certified Public Accountants' (AICPA) Accounting Research Bulletin No. 51, "Consolidated Financial Statements," specifies that:

> ".. For example, separate statements may be required for a subsidiary which is a bank or an insurance company and may be preferable for a finance company where the parent and the other subsidiaries are engaged in manufacturing operations."

This permits nonconsolidation of finance subsidiaries, and increasingly, companies have established captive finance subsidiaries. In many cases, roughly equal amounts of receivables and debt are transferred to the subsidiary and are thereby eliminated from the consolidated balance sheet. In this era of diversified operations, however, the basis for nonconsolidation of finance subsidiaries is increasingly suspect.

From *Financial Executive* (January 1980), pp. 42, 44–48. Reprinted by permission of the Financial Executives Institute.

Sales of Receivables with Recourse

Some view such transactions as the same as a secured borrowing, that is, a loan secured by the pledge of accounts receivables. Because the lender has recourse to the "seller" of the receivables in case of noncollection, this view has considerable merit; the borrowing is reported as a liability and the receivables remain on the balance sheet. Others regard such transactions as a sale of receivables, with the proceeds being applied to reduce existing borrowings. The effect on a consolidated balance sheet is similar to the creation of a finance subsidiary: Receivables *and* liabilities are eliminated from the balance sheet.

Product Financing Agreements

There has been little specific guidance on accounting for transactions involving the sale of a product accompanied by a seller's agreement to repurchase the product at a later date. In late 1978, the Accounting Standards Executive Committee (AcSEC) of the AICPA issued Statement of Position 78–8, "Accounting for Product Financing Arrangements," indicating that sales of a product with an agreement to repurchase should be recognized as a borrowing and not as a sale when certain specified characteristics are present. Under prior practice, however, the sale of the product was often recognized (with profit recognized currently or deferred), the proceeds used to reduce existing indebtedness, and no recognition made in the accounts of the agreement to repurchase. The effect was similar to a borrowing with the pledge of inventory, except that neither the borrowing nor the inventory was reported in the balance sheet of the borrower.

Leases

Financial Accounting Standards Board (FASB) Statement No. 13 provides guidance on accounting for leases. Unfortunately, the objectives sought to be achieved in this Statement will not be attained by application of its criteria for lease classification. While definitive statements about practice under the standard await full implementation in 1980 (when compliance becomes mandatory), early indications are that no significant increase in lease capitalization over prior practice has resulted from its application. Significant numbers of long-term leases that pass substantially all the risks and rewards of ownership of property to the lessee continue to be negotiated and accounted for as operating leases. Those who structure leases may have to work harder (and give up something of value in the process) to achieve a finance lease for the lessor and an operating lease for the lessee for a given lease, but such matters are negotiated daily.

Project Financing Arrangements

In recent years, a number of financing arrangements have been devised for large construction and operating projects. For example, a joint venture is formed by two or more entities, with no one entity owning more than 50 percent of the venture. It is thinly capitalized and highly leveraged, generally with the debt guaranteed by the venturers. Under current accounting practice, as specified by Accounting Principles Board (APB) Opinion No. 18, "The Equity Method of Accounting for Investments in Common Stock," investments in such ventures are accounted for on the equity method, that is, no portion of the debt incurred is reported in the balance sheet of any venturer. Thus, the debt is off the balance sheet. The use of a trust to handle the financing, generally during the construction period of large capital assets, is another device to keep the borrowing off an entity's balance sheet. In late 1978, the Securities and Exchange Commission (SEC), which appears to be increasingly concerned by the spread of off-balance sheet financing, issued Staff Accounting Bulletin No. 28, which required electric utility companies to include in their balance sheets the assets and liabilities of construction period trusts. The equity method of accounting for investments was developed to achieve improved recognition of income from the investment and improved reflection of the economic earning capacity of the investor.

Additional examples of these arrangements are presented in the following section, but each method has one common characteristic: an arrangement whereby some believe—or hope—that the incurred indebtedness need not be reported in the balance sheet of the entity or entities benefiting from the borrowing. Some of the examples presented have been accounted for as off-balance-sheet financings, some as incurred indebtedness, and some were rejected for accounting or other reasons.

Timber Financing

An entity sells its standing timber at cost to a newly created thin-equity company whose sole purpose is to handle this transaction. The entity also enters into a timber-cutting contract with the newly created company, giving the entity the right to harvest certain quantities over a specified period at specified rates. The entity agrees to make certain payments at future dates should the minimum specified timber harvest not be achieved. The newly created thin-equity company finances the purchase of the timber through bank financing secured by the timber and the cutting contracts. The entity proposes to remove the timber from its balance sheet and account for the payments under the cutting contract as they are made. It would disclose the aggregate commitment under the cutting contract in the notes to the financial statements.

Through-Put Arrangement

Company A forms a partnership with Company B, a customer, to own a project and service Company B's product requirements with a through-put contract. Financing, on a nonrecourse basis, is obtained for 80 percent of the project's cost. Company A is the general partner and invests 10 percent of the partnership equity. Company B is a limited partner, owns 90 percent of the partnership equity and accounts for its limited partnership interest on the equity method of accounting, since it has no control (not being the general partner) and is not at risk on the project except to the extent of its equity investment. Company A accounts for its general partnership interest on the equity method because it has only a 10 percent equity interest. Neither company includes any of the 80 percent borrowed funds in its balance sheet.

Take-or-Pay Contract

Several utilities enter into an agreement to construct a synthetic natural gas facility. A contract is signed with an independent party for the construction of the facility. The several utilities guarantee the debt during construction. The utilities also create a new entity to own the facility upon completion. Each utility enters into a take-or-pay contract for the entire output of the facility. None of the individual utilities will own over a 50 percent interest in the new entity. Each utility will guarantee the debt of the facility and pay amounts that will cover all operating costs and debt service requirements. Because this agreement has many similarities to a joint venture, the individual utilities propose to account for it by using the one-line equity method.

Land Option

A developer buys an option on a land parcel and concurrently agrees to spend a significant amount on the development of the land under option. The option requires an initial down payment, with a continuing option payment that equates to interest. The developer proposes to defer recognition of the acquisition of the asset (land) and the related obligation under the option, even though significant amounts of development funds have been capitalized as a part of the cost of the option. In other circumstances, the developer has "sold" lots to customers while the land and related obligation is still under option and not reported on the balance sheet.

Limited Partnership

A company forms a limited partnership to finance acquisition of a property. The company is the general partner and puts in no investment. The limited partners provide 100 percent financing. The general partner guarantees the limited partnership debt and agrees to manage the property for a fee. The payments committed to by the general partner or a third party user will cover all debt service as well as the management fee. The general partner shares profits and losses with the limited partners equally until the borrowed funds are paid. At that point the general partner would receive 90 percent of any partnership profit, including proceeds from sale of the property. The general partner contends no accounting is required because he has no investment in the limited partnership and even if he did, it is improper to apply accounting to investments in corporations and to investments in partnerships.

Servicing Agreement

E arranges for services to be rendered by F. The service involves a form of processing of a commodity owned by E. The processing is performed in a facility owned by F, and located near E's operations. The service agreement generally runs for a period approximating either the estimated useful life of the facility or the period of repayment of debt used to finance the facility. The service agreement provides for E to pay F specified fees whether or not services are actually rendered, and includes other terms that protect and provide a return to F on its investment in the committed facilities. E does not propose to account for its obligations under the servicing agreement until services are rendered and payments are made.

WHY REMOVE DEBT FROM THE BALANCE SHEET?

Many motivations exist to encourage entities to get debt off the balance sheet. While they may fall in a range from praiseworthy to suspect, the methods described previously rely heavily on accounting for the *form* of the arrangements, not for their substance. Frequently the transaction form is soundly motivated, but even more frequently, the form flows from pressures over which the borrower has little, if any, control.

By getting debt off the balance sheet, the character, or quality, of the balance sheet is improved. Ratios that have stood the test of usefulness for generations will therefore appear more favorable to the borrower. The ratio of debt to equity is decreased, and such decrease is viewed positively by many who evaluate balance sheets. More frequently, however, the motive is to prevent an adverse ratio from evolving. The entity may be near a danger point in its debt-to-equity relationship based on historical standards. Additional debt could so impair the ratio that it would trigger other, more adverse, developments. Credit ratings could be altered. Borrowing costs could increase. Future expansion, replacement, or research plans could be imperiled. With all these potential adversities, it is somewhat surprising that few seem to question whether historical relationships for the debt-to-equity ratio continue to be useful to evaluate financial liquidity under current conditions. Some may feel that such questioning is for academics to pursue; why struggle with such an issue when the matter can be solved more simply by removing it from the balance sheet.

Loan covenants pose even more significant stumbling blocks to accounting for financing arrangements according to their substance. Loan covenants often impose specific restrictions on the amount of additional debt a company can incur. Sometimes they specify a debt-to-equity ratio that must be maintained to prevent an existing loan from being placed in default. Loan covenants that were prepared in less-complicated times may not preclude the borrower from incurring additional obligations, such as those arising from leases, captive finance subsidiaries, or any of the project financing vehicles commonly found today. As loan covenants drafters become more sophisticated, however, they require that certain types of off-balance sheet obligations be considered the equivalent of balance sheet debt to meet the loan covenant. Consequently, new and more innovative methods are being developed. Thus, some long-used procedures for getting debt off the balance sheet (e.g., leases) no longer escape loan covenant requirements.

Other motivations may be somewhat less critical, yet of some practical significance. Corporate planning may indicate a level of borrowing over the next several years that will press projected historical debt-to-equity ratios. While a current project may not lead to a critical problem in this area, the goal may be to get the financing for the current project off the balance sheet to provide room for future borrowing. Thus, some entities that today appear to have no real debt-to-equity problems may be using off-balance sheet methods as part of a longer-range financing strategy.

Interest cost reductions are sometimes a motivation, too. The use of a trust method by rate-regulated entities for financing projects during the construction period was principally aimed at removing the interest costs from the regulated entity's accounts during the construction period. Because interest incurred and capitalized by an entity is viewed by some analysts with suspicion, the motivation is not spurious. Likewise, some merchandisers attempt to get non-interest bearing receivables off the balance sheet in order to reduce interest costs and to improve a key ratio in the merchandising industry, the ratio of interest charges to earnings. In other industries, return on assets is considered important. Thus, removal of an equal amount of assets and debt is favorably viewed.

WHY IS OFF-BALANCE SHEET FINANCING PROMOTED?

Why has the trend of eliminating debt from the balance sheet become so pronounced, and what can be done by accounting professionals to find optimum solutions to the inherent business problems of this trend?

One rather apparent explanation is that existing accounting concepts of a liability are so ill-defined that they are inadequate to deal with the increasingly sophisticated financing methods being practiced today. The concept of a liability under historical-cost accounting relies much more on legal notions than on economic notions. If the financing arrangement does not result in legal debt to the reporting equity, that is, if that entity is only a guarantor or is only secondarily liable, a strong argument can be made to exclude the financing from the entity's balance sheet. If financial statements are expected to reveal the economic effects of transactions and other events in which the enterprise engages, reliance on the legal notion of a liability for accounting purposes needs a critical reevaluation. Accountants need to decide if their reporting is to be principally governed by legal notions (and thus by transaction forms) or by economic notions (and thus more often by transaction substance).

Another plausible explanation is that off-balance-sheet financing is a consequence of the inability of historical-cost accounting to deal effectively with inflation. Under historical-cost accounting, the effects of inflation on the economic activities of the enterprise are neither reported nor well understood. One effect is that the balance-sheet carrying amounts of many assets are currently far below their current value, whether measured on a current-cost basis, a discounted cash-flow basis, or some other measure of current value. For example, many companies have adopted the LIFO method of accounting for inventory costs, both to lower taxes and to eliminate the effect of price fluctuations on "inventory profits." Under LIFO, the carrying amounts for inventories during periods of inflation increasingly diverge from the current values of those inventories. The carrying amount of depreciable property often shows a similar disparity.

As this divergence becomes more pronounced, the pressures for getting new financing arrangements off the balance sheet increase markedly. If asset-carrying amounts were reported on their higher current-value basis, a significant portion of the increased basis (generally the amount of increase less the related tax effect) would be added to the shareholders' equity on the entity's balance sheet. Consequently, using traditional debt-to-equity relationships, entities would have additional capacity to carry increased liabilities. Similarly, to the extent that loan covenant restrictions relate to debt-to-equity relationships, such covenants would be more easily met on a current-cost basis and would thereby tend to permit companies to embark on new capital replacement or expansion programs by using traditional financing arrangements.

Thus, what we have today under the historical-cost accounting basis that underlies current practice is a failure to recognize in balance sheets the current value of assets and a consequent pressure to eliminate from the balance sheet liabilities associated with financing arrangements. In effect, accounting compensates for the understatement of asset-carrying amounts by also understating liabilities. The latter understatement is achieved through acceptance of a wide range of off-balance-sheet financing vehicles. For example, one defect in historical-cost basis of accounting during periods of inflation—the understatement of asset-carrying amounts—is partially alleviated by omitting a more or less compensating amount of liabilities. Surely, neither the business community nor the accounting profession can expect that financial statements can long retain any semblance of credibility if users come to understand the extent to which current balance sheets are being misstated. FASB Statement No. 33, "Financial Reporting and Changing Prices," is a first step in achieving greater awareness of how badly inflation distorts the balance sheet and indirectly promotes creation of novel financing vehicles.

GET IT ON THE BALANCE SHEET

Of the various methods used to get debt off the balance sheet, the FASB has dealt only with the subject of accounting for leases, and many view the conclusions of that Statement as ineffective. AcSEC has made recommendations to the FASB concerning various kinds of project financing arrangements. AcSEC has also requested the FASB to amend Accounting Research Bulletin No. 51 by requiring the consolidation of certain finance subsidiaries. The issues involved in the accounting for sales of receivables with recourse are also under active consideration by AcSEC. These AcSEC projects have been well over two years in development, a period that has seen acceleration in the use of off-balance-sheet financings.

All of these approaches, however, are likely to have only minimal long-run effectiveness. The only sound basis for achieving proper accounting for liabilities is to address the underlying concepts involved. It is hoped that the project of the FASB on the conceptual framework of financial accounting will move along more rapidly and will provide suitable bases for achieving more effective accounting for liabilities (as well as for assets, revenues, and expenses). Preparers and users of financial statements will be better served if financial statements reflect the economic—rather than legal—effects of the transactions of the enterprise. Users should no longer be expected to understand that the understatement of assets in times of inflation is partially offset by omitting substantive liabilities.

Getting debt off the balance sheet is only a symptom of a more fundamental problem in financial accounting, which is giving adequate recognition in financial statements to the varied effects that inflation can have. Getting debt back on the balance sheet will not solve all the shortcomings of the current framework of financial accounting, but it will give users a much more complete and dependable basis for evaluating financial position.

Loose Ledgers: Many Firms Hide Debt to Give Them an Aura of Financial Strength

Lee Berton
Staff Reporter, *The Wall Street Journal*

Prodded by financial analysts' complaints, the Securities and Exchange Commission undertook an extensive study last year concerning debt that corporations manage to keep off their balance sheets. The SEC hoped to give analysts, stockholders and bank lending officers a better fix on this so-called off-balance-sheet financing.

But the agency didn't get very far. "We were so bewildered by the variety of transactions and accounting standards in this area, we finally gave up," says Lawrence S. Jones, who worked on the SEC study.

No wonder. Reacting to inflationary distortions, accounting loopholes and heavy debt burdens, corporations have concocted so many ways to hide or disguise borrowings that deciphering their true liabilities is often impossible. Sometimes, debt isn't acknowledged anywhere; at other times, it's there, but finding it would take a financial wizard with hours of free time and a computer.

"It's all done with mirrors," says Loyd Heath, an accounting professor at the University of Washington in Seattle. "Under current accounting rules, companies apparently can call debt whatever they like."

UNFORTUNATE EFFECTS

Calling it something else doesn't merely face-lift a company's balance sheet. It undercuts the usefulness of balance sheets, which list assets and liabilities and provide major clues to corporate cash flow—and does so at a time when balance sheets have increasingly replaced profit-and-loss statements as thermometers of corporate health.

But most investors, bankers and economists aren't sophisticated enough to see through many off-balance-sheet borrowing tactics. So investors may make ill-informed decisions. Banks often don't know that a company seeking a loan already is deep in hock. And economists misjudge how highly leveraged American business really is.

"Off-balance-sheet borrowing techniques are being used much more frequently, and some are so complex that no one knows how high the mountain of total corporate debt is reaching," warns Arthur Wyatt, a partner at Arthur Andersen & Co., a big accounting firm.

That could be dangerous. If, for instance, companies are borrowing more than they otherwise could, they may be stretching their resources too thin, and they, and their banks, will become more vulnerable in economic downturns. If the economy sours and banks start calling in loans, some companies will be hard pressed to repay their debts.

PAYING THE PIPER

"If you try to hide debt, it will eventually catch up with you," says Abraham Briloff, a well-known accounting professor at Baruch College in New York. "In business, there's cash and there's broke, and cash is better."

Debt is being hidden for all sorts of reasons. Financial analysts and corporate executives say the steady increase in corporate debt in recent years is pushing companies to keep additional borrowings off the financial statement. They also blame inflation, which understates assets and thus spurs the search for novel financing vehicles that permit understatement of liabilities. Moreover, many corporate executives who admit to hiding debt say that as long as they are allowed to do so, they would be foolish not to.

Consider Avis Rent-A-Car, a subsidiary of Norton Simon Inc. In 1980, Avis set up a trust to borrow money to buy automobiles, which it then leases to Avis for its rental fleet. Because the trust is separate from Avis and Norton Simon (which was acquired by Esmark Inc. last July), the trust's debt isn't on their balance sheets. The result: Norton Simon kept $400 million in borrowings off its balance sheet for the year ended June 30. Robert D. Walter, Norton Simon's principal accounting officer, says the trust arrangement held Norton Simon's debt down to 56% of equity at June 30, rather than the 140% that it otherwise would have been.

"One of the big advantages of off-balance-sheet financing," Mr. Walter concedes, "is that it permits us to make other borrowings from banks for operating capital that we couldn't otherwise obtain." He adds that Norton Simon didn't give details of the trust in its annual report because that would have required a report "as thick as a Sears Roebuck catalog."

CRITIC'S VIEW

However, Gerry White, a securities analyst who teaches financial analysis at New York University, calls the tactic a "subterfuge." Avis, he says, "isn't leasing the cars but really owns them." And he notes that both the Hertz subsidiary of RCA Corp. and the National Car Rental unit of Household International Inc. buy rather than lease their cars.

Another technique for hiding debt is to sell receivables, bills due to a company. The company continues to collect the bills and passes the payments on to the buyer as they are received.

Current accounting rules stipulate that if the bills are sold with a full guarantee by the seller, they are considered debt—that is, a collateralized loan. But companies can report such debt in footnotes rather than on the balance sheet. And they never have to report receivables sold without a guarantee, even though many accountants view them as debt, too. After all, the accountants say, a company is really borrowing money and then repaying it in installments as it gets paid on the bills.

In Nashua Corp.'s 1980–82 annual reports, the office-products manufacturer listed a total of $41 million of guaranteed receivables but didn't acknowledge those sold without guarantees. Rodney Wentzell, the company's treasurer in charge of selling receivables, won't talk about the sales of non-guaranteed receivables, but he agrees that they should go on the balance sheet as debt. "It would be a lot easier to analyze, and you wouldn't have to look through the fine print," he says.

An increasingly common method of disguising debt among utilities and petroleum and natural-resources companies is the "throughput and deficiency" contract, also known as "take or pay." A corporation enters into a joint venture or agrees with another entity to buy a certain amount of goods from it or to share a facility. The joint venture then borrows money to build the facility, such as a factory, pipeline or refinery, and the payments for the goods or services cover the interest.

Under current accounting rules, a corporation owning more than 50% of the venture generally must recognize all the debt. But if it owns less than 50%, it doesn't have to recognize any of it. Some companies do just that; others list the debt in a footnote.

"That [rule] doesn't make any sense," says Thorton O'glove, a securities analyst who writes a report on the quality of corporate earnings. He says it makes comparisons of companies in the same industry impossible.

Some accountants complain that the rules also create silly distinctions among various industries. If an oil company, for example, owns less than 50% of a pipeline venture, it usually—at most—calls the money borrowed to build the pipeline a "contingent liability" in footnotes. The rules permit that practice on the assumption that the pipeline won't go out of business. But these accountants ask how debt of a pipeline joint venture differs from money borrowed to build a steel mill.

"They're just playing antics with semantics," Prof. Briloff comments. "Debt is debt."

OIL FIRMS' MANEUVERS

A look at three partnership ventures illustrates how oil companies can report debt as they wish. The Louisiana Offshore Oil Port (Loop), a $21 million platform in the Gulf of Mexico, connects with the Louisiana Cap Line (Locap), a $116 million, 83-mile pipeline that in turn runs north into Capline, a $220 million, 663-mile line to Patoka, Ill.

Ashland Oil Co. owns 18.6% of Loop and 21.4% of Locap, and a footnote in its report for the year ended Sept. 30, 1982, lists $150 million in contingent liabilities for its share of debt in the two projects. The report ignores Capline, 19.046%-owned by Ashland. A spokesman says Capline's debt was financed through long-term leases, which are included in capitalized lease obligations on the balance sheet.

Texaco Inc. and Shell Oil Co., also partners in the three projects, disclose nothing in their latest annual reports about the pipeline debts. They simply say that under long-term agreements, they may have to advance funds to help the projects meet their debt obligations if sufficient crude oil isn't shipped. Accounting officials at both companies say they didn't mention the debt because current rules don't require it. They add that the amounts aren't "material"—significant in relation to the company's overall finances—though the definition of materiality is vague.

Over the next year or two, the Financial Accounting Standards Board, the accountants' rule-making body, plans to consider eliminating this debt tactic. But many accountants are skeptical. "Too many huge debt-intensive companies would be hurt," Prof. Heath says. "If the true debt of a big borrower like a power or an oil company was on its balance sheet, it could bury the company in the eyes of its lenders."

Ironically, some tactics to keep debt off the balance sheet evolved from accounting rules designed to make annual reports clearer. For example, one rule says a company needn't consolidate results of a 100%-owned subsidiary if a separate report for the subsidiary seems "more informative." The rule cites the case of a finance subsidiary owned by a manufacturing company.

"Too many are abusing the rule," Mr. O'glove says. "If the subsidiary provides loans for major products of the parent, the debt should be consolidated."

Some accountants cite Insilco Corp., which, among other things, sells precut lumber for build-it-yourself homes and extends loans to the lumber buyers through a 100%-owned finance unit, Miles Homes. If Miles's debt had been included on Insilco's balance sheet in 1982, debt would have consumed 80% of the parent company's capital. Instead, Insilco reported consolidated debt at 31% of capital.

FIGURES INCLUDED

"We did include Miles's separate balance sheet in our annual report, and investors could have figured out the consolidated debt on their own," says A. Eugene Still, Insilco's vice president for finance. "If we consolidated it ourselves, it would have only confused investors. It would look as if Insilco's receivables were completely out of control—which isn't so."

With all the different ways to keep debt off the balance sheet, companies often seem able to do so at will. J.C. Penney & Co., for example, has taken advantage of the flexible rules.

In February 1980, the big retailer sold $273 million of receivables to Citicorp; the agreement guaranteed the bank a return at least equal to the prime rate, the basic rate on business loans. Penney reported the transaction as a sale and used the cash to remove $273 million in debt from its balance sheet.

In November 1981, however, the Financial Accounting Standards Board issued a proposed ruling that such a sale guaranteeing a "floating interest rate" was a collateralized loan and therefore debt. Penney apparently found out about the proposal, and a month before it was issued the company bought back the receivables for $262 million—at an $11 million loss. It then sold the receivables to its own finance subsidiary, J.C. Financial Corp.—again removing them from the balance sheet.

In each of the past three years, Penney has sold to its own finance subsidiary more than $3 billion of receivables.

If Penney had consolidated results of its finance subsidiary for its latest fiscal year, ended last Jan. 31, its debt-to-equity ratio would have risen to 1.52 from the 1.27 reported. "A 1.52 ratio means that the company is highly leveraged and is more vulnerable during an economic downturn," says Frederick Kopf, a retail-industry analyst with Moseley, Hallgarten, Estabrook & Weeden, a brokerage firm.

Penney says it repurchased the receivables that it had originally sold because it would earn more on them by doing so. But some outside accountants aren't convinced. "Intent is an ephemeral quality that's difficult to audit," Prof. Heath says. "But it looks as if Penney's was trying to keep debt off its balance sheet."

The Curious Accounting Treatment of the Swedish Government Loan to Uddeholm

Stephen A. Zeff
Rice University

Sven-Erik Johansson
Stockholm School of Economics

ABSTRACT: This article describes the successful attempt of the Swedish Government and Uddeholm to circumvent the normal accounting treatment for a government loan to a major company that found itself perilously close to defaulting on its long-term loans. While the transaction between the Government and the company was represented as having a loan, the Swedish Parliament enacted legislation requiring that it be accounted for as if it were a subsidy, hence improving the company's balance-sheet "solidity." The events described here illustrate how the economic consequences of a transaction can dictate its accounting treatment, as well as how the accounting profession can eventually persuade political decision makers not to interfere in accounting determinations.

At the end of 1977, Uddeholm, a leading Swedish manufacturer of steel and forest products, had fallen on hard times.[1] Both of these industries were in recession, although a recent devaluation of the Swedish krona seemed to promise somewhat of a recovery in steel. Forest products, however, were in the doldrums, and the company concluded that outside assistance was required.

Uddeholm's consolidated "Result before Appropriations and Taxes" (roughly equivalent to the American "income from continuing operations," but before taxes) had plummeted from a record high of 486 million kronor (MSEK) in 1974 to a

From *The Accounting Review* (April 1984), pp. 342–350. Reprinted by permission of the American Accounting Association.

[1] Based on its 1977 reported results, Uddeholm was 416th in the *Fortune* list of the 500 largest industrial companies outside the U.S., and it was the 20th largest Swedish company appearing in the *Fortune* survey. Its 1977 group sales were 2,598.8 million kronor, or the equivalent of U.S. $581 million.

negative 448 MSEK in 1977. The pretax income figures for the years 1970 to 1977 indicate the roller-coaster trend:

1970	92 MSEK
1971	44 MSEK
1972	32 MSEK
1973	176 MSEK
1974	486 MSEK
1975	238 MSEK
1976	–155 MSEK
1977	–448 MSEK

Flushed with optimism by the enormous pre-tax income of 1974, Uddeholm's management embarked on a major capital investment program. While annual investments in fixed assets between 1970 and 1974 had ranged between 107 and 126 MSEK, the expenditures vaulted to 288, 531, and 477 MSEK in 1975, 1976, and 1977, respectively. The major portion of these outlays was financed by debt. In 1977 alone, Uddeholm doubled its level of long-term borrowings and more than trebled its level of short-term borrowings. The effect of these actions was a deterioration of the company's "solidity" from 34.7 percent on December 31, 1976 to 24.5 percent shortly before the close of the 1977 fiscal year.[2]

Foreign lenders had provided a substantial portion of the increase in Uddeholm's long-term debt between 1975 and 1977, and the loan agreements stipulated that the debt would immediately become due if Uddeholm's solidity were to fall below 25 percent. Furthermore, in the summer of 1977 Uddeholm's management had predicted a loss for the year of 600 MSEK, which, together with the downward trend in the company's solidity, generated fears of unemployment in the region in which Uddeholm was a significant producer. The Government, therefore, came under pressure to lend some aid.

Owing to Sweden's agreements with international organizations and its trading partners, the Government was probably foreclosed from giving a direct subsidy to Uddeholm.[3] The Government did the next best thing: it extended a 600-MSEK loan to Uddeholm. The loan was made to Uddeholm on December 28, 1977, three days before the close of the fiscal year. No funds were actually transferred from the Government to the company; the transaction was more in the nature of a guaranteed line of credit, a loan authorization. The loan was described by the Government as having a "conditional repayment obligation" (i.e., if and when Uddeholm were to declare dividends, negotiations would be initiated regarding the size and timing of the repayments of the principal and accrued interest, giving due consideration to the company's financial position).

Conceivably, such an executory transaction could have been construed as a potential capital contribution ranking with the equity of preferred shareholders.

---

[2] Solidity is defined as owners' equity plus 50 percent of untaxed reserves, in relation to total assets. In Sweden, it is a commonly used index of creditor protection.

[3] In 1977, the company made about a quarter of its steel sales and more than half of its forest products sales to buyers in EEC countries.

Had it been the intention of the Government not to demand repayment until many years into the future, the effect could well have been seen as a capital contribution. However, there are two bases for rejecting this interpretation. First, it was not at all likely that Uddeholm would elect to postpone dividends until many years into the future. And second, as was observed in connection with the complicated repayment plan negotiated by Nyby Uddeholm and the Government (see below), the intention of the Government was to strike a deal with the company to begin repayments as soon as these disbursements would not be in conflict with the aid-action, namely, to promote the survival of the company. There is no suggestion in the repayment agreement with Nyby Uddeholm that the repayments would be postponed indefinitely into the future. Hence, it seems more appropriate to regard the executory transaction as a loan authorization.

But how to account for the transaction? Since a major objective of the Government was to help the company improve its solidity and its earnings picture, the normal accounting treatment for a loan was found to be wanting. Since, in Sweden, accounting practice is strongly linked to tax rules, it was decided that the Riksdag (Swedish Parliament) should amend the Tax Act to declare that a loan such as that made to Uddeholm was taxable. The clear implication was that the status of the loan as a taxable receipt required that the recipient record it as *revenue*. The action was taken by the Riksdag in February 1978—two months before Uddeholm's 1977 Annual Report was published—and the legislation stipulated that, in order to treat a State loan as taxable, Government permission would be required each time such a loan were made. On March 16, 1978, Uddeholm received the Government permission. As a result, the following entry was made, much to the displeasure of the leaders of the Swedish accounting profession:

Receivable due to grant of State loan	600 MSEK
State loan with conditional repayment obligation	
(credit account in Profit and Loss Statement)	600 MSEK

An intended effect of this entry was to increase the company's solidity from 24.5 percent to 28.2 percent as of December 31, 1977. Furthermore, the company's reported "Net Income" (which, in Sweden, is drawn after transfers to and from a number of untaxed reserves) became 67.9 MSEK instead of a sizable net loss. Thus, the company was able to show an increase in its Net Income from 1976 to 1977 of from 26.8 to 67.9 MSEK.

The much more significant index of profitability, "Result before Appropriations and Taxes," was left undisturbed by the unusual accounting for the State loan, as the 600 MSEK credit was entered in the Profit and Loss Statement immediately following the derivation of "Result before Appropriations and Taxes" and prior to the section in which transfers to and from assorted reserves are found. Uddeholm's Consolidated Profit and Loss Statements for 1976 and 1977 are displayed in Appendix A.

The negotiations between Uddeholm and the Government were carried out under severe time pressures. From the beginning, they were based on the premise that the financial aid should be taxable and thus serve to improve the company's solidity. In Sweden, book/tax conformity is, as a rule, required.[4] But it is evident from the published record[5] that, in the course of the negotiations and the discussions in the Riksdag, accounting and taxation issues were accorded less than a careful analysis.

What was the reaction of the Swedish accounting profession? Since the Riksdag had enacted legislation which purported to convey the Government's policy that the State loan should be treated as a credit item in the recipient's Profit and Loss Statement, the Swedish Accounting Standards Board[6] apparently believed that it had no alternative but to accept the Government's view of the matter. In its recommendation on accounting for State financial aid, which was promulgated on November 20, 1979, the Board said:

> Loans with conditional repayment terms specifically tailored for certain companies and for which the obligation to repay the loan is linked, e.g., with the borrower's future result or decision about payment of a dividend to shareholders, are, however, in the view of the Board, in reality to be regarded as contributions subject to conditional repayment terms until the time the condition for repayment is met in the future. These loans may be recorded as income in the company's income statement when they are received and as expenditures when they are repaid provided that the company has obtained specific permission for the corresponding treatment of the loan for fiscal [i.e., tax] purposes [Sec. II(3)].

The Board made it clear that the usual accounting treatment for individually structured loans, however, was as a liability. Hence, the Board's interpretation of the loan as a "contribution" (i.e., a subsidy) and the final clause in its ruling are worthy of emphasis.

What is particularly interesting about Uddeholm's accounting treatment is that the loan was only authorized and not actually paid to the company. During 1977, Uddeholm succeeded in reducing its volume of inventory by 249 MSEK, which improved its cash flow. Hence, the need for cash had diminished considerably by the end of 1977; moreover, the company's reported loss (448 MSEK) for 1977 turned out to be 25 percent lower than what had been predicted in mid-1977. Later actions,

---

[4]A recent handbook issued by the Swedish Institute of Authorized Public Accountants (Föreningen Auktoriserade Revisorer) underscores the heavy influence of tax law in Swedish accounting practice:

> the single biggest factor in distorting Swedish financial statements is the unique stranglehold which Swedish tax law and practice have on the country's accounting and reporting practices. The fiscal legislators have carried to the extreme the basic rule of Swedish taxation that taxable income is principally based on book income.
> ...The primary aim of Swedish financial statements is conformity with the law, in particular as regards the figure of distributable earnings [FAR, 1980, p. 13].

[5]We rely on the 1980 report of the "riksdagens revisorer" (the auditors of the Swedish Parliament), which gives a comprehensive account of the entire affair.

[6]The Swedish Accounting Standards Board is a Government body which was established on July 1, 1976. It has a full-time chairman (a professional accountant) and ten part-time members who represent a variety of interested parties, including industry, trade unions, accountancy bodies, data users, the National Swedish Tax Board, and the Stockholm School of Economics. Swedish legislation refers to general principles of valuation of assets and liabilities to be followed by all firms that must keep accounting records and produce financial statements. A very general rule is that these firms should follow "good accounting practice," and the Board's principal charge is to develop and define this practice.

such as the mergers with Billerud and Gränges Nyby (discussed below), also alleviated the crisis. In fact, from 1977 to 1982, when the entire loan authorization to Uddeholm was terminated, no funds were ever transferred to Uddeholm by the Government. In the American setting, the arrangement consummated in late 1977 between the State and Uddeholm would have been regarded as a wholly executory contract—since the promise to make the loan had not yet been carried out—and no journal entry would have been made. In the Swedish case, not only was an entry made, but the credit was entered in the Profit and Loss Statement rather than as a liability offsetting the receivable (as incongruous as even this treatment might appear).

The outcome of the negotiations between Uddeholm and the Swedish Government led to the invention of an accounting artifice to achieve an improvement in Uddeholm's solidity as well as to enhance its reported net income.

MERGER WITH BILLERUD

In 1978, Uddeholm engaged in a clever transaction with Billerud, another Swedish company with large interests in the forest products industry. Uddeholm agreed to transfer to Billerud all of its assets relating to the forestry, forest products, and chemicals divisions in exchange for Billerud's assumption of a significant portion of Uddeholm's long-term liabilities. The recorded amount of the transaction on Uddeholm's books was in excess of 1,000 MSEK, the effect of which was to boost the company's solidity to 32.6 percent. One consequence of the "merger" (as it was styled in the Uddeholm Annual Report for 1978) was that Uddeholm acquired a 30-percent equity interest in Billerud Uddeholm (the merged entity), which rose to 38.6 percent by the end of 1978, 46.7 percent by the end of 1979, and 49.9 percent by the end of 1980. In this manner, by falling just short of having a controlling interest, Uddeholm avoided inclusion of its former long-term liabilities in its consolidated balance sheet.

Also during 1978, the Swedish Parliament permitted a transfer of 200 MSEK of the 600-MSEK State loan originally made Uddeholm, to Billerud Uddeholm. By the terms of this action, the loan was made available to Billerud Uddeholm beginning on December 31, 1978 and until December 31, 1981. Hence, the new company was given the opportunity of booking the loan authorization as revenue in 1978, 1979, 1980, or 1981, but Billerud Uddeholm elected not to seize this opportunity in any of the years. Since Uddeholm's interest in Billerud Uddeholm was not controlling, a charge of 200 MSEK appeared in the consolidated 1978 Profit and Loss Statement as a result of the loan transfer.

MERGER WITH GRÄNGES NYBY

In 1979, another merger occurred, this time involving the stainless plate, tube systems, and wire divisions of Uddeholm with the Swedish steel company Gränges Nyby, in which Uddeholm received a 90-percent ownership interest. As part of the merger, Gränges Nyby was renamed Nyby Uddeholm. The Swedish Parliament authorized a transfer of 250 MSEK of the State loan from Uddeholm to Nyby

Uddeholm, and, as was the case with Billerud Uddeholm, the loan authorization was declared to be taxable income and, hence, recognizable as revenue in the company's Profit and Loss Statement. Since Uddeholm owned 90 percent of Nyby Uddeholm, the former's expense of 250 MSEK (owing to the withdrawal of the State loan) was offset, in the 1979 consolidated Profit and Loss Statement, by the 250 MSEK revenue recorded in the accounts of Nyby Uddeholm—except for the 10-percent minority interest. During 1979, Nyby Uddeholm requested and received 250 MSEK in cash from the Government and thus became the first of the companies actually to draw on the original 600 MSEK State loan. (Nyby Uddeholm also had received cash from the Government on other State loans with conditional repayment obligations.)

Of the 600 MSEK loan made to Uddeholm in 1977, only 150 MSEK remained on Uddeholm's books at the end of 1981, and it was reported that the Government had given Uddeholm until June 30, 1983 to reduce this final claim, either by drawing the funds or by canceling the receivable. In fact, Uddeholm made an entry canceling the remaining receivable at the close of 1982. The debit was to an expense account not affecting the "Result before Appropriations and Taxes," and the credit was to the receivable from the Government.

CONCLUDING COMMENTS

The overall effect of the unusual agreement between the Government and Uddeholm was a spurious improvement in the company's solidity. Once the company had found other outside entities with which it could enter into substantive economic transactions (in this case, the mergers with Billerud and Gränges Nyby), the Government-induced accounting aid could be transferred to the merged entities or eventually withdrawn. It was all achieved by sleight of hand, because, in the end, Uddeholm never asked for any funds from the Government (although the Government did make a payment to Nyby Uddeholm), and even though the loan authorization was declared to be taxable, Uddeholm's tax position was such that very little, if any, additional tax had to be paid.

Who, then, was adversely affected by this strange accounting treatment? In its Report of the Directors and in the footnotes to its financial statements, Uddeholm provided extensive disclosure in its Annual Reports concerning the State loans; hence, the shareholders were informed. The pertinent extract from the Report of the Directors in Uddeholm's 1977 Annual Report is presented in Appendix B. Similar disclosures were provided in the footnotes in subsequent years.

One supposes that Uddeholm's creditors, both domestic and foreign, were apprised opportunely of the nature and extent of Government aid. Whether the foreign creditors would have preferred Uddeholm to be required to settle all of its debts immediately (as a result of a solidity of less than 25 percent), or to be able to survive the crisis by continuing to service its debts in the ordinary course, is not known. Yet, two concerns may be mentioned. First, since the Swedish Government had assured international organizations and its trading partners that it would not enhance the competitiveness of its own industry by the granting of subsidies, would a Government loan that must, by law, be accounted for as if it had been a subsidy be in violation of the spirit of that accord? Second, a question can be raised about the meaningfulness of accounting measures that place an interpretation on a transaction which would seem to be foreclosed by international agreements made by one of the parties. Furthermore, the transaction could have been construed as a subsidy only if Uddeholm, once having borrowed money from the Government, were never to declare dividends. If it is reasonable to suppose that Uddeholm would one day declare dividends, the transaction did amount to a loan. What are the consequences for the credibility of accounting information—both at the micro and macro levels— when such a transaction is accorded treatment as a subsidy? The Swedish Accounting Standards Board permitted the strange accounting treatment only because the Riksdag had given it no other choice. The dilemma was made possible by the traditional tie between accounting and tax practices in Sweden.

The report of the auditors of the Swedish Parliament indicates that the legislative body did not have adequate knowledge of the secondary effects on accounting and taxation of the State loans approved in 1977 and later years. The auditors have recommended that such secondary effects should be considered in any similar situations arising in the future, and that the Accounting Standards Board should be invited to present its views to the Parliament. Finally, in 1983 the Riksdag repealed the 1977 amendment to the Tax Act which declared that State loans of the Uddeholm-type were to be treated as taxable to the recipient. In the end, therefore, criticism from the accounting profession had an impact on the political decision makers.

APPENDIX A

Uddeholm's consolidated Profit and Loss Statement for 1977 is provided below. As indicated in the text of this paper, the tax law has had a considerable impact on Swedish financial reporting. The various appropriations (either for tax reasons or resulting from the discretion of the Board of Directors) are always presented between the derivation of "Result before Appropriations and Taxes" and "Net Income." Consequently, Net Income is not regarded in Sweden as a useful gauge of financial progress. Instead, attention is focused on the Result before Appropriations and Taxes, and this is the figure that would be most comparable to Income from Continuing Operations, but before taxes, as employed in the United States.

APPENDIX B

The following extract is taken from the Report of the Directors in the 1977 Annual Report of Uddeholm:

> In order to provide a solid base for the prerequisites which would enable Uddeholm to introduce necessary structural changes in the conduct of its business at a balanced pace, a loan of 600 Mkr with conditional repayment obligation was granted to the Company by the Swedish Government in September of 1977.
>
> This loan was placed at the disposal of the Company on December 28th, 1977, as a non-interest-bearing claim on the State. With effect from that date, the loan can be drawn in whole or in part at the request of the Company after approval by the Government.

Consolidated Profit and Loss Statement
MKR*

		1977		1976	
Operations					
Invoiced sales	Note 2	2,598.8		2,162.4	
Other operating receipts		47.9		26.0	
			2,646.7		2,188.4
Production, selling and administration costs			-2,832.3		-2,268.9
Operating result before depreciation			-185.6		- 80.5
Depreciation according to plan.	Note 3		-134.1		-107.1
Operating result after depreciation.	Note 4		-319.7		- 187.6
Price gain on Parent Company's inventories	Note 5		96.8		83.5
Government subsidy for increased stockpiling. . . .			0.8		20.1
Financial receipts and expenditure					
Dividend received		1.1		0.4	
Interest received		10.7		12.7	
			11.8		13.1
Interest paid			-153.1		-87.3
Share of exchange rate differences on long-term transactions chargeable to the year's accounts	Note 1		- 21.0		—
			-162.3		- 74.2
Results after Financial Receipts and Expenditure			-384.4		-158.2

Extraordinary Receipts and Expenditure

Profit on sale of fixed assets	Note 8	44.5		9.6	
Exchange rate differences on long-term transactions	Note 1	− 93.3		—	
Other extraordinary expenditure	Note 9	− 15.0	− 63.8	− 6.5	3.1
Result before Appropriations and Taxes			−448.2		−155.1
State loan with conditional repayment obligation	Note 1		600.0		—

Appropriations

Book depreciation	Note 3	− 64.5		−174.0	
Thereof charged to Working Environment Reserve		3.3		27.6	
Thereof charged to Special Investment Reserve		—		32.0	
Thereof charged to other Investment Reserves		10.1		49.2	
		− 51.1		− 65.2	
Return of depreciation according to plan		134.1	83.0	107.1	41.9
Working Environment Reserve utilized for cost-accounted measures			0.1		1.2
Transfer to/withdrawal from Inventory Reserve			−133.5		167.8
Transfer to Investment Reserve for forestry			—		− 13.0
Change in difference between book value and actual value of pension commitments			2.6		0.0
Writing down of shares and participations	Note10		− 6.0		− 0.5
Other appropriations			− 2.4		—
Result before Taxes			95.6		42.3
Taxes			− 27.7		− 15.8
Minority interest in loss/income			− 0.0		0.3
Net income			67.9		26.8

*Million kronor (MSEK in current usage).

Uddeholm proposes to call for such facilities only to the extent needed in order for the Company to be able to bring future major structural changes to a successful conclusion.

The conditions may be summarized as follows:

• The loan runs with a fixed annual interest rate of 9 1/2% on the amount paid out. Accrued interest is added to the capital.

• The Company may at any time pay accrued interest in full or in part and amortize the loan or reduce its claim on the State.

• Interest payment and amortization of the Company's claim on the State shall otherwise be effectuated during years in which the Company has decided to pay a dividend to its shareholders. If the Board proposes to recommend such dividend to the Annual General Meeting of Shareholders it devolves upon the Company to enter into negotiations in good time with the Sveriges Investeringsbank on how large an amount the Company shall make such payment with or decrease its claim by. In this context due regard shall be given to such factors as reasonable solidity, dividend policy, etc., with a view to the long-term development of the Company. The result of the deliberations shall be reported jointly by the Company and the Bank to the Government. If the Company and the Bank are unable to reach agreement with regard to the size of the amount, the different viewpoints must be presented in the report. The Government will then decide the size of the amount.

• During the period from the Company's 1978 Annual General Meeting of Shareholders and for as long as the loan has not been finally repaid a person appointed by the Ministry of Industry and a deputy shall have a seat on the Board of the Company.

These conditions along with addenda to the Municipal Tax Act approved by the Riksdag in February of 1978, imply that reception of the loan is entered into the accounts as a taxable receipt, whereas interest payments and amortizations will be entered as a deductible cost. This permits treatment of the conditional loan for accounting purposes as follows:

In the 1977 Profit and Loss Statement, the whole loan amount is entered as an extraordinary receipt. The same amount is entered into the Balance Sheet of December 31st both as a claim on the State and among contingent liabilities as a conditional liability. When payment is made to the Company the amount of the claim is reduced correspondingly. The conditional loan thus had no direct bearing on the financial situation during 1977.

REFERENCES

Föreningen Auktoriserade Revisorer FAR, *Survey of Accounting Practices in Larger Swedish Companies, 1980* (Stockholm: Auktoriserade Revisorers Serviceaktiebolag, 1980).

Riksdagens Revisorers Kansli (1980).

"Swedish Accounting Standards Board's recommendation on accounting for state financial aid," promulgated November 20, 1979, Swedish Board of Commerce Code of Statutes (typescript).

Pros and Cons of Defeasance

Michael Blumstein
The New York Times

THE OBJECT

A corporation wishes to strengthen its balance sheet by retiring a large amount of old debt and paying it off with a smaller face amount of new debt paying a higher rate.

THE TECHNIQUE

First, the company buys United States Government securities that will be placed in an irrevocable trust, reserved to make interest and principal payments on the debt to be retired. Because these new Government securities pay a higher interest rate than the debt it will replace, a much smaller amount will, in general, be required to offset the corporate debt.

Second, having set up the trust, the company removes the original debt from its balance sheet. Although the debt is still outstanding, the payments of principal and interest will be made from the trust.

THE PAY-OFF

The corporation has shorn up its balance sheet by reducing its indebtedness. In addition, since a smaller amount of Government securities replaced the debt, the company records a profit on the transaction, namely, the amount by which the face value of the old debt exceeds the cost of the securities that replaced it. This profit is added to the corporation's net income.

THE DRAWBACKS

Defeasance is criticized by some analysts as merely cosmetic accounting, which increases income without improving cash flow. Some critics also contend that there are hidden costs to defeasance because corporations are replacing their own debt with higher quality, more expensive Government securities.

Thanks to some creative accounting blessed by the Securities and Exchange Commission, Wall Street has a new product that it is eagerly peddling to corporate clients.

The name is somewhat forbidding—"in-substance defeasance"—but the pitch is easy: pay off large amounts of old, cheap debt with smaller amounts of new bonds that pay high interest rates and, through some accounting magic, report extra profits and clean up the balance sheet.

"You could see a couple billion dollars of it done in early 1984," said John H. Erdman, a principal at Morgan Stanley & Company. "I can tell you there's a lot of talk about it."

CORPORATE CASH USE QUESTIONED

The issue, however, is whether this new financial maneuver is a poor use of corporate cash and another example of short-term accounting gimmickry to dress up one quarter's profits at the expense of a carefully developed corporate strategy for generating long-term profits. In some cases, analysts think so.

"It's just balance sheet manipulation," said Randolph Westerfield, who teaches corporate financial management at the Wharton School of the University of Pennsylvania. "It's in the cosmetic category. It's more appearance than reality in that it doesn't have any significantly great effects on cash flow, and cash flow is what ultimately determines value."

Others, however, argue that bankers and investors rely heavily on balance sheets, and that making them more attractive is not a bad goal.

Defeasance literally means voiding an agreement. It is not a new financial technique, having been used for years by state and local governments when they wanted to pay off either expensive or restrictive debt but could not buy back all their bonds for one reason or another. However, it was not until July 1982 that the Exxon Corporation introduced the idea to corporate America.

First, the company bought $312 million in United States Government securities. It then put the securities in an irrevocable trust, reserving them for the repayment of principal and interest on $515 million in old long-term Exxon debt. Because the Treasury issues were yielding 14 percent and the old Exxon debt paid only 5.8 percent to 6.7 percent, $312 million in Treasury issues was enough to cover all the obligations of the $515 million in debt that will mature by 2009.

Having in effect paid off, or "defeased," the debt, Exxon then wiped it off the balance sheet and added about $132 million—the after-tax difference between the old debt's face value and the actual cost of purchasing enough Treasury bonds to cover it—to second-quarter earnings. The effect was an increase in that quarter's earnings of about 15 cents a share, to $1.02.

To Exxon, the beauty of defeasance was that it did not have to repurchase its debt, an option companies have always had but one that can be difficult when bondholders do not want to give up their securities.

The Securities and Exchange Commission, however, was not sure it liked the idea and stepped in with a temporary ban the month after the Exxon deal. The commission was concerned about the accounting and whether other creditors could ever take the Government securities in the case of bankruptcy—a question that could still be litigated.

The Financial Accounting Standards Board, the accountants' own watchdog group, then spent more than a year studying defeasance, and voted, 4 to 3, last November to approve. The S.E.C. then unanimously gave its approval late last month.

The excitement on Wall Street has been building ever since, as securities firms seek fees for advice on defeasance and commissions for buying the necessary

Government securities. Bear, Stearns & Company has issued a list of 72 companies with $5.9 billion in outstanding bonds that it says might be defeased.

The Morgan Guaranty Trust Company—commercial banks can arrange these transactions, too—has taken full-page newspaper advertisements that have a bold headline asking, "Considering defeasance?" And the head of Government securities trading at one major investment bank estimated that much more than $1 billion in defeasance deals were done in the last week and a half of 1983.

Few companies, perhaps because of the controversy surrounding defeasance, have announced these deals, although on the last business day of the year, the Atlantic Richfield Company said, without explanation, that it had removed $88 million of debt from its balance sheet by placing Government securities in trust.

HIDDEN COSTS SEEN

This financial maneuver, however, can have some hidden costs, analysts said. Most notably, the corporate debt, in order to be guaranteed and removed from the balance sheet, has to be backed by Government securities. And Government securities, because they are considered riskless, are more expensive than comparable corporate debt.

As a result, companies whose debt is not very highly rated could pay a premium of anywhere from $30 to $450 for every $1,000 worth of debt defeased with Government securities, according to calculations by Roman L. Weil, a professor of accounting at the University of Chicago.

"Shareholders should be suspicious of management that engages in this transaction because of the give-away to bondholders in order to report higher earnings per share," Professor Weil said, referring to the Government securities now backing their bonds.

There is also the question of whether defeasance is a wise use of corporate cash. Analysts say some companies, like Arco, might not need to reduce their borrowings and might better spend their money on repurchasing equity, particularly if the shares are relatively depressed, as they have been in the oil business.

Equity is generally considered the most expensive form of financing because dividends are not tax-deductible, as are interest payments, and because shareholders in the long run demand a bigger return than bondholders.

Buying back debt may also not make much financial sense in today's economic environment in which interest rates are unlikely to drop sharply and may well increase. When Exxon used defeasance in 1982, the timing was good since interest rates then made their historic plunge and the company was able to replenish its coffers with cheaper money. However, if rates were to rise, companies that wanted to expand would end up replacing their cheap debt with more expensive money.

"I doubt very much whether I'd pay off truly long-term debt since it ignores the risk of renewed inflation" and even higher interest rates, said Louis Lowenstein, who teaches corporate finance at the Columbia Law School. "To go paying off long-term dollars is always kind of imprudent."

Nevertheless, not only are the instant profits likely to appeal to some companies, but defeasance also allows them to dress up balance sheets.

Cheap debt, despite its depressed value in the market, is listed on a company's balance sheet at the full face value of whatever is outstanding, and defeasance provides an opportunity to erase these large amounts of debts for smaller amounts of cash.

The result could be better standing with the banks that lend money to the company and the agencies that rate its bond issues. "In a matter of course, we do typically look at face value as opposed to market value," said Roy Taub, chairman of the debt rating criteria committee at the Standard & Poor's Corporation.

Investors who do a cursory investigation of a company when deciding whether to buy shares might also be more favorably impressed by lower debt. "In my work, every day I see people paying a premium for stocks of companies that have a clean balance sheet," said Suzanne W. Wright, an oil industry analyst in First Boston's Denver office.

ACCOUNTING FOR LEASES BY LESSEES

In Statement No. 13, "Accounting for Leases," the FASB attempted to distinguish between leases that were operating programs and those that were financing programs. Arbitrary criteria such as the percentage of the asset's life comprehended by the term of the lease were invoked to differentiate operating from financing leases. Since operating leases are not to be capitalized, while financing leases must be capitalized, potential lessees were not indifferent as between the two classifications.

But the arbitrary cutoffs between operating and financing leases have visited a series of headaches on the FASB. Six interpretations and numerous amendments have been adopted to clarify ambiguities and close loopholes in a pronouncement that has veritably created a new professional class of specialists in how to design a long-term lease contract that will escape the capitalization requirements of Statement 13. A recent FASB research study found "that a majority of the companies surveyed were structuring the terms of new lease contracts to avoid capitalization."[1]

In "Is Lessee Accounting Working?," Richard Dieter, a partner in a major public accounting firm, concludes that the objectives of Statement No. 13 are being lost in a climate in which the Board's arbitrary cutoff rules are being followed to their finest detail. Rather than cling tenaciously to the tenet that assets may be recognized only if the attributes of ownership are approximated, the Board might instead focus on the acquisition of economic resources in exchange for a long-term lease contract. Dieter reviews several of the implementation problems under Statement No. 13, expresses concern over the anomalous results sometimes produced, and, in the end, confesses his frustration with the detailed and arbitrary rules supposedly intended

[1]"FASB-Sponsored Research Report Finds Majority of Leases Structured to Avoid Capitalization," *Status Report* (FASB) (September 1, 1981), p. 1.

to effectuate the objectives sought by the Board. As Dieter writes, "While arbitrary rules may work when the objectives are at the extremes of available options, they rarely work if the position sought is on middle ground."

BIBLIOGRAPHICAL NOTES

Two discussion documents on the subject of accounting for leases are:

An Analysis of Issues Related to Accounting for Leases, Discussion Memorandum (Stamford, CT: FASB, July 2, 1974).
Accounting for Leases, Discussion Paper No. 1 (Melbourne, Australia: Australian Accounting Research Foundation, Second edition, 1983). (First edition was published in 1979.)

A normative research study that was commissioned by the APB is:

Myers, John H.: *Reporting of Leases in Financial Statements,* Accounting Research Study No. 4 (New York: AICPA, 1962).

A major FASB-sponsored empirical study is the following:

Abdel-khalik, A. Rashad (principal researcher): *The Economic Effects on Lessees of FASB Statement No. 13, Accounting for Leases* (Stamford, CT: FASB, 1981).

Is Lessee Accounting Working?

Richard Dieter
Partner
Arthur Andersen & Co.
Chicago

While the objectives of FASB Statement 13 "Accounting for Leases" appear meritorious, the arbitrary rules, sub-rules, subsequent interpretations and amendments (both official and unofficial) for implementing these objectives have created substantial problems for the independent CPA and for financial management. This article analyzes many of the implementation problems; offers reasons why they have arisen; and finally suggests a solution to the dilemma, primarily with respect to accounting for leases by lessees.

The objective of Statement 13, as described in its Appendix (Basis for Conclusions) was that:

> A lease that transfers substantially all of the benefits and risks incident to the ownership of property should be accounted for as the acquisition of an asset and the incurrence of an obligation by the lessee and as a sale or financing by the lessor.

The Board believed that Statement 13 would remove most "if not all, of the conceptual differences in lease classification as between lessors and lessees and that it provides criteria for such classification that are more explicit and less susceptible to varied interpretation than those in previous literature."

Based on actual results of Statement 13 for over two years, its objectives and the assertion of "less susceptibility to varied interpretation" have not been reached. In fact, there continues to be a significant number of long-term leases that pass substantially all risks and rewards of ownership of property to the lessee and yet continue to be accounted for as operating leases. In addition, while drafters of new leases may have to sharpen their pencils a bit, it is common to find agreements negotiated that provide a finance lease for the lessor and an operating lease for the lessee.

STATEMENT NO. 13—AN OVERVIEW

In studying the lease classification rules of Statement 13, one quickly concludes that the major stumbling block to noncapitalization is in overcoming the test of paragraph 7d. While this paragraph represents only one of four distinct tests that, if met, requires a lessee to capitalize a lease, it is the only new rule that is, in most instances, quantifiable. This rule, commonly referred to as the 90 percent recovery test, requires a lessee to capitalize a lease if the present value, at the beginning of the lease term, of the minimum lease payments equals or exceeds 90 percent of the excess of the fair value of the leased property over any related investment tax credit retained by the lessor and expected to be realized by him.

The other lessee capitalization rules, referred to in paragraphs 7a, b and c of Statement 13 are not significant hurdles to overcome. For example, paragraphs 7a and 7b require a lessee to capitalize a lease if "the lease transfers ownership of the property to the lessee by the end of the lease term" or if "the lease contains a bargain purchase option." Both of these tests are substantially unchanged from APB Opinion No. 5 and, except for possible varying interpretation of what constitutes a bargain purchase option, few, if any, leases not capitalized under APB Opinion No. 5 (of which there were very few) would not be capitalized under these rules of Statement 13.

The test in paragraph 7c of Statement 13 is also similar to the underlying thrust of APB Opinion No. 5; however, it does differ in that Statement 13 is more specific. It provides that if the lease term (as defined) equals or exceeds 75 percent of the estimated economic life of the leased property, the lessee is required to capitalize the lease. Most practitioners realize that estimates of useful lives of assets are judgmental and, if an estimate is within a given range, they are not apt to object. Accordingly, a building lease of 30 years will commonly not be required to be capitalized under paragraph 7c, because arguments that a building life often exceeds 40 years is easily sustainable and reasonable. Similarly, estimates of economic lives of 12 to 15 years are not uncommon for equipment covered by an eight-year lease. Thus, for all practical purposes, a lessee is able to overcome the numerical test of paragraph 7c and in clear conscience justify it to himself and his independent auditor. There are, however, extremes that have been taken in this regard, particularly by some major retailers. These assertions and the questions raised by the SEC are discussed in this article.

Nevertheless, the 90 percent recovery test remains the focal point of lease capitalization from the lessee's viewpoint. Accordingly, the implementation problems discussed in this article focus on what the issues are, why there are varying interpretations, to what extremes people are willing to go and what they are willing to give up in negotiating leases that do not meet this test.

One of the best approaches to analyze implementation problems that have beset the practitioner is to study carefully specific issues that the FASB has faced or is facing through issuance of official interpretations and amendments to Statement 13. As of May 1, 1979, FASB had amended Statement 13 four times, had issued six interpretations and had in the exposure stage three additional amendments. In addition, the Board has authorized its staff to develop interpretations on two other lease problems.

PART-OF-THE-BUILDING PROBLEM

Certain perceived measurement problems exist in performing lease classification tests for leases involving only part of a building (e.g., floors of a multi-story office building and retail space in a shopping mall). As a result, FASB devised special rules to assist a user of Statement 13 in obtaining objectively determinable costs or fair market values of leased space. It provided without any specificity that, with respect to the lessee:

> If the fair value of the leased property is not objectively determinable, the lessee shall classify the lease according to the criterion of paragraph 7(c) only, using the estimated economic life of the building in which the leased premises are located.

In practice lessees uniformly asserted that it was never practical to estimate the fair value of a part of a building and thus the 90 percent recovery test was not applicable. Accordingly, only the useful life test was to be applied, and, as discussed previously, this was quickly overcome by applying subjective judgment to estimated useful lives.

Subsequent to the issuance of Statement 13, FASB was asked to clarify when fair value can be objectively determined for a lease involving only part of a building if there were no sales of similar property. The FASB responded by issuing its Interpretation No. 24 in September 1978. It provides that other evidence (e.g., independent appraisal or estimated replacement cost information) may provide a basis for an objective determination of fair value. The Board also acknowledged that (a) it was not imposing a requirement to obtain an appraisal or other similar valuation as a general matter and, (b) a meaningful estimate of fair value "of an office or a floor of a multi-story building may not be possible whereas similar information may be readily obtainable if the leased property is a major part of that facility." This interpretation has had little or no impact on lessee capitalization decisions since Statement 13 continues to be applied literally and information as to fair value remains elusive. Consequently, for the vast majority of leases involving only part of a building or structure, no capitalization is occurring.

RESIDUAL VALUE GUARANTEES

In performing the 90 percent recovery test of Statement 13 a lessee is required to include, in the determination of minimum lease payments, guarantees of the residual value of leased property at expiration of the lease. Lessee guarantees of the residual value, while not uncommon, occur most frequently in leases involving personal property such as automobiles. Since the question of residual value guarantees was not a criterion of lease capitalization prior to Statement 13, it was commonplace to find the residual value guarantee at the end of an automobile lease term equating to the balance of undepreciated cost. Consequently, in performing the lease capitalization tests of Statement 13, many lessees initially found themselves in the unhappy position of having to capitalize most of their automobile leases. Almost immediately after this consequence became known to the car lessors, they set out to amend and rectify lease agreements to overcome the capitalization requirements. This was accomplished primarily through a specific limitation on the amount of the residual value deficiency that a lessee would be required to make up and, in some cases, by limiting the guarantee to situations beyond normal wear and tear.

In addition, the Board assisted lessees in this effort through the issuance of Interpretation No. 19 "Lessee Guarantee of the Residual Value of Leased Property." It dealt with lease provisions that require the lessee to make up a residual value deficiency only in cases where the shortfall in residual value is attributable to damage, extraordinary wear and tear, etc., and whether this type of provision constitutes a lessee guarantee of residual value as that term is used in defining minimum lease payments under Statement 13. The interpretation stated that (1) a residual value guarantee is limited to the specific maximum deficiency the lessee can be required to make up, and (2) a lessee that is required to make up a residual value deficiency attributable to extraordinary wear and tear does not constitute a lessee guarantee of residual value for purposes of defining minimum lease payments.

The practical effect of this interpretation, as it relates to the specified maximum deficiency, can best be demonstrated with an example. Assume a lessee enters into a one-year lease for a current model year Volvo for a monthly rental of $300. The fair market value of the Volvo at the inception of the lease is $10,000. The lessee agrees, at the conclusion of the one-year lease, to make up any residual value deficiency on the car between $3,000 and $8,000. Thus the lessor takes the risk that a one-year-old Volvo would not be worth at least $3,000. In computing minimum lease payments, the lessee would compare the $10,000 to the present value of $3,600 (1 year's monthly payments) and the $5,000 residual value guarantee ($8,000 minus $3,000). The mechanics of the present value computation lead to a conclusion that the minimum lease payments are less than 90 percent of the fair market value of the car at the inception of the lease. While the mechanical test of Statement 13 for capitalization has not been met, it is clear that the lessor has given up very little and yet has been able to achieve an operating lease for the lessee. Thus this interpretation applied literally allows lessees, through a modification of terms that are not economically substantive, to alter substantially the accounting treatment by converting an otherwise capital lease to an operating lease.

CONTINGENT RENT

Statement 13 provides that contingent rentals, from the lessee's viewpoint, are to be charged to expense as incurred, and not considered part of minimum lease payments for the purpose of performing the 90 percent recovery test. Since many leases contain a base rent and an override based on sales, the override rent is excluded from minimum lease payments in determining lease classification. For example, retail space is often leased at a base rate per month plus a fixed or variable percentage of sales over a predetermined amount. Drafters of lease agreements were quick to realize that by a slight reduction in base rent and a minor increase in percentage rent or simply a decrease in the base sales amount, minimum lease payments could be reduced to enable the present value calculation to equal 89 percent of the fair value of the leased property with a miniscule increase in risk to the lessor.

In other circumstances a rental cost is based on the prime interest rate. The following hypothetical example demonstrates the problem. A lease agreement provides that yearly rent will be a function of the prime interest rate times a given principal amount, with a limitation on the absolute amount of rent per year. The limitation would equate to a prime rate of 4 percent. This yearly amount over the lease term would qualify the lease as a capital lease. Nevertheless, the practical interpretation of Statement 13 would be to classify all payments as contingent and consequently the lease would be treated as an operating lease.

Situations such as the above were brought to the Board's attention and in December 1978, it issued an exposure draft of an amendment to Statement 13 providing that:

> Lease payments that depend on an existing index or rate, such as the prime interest rate, shall be included in minimum lease payments based on the index or rate existing at the inception of the lease; any increases or decreases in lease payments that result from subsequent changes in the index or rate are contingent rentals.

This proposed amendment would appear to correct many of the perceived abuses in using the contingent rental clause based on indexes to avoid capitalization.

IMPLICIT INTEREST RATE IN THE LEASE

Statement 13 provides that when a lessee is computing the present value of the minimum lease payments for the purpose of measuring whether a capital lease exists, it should use its incremental borrowing rate unless "it is practicable for him to learn the implicit interest rate computed by the lessor and the implicit rate computed by the lessor is less than the lessee's incremental borrowing rate." If both these conditions exist, the lessee is required to use the implicit rate. By and large, the lessor's implicit interest rate in the lease is lower than the lessee's incremental borrowing rate. This is due to several factors including the lessor's estimate of the residual value. In addition, in determining an appropriate rate of return the lessor considers the additional tax benefits that flow to the lessor (e.g., cash flow benefits of accelerated depreciation for tax purposes); these benefits are not considered in the lease evaluation criteria of Statement 13. As most practitioners realize today, a lessee request from the lessor for the implicit interest rate will "reluctantly" be declined. In most situations, the lessee will not press the lessor because the direction of the answer is known in advance. As a result, many lessees represent to their CPAs that although they have requested information from the lessor, the lessor has refused to respond. Consequently, when performing the 90 percent recovery test, the incremental borrowing rate is used. As is readily apparent, in a long-term lease, when a present value computation is performed using an interest rate of approximately 10 percent (a rate representative of most companies' incremental borrowing rate today), rentals due after ten years have little or no present value.

This problem was brought to the Board's attention and it has proposed to amend Statement 13 to require the lessee, where practicable, to estimate the interest rate implicit in the lease. In so doing, the lessee is forced into an evaluation of the residual value. This unfortunately raises the issue of how to handle inflation, particularly for leases involving real estate. Should the residual value be viewed as a percentage of original cost based on a depreciable life of 30 or 40 years? Should it take into account trends of the past eight years of significant inflation? Should it take an historical approach that shows real estate values have increased at a rate, in many instances, that exceed normal inflation? The Board has not answered these questions in its proposed amendment.

Through the comment letters the Board has received on its exposure draft of the amendment of Statement 13 entitled "Lessees Use of the Interest Rate Implicit in the Lease" it became aware of the problem of estimating residual values. As a result, the Board has directed its staff to address the question of whether expected future increases in value should be considered in estimating residual values. They have also reached the conclusion to defer a decision on the amendment covering the lessee's use of the interest rate implicit in the lease until that question is solved.

In analyzing how the impact of inflation should be considered in determining residual values many would argue that this judgment should be consistent with the other provisions of Statement 13. For example, the Board had emphasized in Statement 13 that upward revisions of residual value are not acceptable. While this appears to relate primarily to the notion that once property is "sold" (capital lease), additional profit recognition by the lessor should not be permitted prior to end of the lease term, it also seems to preclude giving recognition to inflation. It should also be borne in mind that inflation, in general, is not accounted for under the historical cost framework presently used. Others argue that the interest rate (e.g., approximately 10 percent today) used to discount residual values reflects inflation as that rate far exceeds a pure cost of money and therefore in estimating residual values, inflation should also be considered. They further believe that by not assuming inflation for real estate leases, the lease capitalization test and the use of the implicit interest rate of Statement 13 are avoiding economic reality.

THE RETAILERS' ARGUMENTS

Perhaps in no other industry are the potential effects of lease capitalization as significant to the balance sheet as they are to large retail chains. The majority of these retailers lease substantially all their facilities under long-term leases, particularly in shopping malls and strip centers.

Readers of large retailers' financial statements were given a warning of the magnitude of the impact of lease capitalization by the disclosures required under Accounting Series Release No. 147. Most readers assumed that the "noncapitalized financing leases" disclosed in accordance with ASR No. 147 would become capital leases under Statement 13. How wrong they were! In fact, less than one half, and in some cases only a small percentage of the "noncapitalized finance leases" have been treated as capital leases under Statement 13.

For example, one large retailer reported over 160 leases with a present value of approximately $50,000,000 meeting the SEC's definition of a "noncapitalized finance" lease. Reporting under Statement 13, that retailer reported only 50 leases with a present value of $25,000,000 as capital leases. The major reasons for certain "non-capitalized finance leases" not meeting the capital lease test of Statement 13 were (a) option periods were considered in the lease term for purposes of the ASR disclosures but are excluded in Statement 13's tests; (b) the inability to estimate fair market value where the leased premise was part of large shopping mall; and, (c) the exclusion of leases of a property located in government facilities.

The retailing industry has carefully analyzed the criteria for lease classification under Statement 13 and has sought to take consistent and aggressive positions in interpreting the rules. Recently, the Office of the Chief Accountant of the SEC commented that it would be carefully reviewing the assertions and conclusions reached by the industry since it also was taken back by the lack of capitalization of leased stores and facilities under Statement 13 compared to the disclosures of "noncapitalized finance leases" under ASR No. 147.

The following conclusions reached by several large retailers in implementing Statement 13 have led to many long-term leases being classified as operating leases.

Economic Life

Statement 13 defines economic life as:

> The estimated remaining period during which the property is expected to be economically usable by one or more users, with normal repairs and maintenance, for the purpose for which it was intended at the inception of the lease, without limitation by the lease term.

The conclusion reached by certain larger retailers was that the life of the property should be measured in terms of a retail enterprise or otherwise. Since alternative uses (warehouses, etc.) exist, they conclude it is reasonable to assume, for purposes of Statement 13, economic lives of 50 to 75 years. Accordingly, the interpretation leads one to conclude that most real property leases should not require capitalization in accordance with paragraph 7(c) of Statement 13. Literally applied, retailers with a 50-year lease could argue a life of 75 years and fail the capitalization test of paragraph 7c. Without arguing the merits of a 75-year life or the apparent inconsistency with the treatment adopted by nonretailers for economic lives of real property, one wonders whether this interpretation is consistent with the words "for the purpose for which it was intended at the inception of the lease." Namely, is it appropriate to consider the additional useful life as a warehouse that occurs beyond its retail life in determining the economic life under Statement 13?

Part of a Facility

FASB Interpretation No. 24 attempts to rectify a problem of Statement 13, as covered previously, dealing with leases involving only part of building (space in a shopping mall) by indicating that other evidence may provide an objective determination of fair value. One of the factors to be considered is whether the lessee occupies a major part of the facility. The retailers have concluded that a major part would be equivalent to more than 50 percent of the available space which would be an extreme rarity in a shopping mall. Some believe this was not the intent of the FASB and that a more appropriate interpretation would be that an anchor tenant would be assumed to have information to estimate fair market value. This argument appears to have merit, since anchor tenants are an integral part of the mall and the developer's plans, and it would seem reasonable that the anchor tenant would often have this information available, though it may only occupy 10 to 20 percent of the mall space.

LEASES INVOLVING GOVERNMENT FACILITIES

Just prior to finalizing the issuance of Statement 13, FASB added a section under the rules covering leases involving only part of a building. It read as follows:

> Because of special provisions normally present in leases involving terminal space and other airport facilities owned by a governmental unit or authority, the economic life of such facilities for purposes of classifying the lease is essentially indeterminate. Likewise, the concept of fair value is not applicable to such leases. Since such leases also do not provide for a transfer of ownership or a bargain purchase option, they shall be classified as operating leases. Leases of other facilities owned by a governmental unit or authority wherein the rights of the parties are essentially the same as in a lease of airport facilities described above shall also be classified as operating leases. Examples of such leases may be those involving facilities at ports and bus terminals.

This special exemption had a tremendous impact on the airline industry by allowing them to classify their airport terminal space as operating leases. Many took this exemption also to apply to free standing airline hangars, including maintenance hangars, since the property was on government land and subject to the same considerations as airport terminal space. The SEC raised questions on whether the exemption applied to free standing structures since the exemption provided by Statement 13 was in a subsection covering "Leases Involving Part of a Building." This demonstrated that the SEC was also interpreting Statement 13 literally, although in this case it appeared a bit absurd.

In response to problems such as the one cited in the previous paragraph, the FASB issued an official interpretation—No. 23, "Leases of Certain Property Owned by a Governmental Unit or Authority." The interpretation specifies certain conditions that must be met if the leases in question are to be considered operating leases. One of those is that the lessor has the explicit right to terminate the lease at any time. Since such a right often does not exist, at least certain leases in this area may now require capitalization.

The Board, in response to many comments received that these leases should be subject to the same rules as other leases, gave serious consideration to eliminating the exemption entirely. However, it concluded that further consideration of an amendment should not delay the issuance of the interpretation.

WHERE DOES THIS LEAVE STATEMENT NO. 13?

It now appears likely that Statement 13 will rank fourth in number of interpretations and amendments of an authoritative document, ranking behind only APB Opinion No. 15, "Earnings Per Share," APB Opinion No. ll, "Accounting for Income Taxes" and the all time leader APB Opinion No. 16, "Accounting for Business Combinations." In terms of frustration it may rank higher. These distinctions are not without certain redeeming qualities—countless hours of billable professional time are spent in analyzing lease transactions in light of Statement 13, but one wonders whether this is really productive.

Clearly, from a practitioner's viewpoint, Statement 13 has created practice problems and difficulties by forcing one to rummage through rules, amendments and interpretations when analyzing a lease. Conclusions on lease accounting seem to reach the lowest common denominator in practice, so that most practitioners have concluded that the objectives of Statement 13 and substance over form give way to a literal interpretation of the rules of Statement 13. No white knights are appearing to invoke the Board's objectives, since the Board itself, through its amendments and interpretations has opted, for the most part, to apply the arbitrary rules and percentages literally. To answer the question of why Statement 13 has failed to achieve its objective one must first question the objective itself. From the author's viewpoint, it is questionable whether the objective could ever have been expected to be achieved, since the basis of Statement 13 represented a compromise between capitalizing all leases and capitalizing only those where title passes. Thus, Statement 13 is aimed at a position in between, and the break points are arbitrary. While arbitrary rules may work when the objectives are at the extremes of available options, they rarely work if the position sought is on middle ground.

What then is the solution? Would it not be more workable to require capitalization of all leases that extend for some defined period (such as one year), not on the premise that the lease transfers substantially all the risks and rewards of ownership of the property, but that the lessee has acquired an asset, a property right, and correspondingly has incurred an obligation. Using this criterion the necessity for most of the rules of Statement 13 would be eliminated, and the lessee's balance sheet would give a better picture of its assets and liabilities.

What are the possibilities of such a scenario? It is difficult to predict but certain events seem to indicate that a rethinking of Statement 13 is probable. In March 1979, the Board met to consider the underlying concepts in accounting for leases. The subject matter was placed on the Board's agenda in view of the number of amendments and interpretations of Statement 13 and the inordinate amount of time the Board has spent on Statement 13 problems since its issuance. It is generally acknowledged that with the present complement on the Board, and the hindsight of the Statement's difficulties, if Statement 13 were submitted to the Board in its present form, a majority vote to issue would not be sustained.

At its March 6, 1979 meeting, a majority of the Board expressed "the tentative view that, if Statement 13 were to be reconsidered, they would support a property right approach in which all leases are included as 'rights to use property' and as 'lease obligations' in the lessee's balance sheet."

The other recent development comes out of the Board's exposure draft on accounting concepts. Many believe that the Board deviated from the definition of an economic obligation given in that document when it defined a capital lease. Eventually this inconsistency must be removed. If one uses the definition of a liability in the proposed statement on accounting concepts, it is not difficult to reach the conclusion that all leases represent obligations to transfer enterprise resources and should therefore be reflected on the balance sheet.

Statement 13 has not achieved its goal in terms of the degree of lease capitalization that its drafters believed would be accomplished or in eliminating most of the inconsistencies between accounting for leases by lessors and lessees. This practitioner believes the cause of failure is with the objective the Board used—an objective, as has been demonstrated, not capable of practical implementation. The Board should recognize its obligation to rethink the issue and its objective, taking into account its new definition of assets and liabilities, and recognize that while compromise in the setting of accounting principles is necessary in many circumstances, a compromise that doesn't work should be discarded.

ACCOUNTING FOR PENSIONS

The off-balance-sheet-financing question arises also in the area of pension accounting. The question is divisible into two basic issues: (1) In the event that a new pension plan is adopted or an existing plan is amended so that employees' prior work is considered in establishing benefits, then a liability for past (or prior) service is created. Should this liability be recognized on the company's balance sheet, and, if so, at what amount? (2) The rate at which pension plans are funded and that at which the benefits accrue to (and vest in) employees are frequently different. If the actuarial liability to employees (or the amount vested) grows more rapidly than the funding is accomplished, should the differential liability be recognized on the balance sheet?

Pension accounting is currently under very active consideration by the FASB. There have been two discussion memoranda, two sets of public hearings, a preliminary position paper, and a number of research papers written on the subject—all products of the FASB's deliberative process. Pension accounting involves long periods of time, both in the accumulation and payout phases. The period of time during which an individual will be in the company's employ, as well as the employee's life expectancy following retirement, are both uncertain. Obviously, therefore, the amount of a pension liability at any given moment is highly dependent on a number of future events and outcomes. This substantial problem notwithstanding, accountants must develop standards for the measurement of a liability whose disclosure would convey useful information to readers of financial statements. As this measurement would profoundly affect companies' debt-equity ratios, company managements feel strongly about the result of the pension accounting debate.

In "Pension Accounting: The Liability Question," Timothy S. Lucas and Betsy Ann Hollowell, both members of the FASB's research staff, observe that pension plan amendments give rise to liabilities that do not appear on the balance sheet. They argue that it is both desirable and feasible that the additional liability be given accounting recognition. At the conclusion of their article, the authors address the ever-present allegation of adverse economic consequences that are said to flow from accounting recognition of a larger liability.

Two articles taken from *Forbes* suggest different dimensions of the pension accounting problem. In "More Hidden Liabilities," the author discusses the disclosures of potential liabilities that companies may need to make under the Multiemployer Pension Plan Amendment Act passed during the Carter Administration. In "Reading the Tea Leaves," the difficulty of estimating the earning rate on pension fund assets is underscored, together with the opportunity for companies to smooth their reported profits by altering their actuarial assumptions.

The annual *Business Week* survey article, "Pension Scoreboard: A Controversial Glow of Health," reports the surplus or deficit of major companies' pension assets in relation to the benefits that have been legally vested in the employees. Although the picture is not as bleak as it was several years ago, a number of companies still show deficits, although few of these are large in relation to shareholders' equity (net worth). But the FASB's "Preliminary Views," issued in November 1982, expressed a preference for stating a company's liability at the actuarial present value of accumulated plan benefits, plus or minus the effect of estimated changes in future salary levels. In the context of the 100-corporation survey in the *Business Week* article, the column of importance would become the first one, not the second, leading to even more and larger deficits in relation to pension assets. Since the first column (total benefits) does not take into account the possible increase in salary levels, the deficits could be even larger than suggested by *Business Week's* table. Possible economic consequences of such a measurement lack are suggested in the article.

BIBLIOGRAPHICAL NOTES

The FASB's two discussion memoranda and its preliminary views are entered in the literature as follows:

An Analysis of Issues Related to Employers' Accounting for Pensions and Other Postemployment Benefits, Discussion Memorandum (Stamford, CT: FASB, February 19, 1981).
Preliminary Views of the FASB on Major Issues Related to Employers' Accounting for Pensions and Other Postemployment Benefits (Stamford, CT: FASB, November 1982).
An Analysis of Additional Issues Related to Employers' Accounting for Pensions and Other Postemployment Benefits, Discussion Memorandum (Stamford, CT: FASB, April 19, 1983).

Two papers on pension accounting by a leading Canadian accounting practitioner are:

Skinner, Ross M.: *Pension Accounting: The Problem of Equating Payments Tomorrow with Expenses Today* (Toronto: Clarkson Gordon, 1980).
Skinner, Ross M.: "Research and Standard Setting in Financial Accounting—An Illustrative Case," in *Research to Support Standard Setting in Financial Accounting: A Canadian*

Perspective, Sanjoy Basu and J. Alex Milburn (eds.) (Toronto: The Clarkson Gordon Foundation, 1982), pp. 153–202.

A primarily empirical study on pension accounting is:

Harold Danker *et al,* of Coopers & Lybrand, *Employer Accounting for Pension Costs and Other Post-Retirement Benefits,* (New York: Financial Executives Research Foundation, 1981).

An Australian issues paper is:

Hubbard, Graham: *Accounting and Reporting for Superannuation Plans,* Discussion Paper No. 7 (Melbourne, Australia: Australian Accounting Research Foundation, 1982).

An article in which two FASB staff members suggest the implications of the Board's "Preliminary Views" of November 1982 is:

Lucas, Timothy S., and Paul B. W. Miller: "Pension Accounting: Impacting the Financial Statement," *Journal of Accountancy* (June 1983), pp. 90–92, 94, 96, 99–102, 105–106.

Pension Accounting: The Liability Question

Timothy S. Lucas
Project Manager
Financial Accounting Standards Board

Betsy Ann Hollowell
Technical Associate
Financial Accounting Standards Board

Financial reports are not telling the whole story about pensions. But how should that story be told? Should some part of the pension obligation not currently recognized as a liability be included on the balance sheet of the employer? Is there an unrecorded liability for pensions under existing generally accepted accounting principles?

We want to discuss this aspect of pension accounting for three reasons. First, the many questions in the pension accounting area are so complex that they all cannot be effectively discussed at once, and the answer to the liability question does not appear to depend on answers to other questions. Second, and more important, the

Ed. note: Expressions of individual views by members of the Financial Accounting Standards Board staff are encouraged. The views expressed herein are those of the authors. Official positions of the FASB on accounting matters are determined only after extensive due process and deliberation.

question is one of the most significant in terms of the changes from current accounting that could result from the Financial Accounting Standards Board's pension accounting project. That significance can help us to achieve our primary objective—to stimulate thinking about and discussion of the issues involved in the board's project. Third, a majority of the speakers at the FASB's July 13–15 public hearings in New York on its discussion memorandum (DM), *Employers' Accounting for Pensions and Other Postemployment Benefits,*[1] took positions against including pension obligations on employers' balance sheets and provided a variety of supporting arguments. We believe an interesting case can be made *for* recognizing pension liabilities, and that case should be considered and debated by those who are interested in pension accounting questions.[2]

To understand better how the weight of pension liabilities can affect major decisions of management, consider the following report in the press: "Esmark announced recently that it was putting its meat-packing subsidiary, Swift Fresh Meats Division, on the market—and funding the subsidiary's 'sizable' unfunded pension liabilities.

"'They had to do that to make it saleable,' one Esmark analyst commented."

The same article also included a description of another situation: "One instance where pension liabilities were not adequately covered in the original deal—and later came back to haunt a firm—involved the spin-off in 1976 of Facet Enterprises from The Bendix Corp. The divestiture was ordered by the Federal Trade Commission, and Bendix formed Facet as a subsidiary, transferred certain business units to Facet and in 1976 distributed all of the stock of Facet to the common stockholders of Bendix. Included in the transfer to Facet were large unfunded pension liabilities.

"Facet eventually filed suit against Bendix, charging the company was aware of 'highly detrimental financial consequences' the transfer of the obligation would have on Facet."[3]

Facet Enterprises subsequently notified the Pension Benefit Guaranty Corp. that it was terminating the pension plan, which covered some twenty-two hundred employees and retirees. Facet said that terminating the pension plan was necessary to rescue its financially troubled automative parts divisions and that the plan's

[1] Financial Accounting Standards Board Discussion Memorandum. *Employers' Accounting for Pensions and Other Postemployment Benefits* (Stamford, CT: FASB, 1981).

[2] The liability question is one of eight issues addressed in the DM. This article does not attempt to cover other closely related questions, including how to measure the liability if it is to be recorded and the nature of the offsetting debit that arises if a liability is recorded. Measuring or determining the amount of the liability is complex and involves two problems. First, any measure of the pension obligation involves estimating future events, such as how long retirees will live and how many employees will leave before vesting or die before retiring. Second, even after all the estimates are made, there are different attributes of the obligation that may be measured, including vested benefits, accumulated benefits and prior service cost determined under one or more actuarial cost methods. Determining the amount that might be recorded as a liability is beyond the scope of this article, but it involves understanding events related to the growth of the pension obligation as an employee's career progresses from hiring to retirement. The possible choices with regard to the nature of the offsetting debit that arises if a liability is recorded discussed in the DM include recording the debit as an intangible asset or as some kind of charge on the income statement.

[3] Maria Crawford Scott, "Pension Liabilities May Hurt Merger," *Pensions and Investments,* October 13, 1980, p. 4.

unfunded liabilities of about $31 million exceeded the net worth of the three units it covered.

At about the same time, *Fortune* reported

> When Kaiser Steel was considering liquidation last September …some people saw an opportunity for a quick profit in the stock. They believed the sell-off of Kaiser's various properties would fetch considerably more than the $44 per share its stock was going for. This reasoning, however, overlooked the company's unfunded vested pension liability of about $9 per share *and* the even larger amount Kaiser says it would have had to fork over to provide health insurance and other benefits to retirees. When Kaiser's directors eventually voted not to liquidate, they gave as one reason the size of these burdens. The board concluded the liquidation value could actually be *below* the $44 market price.[4]

In these situations, which unfortunately are not unique, a pension obligation had an unexpected and newsworthy effect on the economic potential and well-being of the company. The pension obligation was not suddenly created in any of these situations. It existed all along, but it was not reported as a liability. Although each company had prepared financial statements in accordance with GAAP, the pension situation was not fully understood, even by knowledgeable readers of those statements.

CURRENT PENSION GAAP

Employer accounting for pensions is based, at present, on Accounting Principles Board Opinion No. 8, *Accounting for the Cost of Pension Plans,*[5] as amended by FASB Statement No. 36, *Disclosure of Pension Information.*[6] Opinion No. 8 allows pension cost to be determined under any of a number of acceptable actuarial cost methods. Typically, the method used to determine funding of a pension plan (the annual contribution to the pension fund or trust) is also used for accounting.

Under current GAAP, most balance sheets do not include a line item labeled "pension liability." Nevertheless, under Opinion No. 8 part of the pension obligation is recorded as a liability. The amount of liability recorded (debit expense, credit liability) typically is equal to the amount of liability discharged by the contribution (debit liability, credit cash). This is because contributions to the pension plan are recorded as discharges of the pension liability and because most companies fund pension cost accrued. The resulting net liability—the amount appearing on the balance sheet—is zero. But the amount expensed and contributed to the plan cannot be called an unrecorded liability in the usual sense. It does not appear on the balance sheet only because the transfer of assets to the pension fund is regarded as payment of the liability. If, instead, we view the transfer as a segregation or setting aside of assets, it would be logical to add the accumulated amounts expensed (the liability) and the assets held by the plan to the balance sheet.

---

[4]Mary Greenebaum, "The Market Has Spotted Those Pension Problems," *Fortune,* December 1, 1980, p. 146.

[5]Accounting Principles Board Opinion No. 8, *Accounting for the Cost of Pension Plans* (New York: AICPA, 1966).

[6]FASB Statement No. 36, *Disclosure of Pension Information* (Stamford, CT: FASB, 1980).

But for most employers and most plans another part of the pension obligation has not yet been expensed, recorded as a liability or "discharged" by contributions to the plan. The pension obligation that is not recorded as a liability under current GAAP results, primarily, from plan amendments. Parts of that obligation also may result from establishment of new plans and from cumulative experience gains and losses, but for simplicity we will focus on plan amendments. When a pension plan is amended to increase benefits, the increased benefits usually are granted based on service, including service rendered before the date of the change. In some cases benefits also are increased for former employees who are already retired. After such an amendment, the employer's pension obligation is larger than it was before. It is this incremental obligation that some believe should be recorded as a liability. This view is based on the idea that the employer has an obligation for benefits already earned by employees. The amount of benefits earned (however measured) will not necessarily coincide with the accumulation of prior years' normal costs and amortization of prior service costs recorded under Opinion No. 8.

For convenience, let's assume that we are dealing with a typical company that sponsors a single-employer, defined-benefit pension plan. The plan provides a retirement income benefit of, say, $50 per month for each year of an employee's service. In the current year, the company amends the plan to increase the benefits to $60 per month per year of service for all active employees and for retirees who are receiving pensions. The amendment provides for increased benefits based on all of an employee's years of service, past as well as future. Actuaries will review the change and compute the new, increased amount of contribution the company will pay over a period of years to fund the increased benefits. The accounting question is, When the plan is amended, does a recordable liability arise for that part of the increased benefits attributed to past years of service?

Opinion No. 8 accounting reflects such an amendment prospectively, usually based on the way the cost of the amendment will be funded. No increase in liability is recorded immediately as a result of the event that occurred when the plan was amended. Instead, it is provided for and recorded as expense and a liability a little bit at a time.

Whether a recordable liability arises when the plan is amended depends on what kinds of things belong on balance sheets. Accountants and users of financial statements generally understand the nature of items on balance sheets, including liabilities. That knowledge makes the balance sheet useful. Liabilities such as accounts payable, notes payable and bonds payable all have something in common. And, most important, all accounts, notes and bonds payable are included. If each company had the flexibility to omit some of these items in preparing its balance sheet, disclosing the omitted items in the footnotes, the usefulness of the balance sheet would be reduced. Analysts would doubtless add the "footnote liabilities" to those on the statement and construct their own adjusted balance sheets (as some do today with pension disclosures), but the convenience of having a complete balance sheet would be lost and some users might be misled because they expect all liabilities to be included.

The FASB has begun the process of describing the kinds of things that belong on the right-hand side of a balance sheet by providing a definition of liabilities.

Financial Accounting Concepts Statement No. 3, *Elements of Financial Statements of Business Enterprises,* defines liabilities as "probable future sacrifices of economic benefits arising from present obligations of a particular entity to transfer assets or provide services to other entities in the future as a result of past transactions or events."[7]

The concepts statement also identifies three essential characteristics of a liability inherent in the definition:

> ...(a) it embodies a present duty or responsibility to one or more other entities that entails settlement by probable future transfer or use of assets at a specified or determinable date, on occurrence of a specified event, or on demand, (b) the duty or responsibility obligates a particular enterprise, leaving it little or no discretion to avoid the future sacrifice, and (c) the transaction or other event obligating the enterprise has already happened.[8]

In addition, it discusses other features often found in liabilities: "Liabilities commonly have other features that help identify them—for example, most liabilities require the obligated enterprise to pay cash to one or more identified other entities and are legally enforceable. However, those features are not essential characteristics of liabilities. Their absence, by itself, is not sufficient to preclude an item's qualifying as a liability. That is, liabilities may not require an enterprise to pay cash but to convey other assets, to provide or stand ready to provide services, or to use assets. And as long as payment or other transfer of assets to settle an existing obligation is probable, the identity of the recipient need not be known to the obligated enterprise before the time of settlement. Similarly, although most liabilities rest generally on a foundation of legal rights and duties, existence of a legally enforceable claim is not a prerequisite for an obligation to qualify as a liability if the future payment of cash or other transfer of assets to settle the obligation is otherwise probable."[9]

A careful reading of the above excerpts reveals that the definition of liabilities is primarily a description of current practice; it is not a radical change but a formal description of the kinds of things that we already think of as liabilities. Accountants are likely to agree, for example, that accrued salaries payable is a liability because the company has a responsibility or obligation to employees who have performed services for which they have not yet been paid. The obligation probably will be satisfied by paying the accrued amounts (transferring assets) at a future date, and the event that obligated the company (the performance of the services) has already occurred.

On the other hand, a budgeted expenditure to replace a machine is not a liability, even though the transfer of assets may be virtually certain and the need to replace the machine acute. The budgeted expenditure does not entail the essential obligation—the duty or responsibility to another entity. That obligation will be created by a future event.

The same understanding of a liability (as formalized by Concepts Statement No. 3) can be used in considering the pension liability question. In the example described

---

[7]Financial Accounting Concepts Statement No. 3, *Elements of Financial Statements of Business Enterprises* (Stamford, CT: FASB, 1980), par. 28.

[8]Ibid., par. 29.

[9]Ibid., par. 29.

earlier, when the plan is amended is there an obligation to make a probable future payment? Has the event that obligated the company already happened? It seems clear to us that a case can be made for an affirmative answer to those questions. If so, the pension obligation is similar to other obligations that are recorded as liabilities, and the balance sheet would be incomplete—its usefulness diminished—if the pension liability was excluded, just as it would be incomplete without bank loans or accounts payable.

The news excerpts quoted earlier suggest that economic decisions sometimes are affected by the failure of decision makers to fully understand or consider pension obligations. As noted, the pension obligations that are not recorded and may therefore be overlooked result primarily from plan amendments. The incremental pension obligations that result from a plan amendment are now recorded as liabilities only over future periods. If those obligations were included on the balance sheet as liabilities when incurred, it seems to us, they would be less likely to be overlooked, and the balance sheet would provide a more complete picture of the financial position of the company. We also noted that some analysts adjust present balance sheets to consider some measure of pension obligations. If, as we have suggested, the unrecorded pension obligation looks like other obligations afforded balance sheet status, why do some people still want to exclude pension obligations from balance sheets?

ARGUMENTS FOR AND AGAINST DEFERRED RECOGNITION OF PENSION LIABILITIES

The remainder of this article explores some of the reasons advanced for continuing the present practice of deferred recognition of pension liabilities resulting from plan amendments. Our opinions as to why those reasons have not been convincing also are discussed. The arguments for and against recognition generally apply equally to the obligation resulting from plan amendments and to that resulting from other factors such as experience gains and losses.

The Company's Obligation Is Only To Make Contributions

Some people suggest that the company does not have an obligation directly to the employees but only an obligation to make scheduled contributions to the plan. They conclude that there is no liability if contributions called for (by the actuary) have been made.

We believe this confuses the existence of a liability with its maturity date. If there is an obligation to the plan—an obligation to make future contributions—resulting from past events such as plan amendments and past service, that obligation may qualify as a liability. The fact that the contributions are scheduled for payment in future years does not mean that the obligation should remain unrecorded; most liabilities have scheduled future payment dates. The obligation to the plan and the obligation to the employees are two different ways to describe the same thing. The crucial question is whether there is a present obligation as a result of past transactions or events, not the identification of the obligee.

In addition, the idea that the existence of the pension plan or trust as a separate legal entity somehow avoids what would otherwise be the company's liability leads to other questions. Suppose a company set up a similar trust to be funded over a period of years to pay off a major lawsuit settlement. Should the full amount of the agreed on settlement be recorded as a liability or is it only an obligation of the trust?

It Is Not a Legal Liability

Some argue that the pension liability should be excluded from the balance sheet because it is not a "legal" liability. As the excerpt we quoted from Concepts Statement No. 3 notes, legal status is not required for an obligation to be recorded as a liability. In addition, the meaning of the term *legal liability* in this context is unclear. Pension obligations have been held to be legally enforceable in various circumstances.

It Will Never Have To Be Paid

If a pension plan is assumed to continue in effect, the liability will never be fully paid since there will always be active employees whose pensions are not yet payable. Some people suggest that the pension obligation need not be recorded on this basis.

The same thing may be said, however, of many other liabilities. For example, if a company continues in business, it is unlikely ever to reduce the balance of accounts payable to zero, but it is still considered useful to record and report the total amount of the obligation at the end of each period. This argument seems to be more relevant to funding decisions than to accounting questions.

The Amount of the Obligation Can't Be Measured

Some argue that the pension obligation should be excluded from the balance sheet because it is too uncertain or too hard to measure. They note that several future events must be estimated to calculate the amount of the obligation and that it is expected that these estimates will have to be adjusted as experience unfolds. The need to estimate and project future events is not unique to pensions. Accounting unavoidably involves many estimates and must be able to deal with changes in those estimates. The best current estimate of the amount of the pension obligation, based on the experience and knowledge of the professional actuary, is useful information. Pension accounting is already based on the same estimates; the only difference is that the amounts are spread over a number of future periods.

Spreading the effect of a plan amendment over a number of future periods tends to obscure, rather than report, the effect of the change. The obligation for future pension payments or contributions clearly is greater after a plan amendment than it was before the amendment. Financial Accounting Concepts Statement no. 1, *Objectives of Financial Reporting by Business Enterprises,* states

> Financial reporting should provide information about the economic resources of an enterprise, the claims to those resources (obligations of the enterprise to transfer resources

to other entities and owners' equity), and the effects of transactions, events, and circumstances that change its resources and claims to those resources.[10]

Since the plan amendment is an event that changes the employer's obligation—an event that increases employees' claims to the company's resources—financial statements should reflect that event.

The Increased Benefits Are Granted in Exchange for Future Service

Some suggest that increases in pension benefits are granted in anticipation of future employee services, even though the amount of increase may be computed based on the number of years of prior service. In this view, the employer would be unlikely to increase benefits unless he expected to receive something of value in return. Since the value of past services cannot be enhanced retroactively, the employer must expect to receive benefits in the form of future services. The suggested conclusion is that the liability arises only as the future service is rendered.

The use of this line of reasoning for benefit increases granted to those already retired is based on the idea that current employees will provide services in exchange for benefits paid to other individuals already retired because they expect to receive similar increases after they retire.

The problem with that argument is it does not address whether the employer has a liability—a present obligation to transfer assets as a result of past transactions or events. After a plan amendment becomes effective, that obligation exists. What the employer receives in return for incurring the liability is another issue. An asset can exist as a result of the amendment, for example, if employees are motivated to work harder. Concepts Statement no. 3 has defined assets as "probable future economic benefits obtained or controlled by a particular entity as a result of past transactions or events."[11] Whether an intangible asset exists after a plan amendment is beyond the scope of this article.

Liability Recognition Would Have Economic Consequences

Some suggest that recognizing the unrecorded pension liability would cause some employers to go bankrupt, to be denied access to credit markets or to be unwilling to improve pension plans. These and other predicted economic consequences are perceived as undesirable. They are said to be costs that exceed any possible benefit that might result from changes in pension accounting.

The FASB addressed the relationship between economic consequences and accounting standards in Financial Accounting Concepts Statement no. 2, *Qualitative Characteristics of Accounting Information*:

While rejecting the view that financial accounting standards should be slanted for political

---

[10]Financial Accounting Concepts Statement No. 1. *Objectives of Financial Reporting by Business Enterprises* (Stamford, Conn.: FASB, 1978), par. 40.

[11]Concepts Statement no. 3, par. 19.

reasons or to favor one economic interest or another, the Board recognizes that a standard—setting authority must be alert to the economic impact of the standards that it promulgates. The consequences of those standards will usually not be easy to isolate from the effects of other economic happenings, and they will be even harder to predict with confidence when a new standard is under consideration but before it has gone into effect. Nevertheless, the Board will consider the probable economic impact of its standards as best it can and will monitor that impact as best it can after a standard goes into effect. For one thing, a markedly unexpected effect on business behavior may point to an unforeseen deficiency in a standard in the sense that it does not result in the faithful representation of economic phenomena that was intended. It would then be necessary for the standard to be revised.

Neutrality in accounting is an important criterion by which to judge accounting policies, for information that is not neutral loses credibility. If information can be verified and can be relied on faithfully to represent what it purports to represent—*and if there is no bias in the selection of what is reported*—it cannot be slanted to favor one set of interests over another. It may in fact favor certain interests, but only because the information points that way, much as a good examination grade favors a good student who has honestly earned it.

The italicized words deserve comment. It was noted earlier in this Statement that reliability implies completeness of information, at least within the bounds of what is material and feasible, considering the cost. An omission can rob information of its claim to neutrality if the omission is material and is intended to induce or inhibit some particular mode of behavior.[12]

The board also has recognized its responsibility to limit changes in existing practice to situations in which the perceived benefits exceed the perceived costs of the change.

Economic consequences, however, can work both ways. There also may be economic consequences of failing to change accounting rules that do not reflect economic reality or that are not neutral and unbiased. The costs of not improving accounting are probably as hard to measure as the costs of changes, but they may be significant.

The economic consequences argument against recognizing the pension liability presumes that markets and decision makers will not become aware of the liability if it is not recorded. It also assumes that situation to be desirable. That assumption conflicts with the basic objective of reporting neutral and unbiased information that is relevant to decision makers.

Consider, for example, the suggestion that recording the pension liability will deny some companies access to credit. Decisions to grant or deny credit to a particular company are not made by the FASB; they are made by people, such as bankers, who are concerned with the ability of the company to repay. Credit decisions are based, in part, on accounting information, and those who must decide to grant or deny credit rely on having unbiased information, including information about a company's liabilities. It is inappropriate for the FASB to refuse to recognize a liability that exists just because knowledge of that liability might cause the banker

---

[12] Financial Accounting Concepts Statement no. 2, *Qualitative Characteristics of Accounting Information* (Stamford, Conn.: FASB, 1980), pars. 106, 107, 108.

to deny credit to a particular company. Indeed, that may be a persuasive reason to require recognition of the liability.

CONCLUSION

Based on our work to date, we are not convinced by the arguments against recording a liability when a pension plan is established or amended. We believe that an accounting liability does exist and that including it with other liabilities in the balance sheet will significantly improve the usefulness of financial statements.

CPAs may or may not agree with our conclusion. However, even if they, and the members of the FASB, ultimately do agree, a number of important related questions must be resolved before any change in pension accounting can be implemented, including

• What is the appropriate measure of the liability? Is it vested benefits, accumulated benefits, prior service cost or something else?
• If a liability is recorded, what is the nature of the offsetting debit? Is it expense, an extraordinary charge, an intangible asset or something else?
• How should the assets held by the plan be reflected on the employer's balance sheet? Depending on the measure of the liability, plan assets might exceed the liability for many companies.

These and other related issues are now being considered as part of the FASB's project on employers' accounting for pensions and other postemployment benefits. The answers to the issues may have a significant effect on how financial statements reflect pension activities. We encourage accountants to help in finding answers that improve financial reporting by participating in the board's process.

More Hidden Liabilities

Richard Greene
Associate Editor
Forbes

Just a couple of weeks ago, it looked like the takeover of Leslie Fay Inc.—the $223 million women's apparel manufacturer—was just about reaching the handshaking stage. A private investor, Wilmer J. Thomas Jr. and Wertheim & Co. had offered to buy the firm for $38 million. Then at the eleventh hour, the deal mysteriously fell apart.

The spoiler: a barely noticed amendment to ERISA—dealing with multiemployer pension plans—that will put hundreds of millions of dollars in liabilities on corpo-

From *Forbes* (March 2, 1981), pp. 66–67. Reprinted by permission of *Forbes*. Copyright © 1981. All rights reserved.

rations' books. This amendment, called the Multiemployer Pension Plan Amendment Act (MPPAA), was signed into law by Jimmy Carter last fall. Its intention was to protect individuals participating in these plans from being deprived of their benefits if a number of employers dropped out of the plan, thus leaving large unfunded liabilities. Multiemployer plans represent 25% of all U.S. workers served by defined benefit plans in the private sector. Set up under the Taft-Hartley Act for industries in which a number of companies negotiate with one union, multiemployer plans are notoriously shaky. The industries involved, like mining, trucking and apparel, tend to be labor-intensive industries, some of which can barely afford to fund a pension plan adequately.

Up until now, they really haven't had to worry about anything. "Prior to ERISA, the liability of the employer was limited to some cents-per-hour contribution he had negotiated with the union. Funding could have nothing whatsoever to do with the benefits promised," explains George T. Favetta, vice president of Buck Consultants Inc., one of the country's largest employee benefit consulting firms. "All the employer had to do was put in the amount of contribution stipulated by the contract."

But even after ERISA was put into effect in 1974, employers only had a liability to employees if the plan terminated—if it simply ran out of money and went belly up. But that just meant that employers only had to worry about preventing the plan from falling apart. More important, any individual employer could just run away from the plan at any point, without having to be concerned about leaving behind huge unfunded liabilities as long as the plan didn't go under within five years of his departure.

Although these plans were supposed to be administered by both the company and the union, the companies, for the most part, were pleased to abdicate that responsibility. "These employers just didn't want to get involved in the plans," says Favetta. "So, they would tell their appointees to the board of trustees, 'Leave it to the fellows in the union to run the plan, what do we really care?'"

That's all changed now, with a vengeance. Under the MPPAA, employers must fully fund the contractual benefits for their employees, past and present, if they withdraw from the plan. The idea here was to stop companies from running away and leaving the remaining participants saddled with *their* liabilities. The trouble is that "withdrawal" has been defined so broadly that you can be shot for trying to escape when you're only taking a stroll around the prison yard.

In Leslie Fay's case, for example, the firm was trying to sell its assets to investor Wilmer Thomas and Wertheim. As any good businessman knows, this is just a device to minimize taxes. But MPPAA, like some trigger-happy guard, interprets this as an attempt to escape from the plan. Result: Had Leslie Fay's assets been sold, the company would have had to contribute, over the next five years, enough money to fully fund its share of the underfunded International Ladies Garment Workers Union plan. Although the exact dollar amount involved is difficult to estimate, it could have run as high as $20 million. That made Leslie Fay too expensive and killed the deal.

All sorts of other situations can trigger a technical withdrawal:

• If a firm closes an unprofitable plant, it may have to fully fund the pensions for employees who worked there *in the past*—even if the factory itself has been run by a skeleton crew for years.

• If the union is decertified—an action that is totally out of the hands of any employer—the company may be forced to switch pension plans and face full withdrawal liabilities.

• A gradual reduction in the number of employees may be seen as a "partial withdrawal." Just when a firm is digging itself out of a hole, the MPPAA can hit.

Obviously, this kind of thing is not going to encourage companies to join multiemployer plans. Says Theodore Bernstein, director of benefits for the ILGWU, "We lose employers in the plan mostly when they go out of business. When that happens, we need new members, and to the extent that this amendment inhibits new employers from joining the fund, it's negative."

Dan McGinn, president of the large California actuarial firm that bears his name, goes much further: "Instead of solving or even alleviating the problem of multiemployer pension plans, Congress has created the machinery for their ultimate destruction. This withdrawal liability will inhibit companies from joining plans that will shut off their vital lifeblood. If Congress doesn't act to lessen the impact of the withdrawal liability within five years, a good many multiemployer plans simply will not survive."

Buck's Favetta doesn't think the situation is quite so bad. "What it will do," he says, "is make employers much more aware of the plans. There are certain industries for which multiemployer plans are simply the only right device. But now the employers will have to participate in the running of these plans, and be tougher negotiators when bargaining with the union over benefits."

Whether MPPAA spells doom for the plans, or simply a need for a far more responsible attitude on the part of employers, is an open question. It is very clear, however, that disclosure of such potential liabilities will make a number of large companies mighty uncomfortable. Under FASB Opinion 36, employers may be forced to disclose their share of unfunded multiemployer pension fund liability. This will put participants through much the same pain single-employer pension plan operators went through after ERISA passed in 1974, and *they* had to start making disclosures.

The disclosures will start coming through this year in some companies with the real flood probably arriving next year. The numbers involved will be huge. Conoco, for example, chose to run ahead of the pack. Although the company's officers seem to be regretting that decision now, their disclosure was enlightening: "For the two plans [of which Conoco is a member] combined, these percentages of the unfunded vested liabilities and of the unfunded prior service liabilities would approximate $396 million and $463 million, respectively," reads their annual report. Granted there is some overlap. But even for immense Conoco, with $815 million in earnings last year, that's a substantial liability.

Reading the Tea Leaves

Thomas Baker
Forbes

In the face of disastrous losses for Pan Am and Braniff, Eastern Air Lines looked good in April with a first-quarter profit of $4.1 million. However, had the accountants and actuaries not changed one or two assumptions in Eastern's pension plan it would have been a different story. The airline's pension plan funding in 1981 will be reduced from 1980's $100 million to around $75 million. That's a "saving" of $25 million.

Bet you thought this kind of cookie jar stuff was illegal. Welcome to the rarefied world of actuarial assumptions, where crystal-ball gazing is accepted practice. Simply put, Eastern's squad of actuaries merely penciled in a change in their assumptions of what Eastern's pension fund might earn on its capital in the future. Obviously, if you assume that interest rates will stay high and that you're going to earn more on the money in your fund, then you need to put in less now to meet future obligations. That means you can decrease your annual contribution, as Eastern did.

Is this legitimate? Perfectly. Companies are free to pick any number that feels right to them. "There was a rash of increases in actuarial assumptions in the mid-Seventies, the last bout of high inflation," recalls Ed Davis of Buck Consultants, a New York-based actuarial firm. "People were looking for places to improve earnings. I have to expect that there is going to be another rash."

That's not going to make things any easier for investors trying to compare two companies' pension expenses, or to keep track of how well the pension is funded. Or, for that matter, to compare earnings figures from year to year.

Here's how the change worked for Eastern. Since 1974 the company had been assuming an interest rate of 7% over the long term. The airline knew, roughly, how much money its plan would have to pay out over the next 20 to 30 years, and assuming that it earned 7% on its portfolio over that time, it knew how much it would have to kick in. But now, Eastern and its actuaries have decided that interest rates are going to stay higher than 7% over the next couple of decades, so it raised its assumed rate to 9%—and cut the contribution.

Eastern's treasurer, Charles Glass, says it was the actuaries' idea: "These were recommendations from them." As it happens, Eastern's assumptions aren't much ahead of current practice: A fall 1980 survey by Greenwich Research Associates showed that the average corporate interest assumption was 6.3%, but since then many funds have been steadily ratcheting their assumptions up to the 7%-to-9% range. Crown Zellerbach, for example, changed its rate assumption from 6 1/4% to 8 1/2% last year for reporting purposes (it used a more conservative 7 1/2% internally). That reduced the present value of CZ's anticipated pension payout from

$467 million to $426 million at a time when assets were increasing. That meant the company reported a plan surplus of $85 million. The year before, there was a $77 million shortfall.

Which set of figures is right? It depends on which set of assumptions turns out to be true—if either. What's important to recognize is that company earnings figures can be hoisted up and down by methods and assumptions different for every company.

In an attempt to help, the Financial Accounting Standards Board last year imposed a whole new set of reporting requirements on pension plans (Numbers Game, *Mar. 17, 1980*). The FASB decided that future salary increases shouldn't be taken into consideration when computing how much the plan will have to pay out, and that the interest rate assumption for reporting purposes should be generally higher than many companies use internally.

This FASB ruling only muddied the waters more. One company went so far as to release two sets of figures: one to satisfy the FASB, and then the real numbers—those it uses internally to figure out how to fund the plan. There's a big difference. Under the 10% assumption it thinks the FASB wants, Bethlehem Steel's plan looks just fine: assets of $2 billion and liabilities of $2.4 billion. But with Bethlehem Steel's own 7% assumption, benefit liabilities soar to $3 billion. "If we'd used a 10% interest rate assumption and assumed no salary increases, we would have put much less into the fund," explains Bob Gerst, general manager of employment-cost accounting at Bethlehem Steel. As it was, Bethlehem put $309 million in last year—using its own more conservative 7% figure. "This whole thing is a can of worms, if you ask me," moans Bethlehem's Gerst.

Unfortunately, you can't just impose one rate assumption on everyone. Explains Raymond Perry, a partner at Touche Ross & Co.: "A single assumption is apt to be unrealistic because the experience of companies varies with such things as investment performance and employee turnover."

Now the FASB is preparing for July hearings on pension accounting, and the subject is being thought through again. Among the possibilities: One funding method could be imposed on all companies. But, as Perry said, that would not be realistic. So, which do you prefer: a neat fiction, or an anarchic realism?

Pension Scoreboard: A Controversial Glow of Health

Pension plans of the nation's major businesses are in better shape today than they have been in years, thanks to high real interest rates, the slowdown in wage increases, and stellar returns on pension assets. But being fatter is also intensifying controversies over how—and in whose interest—the plans are managed.

According to *Business Week*'s annual survey of the largest 100 corporations, the

Adapted from *Business Week,* September 17, 1984, pp. 153, 157, 160.

group's 1983 pension assets rose 19%, to $220 billion, up from $185 billion the year before. But only half of this increase is attributable to pension contributions. The remainder represents portfolio managers' good fortunes in both the stock and the bond markets.

Meanwhile, the aggregate vested funding positions—the difference between plan assets and current legal obligations to employees—rose from $37 billion to $58 billion, a heartening 57% enhancement. But while assets grew by $35 billion during the year, promised benefits—a company's liability to present and future retirees— grew by only $14 billion.

Actuaries calculate pension liabilities by estimating future salaries, work force levels, and rates of return on investment. During the period, projected wage inflation moderated, work force levels dropped, and assumed rates of return increased. Therefore, pension plans were projected to cover fewer employees at lower future salaries than previously expected. And by figuring in a higher rate of return, the "present value" of future payments shrank. As a result, many companies are showing vastly improved pension positions. International Business Machines Corp. doubled its pension surplus from $1.6 billion to $3.2 billion. Even struggling U.S. Steel's surplus increased from $855 million to $1.9 billion, while Ford Motor Co. nearly quadrupled its positive position from $170 million to $760 million.

As corporate pension plans have become increasingly overfunded, top management has become more tempted to terminate the program and use excess assets in other ways. It is perfectly legal to do so, says Jerry Spigal, a consulting actuary with Peat, Marwick, Mitchell & Co., "as long as the company pays off every employee's benefits earned to date by buying annuities" on their behalf.

According to the Pension Benefit Guaranty Corp., there were nearly 5,000 plan terminations in the first quarter of 1984, after more than 18,000 terminations in 1983. Recent examples include Cities Service Co., which recaptured $238 million in excess assets; Celanese Corp., which collected $300 million from its overfunded pension plan; and Occidental Petroleum Corp., which pumped $375 million from its pension plan into its general coffers.

Labor unions, to be sure, often balk at the idea of terminating a cash-rich plan. "Unlike a continuing defined benefit plan, where employees can look forward to a percentage of their final pay, annuities are not insulated from inflation," says Spigal. "Or, if you convert to a profit-sharing plan, then you've shifted the investment risk to the employees."

On the other hand, when a plan is severely underfunded, a threat to curtail future benefits in order to balance the books can become a strike issue. Pan American World Airways Inc.—whose underfunding amounted to nearly $500 million, or 115% of its net worth—in early August replaced its defined benefit plan with a cheaper defined contribution plan, sharply cutting payments to pensioners. In retaliation, 12,000 hourly workers walked off the job. A court ordered them back to work six hours later.

Pan Am leads Delta, Eastern Air Lines, and Trans World Airlines in unfunded pension liabilities among the nation's second 100 companies. Also included in that group are hard-pressed companies in the manufacturing and steel industries.

DRAMATIC STEPS

But among the nation's top 100, the number of underfunded plans fell from 13 in 1982 to 5 in 1983. General Motors—with the dubious distinction of having the largest unfunded liability in 1982—slashed its negative position from $1.9 billion to $111 million in 1983. GM dropped to third place on that list in 1983, leaving first and second place to Chrysler Corp. and Bethlehem Steel Corp. Chrysler became the undisputed leader in unfunded pension liabilities for 1983, with its $947 million amounting to 69% of its net worth. Bethlehem Steel—although it was able to reduce its negative figure by 39% from 1982—still tallied a $503 million unfunded liability, representing 38% of its net worth.

However, both Chrysler and Bethlehem have recently taken dramatic steps to slash unfunded liabilities. On July 19, Chrysler's pension fund liquidated $450 million in stocks, transferred in $650 million from the company's general cash account, and purchased $1.1 billion of high-grade bonds that yield 14.2%. That cut its unfunded pension liability in half, because its rate of return increased so sharply. "Most pension plans have a mix of stocks, bonds, and real estate," says Frederick W. Zuckerman, treasurer of Chrysler. "The actuary doesn't know what the return will be, so he arrives at a conservative figure like 8%. But now the actuary can say that our 14.2% return is absolutely assured."

Bethlehem recently boosted the fixed-income portion of its portfolio from 27% to 60%. A company spokesman says the move will slash $50 million in annual pension fund contributions. Believing that interest rates had reached their peak, Bethlehem bought $700 million in bonds on which it locks in an annual interest rate of 14%. In doing so, it immediately cut its unfunded liability in half. And it did so at a time when inflation, at around 4% in the past 12 months, only minimally erodes the purchasing power of a 14% nominal rate. "These real interest rates available on bonds are unprecedented in the history of this country," declares Michael Metz, a bond manager at Oppenheimer & Co.

THE FINE PRINT

Zuckerman says Chrysler would have made the same move in 1981 when rates were also high, but "we had our hands full worrying about survival." He says the only people within the company who were upset with the current bond strategy were the equity managers, who were dismissed. "I didn't fire them because I was angry with them," muses Zuckerman, but "there seem to be a lot of guys who are good this year and terrible the next."

Over the long haul, stocks have provided a higher return than bonds, so most pension funds maintain more than 50% of their portfolios in equities. Analysts say that growing companies will continue to do better with a mixture of stocks and bonds. But for companies in old-line industries with financial problems, the dedicated bond approach—in which bonds are purchased so that interest and principal payments precisely match pension obligations—is a logical step. The strategy could backfire, of course, if inflation returns with such a vengeance that it swamps even a 14% coupon, but it should work well as long as inflation is low and bond yields are high. "We removed from our present and future pensioners the exposure to the vicissitudes of the stock market," says Zuckerman, whose company has obligations to 80,000 current employees and 60,000 retirees.

The overall improvement in corporate pension plans may have knocked the wind out of the Financial Accounting Standards Board's controversial proposal to place pension liabilities on the balance sheet. "They've assumed a low profile lately," observes Carl S. Swope, a vice-president with Johnson & Higgins, an employee-benefits consulting firm.

But the FASB denies that the improved outlook for pensions has sidetracked its proposal to put the figures on the balance sheet. Companies with overfunded plans might also be against the proposal because "large net asset positions have been incentives for takeovers," says Jules M. Cassel, a senior technical adviser with the FASB. Currently, such information is fully disclosed in footnotes to the financial statements, so a corporate predator should be able to sniff out asset-rich pension plans easily. Nevertheless, "people argue that where you put information is almost as important as the information itself," says Cassel, as if management would act differently because information actually on the balance sheet is somehow more significant.

Meanwhile, the board has segregated the disclosure of post-retirement health care and life insurance benefits into a separate project. The corporate community—perceiving that this potential liability would have several times the impact of pensions—vigorously argued against lumping pensions and future life and health insurance benefits together. "The costs of welfare benefits—medical coverage and life insurance—are not prefunded like pension benefits," argued Donald E. Sullivan, a vice-president at Towers, Perrin, Forster & Crosby. The FASB responded by issuing a temporary proposal, essentially for footnote disclosure of medical and life insurance benefits promised, until the matter could be studied further.

LANDMARK DECISION

So despite the greatly lessened anxieties about underfunding of pension plans, regulation as well as legislation and litigation promise to keep the field in ferment for some time. On two fronts, for instance, companies will have to reconsider their treatment of women. The Retirement Equity Act, sponsored by Representative Geraldine A. Ferraro and signed into law by President Reagan, prevents employees from losing their vested benefits because they temporarily stop working—a provision that is expected primarily to benefit women who choose to stay home with their children for a period of years. The law also says that if a vested employee dies before retirement, then the spouse must not be prevented from collecting death benefits.

And the Supreme Court, in what is already deemed a landmark decision in *Arizona Governing Committee vs. Norris,* stated that women and men must be paid equal pension benefits for equal contributions, despite the longer life expectancy of women. The court ruled that the use of sex-based actuarial factors to determine the size of monthly retirement benefit programs violates Title VII of the Civil Rights Act of 1964.

1983's LARGEST CORPORATE PENSION FUNDS

Company		Plan assets millions of dollars
1.	AT&T	$46,380
2.	General Motors	18,128
3.	IBM	10,388
4.	General Electric	10,172
5.	U.S. Steel	8,479
6.	Du Pont	8,182
7.	Ford Motor	8,150
8.	Exxon	7,676
9.	GTE	4,900
10.	Eastman Kodak	3,536

Data: Standard & Poor's Compustat Services, Inc.

1983's LARGEST UNFUNDED PENSION LIABILITIES

AMONG THE TOP 100 COMPANIES RANKED BY SALES

Company	Millions of dollars	As percent of net worth
Chrysler	$947	69.3%
Bethlehem Steel	503	38.3
General Motors	111	0.5
Allied	36	1.1
Nabisco Brands	16	0.9

AMONG THE SECOND 100 COMPANIES RANKED BY SALES

Company	Millions of dollars	As percent of net worth
Intl. Harvester	$698	287.4%
Pan American	499	115.5
American Motors	269	131.0
LTV	220	18.9
Armco	179	13.9
Burlington Northern	153	3.6
Republic Steel	149	12.8
Kaiser Aluminum	123	9.9
Trans World Air	84	11.7
Delta	63	7.0
Eastern Airlines	63	20.0
Dana	35	3.1
Esmark	30	2.7

Data: Standard & Poor's Compustat Services, Inc.

PENSION SCOREBOARD

GLOSSARY

Total benefits

The actuarial present value of pension plan benefits promised to present and former employees based on service rendered to date. Total estimated future benefits are adjusted to reflect the time value of money, using an interest discount factor, and the probability of payment because of death, disability, withdrawal, or retirement, between the reporting date and the expected date of payment. Future salary changes are not considered.

Vested benefits

The estimated current legal obligations of the pension plan— and of the company itself—that eventually must be paid even though the employee leaves the company before retirement or the plan is terminated.

Pension assets

The current value of net assets set aside to pay pension benefits.

Vested funding position

The difference between pension assets and vested benefits. A positive number indicates that vested benefits are fully funded as of the latest plan valuation date; a negative number indicates a current underfunding of vested benefits.

Net worth

The aggregate of preferred stock, common stock, capital surplus, and retained earnings.

Assumed rate of return

The interest rate used by the company in calculating the actuarial present value of accumulated plan benefits.

Pension and retirement expense

The cost of all pension plans and profit-sharing retirement plans of the company and consolidated subsidiaries included as an expense on the income statement for the most recent fiscal year.

NR = not reported;   NM = not meaningful

Data: Standard & Poor's Compustat Services Inc.

536

COMPANY

COMPANY	Total benefits $ mil.	Vested benefits $ mil.	Pension assets $ mil.	Vested funding position $ mil.	Change from 1982 $ mil.	Net worth $ mil.	Assumed rate of return (%) 1983	1982	Pension expense $ mil.
Allied	$2398.0	$2222.0	$2186.0	-$36.0	$33.0	$3181.0	8.0	8.0	$201.0
Aluminum Co. of America	1622.3	1500.6	1580.5	79.9	149.7	3227.5	9.7	9.2	159.2
Ame-ada Hess	59.2	54.6	124.8	70.2	10.6	2525.7	9.0	10.0	4.4
Ame-ican Express	277.0	242.0	505.0	263.0	108.0	4044.0	8.5	8.5	48.0
Ame-ican Stores	175.6	161.6	208.0	46.4	19.8	569.8	7.0	7.0	68.3
American Tel. & Tel.	30100.8	26161.3	46380.3	20219.0	5264.6	62284.9	9.9	10.6	2620.2
Anheuser-Busch	299.8	265.6	418.7	153.1	70.5	2052.5	8.5	8.2	74.0
Ashland Oil	216.6	200.7	411.2	210.5	51.6	1428.6	10.1	9.5	22.2
Atlantic Richfield	1592.0	1498.0	1802.0	304.0	195.0	10888.1	8.0	8.0	136.0
Beatrice	275.0	255.0	394.0	139.0	46.3	2028.0	NR	NR	41.0
Bethlehem Steel	3649.0	3527.0	3024.0	-503.0	327.0	1313.1	10.0	10.0	325.8
Boeirg	2270.0	2022.0	2866.0	844.0	155.0	3038.0	8.5	8.5	208.0
CSX	418.0	404.0	461.0	57.0	17.3	4537.3	9.3	11.0	15.0
Caterpillar Tractor	2510.0	2328.0	2502.0	174.0	325.0	3337.0	7.5	7.5	203.0
Charter	13.2	12.6	19.0	6.5	2.5	614.1	8.5	8.5	NR
Chevron	1059.0	1011.0	1413.0	402.0	179.0	14106.0	8.0	8.0	111.0
Chrysler	3480.6	3021.8	2075.2	-946.6	-45.4	1365.3	9.7	10.2	254.7
City Investing	289.0	262.0	337.0	75.0	53.6	1556.0	7.5	7.5	22.0
Coastal	81.3	71.9	140.0	68.1	47.3	634.0	8.0	5.5	4.5
Coca-Cola	209.1	193.1	280.7	87.6	31.1	2920.8	9.5	10.0	39.0
Colga-e-Palmolive	480.9	444.7	577.3	132.5	43.3	1341.7	7.1	6.7	51.5
Columbia Gas System	390.4	382.4	444.6	62.2	29.4	1728.6	8.5	8.5	31.5
Consclidated Edison of N.Y.	1100.0	975.0	1279.0	304.0	219.0	4365.2	6.0	6.0	111.0
Consclidated Foods	167.7	136.2	153.5	17.3	-13.2	935.0	7.0	7.0	32.5
Continental Group	1051.0	988.0	1043.0	55.0	7.0	1781.0	8.5	9.0	80.0

	Total benefits $ mil.	Vested benefits $ mil.	Pension assets $ mil.	Vested funding position $ mil.	Change from 1982 $ mil.	Net worth $ mil.	Assumed rate of return (%)		Pension expense $ mil.
							1983	1982	
Dart & Kraft	661.2	627.5	958.7	331.2	78.0	2922.7	8.0	NR	43.1
Dayton Hudson	177.0	164.9	221.6	56.6	20.3	1540.2	7.0	7.0	7.4
Dow Chemical	1354.0	1106.0	1330.0	224.0	100.0	5047.0	8.0	8.0	123.0
Du Pont	5630.0	5517.0	8182.0	2665.0	−211.0	11472.0	8.9	9.6	556.0
Eastman Kodak	2421.0	2377.0	3536.0	1159.0	226.0	7520.0	9.0	9.0	132.0
Exxon	5454.0	5151.0	7676.0	2525.0	584.0	29443.1	NR	NR	520.0
Fed. Natl. Mortgage Assn.	7.5	5.8	28.4	22.6	3.6	1275.9	7.5	7.5	0.8
Federated Dept. Stores	27.0	24.6	53.6	29.0	7.8	2333.4	9.0	10.0	64.0
Fleming	17.9	15.2	17.4	2.3	−1.8	262.5	NR	NR	8.8
Fluor	113.7	103.5	123.4	19.9	11.2	1747.2	NR	NR	78.9
Ford Motor	8780.3	7390.0	8150.0	760.0	590.0	7545.3	8.0	8.0	642.8
GTE	2900.0	2500.0	4900.0	2400.0	545.0	6785.0	6.0	6.0	336.0
General Dynamics	1234.7	1142.5	1290.6	148.1	−110.6	1260.6	7.0	7.0	117.5
General Electric	8496.0	7939.0	10172.0	2233.0	711.0	11270.0	7.5	7.5	643.0
General Foods	912.6	860.0	1423.7	563.7	320.5	2040.2	7.5	6.5	80.6
General Motors	21399.4	18239.5	18128.0	−111.5	1803.5	20766.6	9.0	10.2	1714.2
Georgia-Pacific	246.0	219.0	267.0	48.0	20.0	2228.0	6.7	6.5	NR
Goodyear Tire & Rubber	1677.9	1552.5	1834.0	281.5	184.2	3016.2	8.5	8.5	108.2
Grace (W.R.)	261.4	246.2	426.0	179.8	44.9	2182.3	6.5	6.5	37.1
Great Atlantic & Pacific Tea	28.5	21.2	380.0	358.8	37.1	375.8	9.5	10.0	18.2
Gulf	1957.0	1885.0	2419.0	534.0	−151.0	10128.0	NR	NR	186.0
Honeywell	983.3	851.6	1116.7	265.1	252.7	2313.7	8.0	8.0	107.3
Household International	314.7	284.5	485.0	200.5	54.5	1602.3	8.0	8.0	46.7
ITT	1857.7	1687.3	1975.4	288.1	114.4	6106.1	9.0	8.9	258.0
Intl. Business Machines	7452.0	7154.0	10388.0	3234.0	1592.0	23219.0	5.5	5.5	1180.0

Company									
InterNorth	146.6	134.0	300.3	166.3	50.0	1946.6	8.0	7.2	14.2
Johnson & Johnson	268.3	245.1	475.1	230.0	114.9	3026.5	8.5	7.5	59.9
K mart	352.0	269.8	475.4	205.6	74.7	2940.1	7.0	7.0	42.2
Kroger	249.8	228.2	299.1	70.9	32.1	1072.9	NR	7.5	118.9
Lockheed	2189.0	2104.0	2905.0	801.0	99.0	847.3	8.4	8.6	152.0
Loews	236.4	200.3	337.5	137.1	15.3	1688.4	NR	9.0	13.8
Lucky Stores	71.8	59.0	77.7	18.7	14.8	591.1	7.0	6.0	64.9
McDonnell Douglas	1873.5	1651.8	2508.7	856.9	370.6	2067.9	8.0	8.0	197.1
Merrill Lynch	283.6	223.9	267.9	44.0	29.2	1888.0	7.0	7.0	43.2
Minnesota Mining & Mfg.	796.0	623.0	989.0	336.0	159.0	3698.0	8.0	8.0	113.0
Mobil	2940.0	2870.0	3191.0	321.0	169.0	13952.0	6.0	6.0	280.0
Monsanto	1641.0	1463.0	1958.0	495.0	164.0	3667.0	7.5	7.5	131.0
Nabisco Brands	491.6	449.3	433.1	-16.2	14.7	1710.8	9.0	9.0	82.5
Occidental Petroleum	166.9	160.8	237.1	76.3	-268.9	4642.0	8.0	NR	31.3
Pacific Gas & Electric	1220.0	1114.0	1211.0	97.0	114.0	6613.7	7.0	7.0	74.0
Penney (J.C.)	422.0	383.0	822.0	439.0	171.0	3559.0	8.5	8.5	35.0
Peps Co	307.9	235.3	361.6	126.3	45.0	1794.2	7.0	7.0	47.7
Phibro-Salomon	44.0	40.0	75.0	35.0	14.0	2240.0	8.0	8.0	8.0
Philip Morris	463.2	388.9	614.8	225.9	67.6	4033.7	7.5	7.5	94.0
Phillips Petroleum	822.0	691.0	1288.0	597.0	215.0	6149.0	NR	NR	33.0
RCA	1552.0	1481.1	1769.3	288.2	178.2	2540.0	7.0	7.0	186.3
Ralston Purina	239.1	206.1	338.1	132.0	32.0	1104.1	6.0	6.0	21.3
Raytheon	777.4	717.0	869.9	152.9	-13.6	1887.4	7.0	NR	85.1
Reynolds (R.J.) Industries	875.0	745.0	1053.0	308.0	66.0	5854.0	8.0	8.0	98.0
Rockwell International	3150.0	2729.0	3423.0	694.0	345.0	2367.3	7.0	7.0	255.5
Safeway Stores	183.7	179.0	410.8	231.8	79.2	1390.4	8.0	8.0	128.6
Sante Fe Southern Pacific	384.7	368.2	544.6	176.4	98.8	5740.8	NR	10.0	27.1
Schlumberger	201.0	201.0	276.0	75.0	14.0	5818.8	7.0	NR	110.0
Sears, Roebuck	1866.3	1726.8	2144.1	417.3	274.6	9786.9	8.0	8.0	446.0
Shell Oil	1230.0	1121.0	1926.0	805.0	108.0	11359.0	9.0	9.5	84.0

	Total benefits $ mil.	Vested benefits $ mil.	Pension assets $ mil.	Vested funding position $ mil.	Change from 1982 $ mil.	Net worth $ mil.	Assumed rate of return (%) 1983	1982	Pension expense $ mil.
Signal	548.0	499.0	701.0	202.0	151.9	2633.0	7.5	7.5	64.0
Southern	540.2	529.9	820.7	290.8	167.6	5195.2	8.0	8.0	58.5
Sperry	945.9	873.9	1258.9	385.0	59.8	2802.9	8.0	8.0	77.4
Standard Oil (Indiana)	1474.0	1434.0	1635.0	201.0	121.0	12440.0	8.0	8.0	129.0
Standard Oil (Ohio)	875.0	812.0	998.0	186.0	76.0	8100.8	8.0	7.0	91.0
Sun	858.0	787.0	1118.0	331.0	96.0	5236.0	9.0	8.0	75.0
Super Valu Stores	23.5	20.6	26.3	5.7	4.5	384.7	9.0	9.0	15.7
TRW	1014.6	937.2	1361.2	424.0	166.9	1616.0	8.5	8.5	112.7
Tenneco	789.0	707.0	901.0	194.0	160.0	6413.0	7.6	7.2	94.0
Texaco	782.0	725.0	1235.0	510.0	41.0	14726.0	9.4	9.8	175.0
Texas Eastern	98.6	88.3	176.1	87.8	26.6	1422.0	9.5	12.5	18.1
UAL	1570.0	1510.0	2510.0	1000.0	205.0	1597.3	9.0	9.4	258.6
Union Carbide	1457.0	1352.0	2176.0	824.0	298.0	4929.0	9.5	10.0	186.0
U.S. Steel	6955.0	6562.0	8479.0	1917.0	1062.0	5605.0	10.0	10.0	319.0
United Technologies	2351.9	2193.1	3255.2	1062.1	178.3	3783.8	7.8	7.7	215.5
Unocal	660.3	629.3	809.4	180.1	59.1	5180.1	7.0	7.0	54.1
Westinghouse Electric	3113.7	2718.9	2975.2	256.3	358.3	3410.3	NR	8.2	119.0
Weyerhaeuser	438.2	417.9	533.5	115.6	41.4	3238.0	9.5	9.5	42.8
Woolworth (F.W.)	338.0	319.0	397.0	78.0	20.0	1030.0	8.0	7.6	14.0
Xerox	1040.9	1031.2	1109.9	78.7	24.7	4664.4	8.0	8.0	153.3
All-company composite	179867.5	162560.9	220165.4	57604.8	20213.5	510588.5	8.1	8.1	172223.7

STOCK OPTIONS

Stock options are used to compensate managers in a way that, in theory, ties their compensation to the performance of the company. There have been tax advantages attaching to this form of compensation, which have had the effect of reducing the employment cost to the company. Owing to a series of legislative amendments, some of the tax advantages have been limited; nevertheless, this method of compensation continues to be popular. The accounting issue relates to measurement. What is the value of the option granted, and, accordingly, what is the cost to the company of the service acquired from the employee? Options and warrants, rights to buy securities at fixed prices over a period of time, are actively and regularly traded in the securities markets; therefore, we are confident that these rights have value. Employee stock options differ from those that are traded, primarily in that they are not transferable and in many cases may not be exercised for a period of time. In substantially all other respects, publicly traded and employee options are similar. Since employee options do not have a market, the accountant's problem is one of determining their value.

The APB required that the compensation implicit employee stock options be measured by the difference between the option price and the market price on the date of the grant. Yet tax law requires the option price to be no lower than the market price if certain tax benefits are to be available to the employee. As a result, most stock options are assigned an accounting value of zero and no employment expense is reported in the determination of net income.

In "Valuation of Stock Option Contracts," Jerry J. Weygandt proposes an avenue for valuing qualified and nonqualified stock options by use of models developed in the option-pricing literature in the fields of finance and economics. Drawing on the pioneering work of Black and Scholes, Weygandt compares three models in order to approximate a value for warrants. He concludes by proposing empirical tests of which of the three models would be most suited to valuing employee stock options.

Valuation of Stock Option Contracts

Jerry J. Weygandt
University of Wisconsin-Madison

One issue that has frustrated accountants for many years is the difficulty of determining the amount of compensation expense, if any, upon issuance of various stock option contracts to key executives. Many individuals had hoped that the recent APB Opinion related to compensation expense [APB Opinion No. 25, 1972] would have provided a solution to this problem. However, in many respects, it may have compounded the issue since authoritative support is given to certain accounting practices that do not appear in accord with economic reality. For example, as a result of *APB Opinion No. 25,* changes in the market price subsequent to the grant date are used as a means to measure compensation expense where the exercise price or the number of shares issued upon exercise is not known at the date of grant. The result of this "generally accepted accounting principle" may be to remove this type of option as a basis for compensating key executives, because a corporation may be concerned that compensation expense could skyrocket if the market price of the stock increased substantially. In addition, even if the exercise price and the number of shares issued are known at the grant date, the amount of compensation expense recorded by corporations using qualified stock option plans is zero. For nonqualified stock options, the compensation cost is only the difference between the fair market value of the stock and the exercise price. Many other illogical situations could be mentioned.[1] As a consequence, one wonders whether our present accounting treatment in this area provides us with reasonable and appropriate solutions to our measurement problems.

Valuing the stock option as the difference between the market value at the date of grant and the option price is considered by most accountants as a valuation that results in an understatement of the value of the option. Stock options represent compensation for services rendered, and, in some cases, such options constitute a considerable portion of total compensation. Certainly an option to buy stock during an extended future period at a fixed price equal to, or even above, today's prices is not worthless. Since there is no risk of loss to the employer and a possibility,

From *The Accounting Review* (January 1977), pp. 40–51. Reprinted by permission of the American Accounting Association.

[1] Examples are the failure to impute a reduction in value in restricted stock option contracts when measuring the difference between fair market value and option price; the recording of compensation expense in most cases when a cash settlement is made in a phantom plan but an adjustment is ignored if stock is issued; and the recording of compensation expense on a buy-out of a stock option contract. See, e.g., Rogers and Schattke [1972] and Simons and Weygandt [1973].

if not a probability, for great gains exists, the option should possess value that is greater than the spread between the option price and the market value of the stock at the date of grant.

The purpose of this paper is to explore the possibility of using approaches suggested in the finance and economics literature to value stock options at the date of grant. Specifically, by examining the various warrant pricing formulas developed in the recent literature, it is hoped that ultimately a more appropriate valuation can be established for the value of a stock option contract at the date of grant.[2]

SUGGESTED VALUATION APPROACHES

Two approaches are suggested in the accounting literature for valuing stock options at the date of grant[3] at an amount other than the difference between the market price of the stock and the option price. The first [Sweeney, 1960] argues that corporations grant stock options as a substitute for cash compensation. He also proposes that an appropriate method for determining the cost of this substitute compensation involves establishing the total worth of the employee's services to the firm and then allocating a portion to compensation expense each period. The stock option contract is seen as comprising two separate but interrelated transactions: (1) a compensation agreement in which part of the total cash value of the employee's services is paid in cash and (2) a subscription by the employee to a specified number of shares, with investment during the option period of services and a final payment in cash. The employee is thus in a position similar to the investor providing assets (cash) to the corporation in return for stock, except that s/he receives the right to purchase stock at some future time in return for the services provided. The argument that dilution of stockholder equity occurs when shares are purchased for less than market value is countered by

---

[2] For purposes of analysis, the discussion in the remainder of this paper will be limited to nonqualified and qualified stock option plans. Other compensation plans such as restricted stock plans or deferred (phantom) stock plans are not considered, but some of the discussion in subsequent parts of this paper has relevance to these types of plans. Furthermore, it should be noted that the most unusual or complex situations related to option contracts are ignored, such as subsequent increases or decreases in the exercise price after the grant date. Nonqualified stock options offer certain advantages over qualified stock options and have increased in popularity. See, e.g., Louis [1970]. Their major advantages are that they can be effective for any number of years, can be offered at less than fair value, can be treated as a deductible expense for tax purposes by the corporation and are not considered a tax preference item to recipient. Qualified stock options have lost many of their advantages because of the new tax laws, although 49 percent of all large U.S. corporations still use them [*Dun's Review,* February 1974]. A qualified stock option has the following characteristics:

1 Option price must be at least 100 percent of the fair market value of the stock at the time the option is granted.

2 Qualified options by their terms must expire within 5 years from date of grant.

3 Qualified options must be granted within 10 years after the date of adoption of the plan or stockholder approval, whichever is earlier.

4 The stock must be held 3 years from the date the employee acquires the stock in order to qualify for capital gain treatment.

[3] It should be noted that ARB37 (revised) first introduced the grant date. Prior to this point, the entitlement date was considered correct. We are assuming that the grant date is the appropriate measurement date. See, e.g., Dohr [1945]. Some also argue for total nonrecognition—e.g., Dean [1953] and Vatter [1966].

the assertion that the employee is *not* investing less than market value. S/he is merely investing part of his or her consideration in the form of services.

Another approach suggests that the problem be viewed from the standpoint of a corporation granting a marketable *warrant* for shares at a specified price for a given period of time rather than granting a nontransferable employee stock option. Campbell [1961] contended that the problem is similar to that facing the board of directors and financial executives when determining the price for a new issue of stock or debt. Armed with certain subjective data, such as past and projected earnings, dividends and price earnings ratios, as well as economic conditions, it is contended that the accountant can establish a value range for the option. One writer [May, 1961], agreed with Campbell's proposal set forth, although from a different perspective, noting that a relevant surrogate is available in the put and call market regulated by the SEC. Thus, both of these writers point the way in their analyses to an empirical search for a surrogate measure of value for employee stock options. This paper will examine the feasibility of the latter approach. As indicated in the previous section, examination of the theory of warrant pricing provides some interesting insights into the valuing of stock options contracts used as a basis for compensation.

UNDERSTANDING THE WARRANT CONTRACT

To understand warrant analysis, one must have a basic understanding of the following terms. The exercise or option price is the amount required to obtain one share of common. If a difference exists between the selling price of the common and the exercise price at any point, the difference is defined as intrinsic value (never lower than zero). The excess of the warrant price over intrinsic value is defined as the premium (never lower than zero). For example, assume that a company's warrants are selling for $10, the related common stock is selling for $40 and the exercise price for the warrant is $30. In this case, the intrinsic value is $10 and the premium is 0.

It is apparent that the higher the price of the common, the higher the price of the warrant. As the price of the common increases, the likelihood of the warrant being exercised increases. Conversely, the more the price of common falls, the more likely it is that the warrant will not be exercised.

The length of life of the warrant also plays a significant role. Conceptually, the longer the maturity of the warrant, the more valuable is its option. As the maturity date arrives, the instrument will sell for no more or less than its intrinsic value. Figure 1 illustrates the valuation of warrants at various exercise dates.

Line MO represents the maximum value of an option which, in this diagram, is the price of the stock, assuming that the stock acquisition requires nothing other than the warrant. Line MS represents the intrinsic value of the option, since its price never can be lower than zero. Lines T_1, T_2, and T_3 represent different maturity dates of 9, 5 and 1 years, respectively. For example, if the warrant had a perpetual life and the stock were non-dividend paying, the value of the warrant would be the same as the value of the stock[4] [Samuelson, 1965; Samuelson and Merton, 1969; Black and

---

[4]The reason is that the discounted present value of the exercise price is zero at infinity. The stock must be assumed nondividend-paying, or an additional value would be attributable to the stock over and

Scholes, 1973]. It then follows that the closer the exercise date, the closer the warrant's price is to the intrinsic value so that, at the date of exercise, the warrant's price and intrinsic value are the same. It also follows that, holding the maturity date constant, changes in the price of the stock will cause changes in the value of the warrant.

A number of writers have attempted to develop conceptual warrant valuation models that are representative of the true value of the warrant at any point in time [Black and Scholes, 1973; Chen, 1970; Merton, 1973; Samuelson and Merton, 1969]. In addition, other factors, such as volatility of the common stock price, the dividend yield and the interest rate, are considered.

FIGURE 1   Valuation of warrant at different exercise dates

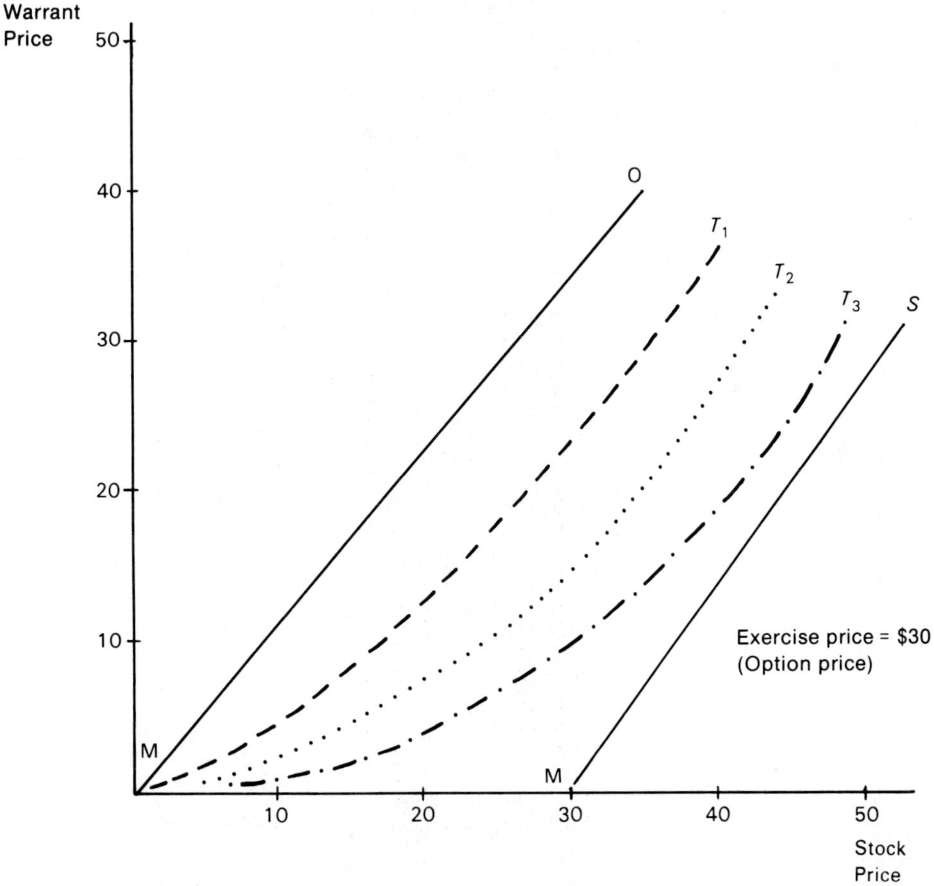

above the value of the warrant. For an analytical solution to this problem, see [Merton, 1973]. It should be noted that in practice the few perpetual warrants do not sell at the price of the common because the assumption of no dividend payment on the common stock is unrealistic.

CONCEPTUAL MODELS

Most of the work in the finance and economics literature related to warrant pricing was stimulated by Samuelson's [1965] original work. He assumed that a warrant must be priced to earn some constant expected return per unit of time (denoted as β), greater than or equal to the expected return per unit of time on the stock (denoted as α), with β given exogenously.[5] A geometric Brownian motion in the probability of stock prices is assumed. Then, given β, a specific relationship between the warrant price and the price of the underlying stock at a given length of time remaining in the life of the warrant can be achieved. In other words, Samuelson assumes that the price distribution is lognormally distributed and that the change in the price of the common stock will be a function of the time horizon. The longer the time horizon, the greater the probability of a larger price increase; or, more precisely, Samuelson shows mathematically that the Kruizenga [1964] formula holds in the short run—that the value of a warrant grows proportionally with the square root of time remaining before elapsing but that, as elapsed time approaches infinity, the value of the warrant approaches the value of the stock.

The problem with the Samuelson formulation is that a closed form expression (an analytical solution) is available only for a perpetual warrant situation, since a finite time case would require mathematics that presently is not developed. Also, the model is difficult to test empirically because the β factor is given exogenously to the model and is not observable. In addition, the assumption of a constant rate of return on the warrant is open to question, because, on intuition alone, the required return on the warrant should be a function of the stock price and the time remaining. This analysis suggests that the risk level on the warrant, and hence its return, should change over time.[6]

In a path-breaking paper, Black and Scholes (B&S) [1973] developed a model that was empirically testable—unlike the earlier works by Samuelson and by Samuelson and Merton. Black and Scholes assume that a perfect hedge can be created such that the return earned on a combination of long in the stock and short in the warrants will lead to a return equal to the risk-free rate of return. To illustrate this concept, assume that an investor purchases common stock for $50 and shorts a certain number of warrants for $20, so that the net investment at this point is $30. Given that this situation is a perfect hedge, the best the investor could earn on this $30 is the risk-free rate of return, since the investor has no risk. The relationship between the stock and the warrants obviously changes over time so that, at any point in time, it may take more or less than one warrant to one share of stock to maintain this hedge. Thus B&S can determine the price for the warrant by having, at any point in time, a measure of the volatility of the stock, the expiration time, the risk-free rate, the stock price and the exercise price. Each of these attributes (unlike the Samuelson model) is observable directly and, therefore, lends itself to empirical testing. The formulation for the B&S model is as follows:

---

[5]Samuelson and others argue that (β) must be greater than (α) because (1) warrants are not adjusted for dividend payments from the common stock and (2) warrants are more price-volatile than the price of the common stock and a risk-averse warrant holder will demand a higher return. [See Chen, 1970].

[6]See also a subsequent paper [Samuelson and Merton, 1969] which incorporates the investor's individual utility function but fails to answer the problems of the previous Samuelson paper.

$$w = xN(d_1) - ce^{-rt^*} N(d_2)$$

where w = the price of a warrant for a single share of stock

x = the current price of the stock

c = the striking price (exercise price) of the warrant

r = the short-term rate of interest

t^* = the duration of the warrant

$$d_1 = \frac{\ln(x/c) + (r + 1/2\sigma^2)t^*}{\sigma\sqrt{t^*}}$$

$$d_2 = d_1 - \sigma\sqrt{t^*}$$

$N(d)$ = the value of the cumulative normal density function

σ^2 = the variance of the rate of return

The B&S model assumes that:

1 The short-term interest rate is known and constant through time.

2 The stock price follows a random walk in continuous time with a variance rate proportional to the square of the stock price. Thus, the distribution of possible stock prices at the end of any finite interval is lognormal. The variance of the rate of the return on the stock is constant.

3 The stock pays no dividends or other distributions.

4 The warrant is "European"; i.e., it can only be exercised at maturity.

5 There are no transaction costs in buying or selling the stock or the warrant.

6 It is possible to borrow, at the short-term rate, any fraction of the price of a security to buy it or to hold it.

7 There are no penalties for short selling. A seller who does not own a security simply will accept the price of the security from a buyer and will agree to settle with the buyer on some future date by paying him or her an amount equal to the price of the security on that date [Black and Scholes, 1973, p. 460].

Although these assumptions are limiting to the extent that Black and Scholes assume a constant variance rate over time and do not include dividends in their formula, remember that accountants are only looking for an approximation of the warrant value and, thus, do not need the preciseness that an option buyer and seller must have.

EXAMINATION OF EMPIRICAL WORK

The empirical work in this area substantially validates the theoretical work of Samuelson and Black and Scholes in that the same variables were found to influence the price of the warrants. One could expect that the price of the warrant would be a function of the exercise price, the price of the associated common stock, the length of time to expiration of the warrant, the volatility of the stock price, the dividend paid on the common and the interest rate. One major study was performed by Van Horne [1969], in which he used two sets of regression studies to test whether these relationships held. The first involved a cross-sectional sample of practically all warrants listed on the American Stock Exchange. Van Horne found, as expected, that the most important component of a warrant's price was the common stock price. The length of time to expiration, the volatility and the dividend variable all had the right sign. The length of time to expiration and the volatility factor were considered significant. Van Horne's regression formula is as follows:

$$P_w/\alpha_w = -.601 + .900 \ (P_s/\chi)_w$$
$$-.941(1/t) + .184(v)$$
$$-.011(\text{Div}/\chi_s) + \mu$$

where P_w/χ_w = market price of the warrant over the exercise price
$\quad\quad\quad P_s/\chi_w$ = market price of the stock over the exercise price
$\quad\quad\quad\quad t$ = length of time to expiration expressed in months
$\quad\quad\quad\quad v$ = volatility (difference between high and low price of preceding year divided by the average price)
$\quad\text{Div}/\chi_s$ = current dividend per share to the total exercise price

The second part of the study involved a regression study using time series analysis. Three perpetual warrants were selected as a basis for this analysis, because the intent was to hold constant the effect of length of time to expiration. In this study, three variables were used in an attempt to explain the price of the warrant: the common stock price, the volatility factor and a rate used to describe the value of funds to investors.[7]

As expected, the price of the stock is significant and is the major reason for the price of the warrant. The results also show that volatility is important and that the greater the volatility, the higher the price of the warrant. In addition, the study indicates that the value of the funds has some significance.

Black and Scholes [1972] also tested their model to determine whether an accurate assessment of actual warrant prices could be predicted. They found that using past data to estimate the variance factor (volatility) caused the model to overprice options on high price-variance stocks and underprice options on low price-variance stocks. It was noted that, while the model tends to overestimate the value of an option on a high variance security, market traders tend to underestimate the value. On the other hand, the model tends to underestimate the value of an option on a low variance security, whereas market traders tend to overestimate the value.

In another study, Shelton [1967] essentially established a zone of plausible prices for warrants as follows: the lower boundary of an option price is the difference between the price of the common and the option price (the option's intrinsic value). If the warrant sold below the intrinsic value, obviously arbitrage would ensue and bid up the price of the warrant. It should be observed that this lower limit has been well-established in the finance literature, and no controversy exists concerning its validity. The more controversial and more useful part of Shelton's analysis, however, related to the ceiling that is set on warrant prices. In general, this aspect of warrant

---

[7] Van Horne reasoned that the greater the value of funds to the investor, the more likely one will prefer the warrant to the stock because the warrant involves less of an investment.

pricing had received little consideration, except to document the fact that the warrant price would not exceed its intrinsic value at the maturity date and that the warrant would not sell for more than the common at any time.

An important finding by Shelton was the fact that the warrant price will equal its intrinsic value generally whenever the common sells for at least four times its exercise value. The reason for this is that once a stock reaches such a value in relation to the warrant, a change in either the price of the stock or the warrant provides little proportional gain relative to one another because they are so high-priced. Secondly, it is highly probable that the common is paying a dividend; and, given the minimum leverage factor available at high prices, it seems unlikely that the warrant price will be higher than its intrinsic value.[8]

Summarizing, then, we find from Shelton that

$$(P_s - P_o) < P_w < \tfrac{3}{4} P_s \text{ if } P_s < 4(P_o) \quad P_w = (P_s - P_o) \text{ if } P_s \geqslant 4(P_o)$$

where P_s = price of the stock
  P_w = price of the warrant
  P_o = option (exercise) price.

This valuation formula by itself does not provide the final answer to the valuation of stock options, but it does provide a zone of plausible prices. The problem becomes much more difficult at this point, because there is a need to find the value of the warrant within the zone of plausible prices. Shelton, using multiple regression analysis, developed the following formulation for warrant valuation:

$$X = \sqrt[4]{\frac{M}{72}}(.47 - 4.25Y + .17L)(A - B) + B$$

where M = the remaining life of the warrant in months (60 months or less for a qualified stock option),
  A = the maximum value of the warrant calculated at 75 percent of the current market price,
  B = the minimum value of the warrants (which cannot be less than zero), calculated by subtracting the exercise price from the current market price,
  Y = the dividend yield of the common stock, and
  L = a symbol of whether the warrant is listed on the American Stock Exchange.

Where does this leave us? The conceptual and empirical work related to warrant pricing has a great deal of consistency in defining the attributes that comprise the

---

[8]It is interesting to note that Shelton's subsequent empirical analysis verifies this statement, and a number of conceptual and empirical studies seem to validate his results. For example, Samuelson [1965] Kassouf and Giguiere [1965] essentially argue independently that the value of the warrant falls in the zone of plausible prices.

price of the warrant. At this point, it is necessary to apply what we know and attempt at least a first step toward developing appropriate values for stock option contracts.

To illustrate, we have developed a price for two hypothetical warrants, choosing two stocks from the New York Stock Exchange: American Telephone and Telegraph and Polaroid. These two stocks provide an interesting perspective, since the price of one stock is stable and the other is volatile.

The information in the tables on page 552 is pertinent.

The values as of 12/31/73 shown on the following page would be computed for the warrants by using the models mentioned earlier: Note that these values are fairly uniform. Although determination of an exact price would be an impossibility, a reasonable assessment of the value of a warrant appears possible. It is interesting to note that the B & S model is, in both cases, higher than the Van Horne or Shelton calculations. This is not surprising because: (1) B & S in their empirical analysis indicate that their model tends to overestimate the value of an option on a high variance security, thereby possibly explaining the Polaroid case and (2) B & S's formulation does not consider dividends, which, at least in the Shelton model, take on great significance, thereby possibly explaining the American Telephone and Telegraph situation.

It should be remembered that this paper is concerned only with nonqualified and qualified stock option plans and does not consider cases such as those in which the exercise price is not known at the date of grant or in which the exercise price changes over time.[10] In addition, the results obtained above directly relate to the valuation of nonqualified stock option plans whose characteristics are essentially the same as those modeled by B & S, Van Horne and Shelton. As indicated in the subsequent sections, additional problems exist related to qualified stock option contracts, which, at present, provide some difficulty.

It is obvious that any substantive conclusions at this point, however, would be tenuous. What appears to be needed is a number of empirical tests to ascertain whether the models presented in this paper will provide a reasonable figure for calculating the option price so that an appropriate cost for compensation expense can be computed. If a consistency can be found among these valuation approaches, or others to be developed, then a set of tables could be developed for the accountant as an aid in finding the proper compensation cost figures.

ADDITIONAL PROBLEMS RELATED TO QUALIFIED STOCK OPTIONS

Qualified stock options have some characteristics that would seem to reduce their value below that of a normal warrant. For example, (1) qualified stock options are

---

[9]We assumed the data for the B & S model [found on page 552] to be: short-term rate of interest 8 percent; variance of the rate of return computed on a 3-year, monthly basis; duration of option is 5 years. All other assumptions related to the models are evident from the formulas presented earlier. As indicated in footnote 2, a nonqualified option can have any length of life, whereas a qualified stock option plan must expire within 5 years.

[10]These problems, however, probably can be modeled, at least for nondividend-paying stocks. For example, if the stock is nondividend-paying and the exercise price is decreasing, the final exercise price

nontransferable and, as a result, cannot be traded like warrants; (2) after the option is exercised, the common stock must be held for 3 years to qualify for capital gains treatment; and (3) the employee, if s/he terminates employment before expiration of the warrant, loses the possible benefits.[11]

A number of approaches can be suggested to resolve this problem. One is simply to ignore these particular features of qualified stock option plans on the basis that any calculation is subjective and, to be conservative, a higher value for the option and, thus, a lower income figure is presented. This is somewhat akin to the issue that the APB faced when handling restricted stock options in *APB Opinion No. 25*. In this situation, they chose to ignore the discount attributed to any restriction on the basis that its determination was a matter of opinion and could not be evaluated objectively. This proposal appears to have little theoretical merit.

A second proposal is to ascribe a proper reduction in value to these features. Such a proposal would not be easy to implement. It is highly unlikely that conditions such as the three mentioned could be modeled easily. However, other avenues appear to exist that might be examined as a basis for ascertaining the reduction in value, if any, that occurs. One such approach is to determine what types of cash tradeoffs a corporate executive makes when s/he receives options versus cash compensation. For example, an executive may take ten extra options in lieu of

---

should be used. If the exercise price is increasing, given a nondividend-paying stock, the warrant holder makes an assessment of the cost and benefits associated with early exercise (higher interest costs) versus exercise at maturity (higher exercise price). For dividend-paying stocks, some assumptions related to price growth, coupled with dividend payments and interest charges are appropriate.

[11] It should be noted that the nontransferability feature is probably not significant, since the beneficial rights under the option can be sold. The market has developed techniques of trading such beneficial rights under any circumstances. See, e.g., a research study conducted for the Investment Bankers Association that addressed this exact question: *Federal Income Taxation of Compensatory Options (Including Warrants) Granted to Underwriters and Other Independent Contractors* (1963). The IBA study found that deferred transferability features had little effect on the valuation of eighty-seven warrants studied. The Investment Bankers study is interesting for other reasons as well. Their study focused on options granted to independent contractors (underwriters, etc.) rather than to employees; their purpose was to present evidentiary proof to the Internal Revenue Service that options granted to independent contractors could be valued at the date of grant.

Regression equations were derived for each of eighty-seven warrants examined. For purposes of comparability, ratios were used instead of absolute prices. The following schedule summarizes the major findings concerning the fluctuations of the market price of the underlying stock from the exercise price and the accompanying fluctuations in the market value of the option:

Ratio of market value of optioned stock to exercise price	Ratio of market value of option to exercise price
80%	28%
90%	34%
100%	41%
110%	48%
120%	55%

An option at least 2 years from exercise was found to sell at approximately 41 percent of exercise price when the market price of its related common stock was at parity with (equal to) the exercise price. A powerful relationship exists between warrant prices and common stock prices; the length of time before expiration is also a significant factor.

The IBA concluded that an experienced appraiser could establish a value for most options, within a reasonable range of perhaps 15 percent, using the guidelines determined in the study. It should be noted that their study is remarkably consistent with the models developed in this paper.

	Range 1973	Closing price 1973	Dividend	Exercise price	Market price (at date of grant)
American Telephone and Telegraph	45⅜ to 55	50¾	$3.08	48	48
Polaroid	65⅛ to 143½	70¼	.32	100	100

	American Telephone and Telegraph		Polaroid	
	Warrant price	% of common stock price	Warrant price	% of common stock price
Black and Scholes	$15.36	(32%)	$49.00	(49%)
Van Horne	15.31	(31.90%)	42.20	(42.2%)
Shelton	12.73	(27%)	42.28	(42%)

$5,000 more in cash compensation; and this choice might help to identify the amount of the cash tradeoff. This amount could be developed from a number of different sources, e.g., from the board of directors, the executive and from compensation materials that provide information as to the pay scale for executive level positions in given industries with given sales levels. Such amounts then could be compared to the general valuation model developed to determine the amount of the reduction in value, if any, that should occur. Another approach might be to examine the market for letter stock, since many characteristics of a qualified option plan are incorporated in these types of transactions. For example, the discount feature related to letter stock may provide some basis for application to qualified stock option plans as well [Jaenicke, 1970]. Efforts in this direction seem worthwhile, for the alternative is to ignore these features altogether (as mentioned above) or simply to set some arbitrary percentage reduction.

CONCLUDING REMARKS

The purpose of this paper was to argue that the accounting profession should investigate further the possibilities of recording compensation expense at the date of grant differently than under present generally accepted accounting principles.[12] The economics and finance literature provides evidence that option contracts can be valued, although an exact evaluation formula still is not devised. However, the literature is remarkably consistent with respect to the variables to consider and the range of values that are appropriate for a given set of conditions. Although an exact figure probably never can be known for any option, it is reasonable to assume that the value for an option can be approximated with a high degree of confidence. In the case of nonqualified stock options, it would seem that the models provide a good answer to our valuation problems. Qualified stock option plans, on the other hand, involve more variables; and it appears that additional research is needed to model their restrictive components.

We are the first to agree that much empirical testing of our approach should be performed before the new model is employed. Empirical validation can be accomplished rather rapidly, however, if resources are directed towards resolution of this issue.

REFERENCES

American Institute of Certified Public Accountants, Accounting Principles Board, "Accounting or Stock Issued to Employees," *Accounting Principles Board No. 25* (1972).
———Committee on Accounting Procedure, "Accounting for Compensation Involved in a Stock Option and Stock Purchase Plans," *Accounting Research Bulletin No. 37* (1953).
Black, Fischer and Myron Scholes, "The Valuation of Option Contracts and a Test of Market Efficiency," *The Journal of Finance* (May 1972), pp. 399–417.

[12] This study has additional significance from another point as well. The Treasury Department recently indicated that one item to be reviewed soon is whether a taxable event occurs when a stock option is granted. This statement may have been prompted by the fact that the Phase 2 Pay Board arbitrarily assigned a value to an option contract of 25 percent of the market value of the stock at the date of the grant. See [Hultar, 1973].

————and Myron Scholes, "The Pricing of Options and Corporate Liabilities," *The Journal of Political Economy* (May-June 1973), pp. 637–653.

Campbell, Edwin D., "Stock Options Should be Valued," *Harvard Business Review* (July-August 1961), pp. 52–58.

Chen, Andrew H. Y., "A Model of Warrant Pricing in a Dynamic Market," *Journal of Finance* (December 1970), pp. 1041–1060.

Dean, Arthur, "Employee Stock Options," *Harvard Business Review* (1953).

Dohr, James L., "Accounting for Compensation in the Form of Stock Options," *The Journal of Accountancy* (December 1945).

Federal Income Taxation of Compensatory Options (Including Warrants) Granted to Underwriters and Other Independent Contractors (Investment Bankers Association, 1963).

Hultar, Robert M., "Trends in Executive Compensation," *The Financial Executive* (November 1973), pp. 78–86.

Jaenicke, Henry R., "Accounting for Restricted Stock Plans and Deferred Stock Plans," *The Accounting Review* (January 1970), p. 119.

Kruizenga, R. J., "Put and Call Options: A Theoretical and Market Analysis" (Ph.D. diss., M.I.T., 1956).

————"Introduction to the Option Contract," in P. H. Cootner, ed., *The Random Character of Stock Market Prices* (M.I.T. Press, 1964).

Kassouf, S. T., "A Theory and an Econometric Model for Common Stock Purchase Warrants (Ph.D. diss., Columbia University, 1965).

Louis, Arthur M., "Hidden Jokers in the New Tax Deck," *Fortune* (July 1970).

May, Wilfred A., "Letter to the Editor," *Harvard Business Review* (November-December 1961), pp. 27–35.

Merton, Robert C., "Theory of Rational Option Pricing," *Bell Journal of Economics and Management Science* (Spring 1973), pp. 141–181.

Rogers, R. Donald and R. W. Schattke, "Buyouts of Stock Options: Compensation or Capital?" *The Journal of Accountancy* (August 1972), pp. 55–59.

Samuelson, Paul A., "Rational Theory of Warrant Pricing," *Industrial Management Review* (Spring 1965), pp. 13–31.

————and Robert C. Merton, "A Complete Model of Warrant Pricing that Maximizes Utility," *Industrial Management Review* (Winter 1969), pp. 17–46.

Shelton, John P., "The Relation of the Price of a Warrant to the Price of its Associated Stock," *Financial Analysts Journal* (July-August 1967), pp. 88–89.

Simons, Donald and Jerry J. Weygandt, "Stock Options Revisited—Accounting for Stock Buy-outs," *The CPA Journal* (August 1973).

Sweeney, Daniel L., "Accounting for Stock Options," *Michigan Business Studies* (1960).

Van Horne, James C., "Warrant Valuation in Relation to Volatility and Opportunity Costs," *Industrial Management Review* (Spring 1969), pp. 17–32.

Vatter, William J., "Corporate Stock Equities," in M. Backer, ed., *Modern Accounting Theory* (Prentice-Hall, 1966).

SECTION SEVEN N

ACCOUNTING CHANGES

The comparability of financial reports between accounting periods is considered to be essential to a reasonable understanding of the activities of an enterprise over time. Indeed, the auditor attests to the fact that the accounting principles employed during the periods covered by the financial statements have been applied consistently. Since there is a general assumption that accounting methods have been and will be applied consistently, when this is not the case there is need for full disclosure that a change in accounting method has occurred. The change in method could affect the income of the period, the carrying value of assets, the owners' equity and/or the liabilities. In short, the change may have a material effect on the financial statements for the current and future years. The change diminishes the value of comparative statements. The accountant is therefore concerned about how to disclose the change as well as the impact which the change will have on comparability between time periods.

When the APB issued Opinion No. 20 in 1971, six of its 18 members dissented. One's difficulty in understanding sections of the Opinion is probably related to the trade-offs that had to be made within the Board in order to arrive at a version that would garner the necessary two-thirds approval for passage. In the Opinion, the Board distinguishes between a change in accounting principle, a change in an estimate, a change in the entity, and corrections of errors. The Opinion describes in some detail the disclosures required to report the circumstances surrounding the change and the effect which the change has on the financial statements.

In their article, "Reporting Changes in Accounting Principles—Time for a Change?," D. Jacque Grinnell and Corine T. Norgaard argue that existing requirements for reporting changes in accounting principles are inadequate. They criticize the "cumulative effect" and "prospective application" methods of accounting for such changes as being disruptive of the year-to-year comparability so essential in financial statements. The authors' preference is for retroactive application. Their argument is that present standards do not even reflect any general principles of disclosure for such changes but instead are an amalgam of arbitrary rules that may not serve the reader of financial statements very well. It is interesting that the authors' policy recommendation—namely, that retroactive application is the best method for reflecting changes in accounting principle, whether voluntary or mandatory—accords with the view expressed by three of the six dissenting Board members in APB Opinion No. 20.

Reporting Changes in Accounting Principles— Time for a Change?

D. Jacque Grinnell
The University of Vermont

Corine T. Norgaard
University of Connecticut

A change in an accounting principle used by a reporting entity may significantly affect financial statement measurements and other related accounting data. Proper interpretation of financial data may be difficult, and the comparability of such data diminished, without adequate accounting and disclosure of the effects of such a change. The objective of reporting the effects of a change in an accounting principle should be to enhance understanding and interpretation of the change.

The adequacy of the current system of reporting the effects of changes in accounting principles has been questioned by the accounting standards executive committee of the American Institute of CPAs. In a letter to the Financial Accounting Standards Board, AcSEC called for a reconsideration of those provisions of Accounting Principles Board Opinion No. 20, *Accounting Changes*.[1] The purpose of this article is to analyze and evaluate the current reporting requirements for accounting principle changes in order to determine whether alternative practices should be adopted.

BACKGROUND

Current treatment of a change in accounting principle is governed by whether the change is voluntary (made at the discretion of management) or mandatory (necessi-

---

From *The Journal of Accountancy* (December 1979), pp. 64–72. Reprinted by permission of the American Institute of Public Accountants. Copyright © 1979 by the American Institute of Certified Public Accountants, Inc.
    [1]Letter from Raymond C. Lauver, chairman, Accounting Standards Executive Committee, to Marshall S. Armstrong, chairman, Financial Accounting Standards Board, March 25, 1977.

tated by a pronouncement of an authoritative body). In the first case, the manner in which the change is reported is governed by APB Opinion No. 20.[2] In the second case, the appropriate treatment is prescribed by each specific pronouncement.

Voluntary Changes

Opinion No. 20 requires that, in general, the change's cumulative effect on retained earnings for years prior to the year of change be computed and reported as part of the change year's income. Pro forma income calculations, together with related earnings per share data, must be disclosed for all periods presented as if the newly adopted accounting principle had been applied retroactively. Disclosure of the new principle's effect on the change year's income and earnings per share must also be made.

Opinion No. 20 cited three specific exceptions to the general cumulative effect treatment, and it requires, for these cases, retroactive application of the new principle through restatement of the financial statements of prior periods.[3] The APB justified these exceptions to the general cumulative effect treatment by stating that certain changes in accounting principles are such that the advantages of retroactive application outweigh the disadvantages. In these cases, the effect of the new principle on income and earnings per share of the change year and of all prior years for which income statements are presented must be disclosed.

In addition, Opinion No. 20 recognized that, in some cases, the cumulative effect may not be determinable, and it cited, as an example, the change in inventory costing from the Fifo to the Lifo method. The prescribed treatment of changes of this type is to disclose the effect of the change on income and earnings per share of the change year and to explain the reasons for omitting the cumulative income effect and pro forma income and per share data for prior years.

In still other cases, while the total cumulative effect on prior years' income is determinable, the identification of the effect with specific prior years may not be possible due to lack of adequate information. An example cited in Opinion No. 20 concerns changing from the completed contract to the percentage-of-completion method of accounting for long-term contracts. In such cases, the reasons for not showing pro forma information for prior years should be disclosed.

Mandatory Changes

APB Opinions.   The accounting and reporting requirements of Opinion No. 20 do not extend to certain accounting principle changes made to implement recommendations of specialized industry pronouncements of the AICPA or to mandatory accounting principle changes made to conform with APB opinions and FASB statements of financial accounting standards.

---

[2] Accounting Principles Board Opinion no. 20, *Accounting Changes* (New York: AICPA, 1971).

[3] The three cases cited are (1) a change from Lifo to another inventory costing method, (2) a change in accounting for long term construction projects and (3) a change to or from the "full cost" method used by extractive industries. See APB Opinion No. 20, par. 27.

When APB Opinion No. 20 was issued in 1971, it permitted AICPA industry audit guides, which dealt with auditing procedures and accounting practices for specialized industries, to prescribe methods of reporting the effects of changing to recommended principles applicable to these specialized industries.[4] Subsequently, the AICPA issued a new series of specialized industry accounting guides, with each guide specifying the manner of reporting the effects of accounting principle changes to conform with its recommendations. The industry accounting guide series has now been replaced by statements of position concerning specialized industry accounting practices. The FASB has issued Interpretation No. 20, *Reporting Accounting Changes Under AICPA Statements of Position,* which states

> For purposes of applying *APB Opinion No. 20,* an enterprise making a change in accounting principle to conform with the recommendations of an AICPA statement of position shall report the change as specified in the statement. If an AICPA statement of position does not specify the manner of reporting a change in accounting principle to conform with its recommendations, an enterprise making a change in accounting principle to conform with the recommendations of the statement shall report the change as specified by Opinion No. 20.[5]

The general policy of the APB was that its opinions, unless otherwise stated, were intended to be applied prospectively, not retroactively. This general policy did not necessarily rule out retroactive application at the election of the accounting entity. For example, Opinion No. 11, *Accounting for Income Taxes,* stated that "the Board recognizes that companies may apply this Opinion retroactively to periods prior to the effective date to obtain comparability in financial presentations for the current and future periods."[6]

In other instances, the APB did rule out retroactive application by provision in the specific opinion. For example, Opinion No. 8, *Accounting for the Cost of Pension Plans,* stated that "the effect of any changes in accounting methods made as a result of the issuance of this Opinion should be applied prospectively... and not retroactively by an adjustment of retained earnings or otherwise."[7] Similar prohibitions of retroactive application are provided in several other opinions.

In still other cases, the APB prohibited the prospective approach by specifically calling for retroactive application. Examples include APB Opinion No. 18, *The Equity Method of Accounting for Investments in Common Stock,* and two related opinions, Nos. 23 and 24, dealing with income tax considerations. In Opinion No. 23, as well as No. 24, the APB stated that "the conclusions of the Board... represent a clarification of current practice" and "accordingly, this Opinion should be applied retroactively...."[8] In elaborating, the board stated further that "adjustment resulting

---

[4]Ibid., par. 4.

[5]FASB Interpretation No. 20, *Reporting Accounting Changes Under AICPA Statements of Position* (Stamford, Conn.: FASB, 1977), par. 5.

[6]Accounting Principles Board Opinion No. 11, *Accounting for Income Taxes* (New York: AICPA, 1967), par. 67.

[7]Accounting Principles Board Opinion No. 8, *Accounting for the Cost of Pension Plans* (New York: AICPA, 1966), par. 49.

[8]Accounting Principles Board Opinion No. 23, *Accounting for Income Taxes—Special Areas* (New York: AICPA, 1972), par. 32.

from a change in accounting method to comply with this Opinion should be treated as an adjustment of prior periods, and financial statements presented for the periods affected should be restated."[9]

In short, all the APB opinions call for either prospective or retroactive application of the provisions, or permit either. In no case, either with respect to opinions issued prior or subsequent to Opinion No. 20, did the APB stipulate the use of the cumulative effect method for implementing a mandated accounting principle change.

FASB Statements.   The method of transition to conform with new requirements is prescribed by each specific statement. The statements selected for comparison in this article are those which are concerned with financial statement measurement alternatives as opposed to mere disclosure of information or statement classification. In cases where changes in accounting measurement principles are mandated, three basic transition methods exist as potential choices for implementing the changes: retroactive application through prior period restatement; prospective application; and the cumulative effect method in accordance with APB Opinion No. 20. All three transition methods have been selected at various times, although retroactive application has been the dominant choice. Further, the choice of transition method has frequently been changed between exposure draft and final statement.

Only once, in the case of Statement No. 5, *Accounting for Contingencies,* was the cumulative effect method prescribed in a final statement as the basis for implementing a mandated accounting principle change. However, in Statement No. 11, *Accounting for Contingencies—Transition Method,* the FASB reversed its position and displaced the cumulative effect method by requiring a modified retroactive application approach for implementing Statement No. 5. The FASB stated that the decision to change the transition method was reached after a "reconsideration of all the circumstances."[10] However, the change was brought about primarily, it would appear, because of inconsistencies in the transition method originally required for Statement No. 5 versus that for Statement No. 8, *Accounting for the Translation of Foreign Currency Transactions and Foreign Currency Financial Statements.* Statements No. 8 and 11 recognized a hybrid approach that combines prior period restatement with the cumulative effect method. "Information presented shall be restated for as many consecutive periods...as is practicable, and the cumulative effect...on the retained earnings at the beginning of the earliest period restated...shall be included in determining net income of that period."[11]

A further modification of the hybrid approach taken in Statements No. 8 and 11 is associated with Statement No. 13, *Accounting for Leases.* In implementing the provisions of Statement No. 13, only prospective application is initially required. Retroactive application is required after 1980, although earlier adjustment is encouraged. After retroactive application is accomplished, post-1976 income

---

[9]Ibid.
[10]Statement of Financial Accounting Standards No. 11, *Accounting for Contingencies—Transition Method* (Stamford, Conn.: FASB, 1975), par. 6.
[11]Ibid., par. 10.

statements and balance sheets as of year-end 1976 and thereafter must be restated when presented. Earlier financial statements, when presented, must also be retroactively adjusted to the extent practicable with the cumulative effect on retained earnings at the beginning of the earliest period restated included in the net income of that period.

In Statement No. 9, *Accounting for Income Taxes—Oil and Gas Producing Companies,* the FASB added an additional shade of gray to the accounting for its mandated accounting principle changes by "permitting" as opposed to "requiring" retroactive application in certain specified situations. If the reporting entity does not choose to restate, it must prospectively apply the new provisions; the cumulative effect method is not permitted as an alternative to retroactive application.

JUSTIFICATION FOR TRANSITION METHODS ADOPTED

Voluntary Changes

When it issued Opinion No. 20, the APB clearly was concerned with abuses developing from a switch in accounting principle when circumstances did not warrant such a switch. The APB stated

> The Board concludes that in the preparation of financial statements there is a presumption that an accounting principle once adopted should not be changed in accounting for events and transactions of a similar type. Consistent use of accounting principles from one accounting period to another enhances the utility of financial statements to users by facilitating analysis and understanding of comparative accounting data.[12]
>
> The presumption that an entity should not change an accounting principle may be overcome only if the enterprise justifies the use of an alternative acceptable accounting principle on the basis that it is preferable.[13]

Accordingly, Opinion No. 20 requires that the justification for a principle change be disclosed in the financial statements in terms of "why the newly adopted accounting principle is preferable."[14]

Since the cumulative effect method highlights, as a special item in the income statement, the retroactive impact on income of an accounting principle change, it may be reasoned that the method was adopted as a punitive measure to inhibit arbitrary or inappropriate principle changes. In fact, three members of the APB dissented to the issuance of the opinion on the basis of their belief that this method was adopted as a disciplinary measure rather than as a way of enhancing the usefulness of financial statements.

Mandatory Changes

While the expressed policy of the APB was that its opinions, unless otherwise stated, were intended to be applied prospectively and not retroactively, the board

---

[12]APB Opinion No. 20, par. 15.
[13]Ibid., par. 16.
[14]Ibid., par. 17.

apparently was not disposed to provide reasons for adopting this policy. It might be presumed that fear of dilution of public confidence in previously reported financial statements was a prime factor militating against retroactive application. As noted earlier, there were some exceptions to this general approach, such as in the case of Opinion No. 11 where the board did permit retroactive application to obtain comparability in financial presentations.

Although no stated policy on transition methods has been adopted by the FASB, there appears to be a growing propensity to select the retroactive application approach unless special circumstances dictate otherwise. The selection of the retroactive application method has been made on the basis that it will provide the most useful information for comparing financial data for periods after the effective date of a particular statement with data presented for earlier periods. This presumption that retroactive restatement through prior period adjustment provides the most useful information is clearly acknowledged in several final statements (including nos. 2, 7, 8, 11, 13 and 19). This view also was acknowledged as the basis for selecting the retroactive application method in the exposure drafts for Statements No. 5 and 12, although the choice of method was later altered in the final statements.

Departures from the retroactive application approach generally have been made on the basis of extenuating circumstances. In Statement No. 5, the cumulative effect method was selected, in part because there might be "significant difficulties involved in determining the degree of probability and estimability that had existed in prior periods."[15] The amendment of that statement by Statement No. 11, as noted earlier, was justified by the FASB on the basis of a "reconsideration of all circumstances," but primarily on the basis of inconsistencies with the treatment required by Statement No. 8. In Statement No. 8, the FASB required the use of retroactive application to the extent practicable since "restatement requires the availability of records or information that an enterprise may no longer have or that its past procedures did not require."[16]

Again in Statement No. 13, based on similar reasoning, retroactive application is required to the extent practicable, but is coupled with a four-year transition period before full implementation is necessitated. The purpose of this four-year grace period is to give companies time to resolve problems of data accumulation and issues relating to restrictive covenants in loan agreements.

In the case of applying Statement No. 12, *Accounting for Certain Marketable Securities,* retroactive application was initially proposed in the exposure draft, but prospective application was ultimately selected in the final statement. The prospective approach was justified as follows:

> The Board has obtained information...that a number of companies have in past years made substantial reclassifications of marketable equity securities as between current and noncurrent assets. With the Board's decision to provide for separate portfolios of current and noncurrent marketable equity securities with different accounting for changes in

[15]Statement of Financial Accounting Standards No. 5, *Accounting for Contingencies* (Stamford, Conn.: FASB, 1975), par. 104.

[16]Statement of Financial Accounting Standards No. 8, *Accounting for the Translation of Foreign Currency Transactions and Foreign Currency Financial Statements* (Stamford, Conn.: FASB, 1975), par. 241.

carrying value of the two portfolios, the number of and seemingly divergent bases for reclassifications that have occurred in recent years would, in the case of retroactive restatement, result in less rather than more comparability.[17]

The FASB also required prospective application of Statement No. 15, *Accounting by Debtors and Creditors for Troubled Debt Restructurings,* on the basis that comparability would not be greatly enhanced by prior period restatement and of the difficulty in generating the information required for restatement.

In summary, a marked contrast in transition methods for implementing voluntary and mandatory accounting principle changes is apparent. While the cumulative effect method serves as the general approach for implementing voluntary changes, this method has not been considered appropriate for implementing mandatory changes. Failure to adopt the cumulative effect method for implementing mandatory changes adds additional credibility to the view that the method was intended as a punitively oriented way of treating voluntary accounting principle changes.

Further, a marked difference in attitude toward implementing mandatory changes exists between the APB and the FASB. The general approach of the APB was one of prospective application whereas the FASB tends to prefer the use of the retroactive approach to the extent practicable.

MANDATORY VERSUS VOLUNTARY ACCOUNTING CHANGES

In determining if it is appropriate to change the existing system for implementing accounting principle changes, a basic question that must be answered is that of whether we should distinguish between voluntary changes and mandatory changes. The AICPA accounting standards executive committee has pointed out three factors in support of more congruence in implementing voluntary and mandatory accounting principle changes: the financial accounting and reporting environment has changed substantially since the issuance of Opinion No. 20; inconsistencies result under the current system; and management may be reluctant to voluntarily adopt different accounting principles considered by it to be preferable.[18]

There can be little doubt as to the validity of the first factor. Since Opinion No. 20 was issued, the range of acceptable accounting and reporting alternatives has significantly narrowed and continues to diminish through the issuance of pronouncements by authoritative bodies. For example, the range of permitted practices has been reduced in the important and controversial areas of research and development costs, leases and investments.

Further, another inhibitor to inappropriate changes in accounting principles has been established by the Securities and Exchange Commission. Accounting Series Release No. 177, *Notice of Adoption of Amendments to Form 10-Q and Regulation S-X Regarding Interim Financial Reporting,* requires the independent accountant to state whether or not a voluntary principle change by a client in certain SEC filings

---

[17]Statement of Financial Accounting Standards No. 12, *Accounting for Certain Marketable Securities* (Stamford, Conn.: FASB, 1975), par. 41.
[18]Letter from AcSEC to FASB.

is to an alternative which in the accountant's judgment is preferable under the circumstances.[19] The SEC holds that the justification of a voluntary principle change by management is inadequate unless it is sufficient to persuade an independent accountant that the new principle results in better measurement of business operations in the particular circumstances.[20] In addition, SEC requirements concerning the reporting of client disagreements with auditors when there is a change in auditors may help to curb abuses brought about by undesirable principle changes.[21]

The contention that inconsistencies arise because of current reporting requirements also is legitimate. For example, if a company adopts a change voluntarily, it may have to account for the results of the change using the cumulative effect method. On the other hand, if another company made the same change, but did so at a later date as the result of an FASB statement, the change would undoubtedly be accounted for in a manner other than that based on the cumulative effect method. Under these circumstances, it appears logical that the manner of implementing accounting principle changes should provide the same result irrespective of whether such changes are voluntary or imposed through an authoritative pronouncement.

A third argument concerns the behavioral effect of the cumulative effect method on management decisions. A company that is considering the voluntary adoption of a different accounting principle could well be penalized by having to absorb a lump-sum charge to income in the year of change. As a result, management may be reluctant to adopt a new principle which it genuinely considers to be preferable. Conversely, management might be motivated to adopt a less desirable accounting principle, if such adoption was to result in a lump-sum credit to income in the year of change.

In summary, one can hardly take issue with the position that voluntary accounting principle changes which endanger the credibility of financial accounting and reporting and facilitate manipulation should be discouraged. However, the objective of restraining inappropriate accounting principle changes should not be accomplished through the imposition of transition rules which seemingly are intended as disciplinary measures, but which may well have a dysfunctional effect. Accounting rules for implementing accounting principle changes should serve to improve, rather than impair, the quality of financial measurements. The professional judgment and expertise of the independent auditor must be relied on as the basis for monitoring the validity of accounting principle changes. Since the issuance of APB Opinion No. 20, the range of available accounting principle alternatives has been reduced and new safeguards have been built into the system to restrain the adoption of inappropriate accounting principle changes. Consequently, little support can be found for

[19]Securities and Exchange Commission, Accounting Series Release No. 177, *Notice of Adoption of Amendments to Form 10-Q and Regulation S-X Regarding Interim Financial Reporting,* September 10, 1975; also see Securities and Exchange Commission, Staff Accounting Bulletin No. 6, *Interpretations of ASR No. 177, Relating to Interim Financial Reporting,* March 1, 1976, and Staff Accounting Bulletin No. 14, *Amended Interpretations Relating to Reporting Requirements for Accounting Changes,* February 3, 1977.

[20]For an excellent discussion of the preferability issue see Lawrence Revsine, "The Preferability Dilemma," JofA, Sept. 77, pp. 80–89.

[21]Securities and Exchange Commission, Accounting Series Release No. 165, *Notice of Amendments to Require Increased Disclosure of Relationships Between Registrants and Their Independent Public Accountants,* December 20, 1974.

the view that voluntary and mandatory accounting principle changes should be accounted for differently.

ESTABLISHING TRANSITION METHOD GUIDELINES

Questions of merit aside, APB Opinion No. 20 does provide a general frame of reference for implementing voluntary accounting principle changes. No similar basic framework exists for implementing mandatory accounting principle changes; rather, transition approaches are established on a case-by-case basis without reference to an established policy. To provide more consistency between voluntary and mandatory changes, and to ensure consistency within the context of mandatory changes, the need exists for replacing that portion of APB Opinion No. 20 concerning accounting principle changes with new guidelines for implementing all accounting principle changes.

Cumulative Effect and Prospective Application Methods

In developing policy guidelines for implementing accounting principle changes, a preference for one of the three basic transition methods must be established. The cumulative effect method has little theoretical support as a general implementation approach. The primary deficiency of the cumulative effect method concerns its failure to maintain comparability of financial measurements over time. This lack of comparability is particularly acute over the three-year period spanning the change year. Income for the year preceding the change year would be based on the old principle; income for the change year would be based on the new principle and also would include the cumulative effect of the change; and income for the year subsequent to the change year would be based on the new principle.

A related criticism of the method concerns that of distortion of the results of current year's operations through inclusion in the change year's income, as a current period item, of the "catch-up" adjustment which is applicable to prior years. The distortion of the change year's income could be avoided, and comparability of income of the change year with that of subsequent years obtained, by including the cumulative effect as an adjustment to the beginning balance of retained earnings for the change year. However, noncomparability with income of years prior to the change year would remain.

Although prospective application avoids the problems of determining and reporting a cumulative effect adjustment, it also is subject to criticism on the basis of noncomparability of results of the change year and subsequent years with those of the years preceding the change year. In addition, the measurement of operating results for the change year, and for a number of years following, is based on a combined use of the old and new principles.

Retroactive Application

While practical problems of estimating and reconstructing past data may exist, the retroactive approach to implementation of accounting principle changes has a conceptual advantage over the other approaches. The retroactive application method is the only approach which provides complete comparability of financial statements generated over time by a company. The FASB has frequently stressed the benefits of retroactive application in terms of providing more meaningful and comparable financial statements. The APB also acknowledged the merits of retroactive application. It stated in APB Opinion No. 9

"A change in the application of accounting principles may create a situation in which retroactive application is appropriate. In such situations, these changes should receive the same treatment as that for prior period adjustments."[22]

While recognizing a difference between accounting principle changes and prior period adjustments, the APB also acknowledged that the same accounting treatment was applicable to both, namely, retroactive application. Subsequently, this Opinion No. 9 position was altered by Opinion No. 20 with the following comment:

"Paragraph 25 of APB Opinion No. 9 is superseded. Although the conclusion of that paragraph is not modified, this Opinion deals more completely with accounting changes."[23]

It is also interesting to note that the APB in the original exposure draft of Opinion No. 20 stated

The Board concludes that where changes in accounting methods are appropriate, consistency of treatment is overriding and that accounting changes, except in the instances explained hereinafter, should be computed and applied retroactively by restating financial statements presented for any period affected by the change.[24]

This position was subsequently changed in a second exposure draft leading to the final opinion.

A major criticism of the retroactive application approach is that it might lead to erosion of public confidence in the independent auditor who reported on the original statements and in financial reporting in general. Conversely, one may argue that, without retroactive application, financial presentations lead to investor confusion and make comparisons difficult or impossible. This, in turn, might lead to greater dilution of public confidence.

While past decisions by users of financial statements were made on the basis of the old numbers which the auditors approved, this does not justify prohibiting retroactive restatement for changes to preferable accounting principles. Financial statements should be viewed as tentative and subject to revision if judgments and subjective assessments are subsequently altered in light of further information and the development of improved accounting methods. Although not directly related to accounting principle changes, there is a precedent for revision in another area of accounting, namely, the audit function. Because of new information or changed circumstances, the auditor, in updating his report on previously issued financial

[22]Accounting Principles Board Opinion No. 9, *Reporting the Results of Operations* (New York: AICPA, 1966), par. 25.

[23]APB Opinion No. 20, par. 5.

[24]Accounting Principles Board Exposure Draft, *Proposed APB Opinion: Changes in Accounting Methods and Estimates* (New York: AICPA, February 16, 1970), par. 11.

statements, may express an opinion different from that expressed in an earlier report.[25]

Past decisions by users of financial statements cannot be altered. It is current and future decisions which are relevant. These new decisions should be based on the best possible information available which includes measurements based on the application of different, if preferable, accounting principles. Ideally, for current decision-making purposes, comparative financial statements should be presented on a consistent basis using that set of accounting principles considered to be the best under the existing circumstances. Of course, a full and complete disclosure of the impact of a principle change on the current and previously issued financial statements is appropriate. If firms and their auditors, relative to voluntary changes, and the FASB and other authoritative bodies, relative to mandatory changes, genuinely believe that a different principle improves the quality of financial measurements, then it should, in most cases, improve the measurement of past as well as current and future results.

In the final analysis, the comparability of financial data which results through retroactive application and restatement is a compelling argument in support of this transition method for implementing accounting principle changes. Having a set of internally consistent statements and related statistics based on a common set of accounting principles is a strong reason for the adoption of this method as the general mode for implementing accounting principle changes.

While the authors believe that retroactive application represents the best approach for implementing accounting principle changes under normal circumstances, it is not practicable to prescribe a single approach for implementing all changes. However, exceptions to retroactive application should be made only when special circumstances exist to justify modification or which preclude its use. For example, the lack of information relating to prior periods or other problems of data accumulation may preclude strict retroactive application; in such cases, a modified or hybrid approach might be in order, possibly along the lines taken in Statements No. 8 and 11, or No. 13. In other rare situations, determining the impact of a principle change on prior years' statements may require arbitrary assumptions, for example, when adopting the Lifo method of inventory costing; prospective application would appear necessary under these circumstances.

Although this discussion has been concerned exclusively with accounting principle changes which influence financial statement measurements, many pronouncements of authoritative bodies deal with information disclosure and statement classification. In these situations, implementation by retroactive application might also serve as the ideal norm, with limited retroactive application or prospective application justified in particular circumstances.

SUMMARY AND CONCLUSIONS

There appears to be little theoretical justification for maintaining the existing framework for implementing voluntary accounting principle changes in a manner

---

[25]Statement on Auditing Standards No. 15, *Reports on Comparative Financial Statements* (New York: AICPA, 1976), par. 6–7. Also found in *AICPA Professional Standards*, "Report With an

different from those which are mandated by authoritative bodies. From a practical viewpoint, the continuing development of new standards by authoritative bodies which tend to reduce the range of acceptable accounting alternatives, and the development of new safeguards by the SEC, serve to restrain alleged abuses stemming from inappropriate accounting principle changes.

The need exists to develop new guidelines for implementing voluntary and mandatory accounting principle changes in a consistent and logical manner. Based on the importance and utility of statement comparability and trend analysis, the retroactive application and restatement approach should serve as the general means of implementing principle changes, with special circumstances dictating departures from this norm.

Updated Opinion Different From a Previous Opinion"(Chicago, Ill.: Commerce Clearing House, 1977), AC sec. 505.06–07.

IMPACT OF CHANGING PRICES ON ACCOUNTING

The enormous literature dealing with the impact of changing prices on accounting may be divided into two broad areas: relative price changes and general price-level (GPL) changes.

While some academics and professionals have advocated one or another kind of relative price change in accounting for decades, the interest in this reform by standard-setting bodies has been much more recent.

Over the same period, academic and professional accountants have also proposed a GPL solution for companies' financial statements. Although many commentators have argued that the GPL and relative price proposals should be seen as complementary, and not as competitive, there is disagreement over this view.

Since the 1960s, there has been a much more active interest by standard-setting bodies in "inflation accounting"[1] (as the general area of controversy involving the impact of changing prices on accounting has come to be called). Beginning in the mid-1960s and terminating rather abruptly in 1975, the standard-setting bodies of the accounting profession in numerous countries confined their "inflation-accounting" proposals to a GPL solution. During that period the standard setters in the following countries issued one or another form of tentative proposal that GPL accounting be given consideration: Argentina, the United States, Chile, the United Kingdom and Ireland, Australia, New Zealand, Mexico, and Canada. But standard setters' enthusiasm for a GPL solution (known as CPP, or current purchasing

---

[1] The term "inflation accounting" is a misnomer when applied to a combination of GPL and relative price solutions. It should be confined to "accounting for inflation," which would refer to GPL accounting. The term "inflation accounting" seems to have entered usage with the publication in the United Kingdom of the Sandilands Report in 1975, and, for reasons that are not clear, it came to be applied to whatever solution might be found to changing general and relative prices.

power, in the United Kingdom) declined precipitately in 1975–1976. It was then that the Sandilands Committee, which had been appointed by the U.K. government to render a comprehensive report on inflation accounting, and the U.S. SEC declared their preference for a relative price solution over any kind of GPL/CPP accounting. In the United Kingdom and Ireland, a provisional exposure draft in favor of CPP accounting was scrapped, and in the United States the FASB shelved its 1974 exposure draft in support of GPL accounting. Even before the report of the Sandilands Committee was published in September 1975, the standard-setting body in Australia had publicly proposed a current value solution. In the light of these developments, the standard setters in most of the countries that had been active on the GPL/CPP front shifted their focus more toward relative price solutions.

In the end, final pronouncements embodying elements of relative and general price-level solutions were issued in West Germany, the United Kingdom and Ireland, the United States, New Zealand, Canada, and Australia. Each country's solution is different in one or more respects from those of the others. In addition, Mexico allows companies to use either relative or general prices. Argentina, Brazil and Chile, all of which have been plagued by hyperinflation, favor a general price-level solution.[2] The EEC's Fourth Directive, which was passed by the Council of Ministers in 1978, allows member states either to permit or require companies to use replacement-cost valuations in their financial statements. The International Accounting Standards Board, confronted by this array of solutions from country to country, has so far declined to take a position, recommending only that companies disclose which approach they have adopted.

In most of the countries, the restated or adjusted figures are to be shown in supplementary financial statements or in footnotes, both as a transitional measure and to minimize the likely disruption that a complete change to relative price accounting or general price-level accounting (or a combination of both) would provoke. In some countries, the nature and pace of accounting reform have been colored by the government's desire to avoid undesirable "economic consequences." It is feared that "current cost accounting," since it would require companies to display lower reported profits (in most instances), could induce managements to press for higher prices in order to recoup their "lost" profits. Governments also fear that an accounting regimen of generally lower reported profits would lead to intensified pressure for a concomitant reform of the corporate income tax law.

The debate over "inflation accounting" reflects not only an advocate's implied conceptual framework (including beliefs about the objectives of financial reporting) but also one's judgment concerning the supposed economic consequences. Hence, the debate has, at times, centered on "technical" issues relating to such matters as asset valuation, income determination, and appropriate disclosures, and at other times on how particular accounting measures could tilt the behavior of affected parties (e.g., management, labor unions, potential and actual investors and creditors, potential and actual competitors, and government). Policy recommendations have also been conditioned by standard-setters' belief or nonbelief in the efficiency of the

---

[2]In Brazil, the standard was imposed by government. In all of the other countries cited above, the standards were set by professional bodies.

capital markets. Unlike most controversial problem areas in accounting, which potentially affect a limited number of accounts, the policy making on "inflation accounting" could have a pervasive effect throughout the financial statements.

In "A History of Inflation Accounting," Paul H. Rosenfield reviews a number of the major areas of controversy in the inflation accounting debate, and he recounts some of the historical milestones in the work of academics and accounting bodies in the search for a resolution of the dilemma. The pace of work accelerated in the 1970s as inflation became a serious problem in numerous industrialized countries. Rosenfield summarizes arguments that have been made for and against "constant dollar accounting" (GPL accounting), and arguments for and against the relative price proposals of "current buying price" (also known as entry value) and "current selling price" (exit value). One can acquire a proper understanding and appreciation of the various proposals and their supporting rationale only by studying the articles and books that have been written by their supporters and detractors. In the Bibliographical Notes, we endeavor to provide citations to works that more adequately develop the arguments on both sides of the several proposed reforms.

In "Inflation Accounting for Debt," Lawrence Revsine examines the practice of building anticipated inflation into negotiated interest rates and its impact on the computation of the FASB's "purchasing power gain on debt." He argues that the real economic gain on debt is only that portion of the purchasing power gain which may be associated with unanticipated inflation. Like Rosenfield, Revsine draws attention to the contrasting views of physical capital maintenance (which Revsine supports) and financial capital maintenance. Since a real economic gain on debt involves a transfer from debtholders to owners, and since the physical capital maintenance viewpoint is oriented toward the entity as a whole, regardless of capital supplier, any such gain would not be classified as "income." By the light of financial capital maintenance, Revsine argues, a real economic gain on debt is properly includible in income, since the viewpoint is that of the residual equity holders.

The final article in this section, "Current Value Reporting of Real Estate Companies and a Possible Example of Market Inefficiency," by Dan Palmon and Lee J. Seidler, offers evidence that investment builders may need to do more than merely revalue their property holdings if they seek to make an impression on the capital market. In 1976–1977, several such companies altered their financial statements to reflect significant increases in the current value of their real properties, and several went to considerable lengths to invest a high degree of credibility in the valuations. Yet the securities market seemed to pay little attention to reappraised asset values until in one instance the company actually sold its properties at the appreciated price, whereupon its share price jumped 20 percent. Did this constitute evidence of market inefficiency? Must companies actually sell their assets at appreciated prices in order to persuade the market of the validity of upward revaluations in their financial statements? An earlier instance of a company's revaluing its real properties in order to apprise an unbelieving market occurred in the 1960s, when Sheraton Corporation of America devised an elaborate plan of "Net Worth Accounting." In its annual reports to shareholders, Sheraton discussed its accounting philosophy at length and argued for an "economic performance" measure (based on the current values of its real properties) as being superior to the traditional accounting notion of net income. (Extracts from Sheraton's 1961 and 1967 annual reports were reproduced on pages 351–375 of Stephen A. Zeff and Thomas F. Keller (eds.), *Financial Accounting Theory: Issues and Controversies* (McGraw-Hill, 1973).)

BIBLIOGRAPHICAL NOTES

Some of the works advocating historical cost, general price level (i.e., constant dollar) systems, relative price systems, or dual combinations thereof, propose general accounting frameworks and are therefore listed in the Bibliographical Notes following the introduction to Section 2. The following works, classified according to valuation concept, are representative of the major normative arguments:

Historical Cost/Nominal Dollar

Paton, W. A. and A. C. Littleton: *An Introduction to Corporate Accounting Standards* (American Accounting Association, 1940). This is a classic work which has had a profound effect on the literature and practice.

Littleton, A. C.: *Structure of Accounting Theory* (American Accounting Association, 1953).

Kohler, Eric L.: "Why Not Retain Historical Cost?" *The Journal of Accountancy* (October 1963), pp. 35–41.

Ijiri, Yuji: "A Defense for Historical Cost Accounting," in *Asset Valuation and Income Determination,* edited by Robert R. Sterling (Lawrence, KS: Scholars Book Co., 1971), pp. 1–14. For a fuller statement of Ijiri's views, see his *Historical Cost Accounting and Its Rationality,* Research Monograph Number 1 (Vancouver, B.C., Canada: Canadian Certified General Accountants' Research Foundation, 1981).

Anthony, Robert N.: *Tell it Like it Was* (Homewood, IL: Richard D. Irwin, Inc., 1983).

Historical Cost/Constant Dollar

Sweeney, Henry W.: *Stabilized Accounting* (New York: Harper & Brothers, 1936). (Reprinted in 1964 by Holt, Rinehart and Winston, Inc., and in 1978 by Arno Press.) This classic work has been highly influential in the movement for GPL accounting in the United States. In his Chapter III, Sweeney exhibits a preference for replacement-cost valuation. His views in support of Current (Entry) Value/Constant Dollar accounting, with a financial-capital-maintenance interpretation, may be found in his several articles, most of which are reproduced in *Asset Appreciation, Business Income and Price-Level Accounting, 1918–1935,* Stephen A. Zeff (ed.) (New York: Arno Press, 1976).

Schmalenbach, Eugen: *Dynamic Accounting,* originally published in 1955 and translated from the German by G. W. Murphy and Kenneth S. Most (London: Gee & Company (Publishers) Limited, 1959). (Reprinted in 1980 by Arno Press.)

Staff of the Accounting Research Division, *Reporting the Financial Effects of Price-Level Changes* (New York: AICPA, 1963). (This work contains an especially rich pair of appendices which refer to actual applications and case studies.)

Current (Entry) Value/Nominal Dollar

Physical Capital Maintenance

Mathews, Russell and John Mc.B. Grant: *Inflation and Company Finance* (Sydney: The Law Book Co. of Australasia Pty Ltd., 1958). (A second edition was published in 1962.)

Revsine, Lawrence: *Replacement Cost Accounting* (Englewood Cliffs, NJ: Prentice-Hall, Inc., 1973).

Current (Entry) Value/Constant Dollar

Real Financial Capital Maintenance

Edwards, Edgar O. and Philip W. Bell: *The Theory and Measurement of Business Income* (Berkeley, CA: University of California Press, 1961). This classic work has had a profound effect on the literature dealing with relative prices and GPL accounting.

Bell, Philip W.: *CVA, CCA, and CoCoA: How Fundamental are the Differences?*, Research Monograph No. 1 (Melbourne, Australia: Australian Accounting Research Foundation, 1982). This monograph compares the author's preferred method with Chambers' Continuously Contemporary Accounting (CoCoA) and with the physical-capital-maintenance interpretation of Current (Entry) Value Accounting (CCA).

Current (Exit) Value/Constant Dollar

Real Financial Capital Maintenance

Chambers, Raymond J.: *Accounting, Evaluation and Economic Behavior* (Englewood Cliffs, NJ: Prentice-Hall, Inc., 1966). (Reprinted in 1974 by Scholars Book Co.) Also see Chambers' "Second Thoughts on Continuously Contemporary Accounting," *Abacus* (September 1970), pp. 39–55; and "Third Thoughts," *Abacus* (December 1974), pp. 129–137.

Sterling, Robert R.: *Theory of the Measurement of Enterprise Income* (Lawrence, KS: The University Press of Kansas, 1970). (Reprinted in 1979 by Scholars Book Co.)

Discounted Cash Flow

Canning, John B.: *The Economics of Accountancy* (New York: The Ronald Press Company, 1929). (Reprinted in 1978 by Arno Press.)

Staubus, George J.: *A Theory of Accounting to Investors* (Berkeley, CA: University of California Press, 1961).

Market Value/Nominal Dollar

Financial Capital Maintenance

MacNeal, Kenneth: *Truth in Accounting* (Philadelphia, PA: University of Pennsylvania Press, 1939). (Reprinted in 1970 by Scholars Book Co.)

Deprival Value (Value to the Business)/Nominal Dollar

Physical Capital Maintenance

Wright, F. K.: "A Theory of Inventory Measurement," *Abacus* (December 1965), pp. 150–155. (Reprinted in Zeff-Keller, Second Edition.)

Solomons, David: "Economic and Accounting Concepts of Cost and Value," in *Modern Accounting Theory*, edited by Morton Backer (Englewood Cliffs, NJ: Prentice-Hall, Inc., 1966), pp. 117–140.

Inflation Accounting, Report of the Inflation Accounting Committee (Sandilands Report) (London: Her Majesty's Stationery Office, Cmnd. 6225, 1975).

Deprival Value (Value to the Business)/Constant Dollar

Physical Capital Maintenance

Stamp, Edward: "Income and Value Determination and Changing Price-Levels: An Essay Towards a Theory," *The Accountant's Magazine* (June 1971), pp. 277–292. (Reprinted in Zeff-Keller, Second Edition.)

Baxter, W. T.: *Accounting Values and Inflation* (London: McGraw-Hill Book Company (UK) Limited, 1975).

Report of the Committee of Inquiry Into Inflation Accounting (Richardson Report) (Wellington, New Zealand: Government Printer, 1976).

Several volumes are available in which the authors review and analyze the competing approaches to relative prices, general price-level applications, or both, and these include the following:

Sprouse, Robert T.: "Adjustments for Changing Prices," in *Handbook of Modern Accounting,* Sidney Davidson (ed.) (New York: McGraw-Hill Book Company, 1970), Chap. 30.

Rosen, L. S.: *Current Value Accounting and Price-Level Restatements* (Toronto, Ontario, Canada: Canadian Institute of Chartered Accountants, 1972).

Hanna, John R.: *Accounting Income Models: An Application and Evaluation* (Hamilton, Ontario, Canada: The Society of Industrial Accountants of Canada, 1974). Examines the experience of Imperial Tobacco Company of Canada, Limited with replacement cost accounting during the years 1961–1968.

Lee, T. A.: *Income and Value Measurement* (London: Thomas Nelson & Sons, Ltd., 1975). (Walton-on-Thames, Surrey, England: Thomas Nelson & Sons, Ltd., 1975). (A second edition was published in 1980.)

Barton, A. D.: *The Anatomy of Accounting* (St. Lucia, Queensland, Australia: University of Queensland Press, 1975), Chap. 21–25. (A second edition was published in 1977; chapters are the same.) (An abridged version of this discussion was published in Barton, Allan: *An Analysis of Business Income Concepts* (Lancaster, England: International Centre for Research in Accounting, University of Lancaster—ICRA Occasional Paper No. 7, 1975).)

Anderson, James A.: *A Comparative Analysis of Selected Income Measurement Theories in Financial Accounting,* Studies in Accounting Research #12 (Sarasota, FL: American Accounting Association, 1976).

Davidson, Sidney, Clyde P. Stickney, and Roman L. Weil: *Inflation Accounting: A Guide for the Accountant and the Financial Analyst* (New York: McGraw-Hill Book Company, 1976). Also contains a discussion of the impact of GPL accounting on the financial numbers reported by major U.S. companies.

Scapens, Robert W.: *Accounting in an Inflationary Environment* (London: The Macmillan Press, Ltd., 1977).

Ma, Ronald and Russell Mathews: *The Accounting Framework: A Contemporary Emphasis* (Melbourne, Australia: Longman Cheshire Pty Limited, 1979), Chap. 16–22.

Whittington, Geoffrey: *Inflation Accounting: An Introduction to the Debate* (Cambridge, England: Cambridge University Press, 1983).

A discussion and description of the operation of a full-scale system of Historical Cost/Constant Dollar accounting is:

Stickler, Alan D. and Christina S. R. Hutchins: *General Price-Level Accounting: Described and Illustrated* (Toronto, Canada: Canadian Institute of Chartered Accountants, 1975).

A discussion and description of the operation of a full-scale system of Current (Entry) Value/Constant Dollar accounting, with a physical-capital-maintenance interpretation, is:

Drummond, Christina S. R. and Alan D. Stickler: *Current Cost Accounting: Its Concepts and Its Uses in Practical Terms* (Toronto, Ontario, Canada: Methuen Publications, 1983).

An elaborate illustration of the operation of a full-scale system of Current (Entry) Value/Constant Dollar accounting, with a real-financial-capital-maintenance interpretation, may be found in:

Edwards, Edgar O., Philip W. Bell, and L. Todd Johnson: *Accounting for Economic Events* (Houston, TX: Scholars Book Co., 1979), Chap. 12. Chapter 13 draws comparisons among the several competing systems.

Several collections of previously published articles on relative price accounting, GPL accounting, or both, have been issued, of which the following are the best examples:

Parker, R. H. and G. C. Harcourt (eds.): *Readings in the Concept and Measurement of Income* (London: Cambridge University Press, 1969).

Dean, G. W. and M. C. Wells (eds.): *Current Cost Accounting: Identifying the Issues—A Book of Readings* (Lancaster, England: International Centre for Research in Accounting, and Sydney, Australia: Department of Accounting, University of Sydney, 1977). (A second edition was published in 1979.)

Three proceedings volumes from conferences held primarily to discuss the "inflation accounting" controversy are:

Sterling, Robert R. (ed.): *Asset Valuation and Income Determination* (Lawrence, KS: Scholars Book Co., 1971).

Sterling, Robert R. and Arthur L. Thomas (eds.): *Accounting for a Simplified Firm Owning Depreciable Assets* (Houston, TX: Scholars Book Co., 1979).

Sterling, Robert R. and Kenneth W. Lembke (eds.): *Maintenance of Capital: Financial versus Physical* (Houston, TX: Scholars Book Co., 1982).

A proceedings volume from a conference sponsored by the FASB at which the effects of changing general and relative prices on decisions by managers, investors, and creditors were examined in the light of possible improvements in financial reporting is as follows:

Griffin, Paul A. (ed.): *Financial Reporting and Changing Prices: The Conference* (Stamford, CT: FASB, June 1979).

For a FASB-sponsored capital markets study which found that "Statement 33 earnings variables provide no incremental information over and above that already provided by historical cost earnings," see:

Beaver, William H. and Wayne R. Landsman: *Incremental Information Content of Statement 33 Disclosures* (Stamford, CT: FASB, 1983).

A History of Inflation Accounting

Paul Rosenfield

Director
Accounting Standards
AICPA

Prior to World War II, except for isolated supplementary information presented by a handful of companies, accounting had generally ignored changes in the general level of prices—inflation and deflation. Ignoring inflation was an article of faith for many years—it was one of the three basic postulates of accounting. (The other two postulates involved going concern and realization.) The Study Group on Business Income noted: "The postulate that fluctuations in the value of the monetary unit may be ignored is probably the longest established of the three mentioned."[1]

However, pressure built after World War II to recognize the effects on depreciation of the substantial inflation occurring then. The American Institute of Accountants (a predecessor of the American Institute of CPAs) committee on accounting procedure resisted the pressure and made the following statement in a letter to the members of the Institute on October 14, 1948:

> Should inflation proceed so far that original dollar costs lose their practical significance, it might become necessary to restate all assets in terms of the depreciated currency, as has been done in some countries. But it does not seem to the Committee that such action should be recommended now....[2]

The idea of ignoring inflation has been challenged in recent years. In *The Basic Postulates of Accounting*, Maurice Moonitz stated as a basic postulate not that fluctuations in the value of money should be ignored but that "accounting reports should be based on a stable measuring unit" and that "the instability of money is notorious...."[3]

WRITE-UPS DISCONTINUED

E. S. Hendriksen noted that during the 1920s "corporations began writing up assets as sound values were considered to be higher than recent costs."[4] Accounting

From *The Journal of Accountancy*, September 1981, pp. 95, 98, 100, 102–104, 106, 108, 110, 112, 114, 116, 118–120, 122, 124, 126. Reprinted by permission of the American Institute of Certified Public Accountants. Copyright © 1981 by the American Institute of Certified Public Accountants, Inc.

[1]Study Group on Business Income, *Changing Concepts of Business Income* (New York: Macmillan, Co., 1952), p. 20.

[2]Committee on Accounting Procedure, a letter to the members of the American Institute of Accountants (New York: American Institute of Accountants, October 14, 1948).

[3]Maurice Moonitz, *The Basic Postulates of Accounting*, Accounting Research Study No. 1 (New York: AICPA, 1961), pp. 44–45.

[4]E. S. Hendriksen, *Accounting Theory*: 3d ed. (Homewood, Ill.: Richard D. Irwin, 1977), p. 61.

Research Bulletin No. 5, *Depreciation on Appreciation,*[5] reported that 67 of 272 companies examined in the period wrote up their assets. However, following the stock market crash of 1929 and the ensuing Great Depression, the write-ups were quickly discontinued; companies that had written up assets wrote them down again, and other companies also wrote down their assets. From 1930 to 1934, 197 of 272 companies examined wrote down their assets, according to appendix B of ARB No. 5.

Rightly or wrongly, accountants were charged with some of the blame for the crash because they had permitted the write-ups. Thus burned, accountants of the day vowed never to be exposed to such a charge again, and they insisted that assets be carried no higher than historical cost. It has been said that that particular generation of accountants would have to die out before reflection in financial statements of increases in prices of assets held above historical cost could again be seriously considered.

By 1936 the American Accounting Association had enshrined that idea in a "fundamental axiom" of accounting: "Accounting is... not essentially a process of valuation, but the allocation of historical costs and revenues to the current and succeeding fiscal periods."[6] A similar thought was expressed by the AIA in the first of six rules adopted by the membership in 1934: "Profit is deemed to be realized when a sale in the ordinary course of business is effected, unless the circumstances are such that the collection of the sale price is not reasonably assured."[7] That idea was reflected by the Accounting Principles Board in APB Opinion No. 6, *Status of Accounting Research Bulletins,*[8] in 1965: "The Board is of the opinion that property, plant and equipment should not be written up by an entity to reflect appraisal, market or current values which are above cost to the entity."

SPECIFIC PRICE CHANGES IN PRIMARY FINANCIAL STATEMENTS

Primary financial statements generally do not now recognize changes in nonmonetary items simply when their prices change but only when their quantities change—when they are bought and sold. As the AICPA task force on conceptual framework stated:

> At present, changes accounted for are almost exclusively transactions and other changes in the quantity factor and not changes in the price factor.... Only in limited situations are changes now recorded based on changes in the price factor alone—essentially only to implement the lower of cost and market rules for inventories and marketable securities.[9]

[5] Accounting Research Bulletin no. 5, *Depreciation on Appreciation* (New York: AIA, 1940), Appendix B.

[6] American Accounting Association, *A Tentative Statement of Accounting Principles Underlying Corporate Financial Statements* (Sarasota, Fla: AAA, 1936).

[7] "Report of Special Committee on Development of Accounting Principles," *Bulletin of the American Institute of Accountants,* November 15, 1934, p. 11.

[8] Accounting Principles Board Opinion No. 6, *Status of Accounting Research Bulletins* (New York: AICPA, 1965), par. 17.

[9] AICPA task force on conceptual framework, *The Accounting Responses to Changing Prices: Experimentation with Four Models* (New York: AICPA, 1979), p. 10.

Price Changes Recognized on Sale

At the time an asset is sold, all the relevant price changes that have taken place are recognized with the change in quantity. Three types of price change are involved:

1 Change in market. The change in price caused by moving from the buying market in which the asset was acquired to the selling market in which it is to be sold.

2 Producer's margin. The change in price caused by the addition of time, place or form utility to the asset.

3 Selling price change. The change in price caused by changes in the selling price of an asset held before sale.

The total change caused by those three factors is the difference between the buying price paid and the selling price received. The contribution of each of the factors cannot be unequivocally determined except arbitrarily. R. J. Chambers described that condition in terms of a black box, in which the separate contributions of the price changes take place hidden from view and only the overall result can be known with certainty.[10]

Price Declines Recognized before Sale

Price changes are usually not recognized before sale. An exception is the recognition of a loss of recoverable carrying amount before sale. A distinction is made between current and noncurrent assets in recognizing loss of recoverable carrying amount. Since current assets are expected to be used or sold relatively soon, evidence of a temporary decline is sufficient to cause a loss to be recognized. Thus inventories are written down to market price if lower than cost even though the market price might later recover. Also, as explained in Financial Accounting Standards Board Statement No. 12, *Accounting for Certain Marketable Securities*, marketable equity securities are

> grouped into separate portfolios according to the current or noncurrent classification of the securities for the purpose of comparing aggregate cost and market value to determine carrying amount.... Changes in the valuation allowance for a marketable equity securities portfolio included in current assets shall be included in the determination of net income of the period in which they occur.[11]

In contrast, since noncurrent assets are expected to be retained for a considerable time, temporary fluctuations in their price or value are generally ignored. "Reductions in the market prices of noncurrent assets are generally not recorded until the assets are disposed of or are determined to be worthless."[12] The carrying amount of a nonmonetary asset that has not become worthless generally is reduced only when there has been a "permanent impairment" in the ability to recover the carrying

---

[10] R. J. Chambers, *Accounting, Evaluation and Economic Behavior* (Englewood Cliffs, N.J.: Prentice-Hall, Inc., 1966), p. 252.

[11] Financial Accounting Standards Board Statement No. 12, *Accounting for Certain Marketable Securities* (Stamford, Conn.: FASB, 1975), pars. 9 and 11.

[12] APB Statement No. 4, *Basic Concepts and Accounting Principles Underlying Financial Statements of Business Enterprises* (New York: AICPA, 1970), par. 183, S-5E.

amount. For noncurrent marketable securities, "if the decline is judged to be other than temporary, the cost basis of the individual security shall be written down to a new cost basis and the amount of the write-down shall be accounted for as a realized loss."[13] For fixed assets, the APB advises: "In unusual circumstances persuasive evidence may exist of impairment of the utility of productive facilities indicative of an inability to recover cost although the facilities have not become worthless. The amount at which those facilities are carried is sometimes reduced to recoverable cost and a loss recorded prior to disposition or expiration of the useful life of the facilities."[14]

Price Increases Recognized before Sale

In exceptional cases, inventories may be carried at their current selling prices, and changes in those prices while the inventories are held may be recognized in income. The AIA states:

> For example, precious metals having a fixed monetary value with no substantial cost of marketing may be stated at such monetary value; any other exceptions must be justifiable by inability to determine appropriate approximate costs, immediate marketability at quoted market price, and the characteristic of unit interchangeability.[15]

Lifo and Accelerated Depreciation

The Lifo method of inventory valuation and the accelerated depreciation methods have been described as partial responses to inflation or changes in specific prices within the historical cost framework. Devices similar to Lifo are used in the United Kingdom and France.

In Great Britain, stock relief allows companies to charge a portion of the increase in book value of inventories as an expense, deductible for income taxes. The amount charged to income was to be "clawed back" (to become taxable) in the future. In 1979, however, the British government eliminated that possibility. U.S. accounting rules required that a provision for the eventual taxability of stock relief be recorded in consolidated financial statements that included British subsidiaries. With the British change, FASB Statement No. 31, *Accounting for Tax Benefits Related to U.K. Tax Legislation Concerning Stock Relief,*[16] was issued in 1979; it allows those provisions to be taken into consolidated income.

A similar mechanism, *provision pour hausses des prix,* is permitted in France. French tax laws also allow a deferral of tax on corporate capital gains if the amounts are reinvested in productive assets within a specified period.

Many countries experienced severe inflation after World War II and introduced various accounting adjustments to compensate. The most common practice in those

---

[13] FASB Statement No. 12, par. 21.
[14] APB Statement No. 4, par. 183, M-5C.
[15] ARB No. 43, *Restatement and Revision of Accounting Research Bulletins* (New York: AIA, 1953), ch. 4, Statement 9.
[16] FASB Statement No. 31, *Accounting for Tax Benefits Related to U.K. Tax Legislation Concerning Stock Relief* (Stamford, Conn.: FASB, 1979).

countries during the late 1940s and 1950s was to revalue fixed assets and sometimes investments using governmental indexes. The revalued amounts were reported in balance sheets and subsequently depreciated for shareholder reporting and income taxes. The changes in asset amounts were usually untaxed or taxed at minimal rates. Such revaluations were made, for example, in Germany, France, Italy and Japan at irregular intervals, principally to allow companies a measure of relief from taxes on inflated asset amounts. In Latin America the practice has become more institutionalized, as has inflation, and assets are revalued on regular intervals, such as every six months.

ASR NO. 190, REPLACEMENT COST ACCOUNTING

In the U.S., the first formal break with the requirement of the past 50 years to maintain historical cost as an upper limit on the amounts at which nonmonetary assets are presented was Securities and Exchange Commission Accounting Series Release No. 190,[17] issued in 1976. It reversed the long-standing prohibition against presenting information on costs, prices or values above historical cost in reports to the SEC.

ASR No. 190 required SEC registrants with inventories and gross property, plant and equipment exceeding $100 million and constituting more than 10 percent of total assets to present in their forms 10 K supplementary information that disclosed

> the estimated current replacement cost of inventories and productive capacity at the end of each fiscal year for which a balance sheet is required and the approximate amount of cost of sales and depreciation based on replacement cost for the two most recent full fiscal years.

The replacement costs involved were current buying prices of assets not owned that are equivalent to modern versions of assets owned. Information must be disclosed on consideration given "to the related effects on direct labor costs, repairs and maintenance, utility, and other indirect costs as a result of the assumed replacement of productive capacity." Thus the SEC requires information on events that occurred during the period plus information on events and conditions that did not occur or exist but might have, or might in the future. (This differs from FASB Statement No. 33, *Financial Reporting and Changing Prices,*[18] which prohibits including in income possible operating economies that would result from replacement.) The commission cautioned investors and analysts against simplistic use of the data presented, "such as adjusting reported income and coming up with a revised income amount." Paragraph 16 of Statement No. 33 says that ASR No. 190 "calls for information that is not suitable for integration into a computation of income."

The requirements of ASR No. 190 were suspended for companies that provided

---

[17] Accounting Series Release No. 190, *Notice of Adoption of Amendments to Regulation S-X Requiring Disclosure of Certain Replacement Cost Data* (Washington, D.C.: Securities and Exchange Commission, March 23, 1976).

[18] FASB Statement No. 33, *Financial Reporting and Changing Prices* (Stamford, Conn.: FASB, 1979).

the current cost information required by Statement No. 33 in 1979. Companies that elected optional delayed compliance with Statement No. 33 until 1980 continued to report under ASR No. 190 in 1979. With full implementation of the FASB requirements, ASR No. 190 requirements should end.

CAPITAL MAINTENANCE CONCEPTS

A major choice in the design of a system of accounting is the choice of the capital maintenance concept. The idea behind that choice is that income should not be reported as having been earned during a period until and unless the capital with which the enterprise started the period has at least been maintained during the period. That view is expressed in a widely quoted definition of expected income of individuals by Sir John Hicks (*Value and Capital*, p. 172):

> The purpose of income calculations in practical affairs is to give people an indication of the amount which they can consume without impoverishing themselves. Following out this idea, it would seem that we ought to define a man's income as the maximum value which he can consume during a week, and still expect to be as well off at the end of the week as he was at the beginning.

The main point of disagreement concerning the choice of a capital maintenance concept is the definition of **capital** that should be used. There is general agreement that capital refers or should refer to the wealth or the net assets of the enterprise. The disagreement lies in how wealth or net assets should be defined for a capital maintenance concept. The two main definitions are "financial capital" and "physical capital." Proposals for responses to changing prices differ based on that choice (see discussion of accounting responses to specific price changes, including arguments for and against them, below).

Under a **financial capital** concept of capital maintenance, income should be reported as an increase in capital over the capital of the enterprise at the beginning of the period in terms of money or general purchasing power. The FASB (Discussion Memorandum, "An Analysis of Issues Related to Conceptual Framework for Financial Accounting and Reporting: Elements of Financial Statements and Their Measurement," pp. 125–126) observed: "Proponents of the financial capital concept or view may disagree about the attributes of assets and liabilities to be measured, but they agree that the capital to be maintained is measured by the amount of cash (perhaps restated for changes in the general price level) invested by owners, either directly or through nondistribution of earnings in the past."

Under a **physical capital** concept of capital maintenance, capital is not merely the wealth of net assets of the enterprise in terms of money or general purchasing power. The FASB Discussion Memorandum comments (p. 127):

> Capital may be viewed as a physical phenomenon. That is, capital is more than a difference between assets and liabilities. It also manifests certain physical properties of underlying assets or their combined capacity to produce goods or services. Proponents of the physical capital concept may disagree about technical details, but they agree that the capital to be maintained is the physical productive capacity of the enterprise and that costs to be recovered are current replacement costs of assets with the same productive capabilities as assets used.

The concept of capital maintenance is in essence a concept needed to **define income**. Agreement on attributes of assets and liabilities to be measured and on the unit of account are sufficient to design a balance sheet presenting financial position at a particular time. Agreement on those issues is insufficient to design an income statement; agreement on a capital maintenance concept is also needed. Such a concept is needed to specify the point from which to start measuring income. As the FASB observed in the Discussion Memorandum cited previously (p. 125):

> Maintenance of capital or recovery of cost is a financial concept or abstraction needed to measure earnings. It is the point or level that divides return of capital or recovery of cost from return on capital or earnings. Returns above that point are earnings; returns below that point are net losses.

ACCOUNTING RESPONSES TO INFLATION

Proposals to respond in accounting to changes in the general purchasing power of money—inflation and deflation—were made in the U.S. as early as the 1920s.

Henry W. Sweeney

Although scattered references on the problems caused by changing prices appeared in the U.S. literature before the 1920s, the first systematic study and exposition of the problems in this country were by Henry W. Sweeney. His work originated in an examination of the responses to the hyperinflation in Germany in the early 1920s. His article "Effects of Inflation on German Accounting," published in the *Journal of Accountancy* in 1927,[19] was the first of a series exploring the subject and applying the concepts to the American scene.

Sweeney's book *Stabilized Accounting*[20] contained the concepts and procedures for general purchasing power accounting that eventually gained support in the U.S., though Sweeney died before he could see the fruit of his labors. The basic ideas have not been changed; present arguments concerning general purchasing power accounting involve details only. In an introduction to the 1964 reissue of *Stabilized Accounting,* William Paton stated that "*Stabilized Accounting*... still clearly points the way."[21]

"Price-level Depreciation"

Interest in proposals to recognize inflation in financial statements in the U.S. has generally appeared only when the inflation rate was considerably higher than usual. Leading practitioners did not address the problem until the late 1940s when the release of pent-up demands dating from World War II caused rapidly increasing prices. Attention was directed, however, to only one aspect of the problem—the effects of rising prices on fixed-asset costs and on related depreciation. "Price-level

---

[19] Henry W. Sweeney, "Effects of Inflation on German Accounting," JofA, Mar. 1927, pp. 180–191.
[20] Henry W. Sweeney, *Stabilized Accounting* (New York: Harper & Bros., 1936, reissued New York: Holt, Rinehart & Winston, 1964).
[21] Ibid., p. xv.

depreciation" was demanded for use in financial statements and, especially, for tax relief.

The debate on price-level depreciation lasted more than ten years. The clamor was so intense that the AIA felt obliged to outlaw price-level depreciation in ARB No. 33, Depreciation and High Costs.[22] As late as 1958, the AICPA (which was known as the AIA prior to this time) published "Survey on Price-Level Adjustment of Depreciation."[23]

Focusing on price-level depreciation involved two difficulties. First, as indicated, it considered only one of the effects of inflation. Some objected. For example, J. Fred Weston stated that "...if some modification in procedures is made because of changing values of money, consistency requires that all important income effects of fluctuating price levels be taken into consideration."[24]

Second, the stated reasons for advocating price-level depreciation were unclear. The arguments switched between a concentration on rises in the general level of prices as reflected in higher fixed asset costs and a concentration on those higher costs per se. The failure of the campaign at least in part reflected that confusion.

Views of the American Accounting Association

The AAA, an organization dominated by teachers of accounting, has sponsored statements on accounting principles since 1936. Although treatment of specific price changes was discussed in the 1936 statement and in each subsequent statement, changes in the general purchasing power of money were not mentioned until the third statement, the 1948 revision of *Accounting Concepts and Standard Underlying Corporate Financial Statements,* which gave passing reference to the problem in a footnote: "Readers of financial statements may be aided in their interpretations by considering the effect of fluctuations in the purchasing power of money."[25]

In 1951 the first quasi-official recognition was given to general purchasing power accounting by the AAA's committee on concepts and standards underlying corporate financial statements in its Supplementary Statement No. 2, *Price Level Changes and Financial Statements.*[26] The committee recommended a thorough test of financial statements stated in units of general purchasing power rather than in units of money. It adopted as two of its premises the cornerstone of the method advocated by Sweeney:

1 ...a general price level index should be used.

2 ...the adjustments should be comprehensive in scope to the end that the effect of price level changes will be reflected in each item to the extent appropriate.[27]

[22]ARB No. 33, *Depreciation and High Costs* (New York: AIA, 1947).
[23]AICPA Technical Services Department. "Survey on Price-Level Adjustment of Depreciation," JofA, Apr. 58, p. 36.
[24]Fred Weston, "Consistency and Changing Price Levels," *Accounting Review,* October 1949, p. 86.
[25]AAA, *Accounting Concepts and Standards Underlying Corporate Financial Statements,* rev. ed. (Sarasota, Fla.: AAA, 1948).
[26]Committee on Concepts and Standards Underlying Corporate Financial Statements, Supplementary Statement No. 2, *Price Level Changes and Financial Statements,* (Sarasota, Fla.: AAA 1951).
[27]Ibid., pp. 28–29.

Supplementary Statement No. 2 initiated a full-scale examination and debate on the merits of general purchasing power accounting. The AAA sponsored a study of the concepts and methods of general purchasing power accounting by Perry Mason.[28] Later committees of the AAA reaffirmed support in their reports in 1957 and 1966.

Study Group on Business Income

In its 1952 report, *Changing Concepts of Business Income,* the Study Group on Business Income, sponsored by the AIA, introduced the idea of units of general purchasing power:

> ...corporations whose ownership is widely distributed should be encouraged to furnish information that will facilitate the determination of income measured in units of approximately equal purchasing power, and to provide such information wherever it is practicable to do so as part of the material upon which the independent accountant expresses his opinion.[29]

By the middle of the 1950s, the inflation rate had reduced, and the interest of practicing accountants waned in the subject of Supplementary Statement No. 2 and *Changing Concepts of Business Income.* A decade passed before interest returned.

Accounting Research Study No. 6

In 1961 the newly formed Accounting Principles Board of the AICPA established a project on general purchasing power accounting. In its minutes, the Board indicated its agreement that "the assumption in accounting that fluctuations in the value of the dollar may be ignored is unrealistic...." Accounting Research Study No. 6, *Reporting the Financial Effects of Price-Level Changes,*[30] which resulted from the project, recommended that enterprises publish supplementary financial statements with all items stated in units of general purchasing power.

Accounting Principles Board Statement No. 3

In 1969 the APB issued Statement No. 3, *Financial Statements Restated for General Price-Level Changes,*[31] recommending that enterprises present supplementary financial statements with all items stated in units of general purchasing power and giving detailed principles and procedures to be followed in their preparation. The recommendation was not adopted in practice because it was not mandatory.

Nevertheless, in its 1973 report, *Objectives of Financial Statements,* the AICPA Study Group on the Objectives of Financial Statements emphasized the need to recognize inflation: "If the value of the unit of measure is unstable, that is, if

---

[28] Perry Mason, *Price Level Changes and Financial Statements, Basic Concepts and Methods* (Sarasota, Fla.: AAA, 1956).

[29] Study Group on Business Income, *Changing Concepts of Business Income,* p. 105.

[30] Staff of the AICPA Accounting Research Division, *Reporting the Financial Effects of Price-Level Changes,* Accounting Research Study No. 6 (New York: AICPA, 1963).

[31] APB Statement No. 3, *Financial Statements for General Price-Level Changes* (New York: AICPA, 1969).

inflation or deflation is so great that direct cash consequences are no longer comparable, such circumstances should be recognized in the financial statements.[32]

FASB Exposure Draft on General Purchasing Power Accounting

Also in the early 1970s the FASB established a project to determine whether enterprises should be required to present supplementary general purchasing power information. The project resulted in a discussion memorandum in 1974 and an exposure draft in the same year, which would have required presentation of supplementary financial information in units of general purchasing power or key items from those statements.

At roughly the same time, the SEC issued Accounting Series Release No. 190, which required certain replacement cost disclosures. To avoid confronting the SEC with what might be considered to be competing disclosure requirements, the FASB deferred action on its exposure draft on general purchasing power accounting.

The FASB and Constant Dollar Accounting

Financial reporting in units of a single specified amount of general purchasing power, as advocated over fifty years ago by Henry Sweeney, is now called constant dollar accounting by the FASB. Previous names for the same method have included "stabilized accounting," "general price-level accounting" and "general purchasing power accounting." Constant dollar accounting is discussed in FASB Statement No. 33.

The detailed principles and procedures for constant dollar accounting are those first presented in APB Statement No. 3 and repeated in the 1974 FASB exposure draft, *Financial Reporting in Units of General Purchasing Power*,[33] with three relatively minor modifications. The principles are as follows (with the modifications indicated—see the following sections entitled "the date," "the index," and "monetary and nonmonetary items"):

The unit of account. The unit of account is defined in terms of a specified amount of general purchasing power, a "constant dollar." The most convenient way to specify an amount of general purchasing power is to designate it as the general purchasing power of a specified national unit of money at a specified date, for example, the general purchasing power of the U.S. dollar at December 31, 1980.

To specify a unit of general purchasing power, it is necessary to specify both the unit of money and the date, because the general purchasing power of each national unit of money differs from the general purchasing power of all other national units of money and because the general purchasing power of each national unit of money changes (the whole cause of the problem).

---

[32]Study Group on the Objectives of Financial Statements, *Objectives of Financial Statements* (New York: AICPA, 1973), p. 14.
[33]FASB Exposure Draft, *Financial Reporting in Units of General Purchasing Power* (Stamford, Conn.: FASB, 1974).

The date.   Information for the current year should be stated in a unit of account defined in terms of the general purchasing power of the dollar in the current year. A five-year summary of selected data should be stated in a unit of account defined in terms either of the general purchasing power of the dollar in the current year or in terms of the general purchasing power of the dollar in a past year called a base year. For the U.S., FASB Statement No. 33 stipulates the base year to be that used by the Bureau of Labor Statistics in calculating the consumer price index for all urban consumers (CPI-U), the index used for changing the unit.

This principle differs from that in APB Statement No. 3 and the 1974 FASB exposure draft, both of which required that all constant dollar information be in a unit of account defined in terms of the current year. The FASB decided that for a five-year comparison, the arguments in favor of the base year and those in favor of the current year are evenly balanced. Thus, the FASB allows the alternative.

The index.   The CPI-U, which must be used in constant dollar accounting according to Statement No. 33, is an index of changes in the prices of consumer goods and services. This differs from the index required by APB Statement No. 3 and the 1974 FASB exposure draft, both of which required the use of the gross national product implicit price deflator (GNP deflator), an index of changes in the prices of all producer and consumer goods and services. The CPI-U and the GNP deflator have generally moved in the same direction and at comparable rates in the long run. The FASB changed to the CPI-U because it has the practical advantages of being calculated more frequently and of not being revised after its initial publication.

Accounting principles unchanged.   Accounting principles used in the financial statements before restatement are retained in the restated financial information except for the definition of the unit of account. The measurements are not changed (although the amounts may change); they are merely restated to a different unit. Historical cost in units of money is restated to historical cost in units of general purchasing power (this is an area that is commonly misunderstood—some erroneously believe the application of an index of general purchasing power to historical cost results in something that is not historical cost); replacement cost in units of money is restated to replacement cost in units of general purchasing power, and so forth. (The FASB says that if depreciation in the primary financial statements has been calculated partly to allow for expected price changes, methods and estimates different from those used in the primary financial statements may be used in the constant dollar calculations.)

The process is restatement, not adjustment. Adjustment, in contrast, retains the unit of account and changes the measurements—for example, adjusting the balance of accrued interest for the passage of time.

Monetary and nonmonetary items.   Monetary items are balance sheet items accounted for in terms of a specified amount of money on hand or to be received or paid in the future that is not affected by changes in prices; nonmonetary items are all other items. Examples of monetary items are cash, accounts and notes receivable, investments in bonds accounted for at the discounted amount of the contractual money proceeds (interest payments and principal payments), accounts and notes payable and long-term debt.

An entity that holds or owes monetary items gains or loses general purchasing power solely because of inflation (or deflation). For example, during inflation, a holder of a given amount of cash loses general purchasing power—the cash progressively commands fewer and fewer goods and services in general. During hyperinflation, such as occurred in Germany in 1923, the general purchasing power of money can virtually disappear. During inflation, an owner of long-term debt gains general purchasing power. The money that will be required to pay the amounts required by the debt progressively represents a smaller command over goods and services in general. The resources the gain represents were received when the debt was incurred—more general purchasing power was received than will have to be paid back. As Cecilia Tierney points out, "...the general purchasing power gains were received in cash when the debt was incurred...."[34] (This is another area that is commonly misunderstood—some erroneously believe that gains of general purchasing power from owing money during inflation are not reflected in increased resources. In this case, the resources reflected by the gains are received at the beginning of the transaction—when the general purchasing power is received by borrowing and incurring a debt.)

Examples of nonmonetary items are inventories, property, plant and equipment, intangibles, goodwill and obligations to deliver goods or services, for example, under warranties. An entity that holds or owes nonmonetary items is not affected solely by inflation or deflation, since inflation and deflation are changes in the value of money, not other commodities. The holder of a nonmonetary item is affected by the relationship between the rate of inflation and the rate of change of the specific price of the item.

According to the definition of monetary and nonmonetary items, foreign money, claims to foreign money, obligations in foreign money and balance sheet deferred income taxes under APB Opinion No. 11, *Accounting for Income Taxes,*[35] are nonmonetary and were so designated in APB Statement No. 3 and the 1974 FASB exposure draft. FASB Statement No. 33, however, treats them as monetary items; it reflects the view that nonmonetary classification of foreign money and deferred income taxes is technically preferable but that classifying them as monetary is a more practical solution.

The gains or losses could conceivably be calculated directly, by multiplying the amounts of monetary items held by conversion factors before and after changes in the general level of prices during the accounting period. That method is cumbersome, however. The recommended practice is to calculate the gain or loss as the balancing amount in the restated financial statements and to check the amount using a schedule similar to a statement of changes in financial position. APB Statement No. 3 illustrates the method.

[34]Cecilia V. Tierney, "General Purchasing Power Myths," JofA, Sept. 77, p. 94.
[35]APB Opinion No. 11, *Accounting for Income Taxes* (New York: AICPA, 1967).

Conversion factors. The amounts of nonmonetary items are analyzed to determine the dates to which the components of the amounts pertain. A conversion factor is computed for each date by dividing the index number for the date used for the new unit of account by the index number for the date of the component. The component amounts are multiplied by the conversion factors to determine the restated amounts.

Monetary items The numbers at which monetary items are presented are retained if end-of-current-year units are used; those numbers are changed if base-year units are used. If the unit of account is defined in end-of-current-year terms, monetary items are stated in terms of money at the same number as in terms of general purchasing power. Cash of $100 at December 31, 1980, for example, is stated at $100 before restatement and $(80) some 100 after restatement.

If the unit of account is defined in base-year terms, the amount of monetary items is multiplied by a conversion factor computed by dividing the index number for the base year by the index number for the balance sheet date. To illustrate, if the base year is 1973 and the index numbers are (73) 107.63 and (80) 162.28, $100 is restated as follows: $100 x 107.63 ÷ 162.28 = $(73)66.32. This means that $66.32 in 1973 would buy the same goods and services in general that $100 would buy at the end of 1980.

Income statements and equity The amounts of items in the statement of income and the statement of changes in equity are restated to the new unit of account. The amounts of items in those statements are restated using conversion factors that pertain to the dates involved in the items, in the same manner as for nonmonetary items described under the "conversion factors" section above.

Foreign consolidation For combination or consolidation, the financial statements of foreign branches, divisions or subsidiaries are first translated and then restated using the general price level index of the country of the parent company. This method is called "translate-restate," in contrast with the opposite method called "restate-translate," under which the foreign financial statements are first restated using the foreign general price index and then translated at the exchange rate at the balance sheet date. FASB Statement No. 33 adopted the translate-restate method.

Supplementary presentation Selected information from restated financial statements is presented as supplementary information outside the basic financial statements. The information is now considered to be experimental and is therefore not incorporated in basic financial statements. FASB Statement No. 33 specifies the items to disclose and the additional informative disclosures required, including information for the current year and a five-year summary of selected data.

Arguments for Constant Dollar Accounting

The justification often given for constant dollar accounting boils down to an assertion that inflation exists and therefore financial statements should reflect that fact. Accounting Research Study No. 6, APB Statement No. 3 and FASB Statement No. 33 in effect rely on that reasoning.

Henry Sweeney defended consumer general purchasing power as the standard resource to use and placed its relevance squarely with the users of the information:

> In the last analysis men normally engage in all the various forms of earning a living in order to be able directly to use and enjoy—i.e., 'consume'—the goods and services that they want. Such goods and services are 'consumption goods.' It is true that men seem to work for money, not for consumption goods. But even then money is desired, by the miser and the lover of power as well as by the average individual, only because it represents ability to buy desirable commodities and services.
>
> But, it may be argued, the things that men buy with money are not always consumption goods. Much of the time they are 'production goods,' such as factory machinery and buildings. When men buy production goods, however, they do so only because in most cases they hope thereby to obtain eventually more of the consumption goods that they want than they could obtain by buying them in the first place.
>
> In consequence of the foregoing, accounting data should ideally be measured with reference to the progress made in obtaining either more consumption goods or greater power over them. These consumption goods are those represented in the cost of living.[36]

Robert Sterling took the argument a step further and held that the standard resource to use should be determined by reference to the basic interest of users—their personal utility:

> We view 'enterprise' as nothing more than a convenient name for the vehicle that humans establish to maximize...their utility.
>
> In view of the motivation of the enterprise, it should be obvious that we think the Consumer Price Index is most appropriate. It is the closest substitute for a utility measurement that is currently available.[37]

Arguments against Constant Dollar Accounting

Many of the arguments against constant dollar accounting reflect confusion of recognition of changes in the structure of prices with recognition of changes in the general level of prices. For example, an editorial in November 1947 *Journal of Accountancy* stated: "It would hardly be helpful to adjust depreciation on steel mills according to index figures based only on changes in prices of cost-of-living items, such as food, clothing, and rents."[38]

Morton Backer and Richard Simpson took the same view: "Specific replacement cost indexes for different classes of assets provide a better indication of the value of these assets than does a general price-level index applied to non-monetary assets."[39]

However, other more substantive arguments are also advanced, including

1 Users do not believe information in units of general purchasing power would

---

[36]Sweeney, *Stabilized Accounting,* p. 4.

[37]Robert R. Sterling, *Theory of the Measurement of Enterprise Income* (Lawrence, Kans.: University Press of Kansas, 1970), pp. 337, 340.

[38]"Depreciation on Replacement Value," JofA, Nov. 47, p. 356.

[39]Morton Backer and Richard Simpson, *Current Value Accounting* (New York Financial Executives Research Foundation, 1973), p. 146.

be more helpful than information in units of money—Several surveys, including those by M. Backer, R. Estes, T. Dyckman, and P. Barker, have suggested that users do not believe constant dollar information would be more helpful.[40]

2 Information in units of general purchasing power would be confusing to users—This argument was advanced by Clyde Stickney and David Green, who said in 1974 that "...users might be confused as to the meaning of the adjusted statements." They admitted, however, that "an educational program could help."[41]

3 Changing to units of general purchasing power does not make a material difference—This argument was advanced by Stickney and Green, because rankings based on rate of return seem to remain unchanged.

4 People are interested in information in terms of money, not in terms of general purchasing power—Lawrence Revsine and Jerry Weygandt implied that argument, citing the "objective of cash flow predictions" in rejecting general purchasing power information.[42]

5 General price level indexes are not sufficiently reliable—Stickney and Green wrote that "substantial uncertainty regarding the accuracy and reliability of the price indices seems warranted."

ACCOUNTING RESPONSES TO SPECIFIC PRICE CHANGES

Specific Price Systems

A number of proposals have been widely discussed and one has been instituted by FASB Statement No. 33 to supplement historical cost based accounting with comprehensive bases that reflect changes in specific prices of assets while they are held. They would change the attribute emphasized from historical cost to others—for example, current buying price or current selling price. Those systems may use a unit of account defined in terms of units of money or in terms of units of general purchasing power.

Current Buying Price Systems

Some authors have advocated accounting systems in which nonmonetary assets are presented in balance sheets at current buying prices and have given arguments supporting those prices as the suitable attribute. (Others have suggested current buying prices as surrogates for other attributes they consider suitable.) The systems have been given various names by the authors, for example, current replacement

---

[40]Morton Backer, *Financial Reporting for Security Investment and Credit Decisions* (New York: National Association of Accountants, 1970), pp. 233–239; R. Estes, "An Assessment of the Usefulness of Current Cost and Price-Level Information by Financial Statement Users," *Journal of Accounting Research,* Autumn 1968, pp. 200–207; T. Dyckman, *Investment Analysis and General Price-Level Adjustments* (Sarasota, Fla: AAA, 1969); and Phyllis A. Barker, "The Value-Added Tax—The Cost to the Businessman," JofA, Sept. 72, pp. 75–79.

[41]Clyde P. Stickney and David O. Green, "No Price Level Adjusted Statements, Please (Pleas)," *CPA Journal,* January 1974, pp. 25–31.

[42]Lawrence Revsine and Jerry J. Weygandt, "Accounting for Inflation: The Controversy," JofA, Oct. 74, pp. 72–78.

cost accounting, current cost accounting and current replacement value accounting. Statement No. 33 uses the term *current cost accounting*. Furthermore, the same name has been used by various authors and standard-setting bodies to refer to more than one system. Nevertheless, two basic systems using current buying prices may be distinguished, one using financial capital as the capital maintenance concept and the other using physical capital.

Current Buying Prices: Financial Capital.   This system presents nonmonetary assets held at the balance sheet date at the current buying prices of similar assets. Total profit from buying at historical cost and selling at selling price is divided into two parts—holding gains and losses and current operating profit. Unlike historical cost accounting, which usually recognizes all the profit at the time of sale, part of the profit is recognized under this system when the assets are held while prices change and part when the assets are sold.

Holding gains and losses are differences (1) between the historical cost of assets when bought during the period and the current buying prices of similar assets when the assets are sold, if sold during the same period, or at the balance sheet date, if held to the end of the period, and (2) between the current buying prices of similar assets at the beginning of the period the assets are held and the current buying prices of similar assets when the assets are sold, if sold during the period, or at the balance sheet date, if held to the end of the period. The difference between the selling prices of goods sold and the current buying prices of similar assets at the dates the assets are sold is called current operating profit and is included in income in the period of sale.

Two widely cited proponents of this system are Edgar Edwards and Philip Bell and the committee to prepare a statement of basic accounting theory of the AAA in a document known as ASOBAT, *A Statement of Basic Accounting Theory.*[43]

Current Buying Prices: Physical Capital.   This system also presents nonmonetary assets held at the balance sheet date at the current buying prices of similar assets. However, changes in the buying prices of similar assets while the assets are held are recorded in equity rather than included in income. Income from ordinary operations includes the difference between the selling prices of assets sold and the current buying prices of similar assets at the dates of sale.

This system is used by some companies in the Netherlands; it was advocated by the Sandilands committee, a governmental committee in the U.K., and by a chief accountant of the SEC[44] among others; and it is permitted by the Fourth Directive of the European Economic Community.

In its December 28, 1978, exposure draft that led to Statement No. 33, the FASB indicated that it had "concluded that a financial concept of capital is preferable." However, paragraph 104 of the final statement said that the board

---

[43]Edgar O. Edwards and Philip W. Bell, *The Theory and Measurement of Business Income* (Los Angeles, Calif.: University of California Press, 1961), and Committee to Prepare a Statement of Basic Accounting Theory, *A Statement of Basic Accounting Theory* (Evanston, Ill.: AAA, 1966).

[44]John C. Burton, "Accounting That Allows for Inflation," *Business Week,* November 30, 1974, pp. 12, 14, and "Financial Reporting in an Age of Inflation," *JofA,* Feb. 75, pp. 68–71.

has subsequently concluded that it should express no preference for either concept at this time and that enterprises should present information that would enable users to assess the amount of income under both [the financial and the physical capital] concepts.

Two arguments for using current buying prices of similar assets in accounting apply equally to the system involving financial capital and the system involving physical capital, arguments concerning costs avoided and sacrifice on deprival.

The first argument holds that the cost avoided by owning an asset is a satisfactory amount at which to present it in the balance sheet. The FASB stated the argument in paragraphs 69 and 73 of the exposure draft that led to Statement No. 33:

> Current cost is normally the most appropriate current measure of the value of an asset to an enterprise; it represents the cash outlay avoided by ownership of the asset....
>
> Current...cost indicates the amount of cash payments avoided by the ownership of the assets concerned; in that sense it often represents the value to the enterprise of an asset which would have to be purchased if it were not already owned.

However, that argument was omitted from the final statement.

The second argument holds that (1) the sacrifice that would be incurred by an enterprise on being deprived of an asset (sometimes called *deprival value*) is a satisfactory amount at which to present the cost of selling or using the asset in the income statement and (2) the sacrifice is the current buying price of similar assets. The FASB implied that argument in paragraphs 70 and 76 of the exposure draft that led to Statement No. 33:

> Current measurements provide useful information about the amount of operating income earned by an enterprise from continuing operations. For example, suppose that a unit of inventory is sold. The effective sacrifice involved in the sale is usually the current cost of the item; the sale usually causes the enterprise to incur the current cost in replenishing its inventory....
>
> ...it may be helpful to indentify the applicable value by assuming that the enterprise has been deprived of the use of the asset and measuring the adverse effects on cash inflows and cash outflows.

However, that argument also was omitted from the final statement.

Two arguments are specific to buying prices with financial capital, arguments concerning separation of income and cost saving.

The first argument holds that

1 Income from buying, processing and selling an asset is caused
   a By actions of the enterprise that may collectively be called production.
   b By holding an asset while market conditions change.
2 Income reporting is improved by separating it into components that represent those two causes.
3 Using current buying prices of similar assets with financial capital gives the required separation.

Edwards and Bell were early proponents of that argument:

> The activities of the business firm in a particular time period resemble an escalator which has the ability to move to one side as well as upward. Any gains which accrue to the firm as

a result of horizontal movements, or holding activities, are capital gains. Any gains made by the firm as a result of vertical movements, or operating activities, are operating profits.

The difference between the forces motivating the business firm to make profit by one means rather than by another and the difference between the events on which the two methods of making profit depend require that the two kinds of gain be carefully separated if the two types of decision involved are to be meaningfully evaluated.[45]

The FASB also advanced that argument in paragraph 118 of Statement No. 33:

The results of holding activities and continuing operations will be affected differently by economic forces and the two measures may therefore be useful in different ways for the assessment of future cash flows. It is easier to take account of the various forces shaping the time patterns of operating income and changes in current cost amounts if the two items are separated as they are in the current cost information provided for by this Statement.

The second argument holds that buying an asset before the buying price of similar assets rises results in a cost saving, which should be reported as a holding gain. That argument was popularized by Edwards and Bell. First, they concede that an increase in the current buying price of a similar asset is not a gain in the usual sense:

It cannot be called a realizable capital gain because the excess is a difference between entry values, not exit values. A realizable capital gain would imply that it could be realized by selling the asset. When current cost figures are being used, it is not at all that clear that a sale of the asset would convert the excess current cost into a realizable value.

Instead, they say the enterprise saved money by buying when it did, and the saving is a gain that should be reported during the periods the assets are held and the prices rise—

...a saving attributable to the fact that the input used was acquired in advance of use. This saving is attributable to holding activities.... we shall...appropriate the term 'business profit' to mean the sum of current operating profit and realizable cost savings.[46]

One argument is specific to buying prices with invested physical capital; it is the general argument for using physical capital as the concept of capital maintenance. The argument is that income should not be reported until capital has been maintained, that the capital to be maintained is the physical operating capacity of the enterprise and that such capacity is maintained when revenue is obtained sufficient to replace assets used up or sold. Thus Morton Backer and Richard Simpson argue that

profit is earned through a matching of revenue and current costs. Adjustments of the book costs of operating assets to their replacement cost is not an element of profit but a restatement of equity. The notion of a 'holding gain' resulting from increases in replacement cost of operating assets...is rejected since in our view this mythical gain must be set aside for replacement of assets.[47]

Lawrence Revsine and Jerry Weygandt state the argument as follows:

[45]Edwards and Bell, p. 73.
[46]Ibid, pp. 93–94.
[47]Backer and Simpson, *Current Value Accounting*, p. 41.

...the crucial question is this: Which of the two inflation accounting alternatives generates an income figure that reflects the amount of resource inflows that could conceivably be distributed as a dividend without impairing the physical operating level of the firm?[48]

A. J. Merrett and A. Sykes argue that "the reporting of a company's profits should properly reflect what is available for distribution to its shareholders, after allowing for such sums as are required to keep the business physically intact."[49]

Arguments against using the current buying price of similar assets consist mainly of arguments counter to those for such use, that is, arguments based on cost avoided, deprival value, separation of income into components, cost saving and physical capital.

An argument against using current buying prices of similar assets is that the justification for current buying prices based on cost avoided has two related defects. The argument is still pertinent, though the FASB dropped that justification—it is still widely used by proponents of using current buying prices.

First, the cost avoided by ownership of an asset is not necessarily, and is not even likely to be, the cost of buying one like it currently. The cost avoided is a comparison of events as they occurred with different events that by definition did not occur. Speculating about events that might have occurred but did not occur is fraught with danger. Who knows what costs would have been incurred if the enterprise had not bought the asset when it did, that were avoided because the enterprise did buy when it did? Maybe no such costs were avoided—maybe the enterprise could have gotten along without the asset. Anything is possible once a part of the past is assumed to have been altered. More likely, costs considerably in excess of current costs were avoided. For example, owning production assets before they are used avoids not only the cash outlay that would have been required to purchase them at the time of use, but it also avoids the cash outlays that would have been required because production scheduling would have been disrupted by a sudden purchase of the assets rather than by their orderly acquisition before use.

Second, the cost avoided by ownership of an asset is an unsatisfactory amount on which to base accounting for it. By definition it involves events that might have but did not occur. Income accounting should be based solely on events that occurred, not partly on events that did not occur. Using such a cost in the balance sheet does not tell anything about the financial position that exists but only about the financial position that might have existed but does not exist. Using changes in such a cost in the income statement does not tell about successes or reverses enjoyed or suffered by the enterprise but only about the successes or reverses that might have been but were not enjoyed or suffered.

Another argument against using current buying prices is that the argument based on sacrifice on deprival (deprival value) is defective. The sacrifice that would be incurred by an enterprise when it sells or is otherwise deprived of an asset may be a satisfactory amount on which to base accounting for it. But that sacrifice is not the cost of replacing it. The sale of an asset does not cause the enterprise to incur the cost of replacing it; that is a separate investment decision.

---

[48]Revsine and Weygandt, "Accounting for Inflation: The Controversy," p. 76.
[49]A. J. Merrett and A. Sykes, "How to Avoid a Liquidity Crisis," *Economist,* August 3, 1974, p. 11.

Prem Prakash and Shyam Sunder summarize previous evaluations of the argument concerning separation of income, provide additional counterarguments and summarize the "case against the income dichotomy." They contend that the holding risks of the firm's assets are usually not separable. If not,

> ...there is no valid reason or empirical evidence to support the claim that [current operating profit] is a better indicator of the long-run profitability of the firm than the total current value income, that [current operating profit] is the appropriate index for ranking the production processes according to their economic desirability, or that [current operating profit] is a more stable predictor of the long-run profitability of the firm than the historical cost profit.[50]

In 1969, I presented arguments against the cost saving argument for current buying prices. I described a cost saving as a comparison between the results of events as they occurred and events as they might have but did not occur:

> If the purchase price paid was less than would have been required at the time of sale or consumption, the enterprise may be said to have saved money. The money it has after the price rise is more than it might then have had if it had waited until after the price rise to buy the asset....[51]

I contended that such a comparison has no place in reported income, which is supposed to be a report on the history of the enterprise.

The physical capital concept of capital maintenance can be implemented only by using current buying prices. Arguments against that concept are therefore arguments against that justification for the use of current buying prices. In 1975, I cited two related defenses for physical capital, one about dividends and the other about survival. I contended that both defenses are faulty and physical capital cannot be justified. As to dividends

> An argument for starting to report net income only when the physical operating capacity of the enterprise is kept at least level...is that increased assets required to keep physical operating capacity at least level can never be paid out as dividends and should therefore not be reported as part of net income....
>
> The problem with the argument linking net income to dividends is that it requires the erroneous assumptions that the only way increases in net assets can improve future dividend paying ability is by directly providing assets in a form available for distribution and that net asset increases permanently tied up in a form which cannot be distributed cannot support increased future dividends. But net asset increases that cannot themselves be realized and paid out can increase future dividends by providing a larger investment base on which to earn assets for dividends. The larger tree can provide more fruit, even though cutting down the tree cuts off the source of fruit.[52]

As to the survival defense....

The implied argument tying survival to the use of physical operating capacity to define the zero point for determining net income or net loss is the following: Keeping the physical

---

[50]Prem Prakash and Shyam Sunder, "The Case Against Separation of Current Operating Profit and Holding Gain," *Accounting Review,* January 1979, p. 19.

[51]Paul Rosenfield, "Reporting Subjunctive Gains and Losses," *Accounting Review,* October 1969, p. 793.

[52]Paul Rosenfield, "Current Replacement Value Accounting—A Dead End," *JofA,* Sept. 75, p. 70.

operating capacity of an enterprise at least level is necessary for an enterprise to survive in the long run. If its physical operating capacity declines during a period, to that extent it is heading for extinction. If its physical operating capacity remains level or increases during a period, to that extent its future survival is enhanced. Net loss should be computed starting down from the point at which the survival of the enterprise is threatened. Net income should be computed starting up from the point at which the survival of the enterprise is not threatened....

[But (a)] a progressive reduction in physical operating capacity accompanied by an increasing unit margin in terms of the standard resource is compatible with long-run survival, [and (b)] prospering does not necessarily start only when survival is assured.... The reason is that assuring survival and prospering may require different kinds of achievement, not simply different amounts of achievement.... Assuring survival requires not only a given amount of resources but also the right kinds of resources or access to them at the right times, especially holdings of or access to cash.[53]

The Current Selling Price System

The current selling price system has been advocated by a few authors around the world. R. J. Chambers has advocated it for many years, for example, in *Accounting, Evaluation and Economic Behavior* and "Second Thoughts on Continuously Contemporary Accounting."[54] It has also been advocated by Robert Sterling, for example, in *Theory of the Measurement of Enterprise Income* and "Relevant Financial Reporting in an Age of Price Changes,"[55] and J. McKeown has suggested "a large scale study" of it.[56]

In brief, the current selling price system presents assets in balance sheets at their current selling prices. It reports gains and losses in income equal to the excess or deficit of the selling prices less the historical costs of assets when they are acquired, plus or minus changes in the selling prices of assets while they are held, caused by price changes, by processing or by other changes that transform the assets into assets that command higher or lower selling prices. The current selling price system is advocated with the financial capital concept of capital maintenance.

Since some resources, such as goodwill, cannot be sold without selling the business or a significant portion of it, the current selling price system does not include such resources as assets.

The current selling price system ignores the realization principle inherent in the historical cost principle, that profit should not be recognized until it is realized in cash or other monetary assets. In contrast, neither of the current buying price systems technically ignores the realization principle, since only holding gains are recognized before realization and those are said to be cost savings, not profit in the ordinary sense.

---

[53]Ibid., pp. 71–72.

[54]R. J. Chambers, "Second Thoughts on Continuously Contemporary Accounting," *Abacus*, September 1970, pp. 39–55.

[55]Robert R. Sterling, "Relevant Financial Reporting in an Age of Price Changes," JofA, Feb. 75, pp. 42–51.

[56]James C. McKeown, "An Empirical Test of a Model Proposed by Chambers," *Accounting Review*, January 1971, pp. 12–29.

Sterling supports the use of current selling price because this "one bit of information is relevant" to the largest number of decisions; "[O]ther bits...are relevant to one or more but not all decisions..."[57] Similarly, Chambers states that

> there is a fit and proper place for all the kinds of information which have been said to be needed for informed judgments and choices on financial grounds. There is a place for original prices—at the original point of purchase. There is a place for replacement prices—not in periodical reporting, but in the course of reflections on future alternatives. There is a place for present values of expected proceeds—again, not in periodical reporting, but in the course of reflections on future alternatives. There is a place for corrections for general price level movements—in the calculation of the capital maintenance adjustment and net income. And there is a place for resale prices in every one of the contexts just mentioned.[58]

Objections to the current selling price system usually center on intentions concerning the assets. For example, Frank Weston stated that

> fluctuations in the market [selling] prices of...investments are not relevant to the determination of income of a life insurance company, since it does not intend to liquidate these investments at the particular year-end.[59]

Also, A. L. Thomas pointed out that different combinations of assets can give different selling prices: "...the amounts reported on current-exit-value balance sheets and income statements will vary with the aggregation method chosen, giving rise to substantial ranges of ambiguity in the reported figure."[60]

Current Cost Accounting Under FASB Statement No. 33.

The FASB now requires (Statement No. 33) that certain enterprises present supplementary "current cost accounting" information on

- Inventories and property, plant and equipment.
- Income from continuing operations
- Changes in specific prices of inventories and property, plant and equipment.

For that purpose, assets and expenses would be measured as follows, according to paragraphs 51–52:

> - Inventories at current cost or lower recoverable amount...at the measurement date....
> - Property, plant, and equipment...at the current cost or lower recoverable amount ...of the assets' remaining service potential at the measurement date....
> - Cost of goods sold...at current cost or lower recoverable amount...at the date of sale....

---

[57]Sterling, *Theory of the Measurement of Enterprise Income*, p. 156.
[58]Chambers, "Second Thoughts on Continuously Contemporary Accounting," pp. 54–55.
[59]Frank T. Weston, "Response to Evidence for a Market-Selling Price-Accounting System," *Asset Valuation and Income Determination. A Consideration of the Alternatives*, Robert R. Sterling, ed. (Lawrence, Kans.: Scholars Book Co., 1971), p. 100.
[60]A. L. Thomas, *The Allocation Problem: Part Two*, Studies in Accounting Research No. 9 (Sarasota, Fla.: AAA, 1974), p. 115.

- Depreciation and amortization expense of property, plant, and equipment ... on the basis of the average current cost or lower recoverable amount ...

Income from continuing operations excludes changes in prices of inventories and property, plant and equipment.

Current Cost Accounting in the U.K.

The Accounting Standards Committee, representing accounting institutes in Great Britain and Ireland, requires certain enterprises to present supplementary "current cost accounts" consisting of a current cost "profit and loss account and balance sheet together with explanatory notes...."[61]

The amounts in the supplementary information would be based on the value to the business of the assets held and changes in their value to the business. Value to the business is stated to be "(a) net current replacement cost; or, if a permanent diminution to below net replacement cost has been recognized, (b) recoverable amount."[62]

The current cost operating profit would be determined by adjusting historical cost profit

a In relation to fixed assets, a depreciation adjustment being the difference between the proportion of their value to the business consumed in the period and the depreciation calculated on the historical cost basis;

b In relation to working capital:

i A cost of sales adjustment being the difference between the value to the business and the historical cost of stock consumed in the period.

ii An adjustment based on monetary working capital.[63]

It is also necessary to use a gearing adjustment, calculated by

a Expressing net borrowing as a proportion of the net operating assets using average figures for the year from the current cost balance sheets; and

b Multiplying the total of the charges or credits made to allow for the impact of price changes on the net operating assets of the business by the proportion determined at [paragraph] a.[64]

Changes in the prices of assets reflected in the current cost amounts are included in balance sheet reserves and are not given a description that implies they are gains or losses. That treatment reflects the physical capital concept of capital maintenance.

The monetary working capital adjustment is explained as follows:

Most businesses have other working capital besides stock involved in their day-to-day operating activities. For example, when sales are made on credit the business has funds

[61] Accounting Standards Committee, Statement of Standard Accounting Practice No. 16, *Current Cost Accounting* (London, Eng.: ASC, 1980).

[62] Ibid., par. 42.

[63] Ibid., par. 49.

[64] Ibid., par. 50.

tied up in debtors. Conversely, if the suppliers of goods and services allow a period of credit, the amount of funds needed to support working capital is reduced. This monetary working capital is an integral part of the net operating assets of the business. Thus, the Standard provides for an adjustment in respect of monetary working capital when determining current cost operating profit. This adjustment should represent the amount of additional (or reduced) finance needed for monetary working capital as a result of changes in the input prices of goods and services used and financed by the business.[65]

The gearing adjustment is explained as follows:

The net operating assets shown in the balance sheet have usually been financed partly by borrowing and the effect of this is reflected, by means of a gearing adjustment, in arriving at current cost profit attributable to shareholders.[65]

Balance sheet amounts would be presented in the supplementary information as follows:

a Land and buildings, plant and machinery and stocks subject to a cost of sales adjustment—at their value to the business.

b Investments in associated companies—either at the applicable proportion of the associated companies' net assets stated under this Standard or, where such information is not readily available, at directors' best estimate thereof. Allowance for premium or discount on acquisition should be made as stated under [paragraph] e below.

c Other investments (excluding those treated as current assets)—at directors' valuation. Where the investment is listed and the directors' valuation is materially different from midmarket value, the basis of valuation and the reasons for the difference should be stated.

d Intangible assets (excluding goodwill)—at the best estimate of their value to the business.

e Goodwill (premium or discount) arising on consolidation—on the basis set out in SSAP [No.] 14 [group accounts]. Where goodwill is carried at an amount established before the introduction of SSAP [No.] 14 it should be reduced to the extent that it represents revaluation surpluses relating to assets held at the date of the acquisition.

f Current assets, other than those subject to a cost of sales adjustment—on the historical cost basis.

g All liabilities—on the historical cost basis.[67]

SSAP No. 16 differs from FASB Statement No. 33's current cost accounting mainly in that SSAP No. 16 calls for a monetary working capital adjustment and a gearing adjustment, whereas the FASB statement does not.

[65] Ibid., par. 11.
[66] Ibid., par. 16.
[67] Ibid., par. 53.

Inflation Accounting for Debt

Lawrence Revsine
Northwestern University

What is the impact of debt on a company during inflationary periods? Investors, lawmakers, and regulators would obviously like to know, but the absence of a consensus regarding the role of debt provides confusing signals to both private sector statement users and government policymakers. While some financial statement interpreters simply ignore debt when computing inflation-adjusted income, others cite the "borrowing gains" that accrue to firms with large amounts of debt outstanding; advocates of this position argue that these gains largely offset any losses incurred in translating historical cost into inflation-adjusted earnings.[1] This view would suggest that firms may not be suffering as severely as inflation accounting numbers indicate.

This article examines three methods of accounting for debt inflation—the Financial Accounting Standards Board's (FASB's) purchasing power gain approach and current cost accounting under both the physical capital maintenance and financial capital maintenance approaches.[2] To determine which method gives the most realistic picture of the effect of debt on the enterprise, we must ask first whether borrowers actually do gain at the expense of lenders during inflation—i.e., whether they capture, in our terms, *a real economic gain*. As we will see, the answer depends upon whether the inflation was or was not anticipated. Furthermore, interpretation of the gain—when it does exist—also depends upon the capital maintenance approach used.

DO BORROWERS ALWAYS GAIN FROM INFLATION?

Irving Fisher characterized observed interest rates as being comprised of two components—(1) a real component consisting of a risk-free rate plus a risk premium and (2) a component corresponding to the anticipated rate of inflation over the period of the debt.[3] While Fisher posited a multiplicative relation between nominal

From *Financial Analysts Journal* (May-June 1981), pp. 20–25, 27–29. Reprinted by permission of the *Financial Analysts Journal*.

Editor's note: The author thanks for their helpful comments Michael J. Murphy, The First National Bank of Chicago, Professor James R. Boatsman, Oklahoma State University and participants at the Harvard University Seminar on Planning, Accounting and Accountability, especially Professors Kasi Ramanathan and Richard F. Vancil.

[1] See, for example, Sanford Rose, "The Stock Market Should Be Twice As High As It Is," *Fortune*, March 12, 1979, pp. 138–144; A. F. Ehrbar, "Unraveling the Mysteries of Corporate Profits," *Fortune*, August 27, 1979, pp. 90–96; and "The More They Owe, The Richer They Get," *Forbes*, May 26, 1980, pp. 114–115.

[2] This article will ignore the potentially complicating factor of income taxes. Inflation gains or losses attributable to taxation are, in any case, a separate issue from the financial reporting issues relating to debt. For a discussion of inflation and tax gains and losses see J. E. Everett, "Inflation and the Investing Borrower," *Australian Journal of Management,* April 1977, pp. 11–33.

[3] Irving Fisher, *The Theory of Interest* (New York: Macmillan Company, 1930).

rates, real rates and inflation, we'll assume for simplicity that the relation is additive. Thus, if the real interest rate for a $1,000 bond of a certain risk level is five per cent, and the anticipated annual rate of inflation over the life of the bond is 10 per cent, the observed nominal rate on the bond should be 15 per cent, or $150. In other words, the lender seeks protection from purchasing power losses by negotiating an additional interest component equal to the anticipated rate of inflation.

With perfectly anticipated inflation, therefore, the decline in the purchasing power of the amount lent is offset against nominal interest in order to arrive at real interest. Using the example of our $1,000 bond, Table I shows the borrower's real cost for one year (i.e., the lender's real return) if the actual, realized rate of inflation is exactly 10 per cent. Here the borrower's gain of $100 simply compensates the lender for the decrease in the purchasing power of the principal to be repaid.

TABLE I

Real Interest under Perfectly Anticipated Inflation

Nominal interest expense ($1,000 × 15% nominal interest rate)	$150
Less: Purchasing power "gain" on debt ($1,000 × 10% inflation)	100
Equals: Real interest expense ($1,000 × 5% real interest rate)	$ 50

In fact, the borrower has not gained at the expense of the lender. Only when the realized rate of inflation differs from the anticipated rate of inflation will there be a real economic gain or loss on debt.

The available evidence provides rough support for the "Fisher Effect." While the relation is not precise, there is a clear correlation between inflation rates and nominal interest rates.[4] The existence of this general relation indicates that lenders at least strive to protect themselves from the adverse effects of inflation on fixed dollar claims. This differentiation between anticipated and unanticipated inflation is central to developing a method for debt accounting under inflationary conditions.

Purchasing Power Gains

The FASB approach to accounting for debt during inflation requires that inflation gains on debt be measured by taking the product of the observed rate of inflation

[4]The empirical evidence is summarized in an excellent paper by Ross M Skinner, "Memorandum on the Significance of Debt Financing During an Inflationary Period" (Paper prepared for the Ontario Committee on Inflation Accounting, 1977).

and the book value of outstanding debt.[5] Using the data from Table I, this computation would result in a *purchasing power gain on debt* (the FASB's terminology) of $100 (10 per cent of $1,000).

The FASB's purchasing power gain on debt will usually not correspond to what we have called the real economic gain on debt.[6] Specifically, at least some portion of the purchasing power gain on debt is not a gain to borrowers at all; instead, to the extent that inflation was anticipated, hence built into the negotiated interest rate, that portion of the borrower's gain is specious. In the extreme case illustrated in Table I, where the observed rate of inflation was perfectly anticipated, no part of what the FASB would consider to be the borrower's gain ($100) represents a real economic gain on debt. In fact, the FASB's purchasing power gain will correspond to the real economic gain only under the equally extreme circumstance where experienced inflation is a total surprise to borrowers and lenders. Obviously, this will rarely occur.

There is a need for clear signals regarding the existence and extent of real economic gains on debt during periods of inflation. Unfortunately, the FASB approach simply does not satisfy this need. Worse yet, the FASB has included the purchasing power gain on debt approach as a required disclosure on both the constant dollar and current cost inflation accounting bases, widening the potential distortion.[7] Therefore it seems imperative that a totally fresh exploration of issues relating to accounting for debt in a current cost framework be undertaken.

CURRENT COST ACCOUNTING FOR DEBT

Rather than focusing on the observed past rate of inflation (the FASB approach), current cost accounting for debt monitors changes in the price of the debt itself. These changes are termed debt *holding gains* (or losses). Whether these holding gains constitute "income" depends upon the concept of capital maintenance selected—physical or financial.[8]

Physical Capital Maintenance

Under a physical capital maintenance approach to current cost income, a firm's income, or "distributable operating flow," consists of "that portion of net operating flows that can be distributed as a dividend without reducing the level of future

[5]Financial Accounting Standards Board, *Financial Reporting and Changing Prices,* Statement of Financial Accounting Standards No. 33 (Stamford, CT: Financial Accounting Standards Board, 1979).

[6]This shortcoming was first explored in the accounting literature in an excellent article by Robert S. Kaplan, "Purchasing Power Gains on Debt: The Effect of Expected and Unexpected Inflation," *The Accounting Review,* April 1977, pp. 369–378. William H. Beaver ("Accounting for Inflation in an Efficient Market," in *The Impact of Inflation on Accounting: A Global View* (University of Illinois, 1979)) examines the impact of inflation anticipation on nonmonetary assets.

[7]FASB Statement No. 33, p. 33.

[8]These capital maintenance approaches are also discussed in Lawrence Revsine, "Let's Stop Eating Our Seed Corn," *Harvard Business Review,* January–February 1981, pp. 128–134.

physical operations."[9] The physical capital maintenance approach requires that resources sufficient to replace and maintain productive capacity remain within the firm; only inflows in excess of this amount constitute income. The concept of physical capital maintenance therefore focuses on the entity's ability to maintain its physical operating level.

This view is consistent with what accountants term the *entity*—rather than the *proprietary*—theory of ownership equity. The entity theory views both creditors and equityholders as essentially similar providers of capital; the focus is on the entity itself, rather than on any particular group providing capital:

> In the entity theory...the business firm is considered to have a separate existence, even personality, of its own.... The entity theory is based on the equation... Assets = Equities .... While some of the items on the right-hand side of the equation are occasionally called liabilities, they are really equities with different rights in the enterprise.[10]

An income statement prepared under the entity theory considers the firm to be distinct from its owners. That is, the approach is intended to reflect income to the firm itself. By contrast, an income statement prepared under the more familiar proprietary theory reflects income to the stockholders (or proprietors) of the firm.

To understand debt accounting under the entity-based physical capital maintenance approach, consider a firm whose balance sheet on January 1, 1980, consists only of the following items:

Fixed Assets	$1,500	Long-Term Debt	$ 750
		Owners' Equity	750
	$1,500		$1,500

For simplicity, assume the firm has no inventories. The fixed asset account is comprised of two assets—one new and the other one year old. Each was purchased new for $1,000, has a two-year life and a straight-line decline in service potential. The firm's debt matures at the end of 1980. The real rate of interest for firms of its risk class is five per cent; however, when the debt was issued, yearly inflation of 10 per cent was anticipated. The nominal rate of interest on the debt is therefore 15 per cent.

Assume that all price changes take place instantaneously on January 2 of each year and that no further price changes occur during the year. As anticipated, overall inflation of 10 per cent occurs in 1980. The replacement cost of the new fixed asset increases by 10 percent on January 2, 1980 (to $1,100) and a 10 per cent increase also

---

[9]Lawrence Revsine, *Replacement Cost Accounting* (Englewood Cliffs, NJ: Prentice-Hall, Inc., 1973), p. 34. Subsequent authors have also employed the terms "distributable" or "sustainable" income to describe an income measure based on maintenance of physical capital; see Sidney Davidson and Roman L. Weil, "Inflation Accounting: The SEC Proposal for Replacement Cost Disclosures," *Financial Analysts Journal*, March/April 1976, pp. 57–66; and Richard F. Vancil and Roman L. Weil, "Current Replacement Cost Accounting, Depreciable Assets and Distributable Income," *Financial Analysts Journal*, July/August 1976, pp. 38–45

[10]Eldon S. Hendriksen, *Accounting Theory*, 3rd ed. (Homewood, IL: Richard D. Irwin, Inc., 1977), p. 490.

applies to the one-year old asset (to $550). Immediately after these price changes, the current cost balance sheet amount for fixed assets will total $1,650—up $150 from the January 1 figure. Because the inflation was fully anticipated, the price of the outstanding debt will remain unchanged.

The firm's current cost income for 1980 using a physical capital maintenance approach will consist of the maximum amount of funds inflow that can be "consumed" without eroding the beginning-of-period physical capital of the firm (i.e., two assets—one that is new and one that is a year old). Assuming the firm receives $1,512.50 in net operating inflows over the year, its current cost income from continuing operations will be:

Net operating inflows (revenues less direct manufacturing costs)		$1,512.50
Current cost depreciation [($1,100/2) + $550]	$1,100.00	
Interest expense[11]	112.50	
		1,212.50
Current cost income from continuing operations		$ 300.00

To see why current cost income is $300 under a physical capital maintenance approach, we make a series of simplifying assumptions. We assume that all new operating inflows are received in cash. We further assume that the firm refinances the debt, pays a dividend equal to its current cost income from continuing operations and buys a new asset for $1,100 on December 31, 1980 to replace the worn-out asset. Under these circumstances, the ending cash balance is zero ($1,512.50 minus interest of $112.50 minus a dividend of $300 minus asset replacement expenditures of $1,100). The December 31, 1980 balance sheet will then show:

Fixed Assets	$1,650	Long-Term Debt	$ 750
		Owners' Equity	900
	$1,650		$1,650

The reported income of $300 is the maximum amount of inflow the firm can consume while still retaining sufficient funds ($1,100) to reestablish the same total physical asset configuration with which it started the year. The inflows ($300) in excess of the amount necessary to reestablish the beginning asset position constitute income. Since the physical capital maintenance approach concentrates on the firm's physical assets (and ignores the sources from which these assets were financed), it is based upon the entity view of income.

[11]Under a "pure" entity view, interest is a distribution of income, rather than an expense. However, for ease of exposition—and to conform to the remainder of the literature—we treat interest as an expense. This modification does not affect our conclusions.

Financial Capital Maintenance

Under the financial capital maintenance approach, the firm's current cost income for 1980 will consist of the maximum amount of funds inflow it can consume without eroding the beginning-of-period market value of its net assets ($1,500). Continuing the previous example, the firm's income will be:

Net operating inflows (revenues less direct manufacturing costs)		$1,512.50
Current cost depreciation [($1,100/2) + $550]	$1,100.00	
Interest expense	112.50	
		1,212.50
Current cost income from continuing operations		$ 300.00
Holding gains ($1,650 − $1,500)		150.00
Total current cost income		$ 450.00

Current cost income computed on a financial capital maintenance basis differs from the current cost physical income measure by $150—i.e., the amount of the holding gains on fixed assets that arose during the period.

In order to see what capital is being maintained under this approach, assume the firm refinances the debt. Now, however, if the firm pays a dividend equal to its financial capital maintenance income of $450, its cash balance immediately before asset replacement is only $950 ($1,512.50 minus interest of $112.50 minus the dividend of $450). Since a new asset identical to the one being replaced now costs $1,100, the firm cannot pay for it with the $950 on hand. However, if we make the simplifying assumption that assets are divisible (e.g., a new, lower capacity asset costing $950 is available on the market) the firm can use the $950 to replace a portion of the physical asset. If this is done, the firm will once again have assets with a total market value of $1,500 (i.e., $950 plus $550). After doing so, its ending balance sheet will be identical to its January 1, 1980 balance sheet. In other words, the firm can consume $450 (current cost income on a financial capital maintenance basis) and still maintain the beginning-of-period net asset market value of $1,500.

This concept of income differs from the previous concept because it strives to maintain beginning-of-period *financial* capital (market value of $1,500) rather than beginning-of-period *physical* capital (two assets). Since the financial capital maintenance approach concentrates on changes in net asset values (i.e., assets minus liabilities, or owners' equity), it is consistent with the proprietary view of income.

CURRENT COSTS AND ANTICIPATED INFLATION

The two examples above show no real economic gain on debt under either capital maintenance approach. This is because anticipated and actual inflation were equal (at 10 per cent) in the examples. Lenders and borrowers were each satisfied with a real rate of interest of five per cent, which is precisely what resulted from a nominal interest rate of 15 per cent in conjunction with 10 per cent inflation. Thus, despite inflation, borrowers did not gain at the expense of lenders. Furthermore, the market price of the debt did not change, hence there was no holding gain on debt to record under either current cost system.

By contrast, the methodology suggested by the FASB would have led to the recognition of a purchasing power gain on debt of $75 (i.e., the book value of the debt multiplied by the 10 per cent inflation). Given the facts in the example, this FASB reported gain would bear no correspondence to the real economic gain on debt.

Financing Adjustment

Despite the fact that perfectly anticipated inflation never gives rise to a real economic gain on debt, some observers have suggested that a debt adjustment is still necessary in an inflationary environment. To understand the basis for the proposed adjustment, consider our physical capital maintenance example. If the firm paid out all its current cost income from continuing operations as a dividend ($300), its debt/equity ratio would fall from 1:1 on January 1, 1980 to 0.833:1 on December 31, 1980. In other words, the physical capital maintenance approach appears to assume that the full burden of inflation in terms of the increase in the price of replacement assets is borne by the shareholders; in reality, assets are also financed in part by debt.

There are many ways to compute a "financing adjustment" that will reflect the burden of inflation borne by debtholders, but the common objective of most is to arrive at an income number that, given certain dividend and financing assumptions, will essentially maintain the debt/equity ratio at or near its initial level. Applying the simplest possible variant to our example would mean that 50 per cent of the $150 asset holding gain would be considered an element of income while the other 50 per cent would be a direct (non-income) credit to owners' equity. Total income to shareholders would then be $375, rather than $300. The philosophy is that the "extra" income of $75 paid out could be immediately financed by additional borrowing, so that owners' equity would be $825 and debt would also be $825. The additional borrowing of $75 would reestablish the debt/equity ratio of 1:1 and also generate the additional cash needed to replace the old asset. Indeed, a greatly modified variant of this approach (based only upon realized holding gains) was proposed by the Canadian Institute of Chartered Accountants (CICA) in an exposure draft on inflation accounting.[12]

The financing adjustment approach raises some interesting, but at the same time perplexing, issues. For example, the financing adjustment is sometimes advanced as a means for reflecting real economic gains or losses on debt. The CICA proposal argues:

> When an enterprise uses borrowed funds to finance productive assets in a period of changing prices, there is, in effect, a transfer of purchasing power between debt holders

---

[12]Canadian Institute of Chartered Accountants, *Current Cost Accounting*, Exposure Draft, December 1979. The Canadian approach, in turn, is similar to the "financial gearing" adjustment advanced in the

and equity shareholders, offset to a greater or lesser extent by interest charges payable to the debt holders.[13]

This transfer of purchasing power argument seems to make the assumption that experienced inflation is primarily unanticipated. Insofar as inflation was anticipated (as in our example), the wealth transfer described by the CICA does not exist and the rationale for the adjustment is unclear. It is therefore preferable to consider the financing adjustment as something other than an attempt to reflect real economic gains or losses on debt.

A more defensible interpretation is that the adjustment represents a hybrid capital maintenance concept that attempts to reconcile between the entity (physical capital) and proprietary (financial capital) views of income. Indeed, the CICA proposal recommends separate disclosure of what it terms "current cost income to the enterprise" (an entity-based physical capital maintenance measure) and "current cost income to the shareholders" (a proprietary-based measure that includes the financing adjustment). However, this interpretation introduces additional problems, since it is not at all clear what is being maintained. For example, if a firm incurs losses, should it be forced to buy back debt in order to reestablish a target debt/equity ratio? What if this buy back dissipates assets needed to maintain physical capacity? The potential conflicts appear numerous.

Another controversial aspect of the financing adjustment is that it "is not represented by cash available for distribution.... To the extent that additional borrowings can be arranged, however, the amount of the financing adjustment can be released for distribution."[14] But it is incongruous to recognize as an element of income an amount that cannot be paid out unless replenished from another source. Indeed, unless the unique nature of this item were clearly understood, it is easy to envision adverse economic consequences despite the existence of efficient securities markets. If the income number that includes the nondistributable financing adjustment influences public opinion and aggregate social decisions, firms might find their tax burdens increased despite the fact that the reported income must be retained within the firm.

Finally, computation of a financing adjustment would require the accountant to make financial policy assumptions. For example, the financing adjustment would increase in proportion to the firm's leverage, but is it realistic to assume that the additional debt issuance implied by the financing adjustment is always feasible for highly levered firms? Furthermore, what evidence is there that the initial debt/equity ratio is the "appropriate" one for the firm, hence deserving of maintenance? What provision exists for adjusting the target ratio as conditions confronting the firm, the industry or the economy change? Any definition of income designed to maintain certain financial ratios introduces a significant alteration in the accounting function that has yet to be justified in terms of purpose or utility.[15]

U.K. by the Accounting Standards Committee's *Exposure Draft No. 24, Current Cost Accounting* (London: Accounting Standards Committee, 1979).
[13] CICA, Par. B.38.
[14] Ibid., Par. B.39.
[15] For additional perspectives on the financing adjustment, see David Tweedie, "Financial Reporting, Inflation, and the Capital Maintenance Concept" (Occasional Paper No. 19, International Centre for Research in Accounting, University of Lancaster, 1979).

UNANTICIPATED INFLATION

Borrowers gain from inflation only when the inflation is unanticipated. Return to our example of a $1,000 bond carrying a 15 per cent nominal rate of interest and consider what happens if the realized rate of inflation turns out to be 14 per cent, instead of the anticipated 10 per cent. Table II shows the borrower's after-the-fact real cost and the lender's real return under these assumptions.

TABLE II

Real Interest under Unanticipated Inflation

Nominal interest expense	
($1,000 × 15% nominal interest rate)	$150
Less: Anticipated decline in the	
purchasing power equivalent	
of the loan principal ($1,000 × 10% inflation)	100
Equals: Target real interest ($1,000 × 5%)	50
Less: Unanticipated decline in the purchasing	
power equivalent of the loan principal	
($1,000 × (14% – 10%)	40
Equals: After-the-fact real interest	$ 10

The unanticipated inflation resulted in lenders receiving less than the target return. Obviously, this also means that borrowers paid a lower than anticipated actual interest cost, with the amount of the difference being the unanticipated inflation multiplied by the loan principal, or $40 in this case. Unanticipated inflation gives rise to a wealth transfer between lenders (bondholders) and borrowers (stockholders). The amount of the lender's loss will precisely equal the amount of the borrower's real economic gain on debt.

A precise measure of the borrower's economic gain would require estimating the anticipated rate of inflation at the time of the original borrowing. Clearly, such estimates would be subject to considerable measurement error. For this reason, it seems impracticable to try to introduce an estimate of anticipated inflation into the FASB's computation of purchasing power gains on debt. On the other hand, ignoring the anticipated inflation altogether is worse still, since that approach to measuring gains on debt is devoid of any conceptual foundation.

The key to the dilemma is, of course, separating anticipated from unanticipated inflation. Some have suggested that unanticipated changes in inflation can be approximated by measuring changes in the market price of debt.[16] Of course, changes in the market price of debt will incorporate other factors in addition to

---

[16] Note that this approach will miss one-time unanticipated inflation that is expected to be followed by a return to previous rates of inflation. The reason is that such one-time effects will probably not result in a change in interest rates, hence will not cause a change in the market price of debt.

changes in inflation expectations—for example, changes in financial risk. Nevertheless, this price change approach seems to provide a reasonable surrogate for measuring real economic gains on debt in a current value system.[17]

Assume the simplest possible scenario, where the observed holding gains on debt are totally attributable to changes in inflation anticipations. Under such conditions, will the downward change in the market price of debt constitute gain in an accounting sense? The answer to this question depends on which capital maintenance concept is used.

Gains under Physical Capital Maintenance

A correctly measured real economic gain on debt merely represents a transfer between two categories of providers of entity capital. Since the physical capital maintenance approach adopts the entity concept of income, which focuses on the entity itself (not on the separate providers of capital), the critical question in determining whether such wealth transfers constitute income under this approach depends on whether or not the entity itself benefits. The question is easily answered: The wealth transfers that arise under unanticipated inflation leave the position of the entity as a whole unchanged.

Consider the case of bonds that have no call penalty and thus can be retired at market value. If unanticipated inflation causes the price of such bonds to fall, the firm could retire the bonds immediately by expending cash equal to the new, lower market price of the bonds. But if the expended cash must be replaced in order to finance future operations, new bonds must be issued at the new, higher interest rate. The total debt-associated cash flows to the entity after refunding will equal the debt-associated cash flows it would have received without refunding. Thus, in the absence of call penalties, etc., the entity has no inducement to refund.

In other words, unanticipated inflation, per se, does not affect the debt-associated total cash flows to the entity as a whole.[18] It merely represents a wealth transfer from bondholders to stockholders within the entity. For this reason, under a physical capital maintenance approach, the income measure will reflect no real economic gain on debt under any circumstances.[19]

---

[17]As suggested by Kaplan, "Purchasing Power Gains on Debt."

[18]The effect of unanticipated inflation on bond prices depends on whether the unanticipated inflation that was actually experienced is expected to persist in future years. If the 14 per cent rate of inflation is expected to continue, then (according to the Fisher Effect) nominal interest rates will climb to 19 per cent and bond prices will fall. On the other hand, if the 14 per cent inflation is considered to be a one-time aberration, and future inflation rates are expected to fall back to 10 per cent, then nominal interest rates will remain at 15 per cent and bond prices will not change. Under either scenario, there is no real economic gain under the entity view.

[19]Those who agree that cash flows to the entity as a whole are unaffected by the so-called inflation gain on debt might still be tempted to report these items under a physical capital maintenance concept. Their argument might go: "So long as accountants specifically identify the 'inflation gain,' what harm can possibly be done in an efficient market setting? Readers who believe that the gain is specious will simply ignore the item."

In my view, this is a highly unsatisfactory approach. Even though I, too, believe in the efficiency of the

Note that the entity view differentiates between a change in the price of debt and a change in the price of an asset. The asset price change is treated as a holding gain and is considered to affect the entity as a whole; by contrast, the debt price change is ignored. Ignoring changes in the market price of debt is analogous to ignoring changes in the market price of outstanding common stock; both are carried at book value for the same reason—i.e., changes in the prices of these securities do not directly affect the entity's cash flows.

To illustrate this point further, let us return to a slightly altered version of the example. Assume that the firm's debt does not mature until December 1981 and that, because of previously unanticipated inflation that is now expected to persist, the December 31, 1980, market price of the firm's debt falls to $700. If the asset's replacement cost new is still $1,100, the firm cannot distribute the change in the price of the debt. If it did try to distribute the price change (in addition to the $300 dividend), its cash balance would fall to $1,050—$50 less than the replacement cost of the asset. The expended funds would have to be replenished to allow the entity to replace the asset and thereby maintain physical capacity. Similarly, because of the increase in current interest rates, the net cash flows associated with refunding the debt must be identical to the cash flows associated with maintaining the existing debt to maturity. Thus, from an entity perspective, holding gains on debt cannot be distributed without reducing physical capacity nor, in the absence of call premium frictions, do they alter the debt-related cash flow stream. Hence they do not qualify as income under a physical capital maintenance approach.[20]

---

securities markets, it is clear that financial results are used as a basis for decision-making in a multitude of economic sectors. While financially sophisticated users may quickly learn the "correct" treatment of inflation gains on debt, the bottom-line number that is reported—even with full disclosure of its components—does have a potentially great effect on other classes of users. A case in point is the public's reaction to oil companies' "windfall profits," which more than likely included large amounts of undistributable (in a physical capital maintenance sense) holding gains on inventories and fixed assets. The general public's use of accounting numbers is of considerable social importance. To include conceptually unsupported items in income under the premise that disclosing the nature of the items will guard against misinterpretation may be acceptable in a financial market setting; however, it is totally unacceptable in a broader social setting.

[20]The effect of changes in interest rates on distributable operating flows must also be considered. Insofar as distributable operating flow is intended to reflect long-run future flows that could be sustained if costs and prices remained at their current levels, then interest expense should be charged to income at current rates. The entry would be:

DR Interest expense (at current rates)	XXX	
CR Cash or interest payable		XXX
CR Equity		XXX

In this view, the "extra" expense represents the cash hold-back that must be anticipated in order to pay future, higher interest costs when the existing debt matures and is refunded.

One might argue that this approach understates distributable operating flow, since a deduction for historical cost interest expense shields sufficient funds from dividends to provide for replacement of the asset itself. While this view is strictly correct as far as it goes, it also leads to an anomaly in interpreting the resulting historical cost interest distributable flow figure. Specifically, if interest is deducted at historical cost, and if we assume a continuation of existing replacement cost operating margins, distributable flow would fall when the debt matures and is refunded, presumably at the existing current rates. Thus the distributable operating flow figure that results when interest is deducted at historical rates seems inconsistent with the FASB's cash assessment criterion (in *Objectives of Financial Reporting by Business Enterprises,* Statement of Financial Accounting Concepts No. 1 (Stamford, CT: FASB, November 1978). It is for this reason that an interest deduction at current rates appears to be preferable.

Gains under Financial Capital Maintenance

Under the financial capital maintenance approach, a wealth transfer between stockholders and bondholders brought about by unanticipated inflation can be said to represent a real economic gain (or loss). This is because the financial capital approach takes the proprietary—rather than the entity—view of capital. Under the proprietary approach, an increase in owners' equity (assets minus liabilities) represents distributable income to the owners. Thus a holding gain on an asset, representing an increase over the beginning market value of the asset, is treated as an element of income. Similarly, a decrease in the market value of debt, representing a decrease in liabilities, constitutes a net increase in owners' equity that may legitimately be treated as distributable income.[21]

Using changes in the market price of debt to measure real economic gains on debt is consistent with the philosophy underlying the financial capital maintenance approach. But such gains must be measured using changes in the market price of the debt, not via the approach suggested by the FASB. Furthermore, if such gains are to be included in income, then the concept must include both asset and debt holding gains to be internally consistent.

Implications

Anticipated inflation never gives rise to a real economic gain on debt from the borrower's perspective. Furthermore, even when the market price of debt does change—thus suggesting unanticipated inflation—it does not automatically follow that there has been a gain on debt. The impact of unanticipated inflation on levered firms depends upon whose perspective—the firm's or the shareholder's—is being considered.

If one wishes to assess the impact of inflation on the exclusive interests of shareholders, then a financial capital maintenance approach is warranted. Under this approach, properly measured unanticipated inflation gives rise to an accounting

---

[21]FASB Statement No. 33 measures holding gains net of overall changes in average price levels. Extending this approach to holding gains on debt would change the *amount* of the gain included in a financial capital maintenance income statement, but not the concepts involved.

The journal entries for current value debt accounting under the financial capital maintenance approach are as follows:

(1)	DR Interest expense (at current rates)	XXX	
	CR Cash or interest payable		XXX
	CR Equity		XXX
(2)	DR Bonds payable	XXX	
	CR Inflation gain on debt		XXX
	CR Equity		XXX

The second entry, of course, would have to be reversed in ensuing years as the market price of the bonds rises as maturity approaches. Notice that Franco Modigliani and Richard A. Cohn, in "Inflation, Rational Valuation and the Market," *Financial Analysts Journal,* March/April 1979, implicitly adopted the proprietary view of income in arguing that equities are undervalued. However, they would charge interest at net, "real" rates, rather than at nominal rates as we have done here. The difference seemingly arises because Modigliani and Cohn adopt an *ex post* income measure, while we adopt the cash flow prediction *ex ante* measure recently promulgated by the FASB in Statement of Financial Accounting Concepts No. 1.

gain on debt, which would appropriately be added to operating income in reporting the short-run inflation-adjusted income to shareholders. Government planners, regulators, taxing authorities and legislative bodies, however, must adopt a broader perspective than that of the shareholder's individual gains. In evaluating aggregate social policy issues, their focus legitimately centers on the entity as a distinct unit, and for this purpose a physical capital maintenance approach is most appropriate.

A failure to understand the distinction between income to the entity and income to the shareholder leads to confusion of the following sort:

> The true profit situation isn't nearly so bleak. Proper inflation adjustment requires some additional rejiggering—on the liability side of the balance sheet—that increases profits. Those adjustments involve the gains *that companies* get when inflation reduces the real value of their dollar denominated liabilities. (Emphasis added.)[22]

From the perspective of the entity as a distinct unit, the wealth transfer that arises from unanticipated inflation has no effect. That is, the transfer affects the suppliers of capital but not the entity itself. Thus the income number intended to reflect aggregate entity performance should not incorporate any gain on debt under inflationary conditions.

[22]Ehrbar, "Unraveling the Mysteries of Corporate Profits," p. 93.

Current Value Reporting of Real Estate Companies and a Possible Example of Market Inefficiency

Dan Palmon
Rutgers University, Newark

Lee J. Seidler
New York University

Many corporations complain that the market underestimates their "real value." (There are few recorded complaints of market overvaluation.) Real estate companies seem to exceed most other industry groups in the volume and fervor of their lamentations in this respect. Of course, efficient market theory suggests that continued undervaluation of a publicly traded stock, with full disclosure of the supposedly causal factors, is improbable. Nevertheless, some recent information and events related to the current value reporting of several real estate companies and subsequent transactions suggest that the continued wailing of the real estate companies may not be entirely baseless.

This article:

1 Reviews the application of present value techniques by several real estate

From *The Accounting Review* (July 1978), pp. 776–790. Reprinted by permission of the American Accounting Association.

companies to satisfy the requirements of SEC Accounting Series Release No. 190 and suggests that in the particular circumstances of this industry, the results may be more valid than in the usual industrial situation, and

2 Examines user reactions to this present value information and other evidence to suggest an example of market inefficiency.

To start, it is useful to define the type of company discussed here. Sometimes referred to as investment builders, these enterprises construct and operate income producing real properties such as shopping centers, hotels, multi-family housing, and office buildings. They should not be confused with retail land sales companies whose accounting was severely criticized in the past. They are not real estate investment trusts (REITs) which provide financing, usually for construction and other interim purposes.

Among the leading investment builders are The Rouse Company, Monumental Corporation and Ernest W. Hahn, Inc., all of which will be discussed in this article.

Although the operations of these companies cover a range of real estate activities, a typical project would involve selecting a site for a shopping center, arranging for a long-term lease of the principal area by a national department store chain, arranging financing, constructing the shopping center, leasing the other stores in the center, and subsequently operating and maintaining the project. Rental revenues are applied to operating expenses and to interest and amortization of the related debt.

As the debt is amortized, and assuming the continued viability of the shopping center, it will almost always be refinanced to provide equity to support new projects. Therefore, a continuously high level of debt is maintained. The 1976 historical cost balance sheet of The Rouse Company, for example, showed:

	(millions)
Debt	$358.4
Other liabilities and deferred credits	20.0
Shareholders' equity	16.0
Total	$394.4

Real estate companies tend to bemoan the conventional financial accounting requirement for depreciation of properties. (Of course, there is no complaint about depreciation for tax purposes.) Certain sayings, such as "real estate tends to appreciate, not depreciate," and "a well-maintained property never depreciates" are taken as axiomatic in the industry. The conventional requirement that a provision for depreciation of properties be made in the financial statements is a key point of contention. Properties are shown at constantly declining historical cost net book values in the balance sheet, when they are often worth considerably more than cost. Reported income is understated because of the same requirement. These two impacts combine to mislead investors in the opinion of the managements, and tend to cause share prices to be unduly depressed.

Managements of real estate companies have not kept their complaints within the confines of the board room. Tishman Realty & Construction was quite willing to state in a prospectus:

> In the opinion of management, the price at which the Common Stock traded in the public securities markets...did not reflect the underlying value of the assets of the corporation [Tishman, 1977, p. 68].

And, as will be discussed in greater detail below, Tishman took rather drastic action to remedy the situation:

> Therefore, management believes that shareholders will realize greater benefit from the sale of a majority of the Corporation's assets than they would if the Corporation continued in existence and the shareholders' only means of realizing the value of their investment were by selling the Common Stock in the public market [Tishman, 1977, p. 68].

Before taking actions such as Tishman's to counter these supposed impacts on share prices, real estate companies disclosed and attempted to emphasize cash flow information, rather than conventional accounting results. The companies argue that net cash flow from operations, after deduction of payments for interest and principal on outstanding mortgages, is a better gauge of their profits than conventional net income figures. The cash flow result does not include deductions for depreciation and deferred taxes and is invariably considerably higher than accounting net income.

The contentions of the real estate companies are as difficult for practicing accountants to accept as for academic theorists. Built of bricks and mortar and with a high portion of their value attributable to land, well-maintained, income-producing properties do not depreciate physically. Indeed, as inflation progresses, the cash flows generated by the properties normally increase. Since the value of a property is the present value of the future net cash flows it can generate, its value increases rather than depreciates. Provisions for maintenance of items such as roofs, air conditioners, *etc.,* are all that are required to match income and expense.

In addition to depreciation requirements, Tishman also blamed the lower of cost or market convention:

> Generally accepted accounting principles have prohibited the Corporation from writing up its operating assets to estimated market values, but have required the corporation to write down its properties held for sale to their estimated disposal value [Tishman, 1977, p. 68].

However, Tishman's comments about properties written down to disposable value suggests that well-maintained, income-producing real estate may well decline in value. Bricks and mortar are stable, but populations migrate and neighborhoods decline. Shopping centers which were originally located in the center of population concentrations find themselves displaced as the population shifts and newer centers are better located. However, systematic accounting depreciation, apparently directed at physical deterioration, fails to capture the essence of these essentially demographic changes.

Even less conventional is the contention of the investment builders that the repayment of debt represents an increase in equity. As the debt is repaid on a property, the company's equity in it increases. Subject only to some delays or accelerations because of money market conditions, the companies regularly refinance the properties, keeping debt levels high. The financing produces cash in hand. This can be, and is used as the equity base for additional property acquisitions. Thus, argue the companies, debt repayment generates unrealized equity and the act of refinancing is the realization.

Therefore, under accrual accounting, it would be logical to recognize debt repayment as an act which generates profit.

The arguments for not considering deferred taxes as expenses are not new, and are quite similar to those set forth by Davidson as early as 1958 [Davidson, 1958].

In effect, the real estate companies argue that their income statements should appear about as follows:

Rental Revenues	XXXX
Less:	
Operating expenses	XXXX
Maintenance	XXXX
Real estate taxes	XXXX
Mortgage interest and amortization	XXXX
Income taxes paid	XXXX
Income	XXXX

As a short cut, some companies merely added back depreciation and deferred taxes to conventional net income, subtract mortgage amortization and present the "cash flow" figure.

The proliferation of different measures of cash flow, the use of "cash flow per share" figures and the resultant possible confusion to investors caused the SEC to issue ASR No. 142, in 1973. This release placed sharp restrictions on the nature of the cash flow information that could be presented by these companies, and in particular, did not allow presentation of cash flow figures on a per share basis.

ASR No. 142 became the *bête noire* of the real estate industry and laments of market undervaluation increased.

The increase in the rate of inflation experienced in the United States during 1974 and thereafter provided both harm and potential aid to the real estate companies. As with all companies, the value of the shares of real estate companies derives from the present value of the estimated future net cash flows to be derived from the net assets. A high proportion of the future cash inflows (rentals) of an investment builder are fixed or determinable, as are most of the future cash outflows (debt amortization). However, as in any solvent business, assets exceed equity. Thus, with higher interest rates, the present value of investment properties (less the present value of future mortgage payments) declines. The share prices of the companies appear to reflect higher interest rates in a distinctly negative manner.

At the same time, however, the promise of continued inflation suggested to corporate management that future cash inflows would rise; that is, their properties should be worth more. However, conventional accounting did not permit any accounting recognition of this apparent increase in value. The situation of the real estate companies can be illustrated by the equation describing present value:

$$\text{Present Value} = \frac{\text{Cash Flow}}{\text{Interest Rate}}$$

Increases in the interest rates lower the present value, and seem to be reflected by the market. Increases in cash flow caused by inflation, raise present value, but the companies believe they are ignored by the market.

Of course, market theory suggests that both factors would be adequately reflected. The company managements are convinced that the market reflects only the negative impact of interest rates and not the positive increment in the values of their properties.

However, the rate of inflation stimulated the Securities and Exchange Commission to action, and in ASR No. 190, the Commission called for supplementary disclosure of replacement cost information by large, publicly held corporations. Actually, the proposals which led to the issuance of ASR No. 190 were promulgated by the SEC in August, 1975. The proposals themselves stimulated action on the part of some investment builders, eager for an opportunity to present legitimately more complete information about the current values of their companies.

Approximately coincident with the ASR 190 proposals, one such company requested the authors of this article to develop a system of accounting and reporting which would be rational and hopefully acceptable, but which would reflect both the current values of the company's properties and the changes in value due to debt amortization, inflation and other factors.

As a preliminary step, we reviewed the operations of the company and its properties, which consisted principally of 20 large shopping malls and about 16,000 rental apartments. Properties are occasionally purchased or sold. When such transactions take place, real estate operators apply a multiple (called a "cap" or capitalization rate) to current annual net cash flows to obtain a valuation. This method, which has been in use as long as any current operators can recall, is a less sophisticated version of a present value calculation. The multiple is the result of dividing 100 by the discount (or capitalization) rate which would be used for present value purposes. That is, if the appropriate interest or discount rate were eight percent, the multiple or cap rate would be 12.5 (100 divided by 8). By multiplying the current cash flow by the cap rate, the real estate operator makes the simplifying assumption that the present net cash flows will continue unchanged for an indefinite period. The multiple used to produce this current valuation is frequently adjusted as interest rates change.

As a practical matter, real estate operators are not so naive as to accept uncritically any *one* year's cash flow. Estimates of future cash flows are also made and may result in an adjustment of the capitalization rate—a crude, but practical solution.

Thus, it became clear that real estate operators make explicit projections of future cash flows in the normal course of their business operations. These projections can be used as the valuation basis for determining the current value of rental properties.

It should be noted that estimates of future cash flows from individual assets can rarely be made for most businesses. Indeed, most productive assets are operated only as one portion of a longer production-sales cycle. It is virtually impossible to associate identifiable cash flows with individual assets or even productive units. Therefore, projections of future cash flows can be made only in the aggregate (company-wide basis or division-wide basis).

Income-producing real estate appears to be an exception to the general situation. Inflows of cash can be traced directly to individual, virtually self-sufficient units, such as shopping centers or apartment buildings. Similarly, outflows (interest, taxes, maintenance, *etc.*) are almost completely traceable to the same separate units. Large elements of both future inflows and outflows of cash are often contractual in nature, such as lease revenues and mortgage interest and principal payments, or are reasonably predictable, such as real estate taxes. The ability to project future cash flows on an asset-by-asset (property-by-property) basis increases the reliability of the resulting projections for the company as a whole.

The management of the company which had consulted us, and its auditors, believed that management has the ability to make reasonably accurate forecasts of net cash flows from specific properties for at least five years into the future. The results of earlier forecasts made for operational purposes, for acquisitions and in connection with a major merger, and comparison of these forecasts with actual reported results substantiated these assertions.

Thus, our initial research indicated that two conditions exist in the operations of real estate investment builders:

1 Cash inflows and outflows can be isolated and traced to specific units, and
2 Managements have a history of making reasonably accurate project-by-project cash flow projections and of using them in normal business operations and decision making.

The existence of these somewhat unique conditions suggested that it might be possible to design an accounting system based on the present value of future net cash flows which was capable of being implemented and used by an investment builder. The authors proceeded to design such a system, the essential elements of which include a present value balance sheet and an income statement which presents both conventional reporting of realized transactions during the period and unrealized changes in present values. An additional financial statement reports, using variance analysis techniques, the sources of change in the present value balance sheet, other than realized transactions. This statement also includes a comparison of predicted cash flows (used in the present value computation) with actual.

The system was designed in considerable detail, and was tested on a retroactive basis on a segment of the company. It appeared satisfactory in all technical respects.

However, the company did not adopt the system for external financial reporting purposes, for two intermingled reasons. Management had significant, and probably warranted, reservations about the substantial amount of "new" terminology incorporated in the system and the financial statements generated by it. There were fears that users of the financial statements would not understand them; present value concepts are not familiar to most shareholders.

At about the same time, another large investment builder, The Rouse Company, proposed to the SEC that it be allowed to publish a current value balance sheet based on valuations provided by real estate appraisers, to serve as conformity to the requirements of ASR No. 190. Rouse had, for three years, been publishing a "value added" table, summarizing the Company's estimate of value in its operating properties. The SEC gave its permission, and the May 31, 1976 annual report of The Rouse Company included "Consolidated Cost Basis and Current Value Basis Balance Sheets," in the conventional financial statements [Rouse, 1976, p. 20]. However, only the balance sheet was presented on a current value basis; the income statement and the statement of changes in financial position were given only on historical cost.

The Rouse financial statements were accompanied by a letter from a property appraiser which concurred with the Company's estimates of current value [Rouse, 1976, p. 26]. The current value balance sheet was mentioned in the opinion of the auditors, who described it as providing "relevant information about the current financial position of the company which is not provided by financial statements prepared on the historical cost basis" [Rouse, 1976, p. 25].

The Rouse system had the twin virtues of more familiar terminology than that of the authors, and had already been accepted by the SEC. Certainly, a bit of sour grapes is involved, but the authors believe that their system constitutes a more complete approach than did that of Rouse. Nevertheless, the Rouse system was not only accepted by the SEC, it became a general model for the reporting of several other companies in the industry.

Rouse issued a seven-month report at December 31, 1976, in order to change to a calendar year. The figures are summarized in Table 1.

On the current value basis, Rouse's net property increased $121,987,000 or 36 percent over the cost basis. This substantial increase was not unusual as illustrated by the examples in Table 2 of other companies that disclosed current value information in their 1976 annual reports.

The current value basis figures also had a significant effect on the shareholders' equity of each of the companies as shown in Table 3.

All of the companies are in the real estate investment or lodging industries except for Trans Union, which also has discrete assets for which future rentals can be predicted.

Ernest W. Hahn, The Rouse Company, and Days Inns calculated their own current values for the properties and had these estimates reviewed by real estate consultants.

For operating property, The Rouse Company and Ernest W. Hahn, Inc. used similar methods of computing current values. Hahn stated in a footnote that management added the company's current value equity in each property to the company's portion of the related property debt and present value of ground lease commitments. Hahn defined current value equity as the company's portion of each property's estimated stabilized annual net cash flow (operating revenues less operating expenses, interest, principal payments on debt, and participation payments to lessors, lenders and partners) divided by a rate of return (ranging 8.5 percent to 10.5

TABLE 1

The Rouse Company Condensed Balance Sheet
December 31, 1976
(in thousands)

	Current value basis	Historical cost basis
Assets		
Operating properties	$411,568	$349,702
Less accumulated depreciation and amortization		59,275
	411,568	290,427
Development costs net of reserve	46,245	46,245
Furniture, Fixtures and Equipment	4,407	3,561
Net property and deferred cost of projects	462,220	340,233
Notes receivable	14,922	14,660
Other assets	51,430	51,430
Total	$528,572	$406,323
Liabilities		
Liabilities and deferred credits*	$390,655	$390,655
Shareholders' Equity		
Book cost	$ 15,668	$ 15,668
Revaluation Equity	122,249	
Total Shareholders' Equity	$137,917	$ 15,668
Total	$528,572	$406,323

*The difference between the book value (historical cost) and current value of liabilities (principally mortgages) is included in the current value of operating properties.

TABLE 2

Net Property—Current vs. Historical Cost
(In thousands of dollars)

Net Property	Current Value	Historical Cost	Increase	Percent Increase
Hilton Hotels	$466,937	$236,961	$229,976	97%
Monumental Properties	549,602	364,248	185,354	51%
Ernest W. Hahn*	413,878	301,820	112,058	37%
Days Inns of America	62,234	38,573	23,661	01%
Trans Union Corp.	854,200	787,200	67,000	9%

*1977 Annual Report.

TABLE 3

Shareholders' Equity—Current vs. Historical Cost
(In thousands of dollars)

Stockholders' Equity	Current Value	Historical Cost	Increase	Percent Increase
Rouse Company	$137,917	$ 15,668	$122,249	780%
Hilton Hotels	460,977	231,001	229,976	100%
Monumental Properties	183,285	12,123	171,162	1411%
Ernest W. Hahn	118,942	20,789	98,153	472%
Days Inns of America	22,041	611	21,430	3507%
Trans Union Corp.	334,935	267,935	67,000	25%

percent), which Hahn's management believes represents current market rates. The same method is used by Hahn's management to determine an appropriate selling price for a property. The Rouse Company determined the estimates of current value by adding each property's equity interest and the outstanding balance of related debt. Rouse defines "equity interest" in a similar manner to Hahn's "current value equity."

For undeveloped land Hahn used estimates of market value where there were recent sales of comparable property. Absent such sales, land was stated at historical cost. Rouse did not disclose how the value of undeveloped land was determined, but stated it as $9,200,000. Rouse also stated that its appraisers did not review the land estimates.

Days Inns determined current values for its leasehold interests, leased fee interests, fee interests and franchise agreements. Its various assumptions were described in detail in the annual report. Each company stated its concept of current value in a slightly different manner. Days Inns defined it as:

> The values of the interest in its various properties is the estimated current investment which investors would make to purchase the Company's interest in each property's future cash flow [Days Inns, 1976, p. 6].

The company holds leasehold interests in 66 motels. Current value was estimated as the present value of each property's cash flow for the remaining lease terms. Estimates of future cash flows were generally based on 1976 occupancy rates and average daily room rates at October 1, 1976. Expenses were estimated at the 1976 percentages they bore to revenues. The resulting net cash flows were then discounted at rates from 15 percent to 19 percent, representing "historical performance and the quality of the individual property."

The interest rates appear quite high, as compared to those used by some other companies, and when combined with the use of 1976 revenue figures, would seem to give an extremely conservative result. Note below, however, our suggestion that some of the interest rates may have been "forced."

Days Inns also owns and leases out 10 motels. The current value of these properties was determined at a 10 percent discount rate. It is interesting to note that in the evaluation of a commercial warehouse, cash flow estimates were reduced, "because of lower than stabilized occupancy at the September 30, 1976 valuation date" [Days Inns, 1976, p. 6].

The company also owns and operates one motel. The value of this property is estimated on the basis of its current income and expenses capitalized at 13 percent. The company's home office building, a portion of which is rented to others on short-term leases, was valued by estimating economic rent, less normal vacancy allowance and expenses, and by capitalizing the potential net income at 9½ percent.

Days Inns franchises motels and restaurants to others, under 20 year agreements. These agreements are not carried in the historical cost balance sheet. However, for current value purposes, the company computed the present value of the future recurring franchise fees and discounted them at 20 percent, giving a value of $9,500,000 which was entered on the current value balance sheet. Thus, the current value computations resulted in the addition of an asset which would not be recognized under historical cost accounting.

Hilton Hotels and Monumental Corporation employed real estate consultants and appriasers to determine independently the current market value for all operating properties and land. These companies felt that the use of appraisers rather than in-house estimates would maximize the apparent reliability of the reported values. The appraisers determined the current values on the basis of discounted future cash flows. Hilton's discount rate is 9 percent to 12 percent while Monumental's rate is undisclosed.

Hilton Hotels Corporation established fair market value as its current value concept:

> Fair market value is frequently referred to as the price at which a willing seller would sell and willing buyer would buy, neither being compelled to sell or buy. Fair market value was arrived at by calculating the present worth of estimated future income streams accruing to the owner utilizing rates of return ranging from 9 to 12 percent and various terms of financing and conditions of sale and profitability factors with respect to individual properties [Hilton, 1976, p. 36].

However, a significant portion of Hilton's income is derived from hotel management. Indeed, to raise capital, the company frequently sells hotels but continues to manage them under long-term agreements. Hilton considered this situation in its present value computation:

> It was assumed that the buyers of the hotel properties would retain management companies to operate the properties and, therefore $3,965,000 in annual pro-forma management fees were deducted from the estimated future earnings stream used to value the hotel properties [Hilton, 1976, p. 36].

Hilton also noted that since owners of Las Vegas properties do not customarily employ third party management, the adjustment was not made for properties in that city.

By subtracting the present value of the future management fees from the fair market value of the properties, Hilton is adjusting for the value added to the properties by its management abilities, in two ways. First, it appears to be stating that a component of the fair market value of the property is the assumption of continuing Hilton management. Without continuing Hilton management, a buyer would be required to develop a management capability, and would reduce the price it was willing to pay for the property by the anticipated cost to develop such a capability.

However, to Hilton, the future management fees are unperformed and unrealized services and, therefore, not appropriately includable in the value of the property.

Trans Union Corporation is the only company reviewed here which is not involved in real estate.[1] However, a major element of Trans Union's business is long term rail car leasing. The company owns a fleet of rail cars and supplies the cars and related maintenance and administrative services to railroads. The rail car fleet generates revenues and costs which are similar in nature to those of a real estate operation. Trans Union noted:

> Since the Company has no requirement for shipping services itself, it perceives the capacity of this fleet to be its revenue earning ability...[Trans Union, 1976, p. 26].

It will be recalled that Days Inns was quoted above as relating the current value of its properties to the amounts that *outsiders* would invest to obtain the cash flows from the properties. Trans Union took a similar approach, but related the computation to the amounts *it* would invest:

> The replacement cost of the rail car fleet is deemed to be that value which the Company would be willing to invest in new cars to obtain an income stream at a level equivalent to that which the fleet is currently earning [Trans Union, 1976, p. 26].

This approach would appear to allow a good deal of subjectivity. However, Trans Union relates its willingness to invest to its actual reinvestment policies, in an apparently unique linkage between financial reporting and internal decision making:

> In practice, replacements of retired cars are not made unless a satisfactory rate of return is obtainable under an acceptable lease arrangement with a credit-worthy lessee. The techniques used to determine replacement costs were based on the decision making process applied to new car additions and involve discounted cash flow calculations applied to lease rentals less executory costs such as maintenance [Trans Union, 1976, p. 26].[2]

Note that Trans Union used conventional techniques of cost indexing for the replacement cost computations on its other assets.

DISCOUNT RATES

In principle, the discount rate used in the previously described computations ought to be the after-tax return expected from comparable investments appropriately risk adjusted. Similarly, the cash flows used in the computations should be on an after-tax basis. The previous discussions of the methods employed by the different companies indicate a wide range of discount rates. None of the companies explicitly

---

[1] Another current value presentation of particular interest is that of Iowa Beef Processors, Inc. In their October 30, 1976 financial statements, Iowa Beef prepared a full set of consolidated current value financial statements along with complete notes. Since their methodology did not involve the use of present value techniques, it is not reviewed in this article.

[2] In a separate section of the annual report, Trans Union also explains its capital budgeting process.

mentions whether the discount rates are pre-tax or after-tax, although as noted below, several consider taxes in one way or another.

The authors discussed these present value computations with senior financial executives of each of the companies.

Several general conclusions emerged from these discussions. Perhaps most important, was that few of the financial executives queried were aware of the pre-tax, after-tax issue as it impacted the discount (or capitalization) rate. One company indicated to us that it had considered taxes by using the following supposedly scientific formula:

$$\text{Current Value of Asset} = \frac{\text{Cash Flow Before Tax}}{\text{Capitalization Rate Before Tax + An Increment to Compensate for no Tax in the Numerator}}$$

Most of the other companies, however, indicated that they had used an "appropriate" discount or capitalization rate. On an "off-the-record" basis, the assistant to the treasurer of one of the companies admitted that the company "knew what the properties were worth" and that the discount rate used was the one which would give the appropriate values. Our other discussions gave us good reason to suspect that similar considerations prevailed at some of the other companies.[3]

Such determinations of the discount rate may seem cynical and certainly unscientific. Nevertheless, they are indicative both of the state of the art and of the nature of the business. The authors' work with one of the companies, described above, convinced us that the officers of that company had clear and accurate perceptions of current market values of properties of the type they bought, sold and operated. And, as noted above, those market values are a function of the value of the future cash flows expected from the properties.

However, with the current environment of financial reporting, and the credibility gap created by the excessively imaginative accounting practices of the 1960s in industries such as franchising, land sales and leasing, a management estimate of value, unsupported by supposedly rigorous calculations and attestation, seems unacceptable. As a result, several of these managements felt obliged to add a supposedly objective methodological base to their work. Alternatively, some managements used outside, supposedly independent appraisers to provide an additional aura of objectivity, although as one treasurer noted, "No outside appraiser knows as much about the values of our properties as we do."

INCOME TAXES

The companies were not consistent in their treatments of income taxes, outside of the discount rate. Monumental Properties and E. W. Hahn discounted pre-tax cash flows and then showed the present value of estimated future tax payments as

---

[3]We would specifically exclude Trans Union from this comment. The Company has previously demonstrated a high level of understanding and utilization of present value techniques for decision making purposes, both for capital budgeting and management of its pension fund.

liabilities. Rouse makes no specific provision for income taxes, but informed us that it is likely to do so in future reports.

Days Inns was unique in providing for both income taxes (capital gains) and commissions that would be payable on disposition of the properties:

> Even though the Company does not anticipate a sale of its property interests, a provision of 3 percent of the estimated gross current value of such interests has been made for estimated sales commissions which would be payable on realization of the current values. Likewise, income taxes have been provided at 33 percent (30 percent Federal and 3 percent state) of the estimated current value in excess of historical cost [Days Inns, 1976, p. 7].

MARKET REACTION

If the laments of the real estate companies about generally accepted accounting principles and the resulting undervaluation of their share prices were correct, then one would expect to see substantial market reaction to the release of the current value figures. Unfortunately for the contentions of the companies, there were no perceptible market reactions.[4]

For example, Monumental Corporation was one of the companies which fulfilled ASR No. 190 requirements through the use of present value-appraisal figures.

Monumental's 1976 financial statements (which included the present value information) were released on April 5, 1977. The share price was unchanged that day and closed at 12⅝. (Bid OTC.) Previous trading during 1977 had been in a range of 11½ to 13½. On April 6, the price rose to 12¾ and was unchanged on April 7. Clearly, there was no significant market reaction to the release of the current value information, although the result suggested that the historical cost figures were substantially below the current value of Monumental's real estate holdings.

The minimal market reaction might be explained by the earlier release of Rouse's figures, which also showed a substantial excess of present value over historical cost figures. Thus, the nature of the Monumental results might have been anticipated, especially since the two companies and their properties are similar.

However, the market had accorded a similarly lethargic reaction to the earlier Rouse figures. There are several possibilities which might explain these market reactions. First, the market might have fully anticipated the figures of both companies. Certainly, the companies had been arguing for some time that their properties were worth more than book value.

Another alternative is that the market did not believe the present value results either actively, in the sense of disbelief, or passively by ignoring them. It is not unusual for corporate managements, suffering from depressed share prices, to maintain that their properties are undervalued by the accountants.

On April 12, 1977, Monumental Corporation announced a plan by which its real estate holdings would be sold and the cash proceeds distributed to the shareholders. The shares jumped more than 20 percent on the date of the announcement to 15⅝

---

[4] We reviewed the prices and activity of the shares of all the companies discussed here, for the period surrounding the release of the current value information. There were no indications of unusual activity.

and closed at the end of April at 18. Despite the generally desultory nature of the market during the remainder of 1977, Monumental shares closed at 22 at the end of the year. Discussions with management and our own review of relevant publications and discussions with financial analysts indicate no other major events, internal or external, to explain the share price change, other than the announcement of the sale of the properties.

Note that the magnitude of the increase in the price of Monumental's shares is understated by the company's corporate structure. Monumental Corporation consists of several units, principally a group of insurance companies and Monumental Properties, the real estate company, which is wholly owned. On a conventional accounting basis, Monumental Properties contributed only 12 percent of reported earnings. Monumental Properties' assets were 33 percent of consolidated assets on an historical cost basis, 49 percent on a current value basis. Therefore, the indisputably large jump in the share price of the total company which was apparently precipitated by the sale announcement related to less than half of consolidated assets.

One financial analyst calculated that if the insurance companies owned by Monumental were consistently valued by the market at average multiples for companies of their type and quality, and the market price were to fully reflect the current values for its properties claimed by Monumental in its replacement cost computation, the share price would be $24 to $26 [Bear, Stearns, 1977]. This estimate may be compared with the year-end price of $22 per share. One possible explanation of the "discount" may lie with uncertainty associated with the tax treatment of the sale of the properties. Monumental proposed to create a trust arrangement which would minimize taxes on the disposition. The company had not yet received a favorable ruling from the Internal Revenue Service by year end.*

Why did the market apparently ignore the well published announcement of the "value" of the properties, but react so favorably to the announcement that they would be sold, for a price which would be close to that earlier announced value?

The essential meaning of the sale announcement is that other real estate operators, rather than Monumental, will manage the properties in the future. The increase in the share price reflects a market estimate that these other operators will pay Monumental an amount which is higher than the value of the properties as seen by the same stock market prior to the liquidation announcement. Why?

One possible explanation is that the potential purchasers are perceived as being better property managers than Monumental. If the buyers of the properties are better managers they will obtain higher returns from the properties than Monumental. Hence, the properties are worth more in their hands than in Monumental's and the purchase price will reflect this increase in value.

This explanation falters, however, on two counts. The potential buyers were not named at the time the sale of the properties was announced. Indeed, there were no specific buyers at hand at the time of the announcement. Therefore, the implication of this explanation could only be that the eventual buyer would be a better manager than Monumental.

Editor's note: On March 30, 1978 Monumental announced receipt of the IRS Ruling. The share price increased from $20 to $24 in the next three days.

However, our experience in the industry and conversations with the managements of other leading companies confirm that Monumental's management is considered to be one of the best in the industry. Clearly, the management of Monumental could not be of such poor quality as to justify such a significant market reaction.

Another possible explanation is that of a liquidity preference by Monumental shareholders. That is, the shareholders would prefer to receive the cash values of the properties immediately, rather than as future dividends. Such an explanation might have some value for a stock which is infrequently traded. However, Monumental shares are quite actively traded (from 15,000 to 50,000 shares per week) and there is no lack of liquidity.

It is possible that the different tax treatments accorded to the ordinary earnings of Monumental Corporation and recipients of its dividends, as compared to the tax treatment accorded to the proceeds resulting from the sale of the properties, could account for the change in the value of the stock. For example, if the Monumental distributions after the sale of the properties were somehow tax free to the shareholders, the liquidation would, in effect, raise the after-tax value of the proceeds. However, no such difference exists. Monumental shareholders will be taxed at capital gains rates on the proceeds from the distribution, in precisely the same manner as they would be taxed if they sold their shares in the normal course of business.

It also might be suggested that a potential buyer of the properties would be in a lower tax bracket than Monumental Corporation, thus producing a relatively higher value to the properties in the buyer's hands. However, Monumental Corporation's tax rate (current) is only 18 percent. It is difficult to envision a buyer with a significantly lower tax rate.

With no other hypothetical explanations readily available, one might question the efficiency of the market in this situation. The current values of the properties were fully disclosed and available to the market. Note, that the computations of current value required by ASR No. 190 were by no means the first indications of the values of the properties. Monumental, in common with virtually all the other property companies, has consistently and enthusiastically disclosed its property holdings in its annual reports for many years. It would not have taken a particularly impressive demonstration of skills in financial analysis to make a determination of the current value of any of these companies.

Thus, one explanation for the instant and significant reaction of the Monumental share prices to the announcement of the property sale might be: the market chose to disregard or disbelieve the earlier evidence of the current value of the properties. Either case is a form of market inefficiency.

ACTIONS OF OTHER COMPANIES

Our suggestion that the behavior of Monumental share prices in the period after the sale announcement suggests an instance of market inefficiency is neither new nor unique. Indeed, the reason for the sale was the conclusion by the management of Monumental that the market was inefficient; that is, that it was not reflecting the values of the properties as the management perceived them to be. Monumental's management had tried other means, short of selling their properties, including disseminating additional materials on the company, holding analysts meetings, *etc.* Finally, management, who are also significant shareholders, concluded that the only way to realize the value of the properties was to demonstrate that value by selling them.

If Monumental's decision to sell its properties in the attendant circumstances was the only recorded instance of such behavior, we would have not much more than an interesting anecdote. However, Monumental was not alone. To the contrary, several other property companies have taken similar actions for the same stated reasons. We have singled out Monumental because the change in its share price was so sudden and significant.

Earlier in this article we pointed out that Tishman Realty Construction arranged to sell its properties in late 1977 for the same reasons given by Monumental.

On December 17, 1976 Arlen Realty & Development Corp. announced plans to concentrate on the development of real estate for sale, rather than retain and operate its properties. *The Wall Street Journal* noted:

> Like other publicly held real estate companies, Arlen has found it difficult to convey to investors the true value of its assets. While a real estate company may have a positive cash flow from its operations, it may report a paper loss because it must expense depreciation and amortization of deferred charges.

In October, 1976, another leading property company, Koger Properties, announced the formation of a series of partnerships to which many of its properties would be sold. Again, market undervaluation was given by management as the reason for the transaction. In its 1977 annual report, Koger noted:

> It is certainly not in our shareholders' interest to see their equity trading far below asset value, particularly if assets can just as easily be sold....
>
> These funds will enter the bloodstream of this enterprise at a price fixed by real estate fair market values, rather than a price based upon the vagaries of the OTC Market!

We reviewed the performance of the share prices of the above-described companies. In all cases, with the exception of Arlen, which was burdened by problems associated with its investment in Korvette's, there were indications of some increase in price which appeared to be associated with the announcements of the sales of the assets. However, none of the price changes approached the dimensions of those associated with Monumental. One possible explanation for the difference in share price behavior is that Monumental gave absolutely no prior hint of its sale, while most of the other companies had earlier given various indications that they were contemplating property sales.

However, our purpose in citing these additional examples was not to examine the behavior of their share prices, but to demonstrate that Monumental's management was not alone in believing that the market was inefficient with regard to the valuation of its shares and most important, that it was not alone in taking the extreme measure of selling off its assets in order to realize the values the market apparently refused to confer on its shares.

CONCLUSION

Obviously, this description of the behavior of the price of Monumental Corporation's shares and of the actions taken by the managements of several companies provides no definitive evidence of market inefficiency. These are only observations which have not been subjected to any rigorous analysis, nor considering the small number of instances, could they be.

They are, nevertheless, provocative. When the managements of several large corporations appear to be so convinced of the existence of market inefficiency in their particular situations that they are willing to liquidate some or all of the corporation's capital assets, further inquiry seems justified.

The problem of a small number of examples may be addressed by considering another similar phenomenon which has received considerable publicity in recent months, namely numerous takeover bids for corporations with offers for shares far in excess of current market prices. Such offers to transfer control of the corporate assets, at prices above "market," appear to represent situations which are similar in nature to that of the real estate companies described above. However, here the initiative comes from a potential buyer rather than a potential seller of corporate assets.

Since there are more takeover offers than dispositions of properties by disgruntled managements of real estate companies, this other area may provide more fruitful opportunities for further research.

REFERENCES

Bear, Stearns & Co., *Arbitrage Research* (April 22, 1977).
Davidson, S., "Accelerated Depreciation and the Allocation of Income Taxes," *The Accounting Review* (April 1958), pp. 173–180.
Days Inns of America, Annual Report, (September 30, 1976).
Hilton Hotels Corporation, Annual Report (December 31, 1976).
The Rouse Company, Annual Report, (May 31, 1976).
Tishman Realty & Construction Co. Inc., Notice of Combined Annual and Special Meeting of Shareholders (October 19, 1977).
Trans Union Corporation, Annual Report (December 31, 1976).

Postscript*

It will be recalled that the article described an unusual increase in the price of the shares of Monumental Corporation after an announcement that the real estate properties of the company would be sold: from 15⅝ to 18 and to 22 by the end of 1977. With the announcement of a favorable tax ruling, the price increased to 24.

By mid-1978, the price rose to 27¾. In August, as originally announced, the company split into two entities. For each share of Monumental Corporation stock, holders received .52 shares of a new Monumental Property Trust and .48 shares of a

---

*The Accounting Review, October 1979, p. 824.

new Monumental Corp. stock, representing the insurance portion of the original company. Prices at August 10, 1978, the first day on which both the new Monumental Corporation and Monumental Property Trust were quoted, were 20 and 38½, respectively, equal to a selling price for each old share of 29⅝ ((20 x .48) + (38.5 x .52)). On December 31, 1978, the new shares closed at 21¾ and 50¼, respectively, equivalent to a 36½ price for the old shares. On February 21, 1979, Property Trust shares were 54 and Monumental Corporation shares were 31¾ (i.e., 43 in terms of the old shares). There were no significant changes in the properties owned by the real estate trust during this period. The increase in the Monumental Corporation insurance company stock is apparently unrelated to the increase in Monumental Property Trust. It appears to have been the result of improved results and rumors of an impending takeover.

Follow-up note to "Current Value Reporting of Real Estate Companies and a Possible Example of Market Inefficiency" (Dan Palmon and Lee J. Seidler; *The Accounting Review*, July 1978).

ACCOUNTING ALTERNATIVES AND THE CAPITAL MARKET

A considerable volume of accounting research in recent years has been aimed at trying to understand the real-world environment in which accounting reports are used and in which accounting is practiced. Perhaps the most prominent of the several approaches to empirical research in accounting has been the capital market study.

Since the mid-1960s, scores of capital market studies have been reported in the accounting literature, largely inspired by developments in finance. Accounting researchers disagree over the usefulness of capital market studies reported to date, whether as valid indicators of capital market behavior or as guides to assist accounting professionals and policy makers.[1] Nonetheless, the studies have been widely read and discussed, they have provoked controversy, and policy makers have apparently relied on them for insights into how the securities market reacts to proposed changes in accounting standards. In the Bibliographical Notes at the end of this introduction, we refer to several works that assess the contribution of capital market research to accounting knowledge.

In the first article in this section, Daniel W. Collins, Warren T. Dent, and Melvin C. O'Connor discuss "The Market Effects of the Elimination of Full Cost Accounting in the Oil and Gas Industry." During 1977–78, the FASB and SEC were trying to decide whether "full cost" or "successful efforts costing" was the preferable method of accounting for the cost of unproductive wells. Strong opinions were expressed on both sides, and the new federal Department of Energy foresaw grave consequences for the pace of oil and gas exploration of a requirement that all companies use

---

[1]In his article reproduced in Section Four, "What Should Be the FASB's Objectives?," William H. Beaver suggests the implications of capital market research for accounting policy making.

successful efforts costing. In the course of the raging controversy, several capital market studies were conducted in order to gauge the effect of the FASB's July 15, 1977 exposure draft favoring successful efforts costing on security prices. Collins, Dent, and O'Connor review and evaluate the studies, together with two studies done in the early 1970s when a committee of the Accounting Principles Board tentatively proposed a similar switch to successful efforts costing. The article reveals disagreements among researchers on how such studies should be conducted. The choice of sample companies, the testing period, and the statistical techniques employed can have an effect on the meaningfulness of the findings. The authors conclude that "empirical evidence suggests that the proposed elimination of full cost accounting has had a measurable negative impact on the equity securities of potentially affected firms." Other researchers, such as Dyckman, would disagree.[2] Whether one agrees or disagrees with the authors' conclusions, the article by Collins, Dent, and O'Connor provides insight into the potential usefulness of capital market studies in the resolution of controversial accounting problems.

In "Briloff and the Capital Market," George Foster studies the impact on the stock market of Abraham J. Briloff's celebrated critiques of company financial reporting. Writing primarily in the weekly financial magazine *Barron's,* Briloff has reproved companies for using deceptive or uninformative financial reporting practices.[3] In his study, Foster tests whether 15 of Briloff's articles published between 1968 and 1976 triggered a stock market reaction. To Foster's surprise, they did. In the last several pages of his article, Foster tries to explain how a supposedly efficient market would find information value in magazine articles based almost wholly on publicly available information. Does Foster's result imply a market inefficiency? Has Briloff brought a "superior insight" to the market? Foster speculates on these and other questions.

BIBLIOGRAPHICAL NOTES

Several authors have discussed and evaluated the contribution of capital market research to accounting knowledge. The following works are worthy of consultation:

Dyckman, Thomas R., David H. Downes, and Robert P. Magee,: *Efficient Capital Markets and Accounting: A Critical Analysis* (Englewood Cliffs, NJ: Prentice-Hall, Inc., 1975).

---

[2]See, for example, Abbie Smith and Thomas R. Dyckman, "The Impact of Accounting Regulation on the Stock Market: The Case of Oil and Gas Companies: A Comment," *The Accounting Review* (October 1981), pp. 959–66. The Dyckman study cited in the Collins-Dent-O'Connor article was eventually published as Thomas R. Dyckman (with the assistance of Abbie J. Smith and The FASB Staff), *The Effects of the Issuance of The Exposure Draft and FASB Statement No. 19 on the Security Returns of Oil and Gas Producing Companies* (Stamford, CT: FASB, March 1979). The Collins and Dent study cited in the Collins-Dent-O'Connor article was published under title, "The Proposed Elimination of Full Cost Accounting in the Extractive Petroleum Industry: An Empirical Assessment of the Market Consequences," *Journal of Accounting and Economics* (March 1979), pp. 3–44. Also see Baruch Lev, "The Impact of Accounting Regulation on the Stock Market: The Case of Oil and Gas Companies," *The Accounting Review* (July 1979), pp. 485–503.

[3]Briloff has written three books in which most of the contents of his articles have been reprised. These books are cited in the Bibliographical Notes following the introduction to Section Three.

Kaplan, Robert S.: "The Information Content of Financial Accounting Numbers: A Survey of Empirical Evidence," in *The Impact of Accounting Research on Practice and Disclosure,* A. Rashad Abdel-khalik and Thomas F. Keller, eds. (Durham, NC: Duke University Press, 1978), pp. 134–173.

Peasnell, K.V.: "Empirical Research in Financial Accounting," in *Essays in British Accounting Research,* Michael Bromwich and Anthony G. Hopwood, eds. (London: Pitman Publishing Limited, 1981), pp. 104–129.

Beaver, William H.: *Financial Reporting: An Accounting Revolution* (Englewood Cliffs, NJ: Prentice-Hall, Inc. 1981). (See Robert S. Kaplan's review of Beaver's book: *Journal of Accounting and Economics* (December 1981), pp. 243–252.)

Abdel-khalik, A. Rashad and Bipin B. Ajinkya, "Accounting Information and Efficient Markets," Chap. 47 in *Handbook of Accounting and Auditing,* John C. Burton, Russell E. Palmer, and Robert S. Kay, eds. (Boston, MA: Warren, Gorham & Lamont, Inc., 1981).

Ricks, William: "Market Assessment of Alternative Accounting Methods: A Review of the Empirical Evidence," *Journal of Accounting Literature* (Spring 1982), pp. 59–102.

Keane, Simon M.: *Stock Market Efficiency: Theory, Evidence, Implications* (Deddington, Oxford, England: Philip Allan Publishers Limited, 1983), esp. Chap. 9.

Two works that suggest the implications of capital market research for financial statement analysis are the following:

Lev, Baruch: *Financial Statement Analysis: A New Approach* (Englewood Cliffs, NJ: Prentice-Hall, Inc., 1974).

Foster, George: *Financial Statement Analysis* (Englewood Cliffs, NJ: Prentice-Hall, Inc., 1978).

A large area of empirical research in accounting involves the application of behavioral research tools to accounting problems. A leading journal in the area is *Accounting, Organizations and Society,* published by Pergamon Press. Several works that summarize and assess much of the research done in the area are the following:

Hopwood, Anthony: *Accounting and Human Behaviour* (Englewood Cliffs, NJ: Prentice-Hall, Inc., 1976). (Originally published in 1974 by Accountancy Age Books, Haymarket Publishing Limited, London.)

Dyckman, Thomas R., Michael Gibbins, and Robert J. Swieringa,: "Experimental and Survey Research in Financial Accounting: A Review and Evaluation," in *The Impact of Accounting Research on Practice and Disclosure,* A. Rashad Abdel-khalik and Thomas F. Keller eds. (Durham, NC: Duke University Press, 1978), pp. 48–105.

Libby, Robert: *Accounting and Human Information Processing: Theory and Applications* (Englewood Cliffs, NJ: Prentice-Hall, Inc., 1981).

Ashton, Robert H.: *Human Information Processing in Accounting* (Sarasota, FL: American Accounting Association, 1982).

Two collections of articles that draw out the behavioral aspects of accounting are:

Bruns, William J., Jr. and Don T. DeCoster, eds.: *Accounting and Its Behavioral Implications* (New York: McGraw-Hill Book Company, 1969).

Schiff, Michael and Arie Y. Lewin, eds.: *Behavioral Aspects of Accounting* (Englewood Cliffs, NJ: Prentice-Hall, Inc., 1974)

The following work "is a comprehensive review of empirical research on the usefulness of financial information to investors and creditors"—especially well suited for readers who are not themselves researchers:

Griffin, Paul A.: *Usefulness to Investors and Creditors of Information Provided by Financial Reporting: A Review of Empirical Accounting Research* (Stamford, CT: FASB, 1982).

A colloquy between an accounting practitioner and two accounting academics on the relevance of capital market research to accounting issues is the following:

Wyatt, Arthur R.: "Efficient Market Theory: Its Impact on Accounting," *Journal of Accountancy* (February 1983), pp. 56-65.
Deitrick, James W. and Walter T. Harrison, Jr.: "EMH, CMR and the Accounting Profession," *Journal of Accountancy* (February 1984), pp. 82-94.

Market Effects of the Elimination of Full Cost Accounting in the Oil and Gas Industry

Daniel W. Collins
University of Iowa

Warren T. Dent
Eli Lilly & Co.

Melvin C. O'Connor
Michigan State University

The SEC's new proposal on accounting for exploration efforts in the oil and gas industry undertakes to shift investors' emphasis away from the published income statement toward one that expenses outlays for exploration immediately and treats the estimated value of the resulting discoveries as current revenue.

What effect will the SEC's proposal have on those companies, primarily engaged in oil and gas exploration and production, who have traditionally presented their performance to investors in terms of statements based on full cost accounting? The following article, written before the SEC issued its ruling, suggests that the shift in emphasis will have an adverse effect on the way the securities market values the shares of full cost companies, making it substantially more difficult for them to obtain funds in the capital market.

A number of academic studies have concluded that elimination of full cost accounting would have little or no adverse effect on full cost firms' equity security prices. When the authors corrected for certain methodological deficiencies in those studies, however, this conclusion was reversed. Price declines during the test periods (centering on the APB's 1971 and FASB's 1977 proposals to eliminate full cost accounting)

From *Financial Analysts Journal* (November-December 1978), pp. 48–57. Reprinted by permission of the *Financial Analysts Journal*.

were much more dramatic for full cost firms. Moreover, the impact on full cost producing companies was greater than the impact on full cost integrated companies.

The major issue before the Financial Accounting Standards Board (FASB) in its deliberations on accounting by oil and gas producing companies concerned the choice between full cost and successful efforts methods of accounting for prediscovery costs incurred in finding new oil and gas reserves. A company using full cost accounting capitalizes unproductive exploration and drilling costs from one field and writes them off against future income from productive reserves in another field, thus minimizing the earnings impact of unproductive exploration activity. A company using successful efforts accounting, on the other hand, immediately expenses the exploration and development costs associated with unproductive efforts.

The Board's decision—as implemented in its Statement 19—was to require successful efforts accounting for all oil and gas producing companies.[1] This mandate will have little effect on most of the large, "integrated" oil and gas producing companies, which already use the successful efforts method of accounting. For many of the smaller oil and gas companies, however, Statement No. 19 will force a change from full cost to successful efforts accounting that will, in most cases, substantially reduce reported equity and earnings.

Those opposing the elimination of full cost accounting argue that the resultant damage to full cost firms' financial statements will hinder their access to the capital markets and ultimately reduce exploration and competition in the oil and gas producing industry. Concerned over such possibilities, the Department of Energy (DOE) held public hearings in February of 1978 for the express purpose of collecting evidence on the competitive impact issue. The Securities and Exchange Commission (SEC), prompted by Congressional mandate (via public law 94–163 of the Energy Policy and Conservation Act of 1975) to establish uniform accounting practices in the oil and gas industry, also held hearings to consider whether it should rely on FASB Statement No. 19. Among the solicited comments it received was one from the Department of Justice:

> The SEC must determine whether the proposed mandated switch would likely affect capital market behavior in ways that would significantly disadvantage the competitive viability of any segment of the oil and gas producing industry....[2]

Clearly, few accounting proposals have generated so much concern over potential *economic* consequences.

Whether or not the proposed elimination of full cost accounting will, in fact, have an adverse effect on the valuation of equity securities is obviously an empirical question. This article reviews and attempts to reconcile the relevant empirical research. Studies by Patz and Boatsman, Dyckman and the Directorate of Economic and Policy Research of the SEC suggest that elimination of full cost accounting

---

[1] Financial Accounting Standards Board, *Statement of Financial Accounting No. 19: Financial Accounting and Reporting by Oil and Gas Producing Companies* (Stamford, CT.: FASB, December 1977).

[2] Department of Justice Response to the SEC, February 27, 1978, p. 20.

would have little or no adverse effect on the returns on full cost firms' equity securities.[3] Subsequent analyses by O'Connor and Collins and Collins and Dent, questioning the sample selection, statistical procedures and associated inferences of these studies, suggest otherwise.[4]

THE ARGUMENT

A study of 36 full cost companies undertaken by Touche Ross & Co. in March 1977 showed that a required switch from full cost to successful efforts accounting would (1) reduce reported earnings by an average of 20 percent, (2) reduce asset carrying values of oil and gas properties by an average of 30 percent, and (3) reduce shareholders' equity by an average of 16 percent.[5] A more recent study by the First Boston Corporation estimated that the switch would result in substantial reductions in pretax income and net income for the restatement period 1973 through 1977, the percentage decreases in net income for those years amounting to 55, 22, 38 and 41 percent, respectively.[6] Subsequent estimates by full cost company managements, disclosed in 1977 10-K reports, bear out these figures.

Given this potentially substantial impact, and the presumption that capital market agents place considerable importance on reported earnings in valuing equity securities, the concern expressed in position papers submitted to the FASB, DOE and SEC is not surprising. The following comments typify the concerns of the investment banking firms—the professionals most directly involved in the marketing of new securities:

Lehman Brothers

In recent years there have been a number of exploration companies who have obtained capital through the issuance of securities to the public. *In my opinion, successful efforts*

---

[3] Dennis Patz and James Boatsman, "Accounting Principle Formulation in an Efficient Markets Environment," *Journal of Accounting Research,* Autumn 1972, pp. 392–403; Thomas R. Dyckman (with the cooperation of Abbie J. Smith), "Financial Accounting and Reporting by Oil and Gas Producing Companies: Report on the Effect of the Exposure Draft on the Returns of Oil and Gas Company Securities" (Report submitted to the Financial Accounting Standards Board, Stamford, Conn., December 1977) and "Report 3 on the Effect of Statement 19, 'Financial Accounting and Reporting by Oil and Gas Producing Companies,' on the Returns of Oil and Gas Company Securities" in Appendix to "Response of the Financial Accounting Standards Board to the Request for Comments from Interested Persons by the Securities and Exchange Commission on Accounting Practices—Oil and Gas Producers" (SEC File No. S7–715, February 24, 1978); Directorate of Economic and Policy Research (J. Richard Zecher), Securities and Exchange Commission, "Full Cost vs. Successful Efforts: A Study of a Proposed Accounting Change's Competitive Impact," February 1978.

[4] Melvin O'Connor and Daniel Collins, "Full Cost vs. Successful Efforts Accounting in the Oil and Gas Industries: A Closer Look at the Potential Market Consequences" (Graduate School of Business, Michigan State University, May 1977) and Daniel Collins and Warren Dent, "An Empirical Assessment of the Stock Market Effects of the Proposed Elimination of Full Cost Accounting in the Extractive Petroleum Industry" (Testimony submitted to Securities and Exchange Commission file S7–715).

[5] Touche Ross & Co. letter to the FASB's Ad Hoc Committee on Full Cost Accounting, March 29, 1977.

[6] First Boston Corporation statement to the DOE Inquiry, February 21, 1978.

accounting would make it either impossible or substantially more difficult and expensive for these companies to finance in either the public or private market.[7]

E.F. Hutton & Company

Requiring companies that use full cost accounting to switch to successful efforts accounting will strip those companies of hundreds of millions of dollars of equity and will substantially reduce their earnings. *This will reduce the ability of these companies to compete for new debt and equity capital at a time when the industry needs unprecedented amounts of capital for exploration and development.*[8]

The First Boston Corporation

In our opinion, the change to the successful efforts method in financial reporting will reduce the ability of small exploration companies to attract sufficient capital to proceed with expanded exploration for domestic oil and gas.... *Weaker balance sheets, lower and increasingly volatile reported earnings as well as pressures to reduce dividends can be expected to decrease the liquidity and marketability and prices of equity securities issued by small exploration companies.* Such reduction in the marketability and prices of equity securities will increase the costs and decrease the availability of this important source of capital to such companies.[9]

Donaldson, Lufkin & Jenrette

We believe that imposition of successful efforts accounting as proposed in FASB Statement No. 19 will *so drastically* and *so illogically* impact the earnings of aggressive independent exploration companies that it will, in turn, impair their access to the capital markets and influence the extent of their future competitive exploration activities.[10]

Those who deny the validity of these claims appeal to the efficient markets literature for contradictory evidence. Professor John Burton, former Chief Accountant of the SEC, made the following observations at the DOE hearings:

...a number of different techniques and research designs have been used to try to isolate the market effect of alternative accounting approaches. The overwhelming preponderance of results in this research has indicated that the market place is highly sophisticated in dealing with accounting differences and that market prices therefore adjust for these differences. Various research efforts have tested for market effect when companies changed accounting principles and among companies using alternative principles and concluded in both cases that no discernible effect can be found unless the change also had

[7] James W. Glanville, Officer of Lehman Brothers, Inc., letter to the FASB, March 4, 1977. Emphasis supplied.

[8] R. John Stanton, Jr., Vice President E.F. Hutton & Company, letter to the FASB, March 3, 1977. Emphasis supplied.

[9] Paul L. Miller, President, The First Boston Corporation, letter to the SEC, October 13, 1977. Emphasis supplied.

[10] John Chalsty, Managing Director, Donaldson, Lufkin & Jenrette Securities Corporation, statement to the DOE hearings, February 21, 1978.

tax implications.... In cases where there was no tax effect, changes in accounting simply resulted in compensatory changes in the multiple...applied to earnings in the market place.[11]

Professor Charles T. Horngren reiterated this view in a *Wall Street Journal* editorial article:

> The doomsday critics of FASB Statement 19 essentially adhere to an extremely narrow view of the role of an income statement, a "bottom-line mentality" that is slowly, surely, and justifiably falling into disrepute.... Essentially, these arguments assume that investors in the aggregate can be fooled by how reported earnings are measured. However, there is considerable evidence that the market is not fooled.... Indeed, the securities markets are highly efficient with respect to accounting changes that are devoid of economic substance.[12]

Most of the research the professors allude to in their statements, however, involved assessing the market effects of *voluntary* accounting changes that caused an *increase* in reported earnings.[13] Is it appropriate to conclude that, because previous research has indicated the market is unaffected by voluntary changes in accounting methods that increase reported earnings, the market will also be unaffected by mandatory changes in accounting method that tend to decrease reported earnings? Can one safely assume that mandatory accounting changes are in general devoid of economic substance?

THE STUDIES

A series of studies have addressed the question of the economic impact of mandatory accounting changes in the specific context of either the FASB or the prior APB (Accounting Principles Board) proposal to eliminate full cost accounting in favor of the successful efforts method. Before considering each of them in detail, we should note a number of features common to all.

Each study used the familiar market model to estimate the relation between an individual security's return and the market's return:

$$R_{it} = a_i + b_i R_{mt} + \epsilon_{it} ,\tag{1}$$

where R_{it} = the return on stock i in period t defined as

$$\log_e [(P_{it} + D_{it})/ P_{it-1}],$$

[11]Pages 2-3 of testimony.

[12]*Wall Street Journal*, March 31, 1978.

[13]The following studies fall into this category: Eugene E. Comiskey, "Market Response to Changes in Depreciation Accounting," *The Accounting Review*, April 1971, pp. 279–285; T. Ross Archibald, "Stock Market Reaction to the Depreciation Switch-Back," *The Accounting Review*, January 1972, pp. 22–30; Raymond Ball, "Changes in Accounting Techniques and Stock Prices," *Empirical Research in Accounting: Selected Studies* 1968, Supplement to *Journal of Accounting Research*, pp. 67–92; and Robert Kaplan and Richard Roll, "Investor Evaluation of Accounting Information: Some Empirical Evidence," *Journal of Business*, April 1972, pp. 225–257. More recently, Tom Harrison ("Different Market Reactions to Discretionary and Nondiscretionary Accounting Changes," *Journal of Accounting Research*, Spring 1977, pp. 84–107) considered the market effects of both voluntary and mandatory accounting changes with earnings effects in both directions.

P_{it} being the ith security's closing price in period t (adjusted for stock splits and stock dividends) and

D_{it} being the cash dividend for security i in period t,

R_{mt} = the return on the market in period t,

a_i and b_i = regression coefficients specific to stock i,

b_i = a measure of the relative market risk (beta) of security i, and

ϵ_{it} = the error, or disturbance, term with assumed mean of zero and variance of σ_i^2 .

With the exception of the SEC study, which used daily data, all studies estimated Equation 1 using weekly data from periods prior to either the APB or FASB proposal issuance and combined least squares estimates of a_i and b_i with actual market returns to forecast returns for test periods following proposal issuances. Forecast, or expected, returns were compared with actual returns for each week (or, in the case of the SEC study, day) in the following manner:

$$u_{it} = R_{it} - a_i + b_i R_{mt} \qquad\qquad (2)$$

The studies used these residual, or "risk-adjusted," returns (u_{it}) to assess the market effects of the proposals in question. To control for other, unspecified events that might have influenced the security returns of *all* oil and gas producers during the test period, each of the studies compared the residual returns of the successful efforts companies with those of the full cost companies.

THE APB PROPOSAL TO ELIMINATE FULL COST ACCOUNTING

On October 22, 1971, the APB Committee on Extractive Industries issued an exposure draft recommending the elimination of full cost accounting. Reaction of full cost firms and members of the investment community was overwhelmingly negative. They expressed concerns similar to those of the investment bankers cited earlier in this article.

In a 1972 study, Patz and Boatsman examined the market reaction to this proposal by comparing the weekly returns of full cost and successful efforts firms over a seven-week period surrounding the issuance of the APB exposure draft.[14] They predicated their analysis on the assumption of an efficient market wherein security prices react in an unbiased and instantaneous fashion to pertinent information. Thus if investors, in fact, attached economic significance to the proposed accounting change, one would expect to find the risk-adjusted returns of full cost firms differing from those of successful efforts firms at, or about, the time of the APB proposal.

Based on a two-way analysis of variance where the indicator variables were methods of accounting (full cost versus successful efforts) and size (measured by total revenues), Patz and Boatsman concluded that, "...the common stock prices of

---

[14]Patz and Boatsman, "Accounting Principle Formulation."

full cost companies were not adversely affected at any time during the impact period."[15] Moreover, they suggested that:

> ...any rule-making body considering elimination of accounting alternatives need not concern itself with arguments that the resulting lower earnings of some firms would substantially affect their security prices and ability to secure capital.[16]

On the surface, the Patz and Boatsman results appear to corroborate the findings of prior studies concerned with voluntary accounting changes.[17] A closer examination of the Patz and Boatsman analysis, however, reveals a lack of homogeneity in the samples that would have hampered the ability to detect a market effect if, in fact, one existed. Specifically, integrated companies were pooled with small producing companies in assessing the market effects of the proposal.

Producing firms are essentially exploration-oriented, having little, if any, interests beyond the exploration for and sale of crude oil, whereas integrated firms are generally involved in many activities in addition to exploration. A switch from full cost to successful efforts accounting would typically affect the earnings of producers more adversely, since exploration costs constitute a relatively larger proportion of their cost structure. But if the reaction to the APB's proposal to eliminate full cost accounting was indeed more pronounced for producing full cost companies than for integrated full cost companies, the Patz and Boatsman study would have neglected to detect the difference.[18]

In an attempt to rectify some of the methodological deficiencies of the Patz and Boatsman study, O'Connor and Collins conducted an analysis of the common stock price activity of oil and gas producing firms over a 21-week period surrounding the APB proposal date.[19] The O'Connor and Collins sample consisted of 78 firms (including all firms used in the Patz and Boatsman analysis) differentiated by their accounting methods and, further, by whether they were primarily producing or integrated companies; this classification yielded 13 successful efforts producers, 13 full cost producers, 26 successful efforts integrated firms and 26 full cost integrated firms. Using risk-adjusted returns computed in the fashion described earlier, the study used a two-way analysis of variance to test for market effect during the seven-week period corresponding to the Patz and Boatsman study.

Figure A presents the average cumulative residual returns of the four subsamples of firms over the 21 weeks centering on the seven-week test period. In interpreting Figure A, assume that each of the four subsamples represents an investment portfolio and that, nine weeks before the APB's announcement, an equal dollar amount had been invested in each security of each portfolio. The various plots then trace the average cumulative returns the respective portfolios would have realized,

---

[15] Ibid., p. 401.

[16] Ibid., p. 403.

[17] E.g., Ball, "Changes in Accounting Techniques" and Kaplan and Roll, "Investor Evaluation of Accounting Information."

[18] That producing companies would be more adversely affected is recognized by Dyckman in his 1977 report to the FASB and is demonstrated analytically by Shyam Sunder in "Properties of Accounting Numbers Under Full Costing and Successful Efforts Costing in the Petroleum Industry," *The Accounting Review,* January 1976, pp. 1–18.

[19] O'Connor and Collins, "Full Cost vs. Successful Efforts Accounting."

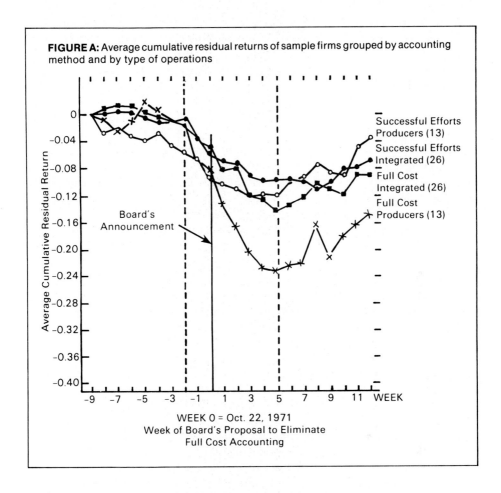

FIGURE A: Average cumulative residual returns of sample firms grouped by accounting method and by type of operations

Board's Announcement

WEEK 0 = Oct. 22, 1971
Week of Board's Proposal to Eliminate
Full Cost Accounting

Successful Efforts Producers (13)
Successful Efforts Integrated (26)
Full Cost Integrated (26)
Full Cost Producers (13)

after abstracting the effects of general market factors, as of any point during the subsequent 21-week period.

The seven-week test period starts two weeks before the Board's announcement, allowing for the possibility that information of the Board's posture with respect to full cost accounting could have leaked to the market before the official memorandum was publicly released. Patz and Boatsman elected to cut off the test period five weeks after the Board's announcement after considering the tradeoff between a period so short as to ignore possible delayed reaction to the news and one so long as to contain extraneous factors (e.g., earnings announcements) that could contaminate market prices. The seven weeks on either side of the test period provide an additional basis of comparison: If investors did not perceive any economic consequences in the Board's proposal, one would expect the relative returns of both successful efforts and full cost firms during the test period to be essentially the same as they were during either the pre- or post-test periods.

The evidence presented in Figure A clearly suggests otherwise. During the seven-week pretest period, there was virtually no difference between successful efforts and full cost firms. Beginning two weeks before the Board's announcement—i.e., during the first two weeks of the actual test period—both successful efforts and full cost firms experienced a marked downward drift in returns. However, the decline was much more dramatic for the full cost firms and, in particular, for the primarily producing full cost firms.

An analysis of variance test on the difference between the residual returns during the seven-week test period and the average returns during the two seven-week periods on either side proved significant at the 0.002 level for accounting method and at the 0.135 level for type of firm. The interaction effect between type of firm and accounting method was significant at the 0.038 level. These results suggest that the APB's proposed elimination of full cost accounting did have a significant adverse effect on the security returns of full cost firms relative to successful efforts firms. Moreover, they suggest that the impact was much more adverse for the full cost producing companies than for the full cost integrated companies.

Whether the depressed residual returns of full cost firms would have persisted had the Board issued a formal opinion is a matter of conjecture, since the APB subsequently retreated from its initial position and never adopted the exposure draft. The fact remains that the APB's tentative position against full cost accounting did apparently alter investors' perceptions of certain firms.

THE FASB PROPOSAL TO ELIMINATE FULL COST ACCOUNTING

Because of the resistance encountered with its October 1971 proposal, the APB tabled consideration of accounting in the oil and gas industry, passing the controversial issue on to its successor, the FASB. On July 15, 1977, the FASB issued an exposure draft on accounting and reporting for oil and gas companies that once again called for the elimination of full cost accounting. With few modifications, this proposal was adopted as FASB Statement No. 19 on December 5, 1977.

Preliminary to the issuance of Statement No. 19, the FASB commissioned Professor Thomas R. Dyckman, Director of Research of the American Accounting Association, to conduct an empirical investigation of the stock market effects of the exposure draft. Dyckman analyzed weekly returns of 113 small independent oil and gas producing companies during the nine-week period following issuance of the exposure draft, comparing the returns of the 72 full cost firms in the sample with those of the 41 successful efforts firms.[20] Based on a week-by-week and cumulative analysis, Dyckman concluded that:

> Our statistical tests do not support the attribution of an information effect to the exposure draft over the entire test period. There is some, but inconclusive, evidence of a possible short-term effect in the two weeks surrounding issuance of the [exposure draft]. This effect did not persist, however.[21]

[20]Dyckman, "Financial Accounting and Reporting by Oil and Gas Producing Companies" (FASB study).

[21]Ibid., Part I, pp. 1–2. After the DOE hearings in February of 1978, Professor Dyckman extended his initial research over a 21-week period centered on the week of the exposure draft issuance and found a

On February 10, 1978, the Directorate of Economic and Policy Research of the SEC issued a report entitled "Full Cost vs. Successful Efforts: A Study of a Proposed Accounting Change's Competitive Impact" (hereafter referred to as the SEC study). Using daily, rather than weekly, data and a smaller sample (37 successful efforts companies and 35 full cost companies), this study reached conclusions similar to Professor Dyckman's:

> This study found an initial adverse securities price impact for those oil and gas companies that would be subject to changes in the reporting of financial results because of the issuance of the FASB exposure draft on oil and gas accounting. However, the study also found a partial reversal of the initial impact. The study concluded that a strong case (could) be made that most of the initial adverse impact traceable to the FASB exposure draft on the trading prices of (full cost) companies had been recovered. On the other hand, the evidence is weak in support of the alternative statement that (full cost) companies suffered a permanent impairment of their capital raising ability as a result of the announcement.[22]

The Dyckman/FASB and SEC studies appear to support the Patz and Boatsman conclusions, which suggest that the proposed elimination of full cost accounting had no apparent adverse effect on the security returns of full cost firms. However, critical assessment of their research raises serious questions about sample selection and statistical procedure. Specifically, a study by Collins and Dent, undertaken as part of the SEC hearings on Statement No. 19, noted that 22 percent (16 firms) of the Dyckman/FASB full cost sample and 23 percent (eight firms) of the SEC's full cost sample were Canadian firms.[23] The basis for including Canadian firms in the samples is suspect, given that both the full cost and successful efforts methods of accounting remain acceptable alternatives for Canadian firms, and that these firms are relatively less dependent than U.S. firms on U.S. capital markets. Moreover, increases in the price of Canadian crude oil during the latter half of 1977, changes in Canadian tax laws providing for a more liberal write-off of exploration costs and a major oil discovery in the West Pembina area of Alberta, where many of the Canadian producers had drilling rights, had positive pricing implications for Canadian firms specifically and could well have offset any potential adverse market reaction to the proposed elimination of full cost accounting in the U.S.

Collins and Dent further questioned the set of successful efforts firms used as the control sample for the Dyckman/FASB study. It would be logical to presume that the reported earnings and/or financial positions of these firms would not be affected in any way by the adoption of FASB Statement No. 19. A review of their annual reports and/or 10-K's, however, revealed that 16 of the 41 successful efforts firms (39 percent) in the original Dyckman/FASB sample indicated that their financial statements would be materially affected in some way by the adoption of FASB No. 19.[24] This raises the question of whether these firms should have been

---

significant adverse market effect for the full cost firms relative to the successful efforts firms. (See Donald J. Kirk, Chairman, FASB, letter to the Department of Energy, March 20, 1978, which includes a copy of Professor Dyckman's letter to the FASB describing the results of this additional analysis.)

[22]Abstract to SEC study.

[23]Collins and Dent, "An Empirical Assessment."

[24]In most cases, the form of successful efforts accounting being used by these companies did not conform to the procedures proposed in Statement No. 19.

included among the control group for testing the potential market effects of Statement No. 19.

From a statistical standpoint, Collins and Dent noted in both Dyckman/FASB and SEC studies a lack of independence in the cross-sectional sample observations arising from the fact that all sample firms were in the same industry and their return measures examined in a common time period. That is, the returns were subject to common, unspecified factors that would have induced correlation among the sample observations. The Walsh and Wilcoxon related samples tests employed in the Collins and Dent analysis, in contrast to those used in the FASB and SEC studies, took specific cognizance of this point, thereby enhancing the likelihood of determining the true effect of the specific accounting change on security returns.[25]

Implementing these and other refinements in sample selection and statistical testing procedures, Collins and Dent compared the market performance of 45 U.S. full cost firms with that of 18 successful efforts firms over three, six and eight-month periods following the issuance of the FASB exposure draft. Figure B shows the difference in average weekly risk-adjusted returns of full cost minus successful efforts firms beginning with the week of the exposure draft issuance (July 15, 1977).

If there were no difference in the market responses of full cost and successful efforts firms, one would expect to observe an approximately equal number of positive and negative spikes of matching magnitude. Figure B indicates, however, a preponderance of large negative spikes. (Assessed over varying time periods, the differences generally were significant at the one and two percent probability levels.) Over the entire test period, the average weekly residual return for the full cost firms was -1.12 percent, while the corresponding return for the successful efforts firms was -0.56 percent.

Figure C displays the cumulative risk-adjusted returns for the two test groups beginning eight weeks prior to the draft issuance and ending 35 weeks after the issuance. In the weeks prior to the issuance of the draft, there was little difference in the performance of the two groups. Following the issuance of the exposure draft, the differences in cumulative risk-adjusted returns became progressively larger, with no evidence of any reversal by the end of the eight-month period.

INTERPRETATION AND CONCLUSION

While several studies have found no evidence of an adverse market effect associated with the proposed elimination of full cost accounting, we believe this finding can be attributed in part to inappropriate sample selection or statistical testing procedures. With correction for these perceived deficiencies, empirical evidence suggests that investors' evaluation of full cost firms was indeed adversely affected by both the APB and FASB proposals to eliminate full cost accounting. How can one explain this response?

For a possible explanation, one must look to how mandatory accounting changes

---

[25] For a description of these testing procedures see Sidney Siegel, *Nonparametric Statistics,* International Edition (Tokyo: McGraw Hill, 1956) and W.J. Conover, *Practical Nonparametric Statistics* (New York: Wiley, 1971).

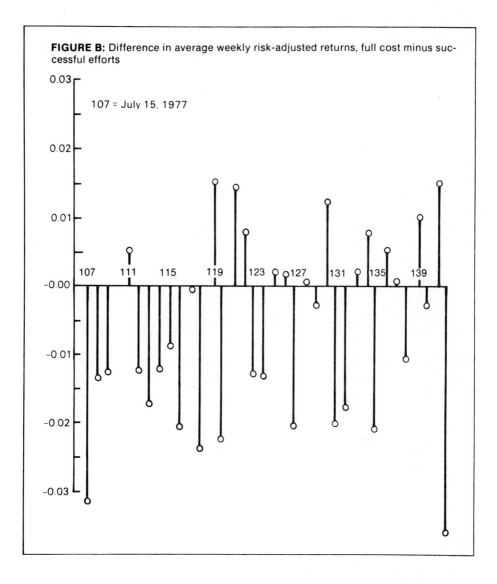

FIGURE B: Difference in average weekly risk-adjusted returns, full cost minus successful efforts

can affect management behavior. Opponents of mandatory successful efforts accounting argued at both the FASB and DOE hearings that the availability of full cost accounting has provided managements the incentive to undertake highly risky and costly exploration activities without fear of being unduly penalized by their financial reports. Indeed, data presented at the DOE hearings by the First Boston Corporation suggest that full cost companies spend a much greater proportion of each revenue dollar on exploration activity than successful efforts firms do.[26]

---

[26]See Exhibit III appended to the testimony of Joseph S. Frelinghuysen, Jr., Vice President and Director, The First Boston Corporation, DOE hearings, February 21, 1978.

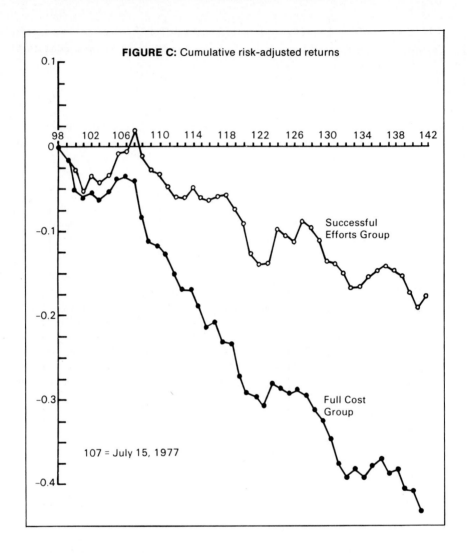

FIGURE C: Cumulative risk-adjusted returns

Managements of the more aggressive exploration full cost companies have indicated that, if full cost accounting were eliminated, they would substantially reduce exploration expenditures in an attempt to cushion the effect of the forced change on their reported financial results.[27] Their behavior would be entirely rational, given that managers perceive that the lower and more volatile earnings figures reported under successful efforts accounting would make it substantially

---

[27] In testimony presented at the DOE hearings (February 21, 1971), Richard Messing, Vice President, Arthur D. Little, Inc., estimated that the elimination of full cost accounting would result in a total reduction in exploratory drilling expenditures of nearly $600 million, which is approximately eight percent of estimated drilling expenditures from all sources.

more difficult for their companies to raise new equity capital. Moreover, managers whose prospects for promotion, bonuses and job opportunities depend in part on the reported net income of their companies can be expected to alter their operating plans to dampen the impact of a mandatory accounting change.

To the extent that the proposed elimination of full cost accounting alters managements' exploration, production and investment strategies, cash flows to full cost firms will change. If investors behave rationally, they will anticipate such occurrence, and their response will be reflected in the equilibrium values of such firms even before the changes actually take place.

Besides affecting management behavior, a mandated change from full cost to successful efforts accounting would probably impose on affected companies certain costs that, in an efficient market, could be expected to lower the value of these firms. For example, in their submission to the SEC, the Federal Trade Commission (FTC) made the following observations:

> As in other industries, entry and expansion in oil and gas exploration is essential to competition, and will be dependent to an increasing extent upon the equity market, particularly the new issues market, as a source of marginal funds. The relative inefficiency of the market for new securities is generally recognized. Due to the short-term nature of a new issues underwriting, underwriters have a felt need to be able to explain quickly the nature of their offering. Successful efforts, however, will generally *increase* perceived information costs, thus discouraging underwritings and raising the cost of capital. Recognizing the time and expense entailed in having to explain the intricacies of accounting practices and their effect upon the 'paper' as opposed to 'real economic' performance of the company issuing the securities, underwriters will tend to demand a higher fee and to set a lower public offering price.[28]

This reasoning led the FTC to conclude:

> The market's negative reaction to the release of the exposure draft, therefore, leads to the conclusion (under the 'efficient market' theory) that (1) there will be increased costs in adjusting to the loss of information, (2) the cost of capital, and thus the growth of affected firms, will be adversely impacted by higher discounting in the new shares market, and (3) 'going public' will prove more costly and thus more difficult.[29]

Empirical evidence suggests that the proposed elimination of full cost accounting has had a measurable negative impact on the equity securities of potentially affected firms. The observed revaluations can be attributed to the effect the mandated accounting change is likely to have on managerial behavior and to the increased costs firms will have to bear in obtaining external financing. These firm-level consequences could have significant implications for national energy exploration. The SEC should therefore carefully weigh all the evidence on the economic consequences of its deliberations and standard-setting in this area.

[28] Federal Trade Commission Response to the SEC, February 27, 1978, p. 25.
[29] Ibid., p. 26.

Briloff and the Capital Market

George Foster
Stanford University

Abraham Briloff is a noted critic of contemporary financial reporting standards.[1] A distinctive feature of his approach is detailed analysis of the financial reports of individual companies. Several observers (e.g., Bernstein [1975]) have cited the "sharp declines" in the prices of companies criticized by Briloff at the time several of his articles were published (notably articles on land developers and computer leasors) as evidence consistent with capital market inefficiency. This note examines the security market reaction to companies criticized by Briloff in his published articles. One concern is whether the cited reactions of the land developers and computer leasors are ex post chosen because of their price drop or whether they are representative of the market reaction to companies cited in Briloff's articles. The evidence presented in Section 2 indicates that companies whose accounting practices are criticized by Briloff, suffer (on average) a price drop of approximately 8 percent on the day the article is published. In Section 3, a variety of explanations for this result are discussed.

1. ARTICLES EXAMINED

Two criteria were used to select the articles to examine: (a) the day the article became "publicly available" must be readily ascertainable,[2] and (b) the accounting practices of specific companies must be criticized. Fifteen articles met these two criteria. A resumé provided by Briloff as well as an independent check of several financial journals were used in selecting the articles. Table 1 (columns 1 and 2) details these fifteen articles and their date and place of publication. The specific companies criticized in each article were noted and security returns on as many as possible collected. In all, security returns on twenty-eight companies cited in the articles were collected.[3] Table 1 (column 3) details these companies.

From *The Journal of Accounting Research* (Spring 1979), pp. 262–274. Reprinted by permission of *The Journal of Accounting Research*.

Editor's note: The assistance of Abraham Briloff in preparing this note is gratefully acknowledged. Coopers & Lybrand provided financial support for the research. Comments from R. Ball, P. Brown, N. Dopuch, D. Emanuel, R. Officer, and R. Orf helped tighten my analysis.

[1] *Unaccountable Accounting* (New York: Harper & Row, 1972) and *More Debits than Credits* (New York: Harper & Row, 1976) illustrate both the breadth and style of his writings.

[2] The appropriate journals were contacted to confirm the "chosen" date of publication. For instance, articles appear in *Barron's* dated on a Monday. *Dow Jones and Company* indicated that *Barron's* is published on Friday nights, for delivery to subscribers on Monday morning. Thus, the earliest date the security market could react to the article is the Monday dated on the journal. See n. 6 for problems in deciding on day 0 for one article.

[3] The basic data source was the *CRSP* daily security return file. Where data were not available from this source, the *ISL* books were used. In several cases, individual companies provided daily returns for the appropriate period.

TABLE 1

ARTICLES OF BRILOFF EXAMINED

Article	Journal/Publication Date	Companies Cited That Are Examined in This Note
1. "Dirty Pooling"	*Barron's* (July 15, 1968)	Gulf and Western; Ling-Temco-Vought (LTV)
2. "All a Fandangle?"	*Barron's* (December 2, 1968)	Leasco Data Processing; Levin-Townsend
3. "Much-Abused Goodwill"	*Barron's* (April 28, 1969)	Levin-Townsend; National General Corp.
4. "Out of Focus"	*Barron's* (July 28, 1969)	Perfect Film & Chemical Corp.
5. "Castles of Sand?"	*Barron's* (February 2, 1970)	Amrep Corp.; Canaveral International; Deltom Corp.; General Development Corp.; Great Southwest Corp.; Great Western United, Major Realty; Penn Central
6. "Tomorrow's Profits?"	*Barron's* (May 11, 1970)	Telex
7. "Six Flags at Half-Mast?"	*Barron's* (January 11, 1971)	Great Southwest Corp.; Penn Central
8. "Gimme Shelter"	*Barron's* (October 25, 1971)	Kaufman & Broad Inc.; U.S. Home Corp.; U.S. Financial Inc.
9. "SEC Questions Accounting"	*Commercial and Financial Chronicle* (November 2, 1972)	Penn Central
10. "$200 Million Question"	*Barron's* (December 18, 1972)	Leasco Corp.
11. "Sunrise, Sunset"	*Barron's* (May 14, 1973)	Kaufman & Broad
12. "Kaufman & Broad—More Questions"	*Commercial and Financial Chronicle* (July 12, 1973)	Kaufman & Broad
13. "You Deserve a Break..."	*Barron's* (July 8. 1974)	McDonald's
14. "The Bottom Line: What's Going on at I.T.T." (Interview with Briloff)	*New York Magazine* (August 12, 1974)	I.T.T.
15. "Whose Deep Pocket?"	*Barron's* (July 19, 1976)	Reliance Group Inc.

2. METHODOLOGY AND RESULTS

Past research has reported that the announcement of such items as annual and interim earnings, dividends, and secondary issues appears to have an observable effect on the capital market; moreover, much of this effect appears to be concentrated in a two-day period surrounding the announcement.[4] Given these results, I decided

---

[4]See Foster [1978, chap. 11] for a survey of this research.

to use daily security returns in the analysis. The period covering thirty trading days before to thirty days after the publication of each article was chosen for examination. Given past research, any security price effect associated with the publication of Briloff's articles should be observable over this sixty-one-trading-day period.

The following model of capital market equilibrium is assumed to describe the pricing of capital assets (see Black [1972]):

$$E\,(\tilde{R}_{it}) = E\,(\tilde{R}_{zt}) + \beta_i[E(\tilde{R}_{mt}) - E(\tilde{R}_{zt})] \tag{1}$$

where R_{it} = return on asset i in period t,

$\quad\quad R_{zt}$ = return on an asset whose returns are uncorrelated with R_{mt} in period t,

$\quad\quad R_{mt}$ = return on the market portfolio in period t, and

$\quad\quad \beta_i$ = relative risk of asset i.

Using (1), the effect of any new information on asset i becoming available in period t can be determined as:

$$\tilde{U}_{it} = \tilde{R}_{it} - E(\tilde{R}_{it}|\tilde{R}_{zt}, \tilde{R}_{mt}, \beta_i). \tag{2}$$

The procedure used to estimate the abnormal return ($\tilde{U}_{it}$) in (2) is based on the "companion portfolio" technique of Black and Scholes [1973]. Specifically, stocks are ranked on an estimate of beta in period $t - 1$ and placed into one of twenty portfolios. The portfolio that stock i is placed in is termed the "companion portfolio" for that stock. The abnormal return on stock i in period t is estimated by "subtracting from the measured return [of stock i] the return on the 'companion portfolio' that has about the same dependence on $\tilde{R}_m$ and $\tilde{R}_z$ as the stock" (Black and Scholes [1973, p. 11]), that is:

$$\tilde{U}_{it} = \tilde{R}_{it} - \tilde{R}_{pt} \tag{3}$$

where R_{pt} = return on "companion portfolio" p in period t.[5] The abnormal returns for each security were then cumulated over the sixty-one-day period examined, to obtain the cumulative abnormal return (CAR):

$$CAR_{it} = \sum_{t=1}^{T} \tilde{U}_{it}. \tag{4}$$

The results are presented in two formats. In Figure 1, the average CAR behavior of the twenty-eight stocks is reported. In Figure 2, the average CAR behavior of the fifteen articles is presented; the average CAR of the stocks in each article is first calculated and then the averages of these CAR's for the fifteen articles determined. The Figure 2 format avoids the possibility that the results in Figure 1 could be

_____

[5]For *CRSP* stocks (twenty-four of the twenty-eight examined), the U^{it}'s were obtained from the "excess returns" tape. For the other four stocks, I assumed a relative risk of one and used the *S & P Composite 500 Stock Index* as the "companion portfolio."

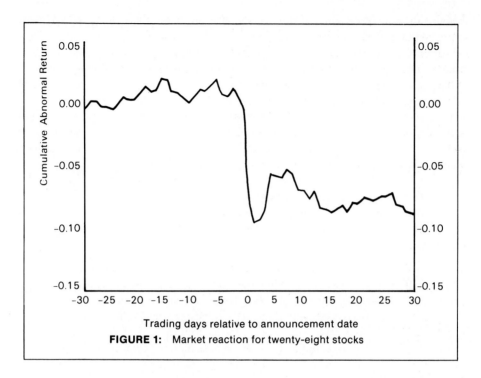

FIGURE 1:   Market reaction for twenty-eight stocks

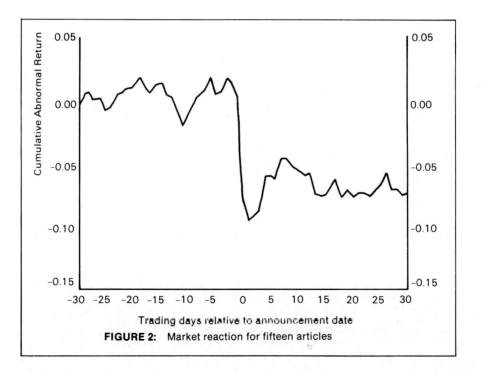

FIGURE 2:   Market reaction for fifteen articles

heavily influenced by one article in which a large number of companies were criticized (and whose stock prices were affected).

The results in Figures 1 and 2 are very similar. I will concentrate subsequent analysis on Figure 2 (which has the advantage that all observations are independent). All tests I report were also done on the Figure 1 data and yielded the same conclusions. The most noticeable feature of Figure 2 is the drop (of .086) in the average CAR on day 0, that is, the day Briloff's article was published. Is this drop a significant one? As a first step, the percent of the fifteen observations with negative abnormal returns on each day was computed. The days with the highest percents were:

Day 0   :93.3% Negative (14 out of 15)
Day + 13 :80%   Negative (12 out of 15)
Day + 27 :80%   Negative (12 out of 15)

Thus, based on the sign of the abnormal return, day 0 is the most extreme observation. If a binomial test is used and independence is assumed (see Siegel [1956]), the probability of fourteen out of fifteen negative observations is less than .01.[6] Days +13 and +27 were also significant at the .01 level. The drops in the CAR on days +13 and +27 were .017 and .014, respectively. Using a binomial test, day +4 exhibited a significant abnormal price increase—the increase in the CAR was .027, with twelve out of the fifteen observations positive. The CAR on day +30 is -.073; this is not significantly different from the CAR on day 0 of -.082. Thus, if a thirty-trading-day postarticle announcement period is used, the significant drop on day 0 appears to be a permanent one.

A more powerful test of significance is the Kolmogorov-Smirnov (K-S) one-sample test, since it takes into account the size as well as the sign of the abnormal return on each day (see Siegel [1956]). The test will be illustrated by reference to day 0. Under the null hypothesis of no negative effect on returns, there should be no clustering of observations with the lowest abnormal return at day 0; the probability of day 0 having the lowest return of the sixty-one returns examined is 1/61. The number of observations with the lowest abnormal return during the -30 to +30 trading-day period at day 0 was first determined. Then the number of observations with the second lowest abnormal return during the -30 to +30 trading-day period at day 0 was determined. This procedure was repeated until all observations had been classified. Seven observations had the lowest abnormal return at day 0; one had the second lowest abnormal return; one the third lowest; two the fourth lowest.... The K-S test compares the actual cumulative distribution with the theoretical cumulative distri-

---

[6] The one article which was associated with a positive abnormal return on day 0 was "Kaufman & Broad—More Questions" (*Commercial & Financial Chronicle*, July 12, 1973). This is the only article for which there was some uncertainty over the centering of day 0. The July 12 date is when the article was first available in the *Commercial & Financial Chronicle*. However, the article was based on an address Briloff gave at the G. Tsai Institutional Investor Luncheon in New York City on July 9, 1973. The abnormal returns for Kaufman & Broad for July 9 were -.017; for July 10, -.055; and for July 11, -.010. Thus, if one uses the address date as day 0, every one of Briloff's fifteen articles I examined was associated with a negative price change on day 0.

bution and concentrates on the maximum difference between the two. Summary results are presented in Table 2. The abnormal return at day 0 is at least within the seven lowest for twelve of the fifteen observations, that is, 80 percent of the cases examined. Under the null hypothesis, .115 (7/61) of the cases would be expected to be in the seven with the lowest abnormal returns. This difference of .685 between the actual and theoretical cumulative distributions is the maximum difference for the sample. A difference of .404 between the two distributions is sufficient to reject the null hypothesis at the .01 level.

I applied the K-S test for each of the sixty-one trading days examined and observed the maximum difference between the actual and theoretical cumulative distributions for each day. A summary of these tests is presented in Figure 3. Only day 0 is significant at the .01 level. The results in Figures 2 and 3 suggest that associated with the publication of Briloff's articles is a significant negative and rapid capital market response.[7]

3. EXPLANATION OF THE RESULTS

What explanation can be given for the results in Section 2? At least five possible ones will be considered: (a) the capital market is inefficient; (b) Briloff, through his superior analytical insights, brings "new information" to the market; (c) Briloff, through his use of "nonpublic" information sources, brings "new information" to the market; (d) the exposés are cues for events such as increased government regulation of industry; and (e) the publication of Briloff's articles coincides with the release of other information about the cited companies.

[7] As a crude test of whether there is any difference in effect over time, I calculated the mean drop in the first eight articles (-.074) and the mean drop in the last seven articles (-.099). These means do not suggest a significant time effect.

TABLE 2

RESULTS FOR KOLMOGOROV-SMIRNOV TEST: DAY 0

	# of Observations with ith Lowest Return	Cumulative % Distribution of Actuals	Cumulative % Distribution under Null	Difference Between (2) and (3)
	(1)	(2)	(3)	(4)
Lowest return	7	.467	.016	.451
Second lowest return	1	.533	.033	.500
Third lowest return	1	.600	.049	.551
Fourth lowest return	2	.733	.066	.667
Fifth lowest return	0	.733	.082	.651
Sixth lowest return	0	.733	.098	.635
Seventh lowest return	1	.800	.115	.685
Eighth lowest return	0	.800	.131	.669
Sixty-first lowest return	0	1.000	1.000	0

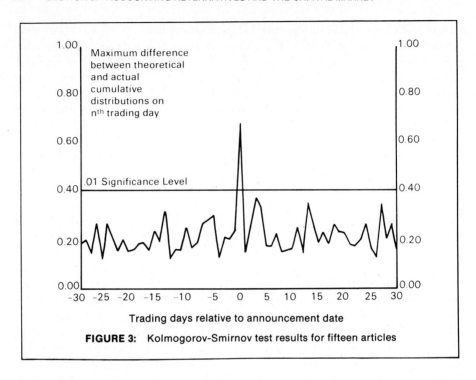

FIGURE 3:   Kolmogorov-Smirnov test results for fifteen articles

Capital Market Inefficiency Explanation

The capital market inefficiency explanation raises the issue of what is meant by an efficient capital market. Definitions of efficiency with respect to a particular information set can be categorized into (a) those concerned with aggregate market variables such as security returns,[8] and (b) those concerned with aspects of individual investor decisions, such as the revision of portfolios.[9] At present, except for some highly specific results (e.g., Rubinstein[1974] and Ng[1975]), our knowledge of the relationship between individual investor behavior and security prices is limited. The implication is that our knowledge of the relationship between the various definitions of market efficiency is also limited. It is quite possible that one may infer (say) efficiency based on an aggregate market definition, but infer inefficiency based on an individual investor definition. When interpreting the results in Section 2, it is important for one to note that the variable examined was security prices. I will restrict my interpretation to a market efficiency definition related to this variable.

Fama[1976] defines a capital market as efficient, with respect to information set

---

[8] For example, see the definition in Fama [1976], discussed subsequently in this note.

[9] For example: "The market is action-efficient with respect to information set A if the optimal position of *any* investor, given the data in *any* information set B, the data in A, and the current price is equal to his optimal position given only the data in B and the price" (Beja [1976, p. 10]). See also Rubinstein [1975] and Beaver [1976] for further discussion of market efficiency definitions.

ϕ_t, if security prices "fully reflect" all the information in that set time t. Notationally, this is expressed as:

$$f(P_{t+1}|\phi_t) = f_m(P_{t+1}|\phi_t^m) \tag{5}$$

where $f(\cdot)$ = The "true" conditional probability distribution of security prices in period $t+1$,

ϕ_t = the information set available at period t,

$f_m(\cdot)$ = the market-assessed conditional probability distribution based on ϕ_t^m, and

ϕ_t^m = the information set used by the market at period t.

Several problems arise in testing whether the equality in (5) holds. First, $f(\cdot)$ is a construct that is not observable. The experimental control I use to proxy for $f(\cdot)$ is the asset-pricing model detailed in (1). Second, the equality in (5) does not specify what would constitute evidence consistent (or inconsistent) with capital market efficiency. It is necessary to assume something about the information set ϕ_t. Note that the definition of ϕ_t includes not only the specific signals in ϕ_t (what some call the "raw data"), but also the implications for $f(\cdot)$ of those signals. If we assume the information provided by Briloff is already costlessly available to all market participants (and the Black asset-pricing model is descriptively valid), then capital market efficiency implies there should be no price reaction to Briloff's articles.

That there is a significant price reaction of the kind detailed in Section 2, however, does not necessarily imply market inefficiency. The descriptive validity of the above-noted assumptions needs further investigation. The assumption that the information set provided by Briloff is already costlessly available to all market participants is an especially troublesome one. At a theoretical level, it is difficult to see what incentives there would be for information acquisition in such a world. Indeed, Grossman and Stiglitz [1975; 1976] argue that if information is costlessly available to all traders, it is possible that no market equilibrium would exist. At an empirical level, the analysis Briloff undertakes appears inconsistent with the information costlessly available to all investors assumption (see below).

"Superior Insight" Explanation

This explanation is based on the argument that Briloff possesses superior skills and is able to earn a (competitive) return from using these skills. The so-called information market, rather than the capital market, is seen as the key to the results (see Gonedes [1976]). Once one recognizes that individuals can earn economic rents from their information production activities, tests of capital market efficiency become more difficult to undertake. It is necessary to predict independently what is the "appropriate" price reaction to releases from such individuals, and then examine if the actual reaction is significantly different from the "appropriate" reaction. Only by independently predicting the "appropriate" price reaction can one devise a test that allows the alternative hypothesis of an inefficient market to be supported by the data. Two important attributes of an "appropriate" price reaction are its timing and its magnitude. To date, most tests have concentrated on the timing issue. A common hypothesis is that if a cue provides information to the market, the response to that cue should be rapid. Thus, once Briloff's articles are placed in the public domain (and are available to all market participants at a negligible cost), market efficiency predicts that any price reaction should be rapid. The data in Figures 1–3 generally support this prediction. On day -1, the average CAR in Figure 2 is .004. It drops to -.082 on day 0 and is at -.073 on day +30.

The other aspect of testing market efficiency is determining the magnitude (i.e., the direction and size) of the price effect one predicts, conditional on an efficient market. Frankly, I have difficulty making such a prediction. The returns to Briloff can take several forms not directly related to security prices (e.g., article and book royalties and an enhanced professional reputation). The readers of Briloff's articles also could find them newsworthy for factors such as their insights into the development of accounting and auditing standards. We can only conjecture whether, based on the information Briloff provides to the capital market, a price drop of 8 percent is (or is not) consistent with an efficient market.

It is important to note that this problem in ex ante predicting the magnitude of the price effect conditional on an efficient market is also apparent (although not always recognized) in many other empirical studies. For instance, Ball and Brown's [1968] study of annual accounting earnings is frequently cited as evidence supporting market efficiency. Though the study may support efficiency with regard to the timing of the price reaction, it is difficult to assert that it supports market efficiency with regard to the magnitude of the price reaction. We have little theory which tells us whether the composite CAR (API) of 8.3 percent which they reported should have been 5, 7, or 9 percent, etc., conditional on an efficient capital market.[10]

"NonPublic" Information Source Explanation

Market efficiency (in the sense of (5)) is always defined with respect to a particular information set. One possible explanation for the results in Section 2 is that the data sources used by Briloff extend beyond the information set "publicly available" in period t. Unfortunately, there is no clear-cut distinction between "publicly available" and "nonpublicly" available information sets.[11] Rather, there is a continuum. At one end of the spectrum are items like annual reports and company announcements that appear to be publicly available at essentially zero cost. Briloff makes extensive use of such items. In nearly all cases they include those of the companies criticized. In some cases they also include those of other companies. For example, in the "Tomorrow's Profit" (*Barron's,* May 11, 1970) article the accounting practices of Telex (a seller of computer disc and tape drives) were criticized. One information

[10]See Foster [1978, p. 357] for further discussion of this point relating to studies which examine the security market reaction to accounting changes.

[11]This lack of a clear-cut distinction makes it difficult to classify studies into one of three forms of market efficiency (weak, semistrong, and strong) outlined in Fama [1970]. Sharpe foreshadowed these problems in his commentary on the Fama paper: "...the definition of semi-strong efficiency is open to dispute (when is information publicly available? which investors are in the public? how soon must the information be available? at what price?)..." [1970, p. 418].

source used was the prospectus of Hudson Leasing Corporation, "a Long Island concern instrumental in financing Telex's leasing activities." This prospectus revealed information about Telex's operations not disclosed in Telex's Annual Report, for example, about its continuing responsibility to maintain the equipment it leases throughout its useful lives.

Further along the information availability spectrum are items such as SEC filings which may be available only at restricted locations or by paying set fees. Briloff also uses these sources. For example, in "Out of Focus" (*Barron's*, July 28, 1969) Perfect Film and Chemical's accounting practices were examined. The use of pooling accounting for the acquisition of a 50.6-percent interest in Plume and Atwood by Perfect Film was criticized. In order to estimate the "net tangible assets" from the acquisition reported on Perfect's books, he used both the Plume and Atwood 1968 Annual Report and documents filed with "the SEC describing the proposed acquisition."

Even further along the spectrum of information availability are company memoranda, etc. Briloff also appears to use this source on occasion. For instance, in "You Deserve a Break..." (*Barron's*, July 8, 1974), he quoted from an August 18, 1973 memorandum from the company's corporate counsel concerning the sale of shares that "McDonald's employees, executives and others" had received from Ray A. Kroc. The memorandum discussed the appropriate forms employees should file if they decided "to sell all or any part of the gift shares."

To gain some overall perspective of the information sources used by Briloff, a "source analysis" of each of the fifteen articles was made. The sources explicitly referred to in each article were noted and classified into one of eight categories.[12] The number of items referred to in each category over the fifteen articles was:

	# of Items	
Annual and interim reports	32	39%
Prospectuses	15	18%
SEC documents	19	23%
Investment analyst/brokerage house reports	3	4%
Convention reports filed with state insurance commissioners	3	4%
Company news releases (letters, etc.) or reports thereof in *Wall Street Journal/Barron's*	7	9%
Company tax returns	1	1%
Company memorandum	2	2%
	82	100%

Based on this "source analysis," my judgment is that it is difficult to explain the drop on day 0 in Figures 1 and 2 by arguing that the major sources Briloff used were not

---

[12] This "source analysis" is obviously not without problems, e.g. (a) I restricted myself to sources Briloff explicitly cited, which may only be a subset of all the sources he used, and (b) I only counted the sources rather than indicated their relative importance to his analysis.

previously readily available or were only available by incurring substantial acquisition costs.

Exposés as Cues for Other Events Explanation

This explanation assumes that due to the effective way Briloff writes (and the medium in which he writes), he acts as a catalyst to parties who can affect the future cash flows of firms (i.e., in addition to any capital market effect flowing from increased accounting disclosure). Consider the "Castles of Sand" (*Barron's*, February 2, 1970) article where the financial reporting and management practices of land developers were criticized. This article could have increased the probability of congressional or SEC investigation into the operations of these companies in this industry.

It is difficult to collect data which directly examine whether this explanation is a major one. Information on how the criticisms of single individuals influence the decisions of congressmen, bureaucrats, etc., is not easily available. However, by examining the content of Briloff's articles, some indirect evidence appears possible. In many cases, Briloff's criticisms are of the accounting decisions of specific companies, without any attempt to elicit governmental, SEC, etc., restrictions on the decisions of these companies. For instance, in "You Deserve a Break," the accounting treatment of "gifts" of McDonald's stock by Ray Kroc to McDonald's employees was criticized. There was, however, no attempt to argue that such "gifts" should not have been made. In only three of the fifteen articles were the criticisms leveled more at the industry level than at the firm level, that is, in "All a Fandangle," "Castles of Sand," and "Gimme Shelter." In as much as criticisms leveled at an industry, rather than at an individual firm, are more likely to generate congressional movements for "reform," the fact that only three articles were exposited at the industry level is not very strong evidence for the "exposés as a cue for other events" explanation. Moreover, the average drop in the CAR on day 0 for these three articles (-.072) was not significantly different from the average drop on day 0 (-.089) for the other twelve articles.

Other Information Releases Explanation

There is always the possibility in any experiment that uncontrolled factors may cause the results observed. In Figures 1–3, day 0 is the date that each article is published. If the publication of each Briloff article coincides with the release of other information about the cited companies, then ambiguity would exist over the cause of the results. The *Wall Street Journal Index* was examined as a check on this possibility. For only four out of the twenty-eight companies examined was there an information item cited on day 0 in the *WSJ Index*. Moreover, for these four companies, it was difficult to make unequivocal inferences that the information item should have a negative effect. For instance, the news release for Great Southwest Corporation (on February 2, 1970—the day the "Castles of Sand" article was published) was "Entered into a joint agreement with C. Brewer and and Co., a unit of International Utilities to develop 285,000 acres in Hawaii." An examination of the items released on day -2, day -1, day +1, and day +2 also revealed little support for this explanation. Thus, if we assume the *Wall Street Journal Index's* summary of information releases about companies is reasonably comprehensive, the "other information releases" explanation does not appear to be a likely one.

4. CONCLUSION

Companies whose accounting practices are criticized by Briloff appear, on average, to suffer an immediate drop in price of approximately 8 percent. Using a thirty-trading-day postannouncement period, this drop is a permanent one. Five possible explanations for this result were examined in Section 3. I argued that three—the nonpublic information sources explanation, the exposés as cues for other events explanation, and the other information releases explanation—were not likely to be the major causes of the immediate price drop. Although the timing of the price reaction is consistent with an efficient market, I am unable (given existing data) to determine whether the magnitude of the price reaction is consistent with the capital market inefficiency explanation or the superior insight (information market) explanation.[13] I hope this analysis illustrates that when one goes beyond "publicly available information," tests of capital market efficiency raise difficult research issues that can leave the results subject to varying interpretations.

REFERENCES

Ball, R., and P. Brown. "An Empirical Evaluation of Accounting Income Numbers." *Journal of Accounting Research* (Autumn 1968): 159–78.

Beaver, W.H. "Market Efficiency." Working paper, Stanford University, 1976.

Beja, A. "The Limited Information Efficiency of Market Processes." Working paper, University of California, Berkeley, 1976.

Bernstein, L.A. "In Defence of Fundamental Investment Analysis." *Financial Analysts Journal* (January/February 1975): 57–61.

Black, F. "Capital Market Equilibrium with Restricted Borrowing." *Journal of Business* (July 1972): 444–54.

———, and M. Scholes. "The Behavior of Security Returns around Ex-Dividend Days." Working paper, University of Chicago, 1973.

Briloff, A.J. *Unaccountable Accounting.* New York: Harper & Row, 1972.

———. *More Debits than Credits.* New York: Harper & Row, 1976.

Fama, E.F. "Efficient Capital Markets: A Review of Theory and Empirical Work." *Journal of Finance* (May 1970): 383–417.

———. *Foundations of Finance.* New York: Basic Books, 1976.

Foster, G. *Financial Statement Analysis.* Englewood Cliffs, N.J.: Prentice-Hall, 1978.

Gonedes, N.J. "The Capital Market, The Market for Information, and External Accounting." *Journal of Finance* (May 1976): 611–30.

Grossman, S., and J. Stiglitz. "On the Impossibility of Informationally Efficient Markets." Working paper, Stanford University, 1975.

---

[13] Note: "Adjusting for the costs of information production activities involves a variety of heady problems in data collection.... It is not clear that any "real world" data are available for attacking these problems—not a very cheery thought for those interested in empirical work" (Gonedes [1976, p. 623]).

————. "Information and Competitive Price Systems." *American Economic Review* (May 1976): 246–53.

Ng, D.S. "Information Accuracy and Social Welfare under Homogeneous Beliefs." *Journal of Financial Economics* (March 1975): 53–70.

Rubinstein, M. "An Aggregation Theorem for Securities Markets." *Journal of Financial Economics* (September 1974): 225–44.

————. "Securities Market Efficiency in an Arrow-Debreu Economy." *American Economic Review* (December 1975): 812–24.

Sharpe, W.H. "Comments" on Fama [1970]. *Journal of Finance* (May 1970): 418–420.

Siegel, S. *Nonparametric Statistics.* New York: McGraw-Hill, 1956.